Spanish in the United States

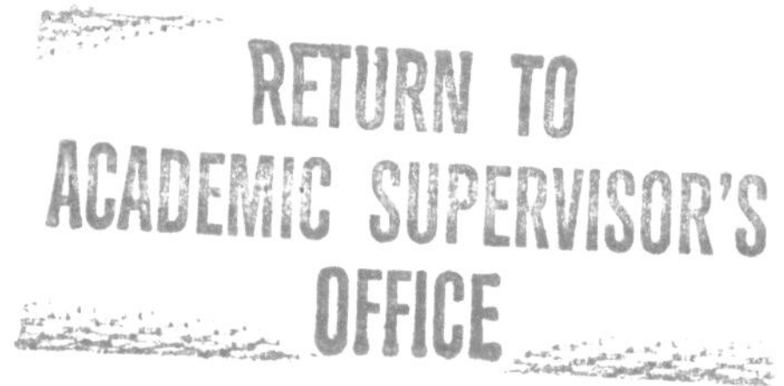

Spanish in the United States

Sociolinguistic aspects

Edited by JON AMASTAE
Department of Linguistics
University of Texas, El Paso

and
LUCÍA ELÍAS-OLIVARES
Department of Spanish, Italian and Portuguese
University of Illinois, Chicago Circle

CAMBRIDGE UNIVERSITY PRESS

Cambridge
London New York New Rochelle
Melbourne Sydney

Published by the Press Syndicate of the University of Cambridge
The Pitt Building, Trumpington Street, Cambridge CB2 1RP
32 East 57th Street, New York, NY 10022, USA
296 Beaconsfield Parade, Middle Park, Melbourne 3206, Australia

First published 1982

Printed in the United States of America

Library of Congress Cataloging in Publication Data

Main entry under title:

Spanish in the United States.

Includes index.

1. Spanish language – Dialects – United States – Addresses, essays, lectures. 2. Languages in contact – United States – Addresses, essays, lectures. I. Amastae, Jon. II. Elías-Olivares, Lucía.

PC4826.S64 460′.1′9 81–15437
ISBN 0 521 24448 X hard covers AACR2
ISBN 0 521 28689 1 paperback

Contents

Contributors

Jon Amastae
Department of Linguistics
University of Texas, El Paso

Garland D. Bills
Department of Linguistics
University of New Mexico

Lucía Elías-Olivares
Department of Spanish, Italian and Portuguese
University of Illinois, Chicago Circle

José L. Galván
English Department
University of California, Los Angeles

Maryellen García
National Center for Bilingual Research
Southwest Regional Laboratory
Los Alamitos, California

Alan Hudson-Edwards
Department of Linguistics
University of New Mexico

Rodolfo Jacobson
Department of Bilingual-Bicultural Studies
University of Texas, San Antonio

José E. Limón
Department of Anthropology
University of Texas, Austin

John H. McDowell
Department of Folklore
Indiana University

Carol W. Pfaff
Department of Linguistics
Freie Universität Berlin
West Germany

Robert Phillips
Department of Spanish
Miami University

Shana Poplack
Department of Linguistics
University of Ottawa

Rogelio Reyes
Multicultural Program
School of Education
University of San Francisco

Rosaura Sánchez
Department of Literature
University of California, San Diego

Alexander Sapiens
School of Education
Stanford University

Carmen Silva-Corvalán
Department of Spanish
University of Southern California

Nicholas Sobin
Department of English
University of Arkansas, Little Rock

T. D. Terrell
Department of Spanish
University of California, Irvine

Guadalupe Valdés
Department of Foreign Languages
New Mexico State University

John T. Webb
Department of Spanish
University of Iowa

Ana Celia Zentella
Black and Puerto Rican Studies
Hunter College
City University of New York

Preface

The beginnings of this book lie in our involvement with the study and teaching of Spanish in the United States during the last several years. The investigation of Spanish in this country has a long tradition. Several studies are quite properly considered classics. In the last ten years at least two anthologies of articles concerning Spanish in the Southwest have appeared, one containing a mixture of older, classic articles and newer studies (Hernández-Chávez, Cohen, and Beltramo 1975) and the other containing only newer articles (Bowen and Ornstein 1976). In addition, over the last ten years interest in Spanish has burgeoned in other sections of the United States, often stemming from dialects other than Mexican, principally Cuban and Puerto Rican. This exploding interest in Spanish here and in other countries has been manifested in journal articles, annual symposia, and one recent conference on Spanish outside the Southwest. We have compiled this volume in the belief that it was time for a volume dedicated to the full range of Spanish dialects in this country and to the spectrum of analytical methods now in use. Some of the articles have been previously published; others are new. Some are by established scholars; others are by relative newcomers to the field who, we believe, will continue to make significant contributions to the study of Spanish in this nation.

We take this opportunity to thank all those who have assisted us in the preparation of this volume. First, we thank Beverly Smith and Joanne Ainsworth, whose encouragement and editorial advice contributed immensely to the volume. We thank the Department of Linguistics and the College of Liberal Arts of the University of Texas at El Paso, and the Department of Spanish, Italian and Portuguese and the Graduate College of the University of Illinois, Chicago Circle, for support and assistance in the preparation of the manuscript.

Finally, we thank the contributors and speakers of Spanish in this country, whose volume this really is.

JON AMASTAE
LUCÍA ELÍAS-OLIVARES

References

Bowen, J. Donald, and Jacob Ornstein, eds. 1976. *Studies in Southwest Spanish.* Rowley, Mass.: Newbury House.

Hernández-Chávez, Eduardo, Andrew D. Cohen, and Anthony F. Beltramo, eds. 1975. *El lenguaje de los Chicanos.* Arlington, Va.: Center for Applied Linguistics.

Introduction

Spanish has been spoken in what is now the United States longer than English has. Spanish settlements in Florida and the Southwest antedate English-speaking settlements in New England by several years. After as many as fifty years of preliminary exploration, San Agustín, in Florida, was settled in 1565; various areas of New Mexico were settled in 1598. Spanish settlements of California were established somewhat later, from 1769 on.

The linguistic study of Spanish in the southwestern United States has a long tradition. It dates back to the pioneering work of Aurelio Espinosa in 1909, which gave not only a basic linguistic description of New Mexican Spanish but also noted many of the phenomena of language mixing that have been studied intensively in recent years. These included borrowing, loan shifts and translations, and code-switching. In many ways this work is the touchstone for current generations of scholars seeking information on southwestern Spanish as well as for those who study Spanish dialectology in general. The tradition has continued, with Espinosa himself writing through the decade of the thirties, and with others such as Bowen and Ornstein in the fifties.

Ornstein (1951) continued the tradition of Espinosa in analyzing features of New Mexican Spanish that can be ascribed to earlier forms, now archaic in standard Spanish, and elements that are new developments arising from internal mechanisms as well as from contact with English. Bowen's (1952) classic study of the Spanish of a small village in north-central New Mexico stands unmatched today as a complete structural analysis of the dialect of one group of speakers. These trends had already been established for Arizona Spanish by Post (1933) and Barker (1947, 1950), who began including significant social factors in his analyses. Barker's work is particularly important for the explicit recognition not only that Spanish itself plays an important social function vis-à-vis English but that within a community it is not homogeneous but heterogeneous and different varieties perform different social functions. Texas Spanish is analyzed by Sawyer (1958) and Lance (1969), the latter concentrating on the systematicity of the language-switching behavior of bilingual speakers.

But Spanish is not now spoken only in the Southwest. In recent years there has been great immigration of Spanish speakers to Florida, New York, Philadelphia, Chicago, and other midwestern cities and to the Pacific Northwest states of Oregon and Washington. Many of these Spanish speakers are Puerto Ricans and Cubans, though many are from other Spanish-speaking countries (the Dominican Republic, Colombia, Venezuela, to name just a few). And of course the Spanish-speaking population of the Southwest has continued to grow through both internal generation and through continued migration, primarily from Mexico.

With the increase in Spanish speakers has come fresh interest in several aspects of linguistic investigation. As Espinosa had begun basic investigation of New Mexican Spanish, so Navarro-Tomás (1948) and López Morales (see López Morales 1968 for references) had examined Puerto Rican and Cuban Spanish. But the more recent increase in numbers of speakers in the continental United States has prompted new interest in their total linguistic situation. In many respects this new interest has reflected developments in the field of linguistics generally, and studies of Spanish in the United States are in the forefront of linguistic investigation.

The significant linguistic activities of the decades of the 1960s and 1970s were the continued development of a linguistic theory first proposed by Noam Chomsky some years earlier and the development of a new subfield, sociolinguistics. The two have occasionally seemed at odds, but each has enriched the other. It is now generally accepted that variation must be incorporated into linguistic theory, just as it is accepted that sociolinguistics is not merely the collecting and cataloging of data.

Sociolinguistics may be very broadly characterized as the study of the language of real speakers in social context. Several trends of sociolinguistic analysis are now evident. One is the study of linguistic variation either within or across social groups, usually with quantitative methods. This trend is associated primarily with the work of Labov (1966). The objective of such investigation often is to discover the mechanisms of and constraints on linguistic variation. These principles of linguistic variation may be either social or linguistic or both. A second broad current is associated primarily with Mackey (1962) and Fishman (1965), who have studied the social functions and interrelationships of language, primarily in bilingual settings. A third general tendency is more anthropological and ethnographic in nature. It developed in investigations of language and culture, texts, myths, and rituals in "exotic" cultures, where different patterns of language use stand out more clearly. This trend is now often labeled the ethnography of communication or the ethnography of speaking (Hymes 1964). The focus of such analysis is the act, or performance, of the speech event and the assumption that speech communities, though heterogeneous, share norms of conduct, or rules, for appropriate speech behavior.

Though much of sociolinguistics has developed in the investigation of black English (Labov 1972) or of the bilingualism of Quebec (Mackey 1962) or of the "exotic" cultures of the Western Apache (Basso 1970) and the Subanum of the Philippines (Frake 1964), a crucible of current work is Spanish in the United States. Investigators are now examining all of the major dialects, in urban and rural environments, among immigrants and natives, from all the points of view just mentioned. The field is extremely rich. It provides a testing ground for theories and methods, and it is the seedbed for new ones.

In compiling this collection, therefore, we have had three broad aims. One was to show the range of Spanish in the United States, which, though originally associated with the Southwest, is now beyond the limits of that area. Significant numbers of Spanish speakers of Mexican background have arrived in the cities of the Midwest. Some of these have followed the trail of migrant agricultural work, which begins in South Texas. Other Mexicans have emigrated to the industrial cities of the upper Midwest directly from Mexico. Still others reside in Oregon and Washington, permanently or temporarily as agricultural workers. Recent years have brought heavy migration of Spanish speakers from a number of Latin American countries. The best-known groups are, of course, Puerto Ricans and Cubans, who are mainly associated with New York and Miami respectively, but large numbers of Spanish-speaking people, especially from Central American countries, can be found in almost every urban center of the United States.

A second aim was to include both established and younger scholars. The work of several of our contributors has received exposure at national and international levels; the work of others has yet to do so. All the contributors will continue, we believe, to make important contributions to the study of Spanish and to the field of linguistics.

A third objective was to illustrate the principal trends and methods in sociolinguistic investigation. Included are quantificational studies of language variation, with focus on the social correlates of and the linguistic constraints on the variation, studies of the social functions of English and Spanish and of specific varieties of Spanish, and an examination in broad terms of the contact of Spanish and English.

Part I, "Varieties and variations of Spanish in the United States," deals with specific aspects of Mexican-American, Cuban, or Puerto Rican Spanish. Part II, "Aspects of language contact and language change," recognizes the fact that Spanish in the United States is a language in intimate contact with another language, and its focus is therefore the effects of this contact. Part III, "Ethnographic aspects of language use in bilingual communities," represents another approach to sociolinguistics, known as the ethnography of communication, which deals with functional aspects of language considered in the overall social situation. In all three parts there is a variety of approaches and authors.

The future will undoubtedly bring increased activity in the investigation of Spanish all over the world. Much basic descriptive work is yet to be done. Whereas a majority of the theoretical linguists of the sixties and seventies concentrated their efforts on English, other languages are now receiving their proper attention. A great deal of sociolinguistic work also remains to be done in Spanish-speaking communities everywhere. The Spanish spoken in Oregon and Washington, for example, is as yet poorly described. The contact of dialects in cities such as Chicago (Mexican, Cuban, Puerto Rican) has yet to be examined. Much remains to be learned about ethnographic aspects of language use in most Spanish-speaking communities. And despite the virtual explosion of work on code-switching, our ignorance of the possibilities of and constraints on this type of language variation is vast. The insights to be gained from such studies will not only increase our knowledge about Spanish but also about language in general in all its aspects: formal structure, variations, social functions, and changes.

References

Barker, George. 1947. Social functions of language in a Mexican-American community. Ph.D. dissertation, University of Chicago.

1950. *Pachuco: an American Spanish argot and its social function in Tucson, Arizona*. Social Science Bulletin No. 18. Tucson: University of Arizona.

Basso, Keith. 1970. To give up on words: silence in Western Apache culture. *Southwestern Journal of Anthropology* 26:213–30.

Bowen, J. Donald. 1952. The Spanish of San Antonito, New Mexico. Ph.D. dissertation, University of New Mexico.

Espinosa, Aurelio. 1909. Studies in New Mexican Spanish. *Bulletin Language Series of the University of New Mexico* 1, no. 2:48–162.

Fishman, Joshua. 1965. Who speaks what language to whom and when? *Linguistique* II:67–88.

Frake, Charles O. 1964. How to ask for a drink in Subanum. *American Anthropologist* 66, no. 6:127–32.

Hymes, Dell. 1964. Introduction: toward ethnographies of communication. *American Anthropologist* 66, no. 6:I–34.

Labov, William. 1966. *The social stratification of English in New York City*. Arlington, Va.: Center for Applied Linguistics.

1972. *Language in the inner city*. Philadelphia: University of Pennsylvania Press.

Lance, Donald. 1969. A brief study of Spanish-English bilingualism: final report. Research Project ORR-Liberal Arts 15504. College Station: Texas A & M University.

López Morales, Humberto. 1968. El español de Cuba: situación bibliográfica. *Revista de Filología Española* 51:111–37.

Mackey, William F. 1962. The description of bilingualism. *Canadian Journal of Linguistics* 7:51–85.

Navarro-Tomás, Tomás. 1948. *El español en Puerto Rico*. Río Piedras: Editorial Universitaria.

Ornstein, Jacob. 1951. The archaic and the modern in the Spanish of New Mexico. *Hispania* 34:137–42.

Post, Anita C. 1933. Some aspects of Arizona Spanish. *Hispania* 16:35–42.

Sawyer, Janet. 1958. A dialect study of San Antonio, Texas: a bilingual community. Ph.D. dissertation, University of Texas, Austin.

Part I

Varieties and variations of Spanish in the United States

The Spanish spoken in the United States comprises many social varieties, some of which have developed as a result of contact with English. The chapter by Sánchez sets up the picture of heterogeneity and complex sociolinguistic situations that will be addressed by the contributions to this volume through different methodologies and theoretical frameworks.

Sánchez presents a comprehensive range of varieties available to Chicano speakers in the Southwest but limits her description to the various phonological and syntactical changes characteristic of the variety that she calls popular Spanish. Her chapter also deals with some of the socioeconomic factors that operate in the development and maintenance of the linguistic situation, such as housing and labor segregation patterns, the constant migration from Mexico, and patterns of education. All these factors have contributed to an asymmetrical pattern of bilingualism in which the varieties of Spanish have lost some of their functions to English in many communities.

A review of some of the most important speech-based projects dealing with phonological aspects of the speech of Cubans and Puerto Ricans is provided by the chapter contributed by Terrell. Most of these projects, including Terrell's own work on Caribbean Spanish, have been influenced by Labov's variable rule model (Labov 1972). After outlining the problem areas that have been studied, Terrell describes the phenomena and attempts to determine how the variables affect other parts of the grammar. He shows how quantitative models have enhanced phonological studies of Spanish in the United States by their helpfulness in demonstrating the extreme variability of the collected data, and he explains the role of extralinguistic factors in accounting for and measuring the extent of that variability.

The influence of English on the Spanish spoken by Hispanics in the United States, especially those who are bilingual, is the most important factor that differentiates U.S. Spanish from that spoken in monolingual Spanish-speaking countries. Though this influence is particularly felt in the lexicon, it appears in other portions of the grammar as well. Phillips examines in his chapter the variation of /b/ in the East Los Angeles area and finds out that a clear-cut complementary distribution of standard descriptions of Spanish is not found in that community, where a voiced labiodental fricative [v] can be found together with the voiced bilabial fricative [b] and the voiced bilabial stop [b]. He attributes [v] in this area to English influence, and argues that [v] is more common among younger Chicano speakers and those who tend to speak English more than Spanish.

As Terrell's chapter indicates, most of the studies dealing with variation in Spanish have dealt with phonology. Only recently have researchers begun to identify variation in syntactic and semantic levels. Syntactic variation in Mexican-American Spanish is the focus of the chapters that follow, by García and Silva-Corvalán.

The chapter by García is an empirical investigation of the locative prepositional phrase in verb phrases of motion. She analyzes data collected from Mexican and Mexican-American speakers in the El Paso–Juárez area of the Texas–Mexico border to illustrate lexical and syntactical variation that suggest that the locative prepositional system of this linguistic variety is undergoing a process of change.

An important point made in García's chapter, which was often overlooked in previous dialectological studies dealing with U.S. Spanish, is that the El Paso speakers model their Spanish usage on the speech of the Juárez working-class speakers. This, and their limited access to standard written Spanish, determines the difference in the variety of Spanish used by them from standard Spanish linguistic norms.

Another case of syntactic variation is examined by Silva-Corvalán, who discusses the factors that determine the expression or nonexpression of the subject in Spanish and the position of the subject with respect to the verb, when it is expressed. Her data are discussed in their discourse context, with the goal of identifying those pragmatic factors that produce the occurrence of the variables.

The last chapter in this section concerns caló, one of the intragroup varieties of Spanish used by Mexican-Americans, especially in the Southwest, and characterized by its lexical innovations. Webb points out some of its many social functions and discusses some of the attitudes and beliefs of caló speakers, as well as some of the grammatical processes of this variety.

Reference

Labov, William. 1972. *Sociolinguistic patterns*. Philadelphia: University of Pennsylvania Press.

1

Our linguistic and social context

ROSAURA SÁNCHEZ

Both material and social conditions determine whether the languages of national and lingual minorities throughout the world thrive, struggle to survive, or cease to exist. Where society is stratified, the social and economic level that the lingual minority occupies will determine the status of the minority language, the extent of its social functions, and the type of social and linguistic interaction between majority and minority language groups. Changes in material and social conditions necessarily produce changes in language and in the status of languages, ensuring their maintenance or loss.

In the Southwest of the United States, the social and linguistic situation of the population of Mexican origin (Chicanos) is intrinsically connected to employment, immigration, and education, factors that have undergone change since 1848, when the Southwest was wrested from Mexico. These have greatly influenced where Chicanos live, how much contact they have with Spanish and English speakers, and thus the degree of preservation of Spanish language varieties and linguistic assimilation.

Chicanos in the Southwest are a national and lingual minority largely of working-class status in contact with a majority English-speaking population that also constitutes the dominant class. Invariably socioeconomic status plays a significant role in determining linguistic and cultural assimilation because material factors combine to produce particular patterns of social relations and attitudes toward a given language. Given the particular population configurations in the Southwest, this process of acculturation and linguistic assimilation is ongoing and incomplete. Thus, at present, the Chicano community includes three different groups: Spanish monolinguals, English monolinguals, and bilingual persons. The bilingual group is the most widespread and the most complex because individuals exhibit various levels of language proficiency in the two languages and various patterns of language choice according to function and domain, as we shall see later. Before exploring the particular Spanish varieties of this population, I will analyze briefly the various factors that create and maintain the present language situation.

According to various statistics, more than 15 million persons in the

United States are of Mexican origin and about 80 percent of these reside in urban areas. In the last forty years this population has been characterized by geographic and occupational mobility, which has taken it out of largely agricultural work into the factory and into service industries. This occupational mobility, however, has not been accompanied by great strides in social mobility, and Chicanos continue to be a low-income population. According to the Bureau of the Census, about 25 percent of all families of Mexican origin have an income below the poverty level. This economic situation is the result of labor segmentation within a capitalist system that has produced a dual labor market: a primary sector with workers who are highly paid and enjoy a certain stability, and a secondary sector characterized by low wages and unstable employment. Workers within the secondary labor market are primarily members of minority groups and women. This dichotomy in the labor market is the most important factor in determining the type of social and linguistic contact between communities because it is the labor process that determines relations of production (i.e., those arising between the owner of the means of production and the workers) and thereby, social relations between groups, classes, and individuals. Thus low-income jobs lead to the concentration of the minority population in ghettos and barrios, where housing is cheap and where one can rely on friends and relatives for assistance during moments of crisis. Those who can earn more money achieve a certain social mobility, moving out of the barrio into higher income bracket English-dominant communities. The concentration of the Spanish-speaking population in certain residential areas is thus a result of poverty and racial discrimination and is largely responsible for the maintenance of Spanish.

The same urbanization and industrialization that have led to segregation and labor segmentation have also produced geographical mobility. Thousands of Chicanos have migrated from towns and rural areas characterized by strong interethnic and family ties to large, sprawling suburbs interspersed with freeways, industry, junkyards, warehouses, and dumps where these bonds are dissolved and where there is often little contact between neighbors. Thus we have a concentrated minority that is segregated from the majority community and within which are conditions that alienate community and family members from each other. This situation both unites and separates the Chicano community. Occupational mobility has also created diversity in the patterns of social relations by bringing highly segregated agricultural workers into a secondary labor market, which usually includes workers from various minority groups. Thus workers in small industries, restaurants, hospitals, maintenance, and other support services are likely to be primarily Chicano and black but may include Asian groups as well. The presence of other minority groups, as well as low-income whites, in these employment categories introduces the Spanish-speaking worker into an English-dominant domain, although some interworker relations may call for Spanish.

Another highly significant factor that influences the linguistic context is the continual flow of workers from Mexico into the United States, which is both documented and undocumented. These workers constitute not only a reserve labor pool but a reserve language pool as well, allowing a constant infusion of Mexican varieties of Spanish into the Southwest. Because both incoming Mexican workers and second-, third-, or fourth-generation Chicanos often reside in the same low-income areas, contact between the two groups has been continuous. Those who have been able to leave the barrio for higher-income areas have little or no contact with these recently arrived Mexicans, nor with other Chicanos, and consequently little contact with the Spanish language. The obvious exception here, of course, are the high-income Mexicans who migrate to the United States, reside in particular high-income areas, like Coronado or La Jolla in San Diego County, and relate socially to other Mexicans of the same income bracket.

The economic factor is thus highly significant as an impediment to the linguistic assimilation of many Chicanos. In general one could say that first- and second-generation Chicanos are likely to make much greater use of Spanish and be Spanish-dominant or Spanish monolingual, whereas the later generations, third, fourth, and subsequent ones, are either English monolingual or English-dominant bilinguals. Yet, the generational factor is not as significant as the segregational factor for people who have stayed in the barrio in contact solely with Spanish-speaking persons. Some persons in Chicano barrios do not speak English at all and some are quite limited in English, although they have lived in this country for many years. It is, of course, possible to be a manual or unskilled laborer without being literate or having any proficiency in English. The presence of these Spanish monolinguals not only reflects the degree of segregation in the Southwest but evidences numerous functions that Spanish continues to have in areas where English is not indispensable.

Education has also contributed to a changing language situation, because instruction in English has facilitated the overlapping of language functions and seriously undermined the use of Spanish as the home language. As educational attainment has increased, formal and informal contact with English has also increased as new roles and situations have opened up for the population. Bilingual education in the public schools, especially of Spanish-language students, could still have a strong impact on the maintenance of Spanish, but unfortunately these bilingual programs have been primarily transitional ones, in which the objective is the rapid acquisition of English in order to place the minority-language students in classes where English is the sole means of instruction.

Occupation, salary, education, and years of residence are all interconnected factors affecting the language choices of Chicanos. Their status in society as primarily low-income working-class persons explains the low status of Spanish in the United States, despite the presence of some middle-class Chicanos in professional, technical, and primary industry categories. Lack of socioeconomic success can lead to disparagement of oneself, one's group, and one's language. It is not surprising, then, that education and the acquisition of English are seen to be the principal vehicles for social mobility and assimilation. For this reason, many parents consciously decide to stop speaking Spanish in the home so that their failure in school will not be repeated by their children. Where change of language in the home is not a conscious decision, the children themselves learn to associate Spanish with conditions of poverty and to resist its use. Language choice is thus both conscious and subconscious, as is evident in many Chicano homes where parents address their children in Spanish and they respond in English.

All of these conditions have produced various types of bilingualism. Using the classification outlined by Glyn Lewis (1972), we can distinguish four types of bilingualism in the Southwest: stable, dynamic, transitional, and vestigial. Stable bilingualism is found at the Mexican border, where Spanish maintains all its functions on the Mexican side, as English does on the U.S. side despite the presence of certain domains, like the commercial areas, where both languages may be used.

In dynamic bilingualism, one of the languages threatens to displace the other as differentiation of social roles and overlapping of language functions occur. This bilingualism, which arises in times of great mobility and instability, when everything is in the process of change, is widespread in Chicano communities and is renewed by each incoming generation of immigrants. Transitional bilingualism, on the other hand, is a more advanced stage, in which one language completely appropriates some of the functions of the other, displacing it little by little until finally only the dominant language remains and only vestiges are left of the other, as evidenced in some expressions or terms reminiscent of another time and culture.

The linguistic context is thus heterogeneous and contradictory, because while Spanish is being displaced in many homes it continues to be maintained as the informal language of home, friendship, and intimacy in many communities. The presence today of an increasingly larger Spanish-speaking community has allowed Spanish to be the second language of several domains in the Southwest. Although it is never the principal language, it sometimes functions as an alternative or secondary code, as evidenced by Spanish versions of billboards, traffic signals, announcements on TV and radio, government and health brochures, rulings, warnings, and school textbooks as well as by bilingual telephone operator services, bilingual salesclerks, and bilingual translators in government and the courts. Ironically, while gaining a certain visibility at the public level,

Spanish has suffered losses of important functions in various spheres. For many Chicanos today, English is the language of the home, the choice for all domains and functions, spoken even in intimacy.

Attitudes of Chicanos toward the Spanish language reflect the full gamut of possibilities, from rejection of the language and the subordinate status that it represents, to defense of it as a symbol of cultural resistance. Maintenance of Spanish is thus considered a bond uniting working-class Spanish speakers in U.S. communities to workers in Latin America. For some middle-class Chicanos and Latinos the maintenance of Spanish means greater opportunities in employment and within the existing political system. Whether it serves as a symbol of resistance or acquiescence to the system, the Spanish language will continue to survive as a living language in the Southwest as long as the material conditions of stratification persist.

Spanish of the Southwest

The Spanish spoken in the Southwest includes a number of varieties reflecting the national origin, as well as its rural or urban nature, the social class, and the education of immigrants from Mexico and Central and South America. This study will deal only with the Spanish varieties of the population of Mexican origin.

Because Mexican immigration, since 1848 but especially since the early part of the twentieth century, originates in various parts of Mexico (despite certain patterns of immigration from certain Mexican regions to particular southwestern states), it is difficult to propose a classification in terms of regional dialects, although studies of dialect have been attempted under the assumption that some variants are peculiar to one state when in fact they are widespread throughout the Southwest. I propose here a study of several sociolinguistic varieties that can be further subdivided by degree of standardization and by rural or urban origin. The linguistic phenomena that characterize these popular Southwest varieties are not exclusive to the Spanish of Chicanos; they can be found in popular varieties throughout the Spanish-speaking world, especially in the popular Spanish of Mexico, the source of our own varieties. Only the *extent* of the borrowing phenomenon can be said to be a distinctive feature of Chicano Spanish. Linguistic borrowing is, of course, widespread whenever two languages are in contact and especially where one is subordinate to the influence of the other. As a consequence of the political and economic influence of English-speaking countries, the English language is a source of loans for many languages including Latin American and peninsular Spanish. Quantitatively, however, the degree of absorption of these loans is greater in Chicano Spanish because of the daily and close contact with the English language.

In a descriptive study, like this one, the function of particular variants within particular contexts is not specified. An analysis of the variables that trigger particular shifts, be they speech acts, turn taking, the presence of particular addressees, or the transmission of particular messages, is also absent. Neither is the aim of this study to propose rules of variability postulating that particular social and linguistic factors trigger certain phonological, morphological, syntactic, and lexical rules. I offer here an inventory of linguistic features that characterize the Spanish of Chicanos, not only in Texas and California but also in the rest of the Southwest. Not all of these features appear in the Spanish varieties of all speakers, but a continuum will be presented that includes numerous variants typical of both rural and urban Spanish varieties in California, Arizona, New Mexico, and Texas. A Chicano Spanish speaker can fall at one or more points along this continuum. Despite urbanization, rural varieties are a major consideration in this study, for most Chicanos have rural roots, whether in the United States or Mexico.

Spanish varieties of the Southwest include both standard and popular codes. Within standard varieties, we can distinguish between formal and informal styles, marked by differences in phonetic and lexical rules. Consider the following examples of both styles:

Formal style:	*Informal style:*
¿Fuiste al cine?	'Tonces 'stábamos hablando inglés.
Ojalá que vayamos.	'Stá bueno.
Lo empujaron.	'Horita no me acuerdo. Lue'o te digo.
Ahora no me acuerdo.	

These standard varieties are the codes used in formal domains, particularly in radio broadcasting, whether in Mexican border stations transmitting to the Southwest or in Spanish-language stations of the Southwest. These standard varieties are generally part of the repertoire of urban Mexican immigrants who have had some schooling in Spanish. Thus education and literacy in Spanish are significant factors determining literacy in Spanish and the acquisition of standard varieties of Spanish. Proficiency in Spanish, however, is primarily oral in the Southwest, especially among second and subsequent generations, because bilingual education is a new component of public schooling and limited generally to non-English-speaking students. Most Chicanos have received no instruction in Spanish.

The rural roots of the Chicano population and the presence of numerous newly arrived immigrants from rural areas in Mexico have served to give the oral Spanish of Chicanos a definitely rural flavor. Differences between rural and urban varieties can also be expressed in terms of rule differences affecting the phonology, morphology, and syntax. Some rules are characteristic of both urban and rural varieties. Particular combinations of these rules can be said to characterize the language of different speakers in the community. As we shall see in the following examples, sex, age, and style are important factors distinguishing between the *vato loco* (the cool dude), the *comadres* (the barrio housewives), the *jovencita* (the young teenage girl) and the Chicano university student.

A *vato loco*:[1]

> Guacha, ¿por qué no me alivianas con un aventón y me dejas en el chante? Y mientras que vas por el Chente, yo tiro clavao, me rastío la greña y me entacucho. Te trais al Chente a mi cantón y le digo a la jefa que nos aliviane con un calmante porque a mí ya me trai la jaspia, y quiero refinar. Le dices al Chente que 'stoy invitao a un borlo y pa' que se desagüite el vato le digo a mi güisa que le consiga una jainita para irnos a borlotear todos. ¿Cómo la ves?

Some *comadres*:

- Fíjate que anoche llegó Juan echándole trancazos a la Filomena. Hizo una rejolina que ¡Válgame Dios! Y pa cabarla de amolar pos no se le antojó a Pedro irse a meter al borlote quesque pa pararle el alta al Juan. A ése ni quién lo paciqüe pero Pedro es mu cabezudo.
- ¿Y a poco se le rajuelió todo?
- Ande, si ni chanza tuvo, porque lo-lo vino la chota y cargó con toos. Diay la Filomena se dejó venir.
- ¿A poco quería que se lo juera a sacar?
- Pos sí. Y como le dije yo, comadre: "No me vengas con lloriqueos. Amárrate las naguas como las meras mujeres y déjalo que se pudra nel bote." No sé pa qué le habló a la ley. Ya no más por no andar dejando.

A *jovencita*:

> *Hey, Mary,* ¿por qué no vienes pa mi casa? Tengo un magazine nuevo *that I got this morning* nel *drugstore*. Tiene todas las *new songs,* muy suaves, de los . . . cómo se llaman . . . *You know* . . . los que cantan ésa que tocaron . . . ahi nel *jukebox when we were at the store*. No, hombre, *not that one, the other one,* la que le gustó *much* a Joe. *I like it too* porque tiene muy suave *rhythm* y las *words* también, muy suaves . . . *yeah . . . what? really????* . . . te llamó? *OOOOhhhhh, Mary*. Ese está de aquellotas.

A Chicano university student:

> Gente orita ya stá despertando y stá dijiendo pos que la única modo de ganarle al gabacho en el juego, este . . . es meternos haciendo cosas de nohotros como de la política y economía, metiéndonos, gente mexicana, que tiene el corazón mexicano, que quiere yudar la gente mexicana . . . Como orita van a tener gente correr en las elecciones de 72 en el estado de Texas. Toavía no han agarrao la persona. Yo creo que es una movida mal porque no tenemos la feria y las conexiones y todo eso. Tenemos que empezar en los pueblos chiquitos. Yo ha hablado con gente que sabe más que yo que cree lo mismo.

[1] Dialogue of Benito Villanueva as recorded by Olga Villanueva, San Diego.

These are all examples of the Spanish spoken in the Southwest. Although all reflect popular varieties, it is evident that standard forms predominate in the oral production. Thus it is the presence of certain morphological and lexical *markers* that characterize popular varieties and that distinguish them from standard varieties. These popular varieties could be classified in terms of place of origin (rural or urban) and in terms of particular subcodes as follows:

Urban:

General:

¿Fuistes al cine?
Cuando vuélvamos, le digo.
¡Qué bueno que haiga venido!
No sabe espelear.
Me llamó pa tras.
Pagaron los biles.

Caló:

Le talonié pal chante.
Aliviáname un frajo.

Code-shifting:

Allí esta más barato *because the one* que me trajo Maggie costaba nomás *one-ninety-eight.*
Y está muy loco el tripe ese porque *mine is a* cábula, *you know*, and liberación también es cábula *and is really a beautiful trip and . . .*

Rural:

General:

Y tamién me gustaba en la noche porque nos juntábanos, un grupo nos juntábanos y nos sentábanos debajo de ese árbol.
¿Qué hicites ayer? ¿Adónde fuites?
Vivemos por la Hill. ¿On tá? Pos tá allí por la ochenta y siete.
Lo vide ayer y me dijo que asina nomás era pero como nomás no trabaja, pos por eso se lo truje a usted pa que me lo arregle.

Each one of these examples contains different types of variants that I shall examine later. As previously indicated, the discourse of any one individual may include standard as well as popular forms. These shifts between varieties function like shifts between styles in many cases and may be grouped within particular repertoires. The findings indicate that although a particular speaker may shift between *está* or *tá*, according to the intimacy or informality of the situation with a given addressee or for a particular speech act or function, rarely do we find a speaker who shifts between *dicemos* and *decimos* according to these same contextual features. Except for cases where there is a conscious effort to make certain shifts as the result of instruction in the Spanish language, a speaker who uses *dicemos* rather than *decimos* will generally use the same form throughout his shifts from informal to formal styles. Lexical shifts are also common for all speakers, especially shifts from loanwords to common Spanish terms, as in shifts from *puchar* to *empujar,* where various factors trigger the change, but again one rarely finds cases, except for those of the conscious learner of new language varieties, where a speaker shifts from *asina* to *así,* that is, from a rural form to an urban form.

In the Spanish version of this article, I attempted to defend Chicano Spanish in view of attacks from various quarters about the inferior quality of its language varieties. Yet despite this defense, the article did not completely escape the tendency to follow certain syntactic notions of norm. Obviously the Bernsteinean notions (1968) of elaborated and restricted codes should have been completely rejected in that article. Popular varieties of language, as demonstrated by Labov (1972), are linguistically complex codes with great syntactic variety, broad vocabularies, and the capacity to serve as the means for transmitting abstract ideas as well as concrete information. Popular codes in the Southwest have numerous functions where they are used as the principal means of communication, such as the home, the neighborhood, centers of recreation, and the church. Because language is a social convention there are instances in which the social context does not require extensive verbal expansion of certain ideas. Once suggested, they are clear to the addressee. Thus it is often not necessary to verbalize certain explanations that are part of general knowledge. Often not more than two or three words are necessary for the meaning to be clear to a friend or family member. The same codes are shared, not only linguistic codes but social ones as well. The mode of explicit or implicit expression depends, of course, on the message to be transmitted and its specific context. All languages also have ready-made expressions of high frequency that can communicate as much as more complex structures, which may be considered unnecessary in informal contexts. In English, for example, there are numerous expressions containing the verb *get.* It is thus nothing strange that informal Spanish has a number of similar expressions containing the verb *agarrar.* These expressions, common in many Spanish-speaking nations and thus not unique to Southwest Spanish, are quite frequent in Chicano communities. Consider the following examples collected from taped interviews and personal observations:

1. Tienes que agarrar una tarjeta para registrarte. (conseguir)
2. Yo voy a agarrar tres cursos. (seguir)
3. Agarra al niño. (Tómalo en los brazos)
4. Agarra al niño. (Detenlo)
5. Voy a agarrar el libro. (tomar)
6. Voy a agarrar trabajo. (conseguir, obtener)
7. Ya lo agarraron. (arrestaron)
8. Es muy agarrado. (adj. derived from *agarrar* – tacaño)
9. Ahí no agarran chicanos. (emplean)
10. Me agarró bien fuerte. (abrazó)

11. No puedo agarrar la estación. (sintonizar la emisora)
12. Agarró la paseada. (se tiró al vicio)
13. Ya agarró juicio. (ya entró en razón)
14. Ya le voy agarrando. (entendiendo)
15. Quieres agarrar los derechos de un americano. (disfrutar)
16. Al rato lo agarra el Army. (recluta)
17. ¿No me quieres agarrar una orden? (comprar)
18. ¿No me quieres agarrar este taquito? (recibir, aceptar)
19. Voy a agarrar el bos. (tomar el bus)
20. Me agarró bien fuerte la calentura. (dio)

As these examples indicate, informal expressions are useful for many language functions within contexts in which Spanish is used. Unfortunately, some language functions require particular experiences that have been either totally inaccessible to persons of Mexican origin or accessible only in English. Without formal instruction in Spanish, it is then not surprising that Chicanos have not developed certain academic and technical language varieties in Spanish. The instructors in bilingual education programs often are native Spanish speakers who have not had the opportunity to develop the lexical repertoire necessary for teaching biology, math, history, or government nor the metalanguage necessary to explain certain cognitive concepts. Obviously these additional language skills can be easily acquired by native speakers if teachers are appropriately trained. Unfortunately the problem is even greater, for besides being deprived of the opportunity to develop these formal language skills in Spanish in the public schools, Chicanos are often also deprived of the opportunity to acquire them in English, as indicated by numerous studies of achievement levels in minority schools throughout the Southwest.

Most of the Spanish-language variants that will be described were derived from the language samples provided through taped interviews of seventeen Chicano students at the University of Texas at Austin. These students were originally from San Antonio, Laredo, Brownsville, Austin, Mason, Odessa, Lyford, Seguin, and San Angelo, Texas. Since then I have had ample contact with students in California, whose speech is also discussed here. Texas Chicanos are much more Spanish dominant, however, than those in California because of their greater concentration in the Texas valley and stronger patterns of segregation in housing and education throughout the state. The study, then, is based primarily on the taped interviews, on personal observations of Chicano university students in Texas, on written compositions by Chicano students in my classes, and on my own personal experience as speaker of Chicano Spanish.

Phonetic variants

The phonetic variants that I shall describe are common in the popular Spanish varieties of Chicanos but may be found throughout the rest of the Spanish-speaking world. Some changes, such as apheresis, laxing, and loss of voiced fricatives, are part of the informal style of all Spanish speakers, whether their main language codes are standard or popular.

Vowel changes

The popular Spanish varieties of the Southwest are characterized by vowels so lax, or nontense, that unaccented vowels are often lost. This vowel loss is especially common in initial position if the vowel is unstressed. In polysyllabic words, unstressed noninitial syllables before stressed syllables may be lost. Diphthongization of contiguous hiatus vowels also occurs unless the two syllables are maintained through the introduction of an intervocalic glide. Homologous vowels are generally reduced to one syllable.

Aphaeresis. The loss of an unaccented vowel in initial position often occurs in rapid and informal speech.

Loss of initial low vowel (*a*):

> yudar, cordar, rodillar, silenciar, paciguar, cabar, reglar, hogar, prender, horcar, hora, horita

Sometimes, however, the vowelless form becomes the accepted form. Consequently it is common to hear, even in careful speech, *Se hogó en el río* or *los hogados* in certain varieties of Chicano Spanish.

Other examples:

haber > ber   estar > tar   hacer > cer   había > bía
estoy > toy, stoy   enfermedad > fermedad   hubiera > biera
estuviera > tuviera

Synaeresis. Two syllables are often contracted into one, in this case through diphthongization.

ea > ia	pelear > peliar (desiar, mariar, voltiar, rial, tiatro, golpiar)
aí > ai	caído > caido (traido, ahi, maiz, raiz)
ae > ai	traer > trai (caer > cai, or, sometimes, a contraction: trer, quer)
	trae > trai (cae > cai)
oe > ue	cohete > cuete
oa > ua	toalla > tualla
eo > io	preocupa > priocupa (or sometimes, reduction: procupa)
	peor > pior

Substitution of simple vowel for diphthongs in stressed position.

ie > e	ciencia > cencia (setembre, pacencia, alenta, quero, sente, penso)
ue > o	pues > pos luego > lo'o > lo
	(mueblería > moblería)

ua > a	graduar > gradar
au > a	aunque > anque
ie > i	diez y ocho > diciocho, dicinueve, etc.
ei > e	treinta y cinco > trentaicinco (venticinco, etc.)

Change of high vowels to mid-vowels.

i > e	injusticia > enjusticia (estoria, polecía, decesiva, enmagino, dericion, defícil, ofecina, dejieron)
u > o	rumbo > rombo (complir, tovimos, joventud, imposieron, recoperó, sepoltura, secondaria, caloroso)

Vowels appearing before a nasal may become low mid-vowels:

invitando > anvitando   entonces > antonces   enveces > anveces

Change of unstressed mid-vowels to high vowels. In the speech of some New Mexicans and their descendants, final mid-front vowels become high as well.

e > i	entender > intender (disilucionó, manijar, siguridad, disconfiado, dishonesto, impidir, dicir, siguida)
	leche > lechi
o > u	morir > murir

Apocope. One or more sounds may be lost at the end of a word.

para > pa   clase > clas

Prothesis. A sound is often added to the beginning of a word, in this case a low mid-vowel.

tocar > atocar   yendo > ayendo   gastar > agastar

Contraction of homologous vowels.

ee > e   leer > ler   creer > crer

Syncope. A sound is often lost in the interior of a word, in this case, unstressed syllables before stressed syllables.

desaparecido > desparecido   desapareció > despareció
necesita > necita   desapego > despego   zanahoria > zanoria
alrededor > alredor

Epenthesis. A sound is inserted or developed; in this case, a glide is inserted in intervocalic position.

creo > creyo   veo > veyo   cree > creye   tío > tiyo
mío > miyo   leer > leyer   creer > creyer   oído > oyido
maestra > mayestra   quería ir > quería yir   oí > oyi
destruir > destruyir

For other cases of epenthesis, see the section on consonants.

Laxing of unstressed vowels:

schwa [ə]   pero > pərə   le > lə   me > mə

Metathesis. Two vowels are transposed.

iu > ui   ciudad > swiđađ > swiđá

Consonant changes

In general, consonants in popular Chicano Spanish also tend to be non-tense, with laxing of fricatives, especially voiced fricatives, the aspiration of sibilants and sometimes of the voiceless labiodental fricative *f*, and the simplification of consonant clusters. These consonantal changes are also common in the informal popular varieties of the rest of the Spanish-speaking world. Some are particularly prevalent in rural Spanish.

Aspiration of the sibilant -s- *in any position.* This occurs especially in rural Spanish varieties in north central Mexico and Texas.

nosotros > nohotros   puertas > puertah   decir > dihir
este > ehte   Sí, señor > hí, heñor

Aspiration of the voiceless labiodental fricative f.

fuimos > juimos   fue > jue   fuerte > juerte

Aspiration of what is now only an orthographic h *in urban Spanish.* This aspiration was common in sixteenth-century Spanish.

Se fue de hilo > Se fue de jilo.   Se huyó > Se juyó.
Se halló . . . > Se jalló . . .

Loss of voiced fricatives in intervocalic and final positions.

1. Intervocalic [ƀ], [đ], [ǥ]
   todavía > toavía, tuavía   todos > toos   estado > estáu
   lado > lau   luego > lue'o > lo'o > lo   agua > awa
   abuelo > awelo   iba > í:a
2. Intervocalic *-y-*
   ella > ea   ellos > eos   botella > botea   billetera > bietera
   orilla > oría   cabello > cabeo, etc.
3. In final position
   vecindad > vecindá   usted > usté   muy > mu

Interchangeable "grave" voiced fricatives [ƀ] *and* [ǥ].

aguja ~ abuja   boato ~ guato   abuelo ~ agüelo

Simplification of consonant clusters.

ct > t   doctor > dotor
nd > d   andábamos > ađá:mos
mb > m   también > tamién
rr > r   barrio > bario   correr > corer

arrancar > arancar   cierra > ciera
arriba > ariba   agarrar > garar
rl > l   tenerla > tenela   pensarlo > pensalo
rn > n, l   pararnos > paranos,
paralos

Metathesis.

pared > pader   problema > porblema, pobrema
impresiones > impersiones   lengua > luenga
magullado > mallugado   estómago > estóngamo, estógamo

Epenthetic consonants.

lamer > lamber   estornudar > destornudar   querrá > quedrá
podemos > podermos   mucho > muncho
nadie > nadien, naiden   aire > aigre   adrede > aldrede
huelo > güelo

Lateralization.

d > l   de > le   advierto > alvierto   desde > desle
n > l   nos > los   nosotros > losotros   nomás > lomás

Use of "archaic" terms, common in rural Spanish. For example:

semos, asina, ansina, truje, vide, naiden, haiga, endenantes

Stress changes.

mendigo > méndigo (change in stress paralleled by change in meaning)
seamos > séanos, séamos (affects all first person plural, present subjunctive verbs)

Alveo-palatal fricative instead of the affricate. It is common in West Texas, southern New Mexico, Tijuana, and the southern part of California to hear *sh* instead of *ch* in words like *muchacho* (*mushasho*) and *cuchara* (*cushara*). This fricative variant has also been documented in Cuba, Paraguay, and other parts of Latin America.

noche > noshe   choque > shoque   leche > leshe

English interference. There are cases of English interference in the speech of some Chicanos, although generally only in that of nonnative speakers of Spanish. The use of retroflex *r* is one example in the speech of English-dominant Chicanos.

Rule differences between varieties may involve the sound system as well as the morphosyntactic component or the lexicon. Some of the differences involve rule simplification, as we shall see in relation to the verb system.

Verb tenses of indicative mood

Southwest Spanish has maintained the same orientation of tense that we find in standard Spanish, as described by Bull (1965). Verb tenses reflect the focus (simultaneous, anterior, or subsequent) from a particular time axis, whether explicitly or implicitly stated. This verbal tense system continues to function in Southwest Spanish, but the morphology and the tenses associated with particular time orientations have varied. To see the differences we must look at the systemic uses of verb tenses in standard Spanish in terms of two time axes: present and past.

The future tense is seldom used in a systemic way. Generally, to indicate a subsequent action, speakers use the present tense or the periphrastic form with the verb *ir* plus infinitive.

> Saldré mañana = Voy a salir mañana
> Salgo mañana

The future case is retained for nonsystemic cases, as in cases of probability:

> *Será tu papá* (or, *Ha de ser tu papá*) 'It's probably your father'
> *No sé que quedrá* (*querrá*) 'I don't know what he wants (might want)'

The future perfect tense is almost never used. To indicate a distant future point before another moment, the simple future tense plus an adverb are used:

> Para diciembre habrá llegado = Va a llegar pa diciembre

Two tenses are oriented toward the present (present and present perfect), and five tenses are oriented toward the past.

Present tense

The orientation is the same in the Spanish of Chicanos, but there is a tendency to add duration to the tense when the action is in progress, as in the following example:

> *Sí, sí te oigo* = *Sí, sí te estoy oyendo* 'I'm listening'

Present perfect tense

As in other Spanish varieties, the use of the preterit verb plus adverb is more common here than the present perfect tense: *Se ha ido* or *Ya se fue*. Other changes here are morphological in nature and affect the auxiliary verb (*he* > *ha*, etc.) or the past participle (*roto* > *rompido*, etc.).

The following are examples of verb tenses oriented toward the past:

Simultaneous to the past		
Perfect aspect	Preterit tense	comí
Imperfect aspect	Imperfect tense	comía
Anterior to the past	Past perfect tense	había comido
Subsequent to the past	Conditional tense	comería
Subsequent to the past but anterior to a subsequent point	Conditional perfect tense	habría comido

Table 1. *Indicative verb tenses*

	Anterior	Simultaneous	Subsequent
Axis in the present	Present perfect	Present	Present
Axis in the past	Past perfect	Imperfect and preterit	Imperfect

Preterit and imperfect tenses
These two tenses, as in the standard Spanish verb system, indicate actions simultaneous to the past axis. The only changes here are morphological, as we shall see later. There is also a tendency to add duration to the imperfect tense:

Comía cuando entró = Estaba comiendo cuando entró.

Past perfect tense
This tense has the same function as in the standard variety. The only changes, again, are morphological. In some cases the auxiliary is changed from *haber* to *ir*, as in *iba comido* for *había comido*. Is it really from the verb *ir* or is it a case of metathesis: *había* > *bía* >*iba*? Perhaps it is a case of confusion between two forms that suffer laxing of fricatives: *había* > *bía* > *ía*; *iba* > *ía*. Or perhaps it is a case of an *-er* verb conjugated as an *-ar* verb: *habiba* (as in *teniba, sentiba*) > *iba*.

Conditional tense
This tense is also rare except in nonsystemic cases indicating probability in the past: *¿Quién sería?*

In place of the conditional we have the imperfect indicative tense and the imperfect subjunctive tense. The question *¿Qué haría Ud. si tuviera mil dólares?* is often answered with either *Yo iba a México* or *Yo fuera a México*. Thus the function of the conditional tense is maintained, but the form having this function is different.

Conditional perfect tense
As in the conditional tense, a substitution is often made, here by use of the past perfect indicative or past perfect subjunctive tenses. For example, the question *¿Qué habría hecho Ud. si hubiera recibido mil dólares?* is often answered with (1) *Yo fuera comprado un carro*, (2) *Yo (hu)biera comprado un carro*, or (3) *Yo (ha)bía comprado un carro*.

Thus, tenses oriented toward the past are often simplified to the preterit, imperfect, and past perfect tenses. The imperfect tenses also function to indicate a point subsequent to the past. The orientations, therefore, seem to be reduced to two, those indicating an action before some given point and those indicating actions both simultaneous and subsequent to a particular moment. (See Table 1.)

Verb tenses of the subjunctive mood

The subjunctive mood includes four tenses in modern Spanish (present, present perfect, imperfect, and past perfect) that appear in subordinate clauses (noun, adjective, and adverbial). In noun clauses, the subjunctive appears after verbs of influence, verbs of doubt or negation, and verbs expressing an emotional view (*Es ridículo que salga*). In the popular Southwest varieties, uses of the subjunctive follow these general rules except after verbs of doubt, where sometimes it does not appear. On occasion, the use is extended to other verbs: *No sé si venga*. I shall now consider some examples where the subjunctive does not appear.

Indicative tense after expressions of doubt or negation:

> No creo que tiene muchas ganas.
> No creo que es necesario.
> No creo que hay sólo una manera de hablar el español.
> No hay nada que puede hacer.
> No hay nada que yo puedo hacer bien.
> No hay seguridad que hallas trabajo.

In some cases there is never a vacillation between the indicative and the subjunctive, as in expressions like *ójala* (*ojalá*) and *ójali* (*ojalá y*):

> Ójala y venga.
> Ójala que ténganos tiempo.
> El espera que nos pórtenos bien.
> El sueño de mi hermana es que algún día júntenos un poco de dinero.

In clauses introduced by verbs of influence there is no uniformity of use:

> A nosotros los católicos nos dice que estéyamos preparados.
> El podrá decir que ténganos un buen tiempo.
> Le gusta que lo van a buscar.
> Hizo que abandonaban el pueblo.
> Querían que la mujer les hacía la cena.
> Quiere que vamos a San Antonio.
> Perdón que no lo ha entregado.
> A mi mamá le gustaba que volvíamos temprano.
> Pedro no quiso que su hijo se casaba porque pierdía.
> Mandó que paraban de ir.
> Es mejor que fumamos.
> Quería que me paraba.

Overall, the tendency seems to be to retain the subjunctive after expressions of hope and in some cases after verbs of influence functioning as indirect commands: *Quiere que váyamos*; *Dijo que ciérremos la puerta*.

In adjective clauses, the subjunctive is used to modify a nonspecific or indeterminate noun to express contingency or expectation: *Se necesita una mujer que tenga vientiocho años* (any woman that might be twenty-eight years old) versus *Vi una mujer que tiene vientiocho años* (a particular woman who is twenty-eight years old). Unfortunately this construction was not used at all in the taped interviews nor did it appear on compositions. The only example appeared in combination with an adverbial clause where the subjunctive was not used: *Pero con una ocupación como maestra no la puede hacer menos que se casa con alguien que es rico.*

In adverbial clauses, the subjunctive is used where the action is subsequent to a given axis: *El vendrá a las cinco. Entonces iremos > Iremos cuando venga.* Or *Me dijo que vendría a las cinco. Yo comí a las tres > Comí antes de que viniera él.* In the varieties in the Southwest the indicative is sometimes (but not always) substituted for the subjunctive in cases of subsequent action, as indicated by the following examples.

1. Lo mandó pa que juera decirle a Demetrio.
2. . . . antes que me fui.
3. El gobierno gasta miles de dólares cada año para que no plantan varias cosas.
4. Chicano Studies serán necesario hasta cuando la escuela pública enseña, no adoctrina.
5. Cuando la sistema se cambia más, los chicanos no van a tener que depender en los gringos.
6. Antes de que comenzaba a pagar . . .
7. Dice que la vida es una cosa que nos pasa antes que llegamos al fin descanso, la muerte.
8. Cuando acabamos ¿vamos a tener un examen?

The subjunctive also appears in subordinate clauses introduced by *si* where an unreal and improbable condition precedes a conditional probability:

> *Si tuviera dinero, iría.* 'If I had the money, I would go.'
> *Si hubiera tenido dinero, habría ido.* If I had had the money, I would have gone.'

Southwest popular varieties offer several possible combinations. The auxiliary *hubiera* is often replaced by *fuera*. Both the subordinate and independent clauses may take the subjunctive form. In some cases different combinations of indicative and subjunctive forms are used. The following examples are classified according to patterns of use:

Si ______________ , ______________
subjuntivo subjuntivo

1. Si biera tenido un auto, yo te biera visitado.
2. Si tuviera mil dólares, yo fuera a Europa.
3. Te dijiera si supiera.
4. Si ellos llegaran a nuestros escalones, fuera fácil para comenzar una revolución.
5. Si yo fuera sido el papá, yo fuera visto que mi hijo . . .
6. Si yo fuera el papá, yo le fuera dicho al hijo que lo que vía pasado, vía pasado.

7. Si fuéranos tenido bastante más tiempo, se me hace a mí que pudiéranos hablar con esos jóvenes para dicirles que no tuvieran miedo de platicar la verdá.

Si ______________________, ______________________
subjuntivo indicativo

1. Te decía si supiera.
2. Si no fuera por la idea, ahorita no tuvíamos Chicano Studies.
3. Si le biera pasado algo a mi mamá, la familia no puedía, mi papá no puedía mantener la familia.

Si ______________________, ______________________
indicativo subjuntivo

1. Te dijiera si sabía.
2. Le ofreciera trabajo si podía.
3. Le diciera que es muy difícil. Si no le puedía enseñar el mal de sus deseos, entonces le ayudara comenzar algún negocio.

Si ______________________, ______________________
indicativo indicativo

1. Te decía si sabía.
2. Si yo era el papá, yo le decía de la vida.
3. Si yo tenía dinero, iba a las vistas esta tarde.

There are other, unusual uses of the subjunctive. In some cases *haber que* plus infinitive is used as an equivalent of *tendría que*; in other words the impersonal construction with *haber* admits a subject:

> Un buen católico hubiera que rechazar las cosas del mundo.

This same construction also appears as an equivalent of *debería haber* plus past participle:

> Y los gringos van a tener que 'cer lo que hubieran hacido años pasado.

The same phrase appears with *fuera* replacing the auxiliary *hubiera*:

> En vez de hacer el edificio fueran ayudado la gente pobre en Austin.

Sometimes in the substitution of *hubiera* by *fuera,* the verb *haber* is retained in infinitive form:

> Puedo vivir la vida como si no *juera ber pasado*. (como si no hubiera pasado)

Morphology of the verb

Verbs in Spanish are divided into three conjugation groups, according to thematic vowel: *-ar, -er,* and *-ir*. The first conjugation group, verbs ending in *-ar*, is the largest not only because most Spanish verbs belong to it but because it contains all modern loanwords (subsuming the *-ear* group). In the popular varieties of the Southwest, the three conjugation groups have, for all practical purposes, been reduced to two groups, forms ending in

-ir having been taken into the *-er* group. The same phenomenon was observed by Espinosa (1930) in New Mexico. Consider the following examples:

Standard varieties	*Popular varieties*
salgo	salgo
sales	sales
sale	sale
salimos	*salemos*
salen	salen
como	como
comes	comes
come	come
comemos	comemos
comen	comen

The only case where the thematic *-i-* vowel is retained, in the first person plural form, is eliminated in the popular varieties. Numerous instances exist of similar verb regularizations, as in the following examples:

Standard	*Popular*
venimos	vinemos
sentimos	sintemos
vestimos	vistemos
mentimos	mintemos
sequimos	siguemos
pedimos	pidemos
dormimos	durmemos
morimos	muremos

Mid-stem vowels become high vowels (*e* > *i*; *o* > *u*) as the thematic vowel is lowered (*i* > *e*). In some cases these vocalic changes correspond to a regularization of the stem, as is evident below:

pid-o	vist-o
pid-es	vist-es
pid-e	vist-e
pid-emos (< pedimos)	vist-emos (< vestimos)
pid-en	vist-en

Stem vowels that are diphthongized when stressed maintain the diphthong even when the syllable is unstressed; subsequently new forms with diphthongized stems are created or derived:

piens-o	puedo/puedemos	vienen/vieneron
piens-as	cuento/cuentando	juego/juegó
piens-a	pierdo/pierdía	despierto/despiertando
piens-amos (< pensamos)	acuesto/acuestó	duermen/duermieron
piens-an	quiero/quieriendo	

Other stem changes that may occur include verbal forms derived from preterit or other tenses:

tuve/tuvía	quiso/quisiendo	pido/pidía/pidiste/pidía
fui/juíanos	vino/vinía	

The simplification of the verb morphology seems to be a strong tendency. Numerous irregular verbs have become regularized in these Southwest popular varieties, as is common in the popular varieties of other Spanish-speaking areas of the world:

seguí/seguió	decir/deciste	decir-dicir/diciera/dicía
componer/componí	poner/poní	sentí/sentió
producir/producieron	entretener/entretení	caber/cabieron/cabo
eres/ero	costar/costa	ando/andé
tú has/yo ha/nosotros hamos		forzar/forzan

The same regularization is evident in the formation of past participles. Not only are there regular variants of irregular participles but there are also participles derived from new stems:

abrir/abrido (abierto)	escribir/escribido (escrito)
decir/decido/dicido/dijido (dicho)	hacer/hacido (hecho)
morir/morido (muerto)	poner/ponido (puesto)
resolver/resolvido (resuelto)	puedo/puedido (podido)
volver/volvido (vuelto)	romper/rompido (roto)
supe/supido (sabido)	niego/niegado (negado)
tuvo/tuvido (tenido)	

In some cases regular verbs are conjugated like irregular verbs:

entregar/entriego

Or verbs in *-er* are conjugated like *-ar* verbs:

traer/traiba (traía)	tener/teneba (tenía)
caer/caiba (caía)	sentir/sentiba (sentía)

The impersonal *haber* construction is also inflected for number:

Habia muchos accidentes > Habían muchos accidentes

Number inflections are also regularized for second person verb forms. In the Spanish verbal system, the second person morpheme is *-s* and it appears in all conjugated forms except in the preterit, where the morpheme is *-ste*. In Southwest Spanish final *s* is maintained throughout all conjugated second person forms, as occurs in other popular Spanish varieties. Thus the forms *hablaste, viviste,* and *comiste* are *hablastes, vivistes,* and *comistes* in Southwest Spanish. In some of the rural Southwest varieties of Texas and New Mexico, the preterit morpheme is *-tes* rather than *-ste*. Thus we have forms like these:

fuiste > fuites	viste > vites
tomaste > tomates	viniste > vinites

Forms like *fuistes, vistes, tomastes,* and *vinistes* are common in urban varieties.

There are other number inflection changes in rural varieties. The first person plural morpheme, for example, which is *-mos* is changed to *-nos* whenever stress falls on the antepenultimate syllable. Proparoxytones (*esdrújulas*) occur in first person plural forms in the following tenses:

conditional tense: comeríamos > comeríanos
imperfect tense: comíamos > comíanos
imperfect subjunctive tense: comiéramos > comiéranos

As I noted previously, regularization of verb stems is common in these popular varieties of Spanish, affecting not only stem vowels but stress as well. This regularization is especially evident in present subjunctive forms. Once stress is retained in the stem, new proparoxytones arise, as in the following examples:

pueda — piense
puedas — penses
pueda — piense
puédamos (< podamos) — piénsemos (< pensemos)
puedan — piensen

This retention of stress on the stem vowel affects regular verbs as well, even when there is no diphthongization of stem vowels involved:

coma — viva
comas — vivas
coma — viva
cómamos (< comamos) — vívamos (< vivamos)
coman — vivan

Once these verb forms take the stress on the antepenultimate syllable, all undergo changes from *-mos* to *-nos* in rural Southwest varieties:

puédamos > puédanos — piénsemos > piénsenos
cómamos > cómanos — vívamos > vívanos

Other changes in the verb system are easily explained as phonetic changes or the retention of archaic forms. The only other interesting phenomenon noted is frequent use of the reflexive forms to indicate the inchoative aspect of verbs and the willingness with which one undertakes an action (Bull 1965):

Me fui a comer el taco. — Me salí de la clase.
Me fui. — Me vine temprano.
Me tomé el vino. — Me leí todo el libro.

Pronouns

Personal pronouns

The personal pronoun system has also undergone simplification, especially in the speech of young people and in the state of California, where the formal *usted* is rarely used. Strangers and adults are immediately addressed as *tú*. In Texas, on the other hand, the *usted-tú* distinction is maintained throughout the general Mexican-origin population, although young people seem to prefer one second person singular pronoun form. The feminine plural form is also rare, leaving the following pronoun system:

yo	nosotros
tú	ustedes
ella, el	ellas, ellos

An interesting phenomenon is the use of the plural proclitic accusative form when the direct object is singular and the indirect object is plural. Evidently there is a transposition of the plural marker from the dative to the accusative, as demonstrated in the following example:

Les di el libro a ellos. > Se los di (a ellos).
Les di la mesa a ellas. > Se las di (a ellas).

An analogous transposition occurs with the enclitic *nos*, which becomes *no* when it is followed by another clitic pronoun. Bear in mind that a somewhat similar sibilant loss occurs in standard varieties when imperative forms lose the final *s* if followed by an enclitic *nos*: (*Vamos* + *nos* = *Vámonos*; *peinemos* + *nos* = *peinémonos*). The loss of final *s* after *nos* is thus an extension of the vowel loss rule plus transposition:

Nos dio el dinero. > No los dio.
Véndanoslo. > Véndanolos.
Véndanoslos. > Véndanolos.

A similar transposition of consonants is prevalent in imperative verbs, where verb final *n* is transposed to the end of the first enclitic pronoun:

Dénmelo. > Démenlo.
Vénganse. > Véngansen.
Bájense. > Bájensen.

Other pronoun variants are the result of phonetic changes. The unstressed *me*, for example, is often assimilated to a mid-back vowel in its immediate context:

Me lo dio. > Mo lo dio.
No me gusta. > No mo gusta.
Se me olvida. > Se m'olvida.

In some cases *me* is converted into *mi*, if there is an adjacent high vowel:

Me dijo que no. > Mi dijo que no.
Me encontré . . . > M'incontré . . .

Other phonetic changes include the lateralization of nasals, affecting both personal and clitic pronouns. Often both *nos* and *los* appear in the same discourse:

1. Quiere que los sálgamos.
2. Nos dice que los páremos.
3. Pasamos día tras día sin jamás pensar en lo que los pasará.
4. Los encontramos con unos jóvenes.

Interrogative and relative pronouns

In the popular Spanish of the Southwest, the interrogative *qué* is often substituted for *cuál*, especially in informational questions calling for *what* in English. Thus instead of *¿Cuál es tu dirección*? or *¿Cuál es tu número de teléfono*? we often hear *¿Qué es tu dirección*? or *¿Qué es tu número de telefón*?

Inflection for number often disappears in the case of *quién/quiénes*:

¿Quiénes son? > ¿Quién son?

Perhaps this simplification is a result of English influence, where there is only one interrogative form: *who*. As previously indicated, however, simplification is a strong tendency in these popular varieties and could easily explain this loss of number inflection. Nevertheless, the use of *que* for *lo que* sounds somewhat like a literal oral translation from the English:

Esto es todo *que* puedo decir de mi comunidad.

There are other pronominal variants in Chicano communities, which I shall merely note, like the use of *acuál* for *cuál*:

Ahí estaba el Piporro no sabiendo acuál quería.

Frequent in rural Spanish varieties, in the Southwest, and throughout the Americas are compound combinations of indefinite pronouns: *algotro* (*algún otro*), *algotra, algotros, algotras, un otro* (only in the Southwest following the English *another*) and *cada quien* (*cada uno*).

Nouns, adjectives, and adverbs

Gender and number agreement rules are also simplified in these popular Spanish varieties. The norm for standard varieties, for example, calls for the article *el* before feminine nouns in the singular that have an initial stressed low vowel: *a*. In the popular varieties, elision produces *l'* before all singular (masculine or feminine) nouns with a word initial vowel, whether the vowel is stressed or not. Thus we have examples like the following:

el agua > l'agua la amiga > l'amiga la hermana > l'hermana
el oro > l'oro el aguacate > l'aguacate el humo > l'humo

Simplification also occurs in the case of gender inflection. In standard Spanish, where gender is inherent in all nouns, there is no correspondence between ending and gender, that is, all nouns that end in *a* are not automatically feminine nouns. Words like *día, problema, sistema,* and other words derived from Greek and ending in *a* are masculine in gender. In the popular varieties, on the other hand, all words that end in *a* (except for words of high frequency, like *día*) may be converted to the feminine gender. Although gender simplification does not occur in all popular varieties, these are some typical examples:

la sistema   la síntoma   la diploma   la mediodía

Another modification of number inflection is characteristic of some rural popular varieties, especially those used in West Texas and New Mexico. The stress rule in standard Spanish calls for an *-s* plural morpheme after stressed *-á* and *-é*, as in *sofás* or *cafés*. Nouns ending in a consonant, with some exceptions discussed later, take an *-es* plural morpheme, as in *papeles* or *poderes*. In these popular varieties, however, both rules are applied to words ending in stressed *á* and *é* so that the plural morpheme after words ending in stressed vowels is *-ses*, as in the following examples:

pie/pieses   papá/papases   café/cafeses   mamá/mamases

In nouns ending in unstressed vowel plus *s*, with stress on the penultimate syllable, the plural morpheme is zero, as in words like *el lunes, los lunes*. Since Spanish in the Americas is characterized by *seseo* (that is, by the absence of a θ phoneme), words like *lápiz* are pronounced with a final sibilant *s* sound as in *lunes*. It is not surprising then that in West Texas one often hears *el lápiz* and *los lápiz*.

Another feature of popular Spanish, especially among the younger bilingual generations, is the lack of number and gender agreement between nouns and adjectives. It could well be a case of English interference, particularly in written texts where Chicano students are prone to translate from their English literary variety when writing compositions in Spanish. Thus, some cases of lack of agreement arise in written discourse that might not ordinarily appear in oral speech. Let us look at some examples:

los escuelas
muchos cosas
Una mujer hecho para pelear.
Una cadena que está conectado.
El televisor es vieja.
Las personas que son gordas son muy alegre.
Yo creo que el tercer persona es hombre.
No son igual.
Estas dos maneras son universal con nuestra gente.

Sometimes in the same discourse a speaker will select more than one gender for the same word:

las ideales, el ideal   el pared, la pared
el función, la función   el parte, la parte

Agreement between numerals and nouns is also simplified. In popular varieties numbers ending in *ún* tend to take a singular noun: *Tiene veintiún año*, rather than *veintiún años*, as in the standard variety. The apocopated form of *ciento* is also common: *ciento cincuenta* > *cien cincuenta*. With numerals over one hundred there is no agreement with the nouns that follow unless the *cientos, cientas* immediately precede the nouns:

400 mujeres – cuatrocientas mujeres
343 mujeres – trescientos cuarenta y tres mujeres

In addition to inflectional suffixes, derivative suffixes abound in the oral speech of this area. The diminutive *-ito, -ita* affix is used in great abundance not only to indicate small sizes and quantities or short duration but to demonstrate affection or sympathy as well, as is common in other Spanish-speaking areas. For example:

más tardecita, al ratito, un momentito, lo'o lueguito, orita, orititita, muchita (muchachita), muchito (muchachito), el negrito, la tiendita, toitito (todito), toita (todita), frijolitos o frifolitos, carrito

Augmentative suffixes are also frequent in Chicano speech with various functions as in other Spanish-speaking areas. More interesting, to augment a qualitative feature to indicate repeated or prolonged duration or even to reiterate an intention, the adjectives, adverbs, or verbs are repeated or the prefixes *re-* and *rete-*, common in other areas, are used:

Está azul azul.
Está fuerte fuerte.
Está retebonito.
Vino luego luego. Vino lo'o luego.
Ponlo recio recio. (más fuerte)
Iba recio recio. (bien rápido)
Ese hombre no más trabaji trabaji y tú de hoquis. (trabaja y trabaja)
Anda canti canti. (cantando)
Lo vi corri corri. (corriendo)
Estaba chifli chifli. (silbando)
El niño está brinqui brinqui. (brincando)

English interference[2]

As a result of the daily contact between English and Spanish speakers and the dominant role of English in every aspect of society, loanwords are numerous in the Spanish of the Southwest. Although the influence of English is primarily evident in the lexicon, it sometimes occurs in pronunciation and syntax. English has also affected intonation patterns, as is particularly evident in the Spanish of bilingual Chicano students who have had all their academic instruction in English.

[2] This section follows Weinreich's (1968) analysis of loanwords.

We will first look at some examples of morphosyntactic influence. Changes within any language are generally explained in terms of rules already operating within that language. It is, of course, possible to find, for example, uses of possessive adjectives before parts of the body and articles of clothing even where there is no contact with English. Yet bilinguals often translate thoughts from one language to oral production in another, especially when the use of the two is continuous and contiguous within the space of a conversation. These bilinguals are often surprised to find that all Spanish speakers do not automatically use the possessive all the time, as in English:

> *Tengo las manos sucias.* > *Mis manos están sucias.* 'My hands are dirty.'
> *Se pusieron el sombrero.* > *Se pusieron sus sombreros.* 'They put on their hats.'

Translation also seems to be the explanation for the addition of the particle *a* before infinitives. Spanish normally uses the *a* after certain verbs of motion (*ir a, salir a, entrar a, venir a,* etc.) to produce expressions like *Va a venir a comer.* Other verbs, however, like *querer, dejar, deber,* and *poder,* for example, are not followed by *a*, as is evident in sentences like *Quiere comer, Puedo ir,* or *Debe cantar.* In the following examples, verbs and *to be*-plus-adjective expressions normally not accompanied by *a* appear with this preposition as is common in English, where infinitives are introduced with *to*:

1. Querían a comenzar.
2. Déjeme atocar la colcha.
3. Lo quieren a quechar.
4. Quedé de a ir para Mexico.
5. Ofreció a prestárnolas.
6. Porque es difícil a presentar todos los lados.
7. Es importante a yir.
8. ¿Pero es asesinato a quitarlas del cuerpo?
9. Es difícil a leer.

A further extension of this phenomenon is the appearance of an epenthetic *a* before a number of verbs. Thus one student wrote: *No puedo hagastar a tiempo a cambiar el mundo.* And others were recorded as saying: *Tuvimos a registrando*; *Tuvimos a buscando*; *Andamos a vendiendo unos posters.*

Where there are certain correspondences between the English and the Spanish verb systems, the English patterns are frequently followed. In the speech of young Chicanos, the progressive tenses are often the preferred form, where a simple present would do as well. Standard Spanish, of course, also has the progressive tense. The difference here is the *absence* of the present tense in speech to refer to an action in progress. Thus a question like *¿Por qué fumas?* would typically be translated as

'Why do you smoke?' rather than as 'Why are you smoking?' In fact the second translation would sound odd to some Chicano Spanish speakers. Other cases pointing to English interference are the use of *-ing* verbals as nouns. Like many English speakers learning Spanish, Chicano students who are native speakers of Spanish often use these verbals as gerunds rather than simply as participles, as is common in Spanish. English gerunds have to be translated as infinitives in Spanish:

> After *leaving* the office, he went to the drugstore. (Despues de *salir* de la oficina, se fue a la botica.)

In the following examples we will find several cases of Spanish *gerundios* functioning like *gerunds* rather than like participles:

1. Para mis hermanitos viviendo en el proyecto era bueno.
2. El hijo quería poner al papá en una posición de sintiéndose culpable de los problemas del hijo.
3. Autorizando abortos es algo que exige mucho pensamiento.
4. Usándolas es una manera de afirmar su mexicanidad.
5. El ideal de la hombría consiste en nunca permitiendo que el mundo exterior penetre en su intimidad.
6. El dinero que gana lo gasta en tomando.

English interference is more commonly seen in written texts than heard in oral speech. Here the interference arises from lack of practice in Spanish composition as a result of English dominance. This type of interference is evident in the absence of an article before generic and mass nouns in Spanish, where an article is always required. Thus sentences like *Man is mortal* or *Rice is good* must be translated as *El hombre es mortal* and *El arroz es bueno* in Spanish. Chicano students, however, will often omit the article, as in English:

1. Capitalismo es un sistema económico
2. Religión es algo muy personal
3. Gente ya orita está despertando
4. Todos creen que cambios son necesarios.
5. Estadísticas revelan que . . .

Constant translation from one language to another, especially when dealing in Spanish with material that has been learned and rehearsed in English, often leads to the translation of prepositions, such as the preposition *to* before infinitives as we have already seen. Informal English also allows particular prepositions that follow certain verbs to appear in sentence final position with transposed object complements. Literal translations thus appear strange in Spanish, as in the following examples:

1. La muerte es un tema que todos piensan en a veces.
2. Quieren quedar vivos porque su vida es la única vida que están seguros de.
3. . . . significa en realidad lo que nosotros tenemos fe en.

Prepositions are especially difficult to translate, but problems also arise when no preposition is required in Spanish, as in the following example:

> *No estamos pidiendo por mas caridad.* (*pidiendo más caridad*)
> 'We're not asking for more charity.'

The one distinguishing characteristic of Chicano Spanish is the presence of numerous loanwords from the English language. The phenomenon of borrowing is, of course, common throughout the world in areas where languages are in contact. In fact the Spanish language itself has incorporated numerous loans from Arabic, Greek, French, Italian, Germanic languages, and American Indian languages throughout its history, loans that are today generally accepted by all Spanish speakers. The Spanish varieties of Latin America and Spain also have incorporated English loanwords but not to the extent that Chicano Spanish has. Thus the distinguishing phenomenon in the Southwest is quantitative and refers to the *degree* of borrowing rather than to the phenomenon itself. Borrowing is actually quite logical given the dominance of English, and given the exclusion of Spanish from most formal functions, especially in academic and technological fields. Thus, information provided and stored in English is frequently converted into Spanish through morphological and phonological adaptations. In most cases borrowing leads to the incorporation of new meanings into Spanish varieties in the Southwest. Often, equivalent terms exist in Spanish but with different connotations, so that particular meanings can be captured only through these loanwords. Often the whole borrowing process becomes a linguistic game that Chicanos delight in playing. Sometimes the equivalent term in Spanish is not part of the Chicano repertoire and borrowing is the only alternative. Various reasons exist, therefore, for the presence of these loanwords in Chicano Spanish; all provide the Spanish varieties with new meanings, but not all are the result of lexical gaps.

Spanish varieties include a number of verbs borrowed from English. These verbs are generally integrated into the *-ar* conjugation group, with *-ear* (pronounced *-iar*) combinations having a higher frequency, as in the following examples:

shine > chainear	*lock* > laquear	*dust* > dostear
mop > mapear	*quit* > cuitear	*watch* > huachar
spell > espelear	*catch* > quechar	*match* > mechear
miss > mistear	*type* > taipear	

Nouns borrowed from English are provided with number and gender, like all nouns in the Spanish language. A certain uniformity prevails throughout the Southwest in terms of the gender assigned to particular loans, but in some cases there are differences. Thus the term for *plug* may vary between *plogue* (masculine) and *ploga* (feminine). What is *magasín* (m.) for some is *magasina* (f.) for others. Yet for terms of high frequency, gender assignments are generally the same in Texas as in California. In some cases gender differences correspond to differences in meaning. For example, in some areas the term for *truck* is *troque,* whereas in others, it is *troca*. Often, *troque* is the larger vehicle and *troca* is equivalent to *troquita*. Sometimes the gender of a loanword corresponds to the gender given its equivalent in Spanish, as in *puche* (from *push*) for *empuje*: *un puche, un empuje*. Where it is a matter of false cognates, as, for example, *carpeta* for *alfombra* 'carpet,' terms already part of the Spanish language with another meaning (*carpeta* 'portfolio' or 'folder') retain their original gender. The form is often simply supplied with an additional meaning if the standard meaning is familiar. *Yarda* and *mecha,* which normally mean *measurement* and the *wick* of a candle or lamp, respectively, in Chicano varieties refer additionally to English *yard,* the green space in front of a house, and *match*.

Sometimes the equivalent in Spanish is not familiar to the Chicano, or it is seen as not having the same meaning, given the different context of use. The equivalent for *mapiador* (from *mop*), for example, is the uncommon *trapeador*. In fact one student indicated that the action *mapear* 'to mop' involved the use of a mop, whereas *trapear* meant cleaning the floor with *trapos* 'rags'. Thus the introduction of new tools led to the incorporation of new loanwords to reflect new meanings.

Because these popular varieties have a simplified gender and number system, words ending in *a* are automatically feminine. In some cases the final low vowel is derived from final *er* in English, where the schwa is related to the central vowel in Spanish, *-a*. Thus we have examples like the following:

la dipa 'dipper' *la juila* 'wheeler' *la mira* 'meter'
la rula 'ruler'

The gender of some words is determined by its correlation with sex, as in the following examples:

el bosero 'busdriver' *la norsa* 'nurse' *la huayfa* 'wife'
el broda 'brother' *el troquero* 'truckdriver'
el hueldeador 'welder'

New loanwords ending in final *e* or in a consonant are generally masculine:

el fil *el yin* 'gin' *el cloche* *el bil* *el bos* *un daime*
el fone *el estare* *un nicle* *el suiche* *el faite* *el saine*

Phonetically, English sounds are adapted to the Spanish phonological system. English sounds are thus replaced with the segment that more closely resembles it in terms of manner of articulation or point of articulation. Thus, words with English *sh* are generally adapted as *ch-*: *sheriff* > *cherife, shampoo* > *champú*. In some areas of the Southwest, however, the fricative variant *sh* exists, as we indicated previously, allowing the following pronunciations: *sherife, mushasho, shampú.* Words ending in a consonant other than *d, l, r, n,* or *s* are incorporated with an added final vowel, generally *e*, as in *puche, sete, cloche,* but sometimes *a*: *brecas.* Words ending in *er*, although generally incorporated with a final *a* (*meter* = *mira*), may at times reveal a final *e*: *mofle* 'muffler', indicating possible acquisition through the printed word. Words starting with initial *s* plus consonant take an epenthetic initial *e* as in *espelear* 'spell', *esquipear* 'skip', and *estare* 'starter'. English words with aspiration, *h*, have a velar fricative in Spanish: *jaiscul* 'high school'.

Extensions of meaning

The incorporation of loanwords has meant the broadening of the semantic fields by allowing the expression in Spanish of meanings acquired through the English language. Chicano Spanish has made false cognates, where the meaning in English is not equivalent to the meaning in standard Spanish varieties, into true cognates, with equivalent meanings. Sometimes the standard meaning is not familiar to the speaker; at other times the speaker adapts to the new meaning system and simply incorporates an additional meaning for that word. Thus, the word *colegio,* which is a public school in most Latin American countries, becomes synonymous with *college,* to indicate the first four years of university work in an institution without graduate studies. The concept of high school is represented by *jaiscul,* the translated *escuela alta,* or *secundaria.* This incorporation of false cognates as true cognates is widespread. Below are just a few examples:

Chicano Spanish	*Standard Spanish*	*English*
librería	biblioteca	library
carpeta	alfombra	carpet
conferencia	reunión	conference
lectura	conferencia	lecture
suceso	éxito	success
realizar	darse cuenta	realize
parientes	padres	parents

When lexical items in English resemble Spanish items with a few minor differences, the loan is incorporated as a true cognate, leading to phonetic and morphological differences between the loan and the original Spanish equivalent, as in the examples below:

competición 'competition' for *competencia*
población 'population' for *población*
telefón 'telephone' for *teléfono*
perpetual 'perpetual' for *perpetuo*
materialístico 'materialistic' for *materialista*
asistante 'assistant' for *asistente*
exploitación 'exploitation' for *explotación*
practical 'practical' for *práctico*

distincto 'distinct' for *distinto*
farmacista 'pharmacist' for *farmacéutico*
sadístico 'sadistic' for *sádico*
incapable 'incapable' for *incapaz*
correctar 'correct' for *corregir*
directar 'direct' for *dirigir*

Compound phrases
English phrases may be borrowed directly and translated literally to produce previously inexistent combinations, like *objetores concientes* (Weinreich 1968, p. 50) for *conscientious objectors* in Florida Spanish. Loan translations are also common in the Spanish of the Southwest, producing combinations that often make no sense to someone coming from another Spanish-speaking country, unless the necessary English code is part of his or her repertoire. These compound phrases include expressions like the following:

English phrase	*Loan: compound phrase*	*Standard Spanish equivalent*
to call back	llamar pa'tras	volver a llamar
to put back	poner pa'tras	devolver, volver a poner
to have a good time	tener un buen tiempo	divertirse
How do you like it?	¿Cómo te gusta?	¿Qué te parece?
to run for office	correr para un puesto o una oficina	ser candidato
to figure the problems out	figurar los problemas	resolver los problemas
Your town is run by anglos.	Su pueblo está corrido por anglos.	está dirigido, gobernado
he grew more confused	creció más confusido	se puso más confuso

Sometimes the English phrase serves as a model for the loan, especially if the literal translation calls for some modification in Spanish, as in these examples:

to get a college education > *agarrar colegio*
to get a kick out of > *agarrar patada*

Hybrid compounds. In some cases part of the original English phrase is translated, and part of the phrase is a loan:

flour > *harina de flor*
bedroom set > *sete de recamara*
light meter > *mira de la luz*
light bill > *el bil de electricidad, el bil de la luz*
traffic sign > *saine de tráfico*

Often the incorporation of loanwords leads to the displacement of an existing Spanish term or to the less frequent use of particular terms. For example, the incorporation of *huachar* 'watch,' together with the existing *mirar* 'look,' have led to the loss of *ver* in the repertoire of some young Chicano Spanish speakers. In some cases, where various terms have similar denotations but different connotations, the incorporation of loans allows for a richer repertoire. Series like the following are common in Chicano Spanish: *el chó, el mono, las vistas, la película, el cine*: *brecas, manea, frenos*. The Spanish equivalent may not be familiar to some speakers, leading necessarily to the incorporation of loanwords, as in the case of *espelear* 'spell,' when the word *deletrear* is not part of instruction in school.

Code-switching

The discourse of bilingual Chicanos is often composed of shifts from one language to another, initiated not only with turn taking in conversations, but within the same utterances. Chicano speakers are aware of these shifts and often answer that they mix both languages when asked if they speak English or Spanish at home: "Pos hablamos revuelto. Inglés y español." These shifts, triggered by shifts in speech act, theme, or language function, are often considered to be the mode of expression that best captures the bilingual, bicultural situation of the Mexican-origin population residing as a minority within an English-dominant society. Code-shifting is thus common in Chicano short stories, novels, poetry, and essays published in Chicano journals and magazines. In *Magazín,* published for a short while in San Antonio, the following sentence appeared in a story: "Se encerró in the recamara and cried over her mala suerte."

Where shifts occur, each language segment retains the pronunciation and grammatical form of the proper language. Thus sentences like *Me puchó* are not examples of code-shifting, because the loanword *puchar* is a part of Chicano Spanish and follows all the necessary morphological and phonological Spanish rules. A sentence like *Me dio un push,* with *push* pronounced as in English, is a case of code-shifting, because the shift is from one phonological and lexical system to another.

Elsewhere I have discussed shifts as means of conveying different levels of meaning. Here, however, I will briefly examine some linguistic constraints that operate in code-shifting. There is not yet a large set of rules to describe nor a code-shifting grammar to propose, but I will attempt to demonstrate that shifts do not occur at random.

The grammatical systems of both languages are totally different in terms of underlying structures, rules, ordering of rules, and rule transformations. Some rules, however, are somewhat similar at the categorical level. Both languages, for example, form the progressive tenses with an auxiliary verb plus verb plus present progressive morpheme. In some cases, as in the formation of questions, the transformational rules differ significantly, with English requiring reordering of categories and the addition of the verb *do*. Shifts seem to occur where there are similarities in structures but not in cases where the surface structures are entirely different. Thus we find examples like these:

Lo hizo *slowly*. Vino *early*.

but never like these:

**How* lo hizo? **When* vino?

The explanation could be that English requires the particle *do*:

1. How *did* he do it?
2. When *did* he come?

Thus shifts like the following are not possible in Chicano discourse:

1. *Con quién *Peter go*? *for* ¿Con quién va Pedro?
2. *Cuándo *is Mary coming*? *for* ¿Cuándo viene María?

The usual surface form for questions in the Southwest requires placing the verb before the subject: *¿Cuándo viene María? ¿Con quién viene Pedro?* Because some varieties of Spanish, like Caribbean Spanish, allow for the preposition of the subject before the verb (*¿Cuándo mi esposo lee? ¿Cuándo yo comeré? ¿Con quién ella baila?*), it may be that shifts are being determined by surface structure rules operating in this area.[3]

Where surface forms are similar there are no problems, and shifts may occur even in the middle of phrases. As I have mentioned, English has verbal complements – gerunds – which function like nouns, whereas in Spanish only infinitive verbals function like nouns. In code-shifting, Spanish participial constructions function like English gerunds and English gerunds function like objects of Spanish prepositions:

1. *I'm talking about* conociéndonos.
2. está hablando de integration, de *understanding other people's cultures.*
3. Estoy por *lowering the standard.*

Thus it would appear that where surface forms are similar but structural rules are significantly different, the speaker will follow the English rule.

The only examples considered here are those that appeared in the taped interviews. In the analysis that follows, however, I have followed my intuition as well. We will look now at specific uses within noun and verb phrases, as well as at shifts occurring at the clause or sentence level.

Shifts within noun phrases. The noun phrase in both English and Spanish consists of the following: (determiner) noun (adjective clause). In these possible combinations, I have found that a noun in English may be preceded by an article in Spanish:

[3] With thanks to Rosa Kestelman, East Los Angeles College, for the information on Caribbean Spanish.

1. el *wedding*
2. el *building*
3. los *officials*
4. metieron un *suit.*
5. Tenemos un *newspaper.*

Spanish nouns, however, are not preceded by English articles. Thus we did not find sentences like **The muchacho está aquí* nor **A mujer vino.* Only in cases where the press has popularized a term and made it a Spanish loan to English do we find any instance of English article plus Spanish noun:

Most of the barrio va por Gonzalo Barrientos.

English nouns may be modified by adjectives in Spanish:

1. Tiene todo el *building* agujeráo.
2. en cualquier *facet of school life*

An English noun modified by an English adjective can be preceded by an article in Spanish:

Hay un *friendly atmosphere.*

If no article is necessary, the entire noun phrase may appear in English after a Spanish verb:

1. Te dan *greater yields.*
2. Puede dar *better results.*
3. Si hay *run-offs.*

Within the Spanish noun phrase, Spanish nouns may be followed by an adjective clause in English:

Una cosa *that turns me off* . . .

The same occurs within an English noun phrase, where the English noun may be modified by an adjective clause in Spanish.

1. *That's another bitch* que tengo yo con los chicanos, que ponen música americana
2. La *most beautiful thing* que nos ha pasado

Predicate adjectives and predicate nouns. A sentence begun in Spanish, with a Spanish verb, may have an English predicate, as in these examples:

1. Me quedé *surprised.*
2. Te digo que está *prejudiced.*
3. Apá es el *dominant.*
4. La vida no nomás es un *party.*
5. Esa es una cosa que ya estamos *brainwashed* los mexicanos.
6. Es *self-employed.*
7. Parece que soy *sensitive.*

Spanish predicates, however, did *not* occur after English verbs.

> **He is* carpintero.
> **She is* sensible. (i.e., She is sensitive.)

Adjectives in English within a Spanish structure may be modified by Spanish adverbs:

1. No quieren ser muy *"radical."* (radical – in English)
2. Es muy *friendly*.

English adverbs, however, do not appear with Spanish adjectives: Thus we do *not* hear **Es very amistoso*. Nor do English adjectives appear within a Spanish noun phrase, that is, between a Spanish determiner and a Spanish noun: **un friendly hombre*.

Verb phrases. Both English and Spanish have underlying sentences of this type: S → noun phrase + auxiliary + verb + (noun phrases). In examples gathered from the recorded interviews, we found that sentences initiated in Spanish, with Spanish auxiliaries, could be followed by English participles:

1. No está *hurting* a la tierra
2. Te están *brain-washing*
3. Cuando van *aging* . . .
4. Estaban *striking Kelly* (AFB), but not: **He is* trabajando

Shifts occur within the auxiliary phrase itself. In Spanish, the auxiliary phrase could be represented morphologically as follows:

> Aux → tense (aspect) (*haber* + *-do*) (*estar* + *ndo*)

The English auxiliary rule has been variously represented, but here I will follow this morphological model, quite similar to the Spanish rule:

> Aux → tense (*have* + *-en*) (*be* + *-ing*)

The code-shifting grammar is thus creating the following combination:

> Aux → tense (*haber* + *-do*) (*estar* + *-ing*)

with the verb that follows in English.

Subject-verb relations. A Spanish verb may be preceded by a noun phrase that contains a Spanish article plus English noun:

> Dice el *announcer* . . .

Spanish, of course, allows reordering of subject and verb.

Verbal phrases. As in the case of progressive verb phrases, periphrastic phrases used to indicate future or subsequent actions and formed with the verb *ir* plus infinitive may consist of the conjugated verb *ir* in Spanish followed by an English infinitive:

> Si va take una muchacha el *dominant role* . . .

The opposite combination (verb *go* plus Spanish infinitive) does not occur:

> **If you're going to* tomar . . .

Noun phrases after prepositions. Spanish prepositions may be followed by English nouns:

1. Yo estoy hablando de *interaction*, de *power*.
2. Siempre ando con *hate*.

On the other hand, Spanish nouns rarely appear after English prepositions, unless, again, it is the case of a culturally marked term, like *barrio* or *gente*:

> *I'm talking about interaction with* la gente

If the verb combines with a preposition in the English expression (as in *look for, watch over, look up,* etc.), then verb loanwords will retain the preposition in English:

> *What would it be like* si un perrao estuviera afuera watchando *over* quien sale para perseguirlos

Verb complements. Verb complements (direct objects) may appear in English after a Spanish verb:

1. Si no tienen *integrated parties* . . .
2. Tiene todo el *publicity*.
3. Agarra el *moisture*.
4. Te dan *greater yields*.
5. Se caba cuando va al *cemetery*, halla el *grave* de su madre . . .

Vestigial Spanish. One of the more frequent types of code-shifting is the introduction of colloquial Spanish expressions in English discourse. Lewis (1972) has commented that in cases of vestigial bilingualism, after the dominant language has taken over all of the functions of the subordinate language, what remains of the nondominant language is evident in a few vestiges, a few expressions or words from a former period. It is to be hoped that Chicano Spanish will never be reduced to the insertion of phrases like *Órale*! or *Jijo*! in English discourse.

This inventory of some linguistic constraints operating in code-shifting is obviously incomplete. It will now have to be integrated into a semantic and ideological analysis that will indicate the function these shifts have in Chicano discourse.

Conclusion

Code-switching and loss of Spanish among younger generations who prefer communicating strictly in English are indicative of strong pressures to assimilate the dominant language. Yet the presence of major contradictions within U.S. society, which contribute to segregation in residence, education, and employment, guarantee the continued concentration of these populations in certain sectors and thus continued interaction of Chicanos with each other, allowing thereby the maintenance of the Spanish language. Chicano barrios are still bilingual and in some instances Spanish monolingual. With the continuing immigration of Mexicans, popular Spanish varieties of the Southwest are constantly enriched and invigorated, especially where a great deal of social and linguistic interaction exists between new and older residents.

I have tried to describe some of the major characteristics of rural and urban Spanish varieties, from a linguistic and pedagogical perspective, for it is important that Spanish classes for native speakers concentrate on making students aware of the existence of different language varieties and on allowing them to increase their language functions in Spanish to where they can discuss academic, political, and technical topics in Spanish and shift from one Spanish variety to another, according to the linguistic and social context.

I do not pretend to suggest that the characteristics of the Spanish varieties presented here are unique to Chicanos or the Southwest. The popular varieties of Argentina, Chile, Mexico, Peru, Venezuela, and other Spanish-speaking areas share many of the features of Chicano Spanish. In general terms, all popular varieties share certain tendencies and certain rules. But despite similarities each specific context is distinct, and the mode of expression is necessarily different. In that sense, the language of Chicanos is a product of the Chicano community. It is the verbalization of a communal experience.

References

Bernstein, Basil. 1968. Some sociological determinants of reception: an inquiry into sub-cultural differences. In *Readings in the sociology of language*, ed. J. Fishman, pp. 223–39. Paris: Mouton.

Bull, William. 1965. *Spanish for teachers*. New York: Ronald Press.

Espinosa, Aurelio. 1930. *Estudios sobre el español de Nuevo Méjico*. Vol. 2. Buenos Aires: Universidad de Buenos Aires.

Labov, William. 1972. *Language in the inner city: studies in the black English vernacular*. Philadelphia: University of Pennsylvania Press.

Lewis, Glyn. 1972. *Multilingualism in the Soviet Union*. The Hague: Mouton.

Weinreich, Uriel. 1968. *Languages in contact*. Paris: Mouton.

2

Current trends in the investigation of Cuban and Puerto Rican phonology

T. D. TERRELL

Both Cuban and Puerto Rican phonology are receiving increased interest and study in the United States principally because of the large numbers of speakers of these varieties of Spanish: Cubans in Miami and Puerto Ricans in New York. Specifically, interest has grown because these varieties must be used in bilingual programs in these two areas. It is well known that at least on the surface, the phonology of these two varieties of Spanish, as well as other Caribbean varieties, differs substantially from (standard) Latin American Spanish spoken in the highlands areas of Mexico, Colombia, and Peru.

Structural phonological theory offers little in the way of a framework for research into the differences that characterize Cuban and Puerto Rican speech, because its focus is the phoneme, and these varieties of Caribbean Spanish differ little from other American varieties on the phonemic level. The consonantal phonemes of American Spanish are:

voiceless stops: /p/ /t/ /č/ /k/
voiced stop-continuants: /b/ /d/ /y/ /g/
voiceless fricatives: /f/ /s/ /h/
tap: /r/
trill: /rr/
lateral: /l/
nasals: /m/ /n/ /ñ/

The main differences are subphonemic (e.g., /x/ = /h/), although they do often involve cases of partial neutralization of phonemes (e.g., /r/ = /l/ in certain positions) that in other varieties of American Spanish are kept completely distinct. Traditional (abstract) generative phonology offers only the concept of the phonological rule,[1] but most work done with this model has been with morphophonemic processes.[2]

[1] This concept was also available to structuralists (Hockett 1954).
[2] Harris (1969) does include an analysis of phonological process in standard Mexican Spanish; however, processes he analyzed differ in Caribbean Spanish only in detail, not in substance.

Labov's (1972b) variable rule model on the other hand is admirably suited for investigation of Cuban and Puerto Rican Spanish, because almost without exception the phonological rules that differ from standard Latin American highlands Spanish are applied variably in the speech of Cubans and Puerto Ricans; that is, normally no speaker applies a rule all of the time (categorical application) and no speaker fails to apply the rules some of the time (variable rule application). Indeed, all recent large-scale investigations of Cuban and Puerto Rican phonology have used Labov's model.[3] The use of a variable rule model results in both theoretical and methodological differences. First, the model is based on speech: The investigator must have a corpus of recorded speech upon which to carry out the investigation. Second, the model is quantitative: The investigator must examine a large number of cases of the phenomenon in question before drawing descriptive and theoretical conclusions.

The first important speech-based project was that of Roxana Ma and Eleanor Herasimchuk (1971), which formed part of the Joshua Fishman project that studied various facets of the speech of Puerto Ricans in New York City. Vallejo-Claros's (1971) study of Cuban phonology, based on a large corpus collected from interviews with early Cuban refugees (many of whom had been in the United States only a few hours) was the second large quantitative investigation for the Caribbean. The most important project by far, however, was Henrietta Cedergren's monumental work on Panamanian Spanish in 1973. Because of its extremely high standards – both methodological and theoretical – it has influenced almost all work in Cuban and Puerto Rican phonology since its completion.

Work on Cuban Spanish has slowed, although some work is being done with the interviews collected by Vallejo-Claros under the direction of Joseph Matluck and Humberto López Morales.[4] This collection suffers from two defects, however: (1) the interviews are single style – all interviews are semiformal and there are no reading styles used – and (2) the informants are all middle- or upper-class speakers. Robert Hammond has a smaller collection of more relaxed speech that has been used to fill in certain gaps in our knowledge of Cuban speech. Still, there has been no real sociolinguistic survey of the Cuban community in the United States. The influx of Cuban refugees in 1980 is a new rich source of data and the next few years will undoubtedly witness an explosion of research on Cuban phonology. Work with this group is especially exciting because we are in the position of being able to look carefully at phonological change in progress.

Work on Puerto Rican speech, on the other hand, has increased. Due mainly to the impetus of the linguistics program of the University of

[3] For work on Cuban Spanish using generative models, see Bjarkman (1978), Guitart (1976, 1977, 1978, 1979), and Hammond (1976a, 1977).

[4] This collection is part of the Latin American Educated Speech Project (LAESP). For more information see Lope Blanch (1968).

Puerto Rico at Rio Piedras, under the direction of Humberto López Morales with the collaboration of Amparo Morales de Walters and María Vaquero de Ramírez, two large collections of interviews have been gathered – one entirely of middle- and upper-class residents of San Juan[5] and the other a stratified one that includes all socioeconomic levels of the metropolitan area of San Juan.[6] The latter collection is serving as the basis for several projects, and it promises to be important in future work. In addition, Shana Poplack, working at the Center for Puerto Rican Studies in New York, has two collections of Puerto Rican speech – one from working-class speakers in Philadelphia and the other from Puerto Rican speakers living in New York. Her 1979 dissertation is the most important recent analysis of Puerto Rican Spanish. It will not be possible here to examine all of her findings. Especially promising is an analytical procedure that she terms "principal components analysis," by which she tries to explain speaker preferences for groups of surface variants, for example, aspiration of /s/ and velarization of /n/.

The Problems

Four areas have aroused great interest in Cuban and Puerto Rican phonology:

1. Aspiration and deletion of syllable and word final (s):[7]
   niños [niñoh] [niño] 'children'
   esto [ehto] [eto] 'this'
2. Velarization and deletion of syllable and word final (n):
   pan [paŋ] [pã] [pa] 'bread'
   comen [komeŋ] [komẽ] [kome] 'they eat'
3. Lateralization of syllable and word final (r):
   salir [salil] 'to leave'
   verdad [beldá] 'truth'
4. Velarization (uvularization) and devoicing of word initial and intervocalic trilled (*rr*):
   rosa [xosa] 'rose'
   carro [kaxo] 'car'

These rules are being studied on various levels. First, it is necessary to describe the phenomena: Who uses which variants, when, and in what proportions? This is a necessary preliminary step, because with minor exceptions none of the variants is used categorically by any speaker. Second, how these variables affect other parts of the grammar must be determined. This is particularly relevant since (s), (n), and (r) all represent morphemes with various morphological and syntactical functions. And

[5] This also is part of the LAESP.
[6] López Morales (1979b) is based on the latter and Terrell (1978a) on the former.
[7] I use the parenthesis notation (*s*) as in Labov (1972b) to indicate a phonological variable.

Table 1. *Deletion of* (s): *educated speakers* (*in percent*)

	First (s)	Redundant (s)
Havana	3	38
San Juan	8	47

finally, and perhaps most importantly, the data should be used to shed new light on the way the phonological component of a grammar changes.[8]

S *aspiration and deletion*

The phonetic manifestation of syllable and word final (s) is the most thoroughly studied of the four variables. It is interesting to note that although all phonologists have commented on these processes from the time any serious study of Caribbean phonology began, only after the advent of quantitative analysis with the variable rule model was it shown that the rules of aspiration and deletion are applied consistently following a well-defined system of conditioning factors.

The aspiration and deletion of (s) have been thoroughly studied for educated speakers of Havana and San Juan.[9] It is clear that most individuals from this socioeconomic level follow the same system of factors that condition the use of a sibilant [s], the most conservative of the three possibilities, the use of an aspirated phone [h], and the complete deletion of the phoneme.[10]

Deletion is conditioned primarily by two factors – length of the word and position in the noun phrase. Position is a factor used by speakers only in plural markers, that is, the final (s) of nouns (*casa*s), and their modifiers (*grande*s, *lo*s, *mucho*s).[11] Only when (s) is in the first position in the noun phrase (*los libros interesantes, mi*s *primeras lecciones, eso*s *muchachos*) is there a strong tendency to avoid deletion. Table 1 compares deletion rates for educated natives of Havana and San Juan for adjectives in the first position with other adjectives and the plural marker on nouns.[12] It is notable that this tendency to preserve some phonetic realization of the first plural marker in the noun phrase is strong despite the fact that there are other markers that in most cases would make even this (s) redundant, that is, /-e/ in phrases like *mi*(s) *suétere*(s) *azule*(s) or the verb

[8] Terrell (1975b, 1977a, 1977b, 1978c, 1979d) also used Cuban and Puerto Rican speech phenomena to suggest changes in the descriptive model of phonological variability on a theoretical level.

[9] Both projects used the LAESP tapes. See Terrell (1977d, 1978b, 1979a) and Hammond (1979a).

[10] [h] included varying degrees of aspiration, both voiced and voiceless as well as complete assimilation resulting in gemination, e.g., *espero* [eppero].

[11] The (s) of pronouns is much more complex and will not be dealt with here.

[12] The data in many of the following tables appear for the first time in print in this chapter.

Table 2. *Deletion of* (s) *in first position modifiers: educated speakers* (*in percent*)

	Las	Los	Numbers	Other first position modifiers
Havana	1	1	9	5
San Juan	7	5	11	10

Table 3. *Deletion of verbal and lexical* (s): *educated speakers* (*in percent*)

		Monosyllabic words	Polysyllabic words
Havana	Lexical (*s*)	10	44
	Verbal (*s*)	4	65
San Juan	Lexical (*s*)	7	32
	Verbal (*s*)	15	48

marker in phrases like *son la*(s) *casa*(s) *bonita*(s), the *-o-* in *los, esos*, or *algunos*, and quantifiers that are inherently plural when used with count nouns: *muchos, tres*, and so on. In spite of this redundancy, deletion rates are uniformly low in all first position modifiers with /s/ as a plural marker. (See Table 2.) Thus the strategy for the educated speakers seems to be to conserve a phonological manifestation of (s) on the first position modifier in spite of possible redundancy.

In other cases of deletion of word final (s) only the length of the word seems to be important. Educated speakers delete freely if the word is polysyllabic and tend to be more conservative if the word is monosyllabic. This is true for both verbal (s) (*nosotro*s *tenemo*s, *tú tiene*s, *él e*s) and lexical (s) (*ve*z, *entonce*s, *ante*s, *despué*s). (See Table 3.)

This finding forced a reconsideration of the functionalist hypothesis (Terrell 1977a) by which it was claimed that (s) as a grammatical marker would tend to be deleted less than lexical (s) (Terrell 1978c). After considerable work it became obvious that the hypothesis in its strong form was false, because deletion of plural (s) depended on its position in the noun phrase not just on its status as a plural marker. Also, unexpectedly, it was found that verbal (s) behaved exactly like lexical (s), with functional criteria playing absolutely no role.[13]

[13] Some have speculated that verbal (s) of *tú* forms may be freely deleted because in Caribbean Spanish the use of *tú* is almost obligatory in many contexts.

Table 4. *Use of the sibilant in prevocalic position: educated speakers (in percent)*

	First position modifier + stressed vowel	(s) + unstressed vowel
San Juan	85	12
Havana	89	10

The deletion of word internal (s) (*esto, pastilla, pescado*) is not the norm for educated Cuban or Puerto Rican speech. However, even with complete deletion there is normally no loss of message, because in this position the functional load of the contrast is low: *pescado-pecado*, for example. Resnick and Hammond (1975) showed clearly that contrary to popular opinion, in complete deletion there are no compensatory effects on the vowel to maintain the phonological contrast.[14]

If the speaker does not delete (s), he chooses between aspiration [h] and retention of a sibilant [s]. In the Caribbean, aspiration is clearly the preference for educated speakers, even in formal speech situations, although most will pronounce a sibilant when reading aloud. The mental connection between a sibilant in orthography and aspiration in speech is strong for these speakers.

The sibilant is favored over aspiration only in a single context – the (s) of a determiner that is followed by a word beginning with a stressed vowel (*los hijos, los otros, mis hijos, sus ojos*). In this context the (s) is almost categorically retained by educated Cubans and Puerto Ricans. (See Table 4.)

In all other contexts, before a consonant (*este, esto*s *niños*) and before an unstressed vowel (*la*s *amigas*), the norm is an aspirated phone. Only before a pause, either at the end of a sentence or in the middle of an utterance, is there a tendency to reinsert the sibilant, most likely as a result of orthographic influence: *lo*s . . . *loh niño*s, *ehto*s . . . *ehtoh libro*s.

For the lower socioeconomic classes, remnants of this same system seem to be present, but the effects are not as strong. Ma and Herasimchuk (1971) noted a strong tendency to conserve the marker of plurality on the first modifier in the noun phrase (NP), but they also report much higher overall rates of deletion than we see for educated Puerto Rican speakers. In her investigation of Puerto Rican speakers of Philadelphia – all lower working-class or housewives – Poplack (1980b) found that the first marker of plurality in the NP was indeed conserved, but she also found a tendency toward local redundancy – if one marker is preserved others that follow

[14] See also Hammond (1973, 1976b).

Table 5. *Deletion of* (s), *by educational level* (*in percent*)

	Overall plural	First position	Modified noun
Primary	71	49	81
Secondary	63	33	80
University	14	11	44

it are often preserved and if the first is deleted then others that follow it are also deleted. Thus she found more than 1,000 cases of NPs with no surface manifestation of (s) at all. She notes that despite this high incidence of (s) deletion there were few if any cases of confusion. Other markers, both morphological and syntactic, presumably carry the load of plurality marking. Terrell (1979b) supported this finding with his investigation of Dominican speech in which (s) was almost categorically absent. In spite of this complete elimination of (s), the notion of plurality was clearly present and there were almost no cases of ambigüity in discourse. In a typical interview with a university student the following items functioned as plural markers.

1. Absence of a determiner:
   Son hecha(s) *por fábrica*(s) 'They are made by factory(ies)'
   una escuela de monja(s) 'a school (run) by nun(s)'
2. Quantifiers:
   trece año(s) 'thirteen years(s)'
   vario(s) *pueblo*(s) 'various town(s)'
3. *-o*:
   lo(s) *liceo*(s) 'the school(s)'
   en esto(s) *tiempo*(s) *de frío* 'in these time(s) of cold'
4. *-e*:
   el me(s) *de la*(s) *flore*(s) 'the month of the flower(s)'
   a vece(s) 'at time(s)'
5. Plural inherent:
   la(s) *tijera*(s) 'the scissor(s)'
6. Verbal concord:
   Ella tiene alguna(s) *persona*(s) *que le traen ropa* 'She has some person(s) who bring(pl) her clothes.'

Following suggestions by Poplack and López Morales, Terrell (1980) studied the interaction of aspiration and deletion of (s) in a group of speakers from López Morales's San Juan interviews, which consisted of informants with only primary or secondary education. This allowed comparison with earlier studies of educated San Juan speech and with Poplack's mainland Philadelphia and New York speakers. These new data revealed that the deletion of word final (s) is indeed much more advanced among informants without higher education. (See Table 5.)

Clearly, the plural marker on the modifier in first position in the NP is deleted less by all groups, but this particular constraint results in a high number of surface markers only for the highly educated group. Thus, listening to educated speech, one could for the most part depend on hearing [h] as a consistent marker for plurality:

> *con mih amiga* 'with my friends'
> *son solamente para lah invitada* 'they are only for the invited'

Remember, however, that even in the speech of educated persons with a preference for aspiration as the surface representation of (s), this [h] can be considered redundant because the listener could interpret plurality from other markers:

> *l*oh *interesado debe*n *estar aquí a la* once 'those interested should be here at eleven'

In the case of other speakers, however, because the [h] as a surface marker for the plural morpheme is usually not present (overall deletion for individual speakers is 41 percent–93 percent), that is, deletion is now the preferred norm for word final (s), listeners are *forced* to attend to other markers to determine the plurality of noun phrases. For example, a sentence such as,

> *No me gu*(s)*tan esa*(s) *camisa*(s) *azule*(s). 'I don't like those blue shirts.'

spoken by an educated speaker would almost always contain an [h] on *esas*. Because this is not true for other speakers, listeners are forced to attend to the *-n* of the verb, *gustan*, and/or the *-e* of *azule*(s). Note that it is not just those who have high rates of deletion who are forced to attend to these other markers, but also those who continue to produce aspiration as a surface marker for (s), unless they can restrict their interactions to only highly educated speakers, hardly a possibility for most speakers. It is precisely the existence in Puerto Rican society, then, of speakers with widely varied rates of (s) deletion – that is, the heterogeneity of the society – that determines the direction of the change. Note also that this refocusing of attention to the identification of plurality by other morphological, syntactic, and lexical means explains how Dominican speakers could have carried the rule of (s) deletion to completion with subsequent restructuring of the lexicon. Puerto Rican speakers, some of whom delete at the rate of 90 percent and higher, are also obviously in the process of restructuring of the lexicon.

In conclusion, the general system for (s) aspiration and deletion is known and we have a fairly good idea of how Cuban and Puerto Rican speech has evolved to this point as a result of analyzing data from the speech of other areas that have adopted these same phonological rules. What remains is to be able to separate particular local tendencies that have perhaps idiosyncratic explanations from those that are based on universal tendencies in language change.[15]

***Neutralization of* r *and* l**

Navarro-Tomás's monumental study of the Spanish spoken in Puerto Rico was based on data collected in 1927–8, although the book itself did not appear until 1948. It is true that he did not possess the means for recording and later analyzing his data, nor did he have access to a computer to help him sort out the variability he found; still, Navarro-Tomás was an extremely good phonetician and there is every reason to believe that his description of Puerto Rican Spanish in the early part of this century is accurate. We may, therefore, compare the present state of the pronunciation of (r) and (l) with his data in order to describe the change and to determine if it is indeed a change still in progress. Unfortunately no one has yet done a complete sociolinguistic study of the variable, and inferences will have to be drawn from the partial studies that have been completed.

Navarro-Tomás describes the three principal possibilities for the neutralization of syllable and word final (r) and (l). They are (1) pronunciation of both (r) and (l) as a lateral, (2) pronunciation of both as an alveolar flap or fricative (sometimes slightly voiceless) and (3) pronunciation of both as an intermediate sound with features of a flap and a lateral. He reported that contemporary popular opinion regarded the neutralization in favor of the lateral as the primary characteristic of popular speech. In his investigation he found that, indeed, the neutralization in favor of the lateral was the most common (52.5 percent), that neutralization in favor of the flap was also quite common (41 percent), and that the mixed variant was the least common of the three (6.5 percent). He also discovered that although all the variants were found in all parts of the island, each phonetic manifestation had centers of predominant use. Neutralization in favor of the lateral was most common in the eastern part of the island, whereas neutralization in favor of the flap was favored by speakers from the west. Navarro-Tomás supposed that the popular idea that neutralization in favor of the lateral was the norm for Puerto Ricans stemmed from the fact that this was the favored process in San Juan, the capital city.

Navarro-Tomás noted also that the process was irregular lexically; that is, word classes could be split such that certain words would be uniformly affected but others would be affected variably. He also reported individual variation, for example, an individual who pronounced *verdad, tarde*, and *carbon* with a flap and *espalda* with the lateral but *barba, muerte, puerta*, and *tarde* with the lateral and *caldo, soldado*, and *saltar* with the flap. Only in the extremities of the island, the northeast and southwest, were processes applied more uniformly. Word final (r) and (l) (*mar, al*) were

[15] For some speculation see Terrell (1979c) and Poplack (1980a).

subject to rule application following the same patterns as word internal (r) and (l). Complete deletion was rare for the subjects he interviewed. Neutralization between (r) and (l) was found primarily in subjects without formal education. However, even in the late twenties he noted that sporadic cases of the neutralization could be found in the speech of individuals of the highest social circles and educational levels of San Juan.

Navarro-Tomás hypothesized that neutralization originated from a weakening in the articulation of the two phonemes and noted that this neutralization of the contrast was found in wide areas of Spain, the Canary Islands, and Latin America. Historically he noted that evidence for neutralization in favor of /r/ is found in texts of the sixteenth and seventeenth centuries.[16] Navarro-Tomás also rejects the theory that the neutralization is due to black influence (1948, p. 84, n. 1).

Navarro-Tomás also noted several other possibilities for pronunciation of /r/ and /l/. In addition to the two basic phones (a flap or fricative and a lateral), there are modalities based on a nasal and those based on aspiration. He did not, however, find many examples of these. Nor did he find much vocalization with /i/ (*habla*[i̯]), so common in certain areas of the Dominican Republic (Golibart 1977, Jiménez Sabater 1975).

Joseph Matluck (1961), another excellent phonetician, spent a year in Puerto Rico in the late fifties and published his informal observations. Matluck is an experienced observer of phonetic phenomena, and his reports are usually very reliable. Matluck claimed that by the fifties, neutralization in favor of the lateral had gained ground and was even becoming the norm in uneducated speech in the western part of the island. He reported also that the use of the lateral was almost general in the entire southeast. In her review of recent work done on Puerto Rican Spanish, Vaquero de Ramírez (1972) reports that neutralization in favor of /l/, or at least a mixed articulation, is now general and that very few persons conserve an alveolar flap (or fricative) regularly in their pronunciation.

Thus from the observations to date it appears that neutralization of (r) and (l) resulted from the phonetic phenomenon of weakening, which extended from focal points of innovation in separate parts of the island. The spread of the lateral varieties appears to have been stronger and has apparently eliminated the earlier [l] → [r] process. There are several important variables, then, in the development of Puerto Rican /r/ and /l/ neutralization:

1. Geographic area of diffusion
2. Two competing processes
3. One process becoming stronger than the other

[16] Alonso (1967, p. 264) disagrees completely, saying that "Fuera de los trueques aislados entre *-r* y *-l* . . . no hay en lo antiguo, ni en los siglos XVI, XVII, y XVIII denuncia alguna de que estas consonantes se confundieran en nunguna parte. Como el yeísmo . . . son fenómenos documentados para el siglo IX y probablemente, desarrollados también en ese siglo . . ."

Table 6. *Style-shifting by Puerto Rican speakers: word internal* (r) (*in percent*)

	Reading word lists	Casual speech
Flap or fricative	61	25
Lateral	34	39
Assimilation	5	27
Deletion	0	10

Source: Ma and Herasimchuk (1971), section 4, table 1.

4. Conservative pressure of education and orthography; hypercorrection
5. Some stigmatism of [r] → [l] or [l]–[r] by educated speakers

The result is extreme variability both in the lexicon and by individuals. Because the process is strongly stigmatized, it shows strong sociolinguistic and stylistic stratification.

There are two quantitatively based studies in recent years. The largest was Ma and Herasimchuk's (1971) study of Puerto Rican immigrants in New York. They found that style-shifting was indeed quite strong for lower-class speakers. In addition to the lateral variant they found two (new?) processes: complete assimilation to the following consonant (resulting in gemmination) or complete deletion of the (r). Neither of these is yet the norm for any speaker; however, it is interesting to note that apparently both have gained ground at the expense of the standard flap and the lateral. Ma and Herasimchuk noted that the [l] to [r] shift occurred but that lateralization of (r) was much more common. They did not study the use of [r] for [l] and therefore we cannot compare the two processes quantitatively. It is clear, however, from Ma and Herasimchuk's data that the weakening processes postulated by Navarro-Tomás have advanced considerably since the early part of the century.

Shouse de Vivas (1978 and 1979), in her quantitative study of lower-class Puerto Rican speech, studied the linguistic constraints of the neutralization process. (See Table 7.)

Based on her data, my hypotheses are that lateralization is favored by prepausal position and that the (r) of infinitives is lateralized more than in monomorphemic words. If (r) is followed by a consonant, lateralization is favored by a following lateral and stop especially if the stop is dental. Thus, favored contexts are in the words *hablar* and *comer* and internally in words like *verdad, carta*, and *puerta*. On the other hand considerably more work will have to be done using a multivariant analysis because the contexts overlap and it is difficult to sort out competing constraints.

In my own preliminary investigation of (r) and (l) among educated speakers of San Juan, I found extreme variability. (See Table 8.) Cases

Table 7. *Linguistic constraints on lateralization, Puerto Rico (in percent)*

Position	[r] → [l]
Prepausal	60
Other word final	38
Word internal	28
Prelateral	48
Prestop	38
Prenasal	25
Prefricative	8
Prealveolar/dental	39
Other	20
Infinitive	52
Monomorphemic	25

Source: Shouse de Vivas (1978).

Table 8. *Lateralization of* -r: *educated speakers, San Juan (in percent)*

	Syllable final [r] → [l]	Word final [r] → [l]
Total	19	22
Females	9	11
Males	29	33
10 M III	43	52
13 M III	28	47
48 M II	1	10
23 M II	36	32
7 M I	60	52
21 M I	5	4
12 M I	23	44
19 M II	38	23
49 F III	26	28
33 F III	15	17
21 F II	4	0
9 F II	14	26
16 F II	6	8
37 F I	0	0
20 F I	3	6
18 F I	63	52

Note: The code in the first column indicates the interview number and the speaker's sex and age (I = young adult, II = middle aged, III = old).

of [l] to [r] were so rare that I did not tabulate them formally. On the other hand only one informant of the sixteen studied was able to avoid lateralization of /r/ completely. Males showed higher levels of lateralization than females; note in Table 8 that only a single female surpassed the norm for males. This supports the contention of all observers that the process is stigmatized, because correction toward the norm by females is a well-established principle, at least for western European and American societies. Table 8 also exhibits clear evidence that the process of lateralization is a "change from below," because it has rather strongly penetrated even the upper educational levels of San Juan society, a phenomenon that Navarro-Tomás thought to be only sporadic at the beginning of the century. It remains to be seen whether increased education will slow the process and perhaps even reverse it, restoring the [r] in its etymologically correct contexts.

The attempts at a quantitative variable rule analysis of the lateralization of /r/ raises both methodological and theoretical considerations. Shouse de Vivas (1979) experienced problems in applying this methodology to an analysis of the effects of style on (r) lateralization. She found that lateralization was more frequent in formal (L = 44%; N = 354) than in casual speech (L = 34%; N = 1,023). We know that this is not the case: Puerto Rican speakers lateralize less in formal situations. Shouse de Vivas suggests that perhaps lexical inconsistencies can account for these skewed results. Lexical considerations, however, can influence the data only if the rule in question is no longer applied consistently according to phonological constraints. That is, if lexical constraints are more important than phonological contexts in the operation of the rule, then an unequal distribution of specific lexical items in different speech styles – certainly a reasonable expectation – will lead to problems in a variable rule analysis.

In the lateralization of /r/, I suspect that this is exactly what has occurred. The rule [r] → [l] was undoubtedly one of consonantal weakening due to the general tendency of Spanish speakers to weaken the articulation of all consonants in syllable final position. The rule also was probably favored by the presence of a following alveolar consonant as in *verdad, carta, sartén, marzo*. In these clusters, *-rd-, -rt-, -rs-,* it is difficult to execute a complete flap and then articulate the following consonant. If one simply brings the tongue to the alveolar ridge but does not maintain enough tension to execute a flap release and at the same time relaxes the edges of the tongue, the result is a lateralized alveolar stop. These originally mixed variants are, of course, still quite common in Puerto Rican speech. Those who are in the process of acquiring speech, either children acquiring their first language or adults acquiring features from the speech of peers, have trouble identifying this mixed (weakened) phone with phonemes /r/ or /l/ in other positions. The acquirer has one of three possibilities: (1) to posit an underlying /r/ with a variable rule, (2) to posit an underlying /r^l/, (3) to posit an underlying /l/. The data suggest that speakers have done all three: In words in which the variable rule applied most often, *verdad, carta,* that is, very common words with /r/ followed by an alveolar stop, many speakers simply have restructured (or acquired) the word with underlying /l/. Because lexical restructuring can proceed word by word (although both frequency and phonological context are factors), the result can be extreme individual variability in cases in which the rule does not (or cannot) go to completion. In the case of the lateralization of (r) the social stigma of the process, plus the variable influence of orthography on literate speakers, are strong factors in preventing categorical restructuring of the lexicon with /l/.

Returning to Shouse de Vivas's seemingly contradictory data, I can offer a tentative explanation and at the same time draw both methodological and theoretical conclusions. If her speakers have irregularly restructured lexicons, that is, some words with /l/, others with /r/ and a variable rule of (r) lateralization, and if those words with categorical underlying /l/ appear more frequently in formal speech (because of topic, for example), then it will appear that the variable rule in question has operated more frequently than it has. Methodologically, then, in using a variable rule analysis, we cannot simply count surface manifestations of variables and proceed to search for correlations without at the same time considering the status of the rule in question – have speakers begun lexical restructuring? On the theoretical level, it is apparent that the theory of variable rules will have to include a framework that details how lexical restructuring takes place.[17]

There is for Cuba no study comparable to Navarro-Tomás's Puerto Rican study by which to measure change in progress. On the other hand, all indications are that compared with Puerto Rican Spanish, syllable and word final (r) for Cuban speakers is relatively stable. All the variants found in Puerto Rico and in other parts of the Spanish-speaking world have been noted also for Cuban speech, but mostly sporadically. Almendros (1958) (cited in Isbaseşcu 1968, p. 56) claimed that the lateralization of (r) was extended completely throughout the western part of the island, but that it was absent in the eastern half. Isbaseşcu (1968, p. 56) found lateralization in all of the subjects she examined but neglected to specify the extent to which the process was used. Haden and Matluck (1973) as well as Vallejo-Claros (1971) found lateralization of (r) to be sporadic in the educated speech of Havana in the late sixties. López Morales (1970, p. 111) claimed that the fricative [ȓ], not a lateral, was the norm. Furthermore, he believes that the general belief that this neutralization exists on a large scale in Cuba comes mainly from observations made more than a century ago in certain areas of the island. Guitart (1976, pp. 23–5) claims that a phenomenon much more common than lateralization is complete

[17] I do not mean to imply that Labov himself has not worked on such a consideration (see, for example, Labov 1972a).

assimilation to a following obstruent (*caldo* [kaddo] *fuerte* [fuette]), especially for speakers from the Havana area.

There are no sociolinguistic studies of (r) in Cuban Spanish in which speech style and socioeconomic class are considered.[18] The only extensive study is Terrell (1976), but only educated speakers from Havana were included and, in addition, the speech style of the informants was semiformal. The norm for these speakers, as for all Spanish speakers, was the standard flap with some weakening to a fricative pronunciation in syllable and word final positions. All other variants (vocalization, lateralization, assimilation, deletion) were present but not systematic in any individual's speech and were infrequent. On the other hand, personal experience with various Cubans who have recently arrived from Havana leads me to believe that, at least for some individuals, complete assimilation as described by Guitart (1976) has become (always was?) categorical.

In summary then, in spite of the excellent study by Alonso (1967, pp. 213–67) of the distribution of the variants of (r) and (l) (and their neutralization) in the Spanish-speaking world, it is still not possible to offer a panoramic description of the extension and use of lateralization of (r) in Spanish, much less an explanation for the way in which the process was and is being adopted.

Velarization of rr

The velarization (or in many cases, the uvularization) of the trilled (rr), whether intervocalic (*carro*) or word initial (*rosa*), is believed to be a unique characteristic of Puerto Rico, although observers have pointed out that velarization and uvularization of *r* is found in many European languages. Only in Brazilian Portuguese, however, is the distribution close to that in Puerto Rican Spanish.

Navarro-Tomás's description (1948) of (rr) is, as is all his work, detailed and accurate. He posits three types of surface variants: alveolar, either trilled or fricative (usually voiced), velar (or uvular) with a clear tendency to devoice, and a variant that seems to be a mixture of the two, that is, alveolar contact with aspiration. The mixed variant is of special interest, because it may explain the phonetic evolution of the velar sound. Navarro-Tomás describes it as consisting of an articulation that begins with a fricative element that vacillates between alveolar and velar and ends with an alveolar sound somewhere between a trill and a fricative. I transcribe the sound as [hr] and have heard it in Puerto Rico and occasionally in Santo Domingo, where the change may be in its first stages.

Navarro-Tomás found that most of his informants pronounced series of either velar or alveolar allophones, varying somewhat in the particular

[18] Vallejo-Claros's (1971) data are invalid because of inclusion of intervocalic /r/ which never lateralizes.

Table 9. *Use of velar phones for* (rr) (*in percent*)

Low formal education	91
University students (west)	80
Educated, San Juan	41

Source: Hammond (1979b).

series but not mixing the main types. Thus those who used velar allophones did so consistently and did not normally use alveolar allophones. Fifty-nine percent of his informants used velarized phones. Otherwise the fricative variant was common, and the standard trill was the least common of the three. In addition he found that each variant was distributed differently according to area. The velar phone was most common for (rr) in the north and southeast. The standard variants were dominant in the southwest, including Ponce. The mixed variant was popular in the northeast, especially in San Juan. Navarro-Tomás also found that the different modalities were found mixed in the same villages and even in the same families.

At least in the early part of the century, however, Navarro-Tomás noted that the velar phone was held to be inferior to the standard variants. For example, he states that a subject reported that she always used a velar sound for (rr) until taught by a teacher to pronounce it "correctly." All members of a certain family in Mayagüez used a velar for (rr) except one child who had learned to produce an alveolar phone in the schools and was greatly praised by his parents. One wonders, however, if the child used the alveolar phone for (rr) with his peers and, if so, what the reaction was.

In the preliminary notes, which were written some twenty years later, Navarro-Tomás suggests that the situation may have changed somewhat. In the prologue to the 1966 edition, he is of the opinion that the use of velar phones for (rr) has decreased. It appears that he was too conservative. Matluck (1961) reports that in the fifties the same three varieties were used in San Juan but that the velar or uvular variant was the most common. Vaquero de Ramírez (1972) says that the use of a velar phone for (rr) has gained considerably in use according to the latest investigations. In certain areas it is the only variant heard, in others it is used by a majority of the population, and in certain areas it is common but has not yet been completely adopted.

Hammond (1979b) found that the velar variant was the form used by most of the informants he studied. (See Table 9.) Some informants were from small towns and had little formal education, others were university students from the western part of the island and highly educated natives of San Juan. My own study of the use of a velar phone for (rr) was based

Table 10. *Velarization of* (rr): *educated speakers, San Juan* (*in percent*)

		Word initial	Word internal
10	M-III	22	17
13	M III	1	0
19	M II	1	0
48	M II	5	6
23	M II	0	0
7	M I	37	7
22	M I	0	6
17	M I	93	96
49	F III	0	0
33	F III	16	14
21	F II	0	0
9	F II	77	88
16	F II	0	0
37	F I	6	7
20	F I	0	0
18A	F I	58	49

Note: The code in the first column indicates the interview number and the speaker's sex and age (I = young adult, II = middle aged, III = old).

on a larger sample of the same educated speakers from San Juan that Hammond used. I, too, found extreme variability. (See Table 10.)

It is clear that velarization of (rr) has not spread to the educated classes as much as lateralization. In addition, the use of velar phones is extremely variable on an individual basis. Only two informants can be said to use velar allophones regularly – a middle-aged female and a younger male. Nor does it seem to be the case that males use the feature much more than females.

Rosario (cited by Ma and Herasimchuk 1971) states that the velar has currently reached all the towns of the island and is heard constantly in meetings, conferences, and radio and television transmissions. Ma and Herasimchuk found that the mixed variant is found to be used mostly by the educated speaker of San Juan, which leads to the possibility that it may be a partial hypercorrection as well as a stage of development. Thus they classified the variable into two types, principally apicoalveolar and postvelar, both varying in degrees of voicing. They found sharp style correlations but the postvelar phone was the norm for informal conversation.

López Morales (1979b, pp. 107–30), in a study of the subjective evaluation of the velar (rr), found that although a clear majority of those surveyed rejected its use (usually because of its supposed "rural" origin), at least one-third found it to be completely acceptable (most of these pointing out its unique "puertorricanness").

Thus, recent work on the Puerto Rican velarization of (rr) has focused on a description of its distribution and an account of its spread through society and through the island. It should be noted that in past years much more attention was given to an explanation of its origin.[19] It is to be hoped that future research will shed light on both issues.

***Velarization and deletion of* (n)**

Fewer studies have been done with syllable and word final (n) than with (s) or with (r). In part this is because it is exceedingly difficult to distinguish between a weak velar nasal consonant and its deletion with retention of strong nasalization on the preceding vowel.

Navarro-Tomás (1948) reported in the early part of the century that in Puerto Rico the velar nasal (ŋ) was uniformly the only variant used in word final position. Because he used mainly word lists this observation must be restricted to prepausal position. Matluck (1961) reaffirms this observation for the late fifties and adds that the same is true of word final position if the following word begins with a vowel (*en esto*). Matluck claimed that the use of a velar phone is so strong that most speakers do not perceive the velar sound as different from other varieties. Neither of these observers commented on the possible spread of velarization to preconsonantal position either internally or word finally.

In their study of stylistic variation Ma and Herasimchuk (1971) classified the phonetic manifestations of (n) into three possibilities: the standard alveolar (or assimilated) nasal, the velarized variant, and the nasalization of the vowel with concurrent deletion of the consonant. They studied the use of these three variants in word final prevocalic position and in word final preconsonantal and prepausal position. Unfortunately, they did not separate their data for the prepausal and preconsonantal group and thus this particular part of their data is invalid. In prevocalic position they found that the standard alveolar variant was indeed used most of the time (about 58 percent alveolar to 42 percent velar) in formal reading but that the velarization or deletion with vowel nasalization (42 percent velarization and 40 percent deletion, respectively) competed for the norm in informal speech. The standard variant, however, was used about 18 percent of the time even in informal speech. They also did not investigate the use of the velar in word internal position.

López Morales (1979a), in the most recent study of the variable in San

19 Megenny (n.d.) in a University of California, Riverside, manuscript discusses in some detail the controversy of whether the velar *r* has its origins in African or indigenous languages, providing strong evidence against the African origin theory. See also Navarro-Tomás (1948, pp. 94–5), Malmberg (1961, pp. 100–1; 1964, p. 232) and Granda (1966, pp. 181–277).

Table 11. *Pronunciation of word internal* (n) (*in percent*)

Position	Alveolar (or assimilated)	Velar [ŋ]	Deletion [ṽ]
Internal			
San Juan	91	1	8
Havana	84	0	16
Final			
San Juan	66	27	7
Havana	36	26	38

Table 12. *Word final* (n) (*in percent*)

Position	Alveolar (or assimilated)	Velar [ŋ]	Deletion [ṽ]
Preconsonantal (____#C)			
San Juan	81	13	6
Havana	60	1	39
Prevocalic (____#V)			
San Juan	66	27	7
Havana	3	59	39
Prepausal (____#P)			
San Juan	22	69	8
Havana	18	54	38

Juan, and Terrell (1975a), in a study of educated speakers of Havana, both found that the standard assimilated phones are still common variants in Puerto Rican and Cuban speech. (See Table 11.) In particular it is clear that velarization in word internal position is very rare and that standard assimilation of point of articulation is the norm. In word final position the velar is more common; however, it is important to examine the context, because all observers have noted that the following segment conditions velarization. It is clear from Table 12 that the assimilated nasal is still the norm for both groups of speakers in preconsonantal position. The velar, on the other hand, is the norm for both groups in prepausal position (confirming earlier observations by Navarro-Tomás and Matluck). In prevocalic position it is the norm for Cubans and increasingly is being used by Puerto Ricans. Deletion appears to be much stronger for Cubans than Puerto Ricans. In addition, López Morales (1979a) found that in San Juan the use of the velar was not affected by sex or socioeconomic levels but that middle-aged speakers and speakers of urban origin favored the use of velars. On the other hand the use of deletion was favored by lower socioeconomic classes and the young.

The data from these two studies, both of which had unexpectedly conservative results, should be compared with the studies by Ma and Herasimchuk (1971) for lower-class Puerto Ricans and by Hammond (1978) for fast Cuban speech. Both studies report much higher rates of velarization and deletion.

It is obvious that we are still far from an adequate description of the state of development of velarization and nasal deletion in both Cuban and Puerto Rican speech. Velarization is usually considered to be a manifestation of weakening. However it is not clear why weakening should occur most in prepausal and word final prevocalic position. Indeed, it is not clear why this process should spread to implosive preconsonantal position, because in this position also it constitutes dissimilation. Guitart (1976, pp. 75–6) argues that velarization is simply a particular manifestation in the nasals of a general backing tendency for implosive consonants in Caribbean Spanish. Also interesting are the examples Hammond found of restructuring of final (n) to a velar: *marico*[ŋ] to a velar – *merico*[ŋ], *marico*[ŋ]es.

Poplack (1978) also studied the same phenomena in the speech of working-class Puerto Ricans from the Philadelphia area. She found that the three varieties were fairly equally distributed in the corpus: alveolar (assimilated), 37 percent; velar, 32 percent; and deleted (nasalized vowel), 22 percent. Because the data was not broken down by phonological context in her report, it is impossible to use it to explain the difference between López Morales's and Terrell's findings on the one hand and Ma and Herasimchuk's and Hammond's findings on the other. Perhaps more important, however, Poplack extended her study by distinguishing carefully between deletion with preservation of nasality on the vowel, *comen* [komẽ] versus complete absence of nasality, *comen* [kome]. As might be expected complete deletion was not the norm and in fact constituted only 9 percent of the cases examined. In absolute terms, however, this amounted to almost 300 examples of failure to mark the verb for plurality. Poplack examined several factors that might favor or, conversely, impede plural marking of the verb. Neither speech style nor phonological context (following segment and stress) affected application of the rule. On the other hand the *-n* of irregular verbs (*es*, *son*; *habló*, *hablaron*), that is, those forms whose plural marker is distinctive without *-n*, was absent less than in regular forms. Poplack (1978, p. 16) hypothesizes that this may be due "to a notion of 'phonic salience' of the singular-plural opposition."[20]

In any case, another factor was also relevant: the place and presence of disambiguating information. That is, if the NP was not marked for plurality in any way, the probability of omitting the verbal marker *-n* was very low. The highest rate of deletion of *-n* was found when the NP was marked for plurality and *followed* the verb. Poplack (1978, p. 18) postulates that this is perhaps due to a "repair mechanism," that is, "insertion of information after the verb may be used as a 'last resort' in order to avoid producing a sentence which is ambiguous as to number."

It is clear then that the study of phonological processes affecting the nasals has barely begun: We have not even reached the stage of descriptive adequacy necessary before we can begin to reconstruct the diachronic path of change.

Conclusions

The goal in studying phonological variability has two facets. Amado Alonso (1967, p. 215) stated it nicely:

> Una cosa es el establecer y describir cómo es y cómo funciona un sistema fonético o uno o más elementos de un sistema fonético, y otra cosa averiguar o conjeturar cómo han llegado a tal estado desde otro anterior.

From this review of recent research on Cuban and Puerto Rican phonology it is clear that although by using quantitative models great advances have been made, much remains to be completed before there will be much to say about human language in general and specifically how languages change.

References

Almendros, Néstor. 1958. Estudio fonético del español en Cuba. *Boletín de la Academia Cubana de la lengua* 7:171–2.

Alonso, Amado. 1967. *Estudios lingüísticos*. Temas Hispanoamericanos. Madrid: Editorial Gredos.

Bjarkman, Peter. 1978. Theoretically relevant issues in Cuban Spanish phonology. *Chicago Linguistic Society* 14:13–27.

Cedergren, Henrietta. 1973. *The interplay of social and linguistic factors in Panama*. Ph.D. dissertation, Cornell University.

Golibart, Pablo. 1977. Gramática generativa de la vocalización cibaeña. Paper presented at the Second Annual Caribbean Dialect Conference, Santo Domingo.

Granda, G. de. 1966. La velarización de /rr/ en el español de Puerto Rico. *Revista de Filología Española* 44:181–227.

[20] Poplack attributes the observation to Guy and Braga (1976) who found the same effect for Brazilian Portuguese.

Guitart, Jorge. 1976. *Markedness and a Cuban dialect of Spanish.* Washington, D.C.: Georgetown University Press.

1977. Aspectos del consonantismo habanero: reexamen descriptivo. Mimeographed. Paper presented at the Special Session on Spanish American Dialectology of the Ninety-second Annual Meeting of the Modern Language Association.

1978. A propósito del español de Cuba y Puerto Rico, hacia un modelo no sociolingüístico de lo sociodialectal. In *Corrientes actuales en la dialectología del Caribe hispánico*, ed., Humberto López Morales. Río Piedras: Editorial Universitaria.

1979. How autonomous is the natural phonology of Cuban Spanish? Mimeographed. Paper presented at the Ninth Annual Linguistics Symposium on Romance Languages, Georgetown University.

Guy, Gregory, and María Luisa Braga. 1976. Number concordance in Brazilian Portuguese. Paper presented at the annual N-WAVE conference, Georgetown University.

Haden, E. F., and J. H. Matluck. 1973. El habla culta de la Habana: análisis fonológico preliminar. *Anuario de Letras* 11:5–33.

Hammond, Robert. 1973. An experimental verification of the phonemic status of open and closed vowels in Spanish. Master's thesis, Florida Atlantic University.

1976a. Some surface phenomena of liquids in Cuban Spanish rapid speech. Paper presented at the Primer Seminario de Dialectología Latinoamericana of the Ninety-first Annual Meeting of the Modern Language Association, New York.

1976b. An experimental verification of the phonemic status of open and closed vowels in Caribbean Spanish. Paper presented at the First Annual Caribbean Dialect Conference, San Juan.

1977. En torno al consonantismo del español cubano – implicaciones para la fonología generativa. Paper presented at the Second Annual Caribbean Dialect Conference, Santo Domingo.

1978. The velar nasal in Miami Cuban Spanish rapid speech. In *Proceedings from the Third Colloquium in Hispanic and Luso Brazilian Linguistics*, ed. J. Lantolf, F. Frank, and J. Guitart, pp. 19–36. Washington, D.C.: Georgetown University Press.

1979. Restricciones sintácticas y/o semánticas en la elisión de /s/ en el español cubano. *Boletín de la Academia puertorriqueña de la lengua* 1, no. 2:41–57.

1979b. Un análisis sociolingüístico de la *r* velar en Puerto Rico. Paper presented at the Fourth Annual Caribbean Dialect Conference, Universidad Interamericana.

Harris, James. 1969. *Spanish phonology.* Cambridge, Mass.: MIT Press.

Hockett, Charles. 1954. Two models of grammatical description. *Word* 10:210–31.

Isbaseşcu, Cristina. 1968. *El español en Cuba.* Bucharest: Sociedad Rumana de Lingüística Románica.

Jiménez Sabater, Max A. 1975. *Más datos sobre el español de la república dominicana.* Santo Domingo: Ediciones Intec.

Labov, W. 1972a. The internal evolution of linguistic rules. In *Historical linguistics and generative theory*, ed. R. Stockwell and R. Macaulay. Bloomington: Indiana University Press.

1972b. *Sociolinguistic patterns.* Philadelphia: University of Pennsylvania Press.

Lope Blanch, Juan. 1968. El proyecto de estudio coordinado de la norma

lingüística culta de las principales ciudades de Iberoamérica y de la penísula ibérica. In *El simposio de México*, pp. 222–3. Mexico City: Universidad Nacional Autónoma de México.
López Morales, Humberto. 1970. *Estudio sobre el español de Cuba*. New York: Los Américas.
1979a. Velarización de /-N/ en el español de San Juan. Paper presented at the annual N-WAVE conference, Université du Quebec à Montreal.
1979b. *Dialectología y sociolingüística: temas puertorriqueños*. Hispanova de Ediciones. Madrid: Editorial Playor.
Ma, Roxana, and Eleanor Herasimchuk. 1971. The linguistic dimensions of a bilingual neighborhood. In *Bilingualism in the barrio*, ed. J. A. Fishman, R. L. Cooper, R. Ma, et al. pp. 347–464. Language Science Monographs, vol. 7. Bloomington: Indiana University, Research Center for the Language Sciences.
Malmberg, B. 1961. Linguistique ibérique et ibéro-romane: problèmes et méthodes. *Studia Linguistica* 15:100–11.
1964. Tradición hispánica e influencia indígena en la fonética hispanoamericana. In *Presente y futuro de la lengua española*, pp. 227–43. Madrid: Instituto de Cultura Hispanica.
Matluck, Joseph. 1961. Fonemas finales en el consonantismo puertorriqueño. *Nueva Revista de Filología Hispánica* 15:332–42.
Megenny, William. n.d. El problema del [R] en Puerto Rico. Manuscript, University of California, Riverside.
Navarro-Tomás, Tomás. 1948. *El español en Puerto Rico*. Río Piedras: Editorial Universitaria.
Poplack, Shana. 1978. On deletion and disambiguation in Puerto Rican Spanish: a study of verbal (n#). In *Centro working papers*. New York: Centro de Estudios Puertorriqueños.
1979. Function and process in a variable phonology. Ph.D. dissertation, University of Pennsylvania.
1980a. Deletion and disambiguation in Puerto Rican Spanish. *Language* 56, no. 2 (June):371–85.
1980b. The notion of the plural in Puerto Rican Spanish: competing constraints on /s/ deletion. In *Locating language in time and space*, ed. William Labov, pp. 55–67. New York: Academic Press.
Resnick, M. C., and Robert M. Hammond. 1975. The status of quality and length in Spanish vowels. *Linguistics* 156 (August):79–87.
Shouse de Vivas, Dolores. 1978. El uso de [l] en Puerto Rico. Paper presented at the meeting of the Asociación de Lingüística y Filología de la América Latina, Caracas, Venezuela.
1979. The use of the [l] variant of the variable *r* in Puerto Rican Spanish in the New England community. Master's thesis, University of Kansas.
Terrell, T. D. 1975a. La nasal implosiva y final en el español de Cuba. *Anuario de letras* 13:257–71.
1975b. Natural generative phonology: evidence from Spanish. *Second language teaching 75 (including linguistics)*. In *Proceedings of the twenty-sixth annual meeting of the Pacific Northwest Council on Foreign Languages*, part 2, ed. H. Hammerly and Isabel Sawyer, pp. 259–67. Vancouver: Simon Fraser University.
1976. La variación fonética de /r/ y /rr/ en el español cubano. *Revista de Filología Española* 58:109–32.

1977a. Universal constraints on variably deleted consonants. *Canadian Journal of Linguistics* 22:156–68.
1977b. Observations on the relationship between group and individual variation in the development of constraints on variable rules: evidence from Spanish. *Berkeley Linguistics Society* 3:535–44.
1977c. Constraints on the aspiration and deletion of final /s/ in Cuban and Puerto Rico Spanish. *Bilingual Review* 4:35–51.
1978a. Parallelisms between liaison in French and /s/ aspiration and deletion in Spanish dialects. *Montreal Working Papers in Linguistics* 10 (November):31–50.
1978b. Sobre la aspiración y elisión de /s/ implosiva y final en el español de Puerto Rico. *Nueva Revista de Filología Hispánica* 27, no. 1:24–38.
1978c. La aportación a la teoría fonológica de los estudios dialectales antillanos. In *Corrientes actuales en la dialectología del Caribe hispánico*, ed., Humberto López Morales. Río Piedras: Editorial Universitaria.
1979a. Final /s/ in Cuban Spanish. *Hispania* 62:599–612.
1979b. La reestructuración fonémica de /s/ en el español dominicano. Paper presented at the Fourth Annual Caribbean Dialect Conference, Universidad Interamericana.
1979c. Diachronic reconstruction by dialect comparison of variable constraints: s-aspiration and deletion in Spanish. Paper presented at the annual N-WAVE conference, Montreal, Canada.
1979d. Problemas en los estudios cuantitativos de procesos fonológicos variables: datos del Caribe hispánico. *Boletín de la Academia Puertorriqueña de la Lengua Española* 7:145–65.
1980. Sound change: the explanatory value of heterogeneity of variable rule application. Paper presented at Symposium: Spanish in the U.S. Setting, University of Illinois at Chicago Circle, October.
Vallejo-Claros, B. 1971. La distribución y estratificación de /r/, /r̄/ y /s/ en el español cubano. Ph.D. dissertation, University of Texas.
Vaquero de Ramírez, María 1972. Algunos fenómenos fonéticos señalados por Navarro-Tomás en *El español de Puerto Rico* a la luz de las investigaciones posteriores. *Revista de Estudios Hispánicos* 1–4:243–51.

3

Influences of English on /b/ in Los Angeles Spanish

ROBERT PHILLIPS

The Spanish phonemes /b,d,g/ are interesting to the phonologist because they have both voiced stop and voiced fricative allophones [b,ƀ,d,đ,g,ǥ] which are said to be in strict complementary distribution in "standard" Spanish. All of them use the fricative allophone except after a juncture or after a nasal. In addition, the /d/ is said to use the stop allophone after /l/. A contrast with English is especially striking, in that the English voiced fricatives are phonemic in their own right. Of great interest in bilingual speech is how the English inventory affects the "standard" distribution and articulation of the Spanish phonemes. Of the three, the case of the /b/ offers the greatest possibilities for influence: the stop/fricative alternation does not occur in English, and the English voiced fricative is the labiodental [v], while the "standard" Spanish allophone is the bilabial [ƀ].

Los Angeles is a good place to do a study of the influence of English on Spanish. There is a very large Spanish-speaking community (variously estimated at between 400,000 and 700,000 speakers), but English is the dominant language in the area. At the time I did my study,[1] Spanish was not the language of instruction in any public schools in the area. And, although there was one Spanish-language television channel, it was somewhat restricted in its programming.

For this study, I used thirty-one informants, each of them carefully chosen to represent different groups. They were classified by sex, by age, by the relative amounts of Spanish and English they used in their daily life, and by a rough social-class distinction. In order to have uniform data for the phonological section of the study, I devised a checklist of words which I attempted to elicit from all informants. This eliciting was generally done by having the informants translate English words or phrases into

Reprinted with permission from the Texas Western Press. From *Studies in Language and Linguistics 1972–1973*, ed. Ralph W. Ewton and Jacob Ornstein (El Paso: Texas Western Press, 1974), pp. 202–12.

[1] *Los Angeles Spanish: A Descriptive Analysis*. Ph.D. dissertation, University of Wisconsin, 1967.

Spanish. Although the complete study involved, in addition, many examples taken from spontaneous speech, the data presented in this chapter are only from the checklist.

This chapter is divided into two sections. The first studies the distribution of the allophones of /b/ in different phonemic environments. In the second section, I break down the informants by the distinctions mentioned above and discuss how different groups use the allophones in differing ways.

There are three voiced labial allophones in common use in Los Angeles Spanish: [b], the voiced bilabial stop; [ƀ], the voiced bilabial fricative; and [v], the voiced labiodental fricative. The clear-cut complementary distribution of "standard" descriptions of Spanish is not found in Los Angeles, doubtless because of the existence of the English /v/ phoneme. In some cases, the [ƀ] and the [v] are in free variation with each other, but in complementary distribution with [b]; in other cases, all three seem to be in free variation. There is some difference among various groups of speakers on this point.

An example of the confusion was found with the word *vino*. It was elicited preceded by pause, by an /l/ ("el vino"); by a nasal ("buen vino"); and by /s/ ("varios vinos"). Pronounced in isolation, four informants used [b], six used [ƀ], and twenty-one used [v]. Preceded by /l/, three used the stop [b], twelve used [ƀ], and fourteen used [v]. When preceded by the nasal, twelve used [b], eight used the [ƀ], and another eight used the [v]. Finally, when preceded by /s/, of the thirteen who responded (the plural apparently was confusing to the majority of them), one used the [b], seven used the [ƀ], and five used the [v].

One suspects that the spelling of the word may have played some part in the confusion with the /b/ in these phrases, although none of the informants read the words. All of them are at least nominally literate in at least one language; most of them have some acquaintance with the writing systems of both languages. And some of them may have been taught, either by teachers, by priests, or by parental example, that there should be a difference between orthographic *b* and *v*. The fact that there is a phonemic difference in English between the stop /b/ and the fricative /v/ no doubt contributes to the confusion and the rather wide-spread use of the [v] among these persons who are in daily contact with English.

/b/ in intervocalic position

The words on the checklist which have the /b/ in this position were *llover, clavo, globo, recibo, huevo*, and *automovil* (along with its variant /atomobil/). Table 1 shows the number of informants found to use each of the allophones in these words. It is seen here that the [b] intervocalically is rather rare, and may well be due in some measure to the eliciting situation. (However, the informants were led to believe that I was eliciting for lexical items, rather than for pronunciation.) [ƀ] is used more often than

Table 1

Word	[b]	[ƀ]	[v]
llover	0	17	11
clavo	0	28	3
globo	4	18	5
recibo (v.)	5	22	0
huevo	1	27	3
automóvil	1	16	2
/atomobil/	1	1	4
Totals	12	129	28

Table 2

Word	[b]	[ƀ]	[v]
burro	28	0	3
brujo	27	3	1
boda	14	4	14
vaca	9	5	16
vino (n.)	4	6	21
Totals	81	18	55

is the [v]. Out of the six items, no one informant used the [v] more than three times, as the summary chart given at the end of this section of the study shows. The generalization here is that it is very much more common for a fricative to be used intervocalically than a stop; furthermore, the fricative used is more commonly [ƀ] than [v].

***Juncture plus* /b/**

This environment was obtained by eliciting the following words in isolation: *burro, brujo, boda, vaca*, and *vino*. Table 2 summarizes the allophonic variation found. Here there is possible orthographic influence in the case of *vaca* and *vino*, but certainly not in the case of *boda*. I found that all of the informants who used a fricative allophone also used a stop allophone in at least one of the five words.

***Nasal plus* /b/**

The checklist has the following three words in which the /b/ is preceded by a nasal: *hombre, tumba*, and *buen vino*. The allophones were used as shown in Table 3. Here we see that if the nasal is word-interior, the /b/

Table 3

Word	[b]	[ƀ]	[v]
hombre	31	0	0
tumba	28	0	0
buen vino	12	8	8
Totals	71	8	8

Table 4

Word	[b]	[ƀ]	[v]
tres vacas	1	14	15
el vino (n.)	3	12	14
varios vinos	1	7	5
yerba	1	7	25
Totals	6	40	59

following it is always realized as a stop. It is when the word begins with /b/ that variation in the choice of the allophones is possible. (Relative to this, I found that the assimilation of a nasal to the point of articulation of the following consonant behaves the same: it is done regularly if the cluster is word-interior, optionally if the cluster crosses word boundaries. This might suggest the existence of / + / in the Spanish of bilingual speakers.)

Nonnasal consonant plus /b/

In this environment, there is almost no use of the stop allophone, as Table 4 shows. No informant used the stop allophone more than one time; its use in this position is very limited. The [v] does seem to be favored slightly over the [ƀ] in this position.

/b/ plus consonant

The only word in this category on the checklist was *pobre*. Three informants used the [b]; twenty-four used the [ƀ] (it was very weakly articulated by seven of them); and four used the [v].

The foregoing shows that the only really clear-cut case of complementary distribution is when a word-interior /b/ is preceded by a nasal. In that case, only the stop allophone [b] may be used. That the [v] is quite widely used is evident, although certainly not to the exclusion of the [ƀ].

Before it will be possible to examine how different groups of informants used the different allophones, I should give an explanation of the way in which I classified the informants. There were, obviously, two sexes. I divided the informants three ways by age: under 25; 25–50; and over 50. I also classified the informants by the amount of Spanish they used in daily life. The three groups were those who clearly favor Spanish; those who clearly favor English; and those for whom neither language is dominant. Finally, I classified them into "lower" and "upper" social standing. This social class is a relative one, comparing the informant with the Mexican–American community as I know it, taking into account such things as education, place of residence, occupation, and income.

In order to have an easy way to identify the essential characteristics of each informant, I devised a four-digit identification system in which each of the digits would give the above information. The meaning of each digit is given as follows:

1--- male
2--- female
-1-- under 25
-2-- between 25 and 50
-3-- over 50
--1- speaks predominantly Spanish
--2- speaks both languages about equally
--3- speaks predominantly English
---1 roughly in the lower half on the social scale
---2 roughly in the upper half on the social scale

Thus, informant number 1231 would be a male between 25 and 50 who speaks predominantly English and who is in the lower half of the Mexican community of East Los Angeles. (All of the informants speak Spanish natively and speak it regularly. Most of the informants were born in Los Angeles; those who were not have lived there for a minimum of ten years. One informant cannot be said to speak English; the others can speak English in varying degrees.)

This classification system allows for thirty-six possible informants if all combinations of factors can be found. I did find informants for all eighteen female combinations. However, I was able to secure only thirteen willing informants for the eighteen possible male combinations. The five "slots" left empty were 1111, 1112, 1212, 1311, and 1321.

Table 5 shows informant-by-informant how many times each used each of the allophones in the various environments. It is from this table that the data in the second section of this study were developed.

To study how the different groupings of informants used the different allophones, in an attempt to find patterns, it is easier – and probably more meaningful – to work with percentage figures, especially since all groupings are not of equal size. Although a true statistical analysis would

Table 5

Inf	Intervocalic			Juncture plus /b/			Nasal plus /b/			Consonant plus /b/			/b/ plus consonant		
	[b]	[ƀ]	[v]	[b]	[ƀ]	[v]	[b]	[ƀ]	[v]	[b]	[ƀ]	[v]	[b]	[ƀ]	[v]
1121	0	3	1	2	0	3	2	0	0	0	1	1	0	1	0
1122	0	5	0	2	0	3	1	0	1	0	0	3	0	1	0
1131	0	5	0	3	0	2	1	0	0	0	2	1	0	1	0
1132	2	1	3	1	0	4	2	0	1	0	0	4	0	0	1
1211	0	4	0	2	1	0	2	1	0	0	2	1	0	1	0
1221	0	3	3	2	0	3	2	0	1	0	1	3	0	1	0
1222	0	6	0	4	1	0	2	1	0	1	2	1	0	1	0
1231	0	3	3	1	0	4	2	0	1	0	0	4	0	1	0
1232	0	5	1	3	0	2	2	1	0	0	4	0	0	1	0
1312	0	6	0	4	1	0	3	0	0	1	2	0	0	1	0
1322	1	5	0	4	0	1	3	0	0	1	2	0	0	1	0
1331	1	5	0	2	1	2	3	0	0	0	1	3	0	1	0
1332	2	4	0	3	0	2	3	0	0	0	1	2	0	1	0
2111	0	6	0	2	2	1	2	1	1	0	2	1	0	1	0
2112	0	6	0	3	0	2	3	0	0	0	3	0	0	1	0
2121	0	4	0	1	0	4	2	0	1	0	1	2	0	1	0
2122	1	5	0	3	0	2	3	0	0	0	3	0	0	1	0
2131	0	3	0	2	1	2	1	1	0	0	1	1	0	1	0
2132	1	3	1	1	4	0	2	1	0	0	4	0	0	1	0
2211	0	5	1	3	1	1	2	1	0	0	3	0	0	0	1
2212	0	5	1	3	1	1	3	0	0	0	3	0	0	1	0
2221	0	5	0	2	0	3	2	1	0	0	3	1	0	0	1
2222	2	4	0	5	0	0	3	0	0	0	3	0	0	1	0
2231	0	2	2	2	0	3	2	0	0	0	1	2	0	1	0
2232	0	3	3	2	0	3	2	0	1	0	0	4	0	0	1
2311	0	6	0	2	3	0	2	0	0	0	2	0	0	1	0
2312	0	5	0	4	0	1	3	0	0	1	2	1	1	0	0
2321	0	4	2	2	1	2	2	0	1	0	2	2	0	1	0
2322	2	4	0	4	1	0	3	0	0	1	1	0	1	0	0
2331	1	2	3	3	0	2	3	0	0	1	0	2	0	1	0
2332	0	2	3	3	0	2	3	0	0	0	1	3	1	0	0

Table 6

	Intervocalic			Juncture plus /b/			Nasal plus /b/			Consonant plus /b/		
	[b]	[ƀ]	[v]	[b]	[ƀ]	[v]	[b]	[ƀ]	[v]	[b]	[ƀ]	[v]
Percent	8	76	16	52	12	36	82	9	9	6	52	42
Number	13	129	27	80	18	55	71	8	8	6	53	42

Table 7

	Intervocalic [v]	Juncture plus /b/ [v]	Nasal plus /b/ [v]	Consonant plus /b/ [v]
Norm %	16	36	9	42
Men %	15	41	12	52
Women %	16	32	8	33
Number	27	55	8	42

Table 8

	Juncture plus /b/ [b]	Nasal plus /b/ [b]
Norm %	52	82
Under 25	40	73
25–50	55	75
Over 50	62	97
Number	80	71

not use percentage figures, I believe that meaningful relationships can be shown by them. In all cases, however, I give the actual numbers concerned, so that the reader can see the size of the sample and the significance the percentages may have.

The norm

Table 6 shows the percentage figures of use of each of the allophones in each of the environments for the whole sampling of thirty-one informants. These percentages will be considered the "norm," against which the different groups will be compared. (In this section of the study, I have chosen to disregard the "/b/ plus consonant" environment, since there was only one such case on the checklist.)

Variations by sex

The only significant variation between the sexes was that the men used the [v] slightly more than did the women in all but the intervocalic position. All four environments are given in Table 7 for comparison.

Variations by age

There were age-differences to be noted both in the use of the stop [b] and in the fricative [v], although the use of the fricative [ƀ] did not show

Table 9

	Juncture plus /b/ [v]	Nasal plus /b/ [v]
Norm %	36	9
Under 25	46	15
25–50	38	9
Over 50	24	4
Number	45	7

Table 10

	Intervocalic [v]	Juncture plus /b/ [v]	Consonant plus /b/ [v]
Norm %	16	36	42
"Spanish"	5	16	8
"Half-half"	14	37	37
"English"	29	57	62
Number	30	54	42

significant differences among the age groups. Table 8 shows the use of the [b] after a pause or after a nasal (the two places "standard" Spanish uses the [b]). Here it is seen that the older persons follow the "rules" of "standard" Spanish more regularly than do the younger speakers. In the use of the [v] in the same two positions, we find that the younger speakers tend to use the [v] more as shown in Table 9. From the chart showing the use of [b], we expect the younger speakers to use a fricative allophone more than do the older speakers. The interesting thing is that they stay remarkably constant in the use of the [ƀ] in these two environments, using it 14 percent after juncture and 12 percent after a nasal.

Variation by language predominance

Here is the most concrete evidence of difference among the groups. Those who speak mainly Spanish use the [v] much less than those who speak mostly English, and the ones who use both tend to be half-way in between. (See Table 10.) (The only environment in which this was not followed exactly was with the nasals; since there were only eight examples of [v] among all informants, those data are omitted here.) This constitutes undisputed evidence that those who speak English most use the [v] the most. Those who speak predominantly Spanish use the [v] comparatively

Table 11

	Juncture plus /b/ [b]	Nasal plus /b/ [b]
Norm %	52	82
Lower	43	75
Upper	61	88
Number	80	71

Table 12

	Intervocalic [v]	Juncture plus /b/ [v]	Nasal plus /b/ [v]	Consonant plus /b/ [v]
Norm %	16	36	9	42
Lower	20	44	13	56
Upper	13	28	6	33
Number	27	36	8	42

few times (no more than 16 percent), while those who speak predominantly English go as high as 62 percent. While not all things are equal (we have seen that sex plays a very small part, and that age plays a slightly larger part), one cannot help but feel that this points to a very definite influence of English on the Spanish of these bilinguals.

Variation by social class

Here there is a small inference that those who are classified as in the "upper" half tend to use the [b] a bit more according to standard distribution, and those in the "lower" half tend to use the [v] more. I am not positive that these figures are terribly significant, but they seem to point to a tendency.

After juncture and after a nasal, the "uppers" use the [b] a bit more than do the "lowers" as Table 11 shows. In all environments, the lower-class informants used the [v] more than did the upper-class informants. The two in which the percentages seem to be significant are after juncture and after a consonant. All four environments are given in Table 12.

Disregarding environments

I put the figures together, disregarding the phonetic environments, to see if larger groupings of the data would confirm the assertions made in Tables 6–12, and they indeed do. If we take the groups given in the tables, and

Table 13

	[b]	[ƀ]	[v]
Norm	32	43	25
Men	31	40	29
Women	33	44	23
Numbers	173	232	135

Table 14

	[b]	[ƀ]	[v]
Norm	32	43	25
Under 25	26	46	28
25–50	29	42	29
Over 50	42	40	18
Numbers	173	232	135

Table 15

	[b]	[ƀ]	[v]
Norm	32	43	25
"Spanish"	33	58	9
"Half-half"	34	42	24
"English"	29	34	37
Numbers	173	232	135

Table 16

	[b]	[ƀ]	[v]
Norm	32	43	25
Lower	26	42	32
Upper	38	42	20
Numbers	173	232	135

take the totals of the number of times they used the various allophones, the same patterns emerge. (Note that in all of them the ''norm'' and actual numbers stay the same.)

Sex. The men tend to use [v] more than the women; the women use [b] and [ƀ] more than the men (Table 13).

Age. The older people us [b] more than the others; those under 50 use a fricative more than the older ones; and the older people use [v] less than the other two groups (Table 14).

Language predominance. Those who speak predominantly Spanish use [v] much less than the others (Table 15).

Class. Some class differences are noted in the use of [b] and [v] (Table 16).

The conclusions which I draw from all of this, in summary, are that very rarely is the nice, neat complementary distribution of ''standard'' Spanish found in the allophones of /b/ in Los Angeles Spanish. Indeed, the only ''rule'' followed strictly is that the stop [b] is used after a word-interior nasal consonant. There are certain groups which have more of a tendency to use the [v] allophone, and they are the two groups which I would expect to be most influenced by English: the younger speakers and those who speak English more than Spanish.

4

Syntactic variation in verb phrases of motion in U.S.-Mexican Spanish

MARYELLEN GARCÍA

This chapter investigates one area of Spanish grammar that is variable for Mexican-Americans living on the Texas-Mexican border, the prepositional phrase that follows verbs of motion and introduces a locative, as in: *Fuimos a San Francisco el verano pasado* 'We went to San Francisco last summer.' In standard Spanish, the preposition *a* indicates the goal orientation of the verb, whereas *para* in the locative prepositional phrase emphasizes the directional aspect of the motion, as in 'Tomorrow we leave for San Francisco,' *Mañana salimos para San Francisco*. Empirical investigation of the locative prepositional phrase in verb phrases of motion was undertaken in the Spanish-language speech community of the El Paso–Juárez area in the summer of 1977. The data collected from fifty-nine Mexican and Mexican-American Spanish speakers in that broad community show two related phenomena that are indicative of changes in the locative prepositional system: (1) the lexical variation between *a* and *para* in verb phrases of motion, and (2) syntactic variation involving locative and infinitive phrases that occur within verb phrases of motion.

The linguistic variables

I will distinguish two syntactic environments as the units of analysis: the prepositional phrase and the verb phrase. The lexical variation between *a* and *para* occurs in prepositional phrases preceded by a verb of motion, either transitive or intransitive, which introduce a locative noun phrase (NP) or adverb. The previous description allows for the expansion of the

The fieldwork on which this chapter is based was supported by a Ford Foundation fellowship. Additional work was supported in part by the National Institute of Education, Department of Education (formerly HEW) pursuant to SWRL (Southwest Regional Laboratory) Educational Research and Development, contract NIE-0076. I am grateful to SWRL's directorate for its professional support and to my colleagues at SWRL for their helpful suggestions, especially Robert Berdan, David Snow, Bruce Cronnell, and Victor Rodríguez. Bruce Osborne also provided invaluable feedback on an earlier version of this chapter, a paper presented at the Conference on Non-English Language Variation, held in Louisville, Kentucky, October 12–13, 1979.

linguistic environment:

	Verb of motion + prep. + {(adverb) NP / adverb}	
1.	a/para + proper noun	*Ibamos a El Paso.* *Ibamos para El Paso.* 'We were going to El Paso.'
2.	a/para + common noun	*Se fueron al pueblo.* *Se fueron para el pueblo.* 'They went to the town.'
3.	Ø/para + loc. adverb	*Iba allá.* *Iba para allá.* 'He/She was going there (that way).'
4.	Ø/para + loc. adverb + proper noun	*Vamos allá a Chihuahua.* *Vamos para allá para Chihuahua.* 'We're going there to Chihuahua.'
5.	Ø/para + loc. adverb + common noun	*Vamos allá al desierto.* *Vamos para allá para el desierto.* 'We're going there to the desert.'

By focusing on lexical variation within a relatively limited environment, the locative prepositional phrase, one can study the immediate syntactic contexts in which *para* occurs for evidence of its semantic bleaching in this speech community. In local usage, locative *para* is used variably with *a* to indicate the goal of the motion and may be serving the purely syntactic function of introducing any locative noun.

For the syntactic variation that permutes the order of a locative prepositional phrase and a following infinitive, the linguistic environment is the entire verb phrase. The types of sentences that exhibit this permutation have a main verb of motion followed by a goal-oriented locative phrase, and they contain an infinitive complement. Sentences 6 and 7 are examples of the input for the variable permutation rule. The linguistic variable for syntactic variation is:

verb of motion + *a* + locative + infinitive

6. *Me gusta ir a Juárez a hacer mis compras.* 'I like to go to Juárez to shop.'
7. *Los fines de semana, vamos a Juárez a bailar.* 'On weekends, we go to Juárez to dance.'

By looking at the broader context in which the lexical variation takes place, that is, the entire verb phrase, one sees syntactic variation consisting of the permutation of whole locative and infinitive phrases within the verb phrase. This variable permutation rule allows for the occurrence of *a* plus the locative after infinitives, an environment in which *en* plus the locative may also occur. Sentences 8 and 9 illustrate the two types of locative selection:

8. *Vamos a nadar a la piscina.* 'We are going to swim to (lit.) the pool.' (*piscina* is part of higher sentence; permutation rule has applied)

9. *Vamos a nadar en la piscina.* 'We are going to swim in the pool.' (*piscina* is generated by the infinitive, not the higher sentence)

As a result of this conditioned variation, lexical variation between *a* and *en* before locative nouns sometimes occurs in environments where other Spanish dialects allow only *en*.

Examples from the data are provided throughout to illustrate the observed lexical and syntactic variation, variation that indicates probable future changes in the locative prepositional system for this dialect.

The speech community

The Spanish-language community of the El Paso–Juárez area includes both Mexicans and Mexican-Americans, who interact often for economic and social reasons. Many people live on one side of the border and work on the other. Others cross the border to shop or for entertainment. Many have their immediate families or other close relatives and friends on the other side. However, the use of English in public domains (e.g., in government and education) in the United States is in contrast to the use of Spanish in all domains, public and private, in Mexico. Therefore, although the El Paso and Juárez community may be cohesive socially and economically, linguistically the Spanish speakers in the two cities form more than one community.

Many of the Spanish speakers in the area share a nonstandard dialect of Mexican Spanish; only a few of the contributing factors can be suggested here.[1] One is the great number of poor and working-class people in Juárez. The north is seen as the place for economic opportunity and thus attracts many rural and working-class people from other parts of Mexico, who bring their rural and regional dialects into the community.

Because most of the poor and working-class people in Juárez usually leave school before the sixth year in order to work to support their families, they have little exposure to a literary standard Spanish and also limited contact with speakers of the standard dialect, who usually continue on in school. Thus, distance is maintained between the working class and the middle and upper classes and as a result between the working class and the standard language. The Juárez working class may serve as a model for El Paso Spanish speakers because much of their contact with Mexicans is with people in service professions either in El Paso or in Juárez. Within El Paso, people in Spanish-speaking neighborhoods maintain norms that were brought over in the late nineteenth and early twentieth centuries by rural immigrants and workingmen responding to the call for workers on the railroads, in industry, and in agriculture and fleeing from the Mexican Revolution.

[1] Language norms in themselves can be one basis on which to define a speech community. Both Labov (1972, p. 158) and Bailey (1973, p. 65) indicate that the way a group of people evaluate certain linguistic features of their language can characterize them as a speech community. Some linguistic norms for Spanish-speaking Mexican-Americans in the Spanish-language community of El Paso are discussed in García (1977).

Functioning in a society where the dominant language of commerce and government is English, Spanish speakers in El Paso are not subject to the normative pressures of a monolingual Spanish-speaking society. Their schooling in El Paso emphasizes literacy in English rather than Spanish; this limits the numbers of those who have access to a written standard. For reasons such as these, the language norms for the El Paso community can be expected to differ not only from the norms of standard Spanish but from those of the Juárez working class as well. The variation between the locative prepositions *a* and *para* may prove to be one of the characteristics of the nonstandard dialect of this community.

Lexical variation between *a* and *para*

The change to be discussed here is the usage in El Paso–Juárez of *para* before nouns that name a destination without also focusing on the indeterminacy with regard to reaching the destination. Both prepositions *a* and *para* can occur before locative nouns in the Spanish language in general, but they serve different functions. When the preposition is *a*, the locative phrase communicates motion directly to a destination in standard dialects. When *para* introduces the locative noun, the motion is "toward" or "in the direction of" that place and does not focus on the destination itself in standard dialects. In his pedagogically oriented book on prepositions, Luque de Durán presents examples of sentences that illustrate the directional use of *para* (1974, p. 87):

10. *Salimos para Madrid dentro de dos días.* 'We (will) leave for Madrid in two days.'
11. *Ibamos para la oficina cuando nos encontramos con unos amigos.* 'We were going toward the office when we met up with some friends.'
12. *Ya han partido para su ciudad.* 'They've already left for their city.'
13. *Corrimos para el lugar del accidente.* 'We ran toward the site of the accident.'

In the nonstandard dialect under investigation, that of working-class Mexicans and working-class and some middle-class Mexican-Americans, the variation between *a* and *para* in this environment indicates that *para* is also being used to focus the motion on the destination itself, as *a* does.[2]

[2] The reduced variant *pa'* is often used to characterize peasant speech in novels. In the following examples, taken from novels with a Mexican setting, the locative phrase invites the interpretation of "motion to."

> "Ña Dolores, donde anoche se jue pa la Cofradía" (Azuela, *Los de abajo*, 1927; in Alvar 1960, p. 621). 'Doña Dolores, where last night she went to the Cofradía.'
>
> "El Oaxaqueño qu'staba aquí se jue pa Tapachula y no pudimos dar con otro en todo el Sosconuso" (spoken by a *mestizo* 'mixed blood' in a novel set in Chiapas; in Alvar 1960, p. 625). 'The man from Oaxaca who was here went to Tapachula and we couldn't find another in all of the Sosconuso.'

Although the nonprescriptive usage of *para* (to indicate motion directly to the destination) is stigmatized as "rural" by speakers of standard dialects in Mexico, the same stigma has not been characteristic of this usage in the United States, perhaps because most of the Mexican immigration over the years has been of rural and working-class people. A pilot study for the present investigation (García 1979) indicates that *para* in locative phrases is much more acceptable for Mexican-American university students than for Mexican students in El Paso–Juárez. Two other empirical investigations, that of Phillips on Los Angeles Spanish (1967) and of Ross on the Spanish of rural Colorado (1975), conclude that in those areas *para* is the more frequently used variant in locative phrases. Within the United States, then, this usage of *para* in locative contexts is not stigmatized and has gained such acceptance that the shift from *a* to *para* has already become the observed norm for some Mexican-American Spanish language communities. The evaluation of *para* as nonstigmatized in the United States may influence its greater use by Mexican-Americans than for Mexicans in El Paso–Juárez.

Given that social context, I wish to explore the linguistic factors that may be influencing the lexical variation between *a* and *para*. One linguistic reason for the variation may be that *a* identifies goals other than physical destination in the discourse. A common function for *a* after a motion verb is to introduce an infinitive to indicate an activity, for example, *Fuimos a bailar,* 'We went to dance.' To serve a similar function, *a* can introduce a noun that names a physical place, to suggest a purpose or activity associated with that place, as in examples 14, 15, and 16 taken from the interviews. (The code preceding the example gives the speaker's initials, age, sex, and nationality.)

14.	LP, 18m, mx	*Sí, como llego a los autocines, y, a los bailes.* 'Yes, like I go to drive-ins, and dances.'
15.	MA, 23m, ma	*Pues, desde chico íbamos a los parques.* 'Well, from the time I was little we used to go to the parks.'
16.	FR, 55m, ma	*Llevo a mis niños al cine. Como ayer fuimos al cine.* 'I take my children to the movies (i.e., theater). Like yesterday we went to the movies.'

Another type of noun, such as *school,* or *college,* can either name a physical location or stand for the related concept, such as *go to school* in English:

17.	AG, 40m, ma	*O, aunque se requiere haber ido a la escuela . . .* 'Or, even though having gone to school may be required . . .'
18.	MA, 23m, ma	*Fueron a U.T. Austin.* 'They went to U.T. Austin.'
19.	MD, 60f, ma	*'Taba yendo a la vocacional.* 'He was going to vocational school.'

20. MG, 40m, ma *Y ya desde muy chica sabe que va ir al colegio.* 'And already at this young age she knows that she'll go to college.'

Still another type of noun, such as *the army,* or *the service,* names groups or entities that people join. Used after verbs of motion they may indicate actual physical movement of someone from one place to another or a change of personal status, as in examples 21 through 24:

21. BS, 34m, ma *Iba a entrar al varsity, yo.* 'I was going to join the varsity.'
22. CG, 54m, ma *Fui al servicio.* 'I went into the (military) service.'
23. MD, 60f, ma *Se fue al servicio.* 'He went to (joined) the service.'
24. JA, 48m, ma *Probablemente si no hubiera ido al ejército . . .* 'Probably if I hadn't gone into (joined) the armed service . . .'

Possibly because discourse context allows for the interpretation of the nouns that *a* introduces as either physical location or as verb phrase complements naming activities, *a* also occurs in this dialect before nouns that have no locative meaning in themselves and that are not acceptable in standard dialects to introduce events or activities. These are nouns associated with an event, although they do not usually behave like events syntactically. However, examples 25–27 show acceptable ways in the El Paso–Juárez community of referring to activities.[3]

25. LR, 58m, mx *No voy siempre, pero cuando puedo financialmente, voy a los toros.* 'I don't always go, but when I can financially, I go to the bullfights.'
26. MA, 23m, ma *Y vamos a los perros allá en Juárez.* 'And we go to the dogs (i.e., dog races) there in Juárez.'
27. SS, 68f, ma *Y no íbamos a las mercancías a la calle de El Paso, a la Mesa.* 'And we go to the merchandise (i.e., shopping) to El Paso Street, (or) to Mesa (Street).'

In light of the previous discussion, I suggest that *para* in locative phrases is losing its semantic feature of indeterminacy and is generalizing in function to indicate the concrete goal of the motion, whereas *a* is used to specify goals that can be interpreted either concretely, as a location,

[3] It is interesting to note that the noun in this type of phrase is often plural. A similar use of the plural by a Mexican-American woman in the Midwest was noted in García (1977, p. 204). Two examples of the plural are taken from the typescript of that interview (p. 207):

> Lines 7 and 8: Porque nosotros migramos de Tejas pa' . . . pa' Ohio para los trabajos.
>
> Lines 24 and 25: . . . allá cada año salíamos a la . . . a las pizcas, a pizcar algodón a diferentes partes.

It is unclear from these data and from those provided by the larger El Paso–Juárez corpus whether the interpretation of the noun phrase that the use of the plural invites, that of an activity, is best explained by the semantics of the lexicon or of the discourse.

or figuratively, as a related activity or event. In the data analyzed here, four categories of nouns emerge: (1) those locatives closely associated with certain activities, such as *autocines* 'drive-ins' with seeing a movie; (2) those nouns that have concrete referents but can stand for a related activity when they complete the meaning of a verb, as in *ir a la escuela* 'to go to (attend) school'; (3) those more abstract nouns that identify groups of people or entities, such as the military service, as in *ir al servicio* 'join the service'; and finally (4) those concrete nouns that have no locative features in themselves and appear to name events when used after verbs of motion, such as *ir a los perros* 'go to the dogs' to mean attending the dog races.

Verb phrase permutation rule

The entire verb phrase is the linguistic environment that exhibits syntactic variation between locative and infinitive phrases, a syntactic variation that also seems to contribute to lexical variation in the locative prepositional system. The variation occurs in verb phrases that begin with a verb of motion and contain an embedded infinitive phrase. This general environment identifies two types of surface structures, as illustrated in examples 28 and 29:

28. Motion verb + locative + infinitive
    Vamos a Juárez a comprar el mandado. 'We're going to Juárez to buy the groceries.'
29. Motion verb + infinitive + locative
    Vamos a comprar el mandado en Juárez. 'We're going to buy the groceries in Juárez.'

The remainder of the discussion proceeds from the notion that the selection of locative prepositions for the embedded verbs (infinitives) is governed by the semantics of the discourse and by the semantic features of the verb. Discourse semantics seems to be the more important of these two factors. When locale is mentioned, whatever the topic of the discourse might be, the speaker may intend the locative either as the goal of the motion (to a place) or as the place within which an activity (described by the verb) occurs. Furthermore, within the sentence, the semantic features of the verb contribute to the selection of locative prepositions. Verbs that indicate the physical movement of an object from one place to another take the locative preposition *a* to introduce the goal. Most verbs that name an activity take the locative preposition *en* 'in,' to situate it within physical boundaries (hereafter referred to as a stative locative function). The sentences in example 30 illustrate the preposition selection expected in standard dialects after embedded infinitives. Table 1 illustrates the prepositional distribution possible for the verbs in examples 28, 29, and 30.

Table 1. *Preposition distribution*

Verb	Motion verb	Locative goal	Physical boundary
comprar	no	—	en
vivir	no	—	en
cambiarse	yes	a	—
mandar	yes	a	en

30. Motion verb + infinitive + locative
  a. *Voy a vivir en El Paso.* 'I'm going to live in El Paso.'
  b. *Vamos a cambiarnos a El Paso.* 'We're going to move to El Paso.'
  c. *Vamos a mandar la caja a México.* 'We're going to send the box to México.'
  d. *Vamos a mandar la caja en México.* 'We're going to send (mail) the box in México.'

A number of alternatives for locative selection exist for verb phrases of motion with embedded infinitives, complicated by the fact that the embedded infinitive can also be a motion verb. First, the matrix verb phrase can contain a locative goal, in which case the preposition used is *a*.[4] Second, the embedded infinitive can also be a verb of motion and so the infinitive phrase can also contain a locative goal introduced by *a*. Third, some verbs (e.g., *mandar*) can take either a goal locative phrase or a stative locative phrase, using *a* for the former and *en* for the latter. Fourth, nonmotion verbs (e.g., *vivir, comprar*), not requiring a goal, allow only stative locatives, taking the preposition *en*.

With this appreciation of the complexity of possible alternatives, we are better able to look at the variation in the locative prepositional system in examples from interviews in the El Paso–Juárez area. Example 28 illustrates the surface structure: verb of motion plus locative plus infinitive, wherein the verb of motion has generated the immediately following locative. Examples 31, 32, and 33 also exhibit this surface structure and imply the same transformational history.

31. CB, 37f, mx *Estábamos pensando ir a Cloudcroft unos días a rentar allí unas cabañas.* 'We were thinking of going to Cloudcroft for a few days to rent some cabins there.'

[4] One such verb included in the table is *cambiarse*, here meaning 'to move (one's household).' This particular verb seems to have a two-part locative, which prohibits situating the activity in a single location. That is, a move involves going from one place to another; in Spanish this calls for the prepositions *de* 'from' and *a* 'to.' Thus, it is possible to say, *Me cambié de Sunset Heights a Coronado* 'I moved from Sunset Heights to Coronado,' but it would be anomalous to say **Me cambié de Sunset Heights a Coronado en El Paso* 'I moved from Sunset Heights to Coronado in El Paso,' or worse, **Me cambié en El Paso* 'I moved in El Paso,'

32. LP, 53f, mx *Mi hermano fue el único que fue a Chihuahua a estudiar.* 'My brother was the only one who went to Chihuahua to study.'
33. AM, 59f, ma *Y llevamos a las dos chamacas a Juárez a comer.* 'And we took our two daughters to Juárez to eat.'

The next set of examples, also taken from the El Paso–Juárez data, exhibit the order infinitive plus locative as shown in example 29. They may be evidence for the variable permutation rule, which seems to be widespread in this dialect, operating on the surface order: verb of motion plus locative plus infinitive, and changing it to: verb of motion plus infinitive plus locative.

34. LR, 58m, mx *Lo llevo a ver correr los perros a Juárez.* 'I take him to see the dogs run in/to/at Juárez.'
35. LP, 53f, mx *Siempre, siempre era una ilusión por venir a vivir para acá a los Estados Unidos.* 'It was always, always a dream to come to live here in/to/at the United States.

It is proposed here that the locatives found in sentences 34 and 35, *a Juárez* and *para acá a los Estados Unidos,* are generated by the matrix verbs, which in both cases are verbs of motion, and that their appearance in surface structure after the infinitive is the effect of a rule that simply permutes the order of a locative and a following infinitive. In independent clauses, or embedded after nonmotion verbs, the verbs in these infinitive phrases would allow only stative physical locatives, taking the preposition *en* as in examples 36 and 37:

36. *Quiero ver correr los perros en Juárez.* 'I want to see the dogs race in Juárez.'
37. *Vivo acá en los Estados Unidos.* 'I live here in the United States.'

The fact that *a* is the locative preposition after the infinitive in sentences 34 and 35 indicates that the locative was not generated by that verb but by the matrix verb, thereby providing evidence for the permutation rule. That the locatives in examples 31, 32, and 33, taken from the same community, have not permuted their order indicates that this rule is variable rather than categorical in the grammar of this community of Spanish speakers.

The permutation rule seems to account for some of the variation in the locative prepositional system in this community. Verb phrases that have undergone the rule exhibit a residual *a* plus locative after infinitives that could not have generated them. This placement of the locative phrase (that is, after the infinitive) results in the occurrence of *a* in the same environment as *en*, when *en* is part of a locative phrase generated by the infinitive itself.[5] Thus, occurrences of *a* after infinitives resulting from a

[5] The latter type of infinitive phrase, with a stative locative phrase introduced by *en*, occurs when the matrix verb is not one of motion and occurs variably in this dialect with a matrix verb of motion.

surface structure permutation, and occurrences of *en* generated by the infinitive verb, may be perceived by speakers as free variation between the lexical alternates *a* and *en* before locative nouns. Data from members of this community indicate that the conditioned syntactic variation is being treated as lexical variation. Locatives that serve the function of stative physical location, which standard Spanish introduces with *en*, are sometimes introduced by *a* in this dialect.

38. AO, 21f, mx *Pos acá a Estados Unidos, casi no conozco, fíjate.* 'Well, here in the United States, I've hardly traveled, can you imagine?'

39. MQ, 68f, mx *Y a quedar un rato allí a la plazita y a dormir.* 'And to stay there a while, in the plaza, and sleep.'

Residual instability in the prepositional system

The data discussed thus far indicate instability in the locative prepositional system for this dialect, the lexical variation between *a* and *para* involving different semantic distinctions from those in the standard dialect and the variable permutation rule between locatives and infinitives accounting for perceived lexical variation between *a* and *en*.

The residual instability in the system is exhibited in the use of syntactic alternatives to express the 'direction toward' meaning of *para* and in the apparent overgeneralization of the rules for the selection of the prepositions *a, en,* and *para* for some speakers. The 'direction toward' meaning is expressed by *hacia* 'toward' and by syntactic paraphrases such as *para el rumbo de* and *para le lado de,* which mean, roughly, 'in the direction of.'

40. CA, 39m, mx *Para el rumbo de México adonde, por ejemplo, donde andaba yo el domingo, ¿verdad? en la madrugada.* 'In the direction of Mexico where, for example, I was, right? in the dawn.'

41. DM, 44f, ma *. . . predomina el, el mexicano para el rumbo de Sunland Park, para Smeltertown.* '. . . the Mexican (person) predominates in the area of Sunland Park, or towards Smeltertown.'

42. AM, 59f, ma *. . . y pa' el lado de Elephant Butte, pa' ca.* '. . . and in the direction of Elephant Butte, this way.'

The environments for the apparently random prepositional variation are similar to those in which the variation is rule governed. Thus, I hypothesize that the constraints on prepositions have become less restrictive for certain speakers, some generalizing the semantic constraints, as when *pa'* introduces a proper name rather than a locative in example 43, and others generalizing the syntactic constraints on lexical variation (between *a* ~ *para* and *a* ~ *en*) as in examples 44 and 45.

43.	AR, 61m, ma	a → para	/——Name	*Y yo me cambiarme* pa' *Romero* . . . 'And change my name to Romero . . .'
44.	MQ, 68f, mx	para → a	/——INF	*Y me dan una carta* a *poder ir* . . . 'And they give me a card so (I) can go . . .'
45.	AO, 21f, mx	a → en	/——NP	*Me vendría aquí* en *El Paso*. 'I would come here to el Paso.

Summary

To summarize briefly, we see that the linguistic environment at the level of the prepositional phrase identifies the relevant locus for the lexical variation between *a* and *para*, whereas the verb phrase expansion of that basic environment identifies a broader context for the investigation of syntactic variation.

A variable permutation rule has been suggested for this Spanish-language community wherein verb phrases of the structure verb of motion plus locative plus infinitive permute their order to verb of motion plus infinitive plus locative, often leaving residual phrases of the type *a* plus locative after infinitival verbs, which could not have generated them independently. The permutation has resulted in environments where *a* plus locative and *en* plus locative can both occur; this conditioned variation between the two kinds of prepositional phrases provides a reason for apparent lexical variation between *a* and *en* plus locative in environments not conditioned by a motion verb.

It is expected that future investigation of these phenomena in the present corpus will expand our understanding of this type of linguistic change by providing more precise sociolinguistic correlates to the variation observed here.

References

Alvar, Manuel. 1960. *Textos Hispánicos dialectales*. Madrid: Selecciones Gráficas.

Bailey, Charles-James. 1973. *Variation and linguistic theory*. Arlington, Va.: Center for Applied Linguistics.

García, Maryellen. 1977. Chicano Spanish/Latin American Spanish: some differences in linguistic norms. *Bilingual Review* 4:200–9.

1979. Pa(ra) usage in United States Spanish. *Hispania* 62:106–14.

Labov, William. 1972. *Sociolinguistic patterns*. Philadelphia: University of Pennsylvania Press.

Luque de Durán, J. 1974. *Las preposiciones: valores generales*. Vol. 1. Madrid: Sociedad General Española de Librería.

Phillips, Robert, N., Jr. 1967. Los Angeles Spanish: a descriptive analysis. Ph.D. dissertation, University of Wisconsin.

Ross, L. R. 1975. La lengua castellana en San Luis, Colorado. Ph.D. dissertation, University of Colorado.

5

Subject expression and placement in Mexican-American Spanish

CARMEN SILVA-CORVALÁN

This chapter presents a study of the factors that determine the expression or nonexpression of the sentence subject in Spanish and the position of the subject with respect to the verb when it is expressed.[1] The data are discussed in their discourse context in order to identify the discourse or pragmatic factors that may determine the occurrence of these variables and are further analyzed quantitatively in order to investigate the statistical significance of the results.

The study is based on recorded interviews of a group of Mexican-American Spanish speakers living in West Los Angeles (WLA). (See Figure 1.) Their ages fall into three groups: fourteen through twenty-nine, thirty through forty-nine, and fifty and over.

No studies of this linguistic issue as it is observed in speech have previously been made. A quantitative study of the position of the subject in the poetry of Miguel de Unamuno was made by Nicole Van den Broeck-Delbecque (n.d.), and one of the expression of first person subject pronouns was made by Bentivoglio (1980).[2] I will compare the results later in the chapter.

Brief mention of the question of subject-verb (SV) order is made by the Spanish Academy of the Language, which states that the regular SV order may be altered for stylistic purposes (Real Academia Española 1973). Gili y Gaya (1951) also refers to this issue, adding that the various orderings of constituents in a sentence should be studied with reference to situation, personal style, phonetic features, and relative importance of the constituents. However, he does not state his definition of these terms,

I would like to thank Flora Klein, William Labov, Sandra Thompson, and Benji Wald for their many helpful comments on an earlier version of this chapter. All errors and misinterpretations remain, of course, mine.

Research for this work was supported in part by a grant from the Institute of American Cultures, University of California, Los Angeles.

[1] For the purposes of this study, I have defined *subject* as the NP that agrees in person and number with the verb.

[2] Since this study was originally written (Silva-Corvalán 1977), another quantitative study of the same issue, though limited only to the use of *yo* 'I' and *nosotros* 'we,' has been done by Bentivoglio (1980) based on spoken Venezuelan Spanish.

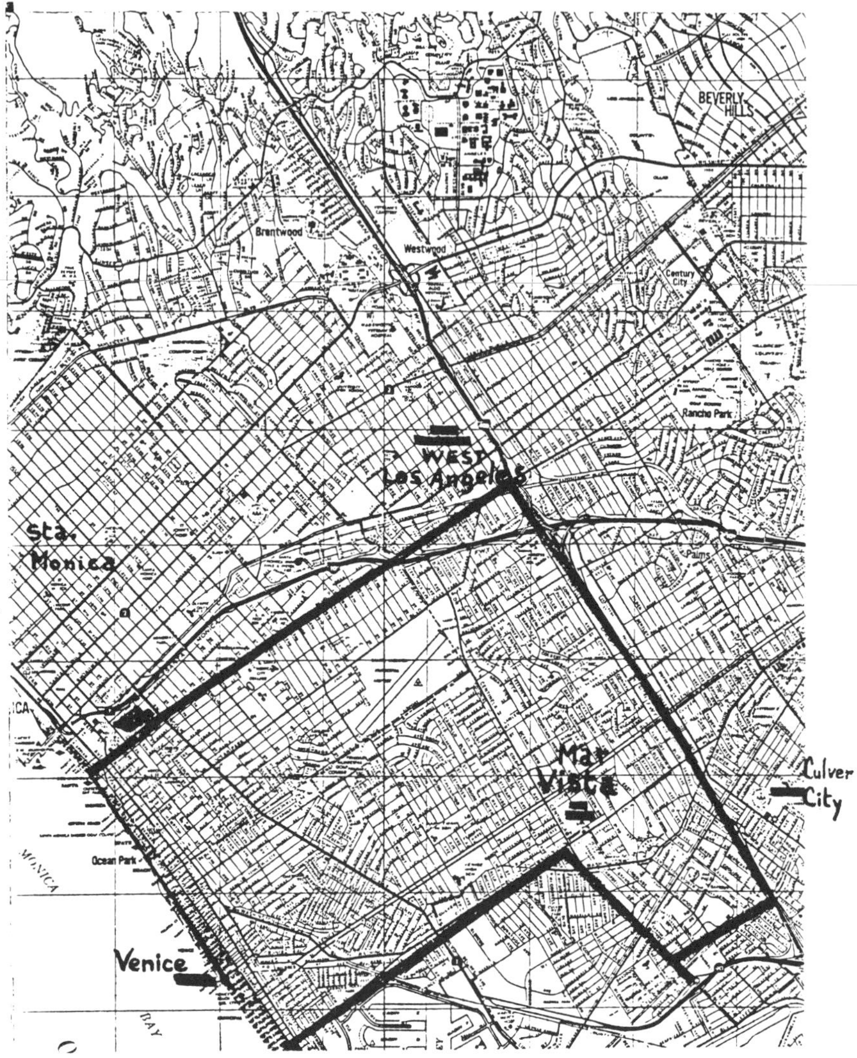

Figure 1. Map of West Los Angeles

nor does he discuss them any further in relation to subject expression and positioning.

The problem of word order variability in Spanish has also been tackled by Henri and Renée Kahane (1950). The Kahanes concerned themselves with a strictly descriptive and quite exhaustive study of the position of the subject in colloquial Mexican Spanish. Most of their data is taken from written material, however, and only some of it from direct conversation. They conclude that the position of the "actor" (i.e., the subject) is mostly in "free variation," although the number of elements in the sentence tends to constrain its variability as follows: (1) In binary expressions the position of the subject is free; (2) in ternary expressions the position of the subject is usually determined by the position of the third element – if it is initial, the subject is in final position, and vice versa; (3) in a quaternary expression the position of the subject is free.

The Kahanes' study constitutes a valuable contribution and serves as a point of departure for any further studies of the issue of subject placement variation. A basic inadequacy in their analysis, however, is its intrasentential approach. The position of the subject is analyzed only with reference to the other elements in the sentence and not with reference to what may precede or follow it in a wider linguistic context. This restricted view led them to conclude that the position of the subject in Mexican Spanish follows a system whose main characteristic is its flexibility. Later in this chapter I will attempt to show that this flexibility also follows a system and that this system can only become apparent if the position of the subject within a sentence is viewed within the discourse context in which the sentence occurs.

The question of the relative position of the "thing-subject" (i.e., a subject whose referent is [-animate]) and the verb in existential sentences in Spanish has been dealt with by Hatcher (1956). She notices that VS is the most usual order in these types of constructions not only in Spanish but in various other languages such as English, Dutch, and German:[3]

> *Falta una maleta* . . . ('misses a suitcase') 'A suitcase is missing.'
> *Empezó el año*. ('began the year') 'The year began.'
> *Pasó el tren*. ('passed the train') 'The train passed.'
> *Entra la luz*. ('enters the light') 'The light enters.'

Hatcher also asserts (but does not discuss further in her paper) that these sentences can occur in what she calls the normal order, SV. She realizes that one of the problems in Spanish lies in the definition of what constitutes an existential sentence, because the concept of existence of the subject is represented by a far larger number of intransitive verbs than in other languages. This difficulty is caused by the enormous lexicological variety of these verbs "which, in their context, tell us only or mainly that the subject exists or is present; is absent, begins, continues, is produced, occurs, appears, arrives" (p. 7). Although Hatcher devotes her paper to a description of the existential sentence in Spanish, she does not deal with examples of postverbal subjects in nonexistential sentences nor with cases of existential sentences where the subject occurs before the verb. As I said in relation to the Kahanes' work, it may be possible to explain these apparent exceptions if they are studied in the discourse context in which they occur. Hatcher takes her data from written Spanish and gives the examples in isolation. She suggests, however, that the

[3] In these three languages, the position left empty by the subject is filled by a dummy subject, a constraint that is not required in Spanish.

relation of the predication to the context may be helpful in explaining the two types of order (SV, VS) and that this approach may help to explain other word-order phenomena. In addition to context, she proposes to consider subthemes and "point of view" as further criteria of analysis.[4]

Hatcher's point-of-view approach is illustrated by one of the techniques used by Bolinger (1952 and 1954–5) in his studies of the relationship between word order and presupposed versus new information: The sentence *Trabaja Juan* 'Juan works' answers the question *¿Quién trabaja?* 'Who works', whereas the sentence *Juan trabaja* answers the question *¿Qué hace Juan?* 'What does Juan do?' The two orders, VS and SV, are determined by the information requested by the question so that the normal order of the constituents in the answer is one where the presupposed element precedes the nonpresupposed element or "point" of the answer. Bolinger's treatment is perceptive and motivating, but because it is based on made-up data it fails to capture the complexities of the issues under consideration as observed in real discourse.

Transformational grammar has offered no new insights into the question of the option between expressing or not expressing the subject in Spanish. Within this framework of analysis, it has been postulated (Hadlich 1971; D'Introno 1979) that underlying subject pronouns undergo an optional rule of deletion when the pronoun is marked "minus emphatic," but no explanation of what is meant by the notion of emphasis is given independently of the circular observation that expressed subject pronouns are emphatic.

In sum, these studies have left unsolved the question of the factors that determine the expression and placement of the subject in Spanish even though some of them have contributed valuable insights. On the other hand, none of these studies has tackled the problem of how and for what purposes speakers of Spanish use the different subject-coding possibilities in spontaneous speech. As a first approach to this general question, this chapter concerns itself specifically with the identification of the discourse factors that may determine the position of the subject with respect to the verb in spoken Mexican-American Spanish, an issue that also touches on the question of the factors that may determine the expression of pronouns in the subject noun phrase.

The sample of speakers

It was decided at the outset that the choice of speakers would be restricted by the following criteria:

[4] By "point of view" Hatcher means that each predication may be "conceived as answering an underlying question asked from the point of view of some one element of the sentence" (1956, p. 5). Intransitives can answer the questions What does the subject do?, What happens, what is the situation?, or What exists, begins, comes in, etc.? Some of the subthemes of the existential theme that Hatcher mentions are: rise, beginning, production, and arrangement.

1. The speakers should be able to converse with the interviewer in Spanish.
2. They should have been living in West Los Angeles for a minimum period of ten years. (This restriction was introduced in order to minimize speech differences due to place of origin.)
3. The speakers should not be college educated. (By restricting the level of education of the sample, I expected to avoid possible interference from literary Spanish.)
4. The sample should include a minimum of twenty-four speakers, divided according to the following categories:

Age	*Sex*
50 +	4 males, 4 females
30–49	4 males, 4 females
14–29	4 males, 4 females

The age and sex specifications were introduced so that the sample could be a source of data for the study of variables sensitive to social external factors. The personal experience of interviewing about seventy Mexican-Americans of WLA provided me with invaluable information about their values and social characteristics.

Social aspects of the sample

The WLA Mexican-American community as a social group

For the purposes of this study, the term "Mexican-American" refers both to a person born in Mexico who has resided in the United States for a minimum of ten years and to a person of Mexican ancestry born and brought up in the United States. Mexican-Americans include, therefore, the population often referred to as Chicanos – people of Mexican ancestry who are citizens of the United States.

The Mexican-American community of WLA is relatively new. Through the interviews I determined that only a small percentage of those over the age of thirty were natives of the area. Two of the speakers interviewed have lived in WLA for more than sixty years. One was born in Culver City and the other one was brought to Santa Monica at the age of two. They stated that although there have always been Mexicans in the area, the bulk of them started coming to WLA after World War II, that is, about thirty years ago. This agrees with my data, which indicate an average period of residence of twenty-four years for Mexican-Americans over the age of thirty. Most of the speakers said that the migration of Mexican-Americans into WLA is increasing steadily. One said, "Todos los domingos veo pasar caras nuevas" 'Every Sunday I see new faces going (to church)'.

The census of 1970 breaks down the information for "persons of Spanish language or Spanish surname" for Culver City and Santa Monica but not for Venice. According to the census, of the 1970 population of Spanish speakers or of persons with a Spanish surname in Culver City and Santa Monica only 33 percent and 32 percent, respectively, were there in 1965.

Mexican-Americans have come to WLA from a variety of places and for a single reason: to find job opportunities and better living conditions. Some of these Mexican-Americans lived for varying periods of time in Texas, Arizona, New Mexico, or in other places in California before coming to WLA; others came directly from Mexico. They constitute a homogeneous social community in that they have the same types of manual, semiskilled jobs, they have a similar economic status, they share cultural values and traditions that reflect a blending of their Mexican background and their experience of American life, and they share language norms.

The WLA Mexican-Americans as a Spanish-speaking community

It is possible to refer to the Spanish spoken in WLA as a "dialect of Spanish," given a definition of "dialect of a language" as based on sociogeographic rather than on strictly linguistic considerations. Wald (1973, p. 40) defines a speech community as "a set of speakers who share a set of norms." The importance of this definition is that the set of norms be shared by the members of the community.

It is beyond the scope of this study to identify the phonological, lexical, and syntactic features that may characterize the WLA dialect of Spanish. However, it is possible to point out some sociolinguistic norms that are shared by the participants in the community[5] and that relate to its being embedded in an English-speaking environment:[6]

1. The members of the community in the age group of fifty and over use Spanish as a means of communication. The males of the population are able to produce some sentences in English as a result of having to understand and use some English at work. One of the speakers (sixty-eight years old) characterizes the situation in the following words:

   El inglés que yo hablo es muy quebrado, muy pobre. Unicamente dedicado al trabajo. Según el trabajo que desempeñe es el inglés que hablo. Mas que cuando se trata de una conversación, un trato así, ya necesito que 'aiga alguien, que algunas palabras yo no las entiendo. O si las entiendo, no las puedo decir.

   'I speak a very poor, broken English. Just the language of work. The type of English I speak depends on the job I may have. But when I have to talk,

[5] There is no doubt that some or all of these features may be found in other Mexican-American Spanish-speaking communities throughout the United States.

[6] I cannot possibly expect to capture the complexity of the bilingual situation in these general comments. My characterization of these sociolinguistic norms is based on an impressionistic knowledge of the situation, gained through direct contact with the community. There may certainly be exceptions to the situations discussed, but I suspect that the exceptions would not amount to more than 10 or 15 percent of the speakers.

to hold a conversation, I need someone, because I don't understand some of the words. Or if I understand them, I can't say them.'

Women, on the other hand, state that they cannot speak any English and that their understanding of this language is limited to what they hear at home from members of the younger generations. This situation is reflected in the following exchange between the interviewer (C) and one of the speakers (a woman fifty-three years old):

L: Este es uno de mis hijos. iay! ¡Estos muchachos que no saben ni saludar!
C: ¡Pero qué grande! Porque yo le conocí a uno chiquito el otro día. ¿Se acuerda?
L: Sí. El niño chiquito tiene siete años y tengo otro de dieciseis años.
C: Es como el hijo mío, él. ¿Qué edad tiene él?
L: El ya los diecinueve.
C: Ah, no. El mío tiene quince. Pero se ve alto así como él.
L: Sí, pues. Si el otro que tengo también tiene, anda en dieciséis y está, casi está igual no más.
C: ¿Y él habla español también, o no?[7]
L: Pues, sí hablan. Batallan mucho. Yo no sé, yo no les hablo.
C: ¿Ud. les habla en inglés a ellos?
L: No, no, no. No sé. No sé hablar inglés.
C: Puro español no más.
L: Puro español. Y ellos – Bueno, sí, tratan de hablar. Pero no, lo empiezan a tartamudear mucho y ya no pueden. Las muchachas mayores sí son las que hablan poquito más bien español, pero ellos no, y el chiquito también.
C: Así es que nunca pueden conversar mucho, entonces.
L: Pues en, en español no. No, no, no, no pueden mucho.
C: Ellos le hablan en inglés a Ud. y Ud. les contesta en . . .
L: En español, sí. Entran y me piden así – O entran pidiendo cualquier cosa y ya yo les digo en español. O los oigo que anda uno con el otro "Que no has visto esto y que no has visto l'otro". Y yo los oigo ¿Verdad? y ya les digo "Allá está en tal parte". Y ya, ellos van. Así ¿Verdad? Pero, es que a los más mayores, mi esposo no los dejaba hablar inglés en la casa: "No. Pa' que aprendan inglés en la escuela o afuera. Aquí tienen que hablar español pa' que aprendan de todo". No, no quisieron. No, es que siempre andan jugando ¿Verdad? y luego ya se crían más hermanitos y todos – Ellos hablan unos con los, con el otro aquí también en inglés.

L: 'This is one of my children. Well! These children don't even know how to say hello!
C: Look how big he is! Because I met the little one the other day. Remember?

[7] I say *también* 'also', because the seven-year-old child had spoken to me in Spanish.

L: Yes. The little one is seven years old and I have another one who is sixteen.

C: He's like my son, him over there. How old is he?

L: He's nineteen already.

C: Oh, no. Mine is only fifteen. But he looks as tall as him.

L: Yes, well. The other one I have is also, is almost sixteen and he is, he's almost as tall.

C: And does he also speak Spanish, or doesn't he?

L: Well, yes, they do. They struggle a lot. I don't know, I don't talk to them.

C: Do you talk to them in English?

L: No, no, no. I can't. I can't speak English.

C: Just Spanish?

L: Just Spanish. And they – well, yes, they try to speak. But no, they hesitate a lot and they can't. The older girls are the ones who can speak a little bit better Spanish, but they (the boys) can't, and the little one also can.

C: So you can never talk much, then.

L: Well, not in Spanish, no. No, no, no, they can't.

C: They talk to you in English and you answer in –

L: In Spanish, yes. They come in and ask me like this – or they come in asking for something and I tell them in Spanish. Or I hear them talking to each other. "Haven't you seen this and haven't you seen that?" And I hear them, right? and tell them "It's in such and such a place." And they go. Like that, right? But, the older ones, my husband didn't let them speak English at home: "No. They can learn English at school or in the street. At home they have to speak Spanish so that they can learn everything." But they didn't want to. You see, they are always playing, right? and then there are more brothers and everybody – they all speak English among themselves at home too.'

In her words, this Mexican-American speaker pictures the general situation and the attitude of the people over the age of fifty[8] toward the use of the English and Spanish languages in the community. These people want to keep Spanish as the language of the home and English as the language of school and of work.

2. The Mexican-Americans aged thirty through forty-nine also use Spanish as their means of communication. The males report the same as the group aged fifty and over in relation to their use of English. The women in this age group, however, report that they have "some knowledge of English" and that they are able to understand and sometimes even say a few things in English to their children or other English-speaking people.
3. Ideally, Mexican-Americans would want to keep Spanish as the language of the home. In practice, however, the following patterns

[8] In fact, the same attitude is exhibited by those aged thirty through forty-nine.

Table 1. *Results of the responses to the question of language preference*

			1st lang. learned		Language preferred		
Age group	Number	Sex	Sp.	Eng.	Sp.	Eng.	Both
50 +	4	M	4	0	3	0	1
	6	F	6	0	6	0	0
30–49	4	M	4	0	4	0	0
	5	F	5	0	4	0	0
14–29	4	M	4	0	0	2	2
	4	F	4	0	0	2	2

Table 2. *Percentage of Spanish spoken at present*

Age group	96–100	90	80	50–60	– 30
50 +	1	1	1	1	0
	5	1	0	0	0
30–49	0	1	2	1	0
	2	1	1	1	0
14–29	0	0	0	0	4
	0	0	0	0	4

may be observed for the population in the younger group (fourteen through twenty-nine):

a. They use English to communicate among themselves.
b. They use Spanish when forced to by the fact that the listener does not understand English.
c. They would like to be able to talk to their elders only in Spanish but in fact use mostly English.
d. As compared with the men in this group, the women speak Spanish more fluently and shift to English less often, at least in the interview situation. Tables 1 and 2 tabulate the responses obtained from a total of twenty-seven speakers to the question of language use.

The interviews

Labov (1966, p. 603) has stated that a fundamental problem "is that of eliciting casual and spontaneous speech in the context of the formal linguistic interview, which normally evokes careful speech only." With this warning in mind, the interviews for the present study were not structured but conducted in a conversational style. A few questions and topics had been prepared beforehand and were introduced to stimulate the conversation, but on the whole the speakers were left free to talk about anything that was of interest to them.

The speakers were chosen without any preliminary contact, except in the case of members of the same family, who were reinterviewed on different occasions so that an average of fifty minutes of speech could be obtained from each one of them.

The goal of eliciting mostly casual speech was not achieved in every instance. The factors that contributed to this partial failure were: (1) the differences in age and sex between the interviewer and the speakers; (2) the inevitable presence of the tape recorder and the speaker's awareness that he or she was being recorded; (3) the odd situation in which the speaker is talking to a stranger. This third factor seems to be the least influential, however, because the interviewer found little difficulty in establishing almost immediate rapport with the informants and thus overcoming the oddness of the situation.

The analysis

Definition of the variables

The study deals with two different but related variables (A and B) in that they both involve the subject noun phrase (NP): (A) The expression versus the nonexpression or absence of the subject in sentences and clauses with finite verbs, such as in examples 1 and 2, and (B) the alternation between preverbal and postverbal position of the expressed subject, as illustrated in sentences 3 and 4. (The sex and age of the speakers follow the examples.)

Subject expressed:

1. *El inglés que* yo *hablo es muy quebrado*. 'The English that *I* speak is very broken.' (m, 68)

Subject not expressed:

2. *Según el trabajo que desempeñe es el inglés que ∅ hablo*. 'The English that (I) speak varies according to my job.' (m, 68)

Sentences 1 and 2 were said by the same speaker within the same discourse unit. They offer a clear illustration of the alternation between presence and absence of the subject in an almost minimal-pair syntactic structure.

Postverbal:

3. *Allá estaban* los meros hospitales. 'The hospitals were there.' (m, 65)

Preverbal:

4. Todos los chicanos *estaban allá*. 'All the Chicanos were there.' (f, 18)

The data included 338 expressed subjects out of a total of 795 tokens. From an average of sixty minutes of recording for each speaker a speech sample was selected and transcribed to serve as the basis for the linguistic analysis. The selection was done according to three criteria:

1. It should include a sample of connected discourse. This was an important constraint on the selection of the sample, given that it was hypothesized that the expression and placement of the subject were dependent on various discourse factors that needed to be identified through an intersentential analysis.
2. The sample usually included, but was not restricted to, one narrative. Side comments during narration were also included. When the narratives did not contain a sufficient number of subject tokens, dyadic exchanges were selected as part of the sample.
3. The sample for each speaker should contain a minimum of twenty expressed subjects of which a minimum of ten should be nonpronominal.

One basic problem in the analysis of the data was to decide which sentences to include and which to leave out. Given that the variables are studied as they are realized in actual speech, that is, in surface structure, it was decided initially that only finite forms of verbs would be included as possible environments for subject expression. Thus, sentences which may be claimed to have undergone equi-NP deletion were not considered as instances of deleted subjects. For example, the predicate *quiere ir a la playa* 'wants to go to the beach' in sentence 5 was analyzed as a single verb phrase (VP) with a complex verbal form *quiere ir* categorized as intransitive. Therefore, sentence 5 has only one NP subject, *María*, which is expressed.

5. *María quiere ir a la playa.* 'Mary wants to go to the beach.'

Some types of finite verb constructions were not included because they are categorically subjectless. These include some idiomatic expressions, illustrated in examples 6 and 7, and subjectless sentences with *haber* (*there is*, *there are*, etc.), *hacer* (with the meaning of *ago*), and *ser* 'to be', as illustrated in examples 8 to 10.

6. *donde quiera* 'everywhere'
7. *como quiera* 'you see that . . .'
8. *Había unas vacas echadas en el suelo.* 'There were some cows lying on the ground.'
9. *hace un año* 'a year ago'
10. *es temprano* 'it's early'

Also excluded were relative clauses whose relative pronoun referent is the subject of the clause, because in these constructions the relative pronoun is in fixed clause initial position:

11. *Vi al policía* que *le pegó.* 'I saw the policeman who hit him.'

It was also decided not to include questions, indirect questions, and exclamations, because the position of the subject in these constructions may obey constraints that are different from those on declarative sentences.

Table 3. *Effect of same reference and switch reference on the number of expressed subjects*

	No. of expressed subjects	*N*	% of expressed subjects
Same reference	77	304	25
Switch reference	261	491	53
Totals	338	795	

Note: $p < .001$.

The quantitative analysis

Only language internal constraints on the occurrence of the variables were investigated. The first parameter used as a possible constraint on both absence and placement of the subject was "same reference" versus "switch reference." Switch reference is established whenever the subject referent of the preceding finite verb, regardless of whether the subject is expressed or deleted, is different from the referent of the expressed subject of the sentence in question. Thus, for example, the subject in example 13, *ellas* 'they' is a case of switch reference because the referent is different from that of the subject of number 12 *yo* 'I', even though the subject is not expressed in 12.

12–14. *Y ya ese día lo conocí,* (13) *porque me, me animaron* ellas (14) *y me llevaron a ese bar.* 'And that day (I) met him, because *they* encouraged me and took me to that bar.' (f, 54)

Same reference is established when the subject referent of the sentence in question is the same as that of the preceding sentence, regardless of whether it is expressed or not expressed, as in number 14. It was predicted that same reference subjects would favor the absence of the subject or its placement in preverbal position when expressed. This prediction was based on the observation that same reference subjects constitute old information, and old information tends to be given initially in most languages (e.g., Turkish, Russian, English, Mandarin Chinese). The results confirmed the prediction. Of a total of 795 tokens, 457 did not have an expressed subject and 338 had the subject expressed, that is, 43 percent of the sample were expressed subjects. Table 3 shows that only 25 percent of the same reference subjects were expressed, whereas of the switch reference subjects 53 percent were expressed.

The results of the cross-tabulation of subject position by same and switch reference also confirmed the predicted outcome. Of the 338 expressed subjects, 144 were postposed and 194 were preposed. The results, illustrated in Table 4, demonstrate that same versus switch reference is an important constraint on subject positioning. Same reference subjects

Table 4. *Effect of reference on the position of the expressed subject*

	No. of expressed subjects in preverbal position	N	% of expressed subjects in preverbal position
Same reference	57	77	74
Switch reference	137	261	53
Totals	194	338	

Note: $p < .002$.

strongly favor preverbal position: they occurred preverbally in 74 percent of the cases. Switch reference subjects display similar percentages in both preverbal and postverbal positions: 53 percent and 47 percent respectively. The overall conclusion that may be drawn from the results of Tables 3 and 4 is that same reference subjects are most frequently not expressed, and if they are, they are most frequently placed preverbally.

At least two questions are posed by the results with respect to our initial hypothesis: (1) Why are same reference subjects expressed at all? and (2) Why are they placed postverbally in 26 percent of the cases? The first question is partly answered later in the discussion of the issue of ambiguity of the verbal form and the topic function of subjects. The second question has not been approached systematically, but identity with the preceding word order and mirror-image ordering in repetitions appear to be possible explanations, as illustrated in examples 15 and 16.

15. *Cuando está* uno *así joven, no, no tiene* uno *pues, responsabilidad de nada*. 'When one is young like this, well one doesn't have any responsibility.' (m, 68)
16. Yo *sacaba muy buenos cheques. Buenos cheques sacaba* yo. 'I got some very large cheques. Some very large cheques I got.' (m, 68)

As stated before, preverbal position for same reference subjects was predicted on the basis that old information tends to come at the beginning of the sentence and new information toward the end. Because a switch reference subject does not necessarily constitute new information, a separate factor group was set up for old information.

Old information was defined as that type of information that the speaker assumes to be "in the consciousness of the addressee at the time of the utterance" as a consequence of having been mentioned or having been clearly implied in the preceding discourse. This definition of old information is based on Chafe (1976, p. 30), but it is somewhat more constrained than Chafe's in that it requires that for a subject to be considered old information, its referent should have been either mentioned or clearly

Table 5. *Expressed subjects, by old and new information*

	No.	%
Old information	285	84
New information	53	16
Totals	338	100

implied in the preceding discourse. By "clearly implied" it is meant a NP that occurs in a situation like the following: The speakers are talking about World War II, and Pearl Harbor is mentioned. One of the speakers then states that "Japan attacked the United States." Given that "Japan" and the "United States" are clearly implied in the preceding conversation about Pearl Harbor, I consider them both to be old information.

As Table 5 shows, 84 percent of the 338 expressed subjects represent old information. This result reflects what seems to be a universal feature of subjects. In "Towards a Universal Definition of 'Subject'," Keenan (1976, p. 318) states that what subjects refer to "is normally known to both speaker and addressee, and so is, in that sense, old information." Spanish confirms this observation.

A further question relates to the effect of old information on the position of the subject, and surprisingly, this effect appears to be fairly low. Sixty-one percent of old subjects are preverbal. The results, illustrated in Table 6, apparently provide counterevidence for the widespread hypothesis that the order of the main constituents of a sentence crucially depends on the question of old and new information, with old information appearing at the beginning of a sentence and new information toward the end. In the present study, the results indicate only a tendency for this to be so.

Later observation of the data in the light of the statistical results for subject placement has indicated that the working definition of old information may be deficient in two respects: (1) This definition, as well as Chafe's, does not allow for "degrees" of newness of the constituents with respect to one another. In fact, Chafe rejects the proposal that some piece of information may be "more or less" present in the consciousness of the addressee and favors a clear-cut dichotomy between old and new information. The data, however, offer many examples where the constituents of a given sentence are linearly ordered according to the relative newness of the information conveyed by them, that is, to how recently their referents may have been mentioned in the preceding discourse in such a way that the most recently mentioned one occurs in initial position. So, even though the speaker has to assume that all these referents must be in the hearer's consciousness at the time of speaking, his syntax does respond to different degrees of "newness." Therefore, an absolute value

Table 6. *Postverbal and preverbal position of expressed subject, by old and new information*

	Postverbal position		Preverbal position		Total no. of expressed subjects
	No.	%	No.	%	
Old information	110	39	175	61	285
New information	34	64	19	36	53
Totals	144		194		338

Note: $p < .001$.

of "old" or "new" for subjects cannot capture the complexity of this question of the linear arrangement of the constituents. (2) Another problem with the definition, related to that already discussed, is that it is not constrained to a specific, "narrow scene" as is, for example, Firbas's (1966, p. 246) definition.[9] It is too general because in some cases it has led us to consider as old some piece of information that could be in the hearer's consciousness at the time of speaking but that the hearer might not relate to the specific, narrow context in which it occurred, as illustrated in the answer to question 17.

17. Q: *¿Quién hizo el queque, tú o tu mamá?* 'Who baked the cake, you or your mother?'
    A: *Lo hice yo.* 'I did.'

In this study I have coded subjects like that in the answer to question 17 as old information to be consistent with the definition. Furthermore, constrained by the dichotomous approach, I have coded subjects as old or new without considering degrees of newness with respect to the other constituents of the sentence. This coding for old-new information appears to be inadequate and may account for the low effect of this factor on the position of the subject.

It has been observed before that subject pronouns are expressed more frequently when the verbal form is ambiguous (Gili y Gaya 1951; Real Academia Española 1973). Consequently, the ambiguity of the verbal form was set up as a possible constraint on the absence of the subject. With respect to the issue of ambiguity, it was found necessary to differentiate in the analysis between: (1) morphologically ambiguous verb, (2) morphologically unambiguous verb, and (3) context unambiguous verb.

A morphologically ambiguous verb is any of the undifferentiated forms

[9] According to Firbas, the notion conveyed by a noun may be known and familiar, but in regard to a "narrow, ad hoc scene, it may appear as unknown, new, contextually independent."

for first and third person singular in all the tenses of the subjunctive mood, in the imperfect of the indicative, and in the conditional forms. A morphologically unambiguous verb is a form that is morphologically differentiated from all others. A morphologically ambiguous verbal form was coded as context unambiguous when it could only co-occur with a subject referent marked by the features "nonhuman"[10] and when in a given discourse unit only the first person singular was a possible subject of the ambiguous forms, that is, when the speaker was talking only about himself. In these cases, it was thought that the discourse provided the clues necessary to disambiguate the subject referent so the verb was classified as contextually unambiguous. The three types of verbal forms are illustrated in examples 18–21.

Morphologically ambiguous:

18. *iba* 'I/(s)he went'
iría 'I/(s)he would go'
fuera 'I/(s)he went' (subjunctive)

Morphologically unambiguous:

19. *voy* 'I go'
va '(s)he goes'

Compare examples 20 and 21, taken from a description by one of the speakers of his job at a ceramics factory. The verbal forms are coded as morphologically ambiguous in number 20, where the speaker is talking about himself and another worker, and as contextually unambiguous in number 21, where the speaker is talking only about himself. The verbal form numbered 7 in example 20 exemplifies a contextually unambiguous form whose subject is nonhuman.

Contextually unambiguous:

20. Así es de que yo *hacía*[1] el plato y había un negrito que lo cortaba. Ese lo *redondeaba*[2]. Y entonces me lo *mandaba*[3] a mí y yo le *ponía*[4] un anillo que *lleva*[5] arriba para, pa' librarlo del calor *era*[6] el anillo ese, pa' librarlo del calor pa' que no se *reventara*[7].
'So I made the plate and there was a black guy who cut it. He rounded it. And then he sent it to me and I put a ring around it so that, that ring was to isolate it from the heat, to insulate it from the heat so that it didn't break.'

21. Entonces, a mí me daban la fórmula y yo, yo – todos los, las *batía*, luego ahí los *mandaba* a los tanques, *ponía* los tanques, los *llenaba*, la *tapaba* y luego lo, lo *comenzaba* ya pa' la hora de irme los *comen-*

[10] The inclusion of ambiguous verbal forms with a nonhuman subject in the category of context unambiguous may not prove to be adequate for other speech samples. In the data, the verbal forms that occurred with these subjects unambiguously referred to nonhuman subjects (e.g., *reventar* 'to blow up,' *derretir* 'to melt') so the context was considered to be unambiguous. But we have to acknowledge the possibility that these verbs may be used metaphorically with human subjects.

Table 7. *Effect of ambiguity of verb on the number of expressed subjects*

	No. of expressed subjects	*N*	% of expressed subjects
Ambiguous verb	72	105	69
Unambiguous verb in context	19	49	39
Unambiguous verb	247	641	38
Totals	338	795	

Note: $p < .001$.

> *zaba* – Me *echaba* otras tres horas, cuatro horas más todos los días. 'Then, they gave me the formula and I, I – all of them, I poured them, beat them, then I sent them to the tanks, I filled them, covered them and then I, I started it when it was time to leave I started it. – I worked about three, four hours overtime every day.'

In a further study of the role of ambiguity in determining the expression and placement of the subject, a finer coding system would probably have to differentiate, for instance, between verbal forms preceded by a reflexive clitic and those that are not, because it is likely that the clitic will serve the disambiguating function that a subject pronoun does.[11] This would be valid only for intransitive pseudoreflexive verbs, because true reflexives without an overt subject remain ambiguous (e.g., *me lavaba* 'I/(s)he washed myself/me'). The results obtained from the cross-tabulations indicate that ambiguity has a stronger effect on the expression than on the positional variable.

The contribution of the ambiguity factor is most interesting with respect to the expression of the subject. Table 7 illustrates the results, which show a clear decrease in the percentage of expression along the scale of ambiguity: Sixty-nine percent of the subjects are expressed with ambiguous verbs, 39 percent are expressed with context unambiguous verbs, and 38 percent with morphologically unambiguous verbal forms. These results indicate that speakers are aware of different levels of ambiguity in discourse. Part of their linguistic competence is their ability to resolve this ambiguity by, for instance, the use of subject pronouns to disambiguate subject reference.

Observe the results illustrated in Table 8. If the verb is morphologically ambiguous, the subject occurs in preverbal position in 64 percent of the total instances of ambiguous verbs. Fifty-four percent of the subjects are

[11] Note that in English same reference subjects may also be unexpressed in coordinate sentences, as in example 21. It seems to me, however, that even here variation between pronoun and zero is more constrained than in Spanish. I do not know of any studies of this type of variation in English.

Table 8. *Effect of verbal ambiguity on placement of expressed subject*

	No. of expressed subjects in preverbal position	*N*	% of expressed subjects in preverbal position
Ambiguous verb	46	72	64
Context unambiguous	15	19	79
Unambiguous verb	133	247	54
Totals	194	338	

Note: $p < .05$.

Table 9. *Preverbal position of expressed subject, by number of arguments*

	No. of expressed subjects in preverbal position	*N*	% of expressed subjects in preverbal position
One argument	55	120	46
Two or more arguments	139	218	64
Totals	194	338	

Note: $p < .002$.

preposed in the morphologically unambiguous group. Surprisingly, however, 79 percent of the subjects are preposed in the context unambiguous group. The results, therefore, may reflect a general tendency for subjects to occur preverbally rather than show the effect of the ambiguity factor on this variable.

The number of arguments in the sentence or clause was set up as another factor influencing the placement of the subject. This factor was included because a preliminary observation of the data appeared to support the study made by the Kahanes (1950) that showed that subjects were quite frequently placed in postverbal position when the verb was intransitive.

Table 9 summarizes the results of the study. In one-argument sentences the subject is preposed in 46 percent of the cases, that is, no clear effect is observed when the subject is the only argument of the verb.[12] The explanation for this distribution must be related to the constraints imposed by same reference and newness of information. In sentences with two or

[12] Included in this group were: (1) intransitive sentences, (2) *se* passive sentences, (3) regular, obligatory, and pseudoreflexive sentences, and (4) transitive sentences with an object clitic and zero object noun phrase (e.g., "ellos *lo* hacen" 'they do *it*').

more arguments on the other hand, 64 percent of the subjects are preposed. One possible explanation for this distribution may be offered with reference to perceptual and discourse factors: if there are two or more NPs in a sentence they are polarized around the verb in such a manner that the subject NP is placed preverbally and the object NP postverbally to prevent a misunderstanding of the functions of these constituents.[13] Furthermore, the subject is preverbal because it is frequently old information (see Table 5), and old information tends to be placed in initial position (see Table 6). The use of a more fixed subject-verb-object (SVO) order may be related to the growing tendency not to mark overtly the direct object with the preposition *a* in spoken Spanish.[14] Thus, from a language with a more pragmatic word order, Spanish appears to be developing into a language whose word order has a grammatical function: that of signaling subject and object.[15] The fact that intransitive subjects behave differently should not be surprising, because in fact there are ergative languages that also differentiate between transitive and intransitive subjects, though by means of other syntactic devices such as case marking or verb agreement.

One other group of factors was included in the study of the positional variable: the presence of an initial adverb, the presence of a postverbal adverb, and the absence of an adverb. Previous observation of the data had led to the hypothesis that the presence of an initial adverb would correspond with a subject in postverbal position. This prediction was made from the observation that initial adverbs usually introduced existential sentences, as illustrated in examples 22–24. Earlier studies (Hatcher 1956 and Silva-Corvalán 1977, 1978) had shown that subjects tended to occur postverbally in these types of constructions, as noted previously.

22. *Atrás venían* los médicos. 'The doctors came behind.' (m, 65)
23. *Luego llegaron* los chicanos. 'Then came the Chicanos.' (m, 17)
24. *Ya venía* la tormenta. 'The storm was coming already.' (m, 40)

The results illustrated in Table 10 confirm the hypothesis that when there is an initial adverb the subject is postverbal in 85 percent of the cases as compared with only 36 percent when the adverb is postverbal and when there is no adverb. These figures need to be investigated further. There seems to be sufficient evidence to support an explanation of the position of the adverb and the subject with reference to the informational

[13] Cf. Venneman (1974) where he postulates that a fundamental moving force behind the change from subject-object-verb to subject-verb-object is the need to disambiguate noun phrase functions in a language that has lost most of its case marking system.

[14] See Silva-Corvalán (1977) for a discussion of word order in two-argument sentences. The percentages are 78 percent of SVO, 7 percent of OVS, 7 percent of VSO, and 8 percent of VOS.

[15] See Thompson (1978) for a discussion of a typology of languages based on the function of word order.

Table 10. *Placement of expressed subject, by position of adverb*

	No. of expressed subjects in postverbal position	*N*	% of expressed subjects in postverbal position
Initial adverb	39	46	85
Postverbal adverb	13	36	36
No adverb	90	251	36
Totals	142	333	

Note: $p < .001$.

weight of these constituents in a particular situation. Thus, the adverb will be initial and the subject postverbal when (1) the adverb is used as an introductory presentational device, much like the dummy subject "there" in English, with a presentational verb that either introduces or reintroduces a subject referent into the discourse, as illustrated in examples 25 and 26; and (2) the adverb points to a place, time, or manner that has been referred to in the immediately preceding discourse, as in examples 27–29.

25. *Pues* ahí *viene* el muchachito *sin calzón, muy zorongo, como si nada.* 'And there comes the little boy without his underpants, easygoing, as if it didn't matter.' (f, 38)
26. Años atrás *vinieron* más, después *entraron* las máquinas, *esas piscadoras.* 'More came years ago, then came the machines, the harvesters.' (m, 69)
27. *Pero el año pasado cuando vamos aquí al Paso, ahí todo eso es unos fíles, millas, y ahí va viendo* uno *la máquina.* 'But last year, when we go to El Paso, everything is fields there, miles, and one sees the machine there.' (m, 69)
28. *Estaba una plaza así como en alto y tenía gradas y así* en una de esas gradas *me acosté* yo. 'And there was a square like this, high, and it had steps and there I lay down on one of those steps.' (m, 40)
29. *Y cuando llegamos a Santa Monica* acá *vivían* muchos japoneses. 'And when we came to Santa Monica many Japanese lived here.' (m, 65)

In the two cases illustrated in examples 25–29, the subject conveys newer information than that conveyed by the adverb and thus is postverbal.

Sankoff's (1978) VARBRUL 2 program was run to permit comparison in a single analysis of the effect of the five factor groups just discussed with respect to both the position and the expression variable. The results of this program for the probability of the subject to be absent are illustrated in Table 11, which shows that the absence of the subject is most favored when the subject is old (.69) and least favored when the verbal form is

Table 11. *VARBRUL output for expression versus absence of the subject*

switch reference = .34	same reference = .66	—
old information = .69	new information = .31	—
ambiguous V form = .28	unambiguous V = .68	context unambiguous = .55
one argument = .45	two arguments = .61	three arguments = .44

Table 12. *VARBRUL output for preverbal versus postverbal subject*

switch reference = .51	same reference = .49	—
old information = .42	new information = .58	—
unambiguous = .72	ambiguous = .28	—
two arguments = .52	three arguments = .48	—
initial adverb = .86	no adverb = .26	postverbal adverb = .33

morphologically ambiguous (.28). All the factors included in the study appear to be significant and may be ordered according to their relative weight in favoring the absence of the subject.

The results obtained for the effect of the various factors on the postverbal position of the subject, illustrated in Table 12, indicate that some of the factors have no effects, namely, switch and same reference, old and new information, and number of arguments. Notice that one-argument sentences had to be excluded, because the VARBRUL program rejected them as a knock-out factor.[16]

Switch reference and new information only slightly favor the postverbal placement of the subject. On the other hand, the occurrence of an initial adverb and unambiguous verbal forms strongly favor this postverbal position. It is interesting to notice that in the environment of an ambiguous verbal form the postposition of the subject is not favored. This suggests that the placement of the subject in front of the verb when it is ambiguous may be a communication strategy used by Spanish speakers to disambiguate subject reference at a point where communicative distress has not yet been created as a result of an ambiguous verbal form.

Contrast and discourse topic

Two other factors bear upon the question of the expression and placement of the subject: (1) contrast and (2) the establishment of the subject as the topic of a discourse unit. These determine both the expression of the subject and its placement in preverbal position.

[16] A knock-out factor is a contextual factor that is not compatible with one of the variants. This factor is always assigned a categorical value of 0 or 1. The difficulties associated with the knock-out constraints are discussed in Sankoff (1978).

I will call a subject NP the "focus of contrast" when the referent of the NP in question stands in opposition to a closed number of clearly identifiable alternatives. The notion of alternatives in opposition, not just a list of alternatives, in that only one of the alternatives in a contrasting situation may be chosen as the right one, is crucial to the definition of contrast. Furthermore, when a subject NP_1 is the focus of contrast, there is always an element, X, that stands in relation to this subject and participates in the contrastive situation in opposition to another element, Y, which stands in relation to the subject NP_2 contrasting with NP_1. For example, in "My father met him but my mother didn't," "my father" (NP_1) and "my mother" (NP_2) are in contrast and so are "met him" (X) and "didn't" (Y), which are related to NP_1 and NP_2, respectively. Furthermore, elements in contrast belong to the same semantic field. They share general semantic features, such as animacy, agency, action, time, or place. Thus, it would not be possible to contrast time and place, for instance, or animacy and action.

It is axiomatic that languages may express contrast by means of several phonetic and syntactic devices. Here, I will discuss the preverbal placement of the subject NP (and tangentially of other sentence constituents) in situations of contrast. I will refer exclusively to the question of word order, because no study of other syntactic or phonetic features has been made. My analysis of the relationship between word order and expression of contrast implicitly claims, however, that given the same intonational and stress pattern (with falling intonation and no special stress on any word) the order SV will be used when the subject is in contrast, and not the order VS.

Observe, for example, sentences (f) and (k) in example 30 in the discourse context in which they occur. The speaker is an eighteen-year-old female and the discourse topic is her boyfriends:

30. (a) Una vez tenía un novio, no novio, amigo, que era half black. Y – (b) Mi papá nunca lo conoció. (c) Mi mamá sí. (d) Mi mamá dijo que estaba guapo. (e) Pero no me gustó. (f) No era, no era lo que yo quería. (g) No me gustó. (h) Pero, mi mamá dijo que estaba guapo pero yo no creo. (i) Yo pensaba que estaba feo. Yo sí. (j) No lo quería. (Pause) (k) Yo, salir con el que yo quiera. (l) Si me gusta, salir. (m) Si son mis amigos, OK.
'(a) I once had a boyfriend, not a boyfriend, just a friend, who was half black. And – (b) My father never met him. (c) My mother did. (d) My mother said he was handsome. (e) But I didn't like him. (f) He wasn't, he wasn't what I wanted. (g) I didn't like him. (h) But, my mother said he was handsome but I don't think so. (i) I thought he was ugly, I did. (j) I didn't want him. (Pause) (k) As for me, I go out with whom I want. (l) If I like him, I go out. (m) If they are my friends, OK.'

The alternatives in opposition in this piece of discourse are: *mi papá*, *mi mamá*, and *yo*. The whole paragraph is clearly contrasting these three participants with respect to what they like and want. In (f) the speaker states what *she* wants as opposed to what *her father* or *mother* want, and in (k) she reaffirms this contrast by stating that she can go out with whomever *she* wants regardless of what her parents may want. The contention that subjects will be placed preverbally in contrastive situations is evidently supported by the SV order of all the sentences in this piece of discourse.

Take, for instance, sentences (b), (c), (h), and (i). Along the lines of our discussion of focus of contrast, two focuses of contrast can be identified in each of these sentences: in (b) and (c) contrast is established between *mi papá* and *mi mamá*, and between *nunca lo conoció* and *sí* (*lo conoció*); in (h) and (i) the contrast is between *mi mamá* and *yo* and between *que estaba guapo* and *que estaba feo*.

In (h) the conjunction *pero* introduces a contrastive clause. The subject of the clause, *yo*, could have been deleted in this case because the verb form unambiguously indicates person and number. If the speaker had intended to give *yo* merely as a piece of further redundant information, she could have placed it in postverbal position. Yet, she expresses the subject and places it preverbally because there is a situation of contrast with *mi mamá* and *yo* is the focus of contrast in the clause. Sentence (h) would have, in fact, been unacceptable with the subject of the clause in postverbal position:

31. *Mi mamá dijo que estaba guapo *pero no creo yo.*

It may also be argued that the SV order of these sentences obeys the principle of old-new information. Though this is indeed so, my contention is that in addition to the fact that the order SV corresponds to old-new information in (b), (c), (h), and (i), the preverbal position of the subject has a contrastive function that requires the expression of the subject.

Sentence (k) illustrates an example of a left-dislocated subject NP. In Spanish, a left-dislocated NP subject does not need to leave a copy behind. Thus, (k) would have also been grammatical with *yo* deleted in the dependent clause, and there would have been no ambiguity as to who the subject of *quiera* was: *Yo, salir con el que quiera*. However, the speaker chooses to express *yo*, and the effect of this is to make the contrast between *yo*, *mi mamá*, and *mi papá* even more prominent.

The same choice between expression or deletion of the subject is possible in example 32, sentence (a), spoken by a young girl of fourteen.

32. Yo conozco algunas (niñas que están en gangs), pero muchas no, no me quieren. Pero yo creo que, que me tienen celo, porque ellas ven que estoy yendo a una buena escuela y, y no so-, yo no soy como ellas porque ellas nunca me han vi-, nunca me has visto agarrarme en un pleito con otra. (a) Y esas que tienen gangs, que yo conozco, cada minuto andan buscando pleitos.
'I know a few (girls who are in gangs), but many don't, don't like me. But I think that, that they are jealous, because they see that I'm going

to a good school and, and I'm not, I'm not like them because they've never seen, they've never seen me start a fight with another one. (a) And those who have gangs, that I know, are always looking for trouble.

Sentences like *que yo conozco* in example 32 will be referred to as parenthetical sentences. Parenthetical sentences are those that are said as a comment or explanation and may or may not be embedded but remain outside the main narrative. *Yo* is expressed in the clause in the example because it is a parenthetical clause, and it is placed in initial position because it is contrastive. The idea that the speaker wants to convey is that "the girls that *I* know who are in gangs are always looking for trouble," leaving open the possiblity that not all girls in gangs are looking for trouble.

Notice that this discourse is similar to that quoted in example 30 in that the speaker is placing herself in a situation of contrast wth other subject referents, *ellas* in example 32. Here, the subject pronouns *yo* and *ellas* could have been deleted in eight sentences, but they are deleted in only two of the eight. I propose that speakers will strongly tend to express pronominal subjects in this type of discourse in which a sustained situation of contrast exists between two or more subject referents even though the verb morphology provides sufficient information to identify these referents. Furthermore, the position of the subject in these sentences will be, as shown by the examples discussed, preverbal.[17]

I have stated before that the establishment of the referent of a subject as the topic of a discourse unit requires the expression of the subject NP.[18] The topic of a discourse unit is what the unit is about; its referent is usually the most frequently mentioned participant in the discourse unit, usually the participant from whose point of view the events are related.

Let us observe the following dialogue between myself and a fourteen-year-old girl.

33. C: ¿Y en qué cosas te entretienes, entonces, después de la escuela?
M: En el trabajo, las tareas. (a) Porque – yo salgo de escuela, (b) y es otra cosa que me gusta porque me quedo entretenida. (c) Porque yo vengo de la escuela como a las tres y media y lueguito me pongo a hacer el trabajo y 'cabo como a las nueve. Y de ahí me acuesto y me levanto otra vez y es lo mismo todos los días porque – en esa escuela dan mucha tarea. Pero, de todos modos estoy aprendiendo mucho, me está haciendo bien.
C: 'And what do you do, then, to entertain yourself after school?'

[17] See Silva-Corvalán (1979) for a detailed discussion of the role of contrast in relation to word order in spoken Spanish.

[18] The notion of discourse unit (DU) is introduced and discussed at length in Wald (1976). Basically, a unit in discourse is defined as consisting of more than one sentence with internal coherence of sense and content spoken by a single speaker. A narrative is a DU, but within a narrative there may be one or more embedded DUs.

M: 'Work, homework. (a) Because – I come from school, (b) and that's another thing I like because it keeps me busy. (c) Because I come from school at about three-thirty and right away start doing my work and finish around nine. And then I go to bed and get up again and it's the same thing every day because – in that school they give you a lot of homework. But in any case I'm learning a lot, and it's doing me good.'

In this discourse there are eight sentences where the subject *yo* could have been either expressed or deleted, but it is expressed in only two of the eight. Notice that these figures reflect a symmetrically opposite situation to the one illustrated by example 32, where in eight sentences only two subjects had been deleted. Of course, the nature of this type of discourse is also different. There is no situation of contrast. Indeed, no other subjects are expressed in the paragraph. The whole discourse unit is about the speaker, *yo*, and the things she does after school. The question is why the speaker expressed the pronoun *yo* at all. The sample supports our hypothesis that the speaker does so to establish herself as the topic of this discourse unit. She takes her turn by answering a question about what she does to entertain herself after school and establishes herself as the topic of the short passage in (a). However, she interrupts (a) to make a parenthetical remark, (b). When she resumes her report she produces a sentence, (c), that is synonymous with the previously interrupted one, echoes its syntax, and completes the meaning of (a).

Example 34 provides further evidence in support of this analysis. The dialogue is between myself and a young woman of eighteen years.

34. C: No. No le pregunté a él yo que pensaba de los blacks. ¿Porque hay muchos problemas en, cuando tú estabas en la Venice High, por ejemplo?

T: Oh, sí, oh. Yo no quiero a los blacks. Me hicieron mucho, a mí. No los quiero, pero. No, he tenido muchos amigos, unos sí y unos no. Ya. Depende quiénes son. Pero casi – Como conozco a un black. No, sin conocerlo digo "No lo quiero." Y después que lo conozca ya, ya mejor. Depende cómo son ellos. Pero, a mí me han hecho muchas cosas.

C: 'No. I didn't ask him what he thought about blacks. Why, are there many problems in, when you were in Venice High, for instance?'

T: 'Oh, yes. I don't like blacks. They did many bad things to me. I don't like them, but. No, I've had many friends, some OK, others not OK. It depends on who they are. But – Like when I meet a black. Well, without knowing him I say "I don't like him." But after I get to know him it's better. It depends on them. But, they've done a lot of bad things to me.'

Here, I have asked the speaker a general question. Her answer reflects the egocentric character of discourse: She places herself *as the topic of the unit* by starting with a sentence about how *she* feels toward blacks

Table 13. *Comparison of the results for written and spoken Spanish (in percent)*

	Written Spanish	Spoken Mexican-American Spanish
Copulative sentences excluded	32	34
Expressed subjects	45	43
Preverbal subjects	52	57

– "Yo no quiero a los blacks," where the subject *yo* is syntactically redundant – and then continues narrating the events in relation to herself.

I showed previously that the expression of subjects is favored by the occurrence of an ambiguous verbal form. It was further shown that subjects are expressed in situations of contrast, in parentheticals, and to establish the referent as the topic of a discourse unit. No notion of emphasis, which has been previously suggested but never well-defined in the literature on Spanish subject pronouns (D'Introno 1979; Hadlich 1971; Gili y Gaya 1951; Stockwell, Bowen, and Martin 1965; Phillips 1976), seems to be necessary to account for the expression of the pronominal subjects discussed here.

Conclusions

In this chapter, I have identified and measured some of the factors that determine the expression or nonexpression of the subject and its preverbal or postverbal placement when it is expressed in the Spanish spoken by Mexican-Americans in WLA.

Discourse rules are not categorical, but a definite regularity exists in the speech behavior of the speakers studied: Same reference subjects are rarely expressed; pronominal subjects are expressed in parentheticals, to establish the referent as the discourse topic, to disambiguate verbal forms, and in situations of contrast. The postverbal position of the subject is favored when the verbal form is unambiguous and when there is an initial adverb. I have shown that the postverbal placement of the subject in this case is related to the relative newness of the information conveyed by the subject as compared with the information conveyed by the adverb.

Some of the percentages obtained on the basis of the data may be compared with those obtained for written Spanish by Van den Broeck-Delbecque (n.d.) and for spoken Caracas Spanish by Bentivoglio (1980). Table 13 indicates that the results for the written and the spoken language are quite similar. Even though Bentivoglio's study concerns itself exclusively with the factors that contribute to the expression of the first person subjects *yo* 'I' and *nosotros* 'we', her percentages for the influence of the

Table 14. *Comparison of two dialects of spoken Spanish with respect to the expression of subjects by same and switch reference (in percent)*

	Expressed subjects	
	Same reference	Switch reference
Mexican-American Spanish	25	53
Caracas Spanish	25	52

switch reference factor on the expression of the subject are almost identical to the percentages for Mexican-American Spanish. Table 14 compares the results.

It is impossible to compare other percentages because each study selected a different set of parameters. Tables 12 and 13 show that these partial percentages are similar enough to allow us to conclude that the constraints on the occurrence of the expression and placement variables are independent of dialect, that is to say, they reflect a general characteristic of the Spanish language.

References

Bentivoglio, Paola A. 1980. Why *canto* and not *yo canto*? The problem of first-person subject pronoun in spoken Venezuelan Spanish. Master's thesis, University of California, Los Angeles.

Bolinger, Dwight. 1952. Linear modification. *Publications of the Modern Language Association* 67:1117–44.

1954–5. Meaningful word order in Spanish. *Boletín de Filología* (Universidad de Chile) 7:45–56.

Chafe, Wallace. 1976. Givenness, contrastiveness, definiteness, subjects, topics, and point of view. In *Subject and topic*, ed. Charles N. Li, pp. 25–55. New York: Academic Press.

D'Introno, Francesco. 1979. *Sintaxis transformacional del español*. Madrid: Cátedra.

Firbas, Jan. 1966. Non-thematic subjects in contemporary English. *Travaux Linguistiques de Prague* 2:239–56.

Gili y Gaya, Samuel. 1951. *Curso superior de sintaxis española*. Barcelona: Ediciones SPES.

Hadlich, Roger. 1971. *A transformational grammar of Spanish*. Englewood Cliffs, N.J.: Prentice-Hall.

Hatcher, Anna G. 1956. Theme and underlying question: two studies of Spanish word order. *Word* 2 (supp.), Monograph No. 3.

Kahane, Henry, and Renée Kahane. 1950. The position of the actor expression in colloquial Mexican Spanish. *Language* 26:236–63.

Keenan, Edward L. 1976. Towards a universal definition of "subject." In *Subject and topic*, ed. Charles N. Li, pp. 303–34. New York: Academic Press.

Labov, William. 1966. The social stratification of English in New York City. Arlington, Va.: Center for Applied Linguistics.

Phillips, Robert N. 1976. Los Angeles Spanish: a descriptive study. Ph.D. dissertation, University of Wisconsin.

Real Academia Española. 1973. *Esbozo de una nueva gramática de la lengua española*. Madrid: Espasa-Calpe.

Sankoff, David, ed. 1978. *Linguistic variation: models and methods*. New York: Academic Press.

Silva-Corvalán, Carmen. 1977. A discourse study of word order in the Spanish spoken by Mexican-Americans in West Los Angeles. Master's thesis, University of California, Los Angeles.

1978. A quantitative study of subject deletion and subject placement in spoken Spanish. Mimeographed. Manuscript, University of California, Los Angeles.

1979. An investigation of phonological and syntactic variation in spoken Chilean Spanish. Ph.D. dissertation, University of California, Los Angeles.

Stockwell, Robert P., J. P. Bowen, and J. W. Martin. 1965. *The grammatical structures of English and Spanish*. University of Chicago Press.

Thompson, Sandra A. 1978. Modern English from a typological point of view: some implications of the function of word order. *Linguistische Berichte* 54:19–37.

Van den Broeck-Delbecque, N. n.d. La colocacion del sujeto en el cancionero de Miguel de Unamuno. Mimeographed. Manuscript, University of Louvain, Belgium.

Venneman, Theo. 1974. Topics, subjects, and word order: from SXV to SVX via TVX. In *Historical linguistics*, ed. J. Anderson and C. Jones, pp. 339–76. Amsterdam: North-Holland.

Wald, Benji. 1976. The discourse unit: a study of the segmentation and form of spoken discourse. Mimeographed. Manuscript, University of California, Los Angeles.

6

Mexican-American caló and standard Mexican Spanish

JOHN T. WEBB

For the *mono*lingual Spanish speaker, caló may be style, flavor, irreverence in discourse; special vocabulary, nonstandard structure, peculiar idioms, taboo expression; hope for inclusion, effort toward exclusion, identifying of empathy, uncovering of hypocrisy; humility in the face of "superiority," pomposity or pride before what is rejected; "real" warmth in a cold environment, hauteur above what is beneath notice; humor, relaxation, nebulousness. For the *bi*lingual, no matter the degree of dominance in Spanish, caló may represent any or all of these qualities, may be a lifeline to self-identity – corporal, social, spiritual – and may even mean survival.

Caló may be compared with slang, but for most speakers it has a greater dependence on attitude, overall or temporary. Where slang often posits a standard to be lowered in speaking or writing, many or most caló users have not had the opportunity to steep themselves in establishment-approved norms. If raised in the United States, they only rarely have had instruction in written Spanish. To assume a dignity in language, therefore, they often depend on the shaky standards of the immediate environment, individual or social. Whereas slang may imply a hierarchical and multigraded social structure, allowing enormous and often subtle variation in use (English *posh* assumes certain knowledge of upper-class perception), the caló user usually deals with a black-and-white universe. Most brown-skinned people have felt negative discrimination, find certain avenues not open to them, do not believe that they have been dealt with directly. The caló user has recourse to cultural fraternity (*carnalismo*) and knows the overt and covert means of shunning or exploiting inclusion and exclusion inside and outside the group, community, and culture. Whereas slang may confront generally understood taboos and take responsibility for breaking them, caló even more frequently uses taboos against society, judges taboos as beneath contempt, and unconsciously may even provide taboos with a comfortable role within the expression of a segregated social structure. Yet the use of caló in expression and interpretation provides the speaker, and the group, with a release through wryness, with a potential to sigh and then proceed, to bear up, to have *aguante*.

Definition

The title of this chapter implies relative homogeneity in two major speech varieties, each of which is spoken, at least on occasion, by millions of people. Even when considered theoretically, the varying linguistic strata and the fluctuating economic and political conditions of the speakers would not allow for homogeneity. Still, given some time-and-space definition, we can approach conclusions about who it is that speaks either or both, and how it is that either is spoken.

Spanish and English are involved in major intercultural blending in the Estados Unidos Mexicanos and in the United States of America.[1] This contact and borrowing is most evident along the political border between the two countries, where language in a variety of cultures demonstrates a healthy fermentation that promises to last (see Webb 1980). Mexico, the largest Spanish-speaking country, and the United States, the fourth largest (Spain 1977), have been engaged in an interchange of population and language for some time (see especially Espinosa 1930–46 and Lope Blanch 1968, p. 85–9). "Standard Mexican Spanish" (Lope Blanch 1968, 1972) and "standard American English" have been at least partially affected by each other in lexicon, phonology, morphology, and semantics.[2] Nevertheless, Spanish and English expression are normally distinguishable, even for the speaker relatively unconscious of borrowing and of code-switching (Valdés 1978, esp. pp. 2, 8).

Many studies, including some in the present book, indicate the difficulty of defining the standard Spanish language. Lope Blanch, in his many years of work with Mexican colleagues, has described Spanish in the Americas and the roles of Mexican Spanish within such context (Lope Blanch 1968). I will concentrate, therefore, on attitudes and beliefs of speakers, and relate them to the expression of caló in the United States.

History

The term "caló" has been traditionally reserved in Spain to mean the language of the *gitano*, a member of an ill-defined group formed principally of ethnic Gypsies but also including the travelers who have found refuge among them (Heras and Villarín 1974; Webb 1976, p. 1).[3] The

[1] Historically, there have been lasting contacts of cultures across Eurasia, between Africa and Japan. It is not likely, however, that the New World received any long-range influence from elsewhere before the arrival of Europeans. The mixing of thought processes of the Old and New Worlds affected modes of expression in ways recorded in post-Columbian history and in everyday speech of the present. I hope to help show that this "American" heritage can be a major source of pride in our culture.

[2] Oral communication of William Labov in 1970 indicated Phoenix English leveling of *cat, cot, caught,* probably due to Spanish. I omit syntax from a listing of "interference" areas only because of lack of sufficient evidence that this persists in English for more than one generation.

[3] For many people, *romá* is preferable to the term "Gypsies."

extension of the meaning of the term to include the jargon of delinquents, however, has led champions of Gypsy culture strictly to delimit the boundary between the two (Tineo Rebolledo 1909, pp. 5–6). "Germanía," today usually defined as the speech of delinquents, also has its defenders (Hill 1949, pp. v–vi). This latter word, nevertheless, often refers (as does the term "caló") to a mixture of Hispanicized Romanés (or Gypsified Spanish) and modified old germanía (Pabanó 1915, pp. 186–87, 189, and 191) or to New World expression only casually related to peninsular *caló* or *germanía* (e.g., Llorens 1959). Romanés (the ethnic tongue of the Gypsies) and the language of other "travelers" no longer determines caló in Aztlán (the Southwest), but the vocabulary is continually reinforced through exposure to the Romanés spoken by Gypsies in Mexico and in the United States.[4]

Communication in Aztlán

Caló in the southwestern United States is defined by its speakers in terms of criteria of usage.[5] Two or more of the following must be perceivable for the expression to be considered caló:

1. *Deflation of dignity*. The uttering of such expression will markedly deflate, at least temporarily, the assumed dignity of the wider community's formal speech. The positing of such dignity may be made by the individual, the community, or by both.
2. *Nonconventionality*. The expression implies a strikingly humorous or nonconventional view of reality. The more evident such an implication is, the more lively and likely is the potential for lowering the dignity of formal speech.
3. *Group intimacy*. The expression signals the speaker's special intimacy with a type of language that he views as caló or with a group of people who normally use such speech.
4. *Status recognition*. Terms taboo in ordinary discourse with persons believed by the speaker to be of higher social status (not necessarily according to the community's standards) may continue to be thought caló despite great popularity. Preeminent in this category is the family of expressions headed by the word *chingar*; they retain the flavor of strong taboo, are used by most Spanish speakers only in situations calling for emphasis of ghetto cultural values (even when outside urban settings), and are normally "associated" in the wider community with persons choosing, or restricted to, poverty and delinquency.

4 United States Gypsies (*romá*) call Mexican counterparts /méskaja/; no one knows the total numbers involved. Cf. Hancock 1975; Webb 1976, pp. 9–10; and Pickett 1965–7.

5 Cf. Webb 1976, pp. 234–7, and Webb (in press). "Slang" in standard American English may be compared and contrasted, using criteria of Dumas and Lighter (1978). (I am much indebted to the original version, publicly read in 1975.) As to usage criteria, speakers of Mexican-American caló are usually in agreement with similar Mexican informants and consultants because the most capable users of caló are normally fluent in informal Mexican Spanish.

For the speaker, as well as for the outsider, the concept of caló is an elusive one; expressions at one time considered caló may eventually, through excessive use, become normal in popular Spanish or even in English and thus cease to serve for in-group identification.

Nevertheless, the numbered criteria permit a rough categorizing of caló material. The outsider may classify much of such usage as unsavory or taboo. For the caló speaker, the "antisocial" behavior may serve manifold purposes; caló may be substituted for the well-known conventional equivalent in order (1) to protect the speaker from the discomfort caused by the conventional word(s) (i.e., "embarrassment" when having to submit to values of the dominant culture), (2) to protect the speaker from self-disclosure (e.g., for the police officer trying to infiltrate an urban group) or (3) to create discomfort for the listener (the "outsider"). The use of caló may invite the sympathy of ghetto dwellers who also wish to avoid the intervention of the outsider or to inhibit his ease of action. The outsider is often unable to decipher the nuances of caló, whose interpretation requires a certain amount of inventiveness. For many users, more relevant than a creative tongue is a "creative ear"; the listener's interpretation reaches beyond the perception of thoughts and feelings consciously transmitted by the speaker.

Euphemism as a psychological interdiction also plays a part in caló and must be differentiated, by its relation to the unconscious, from much dysphemism and from purposeful deformation and enciphering in the strictly technical language of delinquents and professional criminals. Furthermore, chance phonological, morphological, and semantic similarities can lead to the formation of new expressions.

The communicating human in Aztlán

Some outlines of usage now become more clear. The individual user of caló may be an English speaker, who sprinkles form and content into English discourse. A more fluent user may be a speaker of informal Mexican Spanish who similarly bejewels speech with caló form and content. At a still deeper level, a fluent speaker of informal Mexican Spanish, living in urban poverty and holding to values of such culture, may speak constantly (or a great deal of the time) in caló, to the point of often being incomprehensible to other Spanish speakers; the speech still may not be used with the intention of excluding outsiders per se. At perhaps the deepest level, caló borders on and blends with delinquent cant and, though often used specifically to screen out those persons who do not share the values of extralegal life, still also serves to promote deflation of dignity, nonconventionality, group intimacy, status recognition, or all of these.

Based on data provided by approximately one hundred informants and consultants found able to provide satisfactory definitions and sentence frames for corroborated caló expressions read from a one-page refined field list (Webb 1976, pp. 18–20), the following seems to be true:[6]

1. Most speakers are young male adults, migrant, born in the southwestern United States, and no longer living with their progenitors (who have had only a primary education, and who wanted their children to speak in Spanish and not in caló). These speakers have completed secondary (or equivalent) education in English and have read Spanish only with difficulty; they exhibit less Spanish interference in English than English interference in Spanish but have experienced at least one year since childhood when the most-used language was Spanish. They prefer speaking Spanish, in which they feel themselves better able to express deep feelings, but they believe their own Spanish to be inferior in quality to that taught in U.S. classrooms (even by nonnative speakers). Though they hold higher education in some awe and consider "better" English to be necessarily advantageous in earning a higher steady income, most see no point in continuing their own formal education, and few have plans to change their lifestyle. The majority have crossed the border into Mexico at least once and feel a cultural pride that leads them to identify themselves as *chicano, mexicano,* or the like, but few have been politically militant for any significant amount of time.

Most of them (despite parental preference and because of peer pressure) feel that caló is a rich part of their cultural heritage; though such language is relatively "new" (i.e., they believe it to be of recent ancestral history), it seems to them well worth preserving. Nevertheless, though they have used caló a great deal in the ghetto neighborhood of their teen years, occasionally in some school or camp, and at least somewhat in the military service or with others of Spanish speech (e.g., persons of Cuban or Puerto Rican background), most have not used it for the past year or more. They are aware that they are replacing it with similar speech in English and believe that both Spanish and caló are being lost more and more rapidly with each succeeding generation. Despite this, most speakers are conscious of feeling more rather than less alienated.

2. At the level of popular, informal Spanish, able informants are easiest to find and are equally divided between women and men (though women are more concerned about confidentiality in being identified as informants). Their average age is twenty-two years.

3. People (mostly males) in their late twenties seem best able to evaluate caló as specifically reflecting the culture of urban poverty and speak it only as called for by situations of in-group communication (normally preferring popular, informal Spanish).

4. Persons competent in the language of antisocial life are most often in their early forties, are Spanish dominant, and are difficult to locate

[6] Cf. Webb 1976, 242–7. Certain terms appear to indicate skill in speaking at particular levels of usage (e.g., *bato* 'guy' in popular language, or *apiñi* 'opium' in technical cant).

(but amazingly cooperative when approached with respect); few if any women at this level seem capable in caló aside from strictly technical delinquent jargon.

5. The speaker's attitude toward caló may vary from seeing its use as a rejection of English and its implied values to regarding caló expression as part of ethnic identification and purposeful acquisition of Spanish (of whatever variety). Little-known standard or well-known nonstandard Spanish may be judged to be caló by the casual user. These extremes, or points on continua in between, may be seen by the speaker as being positive or negative.

6. The most capable speakers are normally less affluent and generally are nonliterate. They are often engaged in extralegal activity, and if they are involved in organized crime, they work for young, "respectable" business leaders, who are necessarily less capable in caló (seen by them as a socioeconomically inferior language) and more capable in English and often also in standard Mexican Spanish.

7. Although the use of caló expressions in "usual" speech may or may not prove an acquaintance with their semantics, or the cultural complex they represent, capable consultants (let alone casual informants) may be found in nearly any occupation in any part of the socioeconomic spectrum (cf. Webb 1976, p. 247).

Caló language in Aztlán

Mexican-American caló is a spoken language, based on the grammar of informal Mexican Spanish. Literate native speakers often have difficulty reading it because it lacks standardized conventions, because its surface structure often allows for great freedom in realization, and because it is seldom written and therefore looks peculiar.

Sometimes its form and content are identical to those of standard Spanish, most often when they strike the fancy of a speaker who perceives them as unusual or undignified. At other times, either form or content or both are seen as restricted to a given family, neighborhood, community, or region and thus may not be judged as being from Southwest, Mexican-American, or general Chicano caló. Occasionally, the growing popularity of a caló expression prevents it from serving to deflate dignity, to imply nonconventionality, to signify group intimacy, or to give status recognition; the expression may then cease to be regarded as caló.

Caló is a type of language used principally by people who move in coordinate multiglossia, if not coordinate multilingualism. The speaker, as he proceeds from approximating to the best of his ability formal or "standard" Mexican Spanish, or both, through informal speech to caló, finds difficulty in explaining himself in terms other than caló. The codes were learned in different contexts, and "translation" from one to another approaches impossibility.

Grammatical freedom in caló

As the reader will have noticed, the processes developed in caló are often the same as those found in many other types of language. The rate or extent of development, however, may surprise or shock even the speaker of informal Mexican or Mexican-American language. One of the most obvious phenomena exploited is that of perceived similarity.

The newcomer to caló may be careful to follow the lead of fluent speakers, but in copying novel formulas he soon discovers that "similar" expressions may carry similar weight. For example, almost any form beginning with *n* may mean an emphatic "no":

> *nada, naday, nadaza, nadazo, nalga, nalgas, nanay, naranja, naranja china, naranjas, naranjas de la china, naranjales, narices, nariz, ne, negrete, negros, negrosina, nel, nela, nels, nelsen, nelson, nene, nenel, nerel, never, néver, ni* (plus almost anything), *nicandro, nicanor, nicaragua, nicle, nicolás, niguas, nil, níquel, nones* (Webb 1976, 218–20).

All of these in deeper caló may be extended to "there is/are not; nothing; not at all; not in any way; there wasn't any."

A familiar and purposeful "disguising" that is similar involves adding to the end of a word (or each syllable of a word) a nonsense syllable beginning with an agreed-upon consonant (or consonant cluster) and continuing the base vowel of the last original syllable: *otro* > *otrofo* or *ofotrofo*. Although this pig-Latin-like play is hypocoristic, the intent, among rapid speakers, may be most serious. *Otro,* of course, is an example of serious semantic extension; "other" may refer to "homophile" ("other" sexual preference) or to the "other" side of the U.S.–Mexican border (according to the orientation of the speaker, in Mexico or in the United States) or to the "other" side of death (cf. English "beyond the grave" or "pass over to the other side").

Semantics may be stretched even more. The caló user can feel quite comfortable with diametrically opposite meanings of the same expression, a situation not uncommon in popular speech, particularly in Spanish (Beinhauer 1968, pp. 173–5). Linguistic or extralinguistic factors may govern which pole of the semantic opposition predominates in any given case. Nevertheless, the speaker is normally conscious of the existence of this potential – "bipolar" – ambiguity. Most people fluent in caló are also sufficiently fluent in Spanish so as to be able to choose synonyms or to paraphrase if this potential ambiguity produces difficulties. So it is that both speaker and listener are often aware of semantic distinction (e.g., *ruco* designates someone older or more intimately known than does Spanish *viejo* 'old'; the person termed *viejo,* unmarked by a caló designation, is felt to be deserving of more exploitation and less respect by caló users). Additionally, they distinguish between the semantic characteristics of a word and the semantic interpretation of a sentence frame for that word together with the semantic identity of components of that frame that are syntactically different: *Le hace agua la canoa al hombre* 'He (the man) is homophile' (standard 'The canoe makes water to the man') is certainly both transitive grammatically and intransitive semantically. (The complete "verb" here is *hacer agua la canoa a*; in Spanish, as in English, a canoe cannot make water).[7]

Transitivity

Because of the particular ways in which object and reflexive pronouns are used in caló as well as in Mexican and Southwest Spanish, they often fail in and of themselves as tests of verbal transitivity. Furthermore, because Spanish noun objects are not distinguished by any special form, only careful semantic analysis of sentence frames yields a satisfactory determination of the fundamental syntactic features of caló verbs (Webb 1976, p. 251).

The combination of verb and clitic pronoun(s) must often be considered a single, unanalyzable verb, similar to English verb plus complement (e.g., *bear it, take it out on*). Beinhauer (1968, p. 316) believes that the attempt to supply pronominal antecedents for certain popular constructs, for example, to refer *las* in Spanish *traérselas* 'to be up to something, be of great difficulty' to Spanish *dificultades* 'difficulties,' goes far beyond what is necessary, even when the alleged antecedent may have played at least a marginal role in the original formation of the expression. Caló employs extensively a Mexican Spanish and Southwest Spanish characteristic – the use of the pronoun *le* (in standard Spanish the third person singular [masculine, feminine, or neuter] dative or masculine accusative pronoun) as a verbal complement lacking any identifiable antecedent or referent. Thus, by using *le* with *tirar* (Spanish 'to throw, knock down, fire; [ex]tend; earn, win; pull, attract' → Mexican Spanish 'to damage, wound' → Southwest Spanish 'to use, deal with'), caló has developed 'to accomplish something' (*Voy a tirarle en la burocracia*), where *le* in isolation appears semantically vacuous. *Le* also lacks any specific referent when used with Spanish *hacer la lucha* 'to make the fight or struggle': *Va a hacerle la lucha* 'He's going to make an effort ("give it a try"), steal (for a living)'; likewise in *talonearle* (← Spanish 'to walk hurriedly and diligently,' Mexican Spanish 'to walk a lot [uselessly]') 'to walk, hurry.' Fluent speakers of Mexican and Southwest Spanish understand *le* as representing a genderless indeterminate referent comprehended by both speaker and listener and therefore unnecessary to state; *tirarle* and *hacerle la lucha* can be "explained" in this way; *talonearle* must be considered as a merely formal extension of an existing construction (Webb 1976, p. 249).

[7] Irrelevant for the present discussion is the fact that *canoa* has the value '(human) rear end' for some speakers.

Similarly, *la* (in standard Spanish the third person singular feminine accusative [rarely dative] pronoun) may become an invariable verbal affix (e.g., *calmarla* 'to [a]wait' ← Spanish *calmar* 'to calm'). The interpretation of *chantarla* ('to be quiet, wait, come to a stop, stand up; leave [alone]; stop [victim]; seat; silence' ← Spanish *achantarse* 'to be quiet, be patient, resign oneself'), for example, as 'to shut up (one's mouth)' presupposes that the referent of *la* is *mu* (f.) 'mouth' or its variants. Nevertheless, few caló speakers understand *mu* as 'mouth'; most take it for a nonstandard pronunciation of Spanish *muy* 'very,' and analyze "chantar la mu" *'to stop the "very"' as a humorous expression, or as *chantar lamú* (*lamú* thus appears to be some sort of mysterious adverb). On the other hand, most speakers of Southwest Spanish, when hearing *chantarla,* are quite content to assume that the expression parallels *chingarla* (= *fregarla*; = Mexican Spanish *regarla*) 'to err, bring (situation) to ruin,' in which the pronoun *la* is vacuous. A search for the antecedent substantive would be pointless in the case of uninhibited colloquial language. As in *alivianarla* 'to help, act better,' the complement is vacuous (in context, representing 'life,' 'luck,' or 'situation'); to ask the informant for an explanation of what *la* stands for is to force a fruitless dissection of a normally unanalyzable construct.

Only *le* and *la* appear to mark special meaning(s) in verbs (I have found no similarly vacuous instances of *lo* [in standard Spanish the third person singular masculine or neuter accusative pronoun]) without carrying any significance of their own. Trejo Dueñes (1959, p. 48) found, for example, that Mexico City delinquents differentiate between *sonarle* 'to beat' and *sonar* 'to rob for a living' (← Spanish 'to sound'); my informants have not confirmed this difference but do contrast *ponerle* 'to rob for a living' (*Le pongo con afán*) with Spanish *poner* 'to put.'

In Caló, even more than in standard Spanish, reflexive pronouns carry an intensifying function that bears little or no relationship to the grammatical subject of the verb (e.g., *chingarse* 'to ruin'). Whereas colloquial Spanish *agujerarse,* for example, may mean logically 'to (put a) needle (to) oneself,' the verb in its reflexive form has become only more intensive in caló, so that in *Te lo agujeras* 'You (really) put the needle to (inject) him,' the pronoun *te* has only an attenuated reflexive (i.e., at most a weak "ethical-dative") value: 'You (really, for your own purpose) inject him.' The reflexive pronoun continues to reflect the person and number of the grammatical subject of the verb but approaches a semantic state of nothingness.

Conclusion

Caló among Mexican-Americans, as it makes colloquial language richer, poorer, or apparently vague, is derived principally from a mixture. A blending in Spain of Gypsy speech Hispanicized and of old delinquent cant comes through Mexican Spanish. In the United States, conforming to the continuum of fluency of persons monolingual in informal Mexican Spanish through various "balances" of multilingualism and even to monolingualism in English, caló now represents a special area of expression available for setting tone and making judgment. English speakers may use isolated forms and contents of caló, establishing or preserving a brotherhood principally in the poverty of large communities. The more fluent a person may be in *in*formal Mexican Spanish, the more likely is his (or her) potential for dominance of language defined (often unconsciously) as caló according to specific criteria of usage. As the criteria (deflation of dignity, nonconventionality, group intimacy, and status recognition) tend to preclude standards associated with the dominant culture (in the United States and in Mexico), and because caló expression is rarely written, such language is necessarily variant from standard Mexican Spanish (this last in the sense of a tongue adhering to school-maintained norms). Although for the most part the form and content of caló are in consonance (occasionally in congruence) with the pattern and system of national languages, an overtone of evasion or defiance of authority is often present. Perception and conception (either or both) shape expression for caló users in ways that often distort connotation and even denotation, and may lead to admirable and spontaneous creation.

References

Beinhauer, Werner. 1968. *El español coloquial*. Trans. F. Huarte Morton. 2d ed. Biblioteca Románica Hispánica. Madrid: Editorial Gredos.

Dumas, Bethany K., and Jonathan Lighter. 1978. Is *slang* a word for linguists? *American Speech* 53 (spring):5–17.

Espinosa, Aurelio M., Sr. 1930–46. *Estudios sobre el español de Nuevo Méjico*. Trans., ed., and annot. A. Alonso and Á. Rosenblat, with additional studies by A. Alonso. Biblioteca de Dialectología Hispano-Americana. Vols. 1–2. Buenos Aires: Universidad de Buenos Aires.

Hancock, Ian F. 1975. Patterns of lexical adoption in an American dialect of Romanés. In *Southwest languages and linguistics in educational perspective*, ed. G. Harvey and M. Heiser, pp. 83–108 (and Webb's discussion, pp. 109–15). San Diego: San Diego State University.

Heras [Febrero], Jesús de las, and Juan Villarín [García]. 1974. *La España de los Quinquis*. Barcelona: Planeta.

Hill, John McMurray. 1949. *Voces germanescas*. Humanities Series 15. Bloomington: University of Indiana.

Kany, Charles E. 1963. *American-Spanish syntax*. 2d ed. University of Chicago Press.

Llorens, Wáshington. 1959. Lenguaje de germanía en Puerto Rico. *Revista de Cultura Puertorriqueña* 2, no. 3 (April-June):10–12.

Lope Blanch, Juan Manuel. 1968. *El español de América*. Madrid: Alcalá.

1972. *Estudios sobre el español de México*. Publicaciones del Centro de Lingüística Hispánica 2. Mexico City: Universidad Nacional Autónoma de México.

Pabanó, F. M. 1915. *Historia y costumbres de los gitanos.* Barcelona: Montaner y Simón.
Pickett, David Wayne. 1965–7. The Gypsies of Mexico. *Journal of the Gypsy Lore Society,* 3rd ser., 44:81–99; 45:6–17, 84–99; 46:60–70.
Spain [national government]. 1977. *es: España cultural* (1 January):1.
Tineo Rebolledo, J. 1909. *Gitanos y castellanos: diccionario gitano-español y español-gitano.* Barcelona: Maucci.
Trejo Dueñes, Arnulfo. 1959. Una contribución al estudio del léxico de la delincuencia en México. Ph.D. dissertation, Universidad Nacional Autónoma de México.
Valdés-Fallis, Guadalupe. 1978. *Code switching and the classroom teacher.* Arlington, Va.: Center for Applied Linguistics.
Webb, John T. 1974. Investigation problems in Southwest Spanish caló. In *Southwest areal linguistics,* ed. G. Bills, pp. 145–53. San Diego: San Diego State University, Institute for Cultural Pluralism.
1976. *A lexical study of caló and non-standard Spanish in the Southwest.* Ann Arbor: University of Microfilms International.
1980. Pidgins (and Creoles?) on the U.S.–Mexican Border. In *A festschrift for Jacob Ornstein . . . ,* ed. E. Blansitt and R. Teschner, pp. 325–31. Rowley, Mass.: Newbury House.
In press. Lexicology and nonstandard Spanish. In *Bilingualism and language contact in the borderlands,* ed. E. Brandt and F. Barkin. New York: Teachers College Press.

Part II

Aspects of language contact and language change

Languages in contact often affect one another in a variety of ways. These effects may appear in the language systems themselves (phonology, morphology, lexicon, syntax) or in the patterns of social use of the language.

Language contact in the United States has often been a transitional bilingualism, where a once bilingual population becomes monolingual in English. This has occurred with most immigrant and many native American groups. However, some groups have maintained their bilingualism longer than others, and it is interesting to study the conditions for language maintenance or loss in the United States. Hudson-Edwards and Bills examine a barrio in Albuquerque, New Mexico, an area that has a long tradition of not just bilingualism but multilingualism. Like many contemporary investigators of language maintenance, they find much language shift. But they also find signs of maintenance, and one cannot help pointing out that for all the studies that show evidence of language shift, there have never been more Spanish speakers in the United States, nor has the position of Spanish been so prominent.

Other chapters in this section deal with the possible effects of English on Spanish. One possible result of contact is language mixing, which can occur on several levels. Reyes discusses many types of language mixing, ranging from lexical mixing to syntactic mixing and including the extreme form of syntactic mixing known as code-switching.

Sobin discusses in detail the type of language mixing that on the surface seems perhaps the simplest type. However, as he shows, there are hitherto unsuspected complexities. Departing from earlier studies, such as Haugen's, he draws an extremely important distinction between *reasons for* borrowing (e.g., sociocultural) and *restrictions on* borrowing (e.g., linguistic). To explain the latter he uses abstract lexical subcategorization features, such as [± active], [± stative], and [± *do so*].

The remaining chapters deal with aspects of code-switching. These include the factors of situation domain, ethnicity markers, and reference. Jacobson emphasizes that although these factors have little predictive value, instances of code-switching can be traced back to these causes.

Valdés presents a case study of the code-switching behavior of a single bilingual speaker, recorded in six different speech situations. Several investigators have found that fluent code-switchers are not deficient in their two languages, as is often alleged, but in fact are extremely proficient in the grammars of both. Valdés finds, however, that the relative proficiency of the interlocutor influences the code-switching behavior of the speaker.

Poplack's analysis of code-switching among Puerto Rican speakers shows that there are various types of code-switching, ranging from relatively simple emblematic- or tag-switching, used to demonstrate ethnic solidarity, to true intrasentential code-switching. It is the latter that requires the greatest degree of bilingual skill and is subject to several syntactic constraints.

Pfaff deals with code-switched language produced by Mexican-American speakers in both California and Texas. Some of the constraints she proposes are functional constraints on the expression of tense/aspect/mood and subject/object relationships. The other major constraint permits only surface structures that are grammatical in both languages.

7

Intergenerational language shift in an Albuquerque barrio

ALAN HUDSON-EDWARDS AND GARLAND D. BILLS

Spanish is clearly the most prominent ethnic language spoken in the United States today. Waggoner (1976, p. 5) reports that in July 1975, 13 percent of the U.S. population aged four and over lived in households in which languages other than English were spoken, and Spanish heads the list of languages spoken in those homes. Indeed, the 8.2 million Spanish speakers represent four and a half times the number of speakers of the next most widely claimed ethnic language, Italian. Furthermore, Spanish appears to be one of the most actively maintained ethnic languages. Among the national Spanish heritage population, 81 percent claim Spanish as their mother tongue, almost half live in households where Spanish is the usual language, and only a slightly smaller percentage, 44 percent, claim to speak Spanish as their usual language. Only Chinese and Korean equal or surpass Spanish in these figures (Waggoner 1976, p. 9). The evidence of numerical strength and retention rates demonstrates that Spanish is among the healthiest of the nation's ethnic languages.

For the Spanish heritage population of the Southwest, the diagnosis based on the same kind of evidence is just as positive. In the five states of Arizona, California, Colorado, New Mexico, and Texas, 17 percent of the total population are of Spanish heritage, and of these, 76 percent are of Spanish mother tongue (Bills and Ornstein 1976, p. 5). Within the Southwest, the healthiest place to be is clearly New Mexico. In this state, 40 percent of the people are of Spanish heritage, with 81 percent of these claiming Spanish as their mother tongue (U.S. Bureau of the Census 1971, p. 105).

Reprinted with permission from Newbury House Publishers. From *A Festschrift for Jacob Ornstein*, ed. Edward L. Blansitt and Richard V. Teschner (Rowley, Mass.: Newbury House, 1980), pp. 139–58.

The data collection for the community survey was carried out by eleven student volunteers from the University of New Mexico: Lori Baca, Tim Baca, Esmeralda Fraga, Josephine Hernández, Gaylord López, Arturo Maes, Cecilia Montoya, Proceso Montoya, Elena Pizarro, Alfredo Vigil, and Charlotte Vigil. We gratefully applaud their contributions and wish to give special thanks to Fred and Lori. We also acknowledge with gratitude the funds for essential supplies and equipment provided by the Faculty Research Allocations Committee at the University of New Mexico.

However, the robustness of Spanish in comparison with other ethnic languages does not necessarily mean that Spanish will survive for many years. On the contrary, it is widely believed that the Spanish heritage throughout the Southwest presents yet another classic example of language shift in progress. Most observers readily perceive the societal shift from dominance in Spanish to Spanish–English bilingualism and, with diminished maintenance of Spanish, to English dominance and eventual English monolingualism. Typically, this perception is documented by demonstrating for successive generations significant changes in ethnic mother-tongue claiming, proficiency, or use. However, the process of language shift is considerably more complex than these statistical analyses alone suggest. The purpose of this study, then, is to probe a complex of data from a barrio of Albuquerque, New Mexico, in an effort to characterize in finer detail the mechanism of language shift.

The community examined here is generally labeled Martineztown or sometimes Martineztown–Santa Barbara in government reports. The more acculturated tend to call it simply Martínez. It is one of the oldest areas of Albuquerque, located near the center of town but somewhat isolated by major boundaries on all sides: interstate highways 25 and 40 to the east and north, Central Avenue to the south, and railroad tracks flanked by industrial–commercial areas to the west (see Figure 1). Martineztown covers some 190 square blocks that include industrial sites, commercial establishments, schools, municipal buildings, churches, a hospital, a large cemetery, residential areas, and considerable vacant land. The residential area is about 20 blocks in length and ranges from 2 to 5 blocks in width. Although the city of Albuquerque is almost identical to the state in its proportions of population of Spanish heritage and Spanish mother-tongue retention, this little barrio of approximately 605 households is estimated to be 96 percent Spanish surnamed by Johnson and Yates (1969, p. 32). The total population of somewhat over 2,000 is reported to be 97 percent "persons of Spanish language or surname" with an equally high percentage of Spanish mother-tongue retention (U.S. Bureau of the Census 1972, p. P-11).

A pilot survey was carried out in 1975 to explore the language situation in this ethnic community. This consisted of interviews in the homes of sixty-one families, a 10 percent sampling. Although the target households were randomly selected in advance, absolute randomness was lost in a few substitutions for refusals and no responses; the close correlation of our results with comparable data in the 1970 census, however, indicates that this slight deviation from randomness had no significant effect on validity. Because of the high proportion of Spanish surnames in the population of the barrio, only local Chicanos were used as interviewers. Two persons, usually a male and a female, conducted each interview, one actually interviewing and the other taking notes on responses. The av-

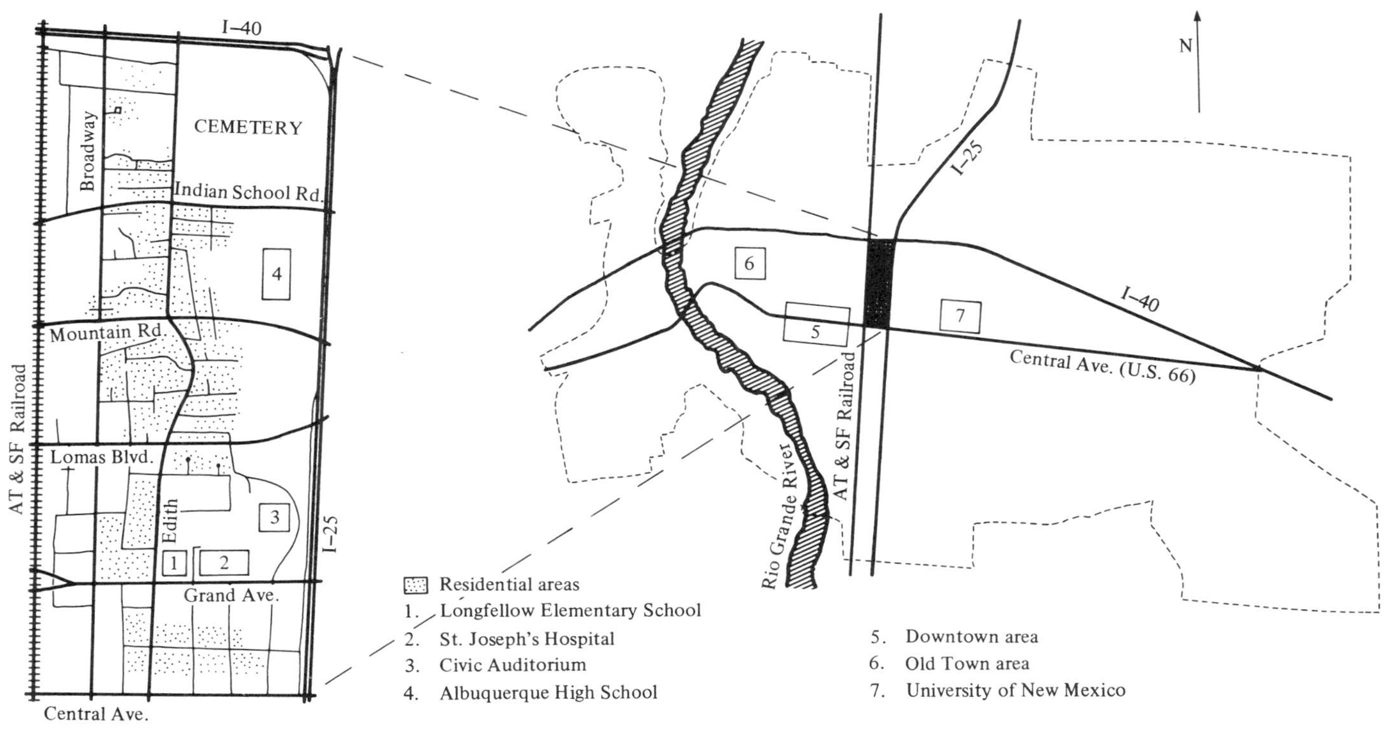

Figure 1. Albuquerque and Martineztown

erage interview lasted approximately thirty minutes and, except for two instances of mechanical failure, all interviews were tape-recorded.

The survey was intended to gather a broad range of basic information, including the spoken language sample in the tape recordings. The survey questionnaire elicited information of three kinds: demographic data, Spanish and English proficiency and use for all household members, and the respondent's attitudes toward the two languages.[1] A brief overview of the demographic data will give a clearer picture of the community and set the stage for the examination of data relevant to language maintenance and shift.

The overwhelmingly Chicano composition of the community reported by Johnson and Yates (1969) and the U.S. Bureau of the Census (1972) is confirmed in our survey. Of the sixty-one households, fifty-six, or 92 percent, were of Spanish heritage. The other five households, all Anglo, were clearly transient elements of the barrio. For present purposes the inclusion of these Anglo households could only have a distorting effect, and the analysis that follows is therefore limited to the Chicano majority, specifically, the 191 individuals in the fifty-five Chicano households for which we have complete tape-recorded interviews.

In her anthropological study of Martineztown ten years earlier, Vincent (1966) emphasized the highly stable nature of the barrio. This impression of stability is precisely one of the most striking aspects revealed by the demographic information collected in the present survey. Almost half of the 191 individuals were actually born into the community and 92 percent were born in New Mexico; fewer than 4 percent were born in Mexico, a sharp contrast to other urban Chicano communities in the Southwest. Of the fifty-five respondents, 72 percent claimed ownership of their homes and only 9 percent reported plans to move from Martineztown. The average age for all individuals is thirty-three years, with one-fourth being over fifty years of age. With regard to education, over one-third of the adults failed to advance beyond the sixth grade, only one in four completed high school, and fewer than one in ten had had any exposure to college. Relatedly, half of the heads of household have no gainful employment, and the employed adults are largely at the low end of the occupational scale. Demographically, then, this Chicano community is poorly educated, blue collar, and 94 percent Catholic. Minimal in-migration and considerable out-migration of young adults gives it the cast of an elderly community with rather small households. In spite of its location in the center of New Mexico's largest urban area, Martineztown – de-

[1] Kravitz (1978) briefly reports on some aspects of the attitudinal data. This pilot project also included a survey of the 145 children in the local elementary school's bilingual education program; a variety of results of this part of the project is reported by Teitelbaum (1976), and Doviak and Hudson-Edwards (1980) provide a penetrating examination of the English of these children.

mographically and in many other ways – has the character of an isolated rural village.

This impression is further enhanced by the strong presence of the Spanish language. The use of language during the interviews, determined primarily by the respondents, sheds some light on the roles of Spanish and English in this community. Fully 58 percent of the interviews were conducted mostly or entirely in Spanish, almost one-fourth in English, and 18 percent in roughly equal measures of the two languages. Though the respondents are not representative of the community, a point to be treated later, this initial piece of objective evidence clearly demonstrates both the prominent role of Spanish and the highly bilingual character of Martineztown.

In the following pages we explore a more comprehensive array of evidence, specifically focusing on Spanish–English proficiency and use and their relationships to generational data. We consider three kinds of variables that blend into the notion of generation: (a) age, somewhat arbitrarily divided into two groups at the twenty-five-year point; (b) composition of household in terms of both number of generations and presence of minor children, yielding a three-point variable to be explained later; and (c) individual generational relationship to the head of household, providing four groups in this community: a "parent" generation composed of parents of household heads, a "senior" generation that includes the heads and their spouses and siblings, a "junior" generation containing the children of heads, and a "grandchild" generation. We utilize just four language variables from our data: (a) mother tongue, (b) speaking ability in Spanish, (c) speaking ability in English, and (d) language use in the home. The following sections explore intergenerational variation for each of these language variables.

Mother tongue

The data presented in Table 1 show that Martineztown is a primarily Spanish mother-tongue community. Fully two-thirds of the individuals for whom information was available either claimed or were reported to have acquired Spanish as their mother tongue. One person in six acquired Spanish and English simultaneously, and a nearly identical number acquired English only. A distinction between those persons providing first-hand information on their own language background and those for whom this information was reported by others shows that 84 percent of the former and only 59 percent of the latter claim Spanish as their single mother tongue. This discrepancy is to be attributed largely to the fact that the average age of the respondents was forty-six, whereas the average age of the other persons reported upon was twenty-seven.

A very clear negative correlation between age and Spanish mother-

Table 1. *Mother tongue by age, composition of household, and generational relationship to head (in percent)*

	Mother tongue			
	Spanish	Both	English	*n*
Total sample	67	18	16	177
Respondent	84	9	7	55
Nonrespondent	59	21	20	122
Age				
1–25 years	38	31	31	81
26 years and over	90	7	3	92
Composition of household				
1 generation	92	8	0	24
2–3 generations, adults	78	11	11	37
2–3 generations, with minors	58	22	21	116
Generational relationship to head				
Parent	100	0	0	3
Senior	87	7	6	87
Junior	44	29	28	80
Adult child	58	27	15	26
Minor child	37	30	33	54
Grandchild	50	25	25	4

tongue reporting is readily apparent in the data in Table 1. Virtually all individuals over twenty-five years of age claim Spanish alone as their mother tongue. Of the eighty-one persons in the younger age group, only 38 percent report their first language to be only Spanish. When age is considered as a continuous variable and mother tongue as a trichotomous one, the correlation between the two is −.48. This negative relationship is not, of course, unexpected. López (1978) reports a smaller but nonetheless negative correlation between age and Spanish as "language of upbringing" for second-generation Chicanos in the Los Angeles area. The Martineztown data include seven persons born in Mexico; if they are removed from the calculation, the correlation between age and the claiming of Spanish as the mother tongue rises slightly to −.50.

The relationship of mother-tongue claiming to the composition of the household is also clear from Table 1. Twenty-four persons in the study sample were reported living in one-generation families. That none of these claimed English only as a mother tongue and that only 8 percent claimed English and Spanish both is no doubt due to the fact that all of these individuals were over forty-five years of age. Members of one-generation households claim only Spanish as a mother tongue with considerably greater frequency than do members of multiple generation households:

92 percent for the former versus 62 percent for the latter. However, the difference between the two- and three-generation households is negligible. For them, a more important consideration by far is whether or not there are children under the age of eighteen present in the family. The data in Table 1 indicate that 78 percent of the persons residing in either two- or three-generational households and having no minor children are reported to have Spanish as a mother tongue, whereas the corresponding figure for persons in families with young children is only 58 percent.

Generational status within one's family can also be seen to be a factor affecting the likelihood of claiming Spanish as a mother tongue. Although the present study obtained information on only three parents of heads of households, all three claimed Spanish alone as their mother tongue. Among the next generation, consisting of heads of households, their spouses, and siblings living with them, the overwhelming majority, 87 percent, claimed Spanish also. By the third generation, however, the proportion of persons claiming Spanish only as a mother tongue is virtually halved. It is understandable in the light of the previous discussion of composition of households that grown children in this junior generation were more likely to claim Spanish than were minor children.

Spanish mother-tongue claiming in Martineztown does not appear to be radically different from that reported for the northern rural village of Arroyo Seco, near Taos, New Mexico (Ortiz 1975). Among 178 persons for whom data were obtained in the latter community, some 77 percent, a mere 10 percent more than in Martineztown, were reported to have acquired Spanish alone as their first language. Among those over twenty years of age in Arroyo Seco, virtually all, 93 percent, claimed Spanish as their only mother tongue; the corresponding figure for those over twenty-five years of age in Martineztown is 90 percent. In Los Angeles, California, on the other hand, Spanish is claimed as the "language of upbringing" by only 42 percent of the subjects in a sample of 397 second- and third-generation married Chicano women (López 1978, p. 270). With respect to mother-tongue claiming, Martineztown resembles the rural village far more than it does the large metropolitan area.

Language proficiency

This section examines the data on proficiency ratings for both English and Spanish in Martineztown. As is to be expected, current English ability and current Spanish ability are inversely related, though only partially so, the Kendall's tau correlation coefficient for the two variables being just −.33. The reason for the relatively low correlation becomes apparent from an examination of the data presented in Table 2. Of the twenty-four persons whose English ability was reported to be "weak" (a rating of "none" or "poor"), twenty-one, or 88 percent, claimed to have a "fluent" (a rating of "good" or "very good") command of Spanish. Likewise, of

Table 2. *Relationship between Spanish ability and English ability*

English ability	Spanish ability None/poor	Fair	Good/very good	Total
None/poor	0	3	21	24
Fair	4	3	30	37
Good/very good	24	35	53	112
Total	28	41	104	173

the twenty-eight persons with weak Spanish ability, twenty-four, or 86 percent, apparently spoke fluent English. However, a fluent command of *both* languages was reported for fifty-three individuals, more than twice the number reported to be weak in one or the other language. Thus, while it is clearly the case that a poor knowledge of one language implies fluency in the other, the reverse does not hold true, for Martineztown is populated by a substantial number of effective bilinguals.

Comparable data on language proficiency in other Spanish-speaking communities of the Southwest are not available. However, Skrabanek (1970, p. 275) reports that in the 544 Mexican-American families studied in the Texas counties of Atascosa and Bexar, "not one person . . . old enough to talk was found who did not speak Spanish fluently, and an overwhelming majority speak Spanish more fluently than English." Also, in Arroyo Seco, New Mexico, Ortiz (1975, p. 154) found that 53 percent of the individuals in his study reportedly feel more comfortable speaking Spanish than English, 41 percent are equally at ease in both languages, and only 6 percent are more comfortable speaking English. Insofar as these data may be interpreted as a reflection of relative language proficiency, they may be compared with the data in Table 2, which show the fifty-four persons, or 31 percent of the Martineztown subjects for whom information was available, rate their Spanish ability superior to their English ability, while fifty-six persons, or 32 percent, rate their English on a par with their Spanish, and sixty-three persons, or 36 percent, rate their English better than their Spanish. Though predominantly of Spanish mother tongue, the people of Martineztown show a marginal tendency toward English dominance.

Not surprisingly, the mother-tongue data correlate more strongly with Spanish ability than with English ability. These relationships are clearly displayed in the cross-tabulations presented in Table 3. With regard to speaking ability in Spanish, almost 80 percent of the 114 Spanish mother-tongue claimants are reported to be fluent in Spanish. Among those claiming both English and Spanish, the modal response is "fair." Finally, the majority of the English mother-tongue claimants are reported to be weak

Table 3. *Relationship between mother tongue and Spanish and English ability* (*in percent*)

	Mother tongue		
	Spanish	Both	English
Spanish ability			
None/poor	5	16	59
Fair	16	65	22
Good/very good	79	19	18
n	114	31	27
English ability			
None/poor	20	3	0
Fair	30	10	0
Good/very good	50	87	100
n	113	31	26

in Spanish, though it must be added that only 15 percent reported no ability in Spanish at all. On the other hand, English ability correlates less well with mother tongue, for fluent English was reported for the majority in each mother-tongue category, ranging from 50 percent of the Spanish mother-tongue claimants to 100 percent of the English mother-tongue claimants. It is revealing to note that among the bilingual mother-tongue claimants, only one in five acquired fluency in Spanish, whereas almost nine out of ten achieved English fluency. In all, the Kendall's tau correlation for mother tongue and English ability is a modest .38, but for mother tongue and Spanish ability it is a substantial and highly significant .55.

This strong relationship is also readily apparent when the Spanish-ability ratings provided in Table 4 are compared with the mother-tongue reports in Table 1. Thus, for instance, just as 16 percent of the total sample claimed only English as their mother tongue, 16 percent also claim little or no knowledge of Spanish. Similarly, just as 67 percent reported only Spanish as their first language, 60 percent report a fluent command of that language now.

Age is as highly correlated with Spanish ability as it was with mother tongue. The great majority of those over twenty-five years of age claim at least a good knowledge of Spanish. Those twenty-five and under are fairly evenly distributed on this three-point ability scale, but it must be noted that only 5 percent of this younger group were reported to have no knowledge of Spanish at all. Overall, when Spanish proficiency is treated as a five-point variable and age as a continuous one, the correlation between the two is a very high .63.

Household composition and individual generational status show the

Table 4. *Spanish ability by age, composition of household, and generational relationship to head (in percent)*

	Spanish ability			
	None/poor	Fair	Good/very good	*n*
Total sample	16	25	60	177
Respondent	4	17	80	54
Nonrespondent	21	29	51	123
Age				
1–25 years	33	36	31	83
26+ years	1	12	87	89
Composition of household				
1 generation	0	8	92	24
2–3 generations, adults	5	24	70	37
2–3 generations, with minors	22	28	49	116
Generational relationship to head				
Parent	0	0	100	4
Senior	5	10	85	87
Junior	29	39	33	80
Adult child	12	50	38	26
Minor child	37	33	30	54
Grandchild	25	75	0	4

same kinds of relationship with Spanish ability as might be predicted from the mother-tongue data. Members of two- and three-generation homes with minor children less frequently claim Spanish fluency than do members of comparable households without minor children. The latter, in turn, report less proficiency in Spanish than members of single-generation homes, almost all of whom maintain fluency in the language. Similarly, while all four of the parents of heads of households report fluent Spanish ability, only 85 percent of the latter and their generational peers do so. Finally, among the junior generation, only 33 percent maintain a fluent command of Spanish. Recall, however, that 44 percent of this junior generation reportedly first learned to speak in Spanish. There is a strong suggestion here that as many as one-fourth of these Spanish mother-tongue claimants in the junior generation either did not continue to acquire Spanish to the level of mature native speakers or else, having done so, subsequently shifted to English at some cost to their Spanish ability.

The high rate of English fluency in Martineztown is shown in Table 5. Almost two-thirds of the sample as a whole is reported to have at least a good command of English. For reasons discussed earlier, persons reporting on their own behavior typically claim lower proficiency in English for themselves than for other members of their households. As is to be

Table 5. *English ability by age, composition of household, and generational relationship to head (in percent)*

	English ability			
	None/poor	Fair	Good/very good	*n*
Total sample	15	21	64	177
Respondent	17	34	49	53
Nonrespondent	14	15	71	124
Age				
1–25 years	5	10	86	84
26+ years	24	32	44	88
Composition of household				
1 generation	42	42	17	24
2–3 generations, adults	19	25	56	36
2–3 generations, with minors	8	15	77	117
Generational relationship to head				
Parent	75	0	25	4
Senior	22	32	47	88
Junior	4	11	85	81
Adult child	0	8	92	25
Minor child	5	13	82	56
Grandchild	0	0	100	3

anticipated, a fluent knowledge of English is claimed almost twice as frequently for younger members of the community as it is for persons over twenty-five years of age. Once again, the expected relationship with household composition is apparent. Of those persons living in families with minor children, 77 percent are reported to be fluent in English whereas only 56 percent of those living in multiple-generation households without young children are reported to be as fluent. Lastly, cross-tabulation of English ability with generational relationship to the head of household shows that members of the parent generation are less fluent in English than members of the senior generation, while the latter, predictably, are less fluent than their own children.

There is, however, one minor reversal in Table 5 that sheds some light on the processes involved in language shift in a bilingual community. That is, the adult members of the junior generation are reported to have greater English fluency than the younger members. Given the negative relationship between age and English ability mentioned just above, it might reasonably have been predicted that grown children would have *poorer* English than minors. Indeed, the contrary prediction for Spanish ability is borne out in the data of Table 4, namely, that the older children report better Spanish than the younger children. The data on the claiming of

Table 6. *Home language use by age, composition of household, and generational relationship to head* (*in percent*)

	Home language			
	Spanish	Both	English	*n*
Total sample	46	19	35	178
Respondent	64	24	13	55
Nonrespondent	37	17	46	123
Age				
1–25 years	12	18	70	83
26+ years	74	21	5	91
Composition of household				
1 generation	88	13	0	24
2–3 generations, adults	68	24	8	38
2–3 generations, with minors	29	19	52	116
Generational relationship to head				
Parent	67	33	0	3
Senior	66	23	11	88
Junior	23	16	60	81
Adult child	48	22	30	27
Minor child	11	13	76	54
Grandchild	0	0	100	4

English ability within the junior generation suggest that the pattern of age grading is reversed because of the more extensive contacts of the grown members of this generation with the larger English-speaking community. A similar explanation could, of course, be advanced for the differential between grown and minor children in Spanish ability, but a more plausible interpretation is that the pattern of age grading in Spanish ability in fact reflects genuine language shift across time. In other words, age stratification in the case of English ability may be said to represent a developmental acquisition process, but in the case of Spanish ability it seems to represent diachronic shift.

Home language use

Additional insight into the process of language shift as well as maintenance is provided by the data on language use in the home, presented in Table 6. Despite the relatively high rate of claims of Spanish as a first language and of fluency in Spanish, fewer than half of the individuals in the sample were reported to use Spanish as the primary home language. A further 19 percent use English and Spanish equally, and over one-third use English more than Spanish.

The relationship between age and English use in the home is rather more dramatic than might have been expected. Although more than two-thirds of those twenty-five years of age or younger claim to use English mostly or exclusively in the home, only 5 percent of those over twenty-five do so. In fact, three-fourths of those over twenty-five years of age reportedly use Spanish as the principal home language and fully one-third of this age group use Spanish to the total exclusion of English in the home.

Generational range in the household and the presence or absence of young children are also factors related to the maintenance of Spanish as a language of the home. Both factors contribute independently, and in the predicted directions, to the home use of Spanish, though once again the presence or absence of minor children is the more critical variable. Combining the data for single-generation and multiple-generation adult households, three out of four of the individuals living in homes without minor children reportedly use mostly or only Spanish at home. Among those living in either two- or three-generation households with young children present, only 29 percent use Spanish more than English.

Analysis of home language use by generational relationship to head of household reveals the same asymmetrical distribution of languages that has come to be expected of families caught up in the process of language shift. Of the three parents of heads of household in this sample, one uses Spanish and English equally, one uses Spanish mostly, and the third uses Spanish exclusively. The generation of the head of household differs from the earlier one in that it is the first to have any members at all claiming predominant use of English. The majority of the generation of children, however, claim to use English as the primary home language.

A force counteracting the process of language shift may be signaled by the fact that the adults in the junior generation approximate their parents' language use much more closely than do the minor children. Even though 92 percent of the grown children claimed fluent English, almost half of them use Spanish as the major home language. This apparent manifestation of ethnic language loyalty is not perceivable in the behavior of the minor children, fully 76 percent of whom show predominantly English use in the home. Of the four language variables treated here, it is in home language use that the adults and minors of this generation differ most strongly. One possible explanation for this discrepancy may be attitudinal factors of the sort that Labov (1963) noted on the island of Martha's Vineyard. That is, the older members of this junior generation who made a point of remaining in the community into adulthood are likely to have been those who identified most strongly with the community's values and orientation and, therefore, to have made more of a commitment to the maintenance of Spanish in the home.

Comparative statistics on language use in Albuquerque, or indeed anywhere in New Mexico, are difficult to come by. However, an earlier

Table 7. *Distribution of persons reporting predominant use of Spanish in the home, by location of study (in percent)*

	Location				
	Martinez-town	Los Angeles	Austin	San Antonio	Atascosa County
Heads of households	66	50	59	61	73
Age					
Older	74	—	66	—	—
Younger	12	—	36	24–28	40–48
Generation					
First	67	84	96	—	—
Second	66	15	67	—	—
Third	23	4	49	—	—

socioeconomic survey of the model neighborhood area of Albuquerque, which includes Martineztown, found that 70 percent of the 318 Spanish-surnamed families for whom data were available used Spanish mostly or exclusively in the home (Johnson and Yates 1969, p. 34). This figure approximates quite closely the findings of the present study in regard to heads of households and their parents, though it is substantially in excess of the percentage reported here for the study population as a whole. Elsewhere in New Mexico, Ortiz (1975) notes that in Arroyo Seco parents over the age of forty typically report using Spanish most if not all of the time in domestic situations. Younger parents, however, typically report language use in the home to be more or less equally divided between Spanish and English.

Somewhat comparable statistics are available for several Chicano communities outside of New Mexico. Thompson (1971) reports on Spanish-language use in the home among some 176 imformants living in a Mexican–American neighborhood in Austin, Texas. Skrabanek (1970) reports similar data for 268 Mexican–American households in rural Atascosa County, Texas, and for a further 276 households in San Antonio, in adjacent Bexar County. Finally, López (1978) provides detailed information on 890 Chicano women in Los Angeles, California. The statistics provided by these researchers have been retabulated by the present authors and collated for convenience in Table 7.

The reader is advised that the data from the various studies represented in Table 7 are not strictly comparable in all respects, but are presented there for the purposes of impressionistic comparison. The data for Los Angeles (López 1978) are based on married Chicano women, not on heads of households. In Atascosa County and San Antonio (Skrabanek 1970) and in Austin (Thompson 1971), separate data for language use with parents and with children were averaged together to obtain an approximate overall measure of language use in the home comparable to that used in the present study. Also, both in López (1978) and in Thompson (1971), "generation" is defined as the generational distance from immigration to the United States; in the present study it refers to generational relationship to the head of the household. Finally, the age breakdown is different in all three studies for which data are available: Younger people in the present study are twenty-five years of age and younger, in Skrabanek (1970) they are between ten and twenty-four years of age, and in Thompson (1971) they are between the ages of eighteen and twenty-nine.

In general, it can be seen in Table 7 that the degree of Spanish maintenance in the home on the part of heads of households in Martineztown is highly comparable to that in other locations in the Southwest. Maintenance appears to be lowest in Los Angeles, the most urban of the five locations, and highest in rural Atascosa County. Albuquerque, Austin, and San Antonio, being cities of intermediate size, also show intermediate levels of Spanish use in the home, though Martineztown most closely approximates the rural pattern.

Martineztown seems to be more urban, however, when the comparative data for age are considered. Of the four locations for which usable data are available, Martineztown is most similar in home language use of younger people to the largest urban area, San Antonio, and least similar to the most rural area, Atascosa County. Furthermore, a comparison with the age group data for Austin, a city comparable in size to Albuquerque, suggests an exceptional lack of Spanish maintenance in the home by Martineztown youth.

The percentages of Spanish use reported for each of the generations in the various studies are not strictly comparable due to the different definitions of generational status. However, all three studies for which data are available agree that later generations employ noticeably less Spanish in the home than do earlier ones. In the case of Los Angeles, the drop between the first and second generations is quite dramatic, supporting López's claim that "the pivotal shift [from Spanish to English] occurs during the second generation" (1978, p. 271). By the third generation, Spanish is hardly used at all in the home. In contrast, the data for Austin show a more gradual decline in Spanish use from 96 percent of the first generation who claim to use Spanish most of the time to virtually one-half of the third generation who do so. In the Martineztown context there appears to be no difference in Spanish-language use in the home between the oldest generation and the second oldest, though this is very probably due to the fact that only three persons were identified in the former category. The difference between the second and third generations is more reliable in view of the numbers involved and shows

Table 8. *Interrelationships between types of Spanish claiming, by generation (in percent)*

	Generation	
	Senior	Junior
Total Spanish mother tongue	87	44
Spanish mother tongue claiming fluent Spanish	95	50
Total fluent Spanish speakers	85	33
Fluent Spanish speakers claiming Spanish home language use	75	31
Spanish mother tongue claiming Spanish home language use	76	43
Total Spanish home language use	66	23

a precipitous decline in Spanish use in the home. In this respect, Albuquerque appears to be more akin to the situation in Los Angeles than to that in Austin.

The mechanism of language shift

Comparison between numbers of ethnic mother-tongue claimants in successive generations, as typified for instance in Fishman and Hofman (1966), necessarily does not reveal the full, variegated process that is language shift. More precisely, language shift must be seen as a series of concurrent shifts in the rates of ethnic mother-tongue transmission, individual maintenance of proficiency, and actual use. This process can be viewed in some detail in Martineztown with regard to those two generations for which the greatest amount of data is available, namely, the generation of the heads of households and that of the children of heads of households.

The interrelationships between Spanish mother-tongue claiming, Spanish proficiency, and Spanish home use are displayed for each of these generations in Table 8. Spanish was reported as the first language of 87 percent of the individuals in the senior generation and, of these, fully 95 percent still maintain a fluent knowledge of the language. However, of those members of the senior generation who speak Spanish fluently, only three-quarters actually use it more than they do English in the home. The cumulative effect of this erosion of Spanish vitality is that only 66 percent of the senior generation continue to use it in the home with greater frequency than they do English, thus limiting the opportunity for the immediately succeeding generation to acquire Spanish as a first language.

In fact, only 44 percent of the junior generation are reported to have acquired Spanish as their first language and, of these, only one-half are professed to currently have a fluent command of the language. Once more, it is obvious that there are some in this generation for whom Spanish was claimed as a mother tongue but for whom the environment was not conducive to continued use of it. Many of these speakers, as a result, may never have developed a real facility in Spanish and may, in fact, have witnessed a deterioration of their proficiency with the passage of time. Moreover, of those in the junior generation who did achieve or maintain fluency in Spanish, a mere 31 percent continue to use it as their primary language in the home. In sum, the junior generation is much more prone than the senior one not to develop mature native-speaker competence in Spanish despite having acquired it as a first language and, second, to resort to the use of English as the primary language of the home even in those instances where a fluent command of Spanish was maintained.

The encroachment of English upon the scene may also be viewed in terms similar to those used to describe the decline of Spanish. Fluency in English in the senior generation is not, of course, limited only to those who acquired it as their first language. Although only 6 percent learned English as their first language, 47 percent attain fluency in it; however, only 24 percent of these fluent speakers actually use English as their predominant home language. Among the junior generation, all of those who acquired English before or simultaneously with Spanish now speak it fluently, and 64 percent of those who acquired Spanish first also do so. Moreover, two-thirds of those classified as fluent English speakers currently use it as their main home language.

The inexorable advance of English becomes clearer still when the process of language shift is viewed across linked generations, that is to say, across successive generations within the same family. The hypothesis that later generations would show more Anglophone characteristics than earlier ones was therefore tested individually for thirty-eight multiple-generation families on the items relating to first language, Spanish ability, English ability, and home language use. Out of 141 usable observations, 78 were found to confirm the hypothesis in its most stringent form, namely, that each successive generation within each family observed showed increasingly Anglophone traits. In an additional 10 cases stability was observed between two generations, while a shift in the predicted direction was found in the third. Stability across all generations in the household was observed in 44 instances. Finally, in only 9 cases did a later generation show less Anglophone characteristics than the preceding one and 5 of these were instances where the adults in the family understandably claimed greater English proficiency than their children. Predictably, overall intergenerational stability was most in evidence in the case of mother-tongue and English-proficiency claiming, less so in the case of Spanish-proficiency claiming, and least of all in the case of home language use.

Conclusion

The picture drawn in the preceding pages of this report offers scant consolation indeed to those concerned about the maintenance of Spanish among the urban Chicano populations of the Southwest. True, the language is still very much alive in Martineztown, whether judged in terms of mother-tongue acquisition, current ability, or use in the home. Yet the signs of large-scale shift are everywhere in evidence. The children of heads of households claim Spanish alone as a mother tongue with only half the frequency of their parents' generation. They much less frequently claim a fluent knowledge of Spanish and at the same time much more frequently claim a fluent knowledge of English. They claim to use Spanish as their primary home language with scarcely more than a third the frequency their parents do. While intergenerational loss of Spanish in Martineztown may not be quite as precipitous as in other, larger, urban centers, such as Los Angeles, the sustaining effect of a continuing influx of Spanish-speaking immigrants is not felt in Martineztown to nearly the same degree as in these other areas. Thus, although out-migration of nontraditional youth may help somewhat to preserve the Spanish character of Martineztown in the short run, the longer term prognosis for the survival of the language appears dubious indeed.

Finally, in a more theoretical vein, the results of this study strongly suggest that the process of language shift can be detected in its early stages within a single generation when the proportion of ethnic mother-tongue claimants exceeds the proportion of fluent speakers of the language and when the latter, in turn, exceeds the proportion of those using the ethnic tongue as their primary home language. As López (1978) noted, this process, once begun, accelerates in succeeding generations. Not only are there fewer ethnic mother-tongue claimants to begin with, but a smaller proportion of them advance to the point of mature native-speaker proficiency, and of those who do, a smaller proportion than in the senior generation actually maintain the ethnic language as the primary language of the home.

References

Bills, Garland D., and Jacob Ornstein. 1976. Linguistic diversity in Southwest Spanish. In *Studies in Southwest Spanish*, ed. J. Donald Bowen and Jacob Ornstein, pp. 4–16. Rowley, Mass.: Newbury House.

Doviak, Martin J., and Allison Hudson-Edwards. 1980. Phonological variation in Chicano English: word-final (z)-devoicing. In *A festschrift for Jacob Ornstein*, ed. Edward L. Blansitt and Richard V. Teschner, pp. 82–96. Rowley, Mass.: Newbury House.

Fishman, Joshua A., and John E. Hofman. 1966. Mother tongue and nativity in the American population. In *Language loyalty in the United States*, ed. Joshua A. Fishman, Vladimir C. Nahirny, John E. Hofman, and Robert G. Hayden, pp. 34–50. The Hague: Mouton.

Johnson, Susan S., and Ann S. Yates. 1969. *A joint report on a socio-economic and attitude survey: residents of the model neighborhood and the rest of Albuquerque.* Albuquerque: City of Albuquerque and University of New Mexico.

Kravitz, Merryl. 1978. Grammatical judgements and standard Spanish in a Southwest community. In *The bilingual in a pluralistic society*, ed. Harold H. Key, Gloria G. McCullough, and Janet B. Sawyer, pp. 76–87. Long Beach: California State University.

Labov, William. 1963. The social motivation of a sound change. *Word* 19:273–309.

López, David E. 1978. Chicano language loyalty in an urban setting. *Sociology and Social Research* 62:267–78.

Ortiz, Leroy I. 1975. A sociolinguistic study of language maintenance in the northern New Mexico community of Arroyo Seco. Ph.D. dissertation, University of New Mexico.

Skrabanek, R. L. 1970. Language maintenance among Mexican-Americans. *International Journal of Comparative Sociology* 11:272–82.

Teitelbaum, Herta. 1976. Assessing bilingualism in elementary school children. Ph.D. dissertation, University of New Mexico.

Thompson, Roger M. 1971. Language loyalty in Austin, Texas: a study of a bilingual neighborhood. Ph.D. dissertation, University of Texas, Austin.

U.S. Bureau of the Census. 1971. *Census of population: 1970. General social and economic characteristics.* Final report, PC(1)-C33, New Mexico. Washington, D.C.: U.S. Government Printing Office.

1972. *Census of population and housing: 1970. Census tracts.* Final report PHC(1)-5, Albuquerque, New Mexico, Standard Metropolitan Statistical Area. Washington, D.C.: U.S. Government Printing Office.

Vincent, Maria Girard. 1966. Ritual kinship in an urban setting: Martineztown, New Mexico. Master's thesis, University of New Mexico.

Waggoner, Dorothy. 1976. Results of the survey of languages supplement to the July 1975 current population survey. Paper presented at the Fifth Annual International Bilingual Bicultural Education Conference, San Antonio, Tex., May 4.

8

Language mixing in Chicano Spanish

ROGELIO REYES

Introduction

Consider the following sentences, typical of Chicano speech.

(1) *Cuando yo la conocí* ('when I met her [she said]') "Oh, this ring, I paid so much," *y que todo lo que compran tienen que presumir* ('everything they buy they have to show off').
(2) *A veces* ('sometimes') we take too many things for granted.
(3) *Yo sé, porque* ('I know, because') I went to the hospital to find out where he was at.
(4) *Hizo improve mucho.* 'She improved much.'
(5) *Va a reenlist.* 'He is going to reenlist.'
(6) *Los están busing pa otra escuela.* 'They are busing them to another school.'
(7) Taipeo las cartas. 'I type the letters.'
(8) Puchamos el carro. 'We pushed the car.'
(9) Va a mistir el tren. 'He is going to miss the train.'

In the study of bilingualism, the term "interference" has been used to refer to "those instances of deviation from the norms of either language which occur in the speech of bilinguals as a result of their familiarity with more than one language, i.e., as a result of languages in contact . . ." (Weinreich 1968, p. 1). With such a definition, all nine of the sentences above qualify as examples of linguistic interference. However, this term glosses over different linguistic processes that are involved in the production of these sentences. Moreover, this term seems to imply an involuntary process where the speaker fails to communicate according to the model he is attempting to use. But, in fact, there is evidence that the processes involved in the production of sentences such as (1) through (9) above follow well-defined patterns and are governed by definite constraints which are recognized by the general speech community. Therefore, the use of the term "interference" to refer to these phenomena would seem to be inappropriate.

Reprinted with permission from Indiana University Linguistics Club. From *Studies in Chicano Spanish* (Bloomington: IULC, 1978), pp. 83–96.

Haugen, reviewing his own work, indicates more precision in his use of the term "interference," and he is careful to distinguish it from "borrowing," which he considers "a process of 'code preservation' in which 'the two languages are not superimposed, but follow one another . . .' " (1973, p. 521). He also distinguishes interference and borrowing from "code-switching," which he proposes be used "to refer to the alternate use of two languages including everything from the introduction of a single, unassimilated word up to a complete sentence or more into the context of another language" (1973, p. 521).

Using Haugen's definitions of "borrowing" and "code-switching" as a point of departure, I shall attempt to apply them, modifying them where necessary, to the Chicano bilingual phenomena.[1]

As a source of data for the present study, I have relied mainly on recordings I have made of conversations between myself and other bilingual Chicanos in Oakland, California. The analysis is based on my own competence as a bilingual Chicano. Unless I know otherwise, I assume that whichever sentences are allowable in my own speech are also allowable in the speech of the general Chicano speech community.

Language mixing, type A

Consider sentence (1). Notice that the English segment, "Oh, this ring, I paid so much," constitutes a whole sentence within itself, in which the individual words stand in relation to each other independently of the larger sentence. In this segment of the discourse, the speaker attempts to quote an original English utterance without any deviation from the norms of the system in which it originally occurred. The alternation from Spanish to English is motivated at this point in the discourse by the speaker's intent to quote directly. The segment *y que todo lo que compran tienen que presumir* marks a return to the speaker's normal mode of expression – i.e., Spanish. The syntactic junctures that divide the Spanish and English components of the sentence are easily discernible, and the English component has its own internal syntactic structure.

Example (2) consists of the English sentence *we take too many things for granted,* introduced by the Spanish adverbial phrase *a veces*. As in example (1), the change from Spanish to English occurs at a clearly discernible syntactic juncture and the English segment has its own internal syntactic structure. The motivation for the change from one language to

[1] The question of the intent of the speaker in his use of mixed language patterns is also an important one. In "Bilingualism, Bidialectalism and Classroom Interaction," Gumperz and Hernández-Chavéz (1972) have discussed the question of meaning conveyed through language alternation. However, before very much can be said conclusively about this aspect of bilingual speech, it is necessary to be clear about the linguistic processes with which we are dealing. In the course of the present study the question of meaning will arise, but I shall deal with it only insofar as this serves the purpose of defining the linguistic processes.

the other is not so easily discernible as in example (1), but the internal syntactic structure of the English segment is evident.

In example (3), the alternation from Spanish to English occurs between a Spanish conjunction and an English subordinate clause, which the conjunction introduces. In structure, it is similar to example (2), in which a Spanish adverbial phrase introduces an English sentence.

To summarize, we may make the following generalizations about examples (1), (2), and (3):

(a) The change from Spanish to English occurs at a clearly discernible syntactic juncture.

(b) The English component of the mixed sentence has its own internal syntactic structure.

Language mixing, type B

Now consider example (4). Notice that the English segment in this case consists of the single lexical item *improve*. Syntactically, *improve* is part of a larger unit, on which it depends for its grammatical interpretation. That is, the lexical meaning of the larger unit is contained within the English segment itself, but the inflectional endings normally manifested in Spanish verbal forms in this case are contained in the Spanish form *hizo* – i.e., *improve* is to be interpreted as preterit indicative, third person singular. Therefore, the English segment in this example constitutes an incomplete morphological entity. It is a form without any inflectional identification and depends on the conjugational forms of *hacer* for its grammatical interpretation.

In order to use an English verb in a Spanish context, the Chicano speech community has devised the syntactic frame *hacer* + English bare infinitive, in which *hacer* functions very much like an auxiliary verb that provides the English verbal form with the proper inflectional information for specific syntactic environments – e.g., *ayer yo hice improve* 'yesterday I improved,' *ahora tú haces improve* 'now you improve,' *mañana él va a hacer improve* 'tomorrow he is going to improve,' *yo quería que nosotros hiciéramos improve* 'I wanted us to improve,' *ellos están haciendo improve* 'they are improving,' *ustedes han hecho improve* 'you have improved.' Although the form *improve* conforms fully to the English phonological system, morphologically it appears as an invariable form within the paradigms of the conjugation of the Chicano verb phrase *hacer improve*. The morphological invariability of the English segment in *hacer improve* and in other phrases of the same type – e.g., *hacer draw* 'to draw,' *hacer withdraw* 'to withdraw,' *hacer petition* 'to petition,' *hacer reenlist* 'to reenlist,' *hacer bus* 'to bus' – and its dependence on the forms of *hacer* for its inflectional endings argue in favor of making a basic distinction between example (4) and the preceding examples, which lack these characteristics. However, there are still other examples that remain to be considered before coming to a definite conclusion.

There is another variant of the conjugation of *hacer* + English bare infinitive besides the one represented by example (4). This variant is represented by example (5), *va a reenlist.* Specifically, there is an option to delete the form of *hacer* if the phrase is governed by another Spanish verb that can take only the infinitive – e.g., *va a hacer improve* or *va a improve* 'he is going to improve'; *Quiere hacer improve* or *quiere improve* 'he wants to improve'; *tiene que hacer improve* or *tiene que improve* 'he has to improve'; *lo dejan hacer improve* or *lo dejan improve* 'they let him improve'; *le ayudan a hacer improve* or *le ayudan a improve* 'they help him improve'.

A possible explanation for this option is that in these cases, there is no need to use *hacer,* since the governing verb, expressing tense, mood, number, and person, can only take an infinitive as a complement. Therefore, the expression of the infinitive ending through the auxiliary *hacer* is redundant.

However, let us consider the progressive tenses – e.g., *está haciendo improve* 'he is improving' – where we would expect a similar logic to apply. That is, we would expect the participial form *haciendo* to be deletable also – e.g., **está improve* – since *estar* can only take a present participle as a complement, thus making *haciendo* redundant.[2] However, no such option exists. Instead, we have another option, exemplified by (6) *los están busing pa otra escuela* – with an English present participle – for *los están haciendo bus pa otra escuela,* which is also possible.

The phrase *están busing* represents a variant of *están haciendo bus* – the participial ending is expressed through the ending *-ing* of *busing* in one case, through the Spanish form *haciendo* in the other. Apparently, there is no way that we can reduce both forms to the same frame *hacer* + English bare infinitive, since *busing* is not a bare infinitive. Therefore, we must assume the existence of another frame, *estar* + English present participle. In fact, the existence of this frame is corroborated by its occurrence in the expression of other progressive tenses – e.g., *estaba improving* for *estaba haciendo improve* 'he was improving,' *ha estado improving* for *ha estado haciendo improve* 'he has been improving.'

The Chicano *hacer* + English bare infinitive seems to be based on a syntactic frame of the Spanish language. Chicano phrases like *hacer improve, hacer reenlist,* etc., are probably based on Spanish phrases like *hacer llorar* 'to make cry,' *lograr mejorar* 'to manage to improve,' etc., in which the governing verb always takes an infinitive complement. The function of the Chicano frame, of course, is different, since *hacer* in the

[2] I am not referring here to sentences like *está por venir* 'he is about to come,' or like *están cansados* 'they are tired,' in which the past participle *cansados* functions as an adjective rather than a verb.

Spanish phrase *hacer llorar,* for example, conveys the lexical meaning 'to induce,' whereas in the Chicano phrase *hacer improve* it merely expresses the inflectional endings that are normally expressed by the Spanish verb. It is somewhat comparable to the English tense carrier *do* in sentences like *Yes, I do go.*

Similarly, the frame *estar* + English present participle is probably based on Spanish verb phrases such as *estar mejorando* 'to be improving,' *estar llorando* 'to be crying,' etc., which consist of an inflected form of the auxiliary verb *estar* and a Spanish present participle.

Within the conjugational paradigms of each of these two Chicano syntactic frames, the English verb is morphologically invariable, although the existence of two separate frames gives rise to the variant forms *improve* and *improving.* Thus, the claim to morphological invariability of these English verbal forms holds true in the context of the frames within which the forms occur. However, the statement concerning the dependence of these English forms on *hacer* for their inflection must be restated: In the frame *hacer* + English bare infinitive, the English form depends on *hacer* for its inflection; in the frame *estar* + English present participle, it depends on *estar.*

At this point, let us summarize the characteristics held in common by examples (4), (5), and (6) – in contrast with those of examples (1), (2), and (3):

(a) The English component of the mixed sentence consists of a single lexical item.

(b) The English component of the sentence occurs within a special Chicano syntactic frame and it depends on this frame for part or all of its inflectional interpretation.

Language mixing, type C

Let us now examine examples (7), (8), and (9) and compare their formal characteristics with those of the preceding examples.

In example (7), *taipeo las cartas,* the English verb *type* is adapted phonologically and morphologically to the Spanish language. The English form is modified to fit the Spanish phonological norms: *Type* becomes /taip/ with all-Spanish phonetic segments, to which the vowel /e/ is added in order to form a stem *taipe.* The stem *taipe-* may take any of the endings of the first conjugation – for example:

Present indicative	*taipeo, taipeas, taipea,* etc.
Present subjunctive	*taipee, taipees, taipee,* etc.
Preterit indicative	*taipeé taipeaste, taipeó,* etc.
Imperfect subjunctive	*taipeara, taipearas, taipeara,* etc.

Other examples of this type of phonological and morphological adaptation are *mapear* 'to mop,' *cuitear* 'to quit,' *chitear* 'to cheat,' *chequear* 'to check,' *flanquear* 'to flunk,' etc. These verbs are fully incorporated in the lexicon of Chicano Spanish and are subject to the grammatical rules which govern any other verb of their same class. For all practical purposes, therefore, we can consider these verbs and their inflectional manifestations as belonging to Chicano Spanish. Even monolingual Spanish speakers who live among Chicanos use these forms. However, the source of these forms is English, and this is what constitutes the "interference" or language mixing in this case.

In example (8), *puchamos* represents basically the same phenomenon as *taipeo* – i.e., the phonological and morphological adaptation of an English verb to the Spanish linguistic system. The specific way in which the verb is adapted, however, is different. Most of the adapted English verbs follow the pattern of *taipear*. The form *puchamos,* however, lacks the /e/ that is normally added to the stem: **Pucheamos* would be the expected form if it followed the pattern of *taipear*. Other examples like *puchar* are *huachar* 'to watch, look, see' and *cachar* 'to catch.' Notice that both of these examples have a stem that ends in /č/ – *hua*/č/- and *ca*/č/-, respectively – as does *pu*/č/-. It might be suspected that the final /č/ of the hispanicized stem is what determines the absence of the usual /e/. However, from examples like *pichear* [pičár] 'to pitch' and *suichear* [swičár] 'to switch,' which follows the pattern of *taipear* – e.g., present indicative *pich* [éo], *pich* [éa] s, *pich* [éa]; *suich* [éo], *suich* [éa] s, *suich* [éa] – we conclude that the pattern of *puchar, huachar,* and *cachar* does not depend on the phonological composition of the stem.

In example (9), the form *mistir* 'to miss' represents another adaptation of an English verb to the Spanish morphophonological pattern. The English form *miss* is hispanicized phonologically and morphologically – as are the forms *type* and *push* in examples (7) and (8). But, as in the case of *puchamos,* the specific way in which the verb is adapted is different from that of *taipeo*. In this respect, *mistir* is unique insofar as it is the only example in which an adapted English verb follows the inflectional pattern of the Spanish third conjugation. All other examples conform to the first conjugation. Furthermore, /t/ rather than /e/ is added to the hispanicized form of the verb, resulting in a stem *mist-,* to which the endings of the third conjugation are added – for example:

Present indicative	*misto, mistes, miste,* etc.
Present subjunctive	*mista, mistas, mista,* etc.
Preterit indicative	*mistí, mististe, mistió,* etc.
Imperfect indicative	*mistía, mistías, mistía,* etc.
Imperfect subjunctive	*mistiera, mistieras, mistiera,* etc.

Besides verbs, there are also certain English nouns that are adapted to fit Spanish phonological and morphological contexts – e.g., *la troca* 'the truck,' *la suera* 'the sweater,' *la craca* 'the cracker,' *el raite* 'the ride,' *el traque* 'the railroad track.' These nominal forms – like their verbal analogues *taipear, puchar, mistir,* etc. – follow inflectional patterns that are in accordance with the norms of Spanish morphology. For example, the plural forms of the preceding examples are *las tracas, las sueras, las cracas, los raites, los traques,* respectively.

The diminutive derivatives of the nominal forms also demonstrate morphological adaptation to the norms of Spanish morphology; for example, from *la troca* is derived *la troquita*; from *la suera, la suerita*; from *la craca, la craquita* (the diminutive forms of *raite* and *traque* are *raitecito* and *traquecito* following the pattern of *viaje* 'trip': *viajecito* 'little trip'; *padre* 'father': *padrecito* 'little father'; *madre* 'mother': *madrecita* 'little mother,' etc.).

In summary, examples (7), (8), and (9), have the following common characteristics:

(a) The English component of the mixed sentences consists of a single lexical item.

(b) The English component is adapted phonologically and morphologically to the norms of the Spanish language. Historically, they are the product of language mixing. Synchronically, they are Spanish rather than English forms.

Generalizations

Thus far I have identified three different types of language mixing that occur in Chicano bilingual speech:

(A) Examples (1), (2), and (3), in which
 (a) the change from Spanish to English occurs at a clearly discernible syntactic juncture;
 (b) the English component of the mixed sentence has its own internal syntactic structure.

(B) Examples (4), (5), and (6), in which
 (a) the English component of the mixed sentence consists of a single lexical item;
 (b) the English component of the mixed sentence occurs within a special Chicano syntactic frame and it depends on this frame for part or all of its inflectional interpretation.

(C) Examples (7), (8), and (9), in which
 (a) the English component of the mixed sentence consists of a single lexical item;
 (b) the English component is adapted phonologically and morphologically to the norms of the Spanish language.

If we compare the formal characteristics of the three different types, we see that B and C have a characteristic in common: in both types the English component of the mixed sentence consists of a single lexical item. On the basis of this common characteristic I shall distinguish B and C (as a category) from A, which does not share this characteristic. To refer to these two categories, I propose the use of the term "code-switching" for type A and of the term "borrowing" for types B and C.

The use of the term "borrowing" for the examples of type B might seem to be at variance with Haugen's view, since in his terms code-switching includes "the introduction of a single unassimilated word . . . into the context of another language" (1973, p. 29). This might seem to make examples like *hizo improve mucho* fall under his code-switching category. However, I believe the syntactic analysis of examples (4), (5), and (6) given in this study is evidence that in these examples we are not dealing with single English lexical items alone but rather with a whole syntactic frame of which the unassimilated English form is merely an element. In my opinion, the Chicano syntactic frame makes possible the borrowing of an English lexical item without directly changing its phonological or morphological form. The process is similar to that of type C, except that the borrowed items of type B are adapted to the Spanish context through different means.

In terms of sufficient criteria for these different types of language mixing – that is, in terms of the minimum requirements a mixed language segment must have in order to ensure its proper classification as one of the following statements:

(1) A mixed language segment belongs to type A if the English component is a complete sentence.

Thus, although we need further criteria to be sure of the classification of sentences like example (4), sentences like example (1) offer no problem with respect to their classification.

(2) A mixed language segment belongs to type A if the English segment is separated from the Spanish by an intonational break.

For example, in a recorded segment *So qué chingaos va a poder uno? 'Chando mentiras nomás; son-of-a-bitch.'* 'So what the hell can you do [in order to keep your job]? Just tell lies; *son-of-a-bitch*!' The expression *son-of-a-bitch*! is clearly separated from the Spanish segment by a change in intonation. This marks the English segment as a separate and independent part of the discourse, tantamount to code-switching.[3]

(3) A negative criterion for type A is that no English noun phrase can occur in a Spanish environment.

Thus, a sentence like **Pongan the picket signs* 'Set up the picket signs' is an impossible type of code-switching. Type B, however – e.g., *pongan los picket signs* – could occur in this environment.

[3] The element *so* of the same segment, on the other hand, is not separated from the rest of the sentence by any such intonational break. It is fully integrated with the Spanish segment. Even phonologically it is [so] rather than [sow], as it would be in English. Based on these facts, I would classify *so* in this sentence as type C.

(4) A mixed sentence is to be considered of type B or of type C (depending on the phonological and morphological criteria of [2] and [3]) if the syntactic position of the English component is as in Spanish rather than as in English.

For example, a sentence like *maybe que vengan* 'maybe they'll come' is to be classified as type B because the component *maybe*, phonetically [méybi], as in English, occurs in a position identical to that of *puede ser* in Spanish *puede ser que vengan* 'maybe they'll come.' A position immediately preceding the clause it introduces, as in English, e.g., **maybe vengan*, is nonoccurring.

There is also the possibility of type C in this position, e.g. *chansa que vengan* 'maybe they'll come.' *Chansa,* from the English *chance,* has been modified in this example to function as an adverb. However, the important point here is that the syntactic position of *chansa* is the same as *puede ser* in *puede ser que vengan.* As in the case of *maybe* above, a position immediately preceding the clause it introduces (e.g., **chansa vengan*) is nonoccurring.

Obviously, I have not exhausted here the listing of sufficient criteria for the three types of Chicano language mixing I have identified. I have, however, indicated ways in which such criteria can be devised.

The selection of terms to refer to the two different types of borrowing requires further comparison of their characteristics. As opposed to type C – which involves the phonological and morphological assimilation of the English component into its Spanish environment – in type B the English component retains its original English form. In the latter case, the borrowed item does not become part of the Chicano Spanish lexicon. Type B represents an ad hoc adaptation of English items to Spanish environments.

There are certain constraints on borrowing of type B. Certain English items are never borrowed in this way. For example, we cannot say **hacer eat* 'to eat', **hacer go* 'to go', **hacer sit down* 'to sit down', **hacer see* 'to see', **hacer walk* 'to walk', **hacer drink* 'to drink.' It seems that the Spanish equivalents of most of the borrowed forms of this type belong to a more formal style typical of Chicano speech. Thus, terms such as *mejorar* 'to improve,' *dibujar* 'to draw', *retirar* 'to withdraw,' *dirigir una petición* 'to petition,' have a lower frequency in Chicano speech than *comer* 'to eat,' *ir* 'to go,' *sentarse* 'to sit down,' *ver* 'to see,' *andar* 'to walk,' and *tomar* 'to drink.' This is a possible explanation for the nonoccurrence of the English borrowed forms.

Aside from these constraints, the frames of type B allow for the borrowing of any English verb. The special frames provide the individual speaker with the means to effect the borrowing. Based on these factors, I propose the use of the term "unassimilated borrowing" to refer to type B.

In type C the borrowed item is assimilated into the Spanish of the

Chicano in an integral way. It becomes part of Chicano Spanish in all aspects of that linguistic system. Although new words are constantly being introduced into the Chicano Spanish vocabulary in this manner, borrowing of type C is the result of a common provision accepted by the general speech community. The term "assimilated borrowing" would reflect this aspect of the process.

Conclusion

Since the processes involved in assimilated borrowing are quite straightforward, I shall not repeat here what has already been said about it in the preceding sections. I shall, however, make some concluding statements about code-switching and unassimilated borrowing, pointing out the direction for future study of these bilingual phenomena. It should be borne in mind that the numbered statements below are intended to refer only to Chicano language mixing. Possible universal claims about bilingual phenomena are suggested only at the end of the discussion.

(1) Code-switching is the alternate use in discourse of Spanish and English, in which the alternating segments have their own internal structures and do not depend on the rest of the discourse for their analysis.

This statement is not intended to mean that there is no relationship between the alternate language segments, as is clear from examples such as (3) – *Yo sé, porque* I went to the hospital . . . etc., in which the English segment, although internally complete, is to be analyzed along with *porque* as a subordinate clause, depending on the main clause *yo sé*.

(2) Unassimilated borrowing is the use of an English lexical item, phonetically unassimilated and morphologically invariable, in the context of a Chicano Spanish syntactic frame.

The condition that an unassimilated borrowing be phonetically unassimilated carries with it a corollary condition which may be stated as follows:

(3) In an unassimilated borrowing, the mixing of the phonologies of English and Spanish within the same word cannot occur.

Thus, we have no examples of borrowing such as *[Impr̹uvár], with an English lax [I], retroflex [r̹], labiodental [v] mixed with the Spanish flap [r] of the ending *-ar*.

Along these same lines, it should be pointed out that internally compound forms such as *búsing-los* as in **están búsing-los* for *los están busing* are also excluded. The reason for this is possibly that compound forms of this kind are to be considered single words from the point of view of Chicano Spanish phonology.

An alternative to statement (3) above, might be that stress is what governs the exclusion of mixed phonologies; i.e., that the mixing of Spanish and English phonologies cannot occur within the same stress segment. In other words, if we could find mixing of phonologies within words that have compound stress, e.g., [kṛéyziménte] 'crazily' for *lócaménte,* [íziménte] 'easily' for *fácilménte,* we would have evidence for such an alternative to statement (3). However, I have not been able to find such evidence. Therefore, I shall keep statement (3) without alteration as long as evidence to the contrary is not found.

(4) In unassimilated borrowing, the borrowed item constitutes the head of the main element of the phrase in which it appears, the rest of the frame being in Spanish.

The condition that the surrounding frame of an unassimilated borrowing be in Spanish will prevent constructions such as **pongan the picket signs, *el niño depressed, *voy to improve,* etc., in which the English elements *the, depressed,* and *to,* respectively, constitute the surrounding environment of the main elements of the phrases *picket signs, el niño,* and *improve,* respectively.

This condition, however, does not exclude the possibility of borrowing an English lexical item along with one or more modifiers and considering them as a unit; e.g., *tienen color TV* 'they have a color TV,' *traiba una purple t-shirt* 'he was wearing a purple t-shirt,' *lo hicieron transfer overseas* 'they transferred him overseas.' In some cases, but not always, these compound borrowings are lexical compounds in the source language already and are borrowed *qua* compounds; e.g., *pongan los picket signs* 'set up the picket signs,' *siempre están passing the buck* 'they're always passing the buck,' *hicieron lock out a los huelguistas* 'they locked the strikers out,' *van a lay off a mucha gente* 'they're going to lay off a lot of people.' It is interesting to note in this respect that a sentence such as *hicieron transfer al soldado overseas* 'they transferred the soldier overseas' is possible but not **hicieron lock a los huelguistas out* nor **van a lay a mucha gente off.*

Very tentatively, I would like to suggest that statements (1) to (4) might apply to language mixing as it occurs in other bilingual speech communities. In the present study I have not dealt with the subject other than as it concerns Chicano bilingualism. However, the analysis that has been sketched out here could possibly serve as a basis for the search for linguistic universals in the area of bilingualism in general.

References

Gumperz, John J., and Eduardo Hernández-Chávez. 1972. Bilingualism, bidialectalism, and classroom interaction. In *Functions of language in the classroom,* ed. Courtney Cazden, Vera P. John, and Dell Hymes, pp. 84–108. New York: Teachers College Press.

Haugen, Einar. 1973. Bilingualism, language contact, and immigrant languages in the United States: a research report, 1956–1970. In *Current trends in linguistics* ed. Thomas Sebeok, vol. 10, pp. 505–91. The Hague: Mouton.

Weinreich, Uriel. 1968. *Languages in contact*. The Hague: Mouton. (Originally published in 1953.)

9

Texas Spanish and lexical borrowing

NICHOLAS SOBIN

Introduction

For all of its apparent simplicity, the borrowing of lexical items is really a complex process, undoubtedly carried out for many reasons and subject to numerous restrictions. We can consider here reasons for and restrictions on borrowing lexical items as two separate but interacting sets of factors which influence borrowing. Reasons for borrowing are those pressures which make people borrow terms. Restrictions on borrowing, on the other hand, are factors relating to the ease or difficulty with which a particular item may be borrowed. Essentially this distinction is made by Weinreich (1970) in his separate treatment of these two sets of factors. Investigators such as Weinreich (1970) and Bloomfield (1965) list such reasons for borrowing as the need for a term for a new object, prestige, the need for new synonyms, and the avoidance of homonymy. Less seems to be known about the restrictions on borrowing lexical items. Linton (1940) observes that words referring to things which are concrete may be more easily transferred than words for more abstract concepts. Weinreich claims that, "Other things being equal, morphemes with complex grammatical functions seem to be less likely to be transferred by the bilingual than those with simpler functions" (1970, p. 34). The notion that syntactic category is a parameter relevant to the discussion of borrowing is either explicit or implicit in many works which discuss borrowing. For example, both Haugen (1950) and Weinreich (1970) discuss differences in the frequency of borrowed lexical items as correlating with syntactic category. The borrowing of any lexical item no doubt involves the interaction of reasons for borrowing and various (and as yet mostly undiscovered) restrictions on borrowing. Thus, it is at best difficult to isolate any single

Reprinted with permission from *Papers in Linguistics* 9, nos. 1–2:15–47 (1976).

Thanks are due to a number of Pan American University students for acting as informants. Thanks are also due to Jon Amastae, Lucía Elías-Olivares, Robert T. Harms, Winfred Lehmann, Irene Madero, Sylvia Rendón, Linda Sobin, Paul Willcott, and others for helpful commentary on the data and/or content of this chapter. This chapter was supported in part by funds from AIDP Grant No. OEG–74–2511 and is dedicated to the memories of two dear friends, David DeCamp and Irene Madero.

reason for or restriction on borrowing. Of necessity, most generalizations in this area are really quite tentative. This reservation certainly applies to the statements and claims in this chapter.

This chapter began as an investigation into regularities among lexical items borrowed from English into Texas Spanish in the three major categories, N(oun), V(erb), and Adj(ective).[1] However, it soon became obvious that checking the significance of these regularities would require more general investigation into regularities in the borrowing of lexical items in other languages. Investigation into a number of other languages which have borrowed lexical items reveals regularities consistent with those found in the borrowed lexicon of Texas Spanish (henceforth, T-S). It is claimed in this chapter that on the basis of the evidence found so far, it is not sufficient to differentiate borrowed items along traditional syntactic categorial lines such as N, V, or Adj for the purpose of investigating possible syntactic restrictions on borrowing. Rather, there are finer differentiations of classes of borrowed lexical items describable in terms of semantic/syntactic features. By the term "semantic/syntactic features," I am referring to features of lexical items which play a role in the syntactic (transformational) behavior of sentences containing these items. Thus, this term is specifically related to a transformational view of syntax and is not equivalent to such terms as used by earlier writers. This chapter deals with one such feature, [do so], and its interaction with other more traditional categorial designations.[2]

The rest of this chapter is divided into three major sections. The first presents some representative borrowings from English into T-S and some observations on characteristics of this borrowed lexicon. The second section deals with lexical borrowing into a number of different languages and regularities in those lexicons consistent with the patterns of borrowing into T-S. The third section contains summary remarks, discussion, and conclusions.

Texas Spanish

Representative borrowed lexicon in T-S

The data in this section come from three sources: Cerda, Cabaza, and Farias (1970), Vásquez and Vásquez (1975), and selected residents of the Rio Grande Valley, bilingual in T-S and English, who are students at Pan American University (PAU) in Edinburg, Texas.

[1] The term "Texas Spanish" (T-S) will be used here to refer to the Spanish spoken in the Rio Grande Valley in Texas. T-S is considered by most people in the Rio Grande Valley to be "bad" or "incorrect" Spanish. It is spoken by the majority of the population of the Rio Grande Valley. English, however, must be considered the prestige language in the area.

[2] See Lakoff (1966), Ross (1972), and Sag (1973) for further discussion of this feature.

Of the three categories considered here, N, V, and Adj, the largest group of borrowed lexical items are Ns. Typical examples (given in a broad phonetic transcription) are:

bate 'baseball bat' bil 'a bill or dollar bill' blof 'a bluff'
bloaut 'a blowout' kabús 'caboose' butléger 'bootlegger'
kolektor 'collector' eskurer 'a motor scooter'

This list is taken from Cerda, Cabaza, and Farias (1970). It is only a small portion of the Ns borrowed from English in T-S.

There are a number of Vs borrowed into T-S from English. Following is a representative list of borrowed Vs:

parkyar 'to park blokyar 'to block' wačar 'to watch (out)'
kukyar 'to cook' čusar 'to choose' čopyar 'to shop'
setyar 'to set (hair)' testyar 'to test' waypyar 'to wipe'
kikyar 'to kick' espelyar 'to spell' čityar 'to cheat'
flonkyar 'to flunk' saynyar 'to sign' teypar 'to tape' (either with cellophane or on a tape recorder espatyar 'to spot'
trostyar 'to trust'

All these Vs, except the last two, were among a group of borrowed Vs cited to me by the PAU students. Most of these items can also be found in the dictionaries cited and probably in other articles on the subject.[3]

When the students were asked to try to think of any Adjs borrowed from English in T-S, they could think of none.[4] Upon checking in Cerda, Cabaza, and Farias (1970) and Vásquez and Vásquez (1975), it was apparent that the students thought of none because, if these works are accurate, there virtually are none. Both dictionaries list only one Adj borrowed from English in T-S:

tofudo 'tough'

Characteristics in the borrowed T-S lexicon

There are some regularities or characteristics to be noted about the borrowed lexicon of T-S. First, of the three categories, N, V, and Adj, of borrowed items, N is the largest. In Vásquez and Vásquez (1975), borrowed Ns seem to outnumber borrowed Vs about two to one.

The second characteristic has to do with the category V. Of the categories, V is the second largest. Upon inspection of the Vs borrowed, it is evident, however, that not just any type of V has been borrowed. In particular, all of the Vs borrowed into T-S from English are ones which can be freely replaced by a form of *do so*. Thus we have acceptable the

[3] See, for example, Bowen (1974).

[4] That is, they were asked to think of Adjs which, like the verbs cited, are inflected like normal items in T-S and which are likely to be used by T-S speakers, regardless of their command of English.

sentences of (1) (given with some additional borrowed Vs):

(1) (a) The Germans *spotted* the tanks and the Hungarians *did so* too. (espatyar)
(b) Jack *taught* five courses and Vilma *did so* too. (tičar)
(c) Jack *improved* last year and Vilma *did so* too. (impruvyar)
(d) Jack *quit* and Jill *did so* too. (kwityar)
(e) Jack *trusted* Vilma and Mercedes *did so* too. (trostyar)
(f) Max *touched* the paint and María did so too. (točar)

Compare these sentences with the sentences of (2):

(2) (a) *Vilma *knew* Harriet and Cesario *did so* too.
(b) *Jack *want*ed to leave and Vilma *did so* too.
(c) *Max *wonder*ed who left and María *did so* too.
(d) *Max *tend*ed to like fish and Cesario *did so* too.
(e) *Max *resembl*ed a gorilla and Frank *did so* too.

Further, the *do so* distinction is also made in T-S with parallel grammaticality judgments:

(3) (a) Max *trostió* a María y Cesario *lo hizo* también. 'Max *trust*ed María and Cesario *did so* too.'
(b) Max *espatió* a María y Cesario *lo hizo* también. 'Max *spot*ted María and Cesario *did so* too.'
(c) Max *corrió* y María *lo hizo* también. 'Max *ran* and María *did so* too.'
(d) *Max *supo* la respuesta y María *lo hizo* también. 'Max *knew* the answer and María *did so* too.'

All of the Vs borrowed from English into T-S are replaceable by *lo hizo* in conjoined constructions like those in the examples. Thus, for a second general statement about the borrowed lexicon of T-S, we might say that only Vs replaceable by *lo hizo* in T-S or *do so* in English (which we will henceforth refer to as *do so* verbs) have been borrowed.

Considering the generalization here to involve the *do so* distinction rather than a more Lakoffian (1966) stative/nonstative distinction has a couple of advantages. First, the *do so* distinction would give us an account of the borrowing of "spot," whereas the stative/nonstative distinction would not.

Second, the *do so* distinction is of predictive value in the area of Adj borrowing. Recall that only one Adj, *tofudo* 'tough' has been borrowed from English into T-S. Of further interest is the fact that although *tough* is an Adj in English, the "borrower" of this item did not consider this item to be an Adj. This is evidenced by the *-udo* suffix on this word. *-udo* is a derivational, adjectivalizing suffix. It is placed on words which are not Adjs to make Adjs of them. It would be unacceptable to place the *-udo* suffix on a word which was already categorized as an Adj. Thus, the addition of *-udo* to the items listed in (4) creates unacceptable items:

(4) (a) *grande* 'large'
(b) **grandudo*
(c) *loco* 'crazy'
(d) **locudo*
(e) *mal* 'bad'
(f) **maludo*

Therefore, it appears that the "borrower" of *tough* did not consider the word to be an Adj. It seems safe to say, then, that T-S speaakers have not directly borrowed anything they consider to be an Adj.

Now let us return to our point here. Recall Lakoff's (1966) arguments that Adjs and Vs belong to the same syntactic category (which we might call "verbal") on the basis of shared semantic properties, such as stative and nonstative, as well as identical treatment by a number of transformational rules. If Lakoff is correct on this point, then the second advantage of characterizing the Vs borrowed into T-S as *do so* verbs rather than as nonstative Vs is that in addition to characterizing the correct verbal type, this would also predict that Adjs are not borrowed. This is because neither *Adj* nor *be + Adj* constructions can be freely replaced by *do so*.[5] Thus, even though they contain nonstative Adjs, the sentences of (5) are unacceptable.

(5) (a) *Jack was careful and Jill did so too.
(b) *Jack was polite and Jill did so too.
(c) *Jack was attentive and Jill did so too.

Thus, it would seem that the *do so* distinction is the more revealing one in characterizing Vs and Adjs borrowed into T-S.

Concluding remarks

T-S has borrowed a number of lexical items from English and there are at least two noteworthy characteristics of this borrowed lexicon.[6] First, the largest category of borrowed words is N. Second, of the V and Adj

[5] This fact is also noted by Lakoff (1966, I-11). The term *freely* is important here; be + Adj constructions with nonstative adjectives can be replaced by *do so* but only in progressive constructions: (i) Max is *being careful* and Jill is *doing so* too. (ii) ?*Max has *been careful* and Jill has *done so* too. (iii) *Max *was careful* and Jill *did so* too. Thus, Adjs are not verbals which are freely replaceable by *do so*. Unlike the Adjs, *do so* verbs (along with accompanying structure) can be replaced by *do so* without regard for environments, such as these: (iv) Max is *running* and Jill is *doing so* too. (v) Max has *run* and Jill has *done so* too. (vi) Max *ran* and Jill *did so* too. That is, *do so* verbs are freely replaceable by *do so*. Verbs like *spot* are freely replaceable (and therefore *do so* verbs), since such verbs can be replaced by *do so* in any tense or aspect environment in which the verb can appear: (vii) Jack spotted Jill and Harry did so too. (viii) *Jack spots Jill and Harry does so too. (ix) *Jack spots Jill.

[6] A few other regularities are worth pointing out but they have not been pursued here. One is that nearly all the verbs borrowed are either intransitive or simple object-taking verbs. No verbs with complex restrictions on their selection have been borrowed. Another regularity is that particles are not borrowed in conjunction with verbs but are borrowed in conjunction with nouns. Thus we have *nokyar* 'to knock out' but the noun *nokaut* 'knock out.'

category, only *do so* verbs have been borrowed. The question now arises as to whether or not these patterns of borrowing are accidental or somehow significant and revealing of natural language structure.

Other languages

In order to see whether or not the patterns of lexical borrowing in T-S are significant or not, it is necessary to look at other languages and see if the same pattern or a compatible pattern of borrowing is found. If a number of languages show the same or compatible borrowing patterns, then it is more probable that the borrowing patterns exhibited in T-S and the other languages are significant and warrant more serious consideration.

In dealing with the following data, I will make the assumption (which I think is uncontroversial) that the feature of certain Vs which allows them, along with certain accompanying structure, to be freely replaced by *do so* is a universal property of the meaning of these Vs and not something which is arbitrarily assigned to Vs in every language, requiring independent learning or memorization. Only the claim of universality accounts for the fact that the set of Vs in Spanish which can be replaced by *lo hizo* seems to correspond exactly to the set of Vs which can be replaced by *do so* in English. The probability of this being the case if the *do so* feature were arbitrarily assigned to verbals would be virtually zero. Thus, Vs from the languages to follow will be classified as [+ do so] or [− do so] on the basis of tests in English and independently of syntactic tests for such a feature in the particular languages under consideration, many of which it is presently unfeasible to obtain.[7]

The data to be presented here will be in terms of major categories borrowed. The categories discussed here are N, [$\overset{V}{+}$ do so], Adj, and [$\overset{V}{-}$ do so]. Accepting Lakoff's proposal that Vs and Adjs be categorized in one category, the latter three categories may be considered subcategories of a larger category, verbal. These categories are arranged according to the borrowing patterns discovered in the languages which were investigated. The borrowed lexicons discussed here (except for Ateso) will be individuated according to the borrowing language and the language being borrowed from.

N borrowing

In the categories mentioned, two of the languages investigated have borrowed only Ns from other languages. The first of these languages is Tewa, the language of the Tewa Indians of southern New Mexico. Edward

[7] The feature [do so] is, of course, not to be taken as the actual semantic feature involved here but merely a notation for whatever the feature may actually be which allows free replaceability of certain verbs and other structure by *do so*.

Dozier states, "Spanish loanwords are in general limited to nominal forms. Only two examples of another form class are in the writer's collection: the Spanish conjunctions *si* 'if' and *porque* 'because' . . ." (1964, p. 515). Inspection of the lists Dozier presents bears this out. Of the categories being discussed, Spanish borrowings into Tewa are limited to Ns.

The second instance of the exclusive borrowing of Ns is the list of Old Irish borrowings into Old English, "introduced by Irish missionaries of the seventh century" (Serjeantson 1962, p. 58). The list given by Serjeantson (pp. 58–60) is small, exhaustive, and consists exclusively of Ns.

drȳ 'a magician, sorcerer'
clucge 'a bell'
ancor 'a hermit, anchorite'
stǣr 'history' (ultimately Latin)
ǣstel 'a bookmark' (ultimately Latin)
cīne 'quaternio' (ultimately Latin)
cros 'cross of stone' (ultimately Latin)

N and [$\overset{\text{V}}{+}$ *do so*] *borrowing*

Others of the languages investigated have borrowed only Ns and *do so* verbs. One of the languages to do this is T-S, which was discussed earlier. A second instance of such borrowing is the list of items borrowed from Spanish into Central American Carib from approximately 1493 to 1625. Douglas Taylor (1948, p. 188) lists a number of Ns, two Vs, and no Adjs borrowed from Spanish. The Vs are:

agardaha 'to watch out'   asaluha 'to salt'

Both Vs are *do so* verbs. It is important to note that Taylor claims his lists to be representative but not exhaustive. In subsequent lists of items borrowed into Carib in later periods, he is not reticent to list Vs or Adjs in larger numbers. Thus, insofar as can be told from his lists, Carib borrowing from this period seems to fall in this section.

A third instance of exclusive N and *do so* verb borrowing is the list of borrowed items from Swahili, Luganda, and English into Ateso. Ateso is a language spoken by the Iteso of Uganda and Kenya. Carol Scotton and John Okeju (1973) note that, "By far the greatest number of borrowings, grouping all dialects together, are nouns for objects or concepts new to the Ateso culture" (p. 885). "Borrowed verbs are relatively few; in general, they stand for new concepts, although a few replace Ateso equivalents" (p. 887). It is hard to tell whether or not the list of Vs presented is exhaustive or not. The items listed (p. 887) are:

aki'celewar 'to be delayed' (fr. Swahili)
ai-tund(a) 'to sell' (fr. Luganda)
ai-puga 'to rule' (fr. Lug.)

ai-siom 'to study' (fr. Swa. or Lug.)
ai-wadik 'to write' (fr. Swa. or Lug.)
aki-filinga 'to file letters' (fr. Eng.)
ai-serving 'to serve' (fr. Eng.)

Except for the first item, the others are clearly *do so* verbs. The first item is questionable because (6) is unacceptable:

(6) *Max was delayed and Sheila did so too.

On the other hand, *delay* (a central element in this item) is clearly a *do so* verb, as seen in (7):

(7) The rain delayed the mail and the snow did so too.

Thus, the status of this item as a *do so* verb is genuinely unclear.[8]

Although Scotton and Okeju are interested in enumerating types of borrowing with regard to lexical classification, they do not list or discuss any borrowed Adjs. This would seem to indicate either that Adjs have not been borrowed or that they are very obscure. Thus, from the information obtainable, Ateso would seem to fall in with T-S and Carib (first period) with respect to lexical borrowing.[9]

The borrowings from Latin into Germanic given by Sperber and von Polenz (1966) give a fourth example of the type of borrowing discussed in this section. Again, this list is not claimed to be complete but is claimed to be representative of the data. Indeed, its main purpose is to exemplify the sort of items borrowed. The large majority of borrowed items are Ns for objects. Seven Vs are listed (pp. 18–21), all of them *do so* verbs:

kaufen 'buy' eichen 'gauge, calibrate' pflanzen 'plant'
pfropfen 'cork, plug, graft' impfen 'graft' pflücken 'pluck'
schreiben 'to write'

No Adjs are listed.[10]

N, [$\overset{\text{V}}{+}$ *do so*], *and Adj borrowing*

Other cases of borrowing involve the borrowing of Ns, *do so* verbs, and Adjs but not non-*do so* verbs. One such case is the borrowing of Scandinavian (mostly Old Norse) words into English up to A.D. 1150. The lists given by Serjeantson (1962) are complete as far as can be established. The majority of borrowed items are Ns. The Vs borrowed during this period (pp. 64–74) are:

[8] This item might indicate that the first types of verbs to be borrowed are *do so* verbs *or* verbs which centrally contain a *do so* verb.

[9] Taylor (1948) documents three periods of borrowing into Carib of which 1493–1625 is the first.

[10] Sperber and von Polenz do list adjectives in other lists of borrowed items, e.g. borrowing from French.

ceallian 'to call' farnian 'to prosper' sparrian 'to bar'
eggian 'to egg on' diegan 'to die'
hittan 'to come upon, meet with' tacan 'to touch, take'
flycian 'to marshal, arrange'[11]

Five Adjs were also borrowed during this time. Of these five, only two are not related to a borrowed N (Serjeantson 1962, pp. 64–74). As far as can be told, no non-*do so* verbs were borrowed during this period.

A second case of N, [$\overset{\text{V}}{+}$ do so], and Adj borrowing, also from Serjeantson (pp. 271–81) is the list of items borrowed up to A.D. 650 from Latin into English. This list is also, as far as can be established, exhaustive. Again, the majority of borrowed items are Ns. The Vs borrowed are all *do so* verbs. Typical items are:

scrifan 'to allot, decree' (be)mūtian 'to change, exchange'
pīnian 'to punish, torture' nēomian 'to produce harmony'
(for) stoppian 'to stop up' lafian 'to bathe, wash'
cyrtan 'to shorten'

Some of the Adjs borrowed during this period are:

pællen 'purple, costly' crisp 'curly' pīs 'heavy'
sicor 'safe' cūsc 'chaste, modest'

The number of Adjs borrowed (about nine) is smaller than the number of Vs borrowed (about twenty-six). No non-*do so* verbs seem to have been borrowed during this time.

Another case of this sort of lexical borrowing is found in Michael G. Clyne's work entitled *Transferring and Triggering* (1967). In this work, Clyne attempts to elicit borrowings and switches from Australian English into the German spoken by Germans residing in Australia, which he lumps together under the term "transfers" (1967, p. 19).[12] Because of this lack of distinction between switches and borrowed words, Clyne's listings (pp. 28–50) will include items which would not be included in a list of borrowed items. Even so, Clyne's lists definitely conform to the patterns of borrowing discussed thus far. The largest category of transfers is N. The next largest category of transfers is *do so* verbs (about fifty-six elicited).

[11] (i) Jack called Harry and Jill did so too. (ii) Jack prospered and Jill did so too. (iii) Jack barred their path and Jill did so too. (iv) Jack egged Harry on and Jill did so too. (v) Jack died at ten and Jill did so too. (vi) Jack came upon a band of merry men and Jill did so too. (vii) Jack marshaled a platoon of troops and Jill did so too.

[12] I consider "borrowings" to be words taken into a given language which are frequently known to monolingual speakers of that language and which are inflected as standard items of the same category are. A word which has been "switched" rather than borrowed is one which is not often known to monolingual speakers of the language and which is often not inflected in the language as other items of the same category are. For example, English adjectives often appear in the speech of T-S–English bilinguals, but they are not inflected like other Adjs in T-S and they are only used when speaking to another T-S–English bilingual.

A number of transferred Adjs are also listed (about thirty-one). Concerning these Adjs, Clyne states, "Transferred adjectives are almost invariably left uninflected by my informants – as in English . . . Only isolated instances have been recorded of the inflexion of transferred adjectives – e.g. *righten* and *colourfulle*." (See footnote 12.) About 25 percent of the informants used were, to some extent, German–English bilingual before their arrival in Australia. The elicitor of the data was also known to be German–English bilingual by the informants. A number of the informants used were children. Thus, it seems that a number of items given would not appear on a list of borrowed words. Of all the verbs listed, a few appear to be non-*do so* verbs. They are: *get, understanden, reminden,* and *enjoyen* (Clyne 1967, pp. 35–6).[13] The use of *prefer* is also noted (pp. 81, 124, and 129).[14] Of these Vs, the examples of *get* and *prefer* which are given seem to indicate code-switching rather than borrowing. The example of *get* is preceded by two English morphemes, *farmer* and the English contraction for *has*:

(8) der Farmer's got Schafe. (p. 36)

The examples of *prefer* are inflected like English Vs rather than like other German Vs (including other borrowed Vs) as these informants inflect them:

(9) (a) Ich personlich prefer diese Strasse. (p. 128)
(b) . . . so ich prefer die Self Service shops. (p. 128)

Compare

(c) Oh, ja, ich kaufe auch ein . . . (p. 129)

Clyne noted that *understanden* appeared only once in interviewing two hundred informants. Since the example is not given, it is not possible to say whether the use of this verb indicated a switch or a borrowing. Examples of the uses of *reminden* and *enjoyen* are also not given. Here too, then, one cannot tell whether the use of these Vs was in code-switching or whether they were instances of borrowed Vs. On the basis of information available, I have placed this lexicon in this section. If further evidence indicated that some or all of these non-*do so* verbs have been borrowed, then this lexicon should be included in the next section rather than in this one.

[13] *Were* was also cited (p. 36) as being used by ten-year-olds. Auxiliary verbs are not being considered here, however.

[14] (i) *I *preferred* lobster and Jill *did so* too. (ii) *Jack *understood* Harriet and Jill *did so* too. (iii) ?Jack *understood* what Harriet said and Jill *did so* too. (iv) *Jack *understands* Harriet and Jill *does so* too. (v) ?Jack *reminded* me of a gorilla and his brother *did so* too. (vi) *Jack *reminds* me of a gorilla and his brother *does so* too. (vii) ?*Jack is *enjoying* the beach and Jill is *doing so* too. These sentences indicate that these verbs are not freely replaceable by *do so*.

Several other instances of what may be this type of lexical borrowing that could be mentioned are again found in Sperber and von Polenz (1966). One instance is the list of borrowings from French into German in the sixteenth and seventeenth centuries (pp. 79–82). The majority of items listed are Ns naming objects or people. *Do so* verbs and Adjs are also listed. No non-*do so* verbs are given. The same is true of their list of borrowings from Latin and Greek into German (pp. 71–5) of the humanist period. As with earlier lists from this source, these are exemplary and incomplete. As far as they go, they warrant placement in this section. If further investigation revealed the borrowing of non-*do so* verbs, then these examples would also belong in the following section.

Borrowing of all four classes

Other languages investigated have borrowed items from all four of the categories being considered here. For example, we find the Spanish borrowings into Bolivian Quechua. Bills, Vallejo, and Troike (1969) give a fairly extensive Quechua lexicon and note when an item has been borrowed from Spanish. The largest category of borrowed items is Ns (about 146). The second largest is *do so* verbs (about 45). Next are Adjs (about 17) and then non-*do so* verbs (about 5).

Another language which has borrowed from all four categories is Central American Carib in what Taylor (1948) calls the second and third periods (1625–1786 and 1707–?). The largest category of borrowed items is Ns. Then come the *do so* verbs. Next come the Adjs, most of which appear to be numbers, and finally a few non-*do so* verbs.

It seems probable that in any situation where contact is long and borrowing is extensive, all four categories will be borrowed from.

Gaps

The above is very representative of languages on which data have been found thus far. These languages were chosen arbitrarily and without any consideration for syntactic category of borrowing. This being the case, there appear to be some interesting and significant gaps in the data. Although it is logically possible for all the following to happen, no language investigated has borrowed Vs without borrowing Ns. No language investigated has borrowed Adjs without borrowing *do so* verbs. No language has borrowed non-*do so* verbs without borrowing Adjs. Such gaps seem far beyond chance occurrence. Further, Adjs are fairly common items in everyday speech and not members of some exotic, seldom utilized category. Non-*do so* verbs are also quite common. Some of these appear frequently in hesitation phrases, such as "see?" "you know?" "understand?" They too are not members of an exotic, seldom utilized category. Although most Vs are probably *do so* verbs, verbs like *see, hear, seem, want, perfer, like, dislike, appear, remind, enjoy, know, understand, happen, sound, need,* for example, are not uncommon in spoken language.

Thus, relative rarity of numbers would hardly seem to provide an account of the patterns and gaps in lexical borrowing.[15]

If we utilize Haugen's term "scale of adoptability" (1950, p. 224), the data indicate that Ns are most easily adopted, then *do so* verbs, then Adjs and, of these four categories, non-*do so* verbs are least easily adopted. It is probably the case that if other semantic/syntactic distinctions were being considered, there would be other, finer distinctions within these categories.

Conclusions and discussion

The data viewed so far are most likely only the tip of an iceberg. None the less, a large enough variety of languages has been discussed above to allow us to take seriously the possibility that a semantic/syntactic feature, [do so], distinguishes a class of borrowed lexical items. This will, of course, require a great deal more study to substantiate fully.

Further, if the [do so] classification is a valid one in the differential borrowing of classes of lexical items, then it is hard to believe that it is an isolated example. Future research into differential borrowing should consider classification by other semantic/syntactic features and not just traditional grammatical categories of borrowed lexical items.

It is also worth noting that the borrowing of lexical items from English into T-S is not a random activity but a regular phenomenon, subject to the same restrictions as other languages that borrow or have borrowed lexical items. The notion, popular among some, that T-S is not a language, or that the T-S lexicon is a random mix of English and Spanish is false. The borrowing of English words into T-S is regular and consistent with every other borrowing situation investigated.

Finally, since any real explanation for all of the above is lacking and probably will not be discovered soon, it is worth pointing out another area in which there is analogous data to the borrowing data discussed above and which may, on further investigation, indirectly provide more knowledge about borrowing. That area is child language acquisition. The obvious similarity between borrowing and child language acquisition was noted by Bloomfield in his discussion of "cultural borrowing."[16]

> The child who is learning to speak may get most of his habits from some one person . . . but he will also hear other speakers and take some habits from them . . . Throughout his life, the speaker continues to adopt features from his fellows. [1965, P. 444]

A similar position is taken by Kiparsky (1968, 193–4), who notes the similarity between various historical changes in language and certain

[15] If rarity of use could be shown to be a factor, even this would only place the question one step back; why are certain categories more rare than others?

[16] By this term, Bloomfield means borrowing, "where the borrowed features come from a different language" (1965, p. 444).

stages of child language acquisition.[17] When one looks closely at lexicons being acquired by children, there are some striking similarities between such lexicons and borrowed lexicons. For one, if the figures which Dewey (1971) quotes are correct, then Ns would seem to be by far the most prevalent items in the lexicons of young children.[18] The same is true of the children's lexicons discussed below. The same is also true of all the borrowed lexicons discussed above. Further statements to this effect can be found in Weinreich (1970) and Haugen (1950). Another similarity is to be found in the nature of Ns and Vs acquired by children and borrowed. The Ns are usually "concrete" and the Vs "active." Thus, regarding child language, M. D. S. Braine (1971) says:

> There has been a good deal of Russian work on factors affecting the order of development of categories. The main line of thought . . . appears to be that the order reflects the difficulty of the concepts typically expressed by the categories more than the variety or formal complexity of the grammatical devices signaling them. Categories of more concrete reference develop before those expressing more abstract or relational ideas and before those that are semantically arbitrary [P. 51]

Further on, Braine states:

> The most frequently discussed semantic correlates of categories are the "thingness" of nouns and the "action" character of verbs. Brown (1957) has shown that nouns designate thinglike entities and verbs actions much more frequently in children's vocabularies than in adults'. [P. 55]

Here, too, the borrowed lexicons above appear similar to child language lexicons. Also, Linton (1940) makes mention of the ease with which Ns of concrete reference are borrowed as opposed to Ns of abstract reference. Weinreich (1970, p. 37) assumes the validity of this claim in his own "lexical-semantic" account of the prominence of nouns in borrowed lexicons.

Closer inspections of children's lexicons reveal even greater similarity to borrowed lexicons. As examples, let us consider the following. In an article entitled "The Growth of Phonemic and Lexical Patterns in Infant Language," H. V. Velten (1971, pp. 86–7) presents a list of morphemes

[17] The existence of sequences in the acquisition of lexical items has been documented in a number of works. Bailey, Madden, and Krashen (1974) found among their subjects a "highly consistent order of relative difficulty in the use of English functors or grammatical morphemes across different language backgrounds" (p. 235). In his review of the literature on the order of the development of grammatical categories, Martin D. S. Braine (1971, pp. 50ff.) discusses other researchers, among them Braine, Menyuk, Slobin, Gvozdev, Growne, and Berks, whose research has indicated the existence of sequencing in the development of grammatical categories. A tendency for children to acquire, in order of easiest to most difficult, nouns, verbs, and then adjectives is noted in Dewey (1971).

[18] It should be noted here that assigning syntactic categories to items in children's language is a very tentative matter. See Dewey (1971). The categorical assignments made here and earlier are made on the basis of how the given items would be classified in adult speech. Given the consistent distribution of data along these lines, however, these categories are probably relevant to generalization in this area.

used by his child Joan, whose language development he studied from age eleven months to age thirty-six months. Over two-thirds of the items listed are clearly Ns. There are about fifteen clear examples of *do so* verbs. Some examples are:

fup 'sweep' dat 'cut' zap 'shop' fu 'fall' bus 'push'

The list also contains about ten Adjs. Further, this list contains no non-*do so* verbs. The lexical density of these categories corresponds directly to the patterns of borrowing discussed earlier.

Yuen Ren Chao (1971) in his article "The Cantian Idiolect: An Analysis of the Chinese Spoken by a Twenty-Eight-Months-Old Child" gives a listing of the active vocabulary used by one of his grandchildren at this age (pp. 126–30). In the four categories being considered here, about 150 words appear to be Ns, nearly 70 are *do so* verbs, and nearly 30 are Adjs. Only about 5 non-*do so* verbs are to be found in the items listed. Here again, the density of lexical items in the four categories considered replicates the patterns found in borrowing. N, the category of items most easily borrowed, also displays the greatest lexical density in this and the preceding list. *Do so* verbs, the second most easily borrowed lexical items, make up the second longest list of acquired items in the two lists, and so on. Assuming that the density of lexical items in a given category can be taken as an indication of the difficulty of acquiring that category of item, then it seems that Ns, *do so* verbs, Adjs, and non-*do so* verbs show the same relative degrees of difficulty in borrowing as in language acquisition. Since language acquisition and lexical borrowing are undoubtedly related phenomena, then what accounts for one should account for the other.[19] It seems, then, that child language and borrowing bear research as related and mutually enlightening areas.

[19] At this point it is tempting to conjecture that "concreteness" may be what is responsible for the scaling here, both in borrowing and in child language. The more "concrete" the reference, the more learnable it may be. Other research results would seem to support a "concreteness" hypothesis. James J. Asher (1965) tested the ease of acquisition and length of retention of language among subjects who themselves responded physically to utterances being given in the target language (Russian) as contrasted with subjects who were given the same utterances but who only watched someone else respond to the utterances. Asher reports that, "the group applying the learning strategy of the total physical response had significantly better retention for short, long, and novel utterances" (p. 296). Concerning Asher's results, Susan Ervin-Tripp (1973) says, "Asher has claimed dramatic increases in learning rate and retention when adults were treated like children with respect to learning context, i.e. when they were taught to recognize words referring to actions performed and objects handled" (p. 79). Intuitively, it would seem easiest to teach someone the names for things (concrete nouns) by simply pointing to the object. Action verbs (most *do so* verbs) should be somewhat easy to teach in that they can be acted out. Adjectives would be more difficult to teach because objects usually have more than one property describable by an adjective. It could take more than one object with that property to get across the word for that property. Non-*do so* verbs would be the most difficult to teach in that there are no objects or demonstrations that one can appeal to, to teach such concepts. This could alter our notion of features like "concreteness." Rather than being binary and unique to a particular category (N; see Chomsky 1965), they would be multivalued and cross-categorial.

It is worth reiterating that borrowing is a complex process and that in no sense can the preceding discussion be taken as any general explanation of borrowing. There are no doubt many factors involved in any borrowing, and many things are borrowed which have not been discussed here. It is hoped, however, that the above may indicate the need to consider semantic/syntactic (transformational) distinctions in the further investigation of differential borrowing among syntactic categories.

Appendix

A list of verbs borrowed from English into T-S and not found in Cerda, Cabaza, and Farias (1970) or Vásquez and Vásquez (1975):

blokyar 'to block'
flotyar 'to flood
pinčar 'to pinch'
kwityar 'to quit'
wæksyar 'to wax'
poličar 'to polish'
reypyar 'to rape'
točar 'to touch'
tisyar 'to tease' (hair)
flipyar 'to flip'

flatyar 'to flatten'
čarponyar 'to sharpen'
kikyar 'to kick'
čusar 'to choose'
čarčar 'to charge' (as with a charge account)
čopyar 'to shop'
bročar 'to brush'
waypyar 'to wipe'

mapyar 'to mop'
čevyar 'to shave'
teystyar 'to taste'
espaykyar 'to spike'
forsar 'to force'
lukyar 'to look'
kastyar 'to cast'
ǰokyar 'to joke'
lakyar 'to lock'
čItyar 'to shit'
driŋkyar 'to drink'

References

Asher, James J. 1965. The strategy of the total physical response: an application to learning Russian. *International Review of Applied Linguistics* 2:291–300.
Bailey, Nathalie, Carolyn Madden, and Stephen D. Krashen. 1974. Is there a "natural sequence" in adult second language learning? *Language learning* 24:235–43.
Bills, Garland, Bernardo Vallejo, and Rudolph C. Troike. 1969. *An introduction to spoken Bolivian Quechua*. Austin: University of Texas Press.
Bloomfield, Leonard. 1965. *Language history*. New York: Holt, Rinehart and Winston.
Bowen, J. Donald. 1974. New Mexican Spanish verb forms. *Southwest areal linguistics*, ed. G. Bills, pp. 157–166. San Diego: San Diego State University, Institute for Cultural Pluralism.
Braine, M. D. S. 1971. The acquisition of language in infant and child. *The Learning of Language*, ed. C. Reed, pp. 7–95. New York: Appleton-Century-Crofts.
Brown, Roger W. 1957. Linguistic determinism and the part of speech. *Journal of Abnormal and Social Psychology* 55:1–5.
Castillo, Carlos, and Otto Bond. 1975. *The University of Chicago Spanish-English, English-Spanish dictionary*. New York: Pocket Books.

Cerda, Gilberto, Berta Cabaza, and Julieta Farias. 1970. *Vocabulario español de Texas*. Austin: University of Texas Press.

Chao, Yeun Ren. 1971. The Cantian idiolect: an analysis of the Chinese spoken by a twenty-eight-months-old child. In *Child language*, ed. A. Bar-Adon, pp. 116–30. Englewood Cliffs, N.J.: Prentice-Hall.

Chomsky, Noam. 1965. *Aspects of the theory of syntax*. Cambridge, Mass.: MIT Press.

Clyne, Michael G. 1967. *Transference and triggering*. The Hague: Nijhoff.

Dewey, John. 1971. The psychology of infant language. In *Child language*, ed. A. Bar-Adon, pp. 34–6. Englewood Cliffs, N.J.: Prentice-Hall.

Dozier, Edward P. 1964. Two examples of linguistic acculturation: the Yaqui of Sonora and Arizona and the Tewa of New Mexico. In *Language in culture and society*, ed. Dell Hymes, pp. 509–20. New York: Harper & Row.

Ervin-Tripp, Susan M. 1973. *Language acquisition and communicative choice*. Stanford University Press.

Haugen, Einar 1950. The analysis of linguistic borrowing. *Language* 26:210–31.

1956. *Bilingualism in the Americas*. University: University of Alabama Press.

Kiparsky, Paul. 1968. Linguistic universals and language change. *Universals in linguistic theory*, ed. E. Bach and R. Harms, pp. 171–202. New York: Holt, Rinehart and Winston.

Lakoff, G. 1966. Stative verbs and adjectives in English. In *Mathematical linguistics and machine translation*, Report NSF 17, pp. I-1–15. Cambridge: Computational Laboratory of Harvard University.

Linton, Ralph. 1940. *Acculturation in seven American Indian tribes*. New York: Appleton-Century-Crofts.

Ross, John R. 1972. Act. In *Semantics of natural language*, ed. Gilbert Harman and Donald Davidson, pp. 70–126. New York: Humanities Press.

Sag, Ivan. 1973. On the state of progress on progressives and statives. In *New ways of analyzing variation in English*, ed. C. J. N. Bailey and R. Shuy, pp. 83–95. Washington, D.C.: Georgetown University Press.

Scotton, Carol M., and John Okeju. 1973. Neighbors and lexical borrowings. *Language* 49:871–89.

Serjeantson, Mary S. 1962. *A history of foreign words in English*. New York: Barnes & Noble Books.

Sperber, Hans, and Peter von Polenz. 1966. *Geschichte der deutschen Sprache*. Berlin: de Gruyter.

Taylor, Douglas. 1948. Loan words in Central American Carib. *Word* 4:187–95.

Vásquez, Librado, and Maria Vásquez. 1975. *Regional dictionary of Chicano slang*. Austin: Jenkins.

Velten, H. W. 1971. The growth of phonemic and lexical patterns in infant language. In *Child language*, ed. A. Bar-Adon, pp. 82–91. Englewood Cliffs, N.J.: Prentice-Hall.

Weinreich, Uriel. 1970. *Languages in contact*. The Hague: Mouton.

10

The social implications of intra-sentential code-switching

RODOLFO JACOBSON

The language behavior of the bilingual draws, by definition, on the resources of two rather than a single language. And, while the relative proficiency in each language is not at issue here, the fact that a speaker possesses the ability to communicate in one as well as in the other language makes him different from other speakers in a very specific way. He copes with the whole universe of experience through two language media and he is never quite sure which one he employs at a given moment. It is therefore no small wonder that he not only switches from one to the other language as he moves from situation to situation but at times he does so within the same situation and even within the same sentence. Hence, it is not unusual to hear a person say, for instance,

(1a) I lose my temper porque a mí me da mucho coraje, me da mucho coraje

rather than saying

(1b) I lose my temper because it makes me so furious, so furious

or

(1c) Me enfurezco porque a mí me da mucho coraje, me da mucho coraje

Code-switching of this sort is usually condemned by the monolingual and disavowed by its user, although it can easily be shown – at least in regard to the preceding example – that "I lose my temper" is more expressive than "me enfurezco" and "it makes me so furious, so furious" does not have the power of expression of "a mí me da mucho coraje, me da mucho coraje." Then, why not use both languages to communicate effectively? Surprisingly little has been investigated and written on the language mixed in bilingual societies and even less on Spanish-English code-switching. Edna Acosta-Belén argues that

> there are virtually no studies that define the parameters of "Spanglish," a so-called dialect that is generally described as a particular mixture of Spanish and

Reprinted with permission from *The New Scholar* 6:227–56 (1977).

English and which is presumably used by Spanish-speaking communities in the United States . . . There is a widespread negative attitude towards its use, which creates feelings of inferiority and alienation for those who allegedly use it. [Acosta-Belén 1975, P. 151]

Guadalupe Valdés-Fallis, on the other hand, refers to two such studies (Gingràs 1974 and Lance 1975) but agrees that

at this point there are no definite answers concerning the exact nature of code-switching as it exists in specific Mexican-American communities and many questions are still unanswered. [Valdés-Fallis 1975, P. 143]

It is therefore imperative that researchers in the Southwest begin to address themselves to this aspect of bilingual behavior and attempt to determine what the status of code-switching is and, particularly, which hidden cues may be triggering the surfacing of one or the other language. It is the objective of the present chapter to explore some of the facets of code-switching and to suggest interpretations that appear linguistically, sociologically and psychologically sound. These interpretations have resulted from the analysis of data gathered locally by several students at the University of Texas at San Antonio. (See Appendix.)

Some theoretical considerations

Terms like "Tex-Mex," "Spanglish," and other similar terms have been used indiscriminately to refer to the fact that some speakers of Spanish and English use the resources of both languages when they wish to communicate to one another, especially in informal situations. In the professional literature the term "code-switching" has been used in this context but most sociolinguistic investigators are aware of the fact that not all instances of language mixing can be considered code-switching in the true sense of the word. Lexical borrowings from the other language, regardless of whether or not they are phonologically or morphologically integrated into the receiving language, do not normally reflect code-switching practices. Consider the following statements:[1]

(2) Te acuerdas de la *word?* (CL-4.6)
(3) Terminé el *first semester* del *twelfth grade* . . . (CL-5.4-5)
(4) . . . y van a comer blanquillos, *cookies y orange*. (CL-8.9-10)
(5) . . . y pos lo *mixtea* . . . (CL-9.12)

There is no intent here to alternate between two codes; the English words or phrases merely lend themselves better to convey the speaker's message as he does not seem to have available, at the moment, the correct Spanish idiom.[2] There is even less code alternation involved when the speaker

[1] Codes following the displayed sentences are the initials of the fieldworker, page of the transcription, and line of entry.

[2] I am here treating *mixtea* as an English word although the source *mix* has already been incorporated into Spanish by following Spanish suffixation rules.

shows first language interference in pronouncing or constructing sentences in a second language. True code-switching, on the other hand, occurs when the bilingual alternates between sentences,

(6) I don't need to be called anything else. Ahora, ser americana no me ha quitado sino que me ha agregado mucho más . . . (FM-9.17–19)

or when he switches to his second language within the same sentence.

(7) for example you are the first maestro que tenga cargado [!] y mira a sus niños and salen todos por allí – entonces they have a little bit of order, . . . (WR-2.34–35)

It is mainly this latter kind of alternation that the present chapter intends to examine and analyze in terms of its relationship to various linguistic and sociolinguistic criteria.

The distinction between competence and performance, suggested by Noam Chomsky in the mid 50s, is by now a familiar notion and has been accepted by most language researchers. The use of the two terms is also appropriate in this context if we could assume, for the present, that utterances containing elements from two languages follow specific patterns of co-occurrence and constraints and display therefore the same rule-governed behavior that we normally associate with a uni-language code. Studies along these lines are almost non-existent and Rosario Gingràs' paper, "Problems in the Description of Spanish-English Intrasentential Code-Switching," is one of the very few attempts to examine the code-switching practices of Mexican-American bilinguals from a linguistic viewpoint. Gingràs (1974) argues that

> some sentences . . . have an overwhelming degree of acceptability in comparison to some other sentences . . . which are sentences that seem to have random ordering of linguistic codes . . . [P. 172]

(8a) The man que vino ayer wants to buy un carro nuevo (p. 167)

and

(8b) El man que came ayer wants John comprar a car nuevo (P. 168)

were recorded and played back to a group of Mexican-American and Anglo bilingual informants "to see if acceptability judgments could be elicited for sentences containing examples of code-switching . . ." (Gingràs 1974, p. 170). The very tentative conclusion from that paper suggests that there is indeed a linguistic competence of code-switching, since bilinguals intuitively accept or reject different instances of language alternation. A code-switching grammar could accordingly be designed to determine which mixed sentences are and which are not acceptable.

Early transformationalists proposed a distinction between a matrix and a constituent sentence to account for the embedding of one clause within another,

(9a) The man saw a car on the road (Matrix)
(9b) The man wore a sweater (Constituent S)
(9c) The man who wore a sweater saw a car on the road (Embedded S)

or

(10a) The man wore a sweater (Matrix)
(10b) The man saw a car on the road (Constituent S)
(10c) The man who saw a car on the road wore a sweater (Embedded S)

Sentences with constituents from two languages could be described in a similar fashion by having one language, either one, provide the matrix and the other, the constituent string,

(11a) The man wants to buy a car (Matrix)
(11b) El hombre vino ayer (Constituent S)
(11c) The man que vino ayer wants to buy a car (Embedded S & Matrix)
(11d) El carro es nuevo (Constituent S)
(11e) The man que vino ayer wants to buy un carro que es nuevo (Embedded S_1)
(11f) The man que vino ayer wants to buy un carro nuevo (Embedded S_2)

or

(12a) El hombre quiere comprar un carro (Matrix)
(12b) The man came yesterday (Constituent S)
(12c) El hombre who came yesterday quiere comprar un carro (Embedded S_2)
(12d) The car is new (Constituent S)
(12e) El hombre who came yesterday quiere comprar a car that is new (Embedded S_1)
(12f) El hombre who came yesterday quiere comprar a car new (Embedded S_2)
(12g) El hombre who came yesterday quiere comprar a new car (Embedded S_3)

Either embedding process seems to be valid as long as words that are constituents in one language can freely be substituted by the corresponding words that are the constituents in the other language.

An examination of the data collected in this project reveals that the switching does not necessarily occur at clause level alone. As a matter of fact, phrases, words and other constituents can be alternated as well.

(13) NP I am going to do it because of . . . *sabrosura del change*. (FM-5.7)
(14) VP *Este* group *se levanta(n)*, await, *va*, that way you have an organization going through and they have a system (R-2.19)
(15) VP Al fin me hizo caso a mí y a tu madre y se, you know, *dress'up a little bit*, siquiera un poquito . . . (EC-9.7)
(16) Adj. Phr. (Man) Because I consider it *muy sabroso*. (FM-5.4)
(17) Adv. Phr. (Loc) It was the day you went *al parque*. (WR-1.8)

(18) Marker Phase I bless home, *lo que sea* (FM-2.2)
(19) Marker Phase . . . but even dad brings in some words *y todo* (FM-7.21)
(20) Conj. *Pero* in the case of X, Canales, I'm proud of X . . . (EC-12.16)
(21) Conj. And I'll tell you another thing *que* I'd shoot anybody that comes in my house (FM-1.17)
(22) Conj. *Y* and then she told me one time that she caught herself doing it because it was so much easier sometimes . . . (FM-5.17)
(23) S Mod *Entonces*, now that to me is kind of . . . (FM-7.19)

Alternations at the phrase level occur mainly when noun phrases (13) and adjectival phrases (16 and 17) are objects of the switching. Verb phrase switching is rarer but does also occur (14 and 15). Especially interesting is item (15) where the verb phrase contains a Spanish (the reflexive *se*) and an English element (the past tense form *dress'-up*). Observe that only the Spanish verb is reflexive (se vistió), suggesting that the speaker's frame of mind was Spanish-oriented regardless of the English reflexification. Other instances of phrase level switchings are of the type that Gumperz and Hernández-Chávez (1975) call "ethnic markers" and are illustrated in (18) and (19). Alternations at the word level when these are not lexical borrowings are more often than not conjunctions. The data include some examples of the coordinate conjunctions *pero* (20) and *Y* (22) and to a lesser extent also the subordinate *que* (21). The sentence modifier *entonces* (23), which also occurred, presents another instance of a single word code-switching.

The above is obviously not intended to be a formal nor a full linguistic analysis of co-occurrences and constraints but rather an attempt to include examples of the linguistic nature of some alternations observed in the data. To summarize, the co-occurrence of elements from two languages seems to be favored when entire phrases or clauses are unilingual. Conjunctions, on the other hand, are often conceived of as independent constituents and can occur in one language while the remainder of the clause occurs in the other. All this suggests that constraints do exist but mainly when the constituent structure is broken into units below the phrase level. The one instance where no such blocking occurred (se *dress'-up*) may well have been the result of a slip of the tongue, since the bilingual informants whom we consulted indicated that they would not normally use this construction. Work along these lines is imperative and a more vigorous analysis of code-switching data should help us identify co-occurrence and constraints of what seems to emerge as a social variety used in certain situations by Spanish and English speaking bilinguals in the southwestern United States.

Recent developments in psycholinguistic and sociolinguistic studies have alerted us to go beyond the mere analysis of the code and to investigate aspects of linguistic performance, since both inner and outer factors influence actual speech. From a psycholinguistic point of view, code-switching practices bear a certain relationship to three areas: (1) the acquisition of a second language and the type of bilinguality achieved, (2) the encoding and decoding strategies of code-switching bilinguals, and (3) the attitudinal patterns toward the switching regardless of whether or not the bilinguals actually engage in it.

It has been argued that the acquisition of a second language and the type of bilinguality achieved are closely related to one another. Scholars who study second language acquisitional patterns have stressed, again and again, that we should distinguish the compound from the coordinate bilingual since the former has learned the second language in the home and the latter in an environment outside the home. As for the code-switching tendencies of bilinguals, the evidence seems to indicate that code-switching is favored by compound bilinguals and objected to or, at best, only reluctantly implemented by coordinates. Gingràs (1974) seems to refer to the compound/coordinate distinction because

> . . . judgments on code-switching are influenced by the time of acquisition of the second language: before or after onset of puberty. The Chicano informants all began speaking English by the time they entered the first grade; on the other hand, the non-Chicano informants all acquired their second language as adults. This implies that judgments on code-switching and the actual use thereof are a function not so much of the fact that a person is bilingual, but rather a function of when he became a bilingual. [P. 171]

All this lends credit to Barker's (1975) notion that "where two languages are involved, the functions formerly performed by one language come to be divided by two or more . . ." (p. 171). Although, in the case of the compound bilingual, rather than undergoing a division of functions, he experiences the coalescence of functions regardless of the language employed. In other words, the compound bilingual functions through the medium of two languages just as the monolingual does it through the medium of the only language that he knows. The bilingual's encoding and decoding processes must obviously be based on the understanding of how a truly bilingual community functions. I differ here from the view of other scholars who consider the coordinate bilingual the true bilingual, since neither type impresses me as more truly bilingual than the other. By relating the bilingual's interpersonal relations with the variations in his linguistic behavior, Barker (1975) suggests that the fields of familial/intimate and of Anglo/Mexican-American relations,

> . . . may be represented as a kind of continuum, at one end of which are the intimate relations with others of Mexican descent, while at the other end are the purely formal relations with Anglos. In between are formal and informal relations with people of Mexican descent outside the family circle, and in some cases with Mexicans from Mexico. Paralleling the above described continuum in fields of interpersonal relations is a continuum in language usage, and we find that the

categories of interpersonal relations are reflected by corresponding variations in linguistic behavior. At one end of this linguistic continuum Spanish is dominant in the individual's contacts and at the other end English is dominant. In between are the pochismos, the Pachuco dialect, and the various mixtures of the two languages. [P. 178]

Depending upon the type of bilinguality that speakers have acquired, they will tend to either bring together (compound) or keep separate (coordinate) the two extremes of the spectrum and I cannot think of one or the other approach as being the better. I have recently suggested a similar continuum (Jacobson, 1977) but focused there more specifically on the individual member rather than the community's total range of verbal repertoires. Obviously, the same individual is not expected to shift from Spanish dominance to Pocho to Pachuco to Tex-Mex and further on to English dominance but he will combine different ways of speaking and alternate between such styles as the occasion may suggest to him. In addition, the bilingual who engages in code-switching may achieve the mixing of the two languages by means of two different strategies, his language structure may be basically Spanish but contain English constituents or it may be basically English with Spanish constituents, inserted into it, although I am not yet quite certain as to the extent to which a bilingual is aware of whether he has chosen the former or the latter to convey his message. Encoding and decoding is mainly a subconscious strategy and it is the message on which the speaker focuses rather than the medium – or media – in which he conveys it. Most bilinguals are usually unaware of the fact which language they have chosen to express their ideas but they will certainly remember what the message is that they have conveyed.

The research conducted by social psychologists in Canada and also in the United States has shown that monolinguals and bilinguals hold strong attitudes in regard to the speech varieties that they use. This is even more true with respect to the mixing of two speech varieties. Edna Acosta-Belén (1975) finds

there is a widespread negative attitude towards its [Spanish] use, which creates feelings of inferiority and alienation for those who allegedly use it. [P. 151]

This negative attitude, however, does not seem to exert any refraining force on the code-switching practices as long as these are performed in an informal, relaxed or intimate atmosphere, usually only among members of the same ethnic group. Gumperz and Hernández-Chávez (1975) express this same view when they argue that

in spite of the fact that such extreme code-switching is held in disrepute, it is very persistent, occurring whenever minority language groups come in close contact with majority language groups under conditions of rapid social change. [P. 155]

The bilingual who engages in the mixing of the two languages to the extent that he either denies ever switching at all or refrains from it when he is observed or recorded indicates the low esteem in which the practice is held. This is even the case when the observer is a member of the same ethnic group. A case in point is the comment of one of the fieldworkers in this project to the effect that it had been relatively easy for her, as a Mexican-American and a peer of her informants, to witness code-switching practices but extremely difficult to record these on tape. "The informants were code-switching continuously when the recorder was turned off but when it was on, they would only speak a single language." Therefore interviews designed to collect data on language mixing must be conducted with even greater care than what Labov and his associates suggested (Giglioli 1972, pp. 179–215) because they represent a verbal behavior that is strongly disapproved of by the majority.

In addition to the psycholinguistic concerns of this nature there are a number of sociolinguistic factors that all relate to the code-switching phenomenon. In the literature of the last decade, we find many references to issues that hold a strong relationship to the strategies of certain bilinguals to mix their two languages, not only as they move from topic to topic but also within the same topic. Scholars have discussed in this context the social situation, the norms of interaction, domains, several issues concerning cultural heritage, ethnicity and acculturation and the problem of language choice. The social situation comprises: (1) the interlocutors involved in the speech event, (2) the topic under discussion, and (3) the intent with which the speakers are discussing the topic. Whether or not code-switching is appropriate may result from the appraisal of the situation because if the interlocutors are not those with whom the individual would engage in code-switching, if the topic is too formal for such a strategy and, finally, if the intent is not one of relaxed communication, no mixing is likely to occur. In the bilingual community, as in any other community for that matter, there is a universally shared knowledge in regard to the manner by which its members interact with one another, that is, of their mutually shared interactional norms. Accordingly, the linguistic behavior of the bilingual as well as their own assessment of that behavior has made it clear to us that bilinguals hold very firm views as to when they can and cannot code-switch. These views then, represent the set of norms which they follow at a given moment. In other words, there is a consensus as to where, on the bilingual continuum, they wish to function at a given moment. Their language performance, whichever they have decided on, hinges of course on their ability to be in proper command of their bilingual behavior. Assume that an individual recognizes that, in principle, a monolingual English interaction is called for but that his usual experience leads him to mix the two languages, then his monolingual attitude will merely be reflected by performing less bilingually; that is, he will code-switch less than he normally does. By the same token, if the same individual, under different circumstances, decides that a monolingual Spanish interaction would be appropriate, he may not be entirely successful in his exclusion of English but his speech will tend to be more Spanish dominant than normal.

In order for the bilingual to make a decision of this nature, he must possess a strong awareness for the congruency of a situation and thus be able to correlate a speaker's language variety with one of several social institutions. In the next context of home, peer group, school, church, or employment one such variety is usually appropriate and the others may not be. However, even these domains may still be too broad, since more than one variety may be appropriate in the context of some of these institutions, depending upon the specific circumstances that prevail. Thus, some situations, whatever *domain* they may be associated with, are handled by bilinguals better when the two languages are used in alternation than when they are not. Code-switching, then, assumes a function that is equivalent to that of any other regional or social variety and must be treated accordingly.

Three other notions, "cultural heritage," "ethnicity" and "acculturation," can also be viewed in terms of a continuum, since all three are continually present in the bilingual but their relative potency fluctuates depending on the social situation under consideration. All three are liable to produce reflexes in the speech of bilinguals, either by way of full statements or simple markers,

(24) . . . porque no me contaran como era (FM-9.22–23)
(25) quien tiene el modismo [!] de haberse criado aqui le va [a] sacar la sabrosura de . . , (FM-6.21–22)
(26) . . . He started at . . . bueno . . . this year (EC-12.17)
(27) Perdón, las llaves de García para entrar . . . wow, ¿cuál es? . . . (WR-1.13)

In (24) the speaker switches to Spanish when she justifies her stay in Mexico where she wanted to experience on her own what the Mexican heritage was all about so that others would not have to tell her how it was. The switch to Spanish in (25) carries the meaning of the beauty of one's ethnicity. The person who has been reared here, the speaker argues, appreciates the *sabrosura*, tastefulness, of code-switching. Brief switches to Spanish like *bueno*, (EC 12.17) *lo que sea, y todo, pos, ándale pués* all seem to be ethnic markers, that is, verbal affirmations of Mexican-American ethnicity. However, bilinguals may also wish to affirm the opposite, i.e., the fact that they have made accommodation to the majority society. The interjection *wow* in (27) seems to accomplish just that. Thus, the code-switching bilingual moves forth and back on the continuum of bilinguality to express in words or phrases the extent to which his heritage, his ethnicity and his integration into the society at large vary during the speech performance.

The bilingual, far more than the monolingual speaker, is faced with a series of language-related decisions through which he reveals that he has examined the social situation, he has assessed it to the best of his knowledge, and has made the language choice that the situation demands of him. Whereas this is also true to some extent of the monolingual, the latter makes stylistic decisions deemed suitable for sex, class, context, and so forth, and does not cross language boundaries, nor does he have to engage the unusual strategy of mixing two languages with varying proportions of representation where each resulting mixture opens up socially significant communicative experiences. To engage in intra-sentential code-switching then implies that cues of a psychological or sociological nature have consciously or unconsciously been identified and that a linguistic decision has been made to attend to precisely those cues. It is here assumed that by collecting speech data from bilinguals who interact with other bilinguals and live in a bilingual community where they have acquired the interactional norms that we have discussed above, we are able to identify the cues that trigger the shifting from one to the other language. In other words, we would like to think that as a bilingual switches from, say, English to Spanish or the reverse he has a reason for doing so and that these reasons can be considered psycholinguistic or sociolinguistic cues present either in the bilingual himself or in the bilingual's environment and are reacted to by him as he engages in making the decision or decisions of which language variety to use in each instance.

The present study is based on the above assumption and it is contended that the data collected do indeed reveal why the code-switching occurs in the first place and what social significance the language alternation holds for each participant in the speech event.

The linguistic perspective

I have suggested above that the embedding of a constituent sentence into a matrix sentence and the embedding of a stretch of speech in language B into a stretch of speech in language A bear some mutual relationship. Hence, I will refer in this section to the switching of codes as code-embedding and call the stretch of speech into which "other language" material is inserted, the matrix code, and the stretch of speech that is embedded, the constituent code. Either one of the two languages can supply matrix and constituent codes depending upon the speaker's intent to choose, say, an English or a Spanish frame for his utterance. Consider the following two lines of a conversation between an interviewer and his informant:

(28) EC: Todavía está allá en *University City*?
Mother: No, pero they're going to move him to Windsor . . . (EC-6.13)

The mother responds to the question by beginning her response in Spanish but embeds into the Spanish matrix code the English constituent code "they are going to move him to Windsor . . . ," which is an independent clause. However, note:

(29) Lisa: . . . It's been criticized by Mexicanos of the other side, very, very much because they don't understand it, they can't feel it. If I'm talking to you en español, puro español toda la frase, y de repente . . . (FM-6.15–19)

The whole thought process is in English, it is what we may call an English frame but, for reasons that are here irrelevant, the informant switches to Spanish to complete the utterance. Obviously, it is an example of an English matrix code into which a Spanish constituent code is embedded. The transition occurs at a point where the English construction is reasonably complete, grammatically speaking, since the subject, the verb and the object are fully expressed but to complete the message, the speaker is adding a prepositional phrase and does it in Spanish without interfering with the grammaticality of the English portion of the utterance. Observe, the informant did not say,

(30a) If I'm talking to Ud. en español

nor

(30b) If I'm talking to you in español

but switched when it was grammatically least offensive in both languages. Occasional violations of grammatical constraints, however, occurred in the recordings but were seldom, e.g.,

(31) . . . ya sabía que eran dos, three cans for each machine (R-2.2–3)
(32) . . . for example you are the first maestro que tenga cargado [!] . . . (R-2.34)
(33) Este group se levantan [!], wait, va; that way you have . . . (R-2.17)

The speaker switches here within the grammatical unit, i.e., the phrase, but still without seriously offending the listener's linguistic competence as the literal translation of the word in the constituent code renders a unilingual utterance that is grammatically sound.

Note that

. . . ya sabía que eran dos, tres latas para cada máquina;
. . . por ejemplo Ud. es el primer maestro que tenga cargado[!]
. . . This group stands up, waits, goes; that way you have . . .

do not reflect grammatical violations and since they are unusual occurrences, they do not actually invalidate the view that alternations normally occur at the beginning of a constituent, thus, to prevent the code-switching from violating a grammatical rule of any one of the two languages. Clause-level and phrase-level switches, when they are not borrowings, are limited to adverbs, conjunctions or sentence modifiers. A study with greater emphasis on the purely linguistic perspective of the phenomenon should investigate, in greater detail, which constructions from the two languages can or cannot co-occur in the sentence. On the other hand, these tentative interpretations of the collected data seem to suggest that there are serious constraints when the code alternation involves the violation of a rule in one of the codes. Therefore, Gingràs's (1974) example that was rejected by the Mexican-American bilingual informants,

(34) El man que came ayer wants John comprar a car nuevo [P. 170]

could not have occurred as too many grammatical rules are here violated. The frame here is obviously English, since it is only in English that we can say "wants John to buy," whereas in Spanish it would be "quería que Juan comprara." As a result, "wants John comprar" represents a major violation of Spanish grammar. The same may be said about "a car nuevo" which violates the English adjective positioning rule since an adjective must precede the noun in English. Future studies, it is hoped, will show in greater detail where the boundary between acceptable and unacceptable code-switching utterances lies. A study of this nature would contribute meaningfully to the writing of a Spanish/English code-switching grammar.

The psycho-sociolinguistic perspective

In the preceding section the purely *linguistic* analysis of utterances containing elements of two languages is treated only briefly since this is not the major thrust of the chapter. An analysis of this nature, however, suggests itself as a pressing topic of investigation. The present section intends to consider code-switching, not from the viewpoint of linguistic competence, but of linguistic performance and to consider it first with *psycholinguistic* and then with *sociolinguistic* factors in mind. In other words, the question here is not what grammatical rules can be identified to account for sentences with constituents from two languages, but rather why the code-switching occurs in the first place and which factors or variables make the individual switch from language A to language B or vice versa. It is my contention that the switching from one to the other language is not a random behavior but can be explained as a reflex of psychological and sociological factors of which the speaker may or may not be aware. Regardless of whether or not the person is aware of switching or the factors leading to the switching, these factors must be identified by the researcher as he examines the speech samples of bilinguals who engage in code-switching strategies. Whether psychologically conditioned, these factors are actually cues that trigger language alternation and future research should show the potency of each cue and the conditions under which one cue weakens or even annuls the effect of another. Even this somewhat preliminary research has already shown that several

Table 1. *Toward a theory of code-switching*

A. Semicode-switching	B. Psychologically conditioned code-switching	C. Sociologically conditioned code-switching
1. BORROWING	1. SUBSTRATUM	1. CODE
2. TERMINOLOGY	2. EMOTION	2. DOMAIN
3. CALQUE	3. HESITATION	3. CULTURE
4. ACCESS	4. FALSE START	4. INTERPERSONAL RELATIONS
	5. PREFERENCE	5. TOPIC
		6. METAPHOR

psycholinguistic and sociolinguistic categories and subcategories must be postulated if we wish to come to grips with the nature of code-switching. More specifically, the analysis of the data has supported, first of all, the fact that not all language mixing can be considered true instances of code-switching. It has been previously argued that the borrowing of a word from the other language, regardless of whether or not it has been integrated into the receiving language phonologically or morphologically (borrowing/pochismo), is not an instance of code-switching, nor are loan translations (calque) and words or terms of easiest access. In the latter, the speaker has merely relexified portions of his utterances but without switching to the grammatical system of the second code (easy access). All these instances are best referred to as semicode-switching (see Table 1, A. 1–4) and include four subcategories, (a) borrowing (b) terminology (c) calque and (d) access.

(35) . . . en donde pasa el *expressway?* (EC-1.12)
(36) . . . pa' *lonche* o qué? (EC-3.16)
(37) . . . eh, *bilingual education* en otras palabras. (VC-9.16-17)
(38) . . . I think it is cold right now, *¿no?* (EC-5.11-12)
(39) . . . No, pos yo estaba undecided. (EC-15-.19)

Items (35) and (36) are instances of borrowing, the former without phonological integration into the receiving language and the latter with it. Item (37) contains a technical term, *bilingual education,* which is used in the language in which the term is heard most frequently. The occurrence of *¿no?* in (39) rather than *isn't it?* is remindful of the Spanish *¿no?,* a short form of *¿no es cierto?* and is therefore classified as a calque or a loan translation. *Undecided* and not *indecisa* (39) was at the tip of the informant's tongue. Had she made a stronger effort, she would probably have come up with the Spanish word but in an informal, relaxed situation, there was no apparent need for it and she picked the word to which she had easier access.

From the category of "semicode-switching," on the other hand, are distinguished two other categories, true code-switching in nature, i.e., (1) "phychologically conditioned code-switching" and (2) "sociologically conditioned code-switching" each of which divides again into several subcategories. Table 1 gives the reader the overview of the three major categories and their various subcategories, fifteen in all, that account for the language mixing occurrences identified in this project. "Semicode-switching" and its subcategories have already been considered briefly above. The remainder of this section will therefore be devoted to a discussion of the true code-switching sources, specified under B and C in Table 1. Some of these sources (B) can be said to be psychologically conditioned and others (C), sociologically conditioned. The former are results of individual encoding strategies, that is, they are psycholinguistically conditioned phenomena. The latter reflect responses to certain cues in the social environment, that is, they are sociolinguistically conditioned phenomena.

"Psychologically conditioned code-switching" encompasses five subcategories of which we have recorded numerous examples. Note:

(40a) And I tell you another thing *que* I'd shoot anybody . . . (FM-1.14)
(40b) Te vas *even* con éste así . . . (VC-7.12)
(40c) *Entonces,* now that, to me, is kind of . . . (FM-7.9)

Although the speaker's intent is to speak language B, words or phrases from language A surface unwillingly as a result of the speaker's language dominance. Items (40a) and (40c) are instances where a Spanish conjunction or a sentence modifier surface; in (40b) it is an English adverb that emerges. As a matter of fact, it is conjunctions, adverbs, and sentence modifiers which reveal this unintentional surfacing of the SUBSTRATUM (B.1).

William Labov (1972, p. 208) has shown that the speaker who is embarassed or otherwise emotionally involved in the speech situation pays minimum attention to his speech. Our recordings support his findings as the speakers code-switched to their stronger language when the topic touched upon emotional issues and switched back to the other language as the conversation returned to more general matters. Observe:

(41a) Agárrelo con la mano. Lo que guste.
I just wanted . . . Anda, ahí está. (EC-4, 19-20)
(41b) I lose my temper *porque a mi me da mucho coraje,* (FM-1.15-16)

In (41a), the English-dominant fieldworker switches unwillingly to English to express his embarrassment but returns to Spanish when he has mastered the situation. The contrary occurs in (41b) where the Spanish-dominant speaker code-switches to Spanish to express her indignation more fully. Thus, EMOTION (B.2) appears to be a valid subcategory to reveal one of the speakers' inner cues that are capable of triggering the switch from the weaker to the stronger language.

Hesitation pauses are common among speakers of all languages as the individual grasps for the appropriate word or words to complete his utterance. Speakers, however, differ in the way they fill these pauses, e.g.,

(42) And, *uh*, I've gone out to North Texas . . . (VC-5.21)
(43) . . . she would tell me things – *este* – you know. (FM-5.11)

The English-dominant bilingual usually uses the English-speaking monolingual's hesitation vowel "*uh*" /e/, whereas the Spanish-dominant person instinctively inserts the Spanish-speaking monolingual's "*este*" /este/. Thus HESITATION (B.3) appears as an informative reflex of language dominance.

On the other hand, the speaker who makes a false start in one language often attempts to recast the message in the other language to communicate more effectively and then switches back to the language that had been chosen as a medium of communication in the first place. FALSE START (B.4) as a code-switching source is found in the following two utterances:

(44) Sí, pos tienen ahí hasta unas – *I hadn't . . . I never even seen some of those*. (EC-25.11-12)
(45) It takes – *es más despacio la manera esa*. (EC-25.11-12)

Obviously, (44) illustrates the situation in which a bilingual begins in Spanish but fails to get the message across. He therefore shifts to English and completes his utterance successfully. Item (45) illustrates the reverse: the speaker shifts from English to Spanish for greater ease of communication.

In some instances, however, no obvious psychological source could be identified. The code-switching seems to be the result of the speaker's preference of one code over the other. When the informant responds in English to a Spanish utterance as in

(46) una cortina nada más
What you need is the strip . . . (R-1.16-17)

or when he speaks in Spanish after he is addressed in English as in

(47) See you all later
¿Adónde? *Oyes, X, ven para acá, hijito*. (EC-5.14-15)

both seem to suggest that the respondent merely felt more inclined toward using a language other than the one in which he was addressed. Unless future data suggest a different interpretation, PREFERENCE (B.5) seems to describe effectively those instances that cannot be classified according to the previously suggested "psychologically conditioned code-switching" subcategories.

"Sociologically conditioned code-switching" is the other major code-switching category that was found to encompass six minor categories, say, subcategories which, because of their complexities, had to be subdivided into even smaller units in order to interpret the available data more effectively. Table 2 provides the reader with the complete listing of all subcategories and sub-subcategories of the "sociologically conditioned code-switching" category. Because of the limitations of space the analysis will be confined to significant subcategories rather than an exhaustive treatment of each subcategory.

CODE (C.1) as a code-switching source implies the notion that certain decisions concerning language choice depend entirely upon language matters, such as those specified in Table 2 (a-g). These decisions include (a) in which language one should initiate a response; (b) whether or not one should continue speech in the same code; (c) in which language one should discuss a matter that he has heard before; (d) in which language one should argue a point that regards either one or the other language; (e) whether or not one should quote in the language in which a conversation went on originally; (f) whether or not one should switch to the language in which an argument was advanced; (g) whether or not one should alternate languages because his interlocutor seemed not to have understood; and finally (h) whether or not the existence of a precoined utterance like a proverb or a metaphor warrants the language switch. The following data seem to support the validity of most of the preceding queries.

(48) . . . I wished they'd come more often! *You ought to get on the phone* [Speaker initiates response in the language in which he was addressed but switches later.] – y dijo mamá que vinieran a visitar, ¿yes? (EC-3.20-23)

(49) Every time we go out, I bless it before we go out y todo. [Speaker has switched to Spanish for a reason other than the one under consideration here and now decides to continue using the code to which he has just switched.] *Pero ser precabida.*[3]

(50) And, uh, I've gone out to North Texas [Speaker intends to discuss an experience that is normally discussed in Spanish and switches therefore to that language.] *a levantar el pepino.*[4] (VC-5.21)

(51) Ah, no – it's not a sound problem it's more of a . . . like . . . [Speaker hesitates because it makes little sense to talk about Spanish in English and switches to Spanish therefore.] *como donde acentúa uno la palabra.* (VC-12.9-10)

(52) [Speaker quotes on English-speaking monolingual.] "How long have you been here?" [He switches to Spanish because it is the language in which the conversation is carried on but switches back to English later on when he quotes himself responding in English.] Pos le decía "*twenty-nine, thirty years.*" (EC-10.1-2)

(53) . . . pero the whole thing is that . . . [Speaker recalls a Spanish saying and switches therefore.] *como dicen diferentes países, diferentes cos-*

[3] The use of Spanish could also be justified in terms of a precoined utterance, i.e., *ser precabida vale por dos.*

[4] Here, the use of Spanish could also result from the fact that migrant work is culturally restricted to the Mexican-American and thus evokes Spanish language use.

tumbres. [To continue, speaker switches back to English.] She was born over there, I was born over here. (FM-9.11-13)

DOMAIN (C.2), another code-switching factor, has been here recognized as a valid construct and our data support the findings of Greenfield and Fishman (Ghosh 1972, pp. 64–86) and others who sustain that home or family, neighborhood, church, employment and school all evoke in the speaker very definite language patterns such that the violation of these patterns creates extremely incongruent situations. On the basis of our data, we have succeeded in isolating five domains: (a) home/family, (b) church, (c) employment, (d) school, and (e) business. Neighborhood did not emerge as a separate domain from home/family which may be the result of the scarcity of the data rather than the lack of validity of the domain in question. Note the following code-switching instances in our transcriptions:

(54) . . . since he has been here fifty years *pero mis hermanos no hablan el Español también como yo because* . . . (FM-7.21-23)

(55) X quería "tie" ¿Te acuerdas? *He wants a tie, coat.* ¿A la iglesia? (EC-7.9-11)

(56) ¿No?
Si. *He is going to be training for a manager right now.* (EC-6.7-9)

(57) No, pos a mí también me traen de una ala. *I got an exam Wednesday night and I got to correct some papers for my American History classes* . . . (EC-24.17-20)

(58) Ah, hijo, me están haciendo garras, "cousin." *Insurance.* Oye y *those guys are going to raise the rates,* ¿verdad? (EC-23.10-11)

The home/family domain triggers the switch to Spanish (54), whereas employment (56), school (57) and business (58) work the opposite way, that is, they favor the switch to English. The church domain (55) is as contradictory in the Mexican-American sample as it was in other studies (Ghosh 1972, pp. 64–86). Formal dressing (tie, coat) seems to suggest the population or parishioners at large – hence, English – the parish itself (iglesia) stresses church as a Mexican institution – hence, Spanish.

A person's code is obviously part and parcel of his culture; however, certain cultural facts are not code-related, so that it seemed to make sense to postulate CULTURE (C.3) as a separate code-switch triggering element. In other words, if a speaker wishes to comment upon an issue that is more closely related to culture A, he is prone to switch to the language that the members associated with that culture normally speak. Observe the following examples:

(59) It was the day you went *al parque.* (R-16)

(60) *En México si un* three- or four-year-old, – you have them "recitando." (FM-12.10-11)

(61) *Ándale*, that's probably the best bet. (EC-22.5)

(62) *Oh yeah, uh-huh,* hasta allí si. (VC-4.5)

(63) I went only for one sole reason to Mexico: *porque no me contaran como era*. I went when I was twenty *a la capital*. (FM-9.22-23)

(64) Well, you do a lot of P.R., *cuando vienen las mamases, muy bien, tienes que calmarlas*. (VC-1.3-5)

(65) Ah, bueno, como estás grabando, *I'll take the fifth amendment on that one*. (VC-1.12-13)

(66) Boy, let me tell you that girl Thursday at the "bonco" *tenía tripitas, carne de puerco con pozole* . . . (FM-11.10-14)

Al parque (59) rather than "to the park" suggests a location in the Spanish-speaking barrio or downtown San Antonio area. By the same token, *en México* and not "in Mexico" is seen as the appropriate way of talking about the homeland. Similar to language dominance, we can also talk about culture dominance, such that the Hispanic culture dominant person tends to choose ethnic markers like *ándale* (61) and the Anglo culture dominant prefers markers like *oh, yeah* (62). Mexican heritage is argued more meaningfully in Spanish; hence, *porque no me contaran como era* (63) describes more effectively the desire of a Mexican-American to experience life in Mexico than would, say, "so that others would not have to tell me about it." Likewise, to refer to Mexico City as *la capital* implies a greater understanding of things Mexican than would "la Ciudad de Mexico" or simply Mexico City. *Las mamases* (64) are not just mothers of any children but Mexican-American mothers who, in their majority, are Spanish-speaking monolinguals. Even though the person is speaking Spanish, he could hardly refer to *the fifth amendment* (65) as "la quinta enmienda" and capture at the same time the political significance of this American legal concept. Finally, talking about what some Mexican-Americans call the *bonco* and referring to the Mexican dishes that were served there can be done in no language other than Spanish because how else would you refer to *tripitas, carne de puerco* and *pozole* (66)?

Speakers tend to adjust style and lexicon depending upon the person or persons whom they address, the topics that they select and other elements of the social situation. It is not surprising, therefore, that bilinguals switch from one to the other language to comply with these norms of social interaction. Our data have shown that this is particularly the case when there is a change of interlocutors. Thus, INTERPERSONAL RELATIONS (C.4) often determine whether English or Spanish is appropriate regardless of which language is spoken at a given point in time. This becomes particularly noticeable when a different person is suddenly addressed during the same speech event. Furthermore, not only talking to but talking about certain persons with whom one but not the other language is normally associated may determine the language choice.

(67) [one sibling to the other] X, get it.
[mother to interviewer] Es pa' él. A estas horas, es pa' él. (EC-3.1-3)

(68) [to mother] Con la misma chaqueta por cuatro años.
[mother to daughter] ¿Quién?
[wife (daughter) to husband] You are the one wearing the same jacket. (EC-7.19-21)

(69) [daughter to interviewer] You know what likes the meat most of all? My chin.
[interviewer to daughter] Mis barbas.
[daughter to mother] ¿Cómo está tio Eloy ahorita, 'amá? (EC-3.7-9)

(70) [about Spanish-speaking monolinguals] And now we take some of J.T. up to Grenet[5] pero las mamases no quieren que vengan los niños aquí, – *so it's a privilege* . . . (VC-3.27-4.2)

(71) [about an English-speaking monolingual] And when you are talking to Mrs. Green or . . . do you feel uncomfortable with her?
Uh-huh
Because it has to be all English. (VC-11.18-21)

Items (67-69) illustrate the switch in code depending upon the participants in the speech event. Younger siblings will speak in English to one another (67) but the mother prefers Spanish regardless of the person to whom she talks. The married daughter addresses her husband in English although she responds to a question by her mother in Spanish (68). A younger daughter addresses the interviewer in English – most likely, the language that they normally use in non-experimental situations – but when she addresses her mother she switches to Spanish (69). Items (70–71), in turn, show that the notion of INTERPERSONAL RELATIONS can be expanded to include the language switch that results from talking *about* a person or persons with whom we associate the use of a given language. *Las mamases* (70) only speak Spanish and *Mrs. Green* (71) only English, hence, each is treated in the appropriate language.

TOPIC (C.5) in a more general sense, that is, when it is not limited to interpersonal relations, is best treated independently from the above, since it includes too many topical areas. Topics like (a) occupation, (b) financial matters, (c) mechanical concerns, (d) food, (e) numerical details, and (f) various time-related experiences all appear to be important cues that trigger the use of one language and block that of the other. Note:

(72) . . . and I can relate to them, you know, about *levantando la pera, levantando eso o trabajando en la cebolla* . . . you know. (VC-6.10-11)

(73) . . . *We started out with 900 . . . about 950 kids*
¿Y ahora?
And we've got . . . 'mm, what? 530 . . . (VC-3.14-19)

(74) *It's gonna cost me* por las placas *three hundred.*
Bastantito.
Y cobra como *twelve dollars* cada . . . (VC-8.5-7)

(75) Pero estaba pensando *about the maintenance*. (EC-15.21)

[5] *J. T.* and *Grenet* are names of San Antonio elementary schools.

(76) *Forty-two miles,* fíjate.

(77) *Tengo el complejo de que la mamá mexicana siempre estaba "amase, amase" haciendo tortillas. Cuando me casé* I promised myself I wouldn't. (FM-16.2-4)

Depending upon the nature of the occupation, Spanish or English may be the appropriate code to which the speaker switches. The former migrant worker refers to his duties in the language in which these duties were performed. "Picking up pears" and "working in the onion field" would not have been the same (72). The secretary of a school where English is the medium of instruction feels, in turn, more comfortable talking about her work in English, even though the interviewer tried to make her switch to Spanish by asking her the question "*Y ahora?*" and not "And now?" (73). Money matters evoke English in the speech of bilinguals but may be limited to the portion(s) of the sentence that are strictly cost-related. Thus, *It's gonna cost me* and *three hundred* are in English but "por las placas" in Spanish (b). Mechanical matters, whether trade names, terms or merely applied notions, trigger the use of English. "Mantenimiento" would have produced an image different from *maintenance* (75) in the speaker who talks about his automobile within a broader supraethnic framework. Number, measurements and similar notions are mostly learned in the English-speaking school; hence, *forty-two miles* (76) is more acceptable than "cuarentidós millas," in particular because "kilómetros" would in theory be the correct term to use in Spanish but one that is somewhat unfamiliar to those who were reared outside the metric system. Finally, the memory of the remote past evokes in our Mexican-American informant the use of the language that she only spoke at that time. She refers to *la mamá mexicana* in Spanish but switches to English as she refers to more recent times when she was already married and had become more Anglo/English oriented (77).

METAPHOR (C.6) as a code-switching category brings together, under the same heading, a series of stylistic devices that the bilingual employs quite differently from the monolingual as the switch from one to the other language plays there roughly the same role as do unusual intonation patterns, dialect variations or lexical oddities in the speech of those who know only one language. When the informant asks the interviewer (78) "¿Me aprobó[!] mi sopa?" (EC-5.1-2) and then switches to English saying "*Ah, that's good*" and finally switches back to Spanish telling him that it was not a soup mix from a package, she merely intended to establish the *contrast,* by means of the language switch, between her homemade soup and a soup from a can or a package. *Emphasis* is often created by simply restating in the other language what has just been said in the first one, as in

(79) . . . íbamos allí siempre cada año – *we went there every year.* (VC-6.5-6)

Table 2. *Sociologically conditioned code-switching*

1. CODE
   (a) Initiation of response
   (b) Continued speech (after switching)
   (c) Prior code use
   (d) Code as topic
   (e) Quote
   (f) Courtesy
   (g) Clarification
   (h) Pre-coining
2. DOMAIN
   (a) Home/Family
   (b) Church
   (c) Employment
   (d) School
   (e) Business
3. CULTURE
   (a) Geographic/ecological environment
   (b) Culture-conditioned attitude
   (c) Language-locale association
   (d) Cultural bias
   (e) Cultural heritage
   (f) Persons as cultural exponents
   (g) Social/political institution
   (h) Language as culture
   (i) Culture-related custom
4. INTERPERSONAL RELATIONS
   (a) Siblings
   (b) Spouses
   (c) Peers
   (d) Acquaintances
   (e) Employer-employee
   (f) Teacher-student
5. TOPIC
   (a) Occupation
   (b) Financial matters
   (c) Mechanical interests
   (d) Food
   (e) Numerical details
   (f) Time-related experiences
6. METAPHOR
   (a) Contrast
   (b) Emphasis
   (c) Humor
   (d) Parenthetical Remarks

There can be no question as to whether the addressee understood this simple message, so that it seems to be merely a strategy to underscore the Spanish utterance by restating it word by word in English.

Humor is often suggested as another instance of metaphorical switching (Hymes 1974, pp. 53 and 57) but no significant data were recorded (but see José Limón 1977) that could serve as an illustration, although some code-switching instances classified earlier might have been interpreted in this sense (cf. [69]). Future data will, it is hoped, allow us to also support humor as one kind of metaphorical switching.

Certain *parenthetical remarks*, in turn, were accounted for quite regularly and should therefore be included here.

(80) *Dice* "Why is that?" *Dice* "because if you would stop snoring, then I would be able . . ." (CL-15.18-19)

(81) . . . they got in at Dolores' parents with a – *como se llaman estos fierros* – wrench or something like that . . . (FM-1.1-3)

Upon reporting a conversation conducted in English, the speaker is quoting and not translating (80) but the connecting speech is in Spanish, since it is the language in which the dialogue is carried on. The instances of *dice* are thus inserted as if they were between parentheses to remind the interlocutors to which language they would eventually have to revert as soon as no more quotes in English occur in the conversation. A somewhat different type of parenthetical remark occurs in (81) where the speaker tries, as if it were an inner thought overtly expressed, to come up with the right form. The Spanish question *¿Cómo se llaman estos fierros?* is in a sense off the record and does certainly not suggest that the speaker knew the word in Spanish and not in English, as *fierros* is not the right word and "wrench" comes to the speaker's mind later in response to her inner thought question in Spanish.

In conclusion

It has been the objective of the present chapter to examine a body of data collected by five graduate students at UTSA (See Appendix) and to determine, after a careful analysis of the transcribed utterances (a) whether all instances of language alternations can be truly considered code-switching strategies and (b) whether those that can be so considered exhibit identifiable linguistic patterns and allow psychologically and sociologically sound interpretations. The emphasis here has been placed on the psycholinguistic and sociolinguistic perspectives of the code-switching phenomenon.

The data seem to lend support to the assumption that in fact not all language alternations can be considered "code-switching strategies" proper if we distinguish between utterances containing relexification and others containing sentence constituents from two languages. The former

Table 3. *Informants*

Fieldworker	Sex	Age	Place of birth	Education	Occupation	Socio-economic status ($)
Canales	M	65	Zapata, Tex.	High school diploma	Kelly A.F.B. Technician	15,000+
	F	58	El Encino, Tex.	High school incomplete	Housewife	N/A
	M	25	San Antonio, Tex.	B.S. sec. education	Math teacher	10,000
	F	21	San Antonio, Tex.	High school diploma	Housewife	N/A
	M	21	San Antonio, Tex.	High school diploma	Asst. manager shoe store	7,500+
	F	12	San Antonio, Tex.	Jr. high school	Student	N/A
	M	37	Starr County	B.A. electrical engineering	Engineer	Middle class
Cavallini	F	41	Fowlerton, Tex.	Jr. high school	Beautician	5,000
	F	48	Chicago Hts, Ill. (mother: Lower Rio Grande Valley; father: Spain)	High school diploma	Hair stylist	7,000
	M	29	San Antonio, Tex.	B.S. education	Teacher	10,000
	M	25	Plainview, Tex.	B.A. education	Teacher	10,000
	F	24	Karnes City, Tex.	B.S. education	Teacher	7,500
	F	26	Pearsall, Tex.	B.S. education	Teacher	7,500
	F	44	Laredo, Tex.	M.A. education	Counselor	20,000+

	F	67	Alice, Tex.	Jr. high school	Housewife	7,500
	F	45	Oilton, Tex.	High school diploma	Aide	20,000
	F	37	Von Army, Tex.	High school diploma	Aide	20,000
	M	36	Los Indios, Tex.	High school diploma	Custodian	5,000
	M	43	San Antonio, Tex.	Jr. high school	Custodian	5,000
	F	40+	Floresville, Tex.	High school diploma, some college	School secretary	12,500+
Longoria	F	7	San Antonio, Tex.	Grade 1	Student	N/A 5,000[a]
	M	7	San Antonio, Tex.	Grade 1	Student	N/A 3,000[a]
	M	7	San Antonio, Tex.	Grade 1	Student	N/A 3,000[a]
	F	10	Mexico	Grade 5	Student	N/A 3,000[a]
	F	11	San Antonio, Tex.	Grade 6	Student	N/A 3,000[a]
	F	40+	Hidalgo, Tex.	High school diploma	Aide	10,000+
	F	40+	San Antonio, Tex.	High school diploma	Aide	10,000+
	F	40+	Lockhart, Tex.	M.A.	Counselor	25,000+
	F	40+	San Antonio, Tex.	Jr. college	Substitute teacher	Middle class 15,000
	F	39	San Antonio, Tex.	High school diploma, some college	Secretary aide	Lower middle class 14,000
Martinez	F	35	Laredo/San Antonio, Tex.	B.S. nursing	R.N.	10,000
	M	36	Monterrey	M.A.	Therapist	15,000+
Reneau	M	31	Charlotte, Tex.	Elementary	Janitor	6,000

[a] Parents' income.

have been called here semicode-switching, the latter, true code-switching. The analysis of the examples of true code-switching have yielded some initial evidence that, from the viewpoint of competence, code-switching obeys certain rules of co-occurrence based upon the rules of grammar of the two languages involved in the sense that the code-switching is blocked if it requires the violation of a grammatical rule of either language. As far as linguistic performance is concerned eleven variables have been identified; some psychologically but most of them sociologically conditioned, which seem to act as triggering forces favoring the language alternation. It has not been suggested that the presence of one or more of these variables always produces code-switching, in other words they have no predictive qualities, but only that wherever code-switching occurs it can be traced back to such variables.

Regardless of the tentative findings described here, it has become clear that some utterances produced by Mexican–American bilinguals reveal the resources of the two languages but can only be observed when the social situation is appropriate, that is, when the interlocutors share a high degree of rapport. The utterances so encoded reveal a grammar of their own and do not reflect the speaker's ignorance of either/both languages as has often been suggested. However, since this mixed dialect occurs only in certain social situations, it seems appropriate to define it as a social dialect used by those who not only share the same code but also similar ethnic, cultural and environmental characteristics.

Appendix

Five graduate students from the University of Texas, San Antonio have been indispensable in the collection of the data upon which this paper is based. After an intensive training period in data collection, the fieldworkers recorded a series of conversations of Mexican–Americans from different socio-economic levels, persons with whom they had previously been acquainted, so that it could be expected that the informants would engage in informal interaction and alternate between their two languages as this is normal under such circumstances. The author gratefully acknowledges the efforts made by the participating students Eduardo Canales, Viola Cavallini, Carolina Longoria, Felix Martinez and William Reneau who produced some excellent recordings and transcribed the most meaningful passages of the recorded conversations. These transcriptions made up the corpus of some 75 pages of code-switching dialogues on which the analysis is based.

The fieldworkers set up the various interviews or sessions individually, the number of which depended, to some extent at least, on the former's success in promoting an informal and relaxed atmosphere that might favor code-switching practices. The total recorded time amounted to 690 minutes of speech, but not everything on the tapes was actually transcribed – only those portions of dialogue that contained language mixing, the utterance before and the utterance after; altogether, some three or four lines of verbal exchange.

To ensure the informality of the situation, the fieldworkers only interviewed persons whom they knew well and conducted the sessions in such a way that the least attention would be placed on the manner of speaking. Mr. Canales, for example, accepted a dinner invitation at the home of a family of six and Mr. Martinez, in turn, invited a married couple that he had known for some time to his house. Mr. Reneau sat down with his janitor friend for a talk in the cafeteria and the other fieldworkers, too, selected places for their interviews that were appropriate for creating a relaxed atmosphere. All these settings confirmed the author's assumption that the greater the informality of person or setting, the more the language alternation.

The fieldworkers interviewed a total of thirty-three male and female informants ranging in age from small school children to elderly persons with diverse educational and socio-economic backgrounds. (See Table 3.) At this early stage of the project the variables of age, sex, education and socio-economic level have not been controlled. In a future project, these variables should be controlled and this may then shed some light on the relative frequency with which the bilingual engages in code-switching and on the predictability of this kind of language behavior.

References

Acosta-Belén, Edna. 1975. "Spanglish:" a case of languages in contact. In *On TESOL '75: new directions in second language learning, teaching, and bilingual education,* ed. M. Burt and H. Dulay, pp. 151–8. Washington, D.C.: Teachers of English to Speakers of Other Languages.

Barker, George C. 1975. Social functions of language in a Mexican-American community. In *El lenguaje de los Chicanos,* ed. E. Hernández-Chávez, A. Cohen, and A. Beltramo, pp. 170–82. Arlington, Va.: Center for Applied Linguistics.

Ghosh, Samir K. 1972. *Man, language, and society.* The Hague: Mouton.

Giglioli, Pier Paolo. 1972. *Language and social context.* Baltimore: Penguin Books.

Gingràs, Rosario C. 1974. Problems in the description of Spanish-English intra-sentential code-switching. In *Southwest areal linguistics,* ed. G. Bills., pp. 167–74. San Diego: San Diego State University, Institute for Cultural Pluralism.

Gumperz, John, and Eduardo Hernández-Chávez. 1975. Cognitive aspects of bilingual communication. In *El lenguaje de los Chicanos,* ed. E. Hernández-Chávez, pp. 154–63. Arlington, Va.: Center for Applied Linguistics.

Hymes, Dell. 1974. *Foundations in sociolinguistics: an ethnographic approach.* Philadelphia.: University of Pennsylvania Press.

Jacobson, Rodolfo. 1977. How to trigger code-switching in a bilingual classroom. In *Southwest areal linguistics then and now,* ed. Bates Hoffer and Betty Lou Dubois, pp. 16–39. San Antonio: Trinity University.

Labov, William. 1972. *Sociolinguistic patterns.* Philadelphia: University of Pennsylvania Press.

Lance, Donald. 1975. Spanish-English code-switching. In *El lenguaje de los Chicanos,* ed. E. Hernández-Chávez, A. Cohen, and A. Beltramo, pp. 138–54. Arlington, Va.: Center for Applied Linguistics.

Limón, José. 1978. Agringado joking in Texas-Mexican society: folklore and differential identity. In *New directions in Chicano scholarship,* ed. Ricardo Romo and Raymund Paredes, pp. 33–50. La Jolla: University of California, San Diego.

Valdés-Fallis, Guadalupe. 1975. Code-switching in bilingual Chicano poetry. In *Southwest languages and linguistics in educational perspective,* ed. G. Harvey and M. F. Heiser, pp. 143–60. San Diego: San Diego State University, Institute for Cultural Pluralism.

11

Social interaction and code-switching patterns: a case study of Spanish/English alternation

GUADALUPE VALDÉS

Code-switching, the alternation of two languages, has been studied by a number of scholars, among them Hasselmo (1961, 1966, and 1970), Diebold (1963), Lance (1969) and especially John J. Gumperz (1964, 1969, 1970). In essence, this last scholar's definition of *situational switching* (wherein the participants signal changes in each other's rights or obligations) and *metaphorical switching* (which generates meanings similar to those conveyed by the use of *ty* and *vy*) are presently basic to the study of this phenomenon. At the same time, it is also evident from the work of Hasselmo, Clyne (1967, 1969), Rayfield (1970) and others that not all code-switching lends itself to clear classification. Indeed, as Gumperz himself has suggested, in those situations when either code is permissible, code-switching seems to be merely a question of momentary inclination.

In an attempt to explore this vast grey area, in a recent study entitled "Code-switching and language dominance: some initial findings" (1976), I investigated the code-switching patterns of 26 Mexican–American bilinguals for whom a language dominance profile had been established. I found that, without a doubt, patterns of alternation, frequency, length, etc., were similar for bilinguals of the same type. Moreover, when the base language was Spanish, English switches depended upon the relative proficiency of the speaker in the Spanish language. I suggested in that paper that a series of studies needs to be undertaken of code-switching patterns (of informants for whom some measure of language dominance has been established by the researcher) in order to determine the meaningful use of language alternation for different types of bilinguals.

The purpose of this chapter, then, is to report on precisely such a case study.

Reprinted with permission from the Bilingual Review Press. From *Bilingualism in the Bicentennial and Beyond*, ed. Gary Keller, Richard V. Teschner, and Silvia Viera (New York: Bilingual Review Press, 1976), pp. 53–85.

Research design

A bilingual Mexican-American female, age twenty-four, undertook the following assignment for credit in a Chicano research seminar: to record six situations involving Mexican-American bilinguals in which she herself participated. At that time, the student had no background in linguistics and was simply told that the study would involve an analysis of Spanish/English alternation in the southern New Mexico area. She was not aware that her own speech was of special importance in the research project.

Language proficiency and background of the principal informant

The principal informant, Susie, is a native of southern New Mexico. While she was born in Chihuahua, Chih., she was raised in a small mining town in Grant County, New Mexico, an area which is somewhat isolated from the Mexican border as well as from other regions of New Mexico. Susie's first language was Spanish and as a child she spoke this language at home. She attended public schools in Grant County and was graduated from Western New Mexico University with a degree in mathematics. Currently she is teaching in Anthony, New Mexico, at the junior high school level. At the same time she is a graduate student in Spanish at the University of Texas at El Paso.

Because of her recent interest in the field of Spanish and her exposure to the traditional prejudices of Spanish language instructors, Susie speaks a very careful dialect of standard Mexican Spanish. Only when excited does she use certain *regionalismos* that she has fought to avoid. It is not known whether she has mastered the various speech levels or registers that are characteristic of Spanish speakers who have grown up in a Mexican setting. Her written Spanish is correct, if somewhat stilted, and betrays to some degree a lifetime's use of the English language for abstract and intellectual expression. At the same time, Susie's use of English is spontaneous, casual, and unselfconscious. It is clear that she has mastered a number of registers or styles adequate for use in a variety of social situations.

Tape recordings

The six hour-long tapes were completed as assigned. In each instance Susie simply recorded herself and various friends that she went to visit. In certain cases, especially in the first two tapes, Susie displayed some awkwardness and attempted to actually conduct an interview of sorts. As she became more experienced in the difficulties of stimulating an hour-long conversation by using an interview format, she simply entered into ordinary conversations that included many different topics. The following is a brief description of each of the six social situations and the interlocutors involved in each. This description is summarized in Table 1.

Table 1. *Tape recordings: description*

Tape number	Setting	Interlocutors	Base language
I			
Segment 1	Friend's home (large family)	Guille (female 25) Guille's brother (19) Guille's brother (12) Susie	Spanish
Segment 2	Friend's home (large family)	Guille Guille's mother Guille's father Susie	Spanish
II	Friend's home (young couple)	Former classmate (female 22) Classmate's husband Susie	Spanish
III	Friend's apt. (single woman)	Friend (female 25) Susie	Varies
IV	Friend's home (single woman living with family)	Friend (female 24) Susie	Spanish
V	Susie's apt. (brother, wife and two young children are visiting)	Brother Brother's wife Susie	English
VI	Home of older couple	Male (middle-aged) Female (middle-aged) Daughter (late teens) Susie	Varies

Tape I was recorded at the home of Susie's best friend and fellow student, Guille. The fellow student was also involved in the recording project; however, this recording was made for Susie's benefit. Segment 1 involves an exchange between Susie, Guille, and Guille's two younger brothers, one a teenager and the other a younger boy. This portion of the tape is especially difficult to transcribe as the two young men generally speak simultaneously. Both alternate freely between Spanish and English, although it is apparent that in many instances they prefer English. While Susie, who does most of the talking initially, establishes the base language as Spanish, she switches to English frequently. These switches, however, seem to involve isolated items and often appear to be a response to the young men's teasing.

Segment 2 involves an exchange between Susie, Guille, and Guille's parents. Guille's mother does not speak English. She was born and raised in Mexico and came to the United States eleven years ago. Guille's father reportedly speaks or perhaps understands some English. During this segment, however, he speaks only Spanish. Susie also speaks only Spanish during this second segment, although at some points she expressly asks what specific things she names in English are called in Spanish. She is able to maintain a humorous and very charming conversation in this language, and English switches are almost totally nonexistent.

Tape II was recorded in the home of a former college classmate. The classmate is a female, age twenty-two, who has recently married. There is some initial awkwardness as Susie attempts to conduct a formal interview, but essentially the entire tape is made up of casual conversation touching on current activities, memories, local gossip, etc. The base language is Spanish with frequent English switches by the two principal speakers. The classmate's husband speaks very briefly and does not seem to have been in the room during most of the conversation.

Tape III involves a conversation with a twenty-five-year-old friend who lives in an apartment (or perhaps dormitory). While the friend seems to switch very easily into English, often maintaining an initial switch, most of the conversation uses Spanish as the base language.

Tape IV was recorded at a third female friend's home. This friend and Susie obviously share many activities and have many friends in common. The friend feels very confident in Spanish and although she switches into English naturally and frequently, she comments that in her family much value has been given to speaking Spanish well.

Tape V was recorded in Susie's apartment while Susie's brother, his wife, and their two young children were visiting. The entire conversation uses English as the base language. The children, who are heard laughing and making generally childish noises, do not speak, but they are always spoken to in English. The only Spanish on the tape is that used by the wife and by Susie, who seem to switch in approximately the same proportions. The brother uses Spanish exactly two times during the entire conversation.

Tape VI involves an older couple whom Susie does not know very well. The conversation alternates freely between English and Spanish, with the wife tending to use more Spanish than her husband. The teenager of the family speaks only English and makes it a point to respond exclusively in English to all comments addressed to her in Spanish.

Analysis

All of the recordings were transcribed, and special attention was paid to the context of each conversation. In each instance, the base language was identified. However, in some cases neither language could be described as the base language.

Notes were made on the types of alternation between the two languages

Table 2. *Principal code-switching patterns*

Pattern	Definition
1. Situational switches	Relating to social role of speakers
2. Contextual switches	Situation, topic, etc., are linked to the other language
3. Triggered switches	Switches due to preceding or following item
4. Switching of isolated items	Lexical need?
5. Identity markers	Stress in-group membership
6. Preformulations	Linguistic routines
7. Discourse markers	*But, and, of course,* etc.
8. Metaphorical switches	Obvious stylistic device – used for emphasis or contrast
9. Proper nouns	
10. Quotations and paraphrases	(May be contextual or noncontextual)
11. Sequential responses	Speakers use language last used (following suit)
12. Symmetrical switches	Blend and proportion of language alternation is made to resemble that of other speakers

as they occurred. However, since this study was concerned primarily with the specific patterns characteristic of the principal informant and only tangentially with those of the other speakers, a complete and exhaustive line-by-line study of switching patterns was made for this informant only.

In each case, the setting, context, topic, domain, speaker roles, etc., were considered, and switches were then classified according to the scheme presented in Table 2.

In several cases it was necessary to consult with the principal informant concerning the language use and ethnicity of a specific person quoted or paraphrased, the relationship of a certain topic to a certain domain, etc. In a number of instances several different classifications seemed adequate.

Discussion

Susie's speech contains definite, characteristic patterns of English/Spanish alternation. Here we will present a number of transcribed samples that have been labeled according to the scheme presented in Table 2. After each sample we will comment on the various patterns used, their purpose, effect, etc.

Tape I, segment 1

Susie:	Me caigo y me quiebro . . . ya me quebré aquí y aquí. Me quiebro un pie.	I'll fall down and I'll break . . . I already broke this and this. I'll break a foot.
Male teen:	Un dedo.	A toe.
Susie:	No yo sí brincaba en el **trampoline**[4] ■ **when I was**[3] **a senior.** Hasta por cierto hasta tenían una de esas chiquitas así.	No, I really did jump on the *trampoline when I was a senior.* They even had one of those little ones like this.
Male teen:	¿Un qué?	A what?
Susie:	**Trampoline**[4] de esas chiquitas así como de este ancho. Y nomás tenían un pedacito así donde brinca uno. Y luego nos ponían un cinto y como dos lazos. Entonces brincábamos en el aire y hacíamos una maroma en el aire y caíamos paradas ya en el suelo. Pero nos . . . para en caso de que nos fuéramos a caer nos detenían con el lazo.	One of those little *trampolines* like this, about this wide. And they just had a little place like this where you jump. And then they put a belt on us and something like two ropes. And we jumped up in the air and did a somersault and we landed standing up on the floor. But we . . . so in case we were going to fall they held us with a rope.
Male teen:	(Unclear)	
Susie:	No, porque mira te subes en el **trampoline**[4] y brincas en el aire. Y como brincas bien alto, haces tú la maroma. Como en los **acrobats.**[4] Hasta por cierto salí en un . . . en un . . . de este.	No, because see, you get up on the *trampoline* and you jump up in the air. And since you jump real high, you do the somersault yourself. Like in the *acrobats*. I even was in a . . . in a . . . a uh . . .
Male teen:	Sí, ¿en un qué?	Yes, in a what?
Susie:	Un de . . . en un . . . ¿cómo se dice? Como en un **show.**[4] Era **gymnastics**[4] **show.** Y yo salí haciendo eso.	In a . . . in a . . . what do you call it? Like in a *show*. It was a *gymnastics show*. And I came out doing that.
Male teen:	¿Con tu lazo, con tu lazo? (laughter)	With your rope, with your rope?
Susie:	Pues . . .	Well . . .
Younger brother:	A ver, hazlo.	Let's see, do it.
Susie:	Pero caes en el **trampoline**[4] verdad. Sí pero ésta era . . . mira	But you come down on the *trampoline*, don't you? Yes, but

la ruedita de donde brincas era como de este tamaño. Sí y luego es una **trampoline**[4] así; pero aquí vienen los **ropes**[4] así. Y nomás de ese tamaño. Esa era para brincar. No era **to**[4] ...[■] **it wasn't a**[3 or 2] **big trampoline.** No la puedo explicar.	this was . . . see the little round part that you jump from was about this size. Yes, and then it's a *trampoline* just this size; but here is where the *ropes* go, like this. And it's only that size. That one was to jump (from) . . . It wasn't *to . . . it wasn't a big trampoline*. I can't explain it.

Tape I, segment 1, is characterized by switches of isolated items. The choice seems to involve perhaps a lexical need (trampoline, acrobats) or perhaps a desire to use the term that might be more readily understood by the other two speakers. These initial lexical switches often trigger a following phrase or clause, as in: "No yo sí brincaba en el **trampoline when I was a senior.**" This pattern is very characteristic of Susie's speech.

In this segment it is also evident that as Susie becomes more impatient with the young boy's teasing, the switches become more frequent. While it would be simple to suggest that she is simply at a loss for words in the base language and therefore needs English in order to express herself more fully, it is equally evident from the recording that her "grasping for words" may be the direct result of her momentary frustration at not being able to get her meaning across. Various other exchanges on this tape involve the boys' pretending not to understand and Susie's determination to communicate, all accompanied by her evident impatience and increased use of English switches. A monolingual confronted with a foreigner who does not quite understand his language often resorts to shouting, a useless and often comical device in view of the circumstances. A bilingual faced with another bilingual who does not quite understand his meaning can resort to both raising his voice and increased use of the other common language.

Tape I, segment 2

Susie:	Me escribió uno de Torreón ahora. ¡Ajai!	A guy from Torreon wrote to me today. Horray!
Guille's mother:	¡Cómo andan ay alborotando gente!	Why are you going around getting people excited!
Susie:	Y híjole, más coraje. Fíjese que donde quiera me decían, tienes un acento americano. Les dije, ay es que no han oído a las de allá.	And gee, I was so angry. Everywhere I went I was told, you have an American accent. I told them, oh it's just that you haven't heard the ones from over there.
Guille's mother:	¿Quién, quién te decía?	Who, who told you?

Susie:	Nomás un muchacho me dijo que hablaba bien. Todos los demás, todos los demás me decían, tienes un acento americano oyes. Y luego les decíamos, es que no conocen a las gringas. Y uno me dijo, es que de a tiro eres gringa . . . y que quien sabe que . . . ah . . . y estaba en el baile. Y no le platicamos del baile de la *(name)*.	Only one guy said I talked okay. All the rest, all the rest said, you have an American accent. And then we said, it's just that you don't know the gringas. And one told me, you're really a gringa . . . and who knows what all . . . oh . . . and he was at the dance. We haven't told you about *(name)'s* dance.
Guille's mother:	No hemos platicado nada.	We haven't talked at all.
Susie:	Andaba una albina. ¿Albina se dice? De ésas que tienen de a tiro blanca, blanca y el pelo blanco, blanco, y los ojos como rosas.	An albina was there. Do you say albina? Really white, white and her hair was white, white and her eyes were sort of pink.
Guille:	(unclear) . . . la que no podía ver en el día, esa grandotota.	(unclear) the one who couldn't see in the sun, the big big one.
Susie:	Y luego así muy curiosita. Pero el pelo largo blanco, blanco así. Entonces me decía un muchacho, mira ahí está una de tus compañeras. Dije, ay, esa no es gringa, es albina. Y luego me decía, allí está una de las tuyas. Pues en inglés se dice **albina.**	And then just very strange. But her hair was white, white, like this. Then a guy said, look there's one of your pals. I said, she's not a gringa, she's an albina. And then he said there's one of your people. Well in English you say *albina*.
Guille's father:	¿Pero en español?	But in Spanish?
Susie:	Pues yo digo que albina. Yo tengo uno de ellos. ¿No conoces al David ___?	Well I say that it's albina. I have one of them. Do you know David ___?
Male teen:	Parece gringo pero no es.	He looks like a gringo but he isn't.
Susie:	Sí, tiene los ojos como rojos. Es una familia grande.	Yes, he has sort of red eyes. It's a large family.
Male teen:	Tiene una hermana que es . . . se ve como que no es hermana pero sí es hermana. Se ve poquita más, como más **dark.** Pero es hermana.	He has a sister who is . . . she looks like she's not his sister but she is. She looks a little more . . . sort of *darker*. But she's his sister.
Susie:	El David yo cuando lo vi creía que era gringo. Pero tiene los ojos como rosa, me imagino como de conejo.	When I saw David I thought he was a gringo. But his eyes are kind of pink, I imagine like a rabbit's.
Guille's		

mother:	¿No sería peluca?	Couldn't it have been a wig?
Susie:	A mí me dio risa porque pobre. Andaba bailando uno con ella y luego pos no le podía agarrar el paso y fue y la sentó y sacó a la que estaba sentada con ella. Pos ese mismo que andaba bailando con Eva.	I kind of laughed because poor thing. A guy was dancing with her and then she couldn't follow him so he took her to her seat and asked the girl sitting with her to dance. Well it was the same guy who was dancing with Eva.
Guille's mother:	Creían que eras americana.	They thought you were an American.
Susie:	Les dije, sí como tengo el pelo güero y ojos azules.	I said, oh yes since I have blonde hair and blue eyes.

Tape I, segment 2, is unique in that it contains no English/Spanish alternation as such. On two occasions Susie shows some hesitation as to a particular word in Spanish and inquires about its correct use. In the section transcribed the word is *albina*. In general, however, this segment makes it clear that Susie is indeed capable of sustaining a long and rather elaborate conversation in Spanish without switching into English. It also makes evident a tendency that will become more apparent below: that is, the tendency to reflect the particular language preference of the other speakers.

Tape II

Friend:	Are you hungry?	
Susie:	Uh, uh.	
Friend:	Porque allí hay **Cashews**.[4] ■ **You don't**[3] **like them?**	Because there are some *cashews* there. *You don't like them?*
Susie:	No puedo comer.	I can't eat them.
Friend:	¿Por qué?	Why?
Susie:	(unclear)	
Friend:	Ah pero . . . *yeah*. **You do break out with all that stuff? But your complexion** se ha compuesto mucho.	Oh but . . . *yeah. You do break out with all that stuff? But your complexion* has gotten a lot better.
Susie:	Sí, pues se me quitó, ¿te acuerdas?	Yes, well it went away. Remember?
Friend:	**I know.** De a tiro. No . . . pero no se nota.	*I know*. Completely. No, but you can't tell.
Susie:	Ahí de vez en cuando me salen.	Every now and then I break out.
Friend:	¿Estuvo caro yendo? ¿Como a cuánto todo lo que juites? Como **in the hundreds** yo creo ¿ verdad?	Was it expensive going? About how much was it all the time you went? Like *in the hundreds*, I think, wasn't it?

Susie:	Pues sí, mira, cada vez que iba, bueno, la consulta era **eight**[2] **dollars.** Pero cada vez que iba tenía que comprar las píldoras. Y luego compraba esa cosa que me unto . . . y me salía cada vez que iba como **fifteen**[2] ■ o **twenty**[2] **dollars.**	Well yes, because see, every time I went, well the visit was *eight dollars*. But every time I went I had to buy the pills. And then I bought that stuff that I put on . . . and it came to about *fifteen* or *twenty dollars* each time I went.
Friend:	Pero verdad que **it was worth it?**	But isn't it true that *it was worth it?*
Susie:	Me dijo **that if I flare**[2] **up to go back,**[and] **you know,**[10] **to go back.** ■ Pero[7] ■ **the last time he told me I didn't have**[2] **to go back unless I flare up.**	He told me *that if I flare up to go back, you know, to go back.* But *the last time he told me I didn't have to go back unless I flare up.*
Friend:	**And you haven't? You don't get any more?** ¿De vez en cuando?	*And you haven't? You don't get any more?* Once in a while?
Susie:	**My nose is**[2] **very oily.**	*My nose is very oily.*
Friend:	**Like right now?** 'ta **shiny.**	*Like right now?* it's *shiny*.
Susie:	**Um hum,** es lo primero que se me quema.	*Um hum* it's the first thing that gets sunburned.

Tape II contains several examples of contextual switching, a pattern also very much a part of Susie's general style. In these cases, when speaking about money, she uses English for numerical terms. It is evident that such use does not involve a lexical need but rather is the result of associations which come automatically to Susie when speaking about money. The contextual dimensions of the switches are further made evident in the paraphrasing of the dermatologist. Although Susie often narrates in one language and paraphrases or quotes in another (see transcription of Tape III, segment 2), here the paraphrasing language is definitely related to that spoken by the person being cited. The dermatologist was Anglo and spoke English.

Tape III, segment 1

Susie:	¿Te ha escrito Juan?	Has Juan written to you?
Friend:	Ah . . . Ah . . . ¿sabes que pasó? Me llamó el lunes en la noche. No, no me escribió. Me dijo que había recibido mis cartas . . . y que . . . pues me había empezado a escribir, pero que no podía escribir (unclear) de dos palabras: querida María. **And that was it.**	Oh . . . oh . . . you know what happened? He called Monday night. No, he didn't write. he said he had gotten my letters . . . and that . . . well he had started to write to me, but he couldn't write (unclear) than two words: dear Maria. *And that was it.*

Susie:	**Is he coming[1 1] back?**	*Is he coming back?*
Friend:	**Well that's what he said. He said he's coming down in about two weeks** para ir a una corrida de toros. Dice que **the way he feels right now, you know, he doesn't care who bullfights.** (unclear) Eloy Cabazos **or nobody. Even if it's a calf, I'll come and see it, see somebody bullfight a calf. So he's going to be coming down in about two weeks. And he says he's been real busy** haciendo adobes para una casa que está haciendo y comprando **supplies.**	*Well that's what he said. He said he's coming down in about two weeks* to go to a bullfight. he says that *the way he feels right now, you know, he doesn't care who bullfights.* (unclear) Eloy Cabazos *or nobody. Even if it's a calf, I'll come and see it, see somebody bullfight a calf. So he's going to be coming down in about two weeks. And he says he's been real busy* making adobes for a house he's building and buying *supplies.*
Susie:	Oyes[7], **in two weeks that would be the sixth?**	Listen (hey), *in two weeks that would be the sixth?*
Friend:	**Fourth of July weekend,** pero no me dijo exactmente cuando . . .	*Fourth of July weekend,* but he didn't say exactly when . . .
Susie:	Porque si viene, si van ustedes al **bullfight**[4 or 12] ese día, ese domingo, **I might**[6] ■ **be there, because my friend**[3] **and her husband are bringing her** ■ suegros[4] ■. **Her**[2] suegros **are from** [2]**Tennessee** y los van a traer y quieren llevarlos a una corrida de toros. **So . . . we . . . she wrote to me yesterday and asked**[2] **me to find out if there is a bullfight.**	Because if he comes, if you all go to the *bullfight* that day, that Sunday, *I might be there, because my friend and her husband are bringing her* in-laws. *Her* in-laws *are from Tennessee* and they're going to bring them and they want to take them to a bullfight. *So . . . we . . . she wrote to me yesterday and asked me to find out if there is a bullfight.*

Tape III, segment 1, contains an excellent example of number 11 (a sequential response). Even though the base language is Spanish and only the last sentence of the friend's initial comment is in English (**and that was it**) Susie responds in the last language heard: "**Is he coming back?**" This type of sequential response is very common in Susie although it does not seem to be obligatory.

The final section of this conversation, spoken by Susie, is interesting for a variety of reasons. To begin with, the use of the English switch "**bullfight**" while labeled a number 4 switch, is very evidently also related to the other speaker's use of the same English word. Since the phrase "corrida de toros" has also appeared, it is doubtful that the choice of "bullfight" was made on the basis of a lexical need. Indeed, Susie's switching patterns throughout the entire passage seem to reflect the blend and proportion of those used by the other speaker. The item "**I might be**

there'' can be classified as a simple preformulation or linguistic routine (no. 6), which triggers the following clause: ''**because my friend and her husband are bringing her** suegros.'' *Suegros* is clearly a simple, isolated lexical switch. The sentence following, however, is not a continuation of the triggered switch but rather a contextual switch. The reference is to the in-laws, who are themselves English speaking. The final portion of the passage also contains a contextual switch. In this case the letter is recalled in English because it was written in that language.

Tape III, segment 2

Susie:	[7]Oyes, **when I was a freshman I had a term paper to do** . . . Y [7]este **I waited till the last minute two days before to take notes, to do the typing, to do everything. So I didn't sleep for almost forty-eight hours. And after I turned it in, instead of going home to sleep (it was at the dorm), I had a boyfriend and I went out on a date with him. And all of a sudden, I started acting real** [4]curiosa, **you know. I started going like this.** Y [8]luego decía, **look at the smoke coming out of my fingers, like that, And then** me [8]dijo, **stop acting silly.** Y luego [8]decía yo, ■ [3]mira **can't you see.** Y [8]luego ■ [7]este, **I started seeing like little stars all over the place.** Y volteaba yo [8]asina y le decía **look at the . . . the** . . . no sé era [8]como brillosito así **like stars.** Y [8]luego **he thought I was acting silly and he was getting mad at me. But then he realized that . . . that I was seeing things.** Y luego me [8]llevaron luego, luego al [4]**dorm.** Le tuvieron que hablar a la enfermera y me dieron [4]**tranquilizers,** ■ **because then I started like**	Hey, *when I was a freshman I had a term paper to do* . . . and uh *I waited till the last minute two days before to take notes, to do the typing, to do everything. So I didn't sleep for almost forty-eight hours. And after I turned it in, instead of going home to sleep (I was at the dorm), I had a boyfriend and I went out on a date with him. And all of a sudden, I started acting real* strange, *you know. I started going like this.* And then I said, *look at the smoke coming out of my fingers, like that. And then* he said, *stop acting silly.* And then I said, look *can't you see.* And then uh, *I started seeing like little stars all over the place.* And I turned like this and I said, *look at the . . . the* . . . I don't know, it was sort of shiny like this, *like stars.* And then *he thought I was acting silly and he was getting mad at me. But then he realized that . . . that I was seeing things.* And then they took me right away to the *dorm.* They had to call the nurse and they gave me *tran-*

	screaming[3] **and real weird, you know. And then** . . . Y me regañó tanto la[8] enfermera. Me dijo **don't ever stay up late, I mean**[10 and 12] **don't ever . . . you know . . . sleep at least a couple of hours,** dice,[8] **but don't**[10 and 12] . . .	*quilizers, because then I started like screaming and real weird, you know. And then* . . . And the nurse really scolded me. She said *don't ever stay up late, I mean don't ever . . . You know . . . sleep at least a couple of hours,* she said, *but don't* . . .
Friend:	**You know that happens to me too** . . . (Phone rings and interrupts the conversation).	*You know that happens to me too . . .*

Tape III, segment 2, exemplifies a number of switching patterns that are frequently used by the principal informant. Pattern number 7, for example, the use of discourse markers in one language while speaking in the other (as in the first two sentences of this passage), is most common. The markers used here, *oyes* and *este*, are two great favorites. The isolated switch number 4 is again found in this passage, once in Spanish (*curiosa*) and once in English (tranquilizers); this latter switch is followed by the inevitable triggered switch: "**because then I started** . . ." etc. Once again this passage contains a paraphrase switch number 10 that is definitely related to context. The nurse was Anglo and spoke English.

The most interesting devices in this passage, however, are the stylistic or metaphorical switches that are used to narrate and paraphrase sequentially. Spanish is used for the narration, while English is used to quote or paraphrase the boyfriend and Susie herself. In this case the paraphrasing switch is simply a device which lends emphasis and dramatic effect and is not, as in the nurse's case, contextual. Susie's boyfriend was Chicano and the two normally spoke to each other using Spanish as the base language.

Tape IV

Friend:	¿Qué clase de carro maneja Ernie?	What kind of a care does Ernie drive?
Susie:	No sé.	I don't know.
Friend:	**I saw it yesterday when we went. I thought I saw him. He was wearing his tank top** como la que (traía) el día que lo vi. Este y se me afiguró el mismo. Dije yo no sé si será **because it was a little red car.** No sé qué marca. **But it was a little red car.**	*I saw it yesterday when we went. I thought I saw him. He was wearing his tank top* like the one he had on the day I saw him. And uh it kind of looked the same. I said I don't know if it is *because it was a little red car*. I don't know what make. *But it was a little red car.*

Susie:	Fíjate [7]que **I wasn't . . . I didn't think he was working here this Saturday** porque creo que el [8]otro sábado trabajó . ■. . y yo entré así todo el día me he sentido, me [3]desvelé mucho. Anoche me acosté como a las quince para las tres. Sí y este me sentía muy feo. **You [7]know.■ Remember like you were feeling that day in [3]your stomach, everywhere. Yeah that's how I've been feeling all day. But I think it's the heat** porque el [8]carro . . . Mira me quemo **[9]Alice,■ it was [3]super hot today.**	Look, *I wasn't . . . I didn't think he was working here this Saturday* because I think he worked last Saturday . . . and I went in like this and all day I've felt, I stayed up very late. Last night I went to bed around quarter to three. Yes and uh I felt awful. *You know. Remember like you were feeling that day in your stomach, everywhere. Yeah that's how I've been feeling all day. But I think it's the heat* because the car . . . Look I burn up *Alice, it was super hot today.*
Friend:	**It was one hundred and six.**	*It was one hundred and six.*
Susie:	Pues [6]con razón. Mira me duelen las manos porque las traigo tan quemadas **from [3]holding■ the [3]steering wheel. Anyway, I was in and he was, you know, the one that would let you out. And he was laughing cause he saw me coming in.** Se estaba [8]riendo de mí, **you [7]know.** No me fijé hasta que ya no me dijo. **Oh I didn't [8]think he'd be there.** Platicamos **for about [2]twenty minutes■ and I said I'd [3]better go because** (unclear). No hallé nada. Bueno traje dos [2]libros. Tienen muy poquito de Vallejo pero **you [7]know■ I looked in the [3]magazine articles,** nada. **I was [8]so disappointed.** Mira me estuve . . . desde que te hablé me fui. Me estuve hasta las **one [2]o'clock,** hasta las **five [3]till one when [3]I left.**	Well no wonder. Look my hands hurt because they've gotten so burned *from holding the steering wheel. Anyway, I was in and he was, you know, the one that would let you out. And he was laughing cause he saw me coming in.* He was laughing at me, *you know.* I didn't notice until he told me. *Oh I didn't think he'd be there.* We talked *for about twenty minutes and I said I'd better go because* (unclear). I didn't find anything. Well I brought two books. They have very little on Vallejo but *you know I looked in the magazine articles,* nothing. *I was so disappointed.* Look, I stayed . . . from the time I called you I left. I stayed until *one o'clock,* until *five till one when I left.*

In both Tape III and Tape IV it became evident that the patterns found initially on Tape I had changed considerably. It became evident also, upon examining the blend and proportion of alternation used by the other speakers in each of the tapes, that in each case Susie's particular blend of the two languages seems to resemble that used by the persons she is addressing. In the specific conversation transcribed from Tape IV, a number of patterns examined previously are also present with some small variations. The discourse marker number 7 (*fíjate*) is again a very common one. So too is the English Marker "**you know.**" The use of this last marker in one instance triggers the following sentence: "**Remember like you were feeling** . . ." etc.

Two stylistic devices, which have been labeled number 8, are also present in the first long passage. The first is a parenthetical use, a thought introduced in the middle of a sentence which might normally be set off by commas but which here is simply said in the other language: "porque creo que el otro sábado trabajó." This parenthetical use is very definitely stylistic and one that is handled very skillfully by Susie. In addition, the parenthetical clause triggers two more sentences in the same language.

The second use is very definitely an exclamation: "**But I think it's the heat** porque el carro . . . Mira me quemo **Alice,**" etc. The switch into Spanish takes place as the pitch rises significantly, and the intent is obviously one of emphasis, stressing exactly what the problem seems to be.

The second passage contains a number of interesting patterns. The preformulated "Pues con razón" establishes the base language for the passage in spite of the preceding English utterance by the other speaker. The lexical switch to "**the steering wheel,**" a term that does not come readily to mind in Spanish to many natives of this New Mexico area, evidently produces an anticipational triggering: "**from holding.**" As Haugen (1973) has noted, it is possible that a sentence might be abstractly formed even before the speaker is sure which language is going to come out.

The first clause in this passage identified as number 8 ("Se estaba riendo de mí") is a third type of stylistic switch, involving the repetition of a statement previously uttered in the other language. In this instance the particular stylistic switch is maintained in spite of the discourse marker "**you know.**"

Once again a parenthetical or very personal remark relating Susie's thoughts is emphasized by a language switch: "**Oh I didn't think he'd be there.**"

Also in this passage the use of expressions of time in English seems most consistent. As with money, time is frequently discussed in English as being specifically a concern of the English-speaking domain, but it is not regular in this speaker.

The final contextual switch, "No hallé nada," etc., is significant in that Susie is discussing a poetry class taught in Spanish that very obviously involves the works of César Vallejo. In several of the conversations a discussion of her graduate class work or university professors immediately calls for the use of Spanish, which is, of course, the language of instruction.

Finally, this passage also contains a very familiar discourse marker followed by a triggered switch: "**you know I looked in the magazine articles,**" and a final metaphorical switch: "**I was so disappointed.**" Here again a switch is used dramatically to describe an emotional response.

Tape V

Susie:	**I need to get my hair trimmed.**	*I need to get my hair trimmed.*
Brother:	**Want me to trim it?**	*Want me to trim it?*
Susie:	**Not today.**	*Not today.*
Brother:	**Oh.**	*Oh.*
Susie:	**But I want it straight. When I go down maybe in about three weeks.** Sí [7]porque **I haven't had it trimmed since December.** Y ya me creció [12]mucho de las orillas.	*But I want it straight. When I go down maybe in about three weeks.* Yes because *I haven't had it trimmed since December.* And it's grown a lot on the ends.
Wife:	**You have it straight now.**	*You have it straight now.*
Susie:	**Well** Teresa (unclear) **but she did it kind of bad.**	*Well* Teresa (unclear) *but she did it kind of bad.*
Brother:	(unclear) . . . poco chueco.	(unclear) . . . a little crooked.
Wife:	**You know** ahorita **I saw a girl down at assembly and she had a shag. And it's the first shag** que se me hace que **looks nice on a girl. She had it real short** de acá arriba. **And she had it all to the side.** Pero acá atrás **was long, about as long as this. And she looked real** . . . muy, muy, **she looked real pretty.**	*You know* right now *I saw a girl down at assembly and she had a shag. And it's the first shag* that seems to me *looks nice on a girl. She had it real short* up on top. *And she had it all to the side.* But back here *(it) was long, about as long as this. And she looked real* . . . very, very, *she looked real pretty.*
Susie:	**[7]Well** a veces **you [7]know** me lo quiero cortar. **But if I cut it I go to the other extreme. I cut it so short [12]and I know that if I cut it, then** me [4]pudiera. **You [7]know,**■ **that [8]I'd regret it.**	*Well* at times *you know* I want to cut it. *But if I cut it I go to the other extreme. I cut it so short and I know that if I cut it, then* I'd be sorry. *You know, that I'd regret it.*

Tape V contains a number of interesting segments although the base language throughout is English. Again, it is evident that Susie's particular choice of alternating patterns greatly resembles that used by the female speaker. The male speaker avoided Spanish except for two occasions, one of which is found in this conversation. We have labeled two sentences

number 12, symmetrical switches, because the particular stylistic choice seems unconsciously to involve precisely such a balance.

Tape VI, segment 1

Susie:	**Well I keep starting**[11] **some.** Como por un mes todos[2 or 12] los días escribo y ya dejo. **Last week**[6] empecé otra vez.	*Well I keep starting some.* Like for a month I'll write every day and then I'll stop. *Last week* I started again.
Male:	Quita mucho tiempo.	It takes a lot of time.
Female:	**Yeah.**	*Yeah.*
Male:	Pero con unos tres minutos . . . **but see . . . there are so many things happening in a day** que **one minute, two minutes, three minutes. You have to write only the highlights** nomás.	But with some three minutes *. . . but see . . . there are so many things happening in a day* that *one minute, two minutes, three minutes. You have to write only the highlights* only.
Susie:	Yo hasta empecé a escribir[11] lo que soñaba. **Every morning I would get up**[12] **. . . what I remembered, that I would dream,** escribía. **For about a month I did it and then I got lazy.**	I even started to write down what I dreamed about. *Every morning I would get up . . . what I remembered, that I would dream,* I would write. *For about a month I did it and then I got lazy.*
Female:	(unclear)	(unclear)
Susie:	**And when you want to write it,** porque[8 or 2] yo a veces así **I would wait a week and then try to remember all I did last week. Forget it.**	*And when you want to write it,* because I sometimes like that *I would wait a week and then try to remember all I did last week. Forget it.*
Female:	Ajá. **Daily. Daily.**	Um hum. *Daily. Daily.*
Male:	**Even like that** no le hace cuanta (unclear) tengas, **you still forget it.**	*Even like that* it doesn't matter how much (unclear) you have, *you still forget it.*

Segment 2 was chosen because of the fact that it too illustrates the symmetrical switch discussed above. In this particular conversation, both the male and the female alternate freely between English and Spanish in a proportion which the principal informant reflects almost immediately. Here we have labeled as number 12 a number of switches which, in the light of the patterns exhibited by the other speakers, seem almost imitative.

Tape VI, segment 2

Susie:	**Yeah, you have to learn that from your own mistakes. Like**	*Yeah, you have to learn that from your own mistakes. Like*

	when I started[11] college my first year, you know, staying at the dorm, if I wasn't out, pues estábamos allí platicando en el cuarto. Todas las muchachas se juntaban y luego ya estábamos estudiando a la[2] una. A las dos de la mañana empezábamos a estudiar. ¡Unas desveladas brutas! Y luego ya después aprendí que **there's a time to study and there's the time[6] and the place to . . . you know . . .**	*when I started college my first year, you know, staying at the dorm, if I wasn't out,* well we were there talking in the room. All the girls got together and then we started studying at one. At two o'clock in the morning we started studying. Some really terrible sleepless nights! And then later I learned that *there's a time to study and there's the time and place to . . . you know . . .*
Female teen:	**I've heard too many things about the dorms. The walls are like paper, excuse me, paper thin. You know, gosh like an all-girls' camp. And yet I'd say I'd rather have like a small apartment, you know, maybe have some other girls live with me.**	*I've heard too many things about the dorms. The walls are like paper, excuse me, paper thin. You know, gosh like an all-girls' camp. And yet I'd say I'd rather have like a small apartment, you know, maybe have some other girls live with me.*
Female:	La mujer está más **safe**, más segura y más protegida en los **dorms.**	A woman is *safer*, safer and more protected in the *dorms.*
Susie:	Pero ahora tanto que han cambiado desde que yo fui. Pues ya hace qué . . . cuatro años que fui. Ahora ya las dejan salir. Cuando yo estaba, **we had to be back on weekends by one o'clock and during the week we had to be in by ten thirty.** Pero ahora ya cambió todo. Ahora se pueden estar hasta que les dé la gana. No tienen horas.	But now they've changed so much since I went. Well it's been what . . . four years since I went. Now they let them go out. When I was there, *we had to be back on weekends by one o'clock and during the week we had to be in by ten thirty.* But now everything has changed. Now they can stay out as long as they want. They don't have any hours.
Male:	¿Y es **co-ed?**	And is it *co-ed?*
Susie:	Bueno, **not exactly[6].** Aquí en **State[9]** dicen que es **co-ed[4]. ■ Not exactly[6] though.** Porque como **Garcia[9] Hall, ■ one section is all girls and then[3] all guys. Well there's a division,** un patio[2], ■ entonces[7] (unclear) . . . **for the**	Well, *not exactly.* Here at *State* they say it's *co-ed. Not exactly though.* Because like *Garcia Hall, one section is all girls and then all guys. Well there's a division,* a patio, then (unclear) . . . *for the guys to go visit. But*

guys to go visit. But it has to be a certain time during the day.	*it has to be a certain time during the day.* I think they can
Creo que en la ta[8]rde pueden visitar.	visit in the afternoon.

In this portion of the conversation Susie is primarily speaking to the teenage daughter, who throughout the tape speaks only English. Here Susie's switches are more in keeping with what might be termed her personal switching style than they were in her exchanges with the girl's parents. She begins with a sequential response in English and only makes a contextual switch to Spanish to recall her dorm days and long bull sessions with friends at the university. All of these friends, or those that might be said to be close friends, were Spanish speaking. A final switch in this passage is an excellent example of a linguistic routine: "**there's a time to study** . . ." etc. It is obviously used here deliberately for its unique strength.

The second time Susie speaks in this conversation she also makes a contextual switch; it is similar to previous uses in that the reference is to a specific time.

The final passage contains a number of linguistic routines, such as "**not exactly, not exactly though,**" as well as lexical switches and proper noun use. In one case the use of the proper noun **Garcia Hall** triggers the following sentence.

Finally, the last switch in this passage is again the very familiar parenthetical switch with which Susie often reveals her own thoughts, feelings, or uncertainties.

In essence, then, when Susie is speaking to the daughter of the family, who is not switching at all but maintaining English throughout, she evidently feels perfectly free to switch according to her own stylistic needs and does not present the series of erratic switches which seem characteristic of Tape V and Tape VI, segment 1. However, as opposed to her unswitched Spanish (Tape I, segment 2), which she used when speaking to a monolingual Spanish speaker, here Susie feels perfectly free to switch into Spanish knowing that the daughter understands both languages.

Conclusions

While these brief samples of the six tapes can only offer the reader a vague glimpse into the switching patterns of the principal informant, they can support a number of tentative conclusions:

1. That code-switching as exemplified by the principal informant does not occur simply because the speaker lacks equivalent expressions in the base language chosen;

2. That Rayfield's two conclusions (1970):
   a. "The bilingual has a double stock of rhetorical devices. He takes full advantage of them to emphasize and dramatize his speech . . ."
   b. "The regularity of the patterns of switching shows to what degree the two languages are welded into what might be termed a supersystem, with a bilingual vocabulary, a composite stock of structures, and a phonemic system not identical with that of either of the two languages."

   are very much supported by this analysis;
3. That switching patterns seem to be influenced by the particular proficiency of the other speakers and their preference for one or the other of the two languages or for a specific blend of the two codes;
4. That additional work needs to be undertaken in the study of this phenomenon to include:
   a. The specific patterns for speakers with varying degrees of proficiency in the Spanish language.
   b. The specific patterns for speakers with varying degrees of proficiency in the English language.

References

Clyne, Michael G. 1967. *Transference and triggering*. The Hague: Nijhoff.
1969. Switching between language systems. *Proceedings of the Tenth International Congress of Linguists*. pp. 343–9.
Diebold, A. Richard, Jr. 1963. Code-switching in Greek-English bilingual speech. *Monograph series on languages and linguists*. 15:53–62.
Gumperz, John J. 1964. Hindi-Punjabi code-switching in Delhi. *Proceedings of the Ninth International Congress of Linguists*. pp. 1115–1124.
1967. On the linguistic markers of bilingual communication. *Journal of Social Issues*. 23:48–57.
1969. How can we describe and measure the behavior of bilingual groups? In *Description and measurement of bilingualism*, ed. L. G. Kelly, pp. 242–9. University of Toronto Press.
1970. Verbal strategies in multilingual communication. *Monograph series on languages and linguistics*. 23:129–48.
Hasselmo, Nils. 1961. American Swedish: a study in bilingualism. Ph.D. dissertation, Harvard University.
1966. Linguistic routines and code-switching: some comments on an American-Swedish speech economy. Paper presented at the annual meeting of the Modern Language Association, New York.
1970. Code-switching and modes of speaking. In *Texas studies in bilingualism*, ed. Glenn G. Gilbert, pp. 179–210. Berlin: de Gruyter.
Haugen, Einar. 1973. Bilingualism, language contact, and immigrant languages in the United States: a research report, 1956–1970. In *Current trends in linguistics*, ed. Thomas Sebeok, vol. 10, pp. 505–91. The Hague: Mouton.
Lance, Donald M. 1969. *A brief study of Spanish-English bilingualism: final report, research project ORR-Liberal Arts-15504*. College Station: Texas A & M University. ERIC ED 032 529.

Mackey, W. F. 1965. Bilingual interference: its analysis and measurement. *Journal of Communication*. 15:239–49.
Rayfield, J. R. 1970. *The languages of a bilingual community*. The Hague: Mouton.
Valdés-Fallis, Guadalupe. 1976. Code-switching and language dominance: some initial findings. *General Linguistics*. 18:90–104.
Weinrich, Uriel. 1953. *Languages in contact: findings and problems*. Publications of the Linguistic Circle of New York, No. 1. New York: Linguistic Circle.

12

"Sometimes I'll start a sentence in Spanish *y termino en español*": toward a typology of code-switching

SHANA POPLACK

Ninety-two percent of the Puerto Ricans residing in the continental United States currently claim Spanish as their "mother tongue" (Bureau of the Census 1973). This is true for young as well as older speakers, despite the fact that most of them were either born, raised, or spent a good part of their adult life in an English-speaking society.

Along with signs of vigor and renewal of the language, however, there is also some indication that the use of Spanish is on the wane, especially among the younger generations of speakers who were born and raised in New York City (Pedraza 1978). This situation makes it difficult to foresee whether Puerto Rican Spanish will eventually disappear from the community repertoire, or if through some combination of factors, such as a resurgence of ethnic identity and a continued influx of monolingual speakers from Puerto Rico and other Spanish-speaking countries, it will retain its role.

The present investigation is part of an interdisciplinary study the aim of which is to examine the place of both Spanish and English in a Puerto Rican community in East Harlem through (1) the participant observation of the distribution of both languages in the daily life of the community, (2) the analysis of attitudes of community members toward each of the languages, and (3) the quantitative sociolinguistic analysis of selected linguistic behavior.

Due, among other things, to a circulatory pattern of migration, this appears to be a stable bilingual community rather than a transitional one

Reprinted with permission from *Linguistics* 18, nos. 7–8: 581–618 (1980).

This analysis is part of a research project on Inter-Generational Perspectives on Bilingualism supported by the National Institute of Education under NIE–G–78–0091. The work reported here was carried out while I was a research associate at the Center for Puerto Rican Studies at the City University of New York and has benefited from many fruitful discussions with colleagues there. I am particularly indebted to Alicia Pousada for her contribution to all phases of this study. Frank Bonilla, Don Hindle, and David Sankoff generously contributed their time and insight, for which I am very grateful. Thanks also to Migdalia Rodriguez for her patience and expertise in the preparation of the text. A portion of this chapter was presented at the Linguistic Society of America annual meeting, Boston, December 1978.

in which acquisition of a second language would eventually displace the first (Fishman 1971). This pattern of displacement of the mother tongue has characterized several early twentieth-century immigrant groups in the United States and has usually been brought to completion by the third generation. In contrast, the Puerto Rican community under investigation includes third-generation speakers of both Spanish and English.

A block in the heart of El Barrio, East 102nd Street, perhaps the oldest continuous Puerto Rican settlement in the United States, provides an ideal setting to investigate these issues. Block residents are predominantly (95 percent) Puerto Rican, to the virtual exclusion of all other ethnic groups. If the Spanish language and Puerto Rican culture are to survive in the United States, their chances of doing so are presumably greatest in such an ethnically homogeneous environment. This chapter is an attempt to integrate the results of the ethnographic and attitudinal components of the broader study into a specifically sociolinguistic analysis.

Code-switching

Long-term sociolinguistic observation of East 102nd Street by Pedro Pedraza (1978) indicated that there were three modes of communication among block members: English speaking, Spanish speaking, and code-switching. Although Spanish predominates in certain domains (such as in the home or while playing numbers), its exclusive use in any of these settings was not observed. Similarly, English predominates in official settings, but it is also possible to hear Spanish in these domains. Pedraza further observed that "there were speakers who code-switched because they lacked full command of Spanish and those who code-switched because they lacked full command of English" (p. 33). However, as we will see, it is only by linking ethnographic observations with linguistic analysis that code-switching behavior may be most adequately explained.

Code-switching is the alternation of two languages within a single discourse, sentence, or constituent. In a report on an earlier study of a balanced bilingual speaker (Poplack 1981), code-switching was categorized according to the degree of integration of items from one language (L_1) to the phonological, morphological, and syntactic patterns of the other language (L_2). Because the balanced bilingual has the option of integrating his utterance into the patterns of the other language or preserving its original shape, items such as those in example 1, which preserve English phonological patterns, were considered examples of code-switching in that study, whereas segments such as those in example 2, which are adapted to Puerto Rican Spanish patterns, were considered to be instances of monolingual Spanish discourse.[1]

[1] The reverse pattern, the insertion into an English base of Spanish items with English phonological or morphological patterns is nonexistent in the community.

Table 1. *Identification of code-switching according to type of integration into the base language*

Type	Levels of integration into base language: phon.	morph.	syn.	Code-switch?	Example
1	X	X	X	No	Es posible que te *mogueen*. 'They might mug you.' (002/1)
2	—	—	X	Yes	Las palabras *heavy-duty*, bien grandes, se me han olvidado. 'I've forgotten the real big, heavy-duty words.' (40/485)
3	X	—	—	Yes	[da 'warise] (58/100)
4	—	—	—	Yes	No creo que son *fifty-dollar suede ones*. 'I don't think they're fifty-dollar suede ones.' (05/271)

Note: I have followed Hasselmo (1970) in designating as the "base" language that language to which a majority of phonological and morphological features of discourse can be attributed. X denotes full integration; dash denotes no integration.

1a. Leo un *magazine*. [mægə̣'ziyn] 'I read a magazine.'
1b. Me iban a *lay off*. [lέy ɔ̀hf] 'They were going to lay me off.'
2a. Leo un *magazine*. [maγa'siŋ] 'I read a magazine.'
2b. Me iban a dar *layoff*. ['lei̯of] 'They were going to lay me off.'

In the ensuing sections I will explore code-switching on a community-wide basis, focusing on speakers of varying bilingual abilities. Inclusion in the sample of nonfluent bilinguals requires modifying the previous definition of code-switching. In the speech of nonfluent bilinguals segments may remain unintegrated into L_2 on one or more linguistic levels, as a result of transference of patterns from L_1. This combination of features leads to what is commonly known as a "foreign accent" and is detectable even in the monolingual L_2 speech of the speaker, as in example 3 below, which was rendered wholly in Puerto Rican Spanish phonology:

3. That's what he said. [da 'wari se] (58/100)[2]

In order to consider an utterance such as example 3, which occurs in an otherwise entirely Spanish context, as a code-switch from Spanish into English, I have refined the criteria for identifying a code-switch in terms of the type of integration, shown in Table 1.

The example of type 1, *mogueen*, is phonologically, morphologically,

[2] Numbers in parentheses identify speaker and code-switch.

and syntactically integrated into the base language, although etymologically a loanword from English *mug*. It is here considered an instance of monolingual Spanish discourse. In contrast, type 4 segments are totally unintegrated into the patterns of the base language. This sort of code-switch occurs most typically in the speech of balanced bilinguals. Type 2 follows English phonological and morphological patterns but violates English syntactic patterns. The example shown follows the Spanish syntactic pattern of adjective placement. This type of segment is also considered a code-switch into English, although it is one that violates the "equivalence constraint," to be discussed later. Although type 3 involves phonological integration into Spanish (i.e., it follows Puerto Rican Spanish phonological rules), it is morphologically, syntactically, and lexically English. Thus the example of type 3 is considered a code-switch into English, rendered with a "foreign accent." Spontaneous switches of words, sentences, and larger units at a turn boundary, not involving any change in interlocutors, were also considered to be code-switches if they exhibited types 2, 3, or 4 of integration in Table 1.

Theoretical background

Much of the literature on code-switching (e.g., Gumperz 1971, 1976; Gumperz and Hernández-Chávez 1970; Valdés-Fallis 1976, 1981; McClure 1977) has focused on its social and pragmatic functions. Although there is little doubt that functional factors are the strongest constraints on the occurrence of code-switching, it is clear that linguistic factors also play a role. This chapter demonstrates how the incorporation of both functional and linguistic factors into a single model is necessary to account for code-switching behavior.

Although in some of the earlier literature (e.g., Lance 1975) the occurrence of code-switching was characterized as random, most investigators now appear to agree that in many aspects it is rule-governed, despite the fact that there is little agreement on the precise nature of the rules involved. Proposed grammatical rules have generally taken the form of categorical constraints based on acceptability judgments of invented instances of code-switching (Gingràs 1974, Timm 1975, Gumperz 1976). Although acceptability judgments provide a manageable way to tap community grammar norms, their use is questionable in an overtly stigmatized sociolinguistic marker such as code-switching (Gumperz 1971). Moreover, studies of code-switching performance in two widely separated bilingual communities have independently yielded counterexamples to these categorical constraints (Pfaff 1975, 1976; Poplack 1981).

More important, the proposed constraints are not of the general nature one would wish to ascribe to linguistic universals.[3] In Poplack (1981) two

[3] For example, why should it be possible to switch codes between a subject and a verb only if that subject is not pronominal, as suggested by Gumperz (1976) and Timm (1975)?

syntactic constraints on code-switching were suggested. Together they were general enough to account for all instances of code-switching in the Puerto Rican data on which that study was based as well as the Chicano data on which the majority of the code-switching literature is based; at the same time, they were restrictive enough not to generate instances of nonoccurring code-switches:

1. *The free morpheme constraint.* Codes may be switched after any constituent in discourse provided that constituent is not a bound morpheme.[4] This constraint holds true for all linguistic levels but the phonological, for reasons already explained. Thus, a segment such as example 4 may be produced, in which the first syllable follows the Caribbean Spanish tendency to aspirate /s/ before voiceless consonants, and the second syllable follows English phonological patterns. This should be seen as aiming for, but missing, an English target, rather than a switch between two bound morphemes. However, items such as example 5, where the Spanish bound morpheme *-iendo* '-ing' is affixed to the English root *eat*, have not been attested in this or any other study of code-switching to my knowledge, unless one of the morphemes has been integrated phonologically into the language of the other.

4. una buena ex*cuse* [eh' kjuws] a good excuse
5. **eat*-iendo eating

Included under this constraint are idiomatic expressions, such as *cross my fingers* (sic) *and hope to die* and *si Dios quiere y la virgen* 'God and the virgin willing', which are considered to behave like bound morphemes in that they show a strong tendency to be uttered monolingually.

2. *The equivalence constraint.* Code-switches will tend to occur at points in discourse where juxtaposition of L_1 and L_2 elements does not violate a syntactic rule of either language, that is, at points around which the surface structures of the two languages map onto each other. According to this simple constraint, a switch is inhibited from occurring within a constituent generated by a rule from one language that is not shared by the other.[5] This can be seen in Figure 1, where the dashed lines indicate permissible switch points and the arrows indicate ways in which constituents from two languages map onto each other. The speaker's actual utterance is reproduced in line C. An analysis based on the equivalence constraint may be applied to the by-now classical examples in number 6 that were constructed by Gingràs (1974) and tested for acceptability on a group of Chicano bilinguals.

6a. El *man* que *came* ayer *wants John* comprar *a car* nuevo. 'The man who came yesterday wants John to buy a new car.'
6b. Tell Larry *que se calle la boca.* 'Tell Larry to shut his mouth'

[4] This constraint is confirmed by data from independent studies (Pfaff 1975, 1976; McClure n.d.; Wentz 1977).

[5] A condition similar to the equivalence constraint has been independently suggested by Lipski (1977).

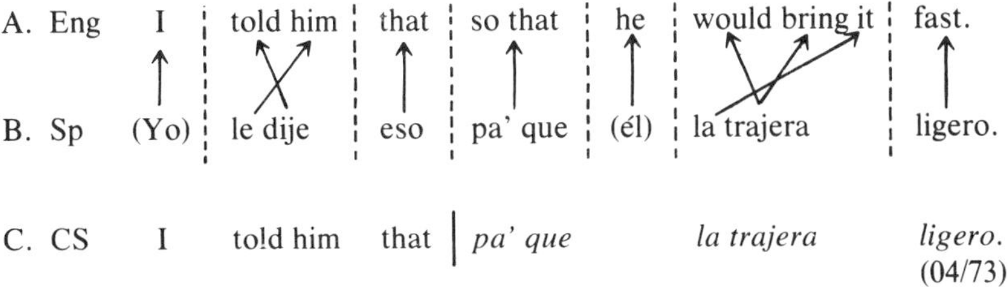

Figure 1. Permissible code-switching points

Gingràs claims that example 6a, in which codes are switched after almost every other word, is "in some very basic sense different" from example 6b, where the switching occurs between major constituents (p. 170). Although it is true, as will be seen later, that major constituents are switched more frequently than smaller ones, I suggest that constituent size only partially explains the difference between the two sentences, and that the important distinction is with respect to the equivalence constraint.[6] The sentence structures in examples 6a and 6b are similar in that both include a verb phrase and a verb phrase complement. In each, the verbs belong to a class that in English requires an infinitive complementizer rule to apply to the verb phrase complement, whereas Spanish makes use of a subjunctive complementizer in this same construction. Sentence 6a violates the equivalence constraint because it applies an English infinitive complementizer rule, which is not shared by Spanish, to the verb phrase complement. Because the code-switch did take place in this invented example, an English rule was lexicalized in Spanish, yielding a construction that could not have been generated by a Spanish rule and that is therefore ungrammatical by Spanish standards. On the other hand, the first portion of sentence 6a was generated by rules that are shared by English and Spanish (i.e., marked for both L_1 and L_2). The L_1 and L_2 versions map onto each other, constituent-by-constituent and element-by-element. A code-switch may therefore occur at any point within the main clause, and the utterance remains grammatical by both L_1 and L_2 standards. Structures in discourse to which a rule from L_1 but not from L_2 must categorically apply were found to be avoided as switch points by the balanced bilingual. There were no cases like sentence 6a in our data, and furthermore, all twenty-six of Gingràs's Chicano informants found it to be unacceptable as well. Constituents whose structures are nonequivalent in L_1 and L_2 tend to be uttered monolingually in actual

[6] Gingràs also claims that it is not obvious whether example 6a should even be considered a code-switch, mainly because "in the formation of the complement it is not clear whether English transformations have applied in an otherwise Spanish structure" (p. 168). Whether or not an invented example should be considered a code-switch is questionable; in any event, it is one that is hardly likely to occur in actual speech, as operation of the equivalence constraint demonstrates.

performance. This occurred in line C in Figure 1 (as well as in Gingràs's example 6b), where the verb phrase complements have undergone the Spanish subjunctive complementizer rule and are also lexicalized completely in Spanish. Ninety-four percent of Gingràs's informants also found sentence 6b to be an acceptable utterance.

An additional site of nonequivalence in sentence 6a is the object noun phrase in the embedded sentence: *a car* nuevo. English and Spanish have nonequivalent rules for adjective movement. In English, attributive adjectives typically precede the head noun, whereas in Spanish they typically follow it. A closed set of Spanish adjectives may also precede the noun. Switching an adjective but not the noun within the noun phrase, by following *either* L_1 or L_2 adjective placement rules for adjectives other than those in the closed set, results in a construction that is judged unacceptable by Timm's Chicano informants (1975, p. 479) and "fairly unacceptable" by Gingràs's informants (p. 172). Such constructions occur very rarely in our own performance data.

Simultaneous operation of the free morpheme and the equivalence constraints permits only code-switched utterances that, when translated into either language, are grammatical by both L_1 and L_2 standards and indicate a large degree of competence in both languages.

One might ask then whether the formulation of these constraints was not simply a consequence of having studied a balanced bilingual speaker: It is not surprising, although it required empirical proof, that an individual with an extensive repertoire in more than one language can manipulate them without violating the grammatical rules of either. But what happens in the case of nonfluent bilinguals? Being clearly dominant in one of the two languages, are they forced to switch into it from time to time because of lack of lexical or syntactic availability when speaking the other?

Weinreich (1953) characterized the ideal bilingual as an individual who "switches from one language to the other according to appropriate changes in the speech situation (interlocutor, topics, etc.) but not in an unchanged speech situation, and *certainly not within a single sentence*" (p. 73, emphasis added). He further speculated that there must be considerable individual differences between those who have control over their switching and those who have difficulty in maintaining or switching codes as required (p. 73).

The phenomenon of code-switching has been a point of contention in assessing community identity. Although intellectuals have seen language mixture to constitute evidence of the disintegration of the Puerto Rican Spanish language and culture (e.g., Varo 1971, Granda 1968), community members themselves appear to consider various bilingual behaviors to be defining features of their identity (Attinasi 1979). The opinion that code-switching represents a deviation from some bilingual "norm" is also widespread in educational circles today (LaFontaine 1975). It is my contention here that code-switching is itself a norm in specific speech situations that exist in stable bilingual communities. Furthermore, as I will demonstrate, satisfaction of this norm requires considerably more linguistic competence in two languages than has heretofore been noted. The present study addresses these issues by analyzing the code-switching behavior of twenty Puerto Rican speakers of varying degrees of reported and observed bilingual ability.

Hypothesis

As documented in Poplack (1981), a single individual may demonstrate more than one configuration or type of code-switching. One type involves a high proportion of intrasentential switching, as in example 7.

7a. Why make Carol *sentarse atras pa' que* ('sit in the back so') everybody has to move *pa' que se salga* ('for her to get out')? (04/439)

7b. He was sitting down *en la cama, mirándonos peleando, y* ('in bed, watching us fighting and') really, I don't remember *si él nos separó* ('if he separated us') or whatever, you know. (43/412)

I refer to this as a more complex or "intimate" type, because a code-switched segment, and those around it, must conform to the underlying syntactic rules of two languages that bridge constituents and link them together grammatically.

Another less intimate type is characterized by relatively more tag switches and single noun switches. These are often heavily loaded in ethnic content and would be placed low on a scale of translatability, as in sentence 8b.

8a. Vendía arroz ('He sold rice') *'n shit*. (07/79)

8b. Salían en sus carros y en sus ('They would go out in their cars and in their') *snowmobiles*. (08/192)

Many investigators do not consider switches like those in example 8 to represent true instances of code-switching but rather to constitute an emblematic part of the speaker's monolingual style (Gumperz 1971, Wentz 1977). It will also be noted that their insertion in discourse has few, if any, ramifications for the remainder of the sentence. Tags are freely moveable constituents that may be inserted almost anywhere in the sentence without fear of violating any grammatical rule. The ease with which single nouns may be switched is attested to by the fact that of all grammatical categories, they have been found to be the most frequently switched (e.g., Timm 1975, Wentz 1977).

It was found that the choice of intimate versus emblematic code-switching is heavily dependent on the ethnic group membership of the interlocutor in the case of the balanced bilingual, who has the linguistic ability to make such a choice. Ingroup membership favors intrasentential code-switching, whereas nongroup membership favors emblematic switching. In other words, the type of switch that all investigators agree to be "true" code-switching was mainly reserved for communication with another in-group member. In considering whether this pattern holds true more generally, we first note that the type of code-switching used by nonfluent bilinguals must be further constrained by bilingual ability. The research to be described examines the extent to which the bilingual competence evinced by the skilled code-switching behavior of a balanced bilingual is shared by the nonfluent bilinguals in the same speech community. This will have ramifications for the possible use of code-switching as an indicator of bilingual ability.

With the inclusion of nonfluent bilinguals in the sample, three alternative outcomes may be hypothesized. The speaker may engage in both intimate (intrasentential) and emblematic switching, regardless of her competence in the two languages, thereby running the risk of rendering utterances that will be ungrammatical for L_1, L_2, or both (and hence providing a principled basis for the claim that code-switching represents a deviation from some norm). On the other hand, the speaker may avoid those intrasentential switches that are syntactically risky. This might ensure grammatical utterances. Such results would weaken the claims that code-switching occurs because of lack of availability in L_2. Logically, there is a third possibility, that the speaker will not switch at all. This need not be considered; although two members of the sample switched only once each in two and one-half hours of speech, there was no one who did not switch at all.

The Sample

Block description

East 102nd Street is located in the heart of El Barrio, one of the oldest and until recently the largest Puerto Rican community in the United States. Although Puerto Ricans have now dispersed to other areas of Manhattan and other boroughs in New York City, it has been estimated that the population on East 102nd Street is still at least 95 percent Puerto Rican.

The block, identified by the census as one of the lowest socioeconomic areas of the city, is largely residential. It consists of sixteen three- to five-story tenements that house some 600 people, and is bounded by major avenues on the east and west. There is a small number of commercial establishments on the block, including two *bodegas*, an *alcapurria* stand, two Hispanic social clubs, a numbers parlor, a pet store, a vegetable market, and a plumbing supply shop. Block life is active. It is not uncommon to see groups of people congregating on the stoops, and in the summer months children play in the streets and adults set up tables on the sidewalks for domino games.

The block has had a stable Puerto Rican population since the 1930s and today includes third- and even fourth-generation family members. Although uncharacteristically homogeneous with regard to ethnicity, block residents are heterogeneous with regard to personal history. About half of the block residents were born and raised in Puerto Rico. These are mostly older people, who tend to be Spanish dominant or monolingual. The younger people were generally born and raised in El Barrio, and most are either English dominant or bilingual. This fact and the low median age of the population (three-fourths are under forty-five years of age) match the general demographic characteristics of the New York City Puerto Rican population in general (U.S. Department of Labor 1975, p. 44).

Extended participant observation of East 102nd Street indicates that block residents may be divided into nine social networks, which, though not mutually exclusive, are seen to reappear consistently in the public life of the block. The informants for this study are drawn from two of the more closely observed of these networks.

Half of the sample belongs to a network centered around the Gavilanes social club. Participants in this network are linked through friendship or familial ties as well as participation in common club activities. The group is male-dominated, and its members are on public display more than other block residents because they are out on the street for large periods of the day. Members range in age from the early twenties to the fifties and most of the males were employed during the period of observation (1975–7). (Only one female in the present sample had paid employment during this time.) The group includes both those born and raised in Puerto Rico, who are Spanish dominant, and those born and raised in New York City, who are English-dominant or bilingual. Group members generally accommodate to the older, Puerto Rican-born members by speaking Spanish.

An additional eight informants belong to a network whose members congregate around the numbers parlor (Banca), a center of lively social activity on the block. Calling the numbers and passing them on by word-of-mouth (in Spanish) is a daily event in block life. Like members of the Gavilanes group, Banca group members range in age from the twenties to the fifties; however, both men and women participate in this network. Friendship and familial ties are less of a factor in linking group members than shared participation in activities in and around the Banca. Members of this network were all born and raised in Puerto Rico and are Spanish-dominant or bilingual. Banca members were for the most part unemployed during the period of observation.

Of the two remaining informants, one does not participate in one network significantly more than in any other, and the second is a recent arrival to the block. Both are Spanish dominant.

The informants

The twenty informants in the sample were selected primarily on the basis of two parameters: age of arrival in the United States and (ethnographically) observed language preference. This choice was made in order to study the effects of bilingual ability and community influence on code-switching. Members of the sample are fairly evenly divided between those who arrived as children (up to six years of age), when parental influence on language use is greatest, or who were born in the United States; those who arrived as preadolescents (aged seven to twelve), when peer influence encroaches on parental influence; those who arrived as adolescents (aged thirteen to seventeen), when peer influence on language choice is greatest (Payne 1976, Poplack 1978a); and those who arrived as adults, when patterns of language use tend to have crystallized.

About half of the speakers were observed to be Spanish dominant, about 10 percent English dominant, and the rest bilingual. With some exceptions these observations confirm the speakers' own self-reports. In addition, several other demographic, ethnographic, and attitudinal factors that could affect language use were studied.

Demographic characteristics of the sample

Eleven of the twenty informants are male, nine are female, and 75 percent of them are between twenty-one and forty years of age. Regardless of age of arrival, all but two have spent ten years or more in the United States, and the majority (60 percent) have been in the United States for more than twenty years. Because duration of stay is probably overshadowed by other influences on linguistic behavior after about two years (Heidelberger Forschungsprojekt "Pidgin-Deutsch" 1977), the level of competence in English of this group is not likely to change much with increased residence in the United States.

Most of the sample (65 percent) have also spent ten or more years in Puerto Rico, either early in life (only one informant was born in the United States), or including extended sojourns after having migrated to the continental United States. There is some correlation between speaker age and time spent in Puerto Rico: The older speakers are generally those who have spent most time on the island. However, the majority of the sample (70 percent) visit the island infrequently: less than every two years. In sum, it is reasonable to expect that these speakers have all also acquired some competence in Spanish, whether it is put to use at present or not.

Sample members report more years of schooling than the general Puerto Rican population in New York City. Seventy percent have had at least some high school education; this includes 20 percent who have either graduated from high school or had some college education.

Slightly less than half of the informants were employed at the time of the study and these mainly in the service sectors of the workforce: baker, cook, medical technician, counterman, and so on. Of these, most (70 percent) are employed off the block.

Language-oriented characteristics of the sample

The informants responded to a language attitude questionnaire, designed to tap various aspects of language skill by self-report as well as community attitudes toward Puerto Rican language and ethnicity.

When asked if they considered themselves "mainly Spanish speakers, English speakers, or bilinguals," slightly more than half (55 percent) of the sample claimed to be mainly Spanish speakers. The others considered themselves bilingual. No one claimed to be mainly an English speaker, reflecting the underrating on the part of speakers of their English language skills. There is doubtless some correlation between this finding and the fact that all speakers report having learned Spanish in early childhood (between the ages of two and seven), with the majority (75 percent) having learned it in Puerto Rico. On the other hand, only two informants learned English in early childhood. Sixty percent of the sample learned English between the ages of seven and twenty-one, and all speakers report having learned English in the United States. When asked to rate their competence in both Spanish and English on a seven-point scale, speakers' ratings are consistent with their verbal self-description. Almost all (95 percent) rate themselves as having more than median proficiency in Spanish, whereas less than half (45 percent) claim this for English. If the hypothesis that code-switching is caused by lack of availability in L_2 were correct, it would appear that members of this sample population would favor switching into Spanish from an English base.

Attitudinal characteristics of the sample

The language attitude questionnaire also seeks to tap speakers' feelings toward language as it relates to Puerto Rican culture and ethnicity. Responses to attitude questions are less readily interpretable than reports of language use. On an ethnic identity scale based on questions about pride in being Puerto Rican, feelings toward assimilation, and characterization of nationality (e.g., Puerto Rican, *Nuyorican*, American, etc.), the majority (65 percent) revealed clear positive identification as Puerto Ricans. When asked to assess how important the Spanish language is to "Puerto Ricanness," 90 percent felt that Spanish is "important" or "very important" to being a Puerto Rican. This attitude was summarized by Sally:

> *si tu eres puertorriqueño* ('if you're Puerto Rican'), your father's a Puerto Rican, you should at least *de vez en cuando* ('sometimes'), you know, *hablar español* ('speak Spanish'). (34/25)

Nevertheless, a majority (60 percent) also felt that Puerto Rican monolingual English speakers did not represent a divisive force in the Puerto Rican community in New York City. When asked if there was "anything you could say in Spanish that you could not say in English," or vice-versa, 60 percent of the speakers felt that there was nothing that could be said in one language that could not be translated into the other. Most of the speakers (75 percent) in this sample are also aware that code-switching is a frequent and widespread phenomenon in their community. When asked if they thought that "few, some, or many speakers mixed languages," three-fourths of the sample thought that many people code-switched. Such awareness of community and individual behavioral norms with regard to code-switching was again voiced by Sally, who provided the title for this chapter.

> Sometimes I'll start a sentence in Spanish *y termino en español* ('and finish in Spanish'). (34/489)[7]

This opinion corroborates Pedraza's ethnographic observation that a majority of block residents code-switched somewhat or frequently.

In sum, although the Spanish language is overwhelmingly considered an integral part of being Puerto Rican, and in spite of the fact that only a minority feel that one or the other of the languages may be better for saying certain things, ethnographic observation, quantitative sociolinguistic analysis, and speakers' own reports all indicate that code-switching is an integral part of community speech norms on East 102nd Street. Code-switches provoked by lack of availability or utilized as an emblem of ethnic identity appear, then, to be only weak factors in speakers' perception of their own behavior.

Methodology

Data collection

The quantitative analyses that follow are based on recorded speech data in both interview and "natural" settings. Pedraza's membership in the Puerto Rican community and his familiarity with the setting and participants allowed him to enter local network situations, such as domino games or *bochinche* 'gossip' sessions, and simply turn on his tape recorder without causing an apparent break in the conversational flow. In addition, he carried out a "sociolinguistic interview" with each informant aiming to elicit casual, undirected speech and administered the detailed attitude questionnaire previously mentioned.[8] Our data, then, range from the vernacular speech of informal, intragroup communication to the more formal discourse used in discussing concepts such as language and culture.

The importance of data collection techniques cannot be overemphasized, particularly in the study of a phenomenon such as code-switching, which cannot be directly elicited. The actual occurrence of a switch is

[7] This lapsus provides ground for interesting speculation, which I leave to the reader.

[8] This questionnaire was developed for the Philadelphia speech community by the Project on Linguistic Change and Variation under the direction of William Labov and was subsequently adapted for use in the Puerto Rican community by the author.

constrained, probably more than by any other factor, by the norms or the perceived norms of the speech situation. The most important of these norms for the balanced bilingual was found to be the ethnicity of the interlocutor (Poplack 1978), once other criteria (appropriateness, formality of speech situation) were met. The balanced bilingual speaker switched four times as frequently with an ingroup interlocutor as with a nonmember and, what is more, used a much larger percentage of intimate switches with the ingroup member. Because the data used in this study are representative of ingroup interaction only, they are presumably characterized not only by a higher rate of code-switching but also by a larger proportion of intrasentential switches than would have been the case if they had been collected by a nonmember.

Coding procedures

Sixty-six hours of tape-recorded speech in which each informant participated in each of the three speech situations provided 1,835 instances of code-switching. Transcription, coding, and analysis of the data were carried out with the invaluable collaboration of Alicia Pousada. The informants appeared on tape, either alone or in a group, from a minimum of two and one-half hours to a maximum of eleven hours. Each instance of a switch was coded as to its syntactic function in the utterance, along with the syntactic categories of the segments that preceded and followed it. We also noted the language of the switch, whether it was preceded or followed by editing phenomena (hesitations, false starts, etc.), whether it constituted a repetition of the preceding syntactic category, whether it was a single noun switch in an otherwise L_2 base, and if so, whether it was an ethnically loaded item.

In each instance, the largest complete constituent next to the switch in the syntactic derivation of the utterance was considered to be the syntactic category of the segment adjacent to the switch. Thus, *con los puños* in sentence 9a was coded as a prepositional phrase preceded by an independent clause and followed by a tag. *Promising* in sentence 9b was coded as a verb preceded by an auxiliary and followed by an object noun phrase, because all of them are dominated by the same verb phrase node. *Que* in sentence 9c was coded as a subordinate conjunction preceded by an independent clause and followed by a subordinate clause. This method was used to determine the syntactic category of the code-switch and the segment following it as well.

9a. But I wanted to fight her *con los puños* ('with my fists'), you know. (43/356)

9b. Siempre está *promising* cosas. 'He's always promising things.' (04/408)

9c. I could understand *que* ('that') you don't know how to speak Spanish, *¿verdad?* ('right?'). (34/24)

Other segments whose syntactic make-up varied but which exercised a consistent function in discourse were coded according to that function. Examples of these are fillers, such as *este* (umm), *I mean*; interjections, *¡ay, Dios mio!* ('oh, my God!'), *shit!*; tags, *¿entiendes?* ('understand?'), *you know*; idiomatic expressions, *y toda esa mierda* ('and all that shit'), *no way*; quotations, put down '*menos*' ('less'). These are segments that are less intimately linked with the remainder of the utterance, insofar as they may occur freely at any point in the sentence. As will be seen, they contrast with the intrasentential switches, which must obey sentence-internal syntactic constraints.

Certain switched segments were larger than a single constituent, as in example 10. Hasselmo (1970) has called this "unlimited switching." These cases, which were relatively rare, required special coding conventions. The only type with nonnegligible frequency involved moveable constituents like *sometimes* and *honey* in example 10. Because these constituents do not form an integral part of the syntactic structure of the sentence, they were relegated to the category of intervening material between the switch and the adjacent syntactic categories, and the switches were considered to have occurred between the independent clause and the adverb in sentence 10a and between the verb phrase and the adverbial phrase in sentence 10b.

10a. No tienen ni tiempo ('they don't even have time') *sometimes for their own kids, and you know who I'm talking about.* (04/17)

10b. Se sentó ('he sat down'), *honey, away from us.* (04/433)

In a case like sentence 11, utterances were divided by sentence boundary. *Pa' muchos sitios* was coded as a switched prepositional phrase in Spanish preceded by an independent clause and followed by a sentence.[9] *With my husband* was coded as a switched prepositional phrase in English preceded by an independent clause and followed by a pause.

11. And from there I went to live *pa' muchos sitios* ('in a lot of places'). Después viví en la ciento diecisiete ('then I lived on 117th') *with my husband.* (42/76)

It will be noted that the analysis of sentence 11 involves a change of base language. The first prepositional phrase is considered a switch into Spanish from an English base, whereas the second is considered a switch into English from a Spanish base. Although speakers who are dominant in one language show a strong tendency to switch into L_2 from an L_1 base, more balanced bilinguals often alternate base languages within the

[9] Note that the sentence itself contains a switch. The switched segment was coded for following syntactic category only if the category was produced in the language other than that of the switch. So an example like *Pa' muchos sitios* was not coded for following syntactic category.

same discourse.[10] An example of this can be seen in 12, which represents a single discourse and where segments to the left of the slashes exhibit a base language different from those to the right.

12. But I used to eat the *bofe*, the brain. And then they stopped selling it because *tenían, este, le encontraron que tenía* ('they had, uh, they found out that it had') worms. I used to make some *bofe*! / Después yo hacía uno d'esos ('then I would make one of those') *concoctions: The garlic* con cebolla, y hacía un mojo, y yo dejaba que se curara eso ('with onion, and I'd make a sauce, and I'd let that sit') *for a couple of hours.* / Then you be drinking and eating that shit. Wooh! It's like eating anchovies when you're drinking. Delicious! (04/101)

Non-code-switches

Certain borderline alternations between L_1 and L_2 were excluded from this study. One type involves switched items that have been referred to by Hasselmo (1970) as socially integrated into the language of the community: segments that are repeated often enough in a certain language to be regarded as habitual. These may or may not be phonologically integrated into the base language and should not be confused with the types of integration shown in Table 1:

13a. Ay, ¡qué *cute* [kju] se ve! 'How cute he looks!' (34/202)
13b. Eso es un *team* [tiŋ]: Palo Viejo. 'That's a team: Palo Viejo.' (37/42)
13c. En ese tiempo había muchos *junkies* [jɔŋki]. 'At that time there were a lot of junkies.' (34/40)

Switches into L_2 designating food names, proper names, and place names were also omitted from this study, except when there was an acceptable L_2 alternative that was not used, for example, *Puerto Rico* [pɔɚ'ɚiykow] ~ [pwɛrtɔ'xikɔ]. Also excluded were translations in response to requests for information, as in example 14a; L_2 segments followed by an explanation in L_1, as in sentence 14b; switches accompanied by metalinguistic comments, as in sentence 14c; and instances of "externally conditioned switching" (Clyne 1972, p. 70) in which the interlocutor switched languages within the same discourse and the informant followed suit, as in example 14d.

14a. A: Lo pusieron un . . . ¿cómo se dice? ¿un tutone? 'They gave him a – what do you call it? a tuton?'
B: *Tutor?* (52/229)
14b. But I used to eat the *bofe*, the brain. (04/101)
14c. I'm one of those real what you call in Spanish *pendejas* ('jerks'), you know. (04/158)

[10] A construct such as "language of the sentence," which according to Wentz (1977, p. 182) is the one in which the determiner and main verb were produced, does not appear to be operative for these data, as they contain a good number of code-switched verbs (sixty, or 3 percent of the data) in a language other than that of the determiner.

14d. A: I had a dream yesterday, last night.
B: *¿De qué numero?* 'What number?'
A: *El cero setenta y cinco.* ('Zero seventy-five.') (34/040)

Quantitative analysis of the data

Our concern here is with both linguistic and extralinguistic questions, and I shall attempt to incorporate the answers into a single analytic model. The linguistic questions concern the surface configuration of the switches. Are there some sorts of constituents in discourse that can be switched and others that cannot? Are there constituents that tend to be switched into one language rather than the other? In what ways do switched items combine with unswitched portions of discourse?

The extralinguistic questions concern the code-switchers. Can the community as a whole be characterized by some code-switching type, or are there speakers who favor certain switch types over others? In the latter case, what are the demographic, attitudinal, and social factors that contribute to the occurrence of one type over another, and what is the comparative effect of each?

To answer these questions the following quantitative analyses were performed on the data: The syntactic category of the switched item was cross-tabulated first with the preceding and then the following syntactic category to ascertain whether certain points (as, for example, the point between determiner and noun) in discourse were more favorable to the occurrence of a switch than others. Also cross-tabulated were switched item by language, to see if certain switch types were favored by one language over another, and switched item by speaker, to see if there was any difference in switching behavior among speakers.

The cross-tabulations revealed that speakers could be divided into two groups: One favored extrasentential switches, and the other tended toward the intrasentential, or more intimate type. The code-switching data were subsequently collapsed into two categories: intrasentential and extrasentential switches. These categories were then cross-tabulated individually with the demographic, attitudinal, and language-oriented characteristics of the informants to discover which, if any, have a bearing on the choice of one code-switch over the other. Tests of association were applied to each of these cross-tabulations to determine the significance of the extralinguistic factors on the occurrence of one code-switch type over the other.

Having determined a dependent variable (in this case, code-switch type), its relevant variants (intrasentential and extrasentential code-switching), and the total population of utterances in which the variation occurs (i.e., the total corpus of switched items), the significance tests made it possible to suggest which extralinguistic factors might reasonably be expected to affect the relative frequency of the two types of code-switches. Because these factors may be correlated among themselves within the sample and have correlated effects on code-switching type, it was then necessary to use multivariate statistical techniques to determine which factors made a significant contribution, independent of the effects of other factors, to the choice of code-switch type. Because of the binomial nature of the data and their uneven distribution among the different possible configurations of factors, a maximum likelihood approach was taken for the evaluation of factor effects, together with log-likelihood tests of significance.

Results

Perhaps the most striking result of this study is that there were virtually no instances of ungrammatical combinations of L_1 and L_2 in the 1,835 switches studied, regardless of the bilingual ability of the speaker.

The hypotheses as to the nature of syntactic constraints on code-switching in the speech of the balanced bilingual, that is, the free morpheme constraint and the equivalence constraint, have been generally corroborated by the present investigation of both balanced and nonfluent bilinguals. There were no examples of switches between bound morphemes of the type **eat -iendo*, mentioned in example 5. A small number (five, or less than 1 percent of the data) of switches within idiomatic expressions did occur, however, as in sentences 15a and 15b.

15a. Estamos como marido y *woman*. 'We are like man and wife.' (< Sp. Estamos como *marido y mujer*.) (05/141)

15b. Mi mai tuvo que ir a firmar y *shit* pa' sacarme, *you know*. 'My mom had to go sign *'n shit* to get me out, you know.' (07/058)

A small number of switches violated the equivalence constraint (eleven, or less than 1 percent of the data). The majority of these (7/11) involved adjective placement, a rule that is not shared by L_1 and L_2. This can be seen in sentence 16a, in which adjective placement follows Spanish but not English rules, and in sentence 16b, in which the reverse is true.

16a. Tenían patas flacas, pechos *flat*. 'They had skinny legs, flat chests.' (09/432)

16b. I got a lotta *blanquito* ('whitey') friends. (34/274)

A strong tendency to avoid nonequivalence is nonetheless manifested in the fact that 88 percent (49/56) of the adjectival forms in the corpus are either predicate adjectives, which have equivalent surface structures in Spanish and English, or members of the subset of Spanish adjectives that precede the noun, as in English. The proportion of switched items that when combined with the rest of the utterance did not follow grammatical rules shared by both L_1 and L_2 is negligible. (Of this small number, *none* of the constructions was idiosyncratic or based on rules that were not drawn from one or the other of the grammars.) This finding is strong evidence that alternation between two languages requires a high level of bilingual competence. Code-switching involves enough knowledge of two (or more) grammatical systems to allow the speaker to draw from each system only those rules that the other shares. Surprisingly enough, this knowledge appears to be shared even by the nonfluent bilinguals in the sample. The way in which these latter speakers are able to fulfill the requirement of grammaticality, despite their limited competence in one of the codes, will be examined later.

Discourse functions of code-switching

The finding that code-switching constitutes the skilled manipulation of overlapping sections of two (or more) grammars is further corroborated by an examination of some of the ways in which a code-switch functions in discourse. One of the characteristics of skilled code-switching is a smooth transition between L_1 and L_2 elements, unmarked by false starts, hesitations, or lengthy pauses. The data show that the transition between the preceding category and the switched item is made smoothly, that is, with no editing, 96 percent of the time, and that between switched item and following syntactic category is made smoothly 98 percent of the time. Other characteristics of skilled code-switching include a seeming "unawareness" of the alternation between languages, that is, the switched item is not accompanied by metalinguistic commentary, it does not constitute a repetition of all or part of the preceding segment, nor is it repeated by the following segment; switches are made up of segments larger than just single nouns inserted into an otherwise L_2 sentence; and code-switching is used for purposes other than that of conveying untranslatable items.

The data for the sample as a whole show that these characteristics are strongly in evidence: The switched item constitutes a repetition of the preceding segment only 5 percent of the time, whereas the following segment repeats all or part of the switched item only 8 percent of the time. Single noun switches constitute only 10 percent of the data; of these, less than one-fourth represent items that are ethnically loaded.

In other words, features known to be characteristic of communication with a nongroup member, such as high percentages of single noun switches used to convey notions that are difficult to translate, are not defining features of intragroup communication.

Linguistic properties of switched segments

Having established that switching occurs in a smooth fashion, I will discuss the nature of the switches themselves. Which constituents are switched, and in what ways do they combine with preceding and following segments? Do certain combinations tend to occur more regularly?

Fifteen syntactic categories whose occurrence is dependent on sentence internal constraints were extracted from the data, along with seven ex-

Table 2. *Code-switching by syntactic category and language*

Syntactic category of CS	No. of CS from Eng. to Sp.	No. of CS from Sp. to Eng.	% of total CS	*N*
Intrasentential				
Determiner	3	0	0.2	3
Single noun	34	141	9.5	175
Subj. noun phrase	44	25	3.8	69
Obj. noun phrase	62	78	7.6	140
Auxiliary	0	0	0.0	0
Verb	6	13	1.0	19
Verb phrase	27	13	2.2	40
Indep. clause	44	35	4.3	79
Subordinate (& relative) clause	53	23	4.1	76
Adjective	3	12	0.8	15
Pred. adjective	6	37	2.3	43
Adverb	14	33	2.6	47
Preposition	2	0	0.1	2
Phrases (prep., adj., advb., inf.)	55	39	5.1	94
Conjunctions (subordinate, coordinate, relative pronoun)	33	16	2.7	49
Extrasentential				
Sentence	201	171	20.3	372
Filler	9	11	1.1	20
Interjection	26	89	6.3	115
Idiomatic expression	8	23	1.7	31
Quotation	20	14	1.9	34
Tag	9	403	22.5	412
Totals	659	1,176		1,835

Note: Nouns and verbs were counted as noun phrases and verb phrases, respectively, if they functioned as such within the utterance.

trasentential, or freely distributable, categories. These are shown in Table 2.

The relative frequencies with which constituents may be switched, indicated in Table 2, largely confirm the findings of other studies (Gumperz 1976, Wentz 1977, Poplack 1981). As can be seen, full sentences are the most frequently switched constituent, making up 20 percent of the data. Extrasentential code-switching types, which require less knowledge of two grammars because they are freely distributable within discourse, constitute about half the data.

Among the intrasentential switches, we find single nouns to be the most frequently switched category, again confirming the findings of other studies. Table 2 also reveals a tendency to switch major constituents, which account for about 60 percent of the intrasentential data, more frequently than smaller ones. This provides additional support for the equivalence constraint, which predicts that whole constituents will be switched rather than elements within them if the syntactic rule for generating the constituent is not shared by both L_1 and L_2.

Language of the switch

Table 2 also shows the frequencies with which the syntactic categories under investigation are produced in each language. As can be seen, with a few exceptions, segments are about as likely to be switched into English as into Spanish, providing further evidence for the suggestion that the code-switching mode proceeds from a single grammar.

The data in Table 2 also provide a test of whether the rate of occurrence of a given syntactic switch category is significantly different from one language to the other. For this a log-likelihood of a rate estimate for the two languages separately was compared with that for the combined data. Significantly more switches from Spanish into English were found for four categories: tags, interjections, single nouns, and predicate adjectives. The last is probably an artifact of sparse data, but the results for tags, interjections, and single nouns have important interpretations.

It is not surprising that bilinguals residing in an English-speaking society should favor English noun switches over Spanish. Interjections and tags, as will be shown, are precisely the switch types that are favored by Spanish-dominant speakers. These speakers not only switch almost uniquely into English from a Spanish base but also are distinguishable from the bilinguals by the type of constituents they switch.

The statistical analysis shows that aside from the four switch types that are favored from Spanish into English, most tend to be switched significantly more from English into Spanish. This result is an artifact of the other, however, and when the tag, interjection, and noun switches are removed from the data, almost all of the remaining switches show no significant rate differences between the two languages.

Combinability of switched segments

In order to ascertain points within the sentence at which segments may be switched, intrasententially switched items were cross-tabulated with segments preceding and following them. In a table generated by the fifteen possibilities of syntactic category preceding the code-switch versus fifteen syntactic categories for the code-switch itself, about 40 percent of the 225 cells were filled; that is, eighty-eight different combinations of some constituent and another switched one occurred. Of the nonoccurrent combinations, 40 percent were syntactically impossible (e.g., auxiliary + preposition); the remainder of the cells were empty due most probably to the distribution of the data – cells corresponding to relatively rare switch types or relatively rare preceding categories, or both, would not be expected to occur with this sample size.

The two most frequently recurring switch points among 681 tokens of intrasentential code-switch plus preceding category were between determiner and noun (19 percent) and between verb phrase and object noun phrase (12 percent). This is not surprising, because evidence already exists that nouns and noun phrases are frequently switched. Other combinations that recur frequently include independent clause and subordinate clause (4 percent), verb and predicate adjective (4 percent), and subject noun phrase and verb phrase (3 percent). The remaining combinations each represent 2 percent or less of the data. Similarly, sixty-three (28 percent) of the possible combinations occurred among the 729 tokens of code-switch plus following category, the overwhelming majority of which also individually represented very small proportions of the data.

Because of the size of the data set, it is statistically unlikely that clearer patterns could emerge from a table with so many cells. With more data, frequencies with which code-switched items precede and follow specific constituents might be able to be predicted. Such frequencies, I hypothesize, would simply reflect the frequency of any given combination of constituents (e.g., adverb + adjective, preposition + noun phrase) in monolingual speech. This hypothesis could only be confirmed by evaluating the frequencies of all the possible constituent combinations in a large sample of monolingual speech, a task beyond the scope of this research.

The present information, however, indicates that there is a rather large number of points within the sentence at which it is permissible to switch codes. This is additional evidence that code-switching requires knowledge of two systems. Note that there is about as much intrasentential as extrasentential switching (Table 2) in the corpus. Although extrasentential switching could presumably be accomplished by alternately drawing on rules from two separate grammars, intrasentential code-switching would appear to depend on the juxtaposition of constituents too intimately connected to be generated separately by rules from two distinct grammars. This, together with the finding that only a very small number of switches are accompanied by breaks in the speech flow, lend strong support to the hypothesis that code-switching is, in fact, a verbal mode distinct from English speaking and Spanish speaking yet consists of the overlapping elements from both.

Differential behavior of informants: language of the switch

Let us now examine the individual code-switching behavior of the informants in the sample. Table 3 shows the frequency with which speakers switch into English. It is striking that the Spanish-dominant speakers switch almost uniquely into English from an unambiguously Spanish base.

Table 3. *Percentage of code-switches into English for Spanish-dominant and bilingual speakers*

Spanish dominants			Bilinguals		
Informant	% of CS from Spanish to English	*N*	Informant	% of CS from Spanish to English	*N*
Eli	100	9	Cal	100	35
Gui	100	35	Edo	99	212
Tera	100	1	Apache	91	63
Isi	100	45	Pearl	57	135
Rosa	100	1	Garra	53	15
Fela	97	69	Candy	52	81
Charlie	94	33	Lola	43	309
Sami	93	93	Melo	39	89
Chito	92	89	Sally	37	354
Shorty	71	40			
Wilda	63	127			
Average	92	542	Average	63	1,293

Note: N = 1,835.

Bilingual speakers on the other hand, cluster around the halfway mark, with some speakers switching more into Spanish from an English base and others the reverse. It is clear that these bilinguals cannot be said to have a single base or dominant language of discourse, but rather two.

Note that three bilingual and two Spanish-dominant speakers (according to self-reports) show patterns that contrast with the other members of their respective groups. As will be seen again later, four of these are speakers whose self-report of language dominance conflicted with our ethnographic and linguistic observations. The fifth, Edo, is in fact bilingual but has strong feelings toward speaking Spanish and has been observed to do so almost uniquely when interacting on the block.

Differential behavior of informants: switch type. Let us now examine another way in which bilinguals differ from Spanish-dominant speakers. The switches in Table 2 were listed according to the presumed degree of bilingual proficiency required to produce them, in decreasing order. Lowest on the scale are taglike switches. These include interjections, fillers, tags, and idiomatic expressions, all of which can be produced in L_2 with only minimal knowledge of the grammar of that language. Next on the scale are full sentences or larger segments, which require much more knowledge of L_2 to produce, although, hypothetically, not as much as is

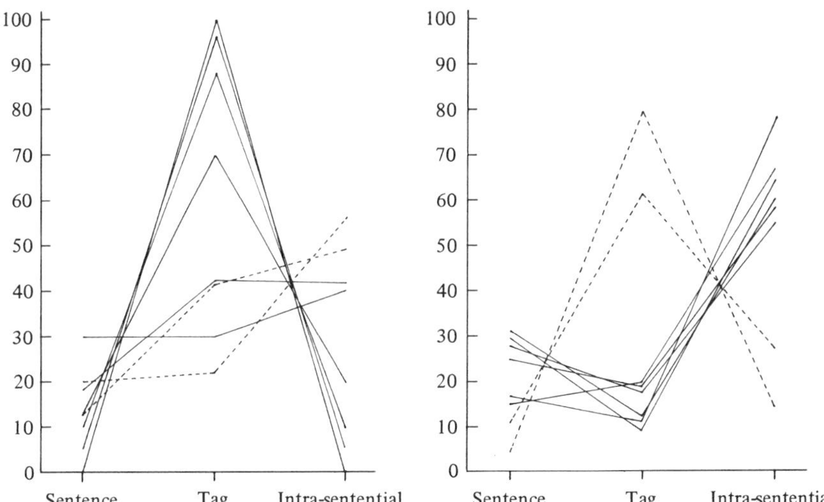

Figure 2. Percentage of switch types for reported Spanish-dominant speakers (N = 1,278)

Figure 3. Percentage of switch types for reported bilingual speakers (N = 531)

required by the third category, intrasentential switches. As suggested, in order to produce this latter sort of switch, the speaker must also know enough about the grammar of each, and the way they interact, to avoid ungrammatical utterances.

Figures 2 and 3 graph the percentages of each of these switch types for the informants in our sample and show that reported language ability (which in all cases but four corresponds to observed ability) is an excellent indicator of code-switching patterns.[11] Figure 2 shows that most of those who report that they know and use more Spanish than English and feel more comfortable with it tend to switch into L_2 by means of taglike constructions, sometimes to the practical exclusion of sentential or intrasentential switches. Those who claim to be bilingual, on the other hand, show a reversal (Figure 3). They strongly favor the switches hypothesized to require most knowledge of both languages, sentential and intrasentential switches. The most favored switch type for bilinguals is clearly intrasentential, whereas the least favored is taglike switching.

The few exceptions to these patterns are represented by the dashed lines on the graphs. Two speakers who claimed to be Spanish dominant in fact show a similar code-switching configuration to the bilinguals, whereas two who claim to be bilingual show patterns similar to the Spanish dominants. Strikingly, these are precisely the cases where ethnographic

[11] Three Spanish-dominant and one bilingual speaker were omitted from these calculations because they each produced fifteen tokens or less.

observation and linguistic analysis were previously found to conflict with self-report, because the speakers underrated or overrated their ability in English. Two additional speakers are actually Spanish dominant but also show a code-switching pattern similar to that of the bilinguals. They do, however, have a greater degree of competence in English than those who follow the "Spanish dominant" pattern. They tend to distribute their switches among the three switch types, rather than show a marked preference for any one, and they may be considered to exhibit code-switching behavior intermediate to the bilinguals and the more clearly Spanish-dominant speakers.

Contribution of extralinguistic factors to the occurrence of code-switch type

Having ascertained that reported and observed bilingual ability is an important factor in predicting the type of code-switch that will be uttered (a chi-square test shows this factor to be significant at the .001 level), I next attempted to determine which other extralinguistic factors might have an effect on the occurrence of intrasentential code-switching. Individual tests were performed on each factor group as well as on each pair of factors within each group to determine their significance.

Sex

The sex of the speaker is a significant factor in predicting code-switch type at the .001 level. Women favor intrasentential switching; over half (56 percent) of their switches are intrasentential, whereas only one-third of the men's switches are of this type.

Age of L_2 acquisition and age of migration to the United States

These two factors were originally examined separately for each speaker. All informants learned Spanish in early childhood, though there was some variation in the age at which English was learned. Because there is a one-to-one correspondence between the age at which the speaker arrived in the United States and the age at which she learned English (not a surprising fact because all speakers report having learned English in the United States), these two factors were subsequently considered as one. On ethnographic grounds we had originally distinguished four ages of arrival/L_2 acquisition: early childhood (two through seven), preadolescent (eight through thirteen), adolescent (fourteen through eighteen), and adult (over eighteen). Tests of association reveal that the difference between learning English/arriving in the United States as an adolescent and as an adult is not significant at the .05 level. Consequently, these two age groups were considered together. All the other age distinctions were significant at either the .001 or the .01 level.

Speakers who learned both English and Spanish in early childhood, the "true" bilinguals, show the highest percentage of intrasentential switching (346/582, or 59 percent). Those who learned English between the ages of eight and thirteen, show only a slightly lower percentage of this type of switch (309/593, or 52 percent), a small difference, but one that is nonetheless significant at the .01 level. Speakers who learned English after the age of thirteen, however, show a much lower percentage of intrasentential switches (196/660, or 30 percent), a drop that is significant at the .001 level.

Reported bilingual ability

As we have already seen in Figure 1, reported (and observed) bilingual ability is an excellent predictor of code-switching type. Bilinguals produce a far greater percentage of intrasentential switches (682/1293, or 53 percent) than those who are Spanish dominant (169/542, or 31 percent). This difference is significant at the .001 level.

Education

Members of the sample were divided into three categories according to their educational attainment: those who had no more than primary school education (first through eighth grades), those who had some high school but did not graduate (ninth through eleventh grades), and those who graduated from high school whether or not they attended some college. An initial test performed on this last group revealed that this factor has an effect on code-switching that is significant at the .001 level. Speakers who had primary school education or less tended to switch intrasententially slightly more (45 percent) than those who had some high school education (41 percent). This difference is not significant. High school graduates, however, switched intrasententially more (60 percent) than either of the other two groups, a significant difference at the .001 level. Upon closer examination, however, it became apparent that although the category contained six speakers, all but five of the tokens (401/406) had been uttered by two bilingual women who had learned English as children. Sex, bilingual ability, and age of L_2 acquisition are the three factors we have already seen to be highly correlated with choice of switch type.

Age

Members of the sample were divided into two groups: younger speakers, those between twenty and forty, and older speakers, those over forty-one. Speaker age was found not to be significant in predicting code-switch type.

Social network membership

All but two informants belong to two ethnographic networks we called the Gavilanes and the Banca groups, both of which include both Spanish-dominant and bilingual speakers. Network membership is not a significant factor in predicting code-switch type.

Ethnic identity

People were divided into those who scored low on a composite index measuring positive feelings toward Puerto Rican identity and those who obtained high scores. Those with positive feelings toward Puerto Rican ethnic identity switched codes intrasententially somewhat more (446/881, or 51 percent) than those who had negative feelings (405/954). This difference is significant at the .001 level.

Continued contact with Puerto Rico

Members of the sample were also divided according to relative frequency of return visits to Puerto Rico. Those who return to the island, where they must speak more Spanish than in New York, more frequently than once every two years, tend to switch intrasententially far less (71/304, or 23 percent) than those who visit Puerto Rico less frequently than once every two years (780/1576, or 49 percent). This difference is significant at the .001 level. Further perusal of these categories, however, indicates that all speakers who migrated to the United States in early childhood (and hence tend toward bilingualism) return to Puerto Rico less frequently than once every two years, and that all those who return more frequently are Spanish dominant, a distinction we have already seen to be significantly correlated with a low incidence of intrasentential switching.

Workplace

A distinction was made between those informants who are employed off the block, where they must presumably interact in English, and those who are either unemployed or employed on the block, where they may communicate in English, Spanish, or code-switching. Those who work off the block switch intrasententially only about a third of the time (167/460), whereas those who remain on the block engage in this switch type half of the time (684/1,375), a difference that is significant at the .001 level. It is conceivable that those who spend the better part of the day in a speech situation where code-switching is not appropriate get less practice in switching and are therefore less skilled at it. More likely, however, since only Spanish-dominant speakers are employed off the block, it is this characteristic that accounts for the low percentage of intrasentential switching by these speakers.

Multivariate analysis of code-switch type

Poorly distributed data, such as those for the factors of education, continued contact with Puerto Rico, and workplace, can be misleading. As we have seen, the apparently significant effect of one factor may really be mainly due to another, language dominance, a fact which is not brought out by looking at one factor at a time. Multivariate analysis can, within limits, separate out these overlapping effects and extract the independent contributions proper to each of several related factors (Rousseau and Sankoff 1978, Sankoff and Labov 1979). It can also provide information on the statistical significance of the distinctions defining each factor group.

Let us now examine the comparative contribution of each extralinguistic factor found by the factor-by-factor analysis to be significant in the prediction of code-switch type: sex, language dominance of speaker, age of arrival in the United States and age of L_2 acquisition, educational attainment, the speaker's feelings toward his own ethnicity, amount of continued contact with Puerto Rico, and location of workplace. To what extent are these extralinguistic factors significant when considered simultaneously? To carry out this multivariate analysis we used VARBRUL 2 (Sankoff 1975) to calculate factor effects and significance levels of factor groups. The factor effects combine to give the probability that a switch will be intrasentential, according to the model $p/(1 - p) = p_o/(1 - p_o) \times p_1/(1 - p_1) \times \ldots \times p_n/(1 - p_n)$, where p_o is a corrected mean parameter and $p_1, \ldots, p_n$ are the parameters representing the effects of factors $1, \ldots, n$ characterizing a given speaker. Factor probabilities vary between 0 and 1, with figures higher than .5 favoring intrasentential code-switching, and figures lower than .5 favoring extrasentential code-switching. The higher the figure, the greater the contribution to rule application, so comparisons can easily be made between various factors and factor groups. The program also calculates the log-likelihood of the model under a given configuration of factor groups. Different analyses can then be compared to see whether the various factor groups contribute significantly to explaining the differential use of code-switching types among speakers.

We have found seven factors that, when examined one by one, seemed significantly to affect code-switch type. Some of these factors, however, are clearly correlated among themselves. To see which ones could be considered to have an independent contribution to choice of code-switch type, we carried out 128 separate analyses, each one corresponding to a different combination of explanatory factors. By examining the log-likelihoods first of the 7 one-factor analyses, then the 21 two-factor analyses, and so on, we could detect which factors contributed a significant independent effect to the explanation of the variation in the data.[12] The result of this was the four-factor analysis depicted in Table 4. Each of the four factors here has a strongly significant independent effect on choice of switch type, but the addition of any of the others – ethnic

[12] I would like to thank David Sankoff for making available a version of the variable rule program that facilitates this stepwise multiple regression procedure.

Table 4. *Contribution of extralinguistic factors to the occurrence of intrasentential code-switching*

Sex		Age of arrival/L_2 acquisition		Language dominance		Workplace	
Female	.59	Child	.55	Bilingual	.68	Off-block	.67
Male	.41	Preadolescent	.55	Spanish	.32	On-block	.33
		Adolescent	.40				

Note: Corrected mean: .36.

identity, education, or continued contact with Puerto Rico – does not significantly increase the explanatory power of the model.

The comparative effect of the factors is of particular interest. As can be seen, reported and observed language dominance is the single factor that most affects the occurrence of this switch type. Bilinguals favor it the most, at .68, whereas those who are Spanish dominant disfavor it, at .32. An almost equal effect is shown by the factor of workplace. Those who work off the block, where they must use English, show a greater tendency to switch intrasententially, at .67, than those who are unemployed or work on the block, where any of the three modes may be used. Table 4 shows that those speakers who acquired both languages in early childhood or preadolescence, a defining feature of the balanced bilingual, switch intrasententially more (.55) than those who learned L_2 at a later age. The table also indicates that women, who are often in the vanguard of linguistic change, favor intrasentential switching more than men.

Discussion

I have shown how to incorporate both linguistic and extralinguistic factors into a single analytical model to account for code-switching performance. The linguistic constraints on this phenomenon, the free morpheme and equivalence constraints, represent the basis on which the foregoing analysis was carried out.

The extralinguistic factors contribute variably to the occurrence of one switch type over another. Long-term familiarity with the members of the speech community and attitudinal and ethnographic studies carried out among them motivate the choice of these factors.

An elementary, but crucial, finding of this study is that there are virtually no ungrammatical combinations of L_1 and L_2 in the 1,835 switches studied, regardless of the bilingual ability of the speaker. This corroborates the hypothesis as to the nature of syntactic constraints on code-switching advanced in Poplack (1978), for both balanced and nonfluent bilinguals.

By showing that nonfluent bilinguals are able to code-switch frequently, yet maintain grammaticality in both L_1 and L_2 by favoring emblematic or tag-switching, I have also demonstrated empirically that code-switching is not monolithic behavior. Three types of code-switching emerge in the speech performance studied, each characterized by switches of different levels of constituents, and each reflecting different degrees of bilingual ability. Multivariate analysis of extralinguistic factors confirms that those speakers with the greatest degree of bilingual ability ("true" bilinguals) most favor intrasentential code-switching, the type I had hypothesized to require most skill. The two Chicano code-switching studies of Gingràs (1974) and Pfaff (1975, 1976) also indirectly support these findings. Gingràs tested a group of Chicano and non-Chicano bilinguals on the acceptability of a series of constructed intrasententially code-switched utterances. The Chicano bilinguals showed much higher rates of acceptance of his grammatical code-switches than the non-Chicanos. This led him to posit that there were probably code-switching norms peculiar to the Chicano community. Although speech communities may be characterized by different code-switching norms, it was also the case that the Chicano group had learned both languages in early childhood, whereas all the non-Chicano informants had learned English as adults. Bilinguals of the first type are precisely those shown to engage most in intrasentential code-switching, a fact that concords with their high rate of acceptance of such switches. Similarly, of three samples of Chicano speakers studied, Pfaff found that those who engaged most in "deep-s" (intrasentential) switching were those whose speech was characterized by use of both Spanish and English.

Previous work (Gumperz 1971, 1976; Valdés-Fallis 1978; Poplack 1978) has shown that code-switching may be used as a discourse strategy to achieve certain interactional effects at specific points during a conversation. The findings in the present study, together with the ethnographic observation that code-switching is a linguistic norm in the Puerto Rican community, suggest that this use is characteristic only of certain types of code-switching, which I call "emblematic," including tags, interjections, idiomatic expressions, and even individual noun switches. On the other hand, a generalized use of intrasentential code-switching may represent instead an overall discourse *mode*. The very fact that a speaker makes alternate use of both codes itself has interactional motivations and implications, beyond any particular effects of specific switches. Indeed, speaker attitudes toward use of Spanish, English, and code-switching, reported earlier in the chapter, do not offer any ready explanation for why a particular segment in discourse should be switched. McClure and Wentz have pointed out that "there is apparently no real social motivation for, or significance attached to, the practice of code-switching [for example] subject pronouns alone" (McClure n.d., p. 266). I agree that there is no "good reason" (Wentz 1977, e.g., pp. 143, 218) for switching subject

a. Intersentential code switching

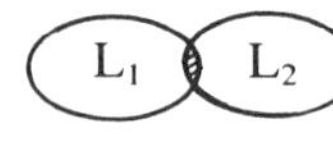

b. Tag-switching

c. Intrasentential code switching

Figure 4. Representation of bilingual code-switching grammars

pronouns, or lone determiners, and so on. Nonetheless, such segments *are* switched by bilingual speakers. It may well be possible in some cases for the analyst to impute situational motivations or consequences to specific intrasentential switches, but the evidence presented here suggests that this has little if any pertinence for the speakers themselves. More important, there is no need to require any social motivation for this type of code-switching, given that, as a discourse mode, it may form part of the repertoire of a speech community. It is then the choice (or not) of this mode that is of significance to participants rather than the choice of switch points. When these conditions are met, any segment in discourse may be switched, depending on the bilingual ability of the speaker and provided that it obeys the equivalence constraint. Thus, I cannot agree that switches of, say, object pronouns are "non-sentences" of any language because "they violate the social motivation for code-alternation in the first place" (McClure n.d., p. 265). They simply violate the equivalence constraint.

The suggestion that code-switching is itself a discrete mode of speaking, possibly emanating from a single code-switching grammar composed of the overlapping sectors of the grammars of L_1 and L_2, is supported by several findings in the present study. I have shown that there is a large number of permissible switch points in the data, rather than a few favored ones. Switching any given constituent in discourse does not necessarily entail continuation in the language of the switch, unless the surface structures are not equivalent in L_1 and L_2. Hence, larger constituents are switched more frequently than smaller ones. It was additionally shown that all constituents are about as likely to be switched into L_1 as into L_2, with the few exceptions contingent upon the bilingual ability of the speaker.

In light of these findings, code-switching behavior may be used to measure bilingual ability. Bilingual speakers might have expanding grammars of the type depicted in Figure 4, representing greater degrees of bilingual acquisition. Further empirical studies of code-switching performance in other bilingual communities would provide comparative data to test these hypotheses.

These findings taken together and interpreted in terms of the equivalence constraint, provide strong evidence that code-switching is a verbal skill requiring a large degree of linguistic competence in more than one language, rather than a defect arising from insufficient knowledge of one or the other. The rule-governed nature of code-switching is upheld by even the nonfluent bilinguals in the sample. Their behavior suggests at least enough passive competence in L_2 to switch codes by means of the few rules they know to be shared by both languages. It is also striking that precisely those switch types that have traditionally been considered most deviant by investigators and educators, those that occur within a single sentence, are the ones that require the most skill. They tend to be produced by the "true" bilinguals in the sample: speakers who learned both languages in early childhood and who have the most contact with the monolingual English-speaking world.

Code-switching, then, rather than representing deviant behavior, is actually a suggestive indicator of degree of bilingual competence.

References

Attinasi, John. 1979. Results of a language attitude questionnaire administered orally to an ethnographically chosen sample of ninety-one residents of a block in East Harlem, New York, 1977–1978. Manuscript. City University of New York, Center for Puerto Rican Studies.

Clyne, Michael. 1972. *Perspectives on language contact*. Melbourne: Hawthorne Press.

Fishman, Joshua. 1971. The sociology of language: an interdisciplinary approach. In *Advances in the sociology of language*, ed. J. Fishman. Vol. 1. The Hague: Mouton.

Gingràs, Rosario. 1974. Problems in the description of Spanish-English intrasentential code-switching. In *Southwest areal linguistics*, ed. G. A. Bills. San Diego: San Diego State University, Institute for Cultural Pluralism.

Granda, Germán de. 1968. *Transculturación e interferencia lingüística en el Puerto Rico contemporáneo (1898–1968)*. Bogotá: Instituto Caro y Cuervo.

Gumperz, John J. 1971. Bilingualism, bidialectalism, and classroom interaction. In *Language in social groups: Essays by John J. Gumperz*, ed. A. Dil, pp. 311–39. Stanford University Press.

1976. The sociolinguistic significance of conversational code-switching. In *Papers on language and context* (Working Paper 46), pp. 1–46. Berkeley: University of California, Language Behavior Research Laboratory.

Gumperz, John J., and Eduardo Hernández-Chávez. 1975. Cognitive aspects of bilingual communication. In *El lenguaje de los Chicanos*, ed. E. Hernández-Chávez, A. Cohen, and A. Beltramo, pp. 154–63. Arlington, Va.: Center for Applied Linguistics.

Hasselmo, Nils. 1970. Code-switching and modes of speaking. In *Texas studies in bilingualism*, ed. G. Gilbert, pp. 179–210. Berlin: de Gruyter.

Heidelberger Forschungsprojekt "Pidgin-Deutsch." 1977. The acquisition of German syntax by foreign migrant workers. In *Linguistic variation: models and methods*, ed. D. Sankoff, pp. 1–21. New York: Academic Press.

LaFontaine, Hernán. 1975. Bilingual education for Puerto Ricans: ¿sí o no? Paper presented at the National Conference on the Educational Needs of the Puerto Rican in the United States, Cleveland, Ohio.

Lance, Donald. 1975. Spanish-English code-switching. In *El lenguaje de los Chi-*

canos, ed. E. Hernández-Chávez, A. Cohen, and A. Beltramo, pp. 138–53. Arlington, Va.: Center for Applied Linguistics.

Lipski, John. 1978. Code-switching and the problem of bilingual competence. In *Aspects of bilingualism*, ed. M. Paradis, pp. 250–64. Columbia, S.C.: Hornbeam Press.

McClure, Erica. n.d. The acquisition of communicative competence in a bicultural setting. National Institute for Education Grant NE-G-00-e-0147 final report.

1977. Aspects of code-switching in the discourse of bilingual Mexican-American children. Paper presented at the Georgetown University Roundtable on Languages and Linguistics, March.

McClure, Erica, and James Wentz. 1975. Functions of code-switching among Mexican-American children. In *Papers from the parasession on functionalism*, ed. Robin Grossman, L. James San, and Timothy Vance, pp. 421–33. Chicago: Chicago Linguistic Society.

Payne, Arvilla. 1976. The acquisition of the phonological system of a second dialect. Ph.D. dissertation, University of Pennsylvania.

Pedraza, Pedro. 1978. Ethnographic observations of language use in el barrio. Manuscript. City University of New York, Center for Puerto Rican Studies.

Pfaff, Carol. 1975. Syntactic constraints on code-switching: a quantitative study of Spanish/English. Paper presented at the annual meeting of the Linguistic Society of America, December.

1976. Functional and structural constraints on syntactic variation in code-switching. *Papers from the parasession on diachronic syntax*. Chicago: Chicago Linguistic Society.

Poplack, Shana. 1978. Dialect acquisition among Puerto Rican bilinguals. *Language in Society* 7, no. 1:89–103.

1981. Syntactic structure and social function of code-switching. In *Latino language and communicative behavior*, ed. Richard Durán, pp. 169–86. Norwood, N.J.: Ablex Publishing Corp.

Rousseau, Pascale, and David Sankoff. 1978. Advances in variable rule methodology. In *Linguistic variation: models and methods*, ed. D. Sankoff. New York: Academic Press.

Sankoff, David. 1975. VARBRUL 2. Manuscript (program and documentation). University of Montreal.

Sankoff, David, and William Labov. 1979. On the uses of variable rules. *Language in Society* 8, no. 2. 189–222.

Timm, L. A. 1975. Spanish-English code-switching: el porqué y how not to. *Romance Philology* 28, no. 4, pp. 473–82.

U.S. Bureau of the Census. 1973. *Puerto Ricans in the United States*. Publication PC (2)-1E. Washington, D.C.: U.S. Government Printing Office.

U.S. Department of Labor. 1975. *A socio-economic profile of Puerto Rican New Yorkers*. New York: Bureau of Labor Statistics.

Valdés-Fallis, Guadalupe. 1976. Social interaction and code-switching patterns: a case study of Spanish/English alternation. In *Bilingualism in the Bicentennial and beyond*, ed. G. Keller, R. Teschner, and S. Viera, pp. 53–85. Jamaica, N.Y.: Bilingual Press.

1981. Code-switching as a deliberate verbal strategy: a microanalysis of direct and indirect requests among bilingual Chicano speakers. In *Latino language and communicative behavior*, ed. R. Durán, pp. 95–108. Norwood, N.J.: Ablex Publishing Corp.

Varo, Carlos. 1971. *Consideraciones antropológicas y políticas en torno a la enseñanza del Spanglish en Nueva York.* Río Piedras: Ediciones Librería Internacional.

Weinreich, Uriel. 1953. *Languages in contact.* The Hague: Mouton.

Wentz, James. 1977. Some considerations in the development of a syntactic description of code-switching. Ph.D. dissertation, University of Illinois, Urbana-Champaign.

13

Constraints on language mixing: intrasentential code-switching and borrowing in Spanish/English

CAROL W. PFAFF

Long-term linguistic and social contact in multilingual communities results in a range of language-mixing phenomena such as borrowing, calquing, and code-switching. These phenomena raise questions both as to the diachronic effect on the language and the synchronic effect on the speaker. From the point of view of language change, we want to know (a) whether and how mixing types are interrelated, (b) whether and under what conditions mixing produces convergence, and (c) to what extent linguistic change in stable multilingual communities proceeds by regular, implicational stages such as have been posited to operate in the development of other mixed languages, e.g. pidgins and creoles. From the point of view of the speaker, we want to know whether a separate grammar of mixing is required to account for mixed varieties, or whether the syntax of mixing follows entirely from universals.

Of course, language mixing originates in response to social motivations, and social factors cannot be ignored in any analysis; however, the realization of mixes is subject to functional and structural syntactic constraints, as well as constraints which reflect semantic and communicational properties of discourse. These constraints bear most directly on the issues of diachronic and synchronic grammar, and are therefore the focus of the present case study of Spanish/English mixture in the speech of Mexican-Americans in the southwestern United States. In the first section, I sketch the background: the sociolinguistics of mixing, previous research, and methodology of the present study. In the second section, I discuss the current controversial distinction between two mixing types

Reprinted with permission of *Language* 55, no. 2:291–318 (1979).

The research reported here was begun in California and carried out primarily in Texas. I am grateful to a number of students at the California State University at Fresno and the University of Texas at Austin who have made their data and intuitions available to me: Consuelo Akin, Elizabeth Hicks, Ana Huerta, Efraín Rodríguez, Alfredo Tepox, Teresa Trejo, Severo Vargas, and Ernesto Zamora. In addition, R. Joe Campbell of the University of Texas at San Antonio has very kindly provided texts of interviews for an on-going survey of San Antonio Spanish. Responsibility for the analysis and conclusions rest with me.

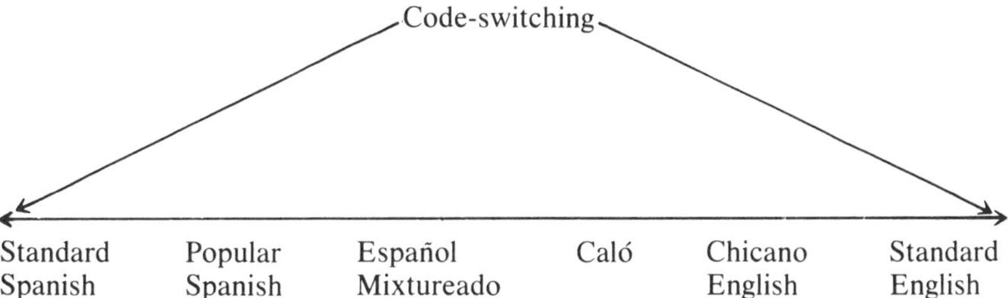

Figure 1. Spanish/English continuum (*Source*: Elías-Olivares 1976, p. 149)

– borrowing and code-switching. In the next four sections, I present a quantitative analysis of syntactic patterns of intrasentential mixing in verb phrases, noun phrases, prepositional phrases, and conjoined clauses, illustrating the operation of proposed constraints to be summarized in the last section.

Background

Sociolinguistic factors

Spanish has been an important language in the southwestern United States for nearly four centuries. After colonization by Spain, the area remained under Spanish, and later Mexican, rule until 1848, when English-speaking immigrants became dominant. Even the early Spanish settlements were never culturally or linguistically homogeneous (Christian and Christian 1966); and in the twentieth century, waves of immigration from Mexico brought more diversity, as workers moved in temporarily or permanently to take agricultural and industrial jobs. At the present time the linguistic situation is extremely heterogeneous, ranging from rural communities in which the population is predominantly Spanish-speaking (common in South Texas), to those which are truly bilingual and to urban communities, particularly in California, where the younger generations are predominantly English-speaking. The consultants for the present study are drawn from communities in the middle of this range: from small towns and cities in central California (Fresno, Selma, Porterville) and from cities in south-central and western Texas (Austin, San Antonio, El Paso).

The verbal repertoire of one of these communities, Austin, has been described in detail by Elías-Olivares (1976). As shown in Figure 1, intrasentential switching represents a variety of speaking superposed on a continuum of Spanish and English. This continuum ranges from standard Mexican Spanish to non-standard local or "popular" Spanish (characterized by a number of phonological changes and morphological regularizations) and to a rather stigmatized variety of Spanish, variously termed Pocho, Tex-Mex, or Español Mixtureado. This variety is highly Anglicized, containing many English loan words and loan translations of English syntactic patterns and idioms. Caló or Pachuco, a variety used especially by adolescents, is characterized by Spanish slang mixed with Anglicisms.[1] Finally, varieties of Chicano English shade into standard colloquial English.

Elías-Olivares suggests (pp. 147–8) that Español Mixtureado is spoken primarily by young people who are competent in English (especially high school students, who favor it as "something different") and by children who have not been sufficiently exposed to both languages, and so have neither internalized separate rules for English and Spanish nor learned the rules for code-switching. Older speakers in Austin look down on Español Mixtureado and code-switching. For them, "good Spanish" means the Spanish of Mexico and, in particular, the avoidance of Anglicisms (p. 152). Similarly, Sawyer (1970, p. 39) notes a tendency for Mexican-Americans in San Antonio to avoid the use of Spanish items in English, even words like *patio, bronco, arroyo*, which are well-accepted in the speech of Anglos in the southwestern United States. Thus there appears to be a "double standard" requiring linguistic purity for both languages.

A countervailing force is found in the positive roles which code-switching plays, reflecting not only speakers' desires to appear competent in both languages, but also to establish solidarity as members of a bilingual community. Elías-Olivares notes (p. 182):

> Speakers have always pointed out that speaking only in Spanish in a [−formal] situation to a Chicano audience will make the audience believe that they are trying to show off. Speaking only in English, on the other hand, will be a signal that the speaker wants to become Anglicized and does not relate to the rest of the bilingual community.

Thus code-switching functions as what Scotton (1976) terms a "strategy of neutrality."

Nonetheless, intrasentential code-switching does not appear to be a totally separate variety, as implied by Figure 1 or by Elías-Olivares' definition of it (p. 178) as "the constant alternation from one linguistic system to another." In my data, even in conversations which impressionistically involve constant alternation, speakers produce a high proportion of turns of speaking entirely in Spanish or entirely in English, as shown in Table 1. Further, the alternation resolves itself into three basic

[1] Phonological characteristics of southwestern Spanish include monophthongization (*cencia* < *ciencia* 'science'); and truncation (*taba* < *estaba* 'I, he was'). Morphological regularization and re-analyses include *pidimos* < *pedimos* 'we ask,' *siéntensen/siéntesen* < *siéntense* 'sit down!' Anglicisms or calques include *yo fui nacido* vs. (*yo*) *naci* 'I was born,' *me vine patrás* vs. *me regresé* 'I came back.' Slang terms include *catiar* 'beat up' and *simón* 'yes.' Further discussion and examples of such features can be found in Elías-Olivares (1976), Rosaura Sánchez (1972), and Hernández-Chávez, Cohen, and Beltramo (1975). Forms such as these are represented in the citations in the text, but have no bearing on the present discussion.

Table 1. *Percentage of switch and non-switch turns in casual conversation*

	Speaker	S	S→E	E	E→S
Family 1	M	64	29	4	2
	Mi	53	16	29	2
	A	31	11	54	4
	Ch	43	21	31	5
	L	8	17	69	6
Family 2	D	49	41	10	0
	E	60	12	28	0
Peers 1	A	25	0	50	25
	B	14	0	43	43
Peers 2	J	33	56	0	11
	F	25	75	0	0

Table 2. *Instances of intrasentential code-switches in speech*

	Single lexical items			Phrases			Clauses	
	noun	verb	adj	NP	PP	VP	coörd. and subord.	rel
Spanish to English	818	71	43	69	36	5	37	3
English to Spanish	14	0	1	4	2	0	27	1

types, as shown in Table 2. In later sections I treat constraints on alternation of single lexical items, phrases, and clauses.

Previous studies

Most earlier work on Spanish/English code-switching has focused on social correlates of language choice. Thus Fishman, Cooper, and Ma (1971), describing the similar situation of Puerto Ricans in New Jersey, discuss the choice of Spanish for topics in home or community domains as opposed to English for work, education, or institutional domains. Gumperz and Hernández-Chávez (1975) and Gumperz (1976) discuss how domain or situational switching has evolved into metaphorical use of Spanish to express a personal or affective orientation to the content of speech, in contrast to a more objective or impersonal use of English. McClure and Wentz (1975) discuss the acquisition of situational and metaphorical switching by children, and point out that competence in these types is attained well before intrasentential switching norms are established.

Until very recently, intrasentential switching was considered syntactically random rather than rule-governed behavior. An early investigation by Espinosa (1917) claimed that the use of regular English words and phrases in the Spanish of New Mexico had no fixed limits, and could not follow regular laws. Labov (1971) claims that, in contrast to phonological and syntactic variation in Black English, alternation between Spanish and English in conversation is random. And, although Lance (1975) gives a short list of 14 switch points, he too suggests that there are no syntactic restrictions on where switching can occur.

However, the recent works of Aguirre (1976), Gingràs (1974), Gumperz and Hernández-Chávez (1975), Gumperz (1976), McClure (1977), Reyes (1974), Timm (1975), and Wentz and McClure (1976, 1977) suggest that there are syntactic constraints on switching; and substantive constraints are proposed by each of these investigators. Except in the work of Wentz and McClure, the conclusions are based on very limited samples of natural conversation of adults; they rely primarily on the investigators' intuitions and on the results of acceptability judgments by Chicano university students, who were simply asked to evaluate or rank-order the grammaticality of lists of sentences. Wentz and McClure have a larger sample of children's speech, and present the results of asking the children to repeat sentences in which Spanish and English were mixed.

While the use of structured elicitation techniques such as acceptability judgments and sentence repetition allows the investigators to control the linguistic environments, there is no guarantee that all crucial factors will be held constant or that the sentences would or could have occurred naturally. (In later sections, I discuss some cases in which the stimulus sentences in these studies include confounding factors.) Furthermore, it is extremely difficult to get reliable judgments on a speech variety that has been traditionally stigmatized, but which has recently come to function as a symbol of bicultural identification or a strategy of neutrality among educated Mexican-Americans. As Rickford (1975) has shown, acceptability judgments often represent stereotypes about verbal behavior rather than reflecting the behavior itself. Evidence that this is true for judgments of conjoined-sentence switching in Spanish/English is discussed later.

Methodology

In contrast to the above studies, the present work is based on an extensive corpus of conversational data from approximately 200 speakers of various ages and social backgrounds, recorded in a variety of social settings by bilingual participant-observers. The conversations represent (a) more or less self-conscious styles – one-to-one interviews with relative strangers, announcements, reports, and questions in public meetings – and (b) casual speech among family members and friends. For purposes of comparison, two examples of conscious code-switching were analysed: the prose sections of a collection of essays and poems (Ricardo Sánchez 1973) and the bilingual class-lecture style of Alurista, a poet and instructor in the Chicano Studies Program at the University of Texas, Austin. (See the appendix for sample passages.)

I have adopted the analytic technique known as "accountable reporting" – i.e., the quantitative analysis of relative frequencies of variable realizations in significant environments. This technique, first applied to sociolinguistic data by Labov, has yielded considerable insight into the constraints on variation in Black and Anglo English, and has subsequently been applied to the description and analysis of variation in other monolingual and multilingual communities by Fishman, Wolfram, Fasold, Cedergren, Sankoff, and Bickerton, to name only a few.

The crucial task in applying accountable reporting is to determine what and how to count: what social and linguistic environments may be relevant conditioning factors.[2] Since my goal is to understand how code-switching fits with other varieties in the linguistic continuum, I have considered single lexical items and morphological adaptations as well as longer sequences of English in Spanish – rather than excluding these as "mere" borrowing, as previous investigators have done (see the next section). "Mixing" is used as a neutral cover term for code-switching and borrowing.

Data are classified in terms of three syntactic criteria: (1) the point of onset of the mix, (2) the syntactic structure or constituency of the mix point, and (3) the duration of the mix. Four conditioning factors are considered: (1) the grammatical function – whether the mix involves nonredundant marking of tense/aspect or case relations; (2) structural conflict – whether the word order, co-occurrence restrictions, optionally or obligatorily expressed relations, and agreement rules of the two languages operate in the immediate environment of the mix; (3) the semantic function – whether the mixed items are interpreted literally or figuratively; and (4) the discourse function of the mix – whether old or new information is being communicated, whether the mix occurs in the main predication or in an aside.

Code-switching vs. borrowing

The question of distinguishing between code-switching and borrowing is an interesting and important one in itself. Although Gumperz and Hernández-Chávez (1975, p. 158) speak of code-switching – even that

[2] As in any empirical research, the theoretical assumptions of the investigator play a major role in the classification, quantification, and interpretation of specific cases. I have counted discontinuous sequences like the following as a single mix –

los – los – uh – Your muscles a veces react 'The – the – . . . sometimes . . .'

– considering the adverbial phrase to have been moved in by a late stylistic rule (cf. Pfaff 1976a). This decision follows from my assumption that mixing is not simply a surface-structure phenomenon. Such cases, however, are rare and do not affect the conclusions drawn here.

involving whole sentences – as a type of borrowing, the two terms are usually construed as making vastly different claims about the competence of the individual speaker. "Borrowing" may occur in the speech of those with only monolingual competence, while "code-switching" implies some degree of competence in two languages. Thus most investigators (including Gumperz 1976) find it appropriate to distinguish between the two. There has been, however, little agreement as to how the distinction is to be made.

Surface morpho-syntax

Classification based on the surface syntax and morphology of the particular utterance considered in isolation has been proposed by a number of investigators. Commonly, single words are classified as borrowing rather than switching, e.g. by Gingràs and by Reyes. The latter further distinguishes (1974, p. 105) between "spontaneous borrowings," which are not morphologically adapted to Spanish, and "incorporated borrowings," which are. Switches, however, are characterized (p. 104) as beginning at "clearly discernible syntactic junctures" and "having their own internal syntactic structure." The following examples illustrate Reyes' distinctions (p. 91).

Code-switching:

(1)a. *Yo sé, porque I went to the hospital to find out where he was at* 'I know, because . . .'
b. *Cuando yo la conocí, "Oh this ring, I paid so much –"* 'When I met her, . . .'

Spontaneous borrowing:

(2)a. *Los están bussing pa otra escuela* 'They are bussing them to another school.'
b. *Va a re-enlist* 'He's going to . . .'

Integrated borrowing:

(3)a. *Taipeo las cartas* 'I type the letters.'
b. *las trocas* 'the trucks.'

Examination of a wider range of examples in actual performance, however, shows that the categories are inherently squishy rather than discrete. There is no reason to attribute different degrees of incorporation or spontaneity to the occurrences of Eng. *train* in 4–6, all of which were produced by a single speaker within the space of a few sentences:

(4) *Estaba training para pelear* 'He was training to fight.'
(5) *No sabía como trainiar* 'He didn't know how to train.'
(6) *Ya no lo trainiará* 'He won't train him any more.'

Second, Reyes' characterization of the starting point for switches as "clearly discernible syntactic junctures" is vague, and fails to distinguish between examples of so-called borrowing like 2b and those like 7, which begin at the same point but intuitively must be regarded as switches:

(7) *No van a bring it up in the meeting* 'They're not going to . . .'

Third, the association of switching but not borrowing with internal syntactic structure ignores the generally recognized possibility of borrowing idiomatic phrases as units, as in

(8) *Lo puso under arrest* 'He put him . . .'
(9) *Yo anduve in a state of shock por dos días* 'I went around . . . for two days.'

Fourth, many frequently borrowed English lexical items have internal syntactic structure, including noun compounds as in 10, verb compounds as in 11, and verb + particle constructions as in 12:

(10) *Va a ver un state executive committee meeting* 'He's going to see a . . .'
(11) *Andamos horseback riding* 'We go . . .'
(12) *¿Por qué te hicieron beat up ese?* 'Why did they beat you up, man?'

Examples like these led other investigators of Chicano Spanish to conclusions different from those of Reyes. Thus Sobin (1976, p. 42) takes the position that some morphologically adapted lexical items are switches rather than borrowings, while Elías-Olivares (1976, p. 187) notes that some items which are neither morphologically nor phonologically adapted to Spanish – notably nouns in business, educational, or otherwise specialized domains associated with the dominant culture – must nonetheless be regarded as part of the Spanish lexicon of some Chicanos.

The indeterminacy of the distinction between borrowing and code-switching rests on the fact that issues which go well beyond the particular utterance are involved. Two types of variation, one social and one linguistic, must be considered: (a) variation in lexical inventories among subgroups and individual members of the Mexican-American speech community, and (b) variation in the functional load of morphological marking for different syntactic categories and in different contexts.

Lexical inventory

To determine fully the status of a given L_2 word in an L_1 utterance, the following questions must be answered: (a) Does an L_1 equivalent exist? (b) If so, is it also in use in the community? (c) Is the equivalent L_1 term known to the individual speaker? (d) Does the individual regard the word as belonging to L_1 or to L_2? Clearly, definitive answers to these questions can be found only through extensive studies of languages in use in the community, on the one hand, and by psycholinguistic probing of individuals, on the other. However, there are often cues in the utterances themselves which indicate the speaker's perception of the foreignness of a word. Cues at the immediate point of language mixing include hesitation, asides, and translation or paraphrase.

Hesitation may occur immediately prior to a switch, as in 13, or precede it by several words, as in 14:

(13) *Los – los – uh – your muscles a veces react* 'The – the – . . . sometimes . . .'

(14) *o limp – limpiar todo – todo el – building* 'or to – to clean all – all of the . . .'

Asides like *as they say* or *como dicen* are also evidence that the speaker is aware of switching to a special term, code, or register:

(15) *Porque eran show calves que los dicen* 'because they were . . . as they call them.'

(16) *Tuve que mandar lo que llaman transcript* 'I had to send what they call . . .'

Translation or paraphrase after or before a mix also indicates its status. In 17, a long paraphrase, continuing overt reference to a perceived lexical gap, follows Eng. *moles*; in 18, the appositional translation *shorthand* indicates that the English word rather than Sp. *taquigrafía* is habitually used in the community, a fact which is corroborated in natural conversation:[3]

(17) *los* MOLES, *en español, usted sabe – los animalitos que parecen ratas pero viven enterrados,* MOLES, *¿cómo se dice la palabra?* 'the moles, in Spanish, you know – the little animals that are like rats except they live underground, moles, how do you say the word?'

(18) *aptitudes necesarias: taquigrafía, o sea shorthand* 'required skills: shorthand, that is . . .'

Functional load

The relationship between morphological adaptation and lexical incorporation is gradient, and depends on the functional load of morphological marking for different syntactic categories. As has also been noted by Elías-Olivares and by Sobin, etymologically English verbs are frequently given Spanish tense/aspect and subject-agreement inflection, but English adjectives are never inflected for gender and number.[4] The predominance of morphological adaptation in verbs has been noted in other language-

[3] Sentence 18 occurred as part of a public service job-opportunities announcement, broadcast over the University of Texas radio station: it is typical of speech which, for social rather than linguistic reasons, attempts to be entirely Spanish but is also constrained to maintain intelligibility. Similar examples have been noted by Ornstein (1975, p. 10) in puristic Spanish-language newspapers in New Mexico.

[4] Sobin (19, pp. 21–2) suggests that *tofudo* 'tough,' the single morphologically adapted English adjective listed in dictionaries of Texas Spanish (Cerda, Cabaza, and Farias, 1953, Vásquez and Vásquez 1975) must have been borrowed originally in some other syntactic category, because the derivational suffix *-udo* cannot occur with underlying adjectives (*mal* 'bad', **maludo*).

contact situations summarized by Haugen, who suggests (1973, p. 536) that this tendency can be explained in functional terms: "The centrality of the verb in the sentence supplements the fact that tense is an obligatory category in (at least) the Indo-European languages." As will be discussed later, it appears that the obligatory nature of tense/aspect marking is a functional constraint on the variable realization of English verbs in Spanish contexts.

Code-mixing and code-changing

McClure and McClure (1975), and Wentz and McClure (1977, p. 706) handle the classification problem more successfully. They use "code-switching" as a cover term for "code-mixing" and "code-changing," defined both socially and syntactically. Code-mixing, they claim, occurs because an L_2 word or expression is more salient or unknown in L_1, the language of discourse; it takes place within constituent boundaries, and results in sentences which belong fundamentally to L_1. Code-changing, however, is principally a stylistic device denoting change in affect, addressee, mode, etc.; it must take place between constituent boundaries, and results in sentences which are sequentially L_1 and L_2.

Though code-mixing and code-changing are theoretically distinct, in practice they are often interrelated, so that code-mixes trigger more extensive code-changes. In the later sections, I discuss examples of triggering of NP, VP, and PP switches, and suggest that structural conflict plays a major role.

Verb mixing: functional lexical and structural constraints

Cases of mixing which involve verbs are linguistically interesting because the grammars of Spanish and English differ in morphological and syntactic marking of underlying relationships, in word order, and in lexical structure. Some of the salient differences in verb morpho-syntax are:

(a) Spanish distinguishes more categories of tense and mood by verb suffix than does English.

(b) Spanish verbal suffixes agree with their subject nouns in person and number; in English, agreement is limited to the irregular verb *be* and to 3sg. present-tense forms of other verbs.

(c) Since Spanish marks subject agreement on verbs, non-emphatic subjects may be deleted, and relatively free word-order permits both subject and object nouns either to precede or follow the verb. English, however, requires an overt subject – which, except when certain focusing transformations apply, regularly precedes the verb.

(d) Placement rules for clitic object pronouns differ. In English, clitic pronouns must immediately follow the verb; but Spanish clitics regularly precede the verb – except in affirmative commands, infinitives, and present participles, where they occur as suffixes.

Table 3. *Instances of English verbs in Spanish contexts*

	Unadapted to Spanish morphology	Adapted to Spanish morphology
1. Participles		
a. *estar* + present participle	7	2
b. *ir, andar* + present participle	10	0
c. *haber* + past participle	2	0
d. *estar, ser* + past participle	3	1
2. Infinitives		
a. periphrastic future	3	0
b. complement-taking verb + stem	8	3
c. *hacer* + stem	3	0
d. nominal, object of preposition	1	1
3. Inflected main verb	5	19
4. Unmarked, tense/aspect marking on other verb in context	3	0

(e) English, but not Spanish, has structurally complex verb–particle constructions like *beat up, make up.*

However, Spanish and English verbal grammar is identical in a significant way: both employ periphrastic verbal constructions in which unconjugated verb forms follow conjugated auxiliaries or complement-taking verbs.

In light of these differences and similarities, we may now examine the realization of etymologically English verbs in Spanish contexts. The results summarized in Table 3 show that morphologically adapted and unadapted English verbs occur in typically different environments, though the difference is not categorical. Unadapted English verbs typically occur as participles, as in 19, or as infinitive (stem) complements, as in 20; but verbs adapted to Spanish morphology occur much more frequently as simple inflected finite forms, as in 21:

Spanish auxiliary + English participle:

(19)a. *Estaba training para pelear* 'He was training to fight.'
b. *¿Donde estás teaching?* 'Where are you teaching?'
c. *porque vas bicycle riding* 'because you're going . . .'
d. *Si va a ir shopping, vaya con Mickey* 'If you're going to go shopping, go with Mickey.'
e. *Yo creo que apenas se había washed out* 'I think it had just . . .'
f. *Le estaba poniendo atención qué estaba recorded* 'He was paying attention to what was recorded.'

Spanish verb + English infinitive complement:

(20)a. *No van a bring it up in the meeting* 'They're not going to . . .'
b. *Va a charter un camión* 'It's going to charter a bus.'
c. *cuando lo comenzó train* 'when he started to train him.'[5]
d. *y que lo quería brincar a ella, que quería rape* 'and that he wanted to jump her, that he wanted to rape.'
e. *El compañero debe de suck on that para que salga la pozona y escupirla* 'His companion ought to suck on that so that the poison can come out and spit it out.'

Morphologically adapted English verbs:

(21)a. *Los hombres me trustearon* 'The men trusted me.'
b. *Taipiamos cada día* 'We type every day.'

Tense/aspect/mood and subject-marking
Such markers illustrate a functional constraint, features of which are presented in the following sections.

Major patterns. The typical participial and infinitival forms of morphologically unadapted English verbs (1a–b, 2a–b in Table 3) occur after Spanish auxiliaries or complement-taking verbs which are inflected for tense, mood, and subject agreement. The statistical predominance of morphologically adapted English verbs in the complementary environment, i.e. as inflected main verbs (3 in Table 3), suggests that morphological adaptation begins in finite forms, then spreads to non-finite participial and infinitival forms, as in these examples:

(22) *porque estaban chiriando* 'because they were cheating.'
(23) *Ella va a ir bien trainiada* 'She's going to go well-trained.'
(24) *No puedo taipiar muy bien* 'I can't type very well.'
(25) *Yo voy a cuitiar ya* 'I'm finally going to quit.'

Verb mixing does not categorically conform to these regular types, however. Morphological adaptation is not freely applicable because of structural and lexical constraints (see later sections), and there are also minor patterns for unadapted verbs.

Minor patterns. The combination of *hacer* + English stem (2c in Table 3) represents an interesting development which has, perhaps, arisen in order to create contexts which conform to the regular infinitival pattern. In 27–28, the standard Sp. *hacer* + infinitive causative construction, illustrated in 26, has been extended to non-causative contexts:[6]

[5] In standard Spanish, the aspectual verb *comenzar* requires the preposition *a* before its complement.

[6] In isolation, 28 is ambiguous with respect to causative/non-causative readings: 'Why did they have you beaten up?' is also possible. In the context (see the Appendix, ex. 5), the non-causative reading is more likely – and, significantly, was the gloss suggested by bilingual participant-observers.

(26) *Me hizo estudiar* 'He made me study.'
(27) *Su hija hace teach allá en San José* 'His daughter teaches there in San Jose.'
(28) *¿Por qué te hicieron beat up?* 'Why did they beat you up?'

This semantic extension of an existing syntactic pattern is reminiscent of the expansion processes of creolization. The use of a semantically general verb "do" or "make" plus a nominalized borrowed verb is a process also found in Japanese adaptations of verbs from Chinese (Lehmann 1975) and English (Sanches 1976).

The use of *hacer* + English stem is rare, and may be geographically or socially restricted. The examples in my corpus are from speakers in California, and the structure is also reported in Reyes' study, based primarily on his own (Arizona) speech. A further example occurs in fiction supposed to represent the speech of New Mexicans (Romero and Romero 1976, p. 35). It is not mentioned, however, in other treatments of the syntax of code-switching (Elías-Olivares, Espinosa, Gingràs, Gumperz and Hernández-Chávez, Lance, Timm). A number of University of Texas students report that they find the construction grammatical but would not use it themselves.[7]

Another minor pattern is the use of unmarked English verbs in Spanish contexts in which they are not immediately preceded by an inflected Spanish verb (4 in Table 3):

(29) *Anda feeling medio nice y start blowing again* 'He goes on feeling rather nice and starts . . .'
(30) *So caminaba de mi casa al bus stop y luego transfer, y luego de ahí al otro bus hasta Kelly Field, y llegaba allá como a los once* 'So I went out of my house to the bus stop, and later from there to the other bus to Kelly Field, and arrived there about 11 o'clock.'

In these cases, the unmarked English verbs *start* and *transfer* occur in conjoined clauses in which the relevant morphological marking occurs on Spanish verbs in preceding (and in 30 also following) main verbs in conjoined clauses.[8]

A final minor pattern for unadapted English verbs in Spanish is the use of morphologically inflected English main verbs (3 in Table 3):

(31) *El perro chewed him up* 'The dog . . .'
(32) *Todos los Mexicanos were riled up* 'All the Mexicans . . .'

[7] Judgments of grammaticality or acceptability, however, are not reliable for less-frequent types of mixing. Ana Huerta (personal communication) reports that informants sometimes reject as impossible the very sentences they have been recorded using.

[8] The third example, *Tú lo underestimate a Chito*, is unclear; because the English 2sg. present mark is Ø, it could also be classified as an instance of inflected main-verb mixing. Note, however, that the subject is overtly expressed, though not emphasized; and the other NP, *Chito*, is overtly marked as object by the 'personal *a*.' This example is also an exception to the clitic pronoun constraint discussed in the next section.

In these cases, tense is marked on the verb: further, the subject is clearly marked as such. In 31, *el perro* must be the subject because the other NP (*him*) is an object pronoun; in 32, the verb is intransitive.

From the preceding discussion of major and minor patterns of verb mixing, it appears that mixing English verbs in Spanish contexts is subject to the following functional constraint:

(33) An English verb not morphologically adapted to Spanish is permitted only in sentences in which tense/mood/aspect and subject are otherwise marked.

However, the major and minor verb mixing patterns are not all productive, synchronic, alternative strategies which speakers can use to conform to the functional constraint in 33. These realization patterns are further restricted by lexical and structural constraints.

Lexical constraints

There is no evidence that morphological adaptation of English verbs is at present a fully productive device for mixing in non-periphrastic contexts. All the etymologically English verbs which occur with Spanish inflection are to be found in dictionaries of Mexican-American Spanish (Cerda, Cabaza, and Farias 1953, Galván and Teschner 1975), and appear to be fully incorporated into the Spanish lexicon of the speakers. Further evidence is provided by Wentz and McClure's report (1975, p. 7) that, in the speech of children, morphological adaptation is restricted to English verbs which are also phonologically adapted to Spanish; they claim to have observed *yo tinqué* but never **yo thinké* for 'I thought.'[9]

Structural constraints

Nor does the use of inflected English main verbs appear to be simply a free alternative which occurs in non-periphrastic environments. Three of the five instances in Table 3 begin with a form of *be*, which clearly is not a lexical gap in Spanish. Example 34 can, perhaps, be dismissed as basically English, switching to Spanish for the NP *la onda* and the conjoined *jambar*:

(34) *Some dudes, la onda is to fight y jambar* '. . . the in thing . . . and steal.'

As will be discussed in the next section, switching of determiner + noun is rare, but in this case is consistent with the status of *la onda* as a quasi-technical slang term.

The remaining two cases of mixes beginning with inflected forms of *be* are 32 (*todos los mexicanos were riled up*) and 35:

[9] Orthographic representations are as given in Wentz and McClure 1976, who provide no finer phonetic transcription. Presumably their use of Spanish vs. English spelling indicates predominance of Spanish vs. English phonology.

(35) *la historia que el Exorcist is based on* 'the story that . . .'

Here the switches can perhaps better be understood as the outcome of structural conflict between Spanish, triggered by the non-Spanish verb + particle structure in conjunction with the English passive as opposed to the Spanish reflexive construction (with *irritarse, basarse*).[10]

In 31 (*el perro chewed him up*), a second structural conflict comes into play: position of the clitic pronoun. In entirely Spanish sentences – or in sentences where English verbs mix into Spanish in a regular pattern of morphological adaptation, like 21a, or a periphrastic construction, like 28 – the clitic pronoun would precede the verb; but in English it must follow the verb and precede the particle. As Wentz and McClure 1976 and Timm 1975 have also noted, the realization of clitic pronouns is subject to the following structural constraint:

(36) Clitic pronoun objects are realized in the same language as the verb to which they are cliticized, and in the position required by the syntactic rules of that language.

To conform to this, the basically verbal mix is extended to the object pronoun.

However, this conflict arises very infrequently. Morphologically unadapted verb-mixes most frequently occur when there is no pronoun object to cause potential structural conflict. As Table 4 shows, 41 out of 45 cases are either intransitive or have noun rather than pronoun objects. In contrast, this bias toward non-pronominal object contexts is not found with

[10] An interesting but rare phenomenon is the switching of particles, but not the verbs, in verb + particle constructions, representing partial syntactic calques. The following are the only examples attested:

(a) *El miércoles en la tarde lo tienes off de todo modos* 'You have Wednesday afternoon off anyway.'
(b) *El miércoles en la tarde se los dan off* 'They give them Wednesday afternoon off.'
(c) *El dentista agarraba off y se iba fishing* 'The dentist took off and went fishing.'
(d) *Sabes los cambian around* 'You know they change them around.'
(e) *Usted me dijo que pusiera todo el mugrero up* 'You told me that I should put all the stuff up.'

The last example is especially interesting because of the actual separation of the particle from the verb. As described above, verb + particle constructions are among the most frequent of verb switches. There are no instances where the verb in a verb + particle construction is switched while the particle is in Spanish. In some cases, English structure is modified to fit Spanish syntax and semantics – a Spanish verb is extended into the domain of an English verb + particle:

(f) *Los franceses levantan el alemán y los alemanes levantan el francés* 'The French pick up German and Germans pick up French.'

In a few cases, an English verb + particle construction has been incorporated as a single unit which functions in the domain of a verb + particle construction from which it is derived:

(g) *Vino Elvis Presley y lo noquió todo* 'E.P. came and knocked him out.'

Table 4. *Realization of clitic object pronouns*

	Postposed English pronoun	Preposed Spanish pronoun	No object pronoun
English verb unadapted switch	3	1	41
English verb morphologically adapted to Spanish	0	13	17

English verbs morphologically adapted to Spanish. This result suggests that switching begins – implicationally, if not historically – in contexts where there is minimal structural conflict.

Noun phrases and NP modification

Under this heading we find a somewhat different set of constraints than those which apply to verbs. The data, summarized in Table 5, can best be understood in light of the following differences and similarities of Spanish and English morpho-syntax:

(a) Spanish, but not English, distinguishes two grammatical genders.

(b) English noun compounds frequently correspond to Spanish N + PP constructions.

(c) Spanish adjectives agree with the nouns they modify in gender and number, morphologically marked for most adjectives; but English adjectives are invariant.

(d) Spanish attributive adjectives frequently immediately follow their head nouns; in English, they typically precede them.

(e) Spanish and English have parallel word order (DET + N) in NPs without adjectives.

(f) Relative clause structures follow the nouns they modify, with parallel syntax in both languages.

As with verbs (discussed in the last section), we find lexical and structural constraints and, in addition, constraints related to the function in discourse (discussed later). There are, however, no parallels to the verbal functional constraints which maintain morphological marking.

Gender/number marking

Gender/number marking is characterized by the following features.

Nouns. While gender is assigned to English nouns used in Spanish, this is not generally associated with inflectional suffixation in the singular; it

Table 5. *NPs and NP modification*

	S→E conversation	E→S conversation	E→S prose
1. Unmodified NP			
a. (D) <u>N</u>	747	12	121
b. <u>D</u> <u>N</u>	10	2	23
c. <u>D</u> N	1	0	0
2. <u>N</u> only in modified NP			
a. (D) A <u>N</u>	68	2	34
b. (D) <u>N</u> A	3	0	0
c. D adv A <u>N</u>	1	0	0
d. D<u>N</u> adv A	2	0	0
3. Adj + N in modified NP			
a. (D) <u>A</u> <u>N</u>	55	0	0
b. (D) <u>N</u> <u>A</u>	3	2	6
c. D <u>adv</u> <u>A</u> <u>N</u>	1	0	0
4. <u>Adj</u> only in modified NP			
a. (D) <u>A</u> N	1	0	0
b. (D) N <u>A</u>	2	0	0
c. (D) N adv <u>A</u>	7	0	0
5. Predicate adjective, substantive, verb complement			
a. "be" <u>A</u>	19	1	2
b. <u>A</u>	14	0	0
c. V <u>A</u>	10	0	0
6. Relative clause			
a. N <u>rel</u>	2	1	0
b. <u>N</u> <u>rel</u>	1	0	0

Note: Underscored constituents are L_2 in L_1 contexts.

should be regarded as syntactic rather than morphological adaptation. The realizations of the plural morphemes of both languages differ only in minor phonological features, often obscured in rapid speech – caused in part by a variable rule which deletes final *-s* in Chicano Spanish (as in Panamanian Spanish, Cedergren 1973, and Puerto Rican Spanish, Ma and Herasimchuk 1971).

Assignment of Spanish gender to English nouns is conditioned by several factors:

(a) Natural gender: masculine for males, feminine for females (*el trainer, un boxer, la maid, esa girl*).

(b) Phonology: some nouns in *-er* are classed as feminine, presumably (as has been suggested by Sánchez 1972) as a result of phonological similarity to Sp. *-a* (*la jira* 'heater').

(c) Morphological class: *-ity* is assigned to the feminine, like *-idad* in Spanish (*la liability, la responsibility, una community*).
(d) Gender of the Spanish equivalent (*la coast* like *la costa*).

However, there is some indication that grammatical gender is beginning to be lost for English nouns borrowed or switched into Spanish; the two-way distinction is neutralized in the masculine. Though at present this neutralization is not widespread, counter-examples to b–d are inevitably masculine: *el divider, unos traditions, el commotion* (cf. Sp. fem. *-ción*), *el tape* 'la cinta.'

Adjectives. As noted previously, adjectives are never inflected for gender and number, whether the gender/number of the antecedent is clear in the immediate context, as in 37 (marked as masc. sg. by the definite article *el*), or unmarked as in 38:

(37) *El cabrón se puso jealous* 'The bastard got jealous.'
(38) *Estaba muy fancy y todo* 'It was very fancy and all.'

Conversely, gender/number marking is maintained on Spanish adjectives in English, even though superfluous to English grammar – as in the following, spoken by a woman:

(39) *I'm not terca* '. . . stubborn.'

That English adjectives are not morphologically adapted to Spanish, in contrast to verbs, rests not only on the fact that gender/number marking is often (as in 37) completely redundant, but more fundamentally on the fact that Spanish gender is primarily a syntactic rather than a functional semantic category.

Word order and lexical integration
Word order and lexical integration can be described as follows.

Nouns. Clearly, mixes of DET with nouns, as in 40–41, and with noun compounds, as in 42 (1a in Table 5), are the most frequent of NP mixes. As is generally acknowledged, they are primarily controlled by lexical gaps or differential availability of lexical items in English or Spanish dominant domains:

(40) *El flight que sale de Chicago* 'the flight which leaves from Chicago.'[11]
(41) *El interest es muy poquito* 'The . . . is very small.'
(42) *Anoche en el executive committee escribimos una carta* 'Last night in the . . . we wrote a letter.'

No structural conflicts arise in such mixes, so no structural constraints are evident.

[11] Proper nouns were excluded when tabulating mixes.

Adjectives. Mixing adjectives outside the modified NP – as verb complements (37), as predicate adjectives (43–44), or as substantive adjectives (45) – involves no structural conflict, and is relatively free, as shown in 5a–c in Table 5.

(43) *No están free* 'They're not . . .'
(44) *Mi papá es muy protective* 'My father is very . . .'
(45) *la más sophisticated* 'the most . . .'

In contrast, mixing adjectives and nouns within the NP is strictly limited, subject to the following surface constraint:

(46) Adjective/noun mixes must match the surface word order of both the language of the adjective and the language of the head noun.

Thus, mixing Spanish and English nouns and adjectives immediately adjacent in the NP is, in general, prohibited. Preposed adjectives are permitted only in those cases – possessive pronouns, ordinal quantifiers, and other limiting adjectives – where Spanish, like English, regularly or frequently preposes the adjective. This constraint holds both for cases in which only the head noun is English, like 47–50 (2a in Table 5), and for cases where both adjective and noun are English, like 51–53 (3a in Table 5):

(47) *mi grandma* 'my grandma.'
(48) *Este Señor McCall tenía – como tres cajas, como tres cases de, de licor* 'This Mr. McC. had – like three cases, like three . . . of, of liquor.'
(49) *el siguiente play* 'the following play.'
(50) *mi único pleasure* 'my only pleasure.'
(51) *Este año en P.E. he ganado three ribbons ya* 'This year in P.E. I've won . . . already.'
(52) *el same night.*
(53) *el next day.*

Similarly, postnominal adjective mixing is permitted if there is structural parallelism between Spanish and English. In 54–56 (4c in Table 5), postposed English adjectives are also preceded by Spanish adverbs:

(54) *Me llevé chile ya roasted y peeled para hacerlo allá* 'I picked up chile already roasted and peeled for making it there.'
(55) *ese color como muy dark maroon* 'that color like very . . .'
(56) *Daban unos steaks tan sabrosos* 'They served some steaks so tasty.'

In 57–58, postposed adjectives occur in relative clauses, structurally predicate adjectives (5a in Table 5) – which, as noted earlier, have parallel syntax in both languages:

(57) *mujeres que son muy ladylike* 'women who are very . . .'
(58) *organizaciones que son muy conservative* 'organizations which are very . . .'

The use of relative clauses and adverbial modification may be conscious or unconscious strategies employed by speakers to avoid ungrammatical mixes within the NP.

Apparent counter-examples. The proposed structural constraint of 46 directly contradicts Aguirre 1976 and Wentz and McClure 1976, who claim that Spanish adjectives postposed to English nouns are grammatical – or, generally, that permitted word orders are constrained only by the placement rules of the language of the adjective. Their claims, however, are based on examples in which the head nouns are all well-integrated into the lexicons of Spanish monolinguals. Thus Aguirre's test sentence (his ex. 38a) was

(59) *Tengo un magazine nuevo* 'I have a new magazine.'

This was rated fully acceptable by seventeen, and somewhat acceptable by two out of twenty judges. Compare this sentence from my own corpus:

(60) *Me huele a toast quemado* 'It smells of burned toast to me.'

This could well be analyzed as not involving mixing at all. Similarly, the cited instances of mixing Spanish adjectives in English contexts might well be regarded as beginning with Spanish head nouns. Aguirre (p. 25) used this test sentence:

(61) *They have a little Chevy convertible nuevo.*

This was regarded as fully acceptable by only nine judges, ten others rating it somewhat acceptable and one rating it unacceptable; but this sentence contains a proper noun which is frequently used by monolingual Spanish speakers. Note also the following example from McClure (1977, p. 98)

(62) *I want a motorcycle verde.*

Sp. *motocicleta* is apparently in the process of phonological convergence toward English: Galván and Teschner (1975, p. 57) give *motorcicleta* as a Texas Spanish variant, and E. Hicks (personal communication) reports *morosaico* in the speech of Spanish monolinguals from Lemming, Texas.[12]

Another apparent counter-example from my own corpus has a clearly Eng. noun, *trunks*, followed by the Sp. adjective *antiguas*:

(63) *Tenía como de esas petacas que dicen como trunks antiguas con records desde que llegaron aquí en mil setecientos* 'It had like these old what they call "petacas," like trunks, with records since they arrived here in 1700.'

In this case, as indicated in the gloss, the postposed adjective should be

[12] Orthographic *r* represents the flap by which Eng. intervocalic *t* in *motorcycle* is realized.

regarded as modifying the Sp. noun *petacas* 'leather-covered cases,' a technical term which is explained by the parenthetical Eng. noun *trunks*. Note that the adjective agrees with *petacas* in gender.

Thus, none of the putative examples of English nouns modified by postposed Spanish adjectives really supports the claim that such switches are grammatical. Clear cases of mixing English nouns and Spanish postposed adjectives, such as would be provided by examples like 64, do not occur:

(64) **I went to the house chiquita.*

Indeed, these have been rated unacceptable in the tests reported by Gumperz (1976, p. 33).[13]

Discourse function and length

It is not the case, however, that length of nominal and adjectival mix is a crucial syntactic constraint, as concluded by Gumperz (1976, p. 33). His findings that longer switches are more acceptable are confounded by his use of test sequences like 65, in which the single-term switches violate structural constraints discussed previously:

(65) the LOST book
the book LOST
the book THAT WAS LOST
the book, THE ONE THAT WAS LOST.

As Table 5 shows, single noun mixes are the most frequent; and single adjectives are permitted in predicate adjective and verb-complement constructions, as well as in appropriate configurations within NPs. The longer relative clause switches (6a–b) which, according to Gumperz' claim, are most acceptable, turn out to be quite rare in actual conversation.

Length of L_2 sequence mixed into L_1 seems instead to be constrained by the function in discourse. The length of mixes within simple NPs and in relative clauses (see the next two sections) is related to factors such as whether old or new information is being communicated, and whether the mix occurs in the main predication or in an aside.

Determiner + noun. These mixes have been claimed to be ungrammatical by Wentz and McClure 1976, who found no instances naturally occurring in the speech of the children they studied. They report that the children were unable to repeat test sequences in which the language of the determiner was different from that of the verb, but identical to that of the head noun.

[13] The two instances of Spanish noun with postposed English adjective (4b in Table 5) are both the phrase *chorizo Mexican* [mɛ́ksikən]. These occurrences (recorded a year apart) are idiosyncratic to the speaker.

In the present corpus, however, DET + N mixes occur, though with low frequency (1b in Table 5). They are predominantly in contexts where they function as technical or quasi-technical terms:

(66) *the minimum foundation que es un sistema para financiero, para financiar las escuelas en el estado de Tejas* '. . . which is a system for financing the schools in the state of Texas.'

(67) *Era el mayor, the mayor* 'He was the mayor.'

(68) *viewing la pobreza in the Southwest* 'viewing the poverty . . .'

(69) *We, los mestizos del mundo tercero, are aware that we are not alone in our struggle* '. . . the mestizos of the third world . . .'

In 66, *the minimum foundation* occurs as a first mention, defined in the non-restrictive relative clause which follows it. In subsequent mentions, the speaker uses the more typical noun-only mix, *el minimum foundation*. In 67, it is clear from the context that the speaker intends reference to the public official designated by Eng. *mayor*, not to the Sp. adjective 'older' or 'greater'; the switch here corrects a "false-cognate" usage. In 67–69 we have literary examples. In 68, Ricardo Sánchez calls up an image of the specifically Mexican or Mexican-American aspects of poverty; in 69, the appositional Spanish NP serves not only to define, but also to emphasize the ethnic and social status of the pronominal subject of the fundamentally English sentence. An example from actual conversation is the previously cited 34 (*la onda is to fight y jambar*). DET + N switches can also be triggered by structural factors, as in the personal pronoun + noun switch of 13 (*los – los – uh – your muscles a veces react*). Here we have a case where the grammatical system of Spanish and English conflict, with no possibility of compromise; Spanish requires definite articles for expressions of inalienable possession, while English uses personal pronouns, or more formally, *one's*. Although mixing is normally fluent and frequently occurs between DET + N with no necessity for repeating the determiner, the speaker here hesitates and repeats the determiner, changing the syntax to conform to English requirements. Such cases indicate that mixing Spanish and English items does not necessarily imply merger of the grammars of Spanish and English; here the rules of both are maintained.

Relative clauses. Full relative clause switching, the long switch examples judged most acceptable in Gumperz' study, occur very rarely in my data (less than 1% of all switches, as can be seen in Table 2). In addition to the non-restrictive relative in 66, we find:

(70) *Tenían los Viva Kennedy Clubs y esos, los, pos, formaron los PASO, which was the Political Association of Spanish-speaking Organizations of Albert Pena, Bob Vale* 'They had the Viva Kennedy Clubs and those, the, well they formed PASO . . .'

(71) *There's lots of reporters reporting on things que ya pasaron* '. . . which have already passed.'

More frequently, relative clause switching involves only part of the clause, either predicate adjectives, as in 58 (*organizaciones que son muy conservative*), or *be-* passives, as in 35 (*la historia que el Exorcist is based on*).

The low frequency of full relative clause switching can perhaps be understood in light of the discourse function of relative clauses, i.e. further identification or parenthetical comment. When further identification involves simple attribution of adjectival qualities, there is no syntactic motivation for switching prior to the adjective itself, since the structures of English and Spanish relative clauses containing predicate adjectives are parallel. However, if a complete predicate assertion is intended, as in non-restrictive relatives, an alternative strategy (which adds still more weight) is to begin an entirely new sentence:

(72) *Because my sister, her husband, él es de México y así los criaron a ellos, you know; his family, ugly, and she's the same, you know?* '. . . he's from Mexico and they raise them like that . . .'

(73) *So yo y un bunche de guys – about twenty guys, and they were from the Ramar gang, ellos vivían allá en Harlandale* 'So I and a bunch of guys . . . they lived there in Harlandale.'

In such sentential switches, which are rather common in casual conversation, switching functions as a framing device, marking the sequence as an aside.

We have seen, then, that morphologically unadapted mixing is constrained to form surface structures shared by both languages. However, as shown by the rarity of the perfectly syntactically acceptable DET + N and full relative clause mixes, it is not the case that mixing is equally probable wherever no surface-structure violations would occur. Similarly, it is discourse, lexical, and social factors (rather than structural ones) that control mixing in constructions where English and Spanish structures are syntactically identical: prepositional phrases and subordinate and coördinate conjunctions (see the following sections).

Prepositional phrases

Prepositional phrases in Spanish and English are structurally parallel: P NP. Theoretically, language mixing could take place in any of the configurations $\text{P }\underline{\text{NP}}$, $\underline{\text{P}}\ \underline{\text{NP}}$, $\underline{\text{P}}\text{ NP}$, where the underscore represent L_2 mixed into an L_1 sequence. As Table 6 shows, however, not all structurally possible mixes are equally probable. English nouns occur freely in Spanish PPs; but mixing of an entire prepositional phrase occurs infrequently, and prepositions alone are never switched.

In addition to the configurational differences, Table 6 shows that the pattern of mixing English into Spanish differs from that for Spanish into English in conversational contexts; $\text{P }\underline{\text{NP}}$ accounts for 85 percent of Eng-

Table 6. *Prepositional phrase switches*

	Conversation S→E	Conversation E→S	Prose E→S
P NP	208	0	51
P NP	36	5	1
P NP	0	0	0

Table 7. *Function of preposition in PP's with switched noun*

	Locative instrumental	Temporal	Figurative
a	18	1	4
con	15	0	1
de	5	0	52
en	61	5	7
para	8	2	6

lish in Spanish, but none of the Spanish in English. In the written corpus, however, P NP accounts for all but one, or 98 percent of the English to Spanish mixes.

Lexical and semantic constraints

Mixing of prepositional phrases is controlled primarily by lexical and semantic factors. P NP mixes, often simply P D N,[14] are instances of NP mixing triggered by lexical gaps or differential appropriateness (discussed previously). The low frequency in conversation of P NP mixes from Spanish to English reflects the fact that Spanish nouns in predominantly English sentences are uncommon in any grammatical function. The prepositions in such mixed PPs (with the exception of *de*, frequently used in adapting English noun compounds to Spanish syntax) are used primarily in literal locative or instrumental senses, as shown in Table 7.

(74) *tiendas de retail* 'retail stores'
(75) *Fuimos del airport* 'We went from the airport.'
(76) *con el bat* 'with the bat.'

P NP mixes, however, are fixed or semi-idiomatic phrases in which prepositions are not generally locative or instrumental, but involve tem-

[14] The notation P NP thus indicates a prepositional phrase in which the mix begins after the preposition, to be distinguished from P NP. It is not intended to imply that an NP such as *el bat* in 76 is syntactically (or lexically) English.

poral or figurative senses, both in Spanish to English (72–79) and in English to Spanish (80):

(77) *Bueno, in other words, el flight que sale de Chicago around three o'clock* 'Fine, . . . the flight which leaves from . . .'

(78) *Lo puso under arrest* 'He put him . . .'

(79) *todos los fondos que requieran para operar la escuela son under your balanced budget* 'All the funds which they require to operate the school are . . .'

(80) *We have it planned for October twenty-ninth a las seis en el Methodist Student Center. Es el Dr. Daniels que es el head de Communication. Va a hablar él de writing style and technique y los que están interesados in this workshop, you know, I can't encourage you enough, people to go. Va a ser el primero y, like I said, we're joining together para tener más poder.*
'. . . at 6 o'clock in the MSC. It's Dr. D. who is the head of Communication. He's going to speak on . . . and those who are interested . . . It's going to be the first and . . . to have more power.'

Structural and social constraints

The P NP *in this workshop* in 80 presents an unusual case in which an idiomatic collocation of verb and preposition is split between two languages.[15] This unusual onset point may be understood as an interaction of structural and social factors. Structurally, Sp. *estar interesados + in* (or *en*) is a calque on Eng. *be interested in*, rather than the standard Sp. reflexive *interesarse en*. The speaker's awareness of the Anglicized structure may have triggered the switch to English – particularly in light of the social setting, a meeting of a Chicano student political organization. Several opposing sociolinguistic forces come into play in this semi-formal, but in-group public event. For these participants, most formal and semi-formal speech is English; but the use of Spanish as the basic medium of communication here is dictated by its social function, reinforcing ethnic and political solidarity. In such settings, however, standard or "good" Spanish rather than Anglicized casual norms would be appropriate. Thus code-switching – which (as noted in the first section) functions generally as a strategy of neutrality – here also specifically provides a socially acceptable means of getting out of an Anglicized structure.[16]

[15] The phonetic similarity of Sp. *en* and Eng. *in* make absolute identification of the mix as either P NP or P NP impossible. But even if 80 were classified as the P NP mix *en this workshop*, the mix would be unusual in including the determiner as well as the noun (cf. the section on DET + noun mixes).

[16] A check of thirty-five San Antonio interviews lends some support to the hypothesis that speakers consciously or unconsciously switch entirely to English to avoid morphologically adapted loans or calques. Sixteen of the twenty speakers who either used recognizable calques or mixed major constituents – clauses or whole phrases – used one or the other but not both. The hypothesis that code-switching provides an alternative to linguistic convergence, serving to keep the two codes separate and "pure" as discussed in the first section, warrants further investigation. Subjective reactions to calquing and switching will provide crucial evidence.

Table 8. *Sentence conjunction switches*

	Free conversation						
	Interview	Meeting	Family	Peers	Prose	Lecture	Total
Conjunction in language of 2nd conjunct							
E→S	10	1	1	7	4	3	26
S→E	9	4	2	3	4	0	22
Conjunction in language of 1st conjunct							
E→S	0	0	0	1	0	0	1
S→E	8	2	2	2	0	1	15

Conjoined clauses

The final case of mixing to be discussed is that of sentences in which one of two coördinate or subordinate conjoined clauses is Spanish, the other English. The syntax of such sentence conjunction is completely parallel in Spanish and English; thus we should expect no structural constraints on switching between conjoined clauses. However, Gumperz (1976, p. 34) has claimed that conjunctions must be in the language of the second of two conjoined sentences, based on judgments on pairs of sentences as indicated below, where italics indicate a switch to the other language:

(81) I was reading a book { *and she was working* / *and *she was working* }

(82) I wanted to stop smoking { *but I couldn't* / *but *I couldn't* }

(83) John stayed at home { *because his wife was at work.* / *because *his wife was at work.* }

Gumperz' claim is not borne out in conversation, though it holds in the literary work of Ricardo Sánchez, and is approximated in Alurista's lecture style, as shown in Table 8.

In addition to sentences like 84–86, which fit the proposed constraint, we also find examples like 87–92, in which the conjunction is in the language of the first conjunct:

(84) *Me estaba defendiendo and then he split* 'He was defending me . . .'

(85) *I keep thinking that Jason probably will be walking cuando cumpla el año* '. . . when he turns one.'

(86) *Ya no podía ir pa'trás cause they had kicked me out of school* 'I couldn't go back anymore . . .'

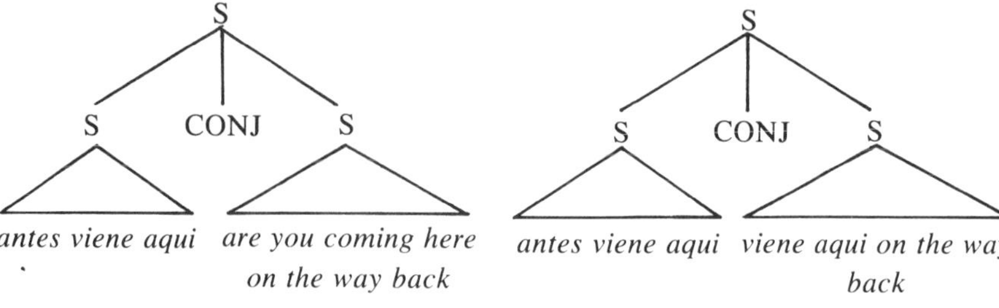

Figure 2. Representation of underlying conjunction of sentences in Spanish and English

Figure 3. Representation of underlying conjunction of two Spanish sentences with a switched PP

(87) *¿Antes viene aquí o on the way back?* 'Are you coming here before or . . . ?'
(88) *They sell so much of it that lo están sacando y many people like it* '. . . they're taking it out and . . .'
(89) *No voy tanto como iba pero I still believe in it, you know* 'I don't go as much as I went but . . .'
(90) *Y él dice que nunca nunca nunca nunca se olvida eso y por mucho tiempo no podía dormir porque it was a bad experience* 'And he says that he'll never never never never forget that and for a long time he couldn't sleep because . . .'
(91) *Trabajé menos porque then I didn't know some of his business* 'I worked less because . . .'
(92) *Como, here you can because viven todos juntos* 'Like, . . . they live all together.'

Elliptical sentences

In a few cases it may be possible to reduce the number of counter-examples to Gumperz' claim by re-analysis of elliptical conjuncts like 87. Two underlying structures are possible. If we analyze 87 as an underlying conjunction of sentences in Spanish and English, as represented in Figure 2, then Conjunction Reduction operates to delete *are you coming here* under identity with *viene aquí*; but the occurrence of *o*, rather than *or* as predicted by Gumperz, remains problematic. But if 87 is analysed as an underlying conjunction of two Spanish sentences with a switched PP in the second, as represented in Figure 3, Conjunction Reduction operates to delete the strictly identical second occurrence of *viene aquí*, and the conjunction *o* is entirely expected.

The grammar of Spanish/English mixing must provide for both analyses. As Pfaff 1976c and Wentz and McClure 1976 independently demonstrate, it is necessary to allow translation equivalents to count as identical to account for elliptical sentences such as these:

(93) A: *¡Estudie ahí!* 'Study there!'
B: *No, I can't.*

(94) A: *¿Vas ir?* 'Are you going to go?'
B: *Well, I want to.*
(95) A: *¿Quién tiene hambre?* 'Who's hungry?'
B: *I am* (Wentz and McClure 1976, p. 657).

Structures like that posited in the second conjunct of the underlying structure in Figure 3 are also found on the surface. As discussed previously, such idiomatic phrases account for a high proportion of whole PP switching within simplex sentences.

Non-elliptical sentences

The above analysis cannot, however, account for non-elliptical counter-examples to Gumperz' claim, e.g. 88–92; and these constitute the majority of the cases. Such cases appear not to be constrained by local syntactic factors. Note, however, that while there is no general constraint against English conjunctions, Table 8 shows (with only one exception, ex. 92) that the counter-example consists of Spanish conjunctions preceding English second conjuncts.[17] This could hardly be accidental, and can be seen as a reflection of the tendency (not constraint) for function words, sentence adverbials, tags, and loosely bound interjections to be realized in Spanish even in predominantly English sentences; e.g.,

(96) *It goes without saying I think que along with the picketing we are doing a boycott.*
(97) *I think the Ramadas aren't real expensive, ¿verdad? They're about twelve or fourteen, o qué* ['or whatever'] *and they're really nice.*
(98) A: *¿No vive aquí?*
B: *Sí, pero we didn't get together yesterday so we were planning to celebrate today.*

As Gumperz and Hernández-Chávez note (1975, pp. 156–7), such forms function socially as markers of ethnic identification, and are frequently employed even by speakers who no longer have effective control of Spanish. Thus it seems that the putative syntactic constraint identified by Gumperz has no structural basis. If it exists at all, it is easily overridden by the solidarity-marking function of using Spanish function words.

Conclusions

In the preceding pages I have considered several aspects of Spanish/English intrasentential mixing. To recapitulate, it appears that speakers

[17] It is interesting to note that this sole counter-example involving an English conjunction occurs in the casual conversation of a male adolescent Californian whose speech is characterized by such other extreme and unlikely mixes as a single English determiner embedded in Spanish:

> *¡Tú crees que un jodido como ése me catiara solo! The pendejo no tiene huevos* 'You think a turkey like that could beat me up by himself? The fool doesn't have any balls . . .'

who code-switch are competent in the syntactic rules of both languages. It is unnecessary to posit the existence of a third grammar to account for the utterances in which the languages are mixed; rather, the grammars of Spanish and English are meshed according to a number of constraints.

Functional constraints

The obligation to express tense/aspect in verb switching gives rise to the following constraint:

(99) Switches to morphologically unadapted English verbs are permitted only when preceded by an inflected Spanish verb, unless tense/aspect is overtly marked elsewhere in the sentence.

But gender/number agreement of adjectives with their antecedents, which is syntactically required but not semantically functional in Spanish, is not maintained in switching to English adjectives. Conversely, syntactically superfluous gender/number agreement is maintained in switching to Spanish adjectives in English sentences.

Structural constraints

Surface structures common to both languages are favored for switches; thus the periphrastic verbal constructions favored by 99 raise no syntactic conflict. Adjective switches, in contrast, are unrestricted when they take the form of predicate adjectives, but are limited within the NP. Postnominal attributive adjectives do not in general occur in NPs with switched adjectives or nouns; prenominally, adjective switching is restricted to typical limiting adjectives, which often precede in Spanish as well as in English.

Semantic constraints

Non-clausal switches tend to start at a point of lexical divergence, e.g. before main verbs, nouns, or adjectives. Whole PP switches involve figurative or temporal meanings; literal locatives switch after the preposition.

Discourse constraints

Violations of the norms of the previous paragraph are associated with discourse and social function. NP switches including the determiner as well as the noun are first-mention or emphasized-mention of technical or quasi-technical terms (including slang). Lone Spanish conjunctions, or Spanish conjunctions preceding switches to English, mark the discourse as Spanish socially.

Structural triggers

In general, longer code-switches are motivated by discourse considerations (parenthetical comments, asides, framing, metaphor etc.) rather than lexical ones. Some longer code-changes, however, are triggered by lexically motivated code-mixes. There appears to be a process, analogous to assimilation in phonology, which results in initiating a switch somewhat in advance of the lexical item which is its head, or in continuing it past the head item. In the present corpus, all instances of such switches occur in contexts where there is structural conflict between Spanish and English: the attachment of clitic pronouns, the DET + N co-occurrence restrictions, or the use of verb + particle.

Mixing and language change

Depending on the socio-political circumstances, language contact and mixing can result in language change of various types – pidginization, creolization, or convergence. The language mixing which is characteristic of the Spanish/English bilingual is essentially different from that in pidgin and creole speaking communities. Loss of gender and number inflection on borrowed adjectives represents the only morphological simplification, and only the limited non-causative *hacer* + infinitive construction represents a creole-like extension of the grammar. This finding that no separate new system is created is to be expected, since speakers are competent in two related languages which have a high degree of structural similarity.

Convergence of various types is found. Calquing, by definition, results in direct linguistic convergence. Borrowing and code-switching also have this effect, but only indirectly. As we have seen, borrowing has affected even the most basic parts of the vocabulary, including numerals and kin terms. Only in the case of verb + particle structures, however, may such relexification prove to be the starting point for more significant convergence; at present no such change is established. Since, in mixing, structural conflict is avoided and surface structures common to both languages are favored, the result is an increase in frequency of formerly less-popular stylistic options in mixed sequences. Further study of the effect of language mixing on syntactic convergence should investigate the extent to which these frequency patterns carry over into speakers' monolingual Spanish and English utterances.

Appendix: Sample texts

(1) Participants are one male (M) and two females (F1, F2), staff members of a state agency in Austin, Texas. Setting: office of M. Situation and topic: casual conversation about families. M is a sociolinguistics student who consciously code-switches in this conversation, but never within a sentence:

M: *Oye, ¿qué está haciendo Jason?* ['Listen, what is Jason doing?'] *Is he walking around?* [6 turns in English.]

F1: *Sí, but the thing is que empezan bien recio* ['that they start pretty fast'] *and then they slack off.*

F2: *Then they go slow.*

F1: *Randy started out bien chico* ['very young']. *The first time he stood up, he was six months old. By the time I really figured out he was walking, bueno ves* ['well, you see'], *but they go slow and sometimes fast and then they slack off.*

F2: *I keep thinking that Jason probably will be walking cuando cumpla el año* ['when he turns one'].

(2) Participants are two adult women from Fresno, California, in phone conversation:

A: *¿Qué pasa?* ['What's happening?'] *Can't you come over today?*

B: *I would love to, but I don't know if we can for sure. Déjame hablarte después que llegue Joe* ['Let me talk to you later after Joe arrives'] *I don't know what to tell you right now.*

A: *Okay y don't forget, llámame después* ['call me later'].

(3) Participants are members of a bilingual family in El Paso, Texas. Parents, married daughter and her husband, and another daughter are engaged in casual conversation in the home of the younger couple. The speaker is the younger man, describing a recent trip to Mexico:

> *A veces queríamos steak* ['Sometimes we wanted to eat steak.'] *Daban unos steaks tan sabrosos* ['They served some steaks, so tasty.']. *Estaba muy fancy y todo* ['It was very fancy and all'].

(4) Speaker is the male president of a Chicano student organization at UT Austin. He is addressing a meeting:

> *Hablé con E.M. de Raza Unida y va a ver un* ['I talked with E.M. of Raza Unida and he's going to see a . . .'] *state executive committee meeting este fin de semana que viene en El Paso* ['the end of the coming week in El Paso'] *y el Travis City delegation va a charter un camión y es treinta dólar ir y vuelta, los que tengan el dinero y están interesados* ['is going to charter a bus and it's $30 going and returning, those who have the money and are interested']. *Va a ser el primero* ['It's going to be the first'] *y like I said, we're joining together para tener mas poder* ['to have more power'].

(5) Participants are two males, engaged in casual conversation on the streets of Porterville, California:

A: *Bueno, ¿por qué te hicieron beat up ese?* ['Well, why did they beat you up, man?']

B: *Pos, nomás porque estaba making up con la morra de Yoli* ['Well, just because I was making up with the chick Yoli'].

A: *Y nomás por eso te catiaron?* 'And just for that they beat you up?'

B: *Simón guy, pero* ['Yeah, guy, but . . .'] *the thing is que uno de los guys andaba con la pinchi Yoli* ['that one of the guys went with the damn Yoli'] *y el cabrón se puso jealous porque nos agarró en la movida chueca* ['and the bastard got jealous because he caught us in an affair'].

(6) Class lecture of Alurista, Chicano poet and instructor at UT Austin:

This is the way we speak. Así hablamos en los barrios en las comunidades ['We talk this way in the barrios in the communities']. *You know, we have to use English to survive and Spanish to preserve our heritage. Why you use one or the other eso tiene que ver mucho con* ['that depends a lot on'] *what kind of impact you give to your words. Ves, hay palabras en inglés que tienen mucha fuerza emocional, como práctica* ['You see, there are words in English that have a lot of emotional force, like practical']. *El idioma anglo-sajón es muy práctico* ['The Anglo-Saxon language is more practical'], *it's a business language.*

(7) Prose of a Chicano writer (Ricardo Sánchez 1973, p. 148):

Why, I questioned myself, did I have to daily portray myself as a neo-gringo cuando mi realidad tenía más sangre y pasión? ['when my reality had more blood and passion?']

References

Aguirre, A. 1976. Acceptability judgements of code-switching phrases by Chicanos: some preliminary findings. ERIC ED 129 122.

Cedergren, Henrietta. 1973. On the nature of variable constraints. In *New ways of analyzing variation in English*, ed. Charles-James N. Bailey and Roger Shuy, pp. 13–22. Washington, D.C.: Georgetown University Press.

Cerda, G., B. Cabaza, and J. Farias. 1953. *Vocabulario español de Tejas*. Austin: University of Texas Press.

Christian, J. M., and C. C. Christian, Jr. 1966. Spanish language and culture in the Southwest. In *Language loyalty in the United States*, ed. Joshua Fishman, pp. 280–317. The Hague: Mouton.

Elías-Olivares, Lucía. 1976. Ways of speaking in a Chicano community: a sociolinguistic approach. Ph.D. dissertation, University of Texas, Austin.

Espinosa, Aurelio. 1917. Speech mixture in New Mexico: the influence of the English language on New Mexican Spanish. In *The Pacific Ocean in history*, ed. H. Morse Stephens and H. E. Bolton, pp. 408–28. New York: Macmillan.

Fishman, Joshua, R. L. Cooper, and R. Ma, eds. 1971. *Bilingualism in the barrio*. Bloomington: Indiana University Press.

Galván, R., and R. Teschner. 1975. *El diccionario del español de Tejas*. Silver Spring, Md.: Institute of Modern Languages.

Gingràs, Rosario. 1974. Problems in the description of Spanish/English intrasentential code-switching. In *Southwest areal linguistics*, ed. Garland Bills, pp. 167–74. San Diego: San Diego State University, Institute for Cultural Pluralism.

Gumperz, John. 1976. The sociolinguistic significance of conversational code-switching. In *Papers on language and context*, by Jenny Cook-Gumperz and John Gumperz (Working Paper 46), pp. 1–46. Berkeley: University of California, Language Behavior Research Laboratory.

Gumperz, John, and E. Hernández-Chávez. 1975. Cognitive aspects of bilingual communication. In *El lenguaje de los Chicanos*, ed. E. Hernández-Chávez, A. Cohen, and A. Beltramo, pp. 154–63. Arlington, Va.: Center for Applied Linguistics.

Haugen, Einar. 1973. Bilingualism, language contact, and immigrant languages in the United States: a research report, 1956–1970. In *Current trends in linguistics*, ed. Thomas Sebeok, vol. 10, pp. 505–91. The Hague: Mouton.

Labov, William. 1971. The notion of "system" in creole languages. In *Pidginization and creolization of languages*, ed. Dell Hymes, pp. 447–72. Cambridge University Press.

Lance, D. Spanish–English code-switching. In *El lenguaje de los Chicanos*, ed. E. Hernández-Chávez, A. Cohen, and A. Beltramo, pp. 138–53. Arlington, Va.: Center for Applied Linguistics.

Lehmann, Winfred P. 1975. Japanese as a consistent OV language. In *Proceedings of a U.S.–Japan sociolinguistics meeting*, ed. Bates Hoffer, pp. 1–12. San Antonio, Tex.: Trinity University Press.

Ma, Roxana, and E. Herasimchuk. 1971. The linguistic dimensions of a bilingual neighborhood. In *Bilingualism in the barrio*, ed. J. Fishman, R. L. Cooper, and R. Ma, pp. 347–464. Bloomington: Indiana University, Research Center for the Language Sciences.

McClure, Erica. 1977. Aspects of code-switching in the discourse of bilingual Mexican-American children. In *GURT 1977*, ed. M. Saville-Troike, pp. 93–115. Washington, D.C.: Georgetown University Press.

McClure, Erica, and M. McClure. 1975. Ethnoreconstruction. *Mid-America Linguistics Conference Papers*, pp. 327–37. Lawrence: University of Kansas.

McClure, Erica, and J. Wentz. 1975. Functions of code-switching among Mexican-American children. In *Papers from the parasession on functionalism*, pp. 421–32. Chicago: Chicago Linguistic Society.

Ornstein, Jacob. 1975. The archaic and the modern in the Spanish of New Mexico. In *El lenguaje de los Chicanos*, ed. E. Hernández-Chávez, A. Cohen, and A. Beltramo, pp. 6–12. Arlington, Va.: Center for Applied Linguistics.

Pfaff, Carol. 1976a. Syntactic constraints on code-switching: a quantitative study of Spanish/English. *Working Papers in Sociolinguistics* 35.

1976b. Functional and structural constraints on syntactic variation in code-switching. *Papers from the parasession on diachronic syntax*, pp. 248–59. Chicago: Chicago Linguistic Society.

1976c. Cross-language reference in bilingual discourse. Paper presented at the Fifth Conference on New Ways of Analyzing Variation, Oct., Georgetown University.

1976d. Processes of language mixing: Spanish/English code-switching. Paper presented at the Internationaler Linguistenkongress, Vienna.

Reyes, Rogelio. 1974. Studies in Chicano Spanish. Ph.D. dissertation, Harvard University.

Rickford, J. 1975. Carrying the new wave into syntax: the case of Black English BIN. *Analyzing variation in language*, ed. Ralph W. Fasold and Roger W. Shuy, pp. 162–83. Washington, D.C.: Georgetown University Press.

Romero, M., and C. Romero. 1976. *Los bilingos*. Santa Fe, N.J.: Sunstone Press.

Sanches, Mary. 1976. Relexification and syntactic change in Japanese. Manuscript, University of Texas, Austin.

Sánchez, Ricardo. 1973. *Canto y grito mi liberación*. New York: Doubleday, Anchor Press.

Sánchez, Rosaura. 1972. Nuestra circunstancia lingüística. *El Grito* 6:45–74.

Sawyer, Janet. 1970. Spanish–English bilingualism in San Antonio, Texas. *Texas studies in bilingualism*, ed. Glenn Gilbert, pp. 18–41. Berlin: de Gruyter.

Scotton, Carol. 1976. Strategies of neutrality. *Language* 52.919–41.

Sobin, Nicholas. 1976. Texas Spanish and lexical borrowing. *Papers in Linguistics* 9:15–47.

Timm, L. 1975. Spanish–English code-switching: el porque y how not to. *Romance Philology* 28:473–82.

Vásquez, Librado K., and María E. Vásquez. 1975. Regional dictionary of Chicano slang. Austin: Jenkins.

Wentz, J., and E. McClure. 1976. Ellipsis in bilingual discourse. *Chicago Linguistic Society* 12:656–65.

1977. Monolingual "codes": some remarks on the similarities of bilingual and monolingual code-switching. *Chicago Linguistic Society* 13:706–13.

Part III

Ethnographic aspects of language use in bilingual communities

Several recent studies have demonstrated how different speech communities throughout the world organize the various sociolinguistic factors that are involved in actual discourse (Gumperz and Hymes 1972; Bauman and Sherzer 1974) and how the range of sociolinguistic variation present in those communities deserves serious consideration. However, studies of the various ways in which languages and varieties of languages are used in Hispanic bilingual communities of the United States, not merely for referential purposes but in functional terms, are scarce. Thus this section should be a welcome introduction for those interested in the discourse behavior of Hispanics, from "El Barrio," New York, to East Austin, Texas.

Fundamental to all the authors of these chapters are basic sociolinguistic concepts developed by Dell Hymes for the description of the relationship between language and social life – speech community, speech event, speech act – as well as a call for a description of language behavior that is ethnographic as well as linguistic (Hymes 1972). This is particularly clear in the chapters by Limón, McDowell, and Zentella.

Several of the authors, who are themselves members of the speech communities they describe, have collected their data in naturalistic settings, as participant observers in the daily interaction of those communities.

Limón's microstudy of the uses of folk Spanish (what Sánchez calls popular Spanish in this same volume) among ethnic nationalist Chicano university students in Texas in the 1960s demonstrates how the use of this variety in those particular meetings exemplifies the way in which a language variety can be used for expressive and meaningful effects. Folk Spanish is a symbol of many meanings, which are described by Limón, such as respect and authority, but at the same time, political resistance and working-class consciousness.

It is important to point out that Limón explains the uses of folk Spanish as part of a more comprehensive framework. His sociohistorical complex of referents allows him to establish some general relationships among language, social class, and social change in Texas-Mexican society that have been instrumental in language maintenance and shift mechanisms. Moreover, as he points out, these relationships have helped language to become a powerful agent in mobilizing people into political action.

The chapter by McDowell also illustrates the fact that speakers select specific varieties from their linguistic repertoires (Gumperz 1964) and utilize them for special purposes, and sometimes for artistic effects. He sets out the ethnographic context for his discussion of Chicano children's verbal folklore in East Austin, Texas, and discovers, not surprisingly, that code-switching is the most functional speech variety within the children's verbal repertoire, in spite of the fact that their verbal art makes use of the entire range of their bilingual resources.

The code-switching strategies of three Puerto Rican third-graders in New York City is the focus of Zentella's chapter. She studies two different types of interactions, a formal interview, and a domino game, and after comparing the code-switching patterns in both situations, she discovers that the most productive and varied form of code-switching is precisely the one exhibited in the domino game, for communicative competence in code-switching is best expressed in the most informal context. Zentella points out the importance of correlating code-switching behavior with the specific rules for interaction as they are perceived by the speakers, a point that is also well-developed by Limón.

The functional allocation of Spanish and English in a more formal type of interaction – a bilingual classroom – is discussed in the chapter by Sapiens. He shows that although the ethnographic context is located in a bilingual classroom in which both languages could equally be used, his analysis of teacher talk indicates that English is the favored language of instruction and classroom control, which raises the question of how well the teacher meets the social and instructional needs of the students.

The last chapter, by Galván, deals with the language used in children's games and the mechanisms of language change. He examines the terminology used by bilingual children to describe marble playing in a South Texas community and relates this to several issues on bilingualism and the shift from Spanish to English.

The diversity of linguistic resources available to bilingual children and adults in Hispanic communities of the United States is present in all the chapters that follow. All the authors attempt in their own different ways to discover the functional uses of the varieties employed and the relationship between the linguistic means and the sociocultural factors through which the speakers interpret the speech events and acts in which they participate.

References

Bauman, Richard, and Joel Sherzer, eds. 1974. *Explorations in the ethnography of speaking*. New York: Cambridge University Press.

Gumperz, John J. 1964. Linguistic and social interaction in two communities. In The ethnography of communication, part 2, ed. J. J. Gumperz and D. Hymes. *American Anthropologist* 66, no. 6:137–53.

Gumperz, John J., and Dell Hymes, eds. 1972. *Directions in sociolinguistics: the ethnography of communication*. New York: Holt, Rinehart and Winston.

Hymes, Dell. 1972. Models of the interaction of language and social life. In *Directions in sociolinguistics: the ethnography of communication*, ed. J. J. Gumperz and D. Hymes, pp. 35–71. New York: Holt, Rinehart and Winston.

14

El meeting: history, folk Spanish, and ethnic nationalism in a Chicano student community

JOSÉ E. LIMÓN

In the second of his two integrated, seminal essays on language and nationalism, Joshua Fishman (1972a, pp. 43–44) notes the special emphasis given to language by nationalist movements:

> Modern mass nationalism goes beyond the objective, instrumental identification of community with language (i.e. with communication) to the identification of authenticity with a *particular* language which is experientially unique and, therefore, functional in a way that other languages cannot match, namely, in safeguarding the sentimental and behavioral links between the speech community of today and its (real or imaginary) counterparts yesterday and in antiquity . . . Nationalism stresses this function, a deeply subjective function, as a summun bonum.

Yet, while noting the significance of language to nationalist sentiment, Fishman laments the "pitifully few studies that focus on a vernacular as a substantive (rather than as a functional) hub of nationalism" (p. 44). He clearly equates "substantive" with "authenticity," "sentimental," and "the deeply subjective."

The present study adds to the minimal work on this theme. In so doing it responds to other, more circumscribed, scholarly needs. For example, in his work on ethnicity markers in speech, Giles (1979, p. 267) tells us,

> we need far more information from a variety of inter-ethnic contexts as to which markers are accentuated and attenuated in intergroup encounters, by whom in both groups . . . and for what purpose, and how these strategies are reacted to in turn by the recipients, in a continuing feedback loop.

We might only add that we also need information from *intra*group contexts with an interethnic symbolic dimension; that is, ingroup contexts marked

The first draft of this study was completed during a 1978–9 postdoctoral year with the Chicano Studies Center at the University of California, Los Angeles. I am grateful to Juan Gomez-Q., director of the center. I am also grateful to Marianna Adler for her critical reading of the final draft.

by the penetrating appearance of outgroup symbolic action, for example, someone speaking the outgroup language.

Mexicans in the United States comprise just such a marked ingroup, and we need to know more about their social uses of language. As Hernández-Chávez, Cohen, and Beltramo (1975) conclude: ". . . in the crucial yet virtually uncharted area of language use among Chicanos, we need to know much more about where and when the different varieties of Spanish and English are used and the social determinants of code selection" (p. xvi). More specifically, in a recent review of sociolinguistic work in this community, Ryan and Carranza (1977) still find that "the extent to which language or speech style is important for ethnic identity among Mexican-Americans has not been addressed specifically by these studies" (p. 77). Finally, studies on contemporary ethnic nationalism within this group have not been concerned with the interactional symbolic uses of language (Gómez-Q. 1978, Reich 1977, Rosen 1974, Segade 1978), although, to be sure, some attention has been given to the use of folk speech in Chicano ethnic nationalist literature (Garza 1977, Ortega 1977, Valdés-Fallis 1975, Ybarra-Frausto 1978).

In this study I primarily examine the social interactional uses of folk Spanish as a political and cultural symbol. The interlocutors are Chicano students at a Texas university, acting in an ethnic nationalist political context. Although my primary focus is on the microcontexts of face-to-face interactions, the full meaning of these symbolic interactions may only be grasped in a macrocontext, that is, by drawing on a history of social change, conflict, language maintenance, and language shift in Texas. This, perhaps unusually lengthy, next section is thus not merely "background." It is the multiple referent – the source of meanings, as it were – for the symbolic uses of language among the Chicano students.[1]

[1] I realize that studies linking the micro and macro "traditions" in sociolinguistics are not common. For me the two approaches seem quite complementary. Hymes, for example, would begin his mode of analysis at the micro level of face-to-face interaction but would eventually want and need to ask questions concerning the larger meanings of language in society – meanings may not be clearly emergent in the descriptive analysis of such microinteractions. Fishman (1972), while affirming the need for this sort of analysis, would be more inclined to begin with the larger metainteractional social forces that impinge upon the speech behavior in any given face-to-face encounter. A rapprochement of these two tendencies seems inevitable and necessary for a full understanding of language in society. Fishman, at least, is explicit on this point: "Just as there is no societally unencumbered verbal interaction so are there no large-scale relationships between language and society that do not depend on individual interaction for their realization. Although there is no mechanical part-whole relationship between them, micro- and macrosociolinguistics are both conceptually and methodologically complementary" (1972, p. 453).

Thus, in linking the ethnography of face-to-face communication in *el meeting* with larger historical forces beyond el meeting, I would like to think that I am one of "those" sociolinguists of whom Fishman says, "it is gratifying to note that for those who seek such ties the links between micro- and macroconstructs and methods exist" (1972, p. 453).

Settlement, social change, and the historical speech community

People of Hispanic and mestizo descent made their first significant appearance in Texas in the early eighteenth century at mission settlements, particularly in San Antonio. This initial and small presence was followed by a more extensive land-grant settlement in 1749 along what is now the Lower Rio Grande Valley from Laredo to Brownsville and the Gulf of Mexico on both sides of the river. By 1848 there were probably some 5,000 Mexicans living north of the Rio Grande, including San Antonio. The population not in San Antonio consisted largely of self-subsistent agriculturalists living in ranching villages organized by extended family and clan units. These people also imported or developed a variety of other cultural behaviors, including food and medical practices, folk Catholicism, a rich folklore, and, of course, language (Paredes 1958, 1976).

We cannot be exactly sure what kind of language was spoken during the period 1749–1848. Eighteenth-century Spanish, to be sure, but certainly already different from that spoken in Spain and the upper classes of central and southern New Spain, given that the northern settlers did not come primarily from those classes. More significant, it was most probably a Spanish already showing the influence of indigenous languages. Perhaps ultimately of greater significance, this area and its language would eventually show the effects of distance and isolation from the centers of political influence and a less than rigorous educational and linguistic standardization.

In the absence of any historical linguistic studies of this early population, we can postulate the evolution of this language up to 1848 and beyond only along the lexical dimensions suggested by Espinosa (1957). Lexically this population probably produced at least four major kinds of changes: semantic changes, as new meanings were given to old terms; coinages, as new terms were produced for new experiences; some transformations, as new terms from other languages were Hispanicized (before 1848, one would suspect that this process was minimal); and finally, a kind of de-evolutionary change, when terms were maintained as archaisms after they had passed from standard academically sanctioned usage in Mexico City and Madrid. Phonological, morphological, and syntactical changes also occurred, as will be evident later. The very likely result by 1848 was a regional dialect of Spanish in which the principal social forces affecting the language were isolation, the lack of education, and a distinctive environment. Further changes occurred as a result of political events beginning in 1821.

Living in a relatively isolated part of New Spain, this population developed a high degree of local self-government, although the people were, of course, subjects of the Spanish Crown at first, citizens of the Republic of Mexico after 1821, and citizens of the United States after 1848, some reluctantly. These political shifts, especially the latter, brought about very significant socioeconomic and cultural changes for this community. As citizens of the Mexican Republic, part of this population was living on the land between the Nueces River and the Rio Grande – the stretch of territory that would be the subject of dispute between Mexico on one side and the soon-to-be-annexed Republic of Texas and its new host, the United States, on the other. The latter would win the war to follow, after its armies successfully invaded Mexico, not without first passing through the Mexican area of South Texas in rather violent fashion.

A greater, long-range consequence of this military victory was the social change in the area, most of it generated and sanctioned by the new political order. At least seven major changes occurred as the area became part of the political economy of the United States from 1848 to the present day: (1) the increase in the Mexican population to some 250,000 by 1910, with some part of the increase created by immigration (census data are very unreliable for this time period for this population) (Nelson-Cisneros 1975, p. 240); (2) the conversion of the area into a capitalist, agriculturally based economic complex, particularly between 1890–1920 (Montejano n.d.); (3) the political and economic transformation of the Mexican population into a landless, labor dependent, racially segregated group (Montejano n.d., Nelson-Cisneros 1975, Zamora 1975); (4) the education of Mexican children by the Texas school systems, albeit in segregated schools until the 1950s (Limón 1974b); (5) the growing hegemony of U.S. popular culture through mass media forms (Limón 1974a); (6) the development of large Mexican enclaves late in this period in urban centers such as San Antonio, Corpus Christi, Dallas, and Houston (Romo 1978); and finally (7) the dramatic expansion of this subject Mexican population by thousands of immigrants fleeing the effects of the Mexican Revolution of 1910, especially along the northern Mexican border states. By 1930 the Mexican population of Texas was approximately 700,000 (Nelson-Cisneros 1975, p. 241).

Language behavior would necessarily show the influence of this period of social change. No doubt, newly arriving immigrants from different parts of Mexico introduced some changes into the language of Mexican South Texas. We should recall, however, that most of these came from the neighboring and culturally similar northern Mexican states. However, another wave of immigrants – those Anglo-Americans coming to South Texas to exploit its economic development between 1890 and 1920 – brought a more crucial change in at least two modes. First, they provided a linguistic resource for many Hispanicized borrowings – *el diche* 'ditch,' *la troca* 'truck,' *lonchar* 'to have lunch,' as in *Vamos a lonchar abajo de la troca despues de limpiar el diche*. (Indeed, one would suspect that much of this borrowing occurred in the workplace.) Over time these borrowings became as Spanish as any other item in the lexicon and thus actually enriched the language (Espinosa 1957). As Elías-Olivares (1979) notes, such a process of relexification adds new words to the Spanish speaker's repertoire. It should not be viewed as interference. The second mode was not as enriching relative to the maintenance of a distinctly Spanish code. The northern American immigrants spoke a language that began to carry prestige as a direct result of their superior political-economic status and its singular institutionalization in the schools. Socioeconomic and educational prestige; the continuing lack of extensive formal education in Spanish; the stigmatization of the culture expressed in that language; and the impact of mass media – all of these social conditions had their effect on language.

As early as 1910, Spanish-language newspapers in the area began to note and criticize the first minor signs of language shift in the population (Limón 1974b, 1978a). These are the first documented beginnings of a now seventy-year period of language shift in Texas induced by all of the factors noted and probably others, such as urbanization from the rural areas of South Texas and the large-scale participation of Mexicans in World War II. Paradoxically enough, the slow integration of schools after World War II probably intensified this process as Mexican children came under increasing peer-group influence of Anglo youngsters, who had the privilege of a prestige language. The results of this period of sociolinguistic change – the contemporary speech community – will be described later. Yet even as I speak of a general language shift in this community, it is very important to note that such a shift occurred slowly, incompletely, and not without resistance.

Continuity, resistance, and accommodation

Different segments of the Mexican population reacted to the new sociolinguistic order in different ways. Some geographical areas seemed to have escaped the most oppressive manifestations of social change largely by absorbing and diminishing its influence in a social fabric of superior numbers. Much more research remains to be done on this point. Nevertheless, it would appear that areas such as Brownsville, Laredo, and Eagle Pass, Texas, and other smaller border communities, continued to maintain a high Mexican demographic dominance, an influential Mexican presence in political and economic affairs and a media and interpersonal influence from across the border. The impact on the Spanish language was less severe in these areas.

In addition to this sort of resistance through structural-cultural continuity, these areas also tended to generate political resistance movements aimed at assisting the rest of the Mexican population in Texas in the face of social-linguistic change. We may note the Cortina movement of 1859 in the Brownsville area (Paredes 1958). We may also note the armed Mexican military attacks of 1915–16 carried out largely against the Anglo-American population. Although clearly organized by Carranza and his forces in revolutionary Mexico, these attacks in Texas had as their goal the establishment of a Spanish-speaking republic of the Southwest. Carranza himself had other, diplomatic, objectives for these attacks, but they clearly drew some of their local leadership and support from the native Texas Mexican population. Further, the Anglo-American authorities visited a savage and indiscriminate retaliation on the actual raiders and the general Texas Mexican populace alike. Many innocent Texas Mexicans lost their lives as a result of hostile American action during this war (Harris and Sadler 1978).

A nonviolent effort to offer unified political-linguistic resistance to Anglo-American encroachment took place in Laredo, Texas, in 1911. Mexicans from throughout Texas met at El Primer Congreso Mexicanista ('The First Mexicanist Congress') to discuss the plight of Texas Mexicans and to propose political and cultural solutions. The Congreso strongly advocated the maintenance of the Spanish language and proposed the formal establishment of Spanish-language schools (Limón 1974b). I say "formal" because the Congreso wanted the upgrading and institutionalization of what older Texas Mexicans today call the "escuelitas" – small, neighborhood, informal schools primarily for small children, where Spanish was taught as well as the necessary English to prepare them for the official American schools. The development and maintenance of these informal folk schools into the 1950s constitute still another form of resistance to language shift.

Economic and linguistic resistance appeared conjunctively from 1900 to 1940. As the Mexican population became both a rural and urban proletariat, the people generated militant labor union activity appealing to their language and culture. Such activity among the working-class sector was found in the Laredo area; the agricultural zone north and northwest of Laredo, known as the Wintergarden; and the growing urban center of San Antonio. The Spanish language was central in the formation of such economic resistance (García 1978, Nelson-Cisneros 1975, Zamora 1975).

Yet even as such linguistically based economic resistance appeared in an urban area like San Antonio, it had to contend with another competing linguistic-political ideology emerging within the community. By the 1920s a sufficiently large middle-class Mexican society had appeared in the city to generate organizations such as the League of United Latin American Citizens (LULAC), which favored an ideology of political accommodation to the new social order and a concomitant acquisition of English as a primary language (García 1978). Such organizations and their new ideology also appeared in the smaller urban areas of the state such as Corpus Christi and in what have been called the "new towns" of the Lower Rio Grande Valley such as Harlingen and McAllen. These were founded and developed by Anglos during the economic growth of 1890 to 1920.

These traditions of resistance and accommodation also affect the interactions that are the chief concern of this study. However, neither language maintenance nor language accommodation movements did as much for their respective causes as the more general social forces operating on the Mexican community. Between 1848 and the present day, education, cultural stigmatization, class mobility, urbanization, World War II, and the mass media have all contributed to general language shift – to a state of transitional bilingualism – always with certain regional and class exceptions producing a somewhat heterogeneous speech community.

The contemporary speech community: a tentative appraisal

Although a perfectly standard and academic form of Spanish may be used by some speakers in Texas in some limited contexts, the Spanish language, in its general use, is much more likely to be a regional dialect. As a dialect, it very likely bears some resemblance to the Spanish of the first settlers from 1749 to 1848, although certainly the social experiences both during this period and afterward have produced changes.

Some lexical possibilities were noted earlier. To these should be added phonological, morphological, and syntactical variation from the standard. In terms of pronunciation the speech is characterized by the reduction of consonant clusters so that the standard *también* is rendered *tamién*; the weakening of single-voiced intervocalic consonants such as /d/ from a fricative in the standard as in *acostado* to its virtual disappearance in the dialect *acostao* (Cárdenas 1975); and the suppression of unaccented syllables (*estoy* → *'toy, para que* → *pa'que*) as well as the use of *x* instead of *f*, as in *afuera* → *ajuera* (Lance 1975). There are morphological and syntactical possibilities for variation. Cárdenas notes "some lack of contrast in the first person plural of the -er and -ir verbs [*decimos* → *dicemos, vivimos* → *vivemos*]" and, syntactically, "a definite preference for the periphrastic *ir a* plus infinitive [vamos ir a comer] in place of the future [comeremos]," whereas "the form *de nosotros* has displaced *nuestro* at all levels of discourse" (p. 3). The result has been the variety that I call "folk" and Elías-Olivares (1979) calls "popular" Spanish. I agree with her that it is "a variety which shares all of the phonological and morphological characteristics of the variety of Spanish used by some educated Latin American speakers in informal situations and by workers and peasants in most situations" (p. 123).

Many factors have produced this regional dialect (Lozano 1976). Probably the single most important factor has been the political denial of formal Spanish language education for this population. If we define "proper" in political terms, we can agree with Lance (1975) that Texas folk Spanish "is very much like that of other people who have not received the amount and kind of education required to instruct the children of the speech community in the proper use of the King's or Academy's language" (p. 38).

Yet, although this dialect has an active presence in the Mexican community of Texas, it is equally clear that (1) not all individuals speak this dialect exclusively, (2) some do not speak it at all, (3) most probably have some English-language fluency, and (4) a few have an exclusive monolingual fluency. I will venture some tentative generalizations on the social significance of this total repertoire based on the work of Elías-Olivares (1979), my own fieldwork on the related subject of verbal folklore (Limón 1978a, 1979, 1980), and my life-long residency in Texas.

In some places English has a comparatively limited social presence. As discussed earlier, some geographical sectors of this population have managed to maintain a high, indeed, overwhelming, Mexican demographic dominance – border areas such as Laredo, Brownsville, Eagle Pass, and some smaller border communities like Rio Grande City. In turn, this dominance has translated into a continuing, highly influential Mexican presence in political and economic affairs. Except for the most legal of proceedings, it would not be at all unusual for such affairs to be conducted almost exclusively in some variety of Spanish, usually folk-popular or northern Mexican standard (Elías-Olivares 1979, p. 133), giving the language an aural prestigious association with visible power. The language also has other functional, institutional roles, for example, in international commerce, church services, campaign oratory, and newspapers, although here one might expect a more formal, nonfolk variety to prevail. Perhaps, more significantly, the local educational systems have rarely offered any direct resistance to the informal use of Spanish in the school setting (the mostly Mexican teachers and administrators often speak it themselves as soon as they leave class), and the Catholic schools have used the language as a medium of instruction, at least historically. To be sure, English is used in highly formal, legal, official settings (the classroom, courtroom, and city council chambers) and for addressing monolingual English speakers (tourists, military, and new arrivals, because resident Anglo-Americans very often acquire Spanish as a second language). Spanish, then, is not restricted to the familial domain but constantly intrudes upon the nonfamilial, formal settings.

We can agree with Sánchez (1978) in her belief that "a form of stable bilingualism exists along the U.S.–Mexican border for a segment of the Chicano (and sometimes non-Chicano) population" (p. 210). One must, therefore, qualify a recent definition of Mexican-Americans as having a low ethnolinguistic vitality (Giles, Bourhis, and Taylor 1977). In these border areas, at least, because of the confluence of demography, social status, and institutional support, the Mexican population continues to enjoy a relatively high ethnolinguistic vitality. In fact, a situation exists that is very close to bilingualism with diglossia (Fishman 1972c). That is, although English is the legally official language (as Spanish is in Paraguay), folk, or standard, Spanish has a socially "official" status and is in constant use throughout all levels and sectors of these border societies (like Guaraní in Paraguay). Both Spanish and English are recognized for intrasocietal communication and both are accorded formal institutionalization. Yet, it might be said that Spanish is accorded greater recognition than English, which is reserved almost exclusively for the most legal settings. As a result of this historically conditional diglossic situation, individuals in these societies have a well-developed ability to maintain a *full* discourse in folk Spanish with some ability and occasions for switching to a more standard variety. In either case, there is a minimal use of English, although some isolated lexical borrowing may occur. Intrasentential code-switching is viewed with some ambivalency and, when it occurs, tends to be Spanish dominant. Speaking too much English outside of "legal" domains carries some stigma (Limón 1978a), although females seem to enjoy greater liberty here (cf. Solé 1978). Such speakers tend to be coordinate bilinguals in their acquisition, use, and attitude toward the two languages.

On the other hand, other communities in Texas, indeed, the rest of the state, might be generally characterized as having bilingualism without diglossia, especially cities like Austin, Houston, Corpus Christi, Dallas, San Antonio, and perhaps even certain large towns very close to the border such as Harlingen and McAllen, established by Anglo-Americans during the 1890–1920 immigration and largely controlled by them up to the present. In such communities, Spanish may not receive the same level of prestige associated with historical primacy, political and economic power, and demographic dominance. These are areas whose Mexican populations are largely the product of recent, essentially post–World War I, internal migration from rural South Texas or international immigration from the turmoil of the Mexican Revolution. The Mexican communities comprise for the most part workers with a clear economic and residential separation from the usually demographically dominant Anglo-American population (Romo 1978). Historically, Mexican culture in these areas has been stigmatized through outright segregation practices. Although small and influential Mexican middle classes have emerged, an accommodationist ideology favoring the use of English has flourished, as the reader will recall, and at times today, the dominant Anglo society will publicly chastize the use of Spanish in formal settings.

Under these minimal social conditions some Spanish continues to be maintained, particularly among the very lower socioeconomic sectors, although largely in familial, interpersonal contexts (Skrabanek 1970). In a field study done in one of the border "new" towns in the 1960s, Madsen (1964, p. 106) quotes an Anglo teacher:

> They are good people . . . Their only handicap is the bag full of superstitions and silly notions they inherited from Mexico. When they get rid of these superstitions and silly notions they will be good Americans . . . A lot depends on whether we can get them to switch from Spanish to English. When they speak Spanish, they think Mexican. When the day comes that they speak English like the rest of us they will be part of the American way of life . . . I just don't understand why

they are so insistent about using Spanish. They should realize it's not the American tongue.

This teacher may still get his or her wish. For possibly even within working-class sectors, and certainly among the lower middle, middle, and upper classes, Spanish, as the exclusive language of conversational discourse, is in an increasingly precarious position (Sánchez 1978). Comparative assessments of ethnic languages under such conditions would also lead one to predict an uncertain future for the language in Texas. Fishman (1972c) notes that in the capitalist industrialization of the West "the means of production . . . have often been controlled by one speech community while the productive manpower was drawn from another." In such cases, "the needs and the consequences of rapid and massive industrialization and urbanization frequently impelled members of the speech community providing productive manpower . . . to learn (or at least be taught) some variety of the language associated with the means of production." Under such conditions lower-class and lower-middle-class immigrants "are particularly inclined to use their mother tongue and other tongue for intra-group communication in seemingly random fashion" and "the language of work (and of the school) comes to be used at home" (p. 148). Finally, "Bilingualism without diglossia thus tends to be transitional . . . Without separate though complementary norms and values to establish and maintain functional separation of the speech varieties, that language or variety which is fortunate enough to be associated with the predominant drift of social forces tends to displace the other" (p. 149).

It is precisely this sociolinguistic process of domain blurring and code-switching that Jacobson (1978) notes in his lower-middle- and middle-class informants in San Antonio, Texas. And, in the Mexican-American community of Austin, Texas, "code-switching is the mode of communication most often used in East Austin especially among third and fourth generation speakers as they feel more at ease using it " (Elías-Olivares 1979, p. 128). Further, Elías-Olivares offers a restraining word of caution to those who believe that newly arriving Mexican nationals will reverse this process of language shift. They, too, soon begin to learn and use English. Like Austin, the Mexican community in Dallas is also heterogeneous and ambivalent about the use of Spanish (Achor 1978).

Summary

So far I have been concerned with setting out some general relationships between language, region, class, and social change with respect to the society and language of Texas Mexicans. My initial tentative claims, then, are these: (1) a dialect of Spanish was established and developed in Texas from 1750 to 1848; (2) the social change induced by the coming of American capitalism, particularly from 1890 to 1920, produced linguistic change; (3) this change affected all Mexicans in Texas, although certain regions offered cultural and political resistance and maintained a high ethnolinguistic vitality; (4) class and racial conflict in other, mostly urban, areas also contributed to language maintenance; although (5) generally in these areas a process of language shift was set in motion producing domain indistinctiveness and code-switching.

Using this historical knowledge as a complex of referents, we can now make some sense of the uses of the Spanish language among ethnic nationalist Chicano students at the University of Texas at Austin in the 1960s. By the 1960s, the social condition of Mexicans in Texas had improved but not enough to stave off the appearance of political resistance once again.

The Chicano student movement in Texas, 1966–75

The Chicano student movement on the University of Texas campus appeared among lower-middle-class and middle-class students primarily from rural and small South Texas towns and large urban areas such as San Antonio, Corpus Christi, and Houston (Limón 1978b). Such students came to the campus in significantly increasing numbers in the 1960s largely as a result of the class mobility of the parental generation, unprecedented financial aid in the post-Sputnik era, and the university's publicity efforts. For many of these students, attending the university represented a geographical, cultural, and class departure from a relatively traditional home and ethnic society. It also meant an entrance into a cultural geographical area with some reputation for anti-Mexican attitudes. These students were also attending a university that historically had represented and embodied the dominant class and cultural interests of Texas.

Nevertheless, in the sixties this academic setting was neither the homogeneous politically conservative bastion of other years nor the quiescent scene of today. Like so many other major campuses at this time, this university was the scene of intense political activism and ideological formulation. This activity was chiefly leftist and critical of the United States for its international policies in Southeast Asia and its domestic attitudes toward minorities and workers. Along with this activism on the left, the campus experienced the culturally nationalist presence of the black civil rights student movement. This activist context stimulated some of the students of Mexican descent to review critically their own political relationship to their home community and to rediscover the essentially oppressed social character of the latter.

This sense of identity with the oppressed became even more pronounced in 1966–7 with the appearance of the primarily Mexican United Farmworkers labor movement. This union and their labor strikers in South Texas during this period continued the tradition of labor economic resistance. As a supporting move for these strikes, union organizers led a march to Austin, the state capital, to petition the governor and legislature for a redress of their economic grievances. The farmworkers appearance in Austin stood as a symbolic reminder to the Chicano students of their sociocultural origins and obligations. As a result, during the fall of 1966 many such students became actively involved in campus support committees on behalf of their kinsmen from South Texas. This initial support effort produced a formal organization in the spring of 1967. Initially known as the Mexican-American Student Organization (MASO), it later changed its name to the Mexican-American Youth Organization (MAYO) and established alliances with similar groups in colleges and universities across the state.

By 1969–70, MAYO had defined itself as an ethnic campus activist group dedicated to political and cultural work on behalf of the Texas Mexican community. Such efforts included continuing support for the farmworkers, campaigning for candidates for elected public offices in Austin, coordination with other statewide groups to induce and support school boycotts, and, most significant for the present study, campus agitation for a Mexican-American studies program at the university, which was finally implemented in 1970.

During the same period, the group was also establishing nationwide contacts with parallel efforts in other states. It was also developing a conscious ideology to guide its work, having rejected the accommodationist ideology of older Mexican-American political groups such as the LULACS. Members of the group attended the famous 1969 Chicano Youth Conference in Denver, which developed the Plan Espiritual de Aztlán. The latter condemned the historical Anglo-American conquest of the borderlands, denounced the present-day policies of cultural genocide, and called for the establishment of a Chicano-controlled Spanish-speaking Southwest, to be named Aztlán, after the ancient Aztec name for the mythic northern lands of their origin. The Texas MAYO group generally adhered to these views and under their influence began to participate in the statewide effort to build the Raza Unida party – a Chicano, third-party electoral alternative in Texas. In addition to these efforts, the students promoted an interest in the identification and revival of their native culture and history principally through art, music, literature, drama, and festival. Finally, these students, like others throughout the Southwest, identified themselves, the larger community, and their ideology with the term "Chicano," taken from folk tradition and given new meanings (Limón 1979).

At the height of its popularity, from 1969 to 1974, MAYO could count on a membership of some 80 to 100 students with perhaps 20 to 30 active members. On certain occasions, they could also draw upon 200 to 300 sympathizers. During this period, the Spanish-surnamed, mostly Mexican-descent student population on the Austin campus numbered from approximately 700 in 1969 to approximately 1,200 in 1974. The events reported in the rest of this study occur during this time. I will define the Chicano student effort as an ethnically based nationalist movement, using Fishman's (1972a) general characterizing criteria. First, the movement involved "the organizationally heightened and elaborated beliefs, attitudes, and behaviors of societies acting on behalf of their avowed ethnocultural interest" (p. 5). Yet, as Fishman points out, it is not really whole societies that act, but rather "proto-elites . . . the essential synthesizers, separators, popularizers and organizers on whom the spread of nationalism depends" (p. 16). Protoelites, such as these Chicano students, try to "create and further . . . broader unity and heightened authenticity" and "plant an awareness of both of these desiderata in a population that is becoming increasingly receptive to unifying and activating solutions" (p. 16). They can do these things because they are, on the one hand, from the ethnic society, and yet they possess or soon acquire a distinctive socializing experience, usually a superior education, that connects them with wider political, sociological, and historical perspectives. Nevertheless, in their effort to heighten and elaborate ethnocultural nationalism, protoelites turn to the history, folklore, and general culture of their society, especially the lower socioeconomic sectors. In the present case, the Chicano movement appealed to such resources as Aztlán, Chicano, preconquest motifs, the Mexican Revolution, and the barrio to build a greater awareness and political-cultural unity among their native population. Occasionally, because of their educationally alienated condition, these *intelligentsia* may fail in their appeal to the masses. Elsewhere I have pointed to one such probable failure of the Chicano movement (Limón 1979). Finally, such elite efforts to construct a national identity from the materials of history, folklore, and culture seem to emerge when ethnic societies find themselves in situations of rapid social change. As such they are a response to the dislocation, fragmentation, anonymity, and oppression that come with such change – a description that I think applies to Mexicans in the post–World War II period and certainly to the Chicano students who left their home communities for the university.

El meeting: speech setting, event, and act

Like any political group, MAYO students came together periodically to plan the goals and strategies of their program. In bilingual colloquial fashion, they referred to these gatherings as "el meeting" as in *Vas a ir a el meeting?* Using Hymes's (1972) model for the description of the interaction of language and social life, I will refer to *el meeting* as a *speech setting,* bringing in the other components of his model as the description proceeds.

The meeting was usually held twice a month, sometimes in a university facility but much more often in the basement of the Catholic Student Center located next to the campus. The center was a familiar place for these, mostly Catholic, students because of their attendance at mass or at the social functions sponsored by the center, especially at the beginning of the semester. Another reason for choosing the center as a meeting place was its value as a source of moral-religious guidance and support in contrast to the secular concerns of the university. This religious-moral dimension, especially as interpreted by younger priests and nuns influenced by Vatican II, resulted in center support for a variety of dissident social causes. The Chicano students found in the center a continuation of the religious authority of the Catholic Church in which they were raised but one with a social-activist inclination. Finally, as a physical locale, the Catholic Student Center afforded a meeting place that was accessible but was not a structural part of the university. Dissident expressive activity, then, occurred in a politically and physically uncompromised location.

Chicano students learned of the meetings through signs posted around the campus, newspaper ads in the *Daily Texan,* and word of mouth. A meeting was not restricted to MAYO members, and very often many of those in attendance were not official members of the organization. About 50 to 100 students attended any given meeting, depending on the issues at hand. Some students prepared political positions beforehand or developed projects that they planned to announce. Others merely attended to find out what was going on in the Chicano scene, perhaps to listen to a guest speaker, and to socialize.

The meeting usually began about 7 P.M. as the Chicano students began showing up and became engaged in various conversations before the meeting was called to order. Conversations ranged from intense political discussion regarding X's candidacy for the MAYO presidency to male-female conversations about a Saturday night date. A small group of men might engage in bantering humor, while across the room a young woman asked someone for some notes for a class she had missed. El meeting was also an occasion for seeing people, exchanging information, and generally, socializing. Eventually, the president would call the meeting to order, the actual proceedings often beginning late – "Chicano Standard Time," some of them would say.

Topically, meeting discourse was substantially concerned with specific issues like MAYO participation in recruiting Chicano studies professors, a scholarship dance, a coalition with an Anglo leftist group, and MAYO participation in a school walkout somewhere in South Texas. Committees were organized around these issues and instructed to develop a course of action and report to the general assembly. The central pragmatic purpose of the meeting was to enlist and organize Chicano students in concrete projects that, in MAYO's estimation, would be of benefit to the greater Mexican community in Texas or to the Chicano student community in particular.

These discussions were the linguistic context – the speech event – in which were embedded the particular speech acts that are the principal concern of this study. However, both event and act must be understood with reference to the speech economy of this particular community, that is, the speech resources and rules present in this society.

Solé (1975, 1978) studied this same student body with quantitative-questionnaire methods. According to her, the university Mexican-American student body reports itself to be highly English dominant in almost all domains except first-generation interaction. Interactions in almost every other domain (peers, younger interlocutors, professors, informal, formal) are conducted either exclusively in English or in heavily English-dominant code-switching. I would generally agree with her based on my own extended participant-observation work in this same community, although certain kinds of folkloric speech acts did lend themselves to a far greater use of Spanish than Solé's methodology was able to capture (Limón 1978b). Nevertheless, she is quite correct – English-dominant discourse was the general linguistic order of the day for these students.

These findings should not surprise us. For the most part, we are dealing with younger, third- and fourth-generation, lower-middle-class and middle-class students. They were the products of the sociolinguistic historical process described earlier. Indeed, their very presence in this elite university was testimony to their high proficiency in English, especially in those often reported instances in which well-meaning parents discouraged the home use of Spanish precisely so that these students could enjoy their academic success. What may surprise us is that el meeting – an ethnic nationalist context – was also highly English dominant according to my own observations and Solé's (1978, p. 33) specific question about this domain. Like Chicano students at the University of Colorado, Boulder (Reich 1977), and at the University of California, San Diego (Sánchez 1978), these students also conducted their political gatherings almost exclusively in English. Yet, I must emphasize the "almost," for Spanish in its folk dialect variety did appear and had a rhetorical-symbolic function when it did so. Such appearances could and did occur in any number of social contexts and domains, but el meeting was most clearly marked by such usages.

I will now present four examples of speech events in these meetings in which folk Spanish is used in extended discourse by four different speakers designated X. Although some code-switching occurs in these X speech acts, it is very minimal and isolated. All other interlocutors are designated A, B, C, D, and so on, and they too, are different people in each event. They are examples of many such events. After each example, I will present a brief analysis of the immediate significance of folk Spanish based on my own sense of the event and on post-event conversations with some of the interlocutors.[2]

Speech event I

(At issue in the following discussion is the question of supporting a predominantly Anglo-American leftist student group in their opposition to U.S. Marine recruitment on the campus.

A: These people have asked for our support on this issue. Is there any discussion?

B: I don't think it's a good thing . . . I am not in favor of working with *gringo* organizations.

C: *Están* radical *los vatos* . . . 'Those guys are radical.'

B: Well, I just don't think it's a good idea. MAYO has enough trouble as it is . . . people think we're radical anyway.

X: *La gente del barrio se aguitan.* 'The people from the barrio will feel bad.'

[2] During the historical period of el meeting, I held various offices in the Mexican-American Youth Organization, including that of secretary; hence, I was very attentive to the discourse as part of my duties. I also took notes in the hope of writing a full history of the Chicano student movement. In the fall of 1972 I began graduate work in anthropology, including course work in sociolinguistics. Between 1972 and 1974 I wrote down the data discussed in this chapter, initially with an interest in the syntactical and grammatical dimensions of code-switching in term papers. I soon shifted my interest as the present issues became more apparent and interesting.

My first attempts to tape-record these kinds of data proved fruitless. I obtained very poor sound quality in a large meeting hall and the level of political sensitivity was such that taping met some skeptical and troubled reactions from the members, although they did not object to note taking. I then began to write down the interactions in my own shorthand form, being especially attentive to (1) instances of extended Spanish usage and (2) code-switching. In "normal" conversations this kind of note taking would have been a nearly impossible task. However, it became quite possible in el meeting because of interesting historical and cultural factors that proved to be a boon to my efforts. The years 1967 to 1970 were a particularly turbulent and emotional time in student politics, and this turbulence necessarily appeared in forums such as el meeting. It was a time of free expression, nonstructure, and speak your own thing. In effect, these political/cultural attitudes meant interruptions, loud discourse, incoherent statements, etc. By the early 1970s however, it was becoming very apparent that this interactional style had its disadvantages for effective, practical political action. Hence, the MAYO membership instituted a rigid set of rules for clear, structured interaction. (1) Members were asked to speak clearly, slowly, audibly and to *all* of the audience, not to the floor, ceiling, or to the president; (2) all speakers were permitted to make full statements; (3) interruptions were not tolerated; and (4) each member wishing to speak had to raise his hand and wait to be called upon. Further, since the presiding officer tried to give the floor to all interested speakers during the course of debate, each speaker knew that he or she might not have the opportunity to speak more than once or twice, hence speakers were very careful in the substance, tone, and tempo of their remarks.

This consciously governed interaction effectively eliminated any conversational overlap, interjections, etc., and encouraged a careful, deliberate mode of address, thereby greatly facilitating my note taking. Nevertheless, I did miss some things in several speech events other than those reported here; I did not feel confident in using them, although they do, in my opinion, verify the notions argued here. I am quite confident that those reported here are extremely close approximations of the linguistic reality that I heard. For the purpose of this discussion, they are reliable evidence.

E: Everybody seems to be forgetting about the war! We need to create solidarity with all groups against the war – it affects *la raza* too!

X: *No hombre, camarada . . . la* girl *está bien . . . 'ta bueno que estamos contra la* war in Vietnam . . . *pero también nosotros tenemos el* Chicano Moratorium *como una manera de dar* opposition . . . *no tenemos que juntarnos con esta gente . . . hay que ver que la gente también le gusta los* marines . . . *hay muchos vatos del barrio que se meten.* 'No man . . . the girl is right . . . all right so we're against the war in Vietnam . . . but we also have the Chicano Moratorium as a way of opposing . . . we don't have to get together with these people . . . we have to see that the people also like the Marines . . . lots of guys from the *barrio* enlist.'

After a few somewhat feeble remarks, the discussion ends with MAYO tabling the suggestion and effectively killing it. My observation of the event and conversations with some of the participants led me to the following assessment: B is a young upper-middle-class woman from San Antonio with low fluency in Spanish. X is from Mercedes, Texas, in the Lower Rio Grande Valley and has solid fluency in English and Spanish. C is from the lower-income Westside of San Antonio, whereas E is from upper-middle-class Houston and has almost no Spanish abilities. As the discussion opens, people's feelings on the issue appear to be very mixed and unclear. B is speaking against the alliance with the leftist group, but she is not judged to be an effective spokesperson, in part because she uses English all the time. E is judged to be a good speaker on behalf of the leftists, except that he too uses English all the time. B starts to speak and is interrupted. X intervenes, upholding B's position, but turns to a folk-Spanish code – a move that he will later acknowledge as a deliberate choice. Others in the meeting besides these interlocutors generally agree that the use of Spanish did influence their decision.

Speech event II

The following discussion concerns a faculty candidate, B, who has been invited to the meeting as part of his visit on the campus.

A: As a faculty member do you see yourself getting involved with Chicano students . . . like with MAYO for example?

B: I don't think I'd have any trouble with that.

C: Have you been involved with a student group at Colorado?

B: Yes, I sponsored MECHA there.

X: *¿Cómo ve usted la cosa de Raza Unida?* 'How do you see the Raza Unida situation?'

B: (No answer, puzzled look.)

(General expressions of slightly disdainful or pained amusement here.)

X: *La Raza Unida. ¿Cree que puede ayudar al partido?* 'The Raza Unida. Do you think you can help the party?'

B: I'm afraid one of the things I'll have to do in Texas is to improve my Spanish.
C: He was just wondering if you could support Raza Unida . . .
X: (Whispering to me) *No vale madre . . . no es Chicano . . . ni siquiera sabe español* . . . 'He's not worth a damn . . . he's not Chicano . . . he doesn't even speak Spanish . . .'
B: Yes, I think I could . . .
X: (Interrupting) Do you think Spanish is important?
B: Yes . . . it's just that I was raised differently.
X: Well, down here we expect people to be able to speak Spanish.

The candidate will be rejected by the students and later by the university (for their own reasons). During the interview, X deliberately switches to Spanish as a test for the candidate. He does so knowing that ". . . down here we expect people to be able to speak Spanish." Actually, he is enunciating a *value* held by these students rather than accurately diagnosing their abilities. Indeed, these students speak English most of the time much like A does. However, in spite of this low fluency, X is able to appeal to a latent value and rhetorically unites the students into rejecting the candidate – a rejection based principally, though not exclusively, on linguistic criteria.

Speech event III

The following discussion concerns the adoption of a resolution supporting a school walkout in southwestern Texas.

A: If we support this resolution, doesn't it mean we should go down there and help them out?
B: I don't think it means that . . . I mean we have classes and stuff . . . I don't think many of us could go . . . it's far.
X: *Qué pronto se les olvida de donde vienen, ¿verdad?* We're talking about *la gente, carnal. Casi todos semos de* South Texas *y este problema está pasando allá y afectando a la raza allí. Apoco venemos a UT y creemos que todos los problemas ya no existen.* 'You sure forget quickly where you came from, don't you? We're talking about the people, brother. Almost all of us are from South Texas and this problem is happening there and affecting *la raza* there. We come to UT and think that these problems no longer exist.'
C: I think we have to be practical . . .
X[1]: *Yo estoy con X . . . 'ta bueno que* we got to study . . . *pero aquí en Austin la vida 'ta bien suave . . . con los* parties *y todo eso* . . . we can't forget *los carnales que no la hicieron aquí – los vatos que están* dropping out *porque las escuelas no sirven . . . el gringo todo el tiempo nos tiene así.* 'I'm with X . . . all right so we have to study . . . but here in Austin life is soft . . . with the parties and everything we can't forget the brothers that didn't make it here . . . the guys who are dropping out because the schools aren't any good . . . the *gringo* always keeps us this way.'

(Loud spontaneous applause and cheering and whistling here followed by the calling of the question and a supporting vote.)

Again, folk speakers X and X^1 have carried a particular issue based not only on the message content but on the form and instrument. In folk Spanish, they seem to use a language variety that appeals to the students. I have no doubt that the same position would have been supported, if it had been expressed in English, but its expression in folk Spanish seems to strike an even more responsive chord in these students, especially when the counterpositions are being expressed in English – ironically, the same English that allows them to be here and at the same time keeps so many of their *carnales* away.

Speech event IV

The following discussion concerns a conference to be sponsored by MAYO.

A: I would propose that we use the BEB . . . it has a large room and small rooms for workshops . . .

X: Mr. Chairman . . . I'm not in favor of that . . . *se me hace que* we should be doing *estas cosas en el barrio pa' que la gente pueda venir . . . acá en la* university *está muy lejos de* East Austin . . . *y como quiera la gente no viene . . . la raza lo ve como un lugar gringo . . .* and besides . . . *la idea es juntarnos con la raza . . . para estar* united. 'Mr. Chairman . . . I'm not in favor of that . . . I think we should be doing these things in the barrio so that the people can come . . . the university is too far from East Austin . . . and anyway the people won't come . . . *la raza* won't come to a *gringo* place . . . and besides, the idea is to get together with *la raza* . . . to be united.'

B: *Todo eso está bien* . . . but it's going to be real hard to get a big place in East Austin . . . and maybe it would be better to have the people on campus . . . *para que sepan que es de ellos también* . . . 'All of this is fine . . . but . . . so that they will know it belongs to them also.'

X: *No . . . pos yo nomás decía que lo importante es el contacto con el barrio . . . pero el carnal dice bien* . . . it could be inconvenient as hell . . . *sólo que el* Municipal Auditorium . . . what about the churches? 'No . . . well I was just saying that the important thing is contact with el barrio . . . unless maybe Municipal Auditorium . . .'

A: Not for something this big.

X: *Ah, 'ta bueno* . . . as long as *la gente puede venir* . . . maybe we could leaflet East Austin. 'Ah, it's all right . . . as long as the people can come . . .'

This interaction is somewhat different from the rest because folk-speaker X concedes the point but not before he is assured that his primary goal – the coming together of the university community and el barrio – has been achieved. My primary interest here is the way that B implicitly acknowledges the rhetorical importance of folk speech by incorporating some of it in his remarks, even though he is not entirely fluent in it. From previous experiences, he has begun to appreciate the rhetorical need for this expressive tool in the argumentation of el meeting. When I questioned him on this particular point, he acknowledged that his partial use of Spanish was in fact in response to the presence of several Xs in the room whom he knew would be arguing for the conference in the barrio.

X: Yeah, with these guys you have to do that [use Spanish] otherwise nobody listens to you . . . it's really funny . . . even though the members don't speak that much Spanish . . . if you don't use some . . . they'll think you're *agringado* . . . these guys [the Xs] are good at it *y te chingan.* ('they'll screw you')

X in this interaction faced two problems. In terms of message content, he had the difficulty of coming up with a building that could house the conference; in terms of message form, he was dealing with an adversary who sounded as though he also could use the folk-Spanish resource. Indeed, as he indicated afterward:

X: Yeah, *el camarada* made sense . . . I don't feel entirely convinced, but I guess it will be all right.
JL: Were you surprised that he used Spanish?
X: *Si, pos* I thought he might be from South Texas . . . and he might be able to persuade *la gente de allá* . . . ('The people from there')

To highlight further the rhetorical use of Spanish as an expressive speech act, note that in the postperformance interview, X reverts to a more ordinary, more "natural" communicative code characterized by a greater use of English. That is, he is no longer performing or engaging in folk rhetoric; he is merely conversing and, even with a fellow lower-middle-class South Texan, he uses English, although as Solé suggests, his choice is undoubtedly influenced by my role as a teacher at the university. According to Solé, such role-differentiated interactions are conducted in English. (Solé 1978, p. 33).

From speech act to genre

When folk Spanish was used in extended discourse during el meeting, it took on the bounded, marked properties of a speech act through the operation of what Hymes would call "instrumentality," "keys," and "norms." "Instrumentality" involves the channel (oral language in this case) and the form of speech (folk Spanish) chosen by the speaker. In this case, the very choice of folk Spanish in an English-dominant context obviously marks that speaker's discourse as distinctive.[3]

[3] Some (few) speakers could conceivably draw on a varied Spanish-language repertoire much like that described by Elías-Olivares (1975) that would include northern Mexican standard, popular, and mixed Spanish. The X speakers would be the only ones likely to have this range. All other speakers were, as Solé notes, highly English dominant in all settings. Yet, of course, this language resource was also varied and could include standard academic, popular Texas, and black English.

"Key" is perhaps more significant still and refers to what literary critics would call tone or mood. What is the tonal choice and effect involved in this particular speech act? The answer seems to be *seriousness*; at least a more pronounced sense of seriousness than in the use of English or English-dominant code-switching. This judgment reflects my own aural sense of the language, my observation of facial expressions, and perhaps most significantly, the testimony offered by the participants. Here are two examples:

JL: Is there any difference in your attitude when you speak Spanish like that? (Referring to a preceding discussion on folk Spanish.)
X: *Pos . . . con español, como que te pones mas serio cuando hablas español en los* meetings . . . even if you have to fake it! 'Well . . . with Spanish, like you get more serious when you speak Spanish . . .'

JL: How do you feel when people use a lot of Spanish in the meeting?
A: What do you mean?
JL: Well, do you like it? Dislike it? How does it affect you?
A: Oh, I think it's great. It sounds good. You know . . . real formal and strong.

"It's great" implies norms of interaction and interpretation. Although in Hymes's sense these have more to do with pragmatic considerations in language use (who speaks when, appropriate contextual use of language), they may also be taken to refer to aesthetic considerations. Folk Spanish is said to be *strong, sound good, bien de aquéllas* (colloquial for real good), *bien bonito* 'real pretty,' but these aesthetic norms also transfer into assessments of personal power. When one uses folk Spanish, according to an informant X, "Como que la gente te pone más atención, porque *si* te entienden . . . aunque no lo hablan mucho . . . y es como si hablas más fuerte en español, te respetan más . . ." ('Like people pay more attention to you because they *do* understand you, even if they don't speak it much, . . . and it's like if you speak strongly in Spanish you get more respect.')

Folk-Spanish speakers dominated el meeting. A prolonged silence after such a speech was not unusual; English-dominant speakers hesitated to speak immediately afterward. Some of the latter reported feeling awed, overwhelmed, or at least subdued by such displays of language.

Considerations of instrumentality, key, and norms lend a distinctive place to folk Spanish in the speech economy of these students. Indeed, it is such a marked, bounded, and powerful mode of discourse that one may think of it as a *genre* of folklore – a bounded, recognized, and broadly traditional way of speaking. Yet, folk Spanish was really its own contemporary and emergent genre defined by its particular speech situation and event. Apart from this context, folk Spanish is rather ordinary language. Other major folkloric forms may acquire a semi-independence from immediate audience reactions and evaluations. Their clear internal structure, metaphorical quality, and linguistically marked openings and closings lend to these major genres the quality of expressiveness and aesthetic formality that is detectable by the individual, perhaps Western, observer examining them even without knowing the context of their performance. Such is not clearly and evidently the case for these folk-speech performances. For example, consider their aesthetic-expressive significance in, let us say, the conversation of a group of older Spanish-dominant Mexicans in the Lower Rio Grande Valley. I suspect there would be very little. These expressive units that are so recognized in el meeting would fade into the ordinary. What is rather plain, ordinary speech in the valley becomes expressive in el meeting. Hymes (1972, p. 65) notes this contextual definition of speech into speech acts as genres.

> By genres are meant categories such as poem, myth, tale, proverb, riddle . . . etc. From one standpoint the analysis of speech into acts is an analysis of speech into instances of genres. The notion of genre implies the possibility of identifying formal characteristics traditionally recognized. It is heuristically important to proceed as though all speech has formal characteristics of some sort as manifestations of genres; and it may well be true . . . The common notions of "casual" or unmarked speech, however, points up the fact that there is a great range among genres in the number of and explicitness of formal markers . . . It remains that "unmarked" casual speech can be recognized as such in a context where it is not expected *or where it is being exploited for particular effect* [emphasis added]. Its lesser visibility may be a function of our own orientations and our own use of it; its profile may be as sharp as any other, once we succeed in seeing it is strange.

In the meetings as well as in other speech situations, folk-speech performers like X seemed to be clearly aware of the expressive dimensions of folk Spanish and of its availability as a genre to be employed in certain kinds of interactional scenes, much like legendry and jokes are considered to be appropriate for specific times and places.[4] Such a traditional performance is available to enhance one's political position in a sociolinguistic environment that values the code even while it has a weak presence in that environment. It is, therefore, no surprise that as part of their planning for their attendance at national Chicano meetings like the 1969 Denver Youth Conference, Texas Chicano students consciously advised each other to use Spanish during these meetings. In the words of one informant X: "La gente de allá no saben usar español muy bien y sales ganando." ('The people from there [California, Colorado] don't use Spanish very well and you come out winning.') Formally (like any folklore genre) folk Spanish was marked, recognized, and available for expressive

[4] The MAYO students also had many meetings off campus with political activists from the East Austin working-class community. In these meetings, all discourse, including formal speeches, discussions, etc., was carried out in what Elías-Olivares would describe as popular or mixed Spanish with very little English used. Predictably enough X speakers were selected by the organization for such liaison contact with the East Austin population.

use; and, functionally (like any folklore genre) it became available as symbolic action to meet certain social needs.

From genre to symbol

I have described – rendered an ethnography of – speaking in a particular speech community and economy by focusing on a speech act – the use of folk Spanish – while taking nearly full account of other necessary components – setting, participants, ends, keys, instrumentalities, norms, and genres. Ultimately, however, a full understanding of folk Spanish as a speech act requires an amplification of the "ends" component. I have already claimed that such speech is an expressive genre with a rhetorical end in relation to these participants, speech economy, and setting. Yet such an analysis is limited. As Hymes (1972, pp. 69–70), himself, notes:

> Functions themselves may be statable in terms of relations among components, such that poetic function, e.g. may acquire a certain relationship among choice of code, choice of topic, and message form in a given period or society.
>
> It would be misleading, however, to think that the definitions of functions can be reduced to or derived from other components. Such a thought would be a disabling residue of behaviorist ideology. Ultimately, the functions served in speech must be derived directly from the purposes and needs of human persons engaged in social action and are what they are: talking to seduce, to stay awake, to avoid a war. The formal analysis of speaking is a means to the understanding of human purposes and needs and their satisfaction; it is an indispensable means but only a means and not that understanding itself.

"Understanding" the full significance of folk-Spanish performance requires that we reconsider the participants, the speech economy, and most significantly, the social and linguistic history of Mexicans in Texas – what folk Spanish "means" in the context of this history. In their use and interpretation of folk Spanish these performers and their audiences rely principally on tradition, that is, on a set of "understood social rules" inherited from the past "which transcend any given social interaction, which tell the performer and the audience what is appropriate in any given context" (Joyner 1975, p. 261). This impinging past may range from the most immediate to more distant events.

To begin with, we should note the social origins of these folk-Spanish speakers designated X, who exert such rhetorical power in the meetings. To a very high degree these predominantly male speakers came from the South Texas border areas with high ethnolinguistic vitality and a tradition of political resistance. Therefore, like Mexican-American adolescents living along the California-Mexico border, these students were highly proficient in Spanish (Aguirre 1979). Those few Xs who are not from these areas were generally from the lower socioeconomic Mexican Westside of San Antonio. Together they made up a group of effective folk-Spanish speakers and, as such, a cadre of leadership for the organization. The latter should not be too surprising nor should the close friendship among these Xs with the same social background and language repertoire. I suspect that they belonged in that total 25 percent of Solé's (1978) respondents who reported themselves to be equally proficient in both languages or Spanish dominant.

On the other hand, the rest of the participants in the meetings generally came from nonborder areas, and/or they had middle-class and upper-class social origins. This general group (represented by A, B, C, D speakers) tended to be very English dominant. Further, as Solé indicates, women in general were highly English dominant. (Solé 1978) Nevertheless, along with the more proficient folk-Spanish speakers, these English dominants also generally subscribed to the ethnic nationalist ideology of the Chicano movement and, in spite of their English dominance, maintained "respect, interest, and nostalgia for the ethnic mother tongue" even after it had become (for them) "substantially dormant or . . . completely lost" (Fishman 1972b, p. 58). As such, they resemble one of Elías-Olivares's informants, a thirty-year-old teacher's aide who believed that her Mexican-American school principal's Spanish was "elevated," "pretty," "correct" (1979, p. 131). Elías-Olivares makes another point that bears directly on the issues of this paper: "Some Chicano teachers in some schools in East Austin look down on the local ways of speaking because most of them come from areas such as Laredo or the Rio Grande Valley in which the standard variety is highly valued and plays a role in the everyday interaction of those communities" (p. 133).

Although the mostly male X speakers from Laredo and the border area did not look down on their fellow ethnic nationalist Chicanos from other areas, they realized that, as border Mexicans, they did possess a powerful linguistic resource and did not hestitate to use it for political ends.

X speakers who used folk Spanish in the meeting appealed to this power, respect, and nostalgia in contextually specific ways, relying primarily upon the *metaphorical* significance of folk Spanish. The use of folk Spanish in the meetings was an example of metaphorical switching for an expressive yet meaningful effect (Bourkis 1979), and its effect depends on its departure from a social consensus on the appropriate or at least the usual code for a certain domain (Scotton and Ury 1977). Yet, the meaningfulness – the tenor – for this extended language metaphor is not to be found primarily in its pragmatic, referential message, if indeed there is one. It is not what is said but the presence of folk Spanish that really counts. As with the Ranamail language in Hemnesberget, Norway, "Social significance attaches to the utterance as a whole; it is not segmentable into smaller component stretches" (Blom and Gumperz 1972, p. 418).

The metaphorical meaning of folk Spanish in this context remains to be specified. To be sure, such switches may be ethnic identity markers "when implicit norms require the use of the majority group's language in inter-ethnic communication" (Giles 1979, p. 258), or they may be used to call forth the personal, familial, and familiar in response to an association of the dominant language with the official and the impersonal (Blom and Gumperz 1972, Brown and Fraser 1979). Yet neither of these explanations is sufficiently specific and satisfying. First, I suspect that the usual and now standard view of a firm code allocation to different domains, such as personal versus impersonal and familiar/familial versus official, does not fully capture one important meaning of folk Spanish in these contexts. Second, although folk Spanish certainly did evoke something like "ethnic identity," we should recall that these evocations occurred during *intra*ethnic speech events and as such they are not merely the linguistic assertion of some vague ethnic identity against nonethnic, dominant-language speakers. These displays of language occur in a nationalist context of shared identity. What, in more specific terms, is the relationship of language to identity in these circumstances?

Let us begin our explication of this folk speech-as-metaphor by considering the first of these general understandings of the use of ethnic languages – their evocation of personal, familiar, familial values. Although I agree with this general association, I believe it takes on a somewhat different meaning in these contexts. My informants' repeated association of adjectives like "formal" and "strong" offers a clue to this meaning. Both through such terminology and through more explicit testimony, my informants linked folk Spanish to the "family," to be sure, but more specifically to parental *authority* in the family, possibly to maleness, to ancestral lineage, and to the general community of Mexicans – *la gente* 'the people.' According to an A, "X sounds just like my father . . . you know . . . he's almost scary." An X verifies this parental symbolism:

X: La idea es . . . tú sabes . . . cada cuando tienes que tratarlos como chavalos (laughter) . . . regañarlos. 'The idea is . . . you know . . . every so often . . . you have to treat them like children [the MAYO students] . . . scold them.'

JL: Is that why you use Spanish?

X: Pos sí . . . es más fuerte . . . en inglés, te oyes todo joto. 'Well yes . . . it's stronger . . . in English you sound all queery (homosexual).'

Obviously, the informant is linking parental authority and maleness, although undifferentiated parental authority was a more likely referent for most of these students. This association of Spanish with parental authority, at least, is strongly supported by a study in which 80 percent of a sample of Mexican-American mothers report that they use Spanish when they want to scold their children (Redlinger 1978). In her study of Mexicans in Dallas, Achor (1978, p. 74) also reports the frequent use of Spanish for scolding children. Finally, the X students often responded to the "excessive" use of English by invoking a traditional folk reproach: "¡Háblame como la gente!" ('Speak to me as the people do!')

Although Spanish may evoke or signal an association with the personal, familiar, and familial, we should also note that it is, at the same time, association with the more official, somewhat impersonal dimensions of that life. It does not seem to be necessarily an evocation of warmth, comfort, and the ludic, but rather of distance, the authoritative, and the serious. Ironically, because of language shift, *English* has become the language of informality and frivolity in addition to that of work and school. Spanish, on the other hand, seems to be linked to serious parental authority, ancestral respect for grandparents (Solé 1978), and perhaps more generally to place, region, and, ultimately, the entire genetic-cultural group – *la raza*. These kinds of values are what make up the primordial factor – paternity – in Fishman's (1977) extended three-part delineation of the way ethnic actors construct a sense of their ethnicity.

Fishman (1977, p. 20) also speaks of "patrimony" and "phenomenology" as two other definitional components in the construction of ethnicity; like paternity, they are inevitably linked to language.

> Ethnicity is not just a state of being (as paternity implies), but it is also a behavioral or implementational or enactment system (as patrimony implies). The paternity dimension . . . is related to questions of how ethnicity collectives came into being . . . The patrimony dimension of ethnicity is related to questions of how ethnic collectivities behave and to what their members do in order to express their membership.

The patrimony – the particular ethnic behaviors selected by this student community for their definition of ethnicity – has to do primarily with region and history. From their perspective, how should Mexicans behave? A number of behaviors were isolated and selected, including a range of expressive behavior having to do with joke narration, food behavior, and dancing (Limón 1978b). Of greater importance, however, was the selection of the themes of counterhegemony and resistance to the historical patrimony available to these students. Such themes are inextricably linked to language. The X speakers and their folk Spanish represent areas in which there is a distinctive Texas Mexican social hegemony – a fact well known to all MAYO members through travel in the border areas while doing political work, visiting friends and family, or shopping in Mexican border towns. The sound of Spanish in el meeting evoked the knowledge that somewhere Mexicans have acted to maintain political and economic influence (unlike the rest of Texas) while keeping their ethnic mother tongue (unlike the rest of Texas). Indeed, this linguistically linked social success is reproduced in the X speakers themselves, who are clearly successful at the university *without having undergone language shift*. Others could say admiringly:

A: The boys from Laredo . . . they speak Spanish so good . . . sometimes I think they think they're too good for us.

B: I really wish I had grown up there [Brownsville] sometimes instead of Houston. Chicanos are *everywhere* and everybody speaks Spanish . . . you'all are so lucky.

Still another important selected aspect of this regional patrimony is the historical political resistance of Mexicans in South Texas both in the border areas and among the San Antonio working class.

As was indicated in the first part of this chapter, this resistance (El Primer Congreso Mexicanista, the 1915 uprisings, the San Antonio labor movement) was often linked to language maintenance. This historical knowledge was brought to bear in the performance and evaluation of folk Spanish by these students. Students came to know this history through informal and formal means. In the early days of the movement (1966–70) certain key books circulated widely among the activists – books like Américo Paredes's *With His Pistol in His Hand: A Border Ballad and Its Hero* and Carey McWilliams' polemical *North from Mexico: The Spanish Speaking People in the United States*. Both give ample treatment to social conflict and resistance in South Texas; Paredes contributes not only to this patrimony but to paternity as well as he discusses the historical primacy of *la gente* – the 1749 settlement of Hispanic mestizos in South Texas. Later, after 1970, the establishment of Mexican-American studies at the university formalized an instructional program that necessarily included discussions of conflict and resistance both in regular classes and in visiting lectures such as those of Victor Nelson-Cisneros (1975) and Emilio Zamora (1975). As an A speaker commented: "I always think of South Texas as a special place . . . all the fighting and the Congreso and stuff . . . they always say Chicanos are passive, well I'm glad somebody fought back."

Whatever else it might mean, the extended use of folk Spanish in this context seems to evoke a general association with a serious, authoritative, parental-ancestral culture and a more specified association with the resistance and hegemony in the border country in conjunction with the working class of South Texas. As language is firmly linked to this social history, so does it come to *mean* resistance and hegemony. This meaning, however, is meaning for these actors. Their construction of their ethnic identity is a selective process in which they attribute meaning to their paternity and patrimony and do so in terms of their present political situation, needs, and expectations. For Fishman, the ordering, selecting, and meaning given to paternity and patrimony is the *phenomenological* aspect of ethnicity construction. In this case, ethnic nationalism is the immediate phenomenological model for the construction of an ethnicity on the basis of an authoritative ancestry (*mi gente, la gente* 'my people, the people'), resistance, and hegemony. It is an ethnic identity constructed from the materials of paternity and patrimony as phenomenologically shaped by the ideological imperatives of ethnic nationalism. It is an ethnicity that was so newly constructed as to need a new name – *Chicano*. Those who came to identify with this name and ideology also developed a clear respect and appreciation for folk Spanish in Texas and elsewhere (Flores and Hopper 1975, Ryan and Carranza 1977).

From symbol to ideology

In the meetings, folk Spanish became powerful rhetoric because it was a powerful metaphor, a multivocal symbol (Turner 1969) evoking and condensing many meanings – ancestral origins, parental and grandparental respect and authority, regional and political resistance, working-class consciousness – all of them coalesced around certain key speakers. Indeed, so many significant meanings are packed into a stretch of discourse in these contexts that the language as the "recorder of paternity, the expresser of patrimony and the carrier of phenomenology" becomes a significant vehicle "and any vehicle carrying such precious freight must come to be viewed as equally precious, as part of the freight, indeed as precious in and of itself" (Fishman 1977, p. 25). Language takes on a politically aesthetic significance: "Speaking well, commanding the language, versatility in language, these often become specifically valued in their own right above and beyond what is spoken about or the purposes of speakers" (p. 25).

It should not be surprising, therefore, that speaking Spanish came to be a valued end in this community. Individuals who did not initially possess great facility practiced their Spanish more often; others set aside a day for speaking only in Spanish with their friends; still others arranged to spend summers traveling in Mexico and other Latin American countries. One suspects that they were after more than just a handy communication skill or an aesthetic mode; it was as if through language, one also acquired a distinctive sociopolitical and cultural understanding.

The calling forth of a political self through the apprehension and learning of language clearly defines language as an inextricable aspect of ideology. Ideologies, epecially figurative metaphorical ideologies like nationalisms, tend to emerge during periods of social change as Fishman (1972a) has already indicated. It is in such times when a society loses its traditional cultural moorings and orientations that ideologies "become crucial as sources of sociopolitical meanings and attitudes" (Geertz 1973, p. 219). Such usually figurative ideologies help to orient actors to their new surroundings; they provide ideas and images needed for an autonomous politics leading to a new cultural order. In the late 1960s and early 1970s, Chicano students in the universities were such actors. They found themselves with the urgent agenda of supporting their still oppressed community and without an immediately identifiable ideology for their efforts. The general implication of Geertz's formulation, however, is that ideology is metaphorically captured by well-bounded symbols – slogans, flags, programs, architecture – and, to be sure, most ideology is of this nature. The Chicano movement certainly created enough such ideological symbols – Chicano, Aztlán, handshakes, songs, dress style, slogans like "Viva la Raza!"

Language, material artifacts, or gestures "transmit" ideology. Language, however, also works in other, more indirect expressive ways. Without necessarily relying on key metaphors or direct referential meaning – as a total system of discourse – it evokes a plenitude of ideological meanings. Nationalist intelligentsia sense this and therefore make language "the mobilizing banner of its literature and politics" (Ross 1979, p. 10). Ross's own "banner" metaphor conveys the idea of an instrument that can "carry" a slogan and at the same time be evocative and meaningful as a total entity. It can wholly call forth the political self and envelop it. Language also works ideologically as aurally keyed, totally enveloping symbolic action (Fishman 1972a, pp. 25–26). As extended communicative discourse, it can acquire symbolic proportions in times of social change because it is

> more *evocative* of the past than unyieldingly *anchored* . . . to it; more indicative of uniqueness than disablingly mesmerized by it. As other symbols of unity and authenticity become problematic . . . the vernacular remains to be reinterpreted in accord with one's own most favored memories and longings as well as in accord with what is considered most dear and most laudable about the ethnic collectivity. [p. 55]

In a context of language shift, the simple sound, rhythm, and diction of folk Spanish in el meeting allowed folk speakers to win small rhetorical victories. However, there may have been yet a larger triumph. At a critical moment of social change and language shift, such sound, rhythm, and diction may well have evoked a socially and linguistically repressed ancestral lineage and political sentiment as much as did any explicit program or slogan. Indeed, language may have been an equally powerful impetus in moving people to political action on behalf of their present-day community. If the historical presence and struggle of the Mexican people in the United States is imbedded and symbolized in language, then that presence and struggle may have been evoked in their young through the very sound of that language – itself the product of historical survival and perseverance. The future maintenance of the Spanish language in Texas and the rest of the Unitred States depends in part on the future political articulation of these revitalized linguistic sentiments.

References

Achor, Shirley. 1978. *Mexican Americans in a Dallas barrio*. Tucson: University of Arizona Press.

Aguirre, Adalberto, Jr. 1979. The sociolinguistic situation of bilingual Chicano adolescents in a California border town. *Aztlan* 10:55–68.

Blom, Jan-Petter, and John J. Gumperz. 1972. Social meaning in linguistic structure: code switching in Norway. In *Directions in sociolinguistics: the ethnography of communication,* ed. John J. Gumperz and Dell Hymes, pp. 407–434. New York: Holt, Rinehart and Winston.

Bourhis, R. Y. 1979. Language in ethnic interaction: A social psychological approach. In *Language and ethnic relations,* ed. Howard Giles and Bernard St.-Jacques, pp. 117–41. Elmsford, N.Y.: Pergamon.

Brown, Penelope, and Colin Fraser. 1979. Speech as a marker of situation. In *Social Markers in speech,* ed. Klaus R. Scherer and Howard Giles, pp. 33–62. Cambridge University Press.

Cárdenas, Daniel N. 1975. Mexican Spanish. In *El lenguaje de los Chicanos,* ed. Eduardo Hérnandez-Chávez, Andrew D. Cohen, and Anthony F. Beltramo, pp. 1–5. Arlington, Va.: Center for Applied Linguistics.

Elías-Olivares, Lucía. 1979. Language use in a Chicano community: a sociolinguistic approach. In *Sociolinguistic aspects of language learning and teaching,* ed. J. B. Pride, pp. 120–35. Oxford University Press.

Espinosa, Aurelio M., Jr. 1957. Problemas lexicográficos del español del sudoeste. *Hispania* 40:139–43.

Fishman, Joshua A. 1972a. *Language and nationalism: two integrative essays.* Rowley, Mass.: Newbury House.

1972b. Language maintenance in a supra-ethnic age. In *Language in sociocultural change: essays by Joshua A. Fishman,* ed. Anwar S. Dil, pp. 48–75. Stanford University Press.

1972c. Societal bilingualism: stable and transitional. In *Language in sociocultural change: essays by Joshua A. Fishman,* ed. Anwar S. Dil, pp. 135–52. Stanford University Press.

1977. Language and ethnicity. In *Language, ethnicity, and intergroup relations,* ed. Howard Giles, pp. 15–57. London: Academic Press.

Flores, N., and Hopper, R. 1975. Mexican Americans' evaluation of spoken Spanish and English. *Speech Monographs* 42:91–98.

García, Richard A. 1978. Class, consciousness, and ideology – the Mexican community of San Antonio, Texas: 1930–1940. *Aztlan* 9:23–70.

Garza, Mario. 1977. Duality in Chicano poetry. *De Colores* 3:37–45.

Geertz, Clifford. 1973. Ideology as a cultural system. In *The interpretation of cultures: selected essays,* pp. 193–233. New York: Basic Books.

Giles, Howard. 1979. Ethnicity markers in speech. In *Social Markers in Speech,* ed. Klaus R. Scherer and Howard Giles, pp. 251–89. Cambridge University Press.

Giles, H., R. Y. Bourhis, and D. M. Taylor. 1977. Towards a theory of language in ethnic group relations. In *Language, ethnicity, and intergroup relations,* ed. Howard Giles, pp. 307–48. London: Academic Press.

Gómez-Q., Juan. 1978. *Mexican students por la raza: the Chicano student movement in Southern California, 1967–1977.* Santa Barbara, Calif.: Editorial La Causa.

Harris, Charles H., III, and Louis Sadler. 1978. The plan of San Diego and the Mexican–United States crisis of 1916: a reexamination. *Hispanic American Historical Review* 58:381–408.

Hernández-Chávez, Eduardo, Andrew D. Cohen, and Anthony F. Beltramo, eds.

1975. *El lenguaje de los Chicanos*. Arlington, Va.: Center for Applied Linguistics.

Hymes, Dell. 1972. Models of the interaction of language and social life. In *Directions in sociolinguistics: the ethnography of communication,* ed. John J. Gumperz and Dell Hymes, pp. 35–71. New York: Holt, Rinehart and Winston.

Jacobson, Rodolfo. 1978. The social implications of intra-sentential codeswitching. In *New directions in Chicano scholarship,* ed. Ricardo Romo and Raymund Paredes, pp. 227–56. Chicano Studies Monograph Series. San Diego: University of California.

Joyner, Charles W. 1975. A model for the analysis of folklore performances in historical context. *Journal of American Folklore* 88:254–65.

Lance, Donald. 1975. Dialectal and nonstandard forms in Texas Spanish. In *El lenguaje de los Chicanos,* ed. Eduardo Hernández-Chávez, Andrew D. Cohen, and Anthony F. Beltramo, pp. 37–51. Arlington, Va.: Center for Applied Linguistics.

Limón, José E. 1974a. Stereotyping and Chicano resistance: an historical dimension. *Aztlan* 4:257–69.

1974b. El primer congreso mexicanista de 1911: a precursor to contemporary chicanismo. *Aztlan* 5:85–117.

1978a. Agringado joking in Texas-Mexican society: folklore and differential identity. In *New directions in Chicano scholarship,* ed. Ricardo Romo and Raymund Paredes, pp. 33–50. Chicano Studies Monograph Series. San Diego: University of California.

1978b. The expressive culture of a Chicano student group at the University of Texas at Austin, 1972–1975. Ph.D. dissertation, University of Texas, Austin.

1979. The folk performance of *Chicano* and the cultural limits of political ideology. *Working Papers in Sociolinguistics* 62. Austin: Southwest Educational Laboratory.

1980. 'La vieja Ines': a Mexican folk game: a research note. In *Twice a minority: Mexican American women,* ed. Margarita B. Melville, pp. 88–94. St. Louis: Mosby.

Lozano, Anthony Girard. 1976. El español Chicano y la dialectologia. *Aztlan* 7:13–18.

Madsen, William. 1964. *The Mexican-Americans of South Texas*. New York: Holt, Rinehart and Winston.

Montejano, David. n.d. Race, class, and culture in Mexican South Texas, 1848–1920. Ph.D. dissertation, Yale University.

Nelson-Cisneros, Victor B. 1975. La clase trabajadora en Tejas, 1920–1940. *Aztlan* 6:239–66.

Ortega, Adolfo. 1977. Of social politics and poetry: a Chicano perspective. *Latin American Literary Review* 5:32–41.

Paredes, Américo. 1958. *With his pistol in his hand: a border ballad and its hero*. Austin: University of Texas Press.

1976. *A Texas-Mexican cancionero: folksongs of the lower border*. Urbana: University of Illinois Press.

Redlinger, Wendy. 1978. Mothers' speech to children in bilingual Mexican-American homes. *International Journal of the Sociology of Language* 17:73–82.

Reich, Alice H. 1977. The cultural production of ethnicity: Chicanos in the university. Ph.D. dissertation, University of Colorado, Boulder.

Romo, Ricardo. 1978. The urbanization of southwestern Chicanos in the early twentieth century. In *New directions in Chicano scholarship,* ed. Ricardo Romo and Raymund Paredes, pp. 183–208. Chicano Studies Monograph Series. San Diego: University of California.

Rosen, Gerald. 1974. The Chicano movement and the politicalization of culture. *Ethnicity* 1:279–93.

Ross, J. A. 1979. Language and the mobilization of ethnic identity. In *Language and ethnic relations,* ed. Howard Giles and Bernard St.-Jacques, pp. 1–4. Elmsford, N.Y.: Pergamon.

Ryan, Bouchard E., and M. A. Carranza. 1977. Ingroup and outgroup reactions to Mexican American language varieties. In *Language, ethnicity, and intergroup relations,* ed. Howard Giles, pp. 59–82. London: Academic Press.

Sánchez, Rosaura. 1978. Chicano bilingualism. In *New directions in Chicano scholarship,* ed. Ricardo Romo and Raymund Paredes, pp. 209–26. Chicano Studies Monograph Series. San Diego: University of California.

Scotton, C. M., and W. Ury. 1977. Bilingual strategies: the social functions of code switching. *International Journal of the Sociology of Language* 13:5–20.

Segade, Gustavo V. 1978. Identity and power: an essay on the politics of culture and the culture of politics in Chicano thought. *Aztlan* 9:85–100.

Skrabanek, Robert L. 1970. Language maintenance among Mexican-Americans. *International Journal of Comparative Sociology* 11:272–82.

Solé, Yolanda. 1975. Language maintenance and language shift among Mexican-American students. *Journal of the Linguistic Association of the Southwest* 1:22–48.

1978. Sociocultural and sociopsychological factors in differential language retentiveness by sex. *International Journal of the Sociology of Language* 17:29–44.

Turner, Victor. 1969. Forms of symbolic action: introduction. In *Forms of symbolic action: proceedings of the 1969 annual spring meeting of the American Ethnological Society,* ed. Robert F. Spencer, pp. 3–25. Seattle: University of Washington Press.

Valdés-Fallis, Guadalupe. 1975. Code-switching in bilingual Chicano poetry. In *Southwest languages and linguistics in educational perspective,* ed. Gina Cantoni-Harvey and M. S. Heiser, pp. 143–60. San Diego: San Diego State University, Institute for Cultural Pluralism.

Ybarra-Fraustro, Tomás. 1978. The Chicano movement and the emergence of a Chicano poetic consciousness. In *New directions in Chicano scholarship,* ed. Ricardo Romo and Raymund Paredes, pp. 81–110. Chicano Studies Monograph Series. San Diego: University of California.

Zamora, Emilio. 1975. Chicano socialist labor activity in Texas, 1900–1920. *Aztlan* 6:221–38.

15

Sociolinguistic contours in the verbal art of Chicano children

JOHN H. McDOWELL

Speech communities, language varieties

The present chapter will map a corpus of juvenile verbal art onto its constitutive sociolinguistic context. I shall concentrate on a series of exemplary texts taken from the flow of peer-group repartee, viewing them collectively as a realization of the latent language repertoire of the encompassing speech community (Mukarovský 1964). At the outset, however, I will pause to recruit the sociolinguistic concepts that will inform the discussion to follow. In particular, I will define language as a socially situated communicative system, composed of speech repertoires describable in terms of registers, varieties, and styles. In adopting a sociolinguistic perspective, I am led to perceive language as a reservoir of linguistic resources, selectively and creatively exploited by native speakers in the pursuit of effective and often artistic communication.

Dell Hymes (1974, p. 51) characterized a speech community as "a community sharing knowledge of rules for the conduct and interpretation of speech." Note that the common knowledge binding any group of speaker-listeners into a community is of two kinds: (1) linguistic competence, or the systemic orders captured in the rules of a grammar, and (2) language use, or the deployment of this competence in actual speech situations. Sociolinguistic analysis, then, is "situated in the flux and pattern of communicative events" and is concerned to "study communicative form and function in integral relation to each other" (Hymes 1974, p. 4). Thus these concepts avoid the apparent sterility of a linguistics divorced from usage as well as the artificiality of a social science only tentatively acknowledging the presence of cognitive structures in human behavior, including speech.

The notion of a speech community directs our attention to a set of related concepts. Speech communities owe their plausibility to common

This research was supported by a grant from the Southwest Educational Development Laboratory for which I wish to record again my thanks. I am indebted also to Leonice Santamaría for her assistance during the fieldwork phase of the project.

bonds of experience and knowledge. Commonality of experience derives from a field for speech interaction, which must be sufficiently intense and regular to permit the establishment of a community. The commonality of knowledge can be stated as a shared inventory of ways of speaking, accompanied by a set of attitudes allowing for the appropriate correlation of codes and settings. This is not to grant the speech community superorganic status: It remains a fiction, a composite built from an immense corpus of observations. But it is a useful fiction, corresponding roughly to some independent reality and capturing some of the critical features of an admittedly indescribable whole.

If we momentarily reify a speech community, we can point to its constitutive ways of speaking, though we must immediately cast these modes of speech as resources shaped and reshaped in the crucible of social intercourse. The existence of ways of speaking is a social fact, and we must attend to this social distribution of knowledge. At the same time it is a richly significant personal fact, and members of speech communities constantly choose among alternative ways of speaking. The particular mode of speech employed to encode a given message may or may not be a matter of deliberate choice. To a great extent, choices of this kind are automatized in ordinary usage patterns. They only become subject to conscious scrutiny when the focus of communication is the code itself (Jakobson 1960, Mukarovský 1964, Havránek 1964). Regardless of forethought and intention, however, we anticipate some mesh between the realized mode of speech and the circumstantial features of the speech moment. Analytically, we can point to issues of a rhetorical nature, leading to the selection of strategic modes of speech, and to issues of an evaluative nature, concerned with internalized attitudes toward modes of speech in the speech repertoire.

What happens when we transport the apparatus developed so far into a bilingual, bicultural setting? The framework of ways of speaking, creatively deployed, stands out all the more palpably for the tangible distinctness of the codes involved. In a monolingual setting the linguistic markers of the different ways of speaking are often quite unobtrusive. In a bilingual setting the alternation of the two languages forces itself upon us; we cannot fail to attend to it. Thus the alternation of Spanish and English among the Chicanos, like the alternation of Spanish and Guaraní in Paraguay, is a starkly manifest linguistic fact (see Rubin 1970). Investigation of speech repertoires in bilingual settings greatly enhances awareness of related phenomena in monolingual settings.

However, the ready availability of certain indicators must not obscure other factors in these complex speech situations. In bilingual speech communities, the subtle linguistic modulations that produce contrasting ways of speaking within each of the cultivated codes must still be confronted. Therefore, attention must be paid to the alternation of languages A and B, but at the same time hierarchies of ways of speaking might be found within language A and within language B. Identifying the alternation of languages A and B, often quite a trick in itself, is only part of the task. In addition, the scope of registers, like formal, colloquial, and slang, must be specified within each of the codes composing the bilingual system.

In many Chicano speech communities, a range of speech styles can be identified within the Spanish portion of the system alone. Thus Elías-Olivares (n.d.) describes these four varieties in the Spanish of East Austin, the major Chicano barrio in Austin, Texas:

1. Northern Mexican Spanish (known as *Español correcto,* among other labels): Example – *se fue a la escuela en su bicicleta.*
2. Popular Spanish (known as *Mejicano*): Example – *se fue* [*hwe*] *a la escuela* [*ehkwela*] *en su bicicleta.*
3. Mixed Spanish (known as *Español regüelto* or Spanglish): Example – *se fue* [*hwe*] *a la escuela* [*ehkwela*] *en su* bicycle.
4. Caló (known as Pachuco talk): Example – *se fue* [*hwe*] *al escuelín* [*ehkwelin*] *en su yonca* (or *chisca*).

Preliminary data indicate that a similar parsing could be done on this same community's English. Candidates for status as Chicano English varieties would include southwestern English vernacular, barrio English (incorporating some degree of Spanish phonological and morphological interference), ghetto English (based on the black English vernacular), and so on (see McDowell 1975).

One prominent speech variety found in many Chicano speech communities is code-switching, involving a rule-governed alternation of Spanish and English within single units of discourse. As Rosaura Sánchez (1977, p. 218) notes, "younger generations residing in Spanish dominant barrios will be characterized by a great deal of code-switching." Analysis of Chicano code-switching between Spanish and English suggests that a grammar could be written to describe it, because native speakers recognize properly and improperly formed utterances (Gingràs 1974), and preliminary characterizations are already available (Jacobson 1977). One interesting dimension of this wedding of codes that has received little attention is the tendency for code-switching to modulate toward creole formation in some settings. Many Chicano children are exposed primarily to the code-switching variety in the Chicano repertoire and have little incentive to separate out the Spanish and English segments of this variety, at least until contact with monolingual settings precipitates this process. Take, for example, the following speech produced by an eight-year-old Chicana in East Austin:

> *Estás lyando tú, es verdad que no tiene* nine years old?

Using Rodolfo Jacobson's techniques, we could label this an instance of intrasentential code-switching, with Spanish as the matrix code and English the constituent code (Jacobson 1977). Yet one might argue in reference to speech of this kind that from the speaker's perspective, we are dealing with a code incidentally derived from two antecedent codes but operating synchronically as a fusion of these two antecedents into a new linguistic system, a Spanish-English creole. There is a need for further investigation of this matter.

The East Austin speech community

The scene is East Austin, a Chicano barrio nestled in between the Colorado River, an interstate highway, and the inevitable railroad tracks. According to the U.S. Census of 1970, fewer than 15,000 Chicanos, primarily of working-class background, resided in East Austin. Various socioeconomic indicators suggest that East Austin could be described as an internal colony, that is, an ethnic enclave set apart by race and language and exploited as a source of cheap labor (Stavenhagen 1968, Acuña 1972, p. iii). I cannot pursue this argument here but must turn instead to a characterization of East Austin as a bilingual speech community.

In addition to the inventory of speech varieties already discussed, there are other, larger considerations. First, the East Austin speech community is a manifestation of compound rather than coordinate bilingualism (Jacobson 1977). The coordinate bilingual "keeps each of his languages quite separate" (Fishman 1971), whereas the compound bilingual favors code-switching. Code-switching is indeed prevalent in East Austin, though not to the exclusion of single-code discourse.

Rosaura Sánchez (1977), drawing on Glyn Lewis's treatment of Soviet multilingualism (Lewis 1972), has developed a four-scale typology of bilingualism among Chicanos in the Southwest:

1. Stable bilingualism, characterized by the geographically contiguous co-existence of linguistic groups, where the bilinguals "resort indifferently to either language in most situations" (Lewis 1972, p. 275)
2. Dynamic bilingualism, where "social mobility, role differentiation and appropriation of different languages for those roles prepares the ground for assimilation" (Lewis 1972, p. 276)
3. Transitional bilingualism, when two languages assume overlapping functions, "a situation which inevitably leads to the exclusive use of one language for those functions" (Sánchez 1977, p. 210)
4. Vestigial bilingualism, marked by "almost complete assimilation, where bilingualism is vestigial and often only symbolic, characterizing a small and diminishing minority" (Lewis 1972, p. 277)

Elements of all four types are present in East Austin, though on balance, the category of dynamic bilingualism best reflects the essential constitution of the speech community. Thus, there appears to be a tendency for the two codes to assume separate social roles: English slated as the language "of literacy, work, education, and recreation, with Spanish limited primarily to intimate domains" (Sánchez 1977, p. 218). But two complications (at least) must be cited in order to do justice to the East

Austin linguistic reality. First, East Austin, situated in the heart of central Texas, lies on the periphery of the United States–Mexico border zone and thereby maintains important ties with the old country. These ties promote the use of Spanish within the community and counteract to a significant extent the encroachment of English. Thus whereas dynamic bilingualism "prepares the ground for assimilation" (Lewis 1972, p. 276), the slide into transitional or vestigial bilingualism is somewhat checked by linguistic replenishment derived from proximity to the border zone.

Another central fact that must be brought into the analysis is the prevalence of code-switching in intragroup communication. Code-switching may indeed facilitate the Spanish monolingual in his quest for English competence, as Sánchez (1977, p. 218) argues, but it is equally true that code-switching provides a continuing role for Spanish within the local speech ecology. Moreover, one senses in East Austin a certain stability in the pattern of prevalent Spanish-English code-switching. Many families evince a three-generation adherence to code-switching as perhaps the most functional speech variety within the repertoire. Here again more detailed investigation is required to resolve essentially empirical questions.

The speech of East Austin children

The Chicano children responsible for the expressive forms to be considered here were denizens of East Austin during 1974, when I found them at play in their peer-groups at neighborhood locations. I worked closely with some fifty children of both sexes, ranging in age from five to eight years; but I consulted, in one way or another, a much larger group, perhaps twice that number, ranging in age from four to twelve years. All of these children were fluent in English, and less than half were fluent in Spanish. I measured their Spanish fluency on a four-part scale:

1. *Fluent*: able to express oneself adequately in Spanish through a rich assortment of grammatical forms – for example, *Mira había este chango que estaba en un palo y este señor estaba yendo pa allá y creía que el chango estaba en un agujero pero no estaba*
2. *Competent*: mastery of some Spanish vocabulary and grammar but some difficulty in the formulation of utterances
3. *Weak*: some familiarity with Spanish but little facility.
4. *Lacking*: only marginal familiarity with Spanish

On this scale, for the fifty children observed in depth, I noted the following distribution:

Fluent	22
Competent	14
Weak	9
Lacking	5

The linguistic capacities of East Austin children cannot be discussed in isolation from attitudes about language that influenced their choice of codes. I found among these children a complex structure of attitudes: (1) shame with respect to Spanish competence, evidently reflecting the pronounced bias of the surrounding Anglo community; (2) pride with respect to Spanish competence, a product of positive attitudes brought from the home as well as from nascent bilingual education programs and the popular television show, "Carrascolendas"; (3) a tendency, sometimes highly pronounced, to reserve Spanish for ingroup communication, a natural result of the highly charged atmosphere regarding Chicano Spanish usage in the state of Texas, and in Austin particularly. (Until the late 1960s spoken Spanish was prohibited on the grounds of any Texas public school, and infractions in the public school system in Texas were subject to corporal punishment.)

The actual verbal code favored by the Chicano children was that of Spanish-English code-switching. Code-switching surfaced even in their relatively formal speech and was the common currency of peer-group interaction. The following conversational gambit is illustrative: an eight-year-old girl had just narrated a spooky story, her nine-year-old brother called her to task for telling lies, and she responded:

> *No es* lies. Just *dije que, este, que el abuelito*
> I mean *el tío se fue pa la casa y ya* feel *algo que le tochaba.*

Note that the situational constraints operating here were likely to produce a bit of informal, everyday speech. Labov (1966) specifies "speech with a third person" as one of the contextual features productive of unmarked speech styles. In the gambit recorded above, the speaker provides a somewhat impassioned plea for credibility and consequently may be supposed to abandon any pretensions to "correct" or "formal" speech patterns. In other words, we have here a piece of casual speech, presumably reflective of the speaker's habitual style in informal or intimate settings.

Code-switching analysis might proceed as follows. Spanish is the matrix code, for three reasons: Spanish lexical items predominate, the English words are lodged in a controlling Spanish syntax, and the Spanish hesitancy marker, *este,* occurs in place of its English equivalents. English, therefore, is the constituent code. Code-alternation transpires at distinct linguistic levels: *lies* is a noun phrase, object of the copula; *just,* an adverbial element within the verb phrase; *I mean,* a sentence retracking unit; and *feel,* an independent verb inserted into the Spanish sentence structure. Jacobson (1977, p. 237) suggests that switching tends to occur when it is "grammatically least offensive in both languages." This may, indeed, serve as a guiding principle in the analysis of Chicano code-switching, though any substantial corpus of examples demonstrates the remarkable fluidity of the system.

Further investigation may show that code-switching in Chicano repertoires cannot be treated as a single language variety. For example, the majority of the children I heard were Spanish-dominant code-switchers, deploying Spanish as the matrix code and English as the constituent code most of the time. But English-dominant code-switching can also be heard in East Austin, sometimes taking the form of English discourse sprinkled with Spanish ethnic markers (Gumperz and Hernández-Chávez 1972). Thus the code-switching treated here as a single language variety may in fact be a composite of two or more closely related speech styles.

The corpus of verbal art

The bilingual Chicano child exploits every potential in his received speech repertoire in formulating utterances exhibiting speech play and verbal artistry. The speech play may freely cross language boundaries, as in the associative sound play produced by a four-year-old boy:[1]

1. nickel, pickle, *eco, chaleco*

Or it may scrupulously adhere to a policy of language segregation. The inherent fascination of the bilingual, bicultural heritage for the East Austin Chicano children is demonstrated by the following exchange on the topic of names between me and a lively group of boys and girls ranging in age from seven through twelve:[2]

2. Raul: Can you say our names in Spanish?
JM: What are your names?
Paula: Paula.
JM: That's Spanish already.
Silvia: Paula. (emphasizing Spanish pronunciation, essentially by stressing the separation of the two adjacent vowels)
Rudi: Say Rudi.
JM: Rudi, ah, Rodolfo.
Adam: Adam.
JM: Adán.
Rosemary: Say Rosemary in Spanish.
JM: Rosamaría.
Adam: Say Mary Jane.
JM: María Juana.
(Laughter)
Adam: What's your name in Spanish?
JM: Juan.
Adam: Juanillo.
Silvia: Juanillo Río.

[1] Performed under the influence of the rhyme reproduced here as example 11.

[2] Parallel name systems were a source of anxiety as well as diversion to the East Austin children. Note the catch on the English "Mary Jane," which becomes "María Juana," that is, almost *marijuana*, in Spanish; and the elaboration of the name "Juan" to "Juanillo" and "Juanillo Rio," a form of name play common in East Austin.

The children were intrigued by the juxtaposition of their name equivalents in Spanish and English, which is, perhaps, reflective of two underlying identities (see Goodenough 1965). The discussion of the verbal art of these children will have to take into account this interest in parallel versions of the same material in two languages, as well as the production of items using the variety referred to here as code-switching. I will use the term "parallel constructions" in reference to verbal forms coexisting in Spanish and English and the term "mixed constructions" in reference to verbal forms incorporating mixed Spanish and English discourse. The verbal art dealt with here exploits the entire range of speech varieties within the East Austin repertoire. Although space does not permit a complete explication of each of the varieties in Spanish and English, I should emphasize here that the children's verbal artistry manifests itself in English-only items, Spanish-only items, and, of course, code-switched items. Even though code-switching may be the predilect speech variety of the children, their ordinary intragroup style, they are by no means confined to this register in their production of verbal art.

Parallel constructions

One major principle structuring the domain of parallel constructions is that if the children possess competence in a certain verbal form in one language, they are likely to possess competence likewise in an equivalent form in the other language. The equivalence may be formal, functional, or referential; it may be due to independent but parallel traditions in the English and Spanish cultural inheritance or to contemporary acts of translation. But whatever the process, the fact remains that the East Austin children maintain parallel versions of their monolingual expressive forms. It would be difficult if not impossible to point to a verbal form, itself composed of solitary Spanish or English discourse, that did not possess an equivalent in the other language. This principle of equivalence between parallel constructions signals the presence of another, more comprehensive principle: namely, that anything that is worth doing in one language is worth trying, at least, in the other language.

Chicano-independent parallel constructions. Parallel constructions derived from autonomous Old World traditions fortuitously copresent in the Chicano millieu will be termed here "Chicano-independent." They may reflect patterns of diffusion in the European setting or the generation of like traditions from like circumstances.

Counting-out rhymes

3. Eenie meenie miney mo
Catch a tiger by its toe,

If it hollers let it go
Eenie meenie miney mo.[3]

4. *Tín marín de don quién fue*
Cúcara mácara títire fue.[4]

Both items (performed by several children, of various ages) are used to determine roles in children's games, thus manifesting a functional equivalence. In each case, the rhyme is recited to emphasize its inherent isochronic pulse, and one member of the group is signalled or touched with each strong metric beat. The person upon whom the final pulse rests is the chosen one. Although the precise referential content of the two rhymes is different, they share a pattern of sensible units alternating with units of nonsense. We may thus speak of a rough formal equivalence in the mode of action associated with the rhyme and in the combination of sense and nonsense. The children readily perceive them as functional equivalents, but unfortunately I have no solid evidence concerning the situational constraints favoring the use of one or the other construct.

Nursery rhymes

5. Pussycat pussycat where have you been?
I've been to London to visit the Queen
Pussycat pussycat what you do there?
I find me a little cat under her chair.[5]

6. *Estaba la pájara pinta*
Sentada en un verde limón
Con el pico le coge la hoja
Con la ala le coge la flor.[6]

These two rhymes (performed in English by a six-year-old girl and in Spanish by a girl of seven) evoke the nursery, the poetic kingdom of the child. They stand in here for a large corpus of pleasing rhymes of innocence performed by the children of East Austin in English and Spanish. Their protagonists are the familiar animals encountered in the child's daily rounds. These rhymes may have a naturalistic bent, as does the Spanish construct; or the animal figures may be anthropomorphized as is the pussycat in the English construct. The prevailing meter is the isochronic pulse characteristic of a great deal of folk poetry.

[3] According to the Opies, this is "undoubtedly the most popular rhyme for counting-out both in England and America; the version common today is Anglo-American in origin, the first and last lines being old British, the middle two from New England" (Opie 1951, p. 156). See also Newell (1883), Bolton (1888), and Gomme (1894–8).

[4] A popular Spanish counting-out rhyme with variants reported from Santo Domingo, Peru, Venezuela, and Puerto Rico (Boggs 1955, pp. 473ff).

[5] A well-known English nursery rhyme, first recorded in 1805 (Opie 1951, pp. 357ff).

[6] Boggs (1955, p. 230) dates this to seventeenth-century Spain, at least, and provides evidence of variants throughout the Spanish-speaking world. The song sometimes accompanies a game.

Game songs

7. Here we go loop the loop
Here we go loop the lie
Here we go loop the loop
All on a Saturday night.

I put my right hand in
I take my right hand out
I give my right hand a shake shake shake
And turn myself about.[7]

8. *Arroz con leche*
Me quiero casar
Con una viudita
De la capital.

Que sepa coser
Que sepa bordar
Que ponga la mesa
En su santo lugar.

Yo soy la viudita
La hija del rey
Me quiero casar
No hallo con quien.

Contigo sí
Contigo no
Contigo mi vida
Me casaré yo.[8]

Example 7 was performed by an eight-year-old girl accompanied by younger children; example 8, by several children of various ages. Each rhyme accompanies a circle game, involving coordinated action on the part of all members of the circle. They are sung, in each case, by all players, though the Spanish construct singles out one player as the luckless widow seeking her spouse. Thus the actual play is different: In the English construct, the game entails a series of coordinated movements performed by all players in unison as they sing in unison; in the Spanish construct, the initial collectivity is ruptured as the widow steps forth, singing the last two verses alone, to pounce upon one player as the make-believe spouse. Note that the principle of equivalence does not extend to the point of producing equivalent songs for the same games. Instead, the natural bond of game form to companion song is retained within each of the two constructs.

[7] Lady Gomme comments: "It is a choral dance, and it may owe its origin to a custom of wild antic dancing in celebration of the rites of some deity in which animal postures were assumed." See Gomme (1894–8) and Newell (1883).

[8] Variants are reported from all corners of the Spanish-speaking world (see Boggs 1955 and Guevara 1965).

Finger games

9. One little pig went to the market
One little pig stayed home
One little pig had roast beef
One little pig had none
One little pig cried wee wee wee
All the way home.[9]

10. *Un elefantito*
Dos elefantitos se fueron
Tres elefantitos se fueron pa trás
Vinieron cuatro elefantitos
Y después se juntaron todos
Eran cinco elefantitos.[10]

These two games call for one player to manipulate the fingers of another player while reciting the words presented in the constructs. In example 9, performed by several children, aged five to eight, the fingers are metaphorically stated as pigs; in example 10, performed by an eight-year-old girl with her younger brother and sister, they are called elephants.

Parody rhymes

11. I went to town
I saw Mr. Brown
He gave me a nickel
I went to go buy a pickle
The pickle was too sour
I trade it for a flower
I saw a fellow
I kicked him in the butt.[11]

12. *Corrí corrí me trompece*
Caí en las lanas de José
Se las metí, se las saqué
Tenía pelitos y me asusté.[12]

Each of these rhymes betrays the healthy irreverence of the child toward the adult world by turning the serious constraints of poetry toward the goal of playful banter. They stand here as representatives of a large class of productions similarly constituted. Example 11 was performed by a seven-year-old girl; example 12, by a group of boys, aged eight to ten.

[9] Widely distributed finger game, first recorded in 1740 (see Opie 1951, pp. 349ff).
[10] I have not yet uncovered any traditional texts, though I suspect it is traditional.
[11] Abrahams (1969, pp. 93–4) reports numerous variants from all over the United States and from New Zealand, dating from 1927 to the present.
[12] Although I have found no exact equivalent, there is an approximation reported in a collection of Mexican riddles (Pauer 1918, p. 541): "Corrí, corrió / Me senté, lo alcancé / Vi un árbol de ciruelas / Cargado de manzanas / Empecé a tirar de piedras / Y cayeron avellanas – La mentira."

Traditional rhyming riddles

13. A riddle a riddle a hole in the middle. A ring.[13]

14. *Una vieja larga y seca*
Que le escurre la manteca. La vela.[14]

Both the English and Spanish oral traditions provide examples of these literary, rhyming riddles. Example 13 was performed by a seven-year-old boy; example 14, by several children older than seven.

Traditional, nonrhyming riddle

15. What has a tongue but cannot talk? A shoe.[15]

16. *¿Qué tiene una cabeza y no tiene ni un cabello? La pelota.*

Each of these two examples (performed by girls aged seven and eleven, respectively) of the "true" riddle in prose, that is, a riddle constituting a genuine test of wits, denies a likely attribute of an object first cited in the riddle proposition.

The parallel constructions so far presented emerge from independent oral traditions fortuitously copresent in East Austin. The distribution of these items in time and space can, for the most part, be documented.

Chicano-dependent parallel constructions. A different class of parallel constructions are those whose equivalence appears to be contemporary. A process of translation, either precise or approximate, is presumably responsible for the existence of parallel constructs, and that process has taken place within Chicano speech communities. The bonded constructs to be discussed here apparently are not derivative from separate oral traditions independent of the Chicano experience. Instead, they apparently owe their existence to cross-fertilization between English and Spanish oral reservoirs in the ambience of the Chicano children's peer group. In some cases the English model seems to have preceded the Spanish. In other cases the reverse is true, an English copy appears to be styled on a Spanish original. This category of parallel construction is termed "Chicano-dependent" because the bonded constructs are rooted in the Chicano ambience.

Children's ditty

17. I'm Popeye the sailor man
I live in a garbage can
I eat all the worms
And spit out the germs
I'm Popeye the sailor man.[16]

[13] This riddle uses a traditional riddling formula. It is recorded in Withers and Benet (1954).

[14] Variants reported in New Mexico, Puerto Rico, Santo Domingo, Chile, and Argentina (see Boggs 1955, Espinosa 1916, Mason 1916).

[15] Included in Taylor (1951, no. 296). See also Farr 1935.

[16] One of the singers, aged six, produced this variant: "Popeye the sailor man / To get in the garbage can / I'll turn on the match / I'll burn off the ass / Of Popeye the sailor man."

18. *Popeye nació en Torreon*
Encima de una sillon
Mató su tía
Con una tortilla
Popeye nació en Torreon.

These two ditties (the first, sung by several children, aged six to ten; the second, by a boy of eleven) are sung to the familiar Popeye tune from the cartoons, which appears to be the source of both variants presented above. Here we may speak of an English original and a Spanish copy. Although the copy is not a precise one, it is nonetheless modeled on an English source. In point of fact, the Spanish variant is as richly evocative of Mexico as the English variant is of the United States. Yet the childish irreverence mentioned above is common to both variants.

Spooky story

19. *Había este chamaquito y esta señora y el chamaquito tenía un chicle y luego se le cayó y luego dijo la señora: "No la levantes porque el diablo ya se la comió." Luego cuando la iba a levantar le dijo eso y luego fue a buscar otro cuando la señora se cayó y le dijo: "Levántame" dijo. Y el chamaquito dijo: "No, porque el diablo ya te lambió." Aquel corrió y la señora ahí se quedó.* (Narrated by a five-year-old boy.)
20. My uncle when he was about your age he used to, every night he go to the railroad tracks, and then there he saw a man and that man was turning on, he was turning on matches in the night, and then he, he said: "What are you looking at?" Then that man got up like that and he didn't have no nose. (Narrated by an eight-year-old girl.)

The oral tradition of Chicano Spanish provides a rich corpus of supernatural tales, involving witches, devils, ghosts, and the like. These stories possess a vitality no longer present in the American English tradition, where these denizens of the supernatural realms have become tame and innocuous through overexposure in popular-culture sources. The children of East Austin tell traditional stories, either in Spanish or in English, that have been orally passed on to them. These tales may also be recited in the code-switching language variety, as we shall see later.

Descriptive riddle

21. What's red? An apple. (Performed by a six-year-old girl.)
22. *¿Qué es blanco y blanco? Un vestido de novia.* (Performed by an eight-year-old girl.)

Modern juvenile riddling in the United States incorporates numerous riddlelike routines that are orthodox descriptions and thus involve none of the trickery associated with true riddles (McDowell 1979). The children of East Austin retain some traditional Spanish riddles, but for the most part their riddling resembles that of their Anglo counterparts. Children's riddling in the United States is heavily invested with popular-culture contributions and the elementary school environment. A great deal of the nontraditional riddling carried on by Chicano children (these descriptive routines being a primary example) derives from Anglo models, whether cast in the original English or in Spanish translations.

Jump-rope rhyme

23. I had a little brother
His name was Tiny Tim
I put him in the bathtub
To teach him how to swim.

He drank up all the water
He ate up all the soap
He died late last night
With a bubble in his throat.[17]

24. *Anoche fuí pa el baile*
Dejé la puerta abierta
Vinieron los ratones
Se comieron mis calzones.[18]

These two constructs (the first, performed by several children, aged seven to ten; the second, by two girls, aged eight and nine) are sung to the same tune, a tune associated with a number of English children's ditties. Jump roping, like riddling, has important ties with the world of the schoolyard, and this again may help account for the production of a Spanish copy from an English original.

Although there may well be additional bonded constructs not mentioned here, this presentation of texts manifesting parallel constructions is now complete. I should emphasize that the texts selected for presentation here do not exhaust the corpus; these texts have merely been chosen to represent classes of bonded constructions. The remarkable conclusion emerging from these materials is that even the compound bilingual, accustomed to conjoining his codes, is able to keep them separate (to coordinate them) under appropriate circumstances. The conditioning factor here is, for the Chicano-independent material, the existence of precoined items (see Jacobson 1977, p. 243) in Spanish and English, and for the Chicano-dependent material, the existence of a precoined item in either of the languages. A second important conclusion is the tendency of a precoined item in one language to trigger the fabrication of a translation in the other language. The term "translation" is used broadly here: literal translations are exceptional, rough translations of form, content, and style being much more common.

All of this is evidence for the assertion that the bilingual Chicano child knows the perimeters of his speech repertoire exceedingly well. If a per-

[17] The first recorded variant was in 1780 (see Opie and Opie, 1951, p. 216). Abrahams (1969, pp. 79–80) reports variants from all over the United States beginning in 1936.

[18] I have found no references to this text in other collections, though it sounds traditional.

son is competent in two languages, one of the options available to him is to produce discourse while systematically segregating the two codes. The children of East Austin have exploited this option, this potential, abundantly, even generating parallel construction where it did not initially exist. The other option is systematically to mix the two codes, an option more in line with the everyday speech of the children. We turn our attention now to the manifestation of this option in the verbal art of East Austin children.

Code-switching

A substantial portion of the verbal art produced by East Austin children utilizes the technique of code-switching. In some cases the code-switching appears to be quite incidental to the verbal gambit, bespeaking the child's ordinary speech style rather than any deliberate form of code manipulation. These instances are collected into the category of "casual code-switching." Other instances of code-switching appear to be more deliberate in character. In some cases the children alternate between Spanish and English in an exploratory fashion, pursuing the various combinations of the two codes in the formulation of acceptable utterances. These are treated here under the label "exploratory code-switching." Finally, in certain verbal productions the switching of codes is the point of the exercise; these locutions employ "pivotal code-switching." Let us review some of the data.

Casual code-switching.

25. What has four legs and a *pico* sticking out? That's a pig, it gots a *pico*. (Performed by a seven-year-old girl.)
26. What's an animal *que* gots two big horns? That's a longhorn. (Performed by a seven-year-old girl.)
27. ¿Por qué comió el *chicken* comida? (no solution provided) (Performed by a five-year-old boy.)
28. ¿Qué es *blue* y *white* con dos *cherries on top*?[19] (Performed by children aged seven and older.)
29. You're not cold, *bato,* you're a fool, aren't you? (Delivered by a nine-year-old boy to his seven-year-old brother.)

All of these but the last one are riddle performances; the last one is a taunt. Some of the characteristic patterns of code-switching in East Austin are present in these examples. The matrix code may be either English (examples 25, 26, 29) or Spanish (examples 27, 28). The constituent code provides key substantives (examples 25, 27, 28), the relative clause marker (example 26), and a term of ethnic solidarity (example 29). The capacity of code-switching to feature a key substantive in the discourse is an instance of foregrounding (see Garvin 1964), a communicative device by no means restricted to bilingual speech communities. Of the five ex-

[19] This riddle was the sensation in East Austin. Reported in Winslow 1966.

amples given above, only example 28 exhibits what is generally thought of as true code-switching. Jacobson (1977) provides the label "semicode-switching" for code-alternation involving merely the insertion of a lexical item from one code into discourse in another code. I am not certain that this distinction is a useful one. It places too much emphasis on syntax at the expense of the semantic structure of discourse.

Exploratory code-switching.

30. . . . este chamaquito estaba *chewing gum* estaba comiendo *gum* y la estaba *chewing* . . .

In starting a narrative, this five-year-old boy presents three formulations of the same message: *a little boy was chewing gum.* The verb phrase (VP) appears in three guises, each one incorporating a distinct form of code-switching:

a. *estaba chewing gum* (gerund and its object appear in English)
b. *estaba comiendo gum* (only the object of the verb appears in English)
c. *la estaba chewing* (object of the verb is preposed here, with the Spanish pronoun in a peculiarly Spanish construction, though the gerund remains in English)

If we view the verb phrase schematically as

Tense be + ing VP Noun phrase
1 2 3 4

we have the following pattern:

(a)		(b)		(c)	
1 =	Spanish	1 =	Spanish	1 =	Spanish
2 =	English	2 =	Spanish	2 =	English
3 =	English	3 =	Spanish	3 =	English
4 =	English	4 =	English	4 =	Spanish

It does not seem arbitrary to attribute to this excerpt an experimentation with code-alternation that transcends code-switching patterns present in the ordinary speech of these children.

31. 1st: Why do the birds fly south? *¿Por qué?* Because it's too far to walk.
2nd: *Porque* it's too far to walk.
3rd: *Porque está* too far *pa anda'*.[20]

In this example (spoken by children from seven to nine years old) we find a social construction of the same kind of experimentation described in reference to example 1. Three formulations of the riddle solution appear. The first involves unswitched English; in the second, the clause marker in Spanish is followed by the solution "it's too far to walk" in English; and in the third, the solution is in Spanish with the predicate noun phrase, "too far," retained in its English form.

[20] The riddle is, of course, traditional (see Ainsworth 1962).

32. Number one *se robó la galleta de la,* cookie jar.
¿Quién yo?–
Sí tú.–
No puede ser.–
Pues luego¿quién?–
Number two *se robó la galleta de la,* cookie jar.

This is a code-switched variant of a singing game known also to the children in its monolingual English original:

33. Number one stole the cookie from the, cookie jar.
Who me?–
Yeah you.–
Couldn't be.–
Then who?–
Number two stole the cookie from the, cookie jar.[21]

All the players (here, boys and girls from six to eleven years old) sing the first line of the sequence as well as the intervening lines 3 and 5. Individual children by turn sing or chant the second, fourth, and sixth lines as the turn at soloist gradually moves around the circle. The framing lines employ code-switching, whereas the dialogue lines in between are maintained in Spanish translations of English originals. This item presents, then, a combination of the two construction types discussed here, parallel and mixed. Although a precoined item in one of the languages often precipitates a translation into a monolingual version in the other language, there is also the possibility of recasting the item in the language variety of code-switching.

Jacobson (1977), the guide through so much of this analysis, writes: "Encoding and decoding is mainly a subconscious strategy and it is the message on which the speaker focuses rather than the medium – or media – in which he conveys it" (p. 233). Surely we must part ways with him here. A great deal of human verbal production exhibits varying degrees of attention to precisely the medium of expression. Bascom (1955, p. 247) defines verbal art as a "concern with the form of expression, over and above the needs of communication." This definition is kindred to the Prague circle's concept of the poetic function, present to some degree in most verbalization, not merely in poetry itself (Garvin 1964). We read in an article by Mukarovský (1964, p. 24): "The striving for beauty need not be limited in its manifestation to the specific forms of the arts. The esthetic needs are, on the contrary, so potent that they affect *almost all* the acts of man." Our investigation of exploratory code-switching indicates that the focus on the medium of expression in a bilingual setting can influence the pattern of code allocation. We turn now to some very suggestive material, those verbalizations in our corpus of mixed construc-

[21] Curiously, I have not found references to this game in oral tradition, though I'm sure they must exist.

tions that display a tendency to elevate the simultaneous availability of two codes to a position of preeminence in the discourse.

Pivotal code-switching.

34. 1st: Knock knock.
    2nd: Who's there?
    1st: Kelly.
    2nd: Kelly who?
    1st: *Qué le importa.*[22]

The trick of the knock-knock joke is to activate a single phonetic string retrospectively subject to discrepant semantic interpretations. What appears to be a first name turns out to operate as the initial segment of some proposition. Here the two separate semantic interpretations are lodged in distinct codes: *Kelly* in English, *qué le* (*importa*) in Spanish. The core semantic of this routine plays upon code-switching.

35. . . . and then she said: "*Sí me cansas.*" And then she told her husband: "*Esposo, que me mates una bruja pa comer*" . . .

In this fragment from a longer narrative by an eight-year-old girl, we find a systematic isolation of Spanish and English, the latter serving to carry narrative transition, the former serving to relay incidents of reported speech. This artistic technique is reminiscent of a point made in the following way by Gumperz and Hernández-Chávez (1972): "Code-switching is also a communicative skill, which speakers use as a verbal strategy in much the same way that skillful writers switch styles in a short story."

36. 1st: *Tun tun.*
    2nd: *¿Quién es?*
    1st: *La vieja Inés.*
    2nd: *¿Qué quería?*
    1st: *Un color.*
    2nd: *¿Qué color?*
    1st: Red.
    1st & 2nd: (laughter)[23]

The insertion of the English word *red* into this traditional Spanish game (performed by boys and girls of all ages) is sufficiently jarring to bring the game to a halt amid the laughter of the two players. Here code-switching is employed as a deliberate violation of the rules of the game, to create a new game, a spoof of the original.

I would argue that in each of the three examples just cited, code-switching is more than an incidental feature of the discourse. It functions instead as a *sine qua non* of the verbal performance; without the code-switching the performance routine would not be the same. In a significant sense

[22] This was a well-known catch among children ages eight to twelve.
[23] This is one of the best-known children's games in the Spanish tradition. Variants are reported from all over the Spanish-speaking world (Boggs 1951, Guevara 1965).

these latter productions are nontranslatable: Their very constitution involves the interplay of the two codes.

Conclusion

The children of East Austin exploit in their verbal play all of the parameters of their bilingual speech repertoire. Verbal art may be couched in monolingual discourse or in discourse involving the alternation of codes. I have not dealt with the utilization of registers within monolingual speech, but clearly the materials presented lend themselves to an analysis of this kind. Thus *español correcto* is evident in some of the traditional items, for example in the consistent use of the subjunctive in example 8. Likewise, the English items from oral tradition incorporate a number of features associated with formal varieties of English, for example, the question, "Where have you been?" in example 5. One detects barrio Spanish in some of the examples, involving greater latitude for on-the-spot formulation: the *chamaquito* of examples 19 and 30; *bato* in example 29; the abbreviated forms *pa anda'* (example 31) and *pa comer* (example 35). The Chicano English vernacular is audible in the locution "turn on matches" in example 20, reflecting interference from the Spanish *prender fósforos*. And the two forms of code-switching, Spanish-dominant (examples 27, 28, 30) and English-dominant (examples 25, 26, 29), are amply represented in our sampling of verbal art produced by the East Austin children.

We have seen that the Chicano children are able to maintain code separation, especially when the impulse to do so is provided by the presence of monolingual items in oral tradition. Perhaps drawing from this model, the children produce monolingual translations of items initially presented to them in only one of the two codes. Yet the tendency toward code-switching evident in their everyday speech asserts itself in the production of verbal art, as might be expected. Code-switching may be an incidental feature of the artistic discourse, or it may assume prominence as a self-motivated scrutiny of linguistic resources, or as the very heart of the verbal performance. The present discussion suggests that the verbal art of some bilingual communities must be viewed as a systematic exploitation of the total range of sociolinguistic resources available in the repertoire of the speech community.

The children of East Austin are the fortunate repositories of two major cultural heritages. Their advantageous position, sometimes obscured by the reigning attitudes in the larger community toward bilingualism, shines forth clearly in the materials presented here. We find in this corpus rhymes and routines in both the Spanish and English languages that have been handed down over many generations to constitute at present a treasury of Chicano verbal art. We also encounter contemporary materials, fashioned in accordance with the traditional molds but reflecting current perspectives and concerns. The classification of the verbal art of East Austin children proposed here, into the categories of parallel and mixed constructions, describes simultaneously the preservation of what is beautiful or useful in tradition and the adaptation of tradition to the expressive needs of the moment. The sociolinguistic context of East Austin has provided the linguistic resources to create a resolutely Chicano expressive profile.

References

Abrahams, Roger, ed. 1969. *Jump-rope rhymes: a dictionary*. Austin: University of Texas Press.

Acuña, Rodolfo. 1972. *Occupied America: the Chicano's struggle toward liberation*. San Francisco: Canfield Press.

Ainsworth, Catherine. 1962. Black and white and said all over. *Southern Folklore Quarterly* 26:263–95.

Bascom, William. 1955. Verbal art. *Journal of American Folklore* 68:245–52.

Boggs, Edna Garrido de. 1955. *Folklore infantil de Santo Domingo*. Madrid: Ediciones Cultura Hispánica.

Bolton, H. Carrinton. 1888. The counting-out rhymes of children: their antiquity, origin, and wide distribution. London: Elliot Stock.

Elías-Olivares, Lucía. 1979. Language use in a Chicano community: a sociolinguistic approach. In *Sociolinguistic aspects of language learning and teaching,* ed. J. B. Pride, pp. 120–35. Oxford University Press.

n.d. Chicano language varieties and uses in East Austin. Manuscript. University of Illinois, Chicago Circle.

Espinosa, Aurelio. 1916. New Mexican Spanish folklore: riddles. *Journal of American Folklore* 28:505–35.

Farr, T. J. 1935. Riddles and superstitions of Middle Tennessee. *Journal of American Folklore* 48:318–36.

Fishman, Joshua. 1971. A sociolinguistic census of a bilingual neighborhood. In *Bilingualism in the barrio,* ed. Joshua Fishman, Robert Cooper, Roxana Ma, et al. Bloomington: Indiana University, Research Center for the Language Sciences.

Garvin, Paul, ed. 1964. *A Prague school reader on esthetics, literary structure, and style*. Washington, D.C.: Georgetown University Press.

Gingràs, Rosario. 1974. Problems in the description of Spanish-English intrasentential code-switching. In *Southwest areal linguistics,* ed. Garland D. Bills, pp. 167–74. San Diego: San Diego State University, Institute for Cultural Pluralism.

Gomme, Lady Alice. 1964. Traditional games of England, Scotland, and Ireland. Reprint ed., New York: Dover Books. (Originally published 1894–8)

Goodenough, Ward. 1965. Personal names and modes of address in two oceanic societies. In *Context and meaning in cultural anthropology,* ed. M. E. Shapiro, pp. 265–76. New York: Free Press.

Guevara, Darío. 1965. *Folklore del corro infantil ecuatoriano*. Quito, Ecuador. Talleres Gráficos Nacionales.

Gumperz, John J., and Eduardo Hernández-Chávez. 1972. Bilingualism, bidialectalism, and classroom interaction. In *Functions of language in the class-*

room, ed. Courtney Cazden, V. John, and Dell Hymes, pp. 84–110. New York: Teachers College Press.

Havránek, Bohuslav. 1964. The functional differentiation of the standard. In *A Prague school reader on esthetics, literary structure, and style,* ed. P. Garvin, pp. 3–16. Washington, D.C.: Georgetown University Press.

Hymes, Dell. 1974. *Foundations in sociolinguistics: an ethnographic approach.* Philadelphia: University of Pennsylvania Press.

Jacobson, Rodolfo. 1977. The social implications of intra-sentential code-switching. *New Scholar* 6:227–56.

Jakobson, Roman. 1960. Linguistics and poetics: closing statement. In *Style in language,* ed. Thomas Sebeok, pp. 350–77. Cambridge, Mass.: MIT Press.

Labov, William. 1966. *The social stratification of English in New York City.* Arlington, Va.: Center for Applied Linguistics.

Lewis, Glyn. 1972. *Multilingualism in the Soviet Union.* The Hague: Mouton.

Mason, J. Alden. 1916. Puerto Rican folklore: riddles. *Journal of American Folklore* 29:423–504.

McDowell, John H. 1975. The speech play and verbal art of Chicano children: an ethnographic and sociolinguistic study. Ph.D. dissertation, University of Texas, Austin.

1979. *Children's riddling.* Bloomington: Indiana University Press.

Mukarovský, Jan. 1964. The esthetics of language. In *A Prague school reader on esthetics, literary structure, and style,* ed. P. Garvin, pp. 31–70. Washington, D.C.: Georgetown University Press.

Newell, William Wells. 1963. *Games and songs of American children.* Reprint ed., New York: Dover. (Originally published 1883)

Opie, Iona, and Peter Opie, eds. 1951. *The Oxford dictionary of nursery rhymes.* Oxford University Press.

Pauer, Paul Siliceo. 1918. Adivinanzas recogidas en México. *Journal of American Folklore* 30:537–43.

Rubin, Joan. 1970. Bilingual usage in Paraguay. In *Readings in the sociology of language,* ed. Joshua Fishman, pp. 512–30. The Hague: Mouton.

Sánchez, Rosaura. 1977. Chicano bilingualism. *New Scholar* 6:209–26.

Stavenhagen, Rodolfo. 1968. Seven fallacies about Latin America. In *Latin America: reform or revolution,* ed. James Petras and Maurice Zeitlin, pp. 13–31. New York: Fawcett.

Taylor, Archer. 1951. *English riddles from oral tradition.* Berkeley: University of California Press.

Winslow, David. 1966. An annotated collection of children's lore. *Keystone Folklore Quarterly* 11:151–202.

Withers, Carl, and Sula Benet. 1954. *The American riddle book.* New York: Abelard-Schuman.

16

Code-switching and interactions among Puerto Rican children

ANA CELIA ZENTELLA

Sociolinguistic and ethnolinguistic research have indicated that a single-style speaker is an anomaly. Both monolinguals and bilinguals have linguistic repertoires with a variety of styles that fulfill many different functions. Monolinguals select among different styles in the same language; bilinguals select among different styles and different languages. Both style-switching and language-switching have been referred to as "code-switching." In this chapter, code-switching refers only to switching between languages.

The communicative competence of speakers in bilingual speech communities includes knowing which of two languages, and which varieties of each, to speak to whom, when, about what, and how. Competent speakers must also know the rules governing the possibility of switching languages during the same speech situation. Every bilingual speech community does not share the same rules concerning code-switching; thus specific linguistic function and the social meaning of code-switching vary in each speech community.

Most of the research on code-switching has focused on adult bilingual patterns (Haugen 1950, Blom and Gumperz 1972, Gumperz and Hernández-Chávez 1975, Pfaff 1975, Timm 1975, Elías-Olivares 1976, Valdés-Fallis 1976). To date, we have only pieces of description and fragments of a theory of acquisition of code-switching by bilingual children. There are many gaps in our knowledge. For example, we know that children switch according to the perceived dominance of the person they address and that older children seem to be better switchers (Shultz 1975, Centro 1976, Cohen 1976, Genishi 1976, McClure 1977); that is, they can manipulate their codes for a wider variety of stylistic purposes and situational demands, but no research documents how children develop this ability over the years. Most important, we know that the children learn their com-

This chapter is the result of the suggestions, guidance, and personal example of Shirley Brice Heath; she has my sincere gratitude and *respeto*. It was supported by a grant from the Southwest Educational Development Laboratory and appeared as *Working Papers in Sociolinguistics*, No. 50.

municative competence as members of a speech community, but the code-switching rules and behaviors of a speech community have not been compared with those of the child in the classroom. Research is hampered because of the multiplicity of variables to be considered and the slow emergence of a comprehensive theoretical framework. It is difficult to compare the research that exists because the definitions of code-switching are not equivalent, and the methodology differs in addition to the age, sex, ability, and so on, of the speakers. Some researchers include borrowings in their tabulations (Pfaff 1975; McClure 1977), others reject them (Gumperz 1976), and most do not specify how they deal with them. Some describe and some quantify. The unit of observation ranges from the sentence to the utterance (defined as a turn at speaking by Cohen and Shultz) to the episode that ranges from seconds to one-half hour. Only McClure distinguishes sentences made at sentence boundaries from sentence internal switching among children.

Code-switching and interaction rules

This chapter points to yet another neglected aspect in the study of code-switching: How the specific interaction rules, as perceived by the participants, correlate with code-switching. As Bruck and Shultz (1977) suggest, "not one, but a complex interaction of many social variables (e.g., activity, addressee, classroom teacher's language) must be considered in the discussion of language use patterns" (p. 85). The fact that a speaker with X characteristics speaks to a hearer with Y characteristics, in a particular place, about a particular topic, during a specific type of interaction, cannot be disentangled, nor can the conversation be duplicated N times, subject to experimental controls. When McClure (1977) states that the "greatest degree of code switching is manifested in free conversation, strongly inhibited in interrogation and narration" (p. 105), we know that this must be influenced by the parameters she recognizes: participants, topic, discourse type, and setting. I maintain that communicative competence in code-switching is also affected by the participants' definition of the interaction and knowledge of appropriate rules for the interaction. Even where there is "no consistent association of language with setting or activities" (Genishi 1976, p. 71), different rules apply during communicative tasks from those used in naturalistic situations. When asked to describe something or to tell another child to make something, bilinguals code-switched when not talking directly about the task but persisted in one language during the task, even when they needed to make the instructions clear. This may be a reflection of the bilinguals' notion of correct teacher/authority behavior, an awareness documented in monolingual peer teaching (Cazden 1977).

Social psychologists define human interaction as "sharing common properties determined by the setting in which communication occurs and the structural relationships between the participants'' (Siegman and Pope 1972, p. 24), but students of language in its social setting must add that verbal human interaction occurs by means of a shared system of phonological, morphological, syntactic, and semantic rules and shared rules about the correct ''ways of speaking'' (Hymes 1974a and 1974b). Because social and linguistic phenomena are always present, any approach to the study of code-switching must correlate social variables and the rules of the setting of the interaction with the syntactic patterns chosen by the speakers. Code-switching itself helps to create a conversational dynamic that only the analysis of conversations can reveal:

> What we need are detailed investigations of speakers' use of code switching strategies, in actual conversational exchanges, to show that they exhibit some form of linguistic patterning, that they contribute to the meaning of constituent messages and that participants in the interaction agree on their interpretation. [Gumperz 1976, p. 14]

Research setting

This chapter analyzes the code-switching strategies of three third-graders in two interactions: (1) an individual interview with the researcher, an adult female member of the New York Puerto Rican speech community, and (2) a domino game in which all three children participate. The research was conducted in a public school in a low-middle-income area in the Bronx, New York City. The subjects are in the only third-grade bilingual class in the school, which is 60 percent Puerto Rican and 40 percent black. All the teachers in the bilingual program are Puerto Rican.[1] As a participant observer, the investigator collected the data during seven days with the class over a period of four months.[2] No effort was made by the investigator to speak one language more than another in the class, although, given the ages (seven through ten) and language dominance of most of the children, Spanish predominated. The participant observer was another teacherlike figure whom the children called upon for academic and personal help. She also took children out of the room upon occasion, brought the class presents, and was called by her first name. The most salient characteristic of the investigator was that she was always accompanied by a tape recorder, and she frequently checked on another left under children's desks.

The research described here is based on three interviews that range between ten and twenty minutes in length with a seven-year-old boy, Juan, an eight-year-old girl, Ana, and a ten-year-old girl, Nora, and on two domino games in which the same children are the only players. Thirty-

[1] The code-switching patterns of the third- and sixth-grade teachers and classes are compared in Zentella (1981a.)

[2] Another seven days were spent with the sixth-grade class, and some of the results of that data are also included. Pseudonyms have been used for both students and teachers.

one interviews were conducted in the class (nineteen in the third grade, twelve in the sixth grade); twelve domino games were recorded. The findings presented here are representative of the patterns in all the interviews and domino games. The interviews were conducted by the investigator in both Spanish and English and took place in a quiet corner of the classroom. A microphone was attached to the child's shirt or blouse, and all interviews were recorded. The children were taken to a small room on another floor of the school for the domino games. The tape recorder was placed under the table and the microphone was taped to its edge; the investigator sat in a corner, seemingly busy with paperwork but actually taking notes on the conversations.

The subjects

The children are quite different in several ways. Juan is a seven-year-old boy who had come from Puerto Rico two months before the interview took place. He lives with his mother and younger brother, who speak only Spanish. His father speaks English and wants him to learn it. Juan does not know how to read or write at grade level in Spanish. The Aspira exam placed him in the 7th percentile in the Spanish version of the test, and in the 1st percentile in the English part.[3] Ana is eight years old and was born and raised in the United States. She lives with two older sisters and her parents; she speaks English to all of them except her mother. Ana was rated as a fluent bilingual by both the teacher and the investigator. She scored above the 21st percentile in English on the Aspira exam, the cut-off point for admission to the bilingual programs, but was placed in the bilingual class at her parents' request. Over 90 percent of the class rated her the best Spanish speaker. Ana is a very good student and is very competitive; she spent an afternoon crying after she had been unable to finish a spelling test because she mistakenly wrote a complete sentence for each word. A month after the interview, Ana was placed in a monolingual class, much to her teacher's distress.

Nora, ten years old, is taller than most of the children in the class, and older than all the children. She repeated a grade in another school. Nora was born in the United States and has never been to Puerto Rico. She speaks English to her two older sisters and Spanish to her mother, younger brother, and two younger sisters. This pattern is typical of most of the children in the class. Only four children (three third-graders and one sixth-grader) reported speaking only Spanish to their siblings. Three others speak only English to their brothers and sisters, and the majority (22/29) reported that they speak both languaes at home:[4] They speak Spanish to

[3] The exam is a result of the Consent Decree signed by the Puerto Rican Educational Agency Aspira of New York, and the New York Board of Education in 1974. Spanish-surnamed children take the exam and those who place below the 21st percentile in English are supposed to be admitted to bilingual programs.

[4] Twenty-nine of the thirty-one children interviewed were asked this question.

those younger than they and English to the older children. Two-thirds of the mothers are Spanish monolinguals but 50 percent of the fathers speak English and Spanish.

Nora placed in the 11th percentile in Spanish and in the 8th percentile in English, but both teacher and interviewer rated her dominant in English. Nora was the only child interviewed who voiced insecurity about her linguistic ability: "Yo no hablo bueno [sic] en español o inglés" ('I don't speak good in Spanish or English') . . . "Sometimes I don't know what Mrs. G. saying [sic] in Spanish. And sometimes I don't in English." Her English shares many characteristics with black English vernacular, although she does not have English-speaking black friends. The same phenomenon has been observed in Philadelphia's Puerto Rican youth (Poplack 1977).

The children also differ in their stated language preference. Although Nora says she prefers Spanish at one point, at another she claims not to speak it to Ana "because it's too hard to speak Spanish." Ana likes both languages equally well, although she rates herself English dominant. After contradicting himself twice, Juan says he prefers English, because he wants to meet new friends and speak to his father and other members of the family in English:

I:	*¿Y qué idioma te guhta*[5] *hablar más?*	'What language do you like to speak most?'
N.	*Un poquito inglés.*	'A little English.'
I:	*Mm, ¿y por qué?*	'Mm, and why?'
J:	*Porque así puedo conocer amigos.*	'Because that way I can meet friends.'
I:	*Ah, sí, ¿y cuál idioma te guhta mejor?*	'Oh yes, and which language do you like best?'
J:	*Mejor me gusta el ehpañol . . .*	'Best I like Spanish . . .
I:	*Ajá.*	'Yes.'
J:	*Pero el máh que me guhta eh el inglés.*	'But the one I like the most is English.'
I:	*El máh que te guhta.*	'The one you like best.'
J:	*Sí.*	'Yes.'
I:	*¿Porque?*	'Why?'
J:	*Porque eh mejor. Eh máh fácil decir lah palabrah en ehpañol que en inglés.*	'Because it's better. It's easier to say the words in Spanish than in English.'
I:	*No te oigo, ¿cómo?*	'I can't hear you, what?'
J:	*Que eh mejor lah palabrah, mm, eh mejor lah palabrah decirlah en ingléh que en español.*	'That it's better the words, mm, it's better to say the words in English than in Spanish.'
I:	*¿Cómo eh mejor?*	'How is it better?'
J:	*Pueh así puedo hablar con mi*	'Well that way I can talk with

[5] Aspirated *s* at the end of syllables = h. Deletion of *s* at the end of syllables is marked by a double dagger (‡).

papá, puedo hablar con el sobrinito, puedo hablar con la sobrinita de él, puedo hablar con mi tía.	my father, I can talk with his little nephew, I can talk with his little niece, I can talk with my aunt.'

Juan's choice of English and Nora's choice of Spanish are characteristic of a general pattern. The younger children preferred English, but the majority of the sixth-graders interviewed preferred Spanish. The biggest disparity between language preference and dominance occurred in the third grade; 47 percent (9/19) rated themselves as English dominant, but 63 percent (12/19) chose English as their favorite language. (See Table 1.) The analysis of the interviews and the domino games indicates that a truly accurate description of dominance and preference must take different speech events into account.

The interviews

The interviews were conducted in both Spanish and English; the interviewer began in Spanish and then switched to English without warning. The children were asked about their personal backgrounds and favorite games and television programs, and an attempt was made to elicit a narrative in each language either about a memorable family gathering or an accident. It cannot be ascertained whether or not the children perceived the conversation as an interview. Psychologists assume that any interview in this society presupposes an "asymmetrical relationship" between the interviewer and interviewee, because the interviewer is in control of the question that the interviewee is expected to answer (Seigman and Pope 1972, p. 2; see also Matarazzo 1963; Frahm 1970; Good and Brophy 1970; and Lewis and Freedle 1972). Sociolinguistic research and accommodation theory have demonstrated that topics such as language, older and higher ranked interviewers, and the presence of a tape recorder all signal a more formal situation for adults, in which greater attention is paid to speech (Labov 1972; Giles and Powesland 1975). Irvine's (1978) suggested characteristics of formal speech were realized in the following ways in the interviews:

Increased structuring and predictability of the code, for example, phonology: presence of syllable final *s* in Puerto Rican Spanish
Adherence to co-occurrence rules, for example, absence of code-switching
Invoking of positional identities, for example, appropriate use of tú/Ud. verb forms.
Emergence of a focus on the speaker's turns and topics, for example, observance of turn-taking rules and answering the interviewer's questions

The interviews with Juan, Nora, and Ana reflect different degrees of

Table 1. *Language proficiency self-rating and preference*

	Self-rating			Preference		
	3rd grade	6th grade	Total	3rd grade	6th grade	Total
Spanish	9	5	14	6	6	12
English	9	6	15	12	4	16
Both	1	1	2	1	2	3
Total	19	12	31	19	12	31

recognition of these variables. Juan is oblivious to all of them. One indication of this is the sheer volume and naturalness of his responses. Even in the part of the English interview that he does not understand, he is eager to expand his answers. In terms of phonology, Juan, Ana, and particularly Nora, have a high degree of aspirated or zero realization of syllable final *s*, realization of which is a marker of formality (Ma and Herasimchuk 1971; Alvarez et al. 1977). The seven-year-old's interview also contained many light moments and unpredictable features, for example, lapses into babylike lisping when he could not pinpoint the day of his arrival and "Ay Dios mío" 'O my God' as a preliminary answer to a question about his birthplace. He speaks with adult intonation and gestures as well as using a child's sound effects for an airplane and a home run. The effect is a humorous one, a frequent result of the breaking of co-occurrence rules. There is little overt recognition of the difference in status between the seven-year-old and the interviewer: He addresses her as "tú" at the very beginning of the interview, ignores questions and attempts to redirect the topic on two occasions, and is the only child to reverse the roles to ask the interviewer a question. The most striking example of an unexpected response concerned the age of his brother, Ollie (O):

I:	*¿Tú tienes otro hermanito chiquito?*	'Do you have another younger brother?'
J:	*Sí.*	'Yes.'
I:	*¿Cuántos años tiene él?*	'How old is he?'
J:	*¿O – ? Yo no sé porque él salió (twice) como mi papá y yo salí como mi mamá.*	'O – ? I don't know because he came out like my father and I came out like my mother.'
I:	*Sí.*	'Yes.'
J:	*Ve, mi mamá salió blanca y yo salí blanco y mi papa salió – mm – m – trigueño y O-ito salió trigueño.*	'See, my mother came out white and I came out white and my father came out – mm – m – olive skinned and little O came out olive skinned.'

I:	*Mm.*	
J:	*Cuando él salió no tenía ni un pelito.*	'When he came out he didn't even have one little hair.'
I:	(laughing) *¿Cuántos años tiene?*	'How old is he?'
J:	*Cinco.*	'Five.'

Race seems to be an important topic to Juan, and the fact that he takes advantage of the interviews to bring it up provides evidence that "the two-person group is the most frequent interpersonal structure for the transmission of private information" (Heller 1972, p. 9). He mentions race again when he describes a family friend: "Era negro negro, no hablaba inglés, pero era negro" ('He was black black, he didn't speak English, but he was black').

Because Juan is monolingual, there are no examples of code-switching in the interview except for "miss" (discussed later), but the English portion reveals discourse tactics that the monolingual calls on to conduct a conversation in a language he does not know. The primary rule seems to be "don't answer anything unless you're very sure of getting it right," and his answers also seem to reflect several "cognitive strategies" documented for other incipient bilinguals (Wong Fillmore 1976):

1. Assume the talk is about something relevant and guess on this basis.
2. Listen for and use formulaic expressions.
3. Look for recurrent parts.
4. Generalize to other forms.

When faced with twenty questions in English, Juan did not respond verbally to six, nodded correctly to one, ignored two by responding with his own topic, gave two wrong answers in Spanish, came close with two other answers, and responded correctly to seven questions. He has apparently learned to listen for cognates and to deduce the question from the context or key words, for example, he did not respond to "dominoes" or "TV" until they were changed to "dóminoh" (Spanish pronunciation) and "TV" was switched to "television," which although it was pronounced in English sounded more like the Spanish /televiysyon/.

I:	Juan. Do you know how to play dominoes? (Juan doesn't answer) (repeat) Dóminoh (Spanish)	
J-I:	*Sí, un poquito.*	'Yes, a little.'
I:	Do you watch TV? (silence) What's your favorite TV program? (silence)	
J-I:	*Eso fue –*	'That was – (attempts to continue previous narrative)
I-J:	On the television, do you watch television? (Nod) What's your favorite TV program? Do you watch –	

J-I:	*El cinco.*	'Five.'
I-J:	Channel five? (nod)	
J-I:	*¡Espiderman!*	'Spiderman!'
I-J:	Which?	
J-I:	*Espiderman.*	'Spiderman.'
I-J:	Spiderman, yeah.	
J-I:	*Y el budi.*	'And "el budi."'
I-J:	Which is that?	
J-I:	*El que hace lulululuo, ¿sabe?*	'The one who goes looloolooloo, you know?'
I-J:	Ohh. I don't know his name.	
J-I:	*Mmm, es el pájaro loco.*	'Mmm, it's Woody Woodpecker.'
I-J:	Oh, Woody Woodpecker!	
J-I:	*Ese, y Flintstone.*	'That's the one. And Flintstone.'
I-J:	Flintstones. They're good.	
J-I:	*Hay otro mah que tiene un perro de electricidad, no ése no me guhta, me guhta el de una mujer que hace magia.*	'There's another one who has an electric dog, no I don't like that one, I like the one about a woman who does magic.'

"Baseball" was the third cognate that triggered a response. It is interesting to note that although the language of the interview switched abruptly, Juan did not react against it or request Spanish. Only one child of the thirty-one interviewed asked for the language he knew best (English). Juan accurately described what he does when somebody speaks to him in English:

> *Bueno, digo lo que sé, porque si no puedo decirlo, digo lo que sé.*
> 'Well, I say what I know, because if I can't say it, I say what I know.'

The only English word in Juan's entire interview is "miss," that is, teacher:

I:	*¿Qué eh lo que máh te guhta?*	'What do you like most?'
J:	*Lo que está dando la ma – la* miss *ahora, eso.*	'What the teach – the miss is giving now, that.'

He switches in midstream from "la ma –" (*-estra* = teacher) to "la miss" perhaps because that is how teachers are addressed in Puerto Rico, and perhaps because it is one of the few English words he is sure of. In the domino game, however, he experiments with several English sounds and words (discussed later).

As in other studies of code-switching, the children in these interviews "followed the leader" in their choice of language, that is, they responded in the language spoken to them if at all possible. Seventy-four percent (23/31) followed the switch in language during the interview, and half that number switched immediately when the interviewer did. The others followed suit two to ten questions later. Only eight children never switched: One is a monolingual English speaker and four others arrived from Puerto Rico or the Dominican Republic within the year. Of the remainder, two were English dominant and one was Spanish dominant.

Ana and Nora switched immediately, and Ana switched back and forth with the interviewer four times. In the interview, Ana would seem to be a perfect example of Weinreich's "ideal bilingual" who "switches from one language to the other according to appropriate changes in the speech situation (interlocutors, topic, etc.), but not in an unchanged speech situation, and certainly not within a single sentence" (1953, p. 73). In contrast to Juan, she also gives indications of considering the interview a formal situation, for example, higher incidence of syllable final *s*, observance of language choice and turns of the interviewer, and few co-occurrence violations. She answers with minimum responses and only expands two answers. She is soft-spoken throughout the interview except for one loud aside, "Shut up," to someone who calls her. Ana only switches out of Spanish for two noun phrases (NPs). One is a smooth code change for an unknown term. "Es mi half sister," which translates the Spanish term *media hermana*.[6] Ana hesitates before the only other loan, "Christmas." This is frequently borrowed by U.S. Puerto Ricans without hesitation, but there are three possible forms for the holiday: Navidad (Spanish), /kriyhma $\overset{\emptyset}{\text{(h)}}$/ (English loan with Puerto Rican Spanish phonology), and /krisməs/ (the English version). Ana chose the last, which required a complete change in phonology. Nora chose the same form the first time she referred to the holiday, but when the interviewer did not understand it, she switched to the second. The Spanish phonology was more consistent with the Spanish interview, and she referred to the holiday in that way for the rest of the interview, that is, three more times. Nora also borrowed /hapiy beldey/ with Spanish phonology for "birthday," as did three others; for these children the English felicitation replaces the Spanish for both the day of birth and the greeting on that day: for example, "Cuando eh Kriyhmah eh mi hapiy beldey" ('when it's Christmas, it's my birthday'). The only other English word in Nora's interview is "shelves":[7]

> *Mi †mana compró un – ¿tú sabeh esa cosa bien grande pa† poner un radio, que tiene* shelves? 'My sister bought a – you know that real big thing where you put a radio, that has shelves?'

Nora's incomplete control over Spanish is obvious in the nonstandard

[6] A Spanish-dominant sixth-grader's (twelve years old) version of the same phrase did not follow the Spanish and English word order – "Tengo tres hermanas step" ('I have three step sisters'/ *Tengo tres medias hermanas*) but broke up the expression and placed "step" in the Spanish adjectival slot.

[7] Omitted syllables or letters are marked with a dagger (†).

Table 2. *Comparison of third- and sixth-grade code-switching in interviews*

	n^a	Sentence internal (%)	Full sentence (%)	Loans (%)	N/NP (%)	English (%)	Spanish (%)
Sixth grade	56	87	11	48	45	81	19
Third grade	61	93	7	41	41	60	40

[a] Stylistic switches within the speaker's turn.

verb form *ponieron*, and her omission of an object in a relative clause: (*la*) *que tiene trece* 'the one) who is thirteen.' She also mispronounces two nouns: "altra presón" for *alta presión* 'high blood pressure,' and "prefume" for *perfume* 'perfume.' During the English part of the interview, Ana never switched to Spanish, and Nora did so only once, to describe her mother's ailment in the only term she had heard for it:

N: I went to the hospital once with my mother cause sometimes she got alta-altra-per-altra presón.
I: *¿Alta presión?* 'High blood pressure?'
N: Yeah, that's what she gots.

Nora consciously honors the language choice of the interviewer. She suppresses a Spanish term when explaining dominoes in English, which gives the impression that she does not know the formulaic expression for passing, but during the game itself she instructs the others on its use:

Interview:
I: What happens if you don't have the right domino?
N: You say – "No."
Game:
(129)[8] N-J: *Cuando tú no tienes, tú dices "paso." Dilo.* 'When you don't have you say "I pass." Say it.'

The limited use of code-switching within their turn at speaking by Nora and Ana is the pattern of most of the interviews. The largest percentage of stylistic sentence internal switches in both third- and sixth-grade interviews were loans, usually nouns and noun phrases. (See Table 2.)

Although we cannot accurately compare these figures with the code-switching recorded during classes at the children's desks because different students are involved for different periods of time, it is interesting to note that during classes there was a lower incidence of code-switching within

[8] The number in parentheses before an example refers to the line in the transcription of the domino game in the Appendix.

Table 3. *Comparison of third- and sixth-grade code-switching at desks*

	n^a	Sentence internal (%)	Full sentence (%)	Loans (%)	N/NP (%)	English (%)	Spanish (%)
Sixth grade	46	37	61	24	13	59	41
Third grade	21	43	57	24	14	42	58

[a] Stylistic switches within the speaker's turn.

the students' turn and that the majority was at sentence boundaries. The percentage of loans and N/NPs was much lower. (See Table 3.)

The higher percentage of loans and of N/NPs in the interview may be the result of the fact that the interviewer selects the topic and leads the speaker into discussions of his or her choice. In order to honor the language of the interview, the speaker must temporarily change to the other language for an unknown term. The speaker might avoid this switch for a single item in spontaneous conversation by shifting to the other language in anticipation of it, that is, at the boundary of the sentence that includes the term. Without larger samples of speech for the same speaker in different situations, we can only speculate that Nora would have chosen to say the sentence with the word "shelves" in it in English or might have continued on in English once she had switched, in a discussion with her friends.

Avoidance by bilinguals of constructions that they do not control, for example, Spanish subjunctive, has been documented by Lavandera (1978) for Cocoliche speakers. She also argues that bilinguals are uneasy in a monolingual setting in either language because they feel constrained against using their complete repertoire. If this is so, we can expect bilinguals to code-switch more with other bilinguals in situations that they do not perceive as requiring only one language, not only as an affirmation of shared identity but also because they are thereby able to express themselves more fully. Some corroboration of this occurred during fieldwork conducted by four fluent Spanish-English speakers in the Philadelphia Puerto Rican community: The only code-switching was directed to the Puerto Rican interviewers, during informal sessions (Alvarez et al. 1977). Poplack (1978) also confirms this.

The domino game

It was hypothesized that among these children, as among the Mexican-American children studied by McClure (1977), "the greatest degree of code-switching (would be) manifested in free conversation" (p. 105). Spe-

Table 4. *Speakers' language choices in domino game*

	Nora	Ana	Juan	Total
English	27	62	3	92
Spanish	69	24	73	166
Both	5	7	1	13
Total	101	93	77	271

cifically, it was necessary to compare the code-switching patterns of the same children in both formal and informal situations. The language choices and syntactic constraints produced in the interviews were contrasted with those exhibited in a domino game in which Nora, Juan, and Ana interacted. The two situations differed in at least four important ways:

1. *Physical setting*: The domino game took place outside of the classroom.
2. *Age/rank of participants*: No adults were involved.
3. *Number of participants*: The dyad was replaced by a triad.
4. *Interaction setting*: The game allowed spontaneous speech in which the children observed different conversational turn-taking rules, somewhat affected by the nature of taking turns in the game.

Analysis of the domino game provides a different picture of the communicative competence of the children from that presented in the interviews. Although the presence of the Spanish monolingual boy necessarily demanded situational switching when he was addressed directly or when an attempt was made to include him in the conversation, the code-switching that emerged is more varied and displays more of the twelve "patterns" that have been observed among fluent Chicano adults in conversations among themselves (Valdés-Fallis 1976).

Although most Puerto Rican children usually see adults (male) play dominoes in Spanish, in this domino game, as in the twelve others recorded, language choices (see Table 4) were a complex result of speaker and hearer proficiency and preference, linguistic security in the situation, knowledge of the rules of the game, history of relations between the participants, and stylistic strategies.

I have already outlined the linguistic proficiency and preference of the three children. Juan and Nora know how to play the game; Ana does not. This situation is unusual for her. In the game, she uses her knowledge of both languages to reaffirm her friendship with Nora and to maintain her distance from Juan, who made the mistake of trying to teach her how to play. Nora, for all her linguistic insecurity, is the link among the players

Table 5. *Language choices of participants to each other in domino game*

	J-A	J-N	N-J	A-J	N-G/E[a]	J-G	A-G/E	N-A	A-N	Total
English	2	0	1	8	3 (nos.)	1	8	23	46	92
Spanish	10	34	49	18	12	29	1	8	5	166
Code-switch	0	0	1	1	0	1	1	3	5	12
Total	12	34	51	27	15	31	10	34	56	270[b]

Note: J -Juan; A = Ana; N = Nora.
[a] G/E = remarks to the Group and to self (Egocentric).
[b] Plus one code-switch by N, addressee unknown = 271.

because she knows both languages *and* the game. Juan is confused about the rules throughout the game and is at a disadvantage because he is the only monolingual, but the situation prompts him to experiment with English.

As expected, both Nora and Ana usually address Juan in Spanish, but Nora is the most sensitive to his position. (See Table 5.) Nora speaks only Spanish to Juan except once when she is in the midst of counting in English, which triggers an English response to him:

(90)	N-G:	*Ana ganó.*	'Ana won.'
(91)	J-N:	*Ahora tenemos que contar to† esto. Tenemos que contar lo que tenemos juntos. Ella, porque ella fue la que ganó.*	'Now we have to count all this. We have to count what we have together. She [i.e., A gets the points], because she was the one who won.'
(92)	N-J:	I know. Two, three, four, five . . . (N counts in English)	

All of her other comments to him are in Spanish, although one contains English discourse markers, which we shall return to later.

Nora's consistent choice of Spanish for Juan reflects her acknowledgment of his handicap, underscored by the fact that he is her junior, a fact that Juan himself defers to when he suggests that she go first because she is the oldest:

(6)	N-J:	*Déjalo así. ¿Quién va primero? Tú vah primero.*	'Leave it like that. Who goes first? You go first.'
(7)	J-N:	*No porque tú eres la más grande.*	'No, because you're the biggest.'
(8)	N-J:	No, no.	

In contrast, 30 percent of Ana's comments to Juan are in English (8/27), and all but one are commands, contradictions, and insults (three were "shut up"). As the following example demonstrates, Ana's Spanish remarks to Juan, on the other hand, show concern or advice, that is, the "caretaking" function cited by McClure. This section is also an example of Ana's command of situational code-switching for addressee shift:

(275)	N-J:	No (re: domino put down by J).	
(276)	J-N:	*Sí.*	
(277)	A-N:	Yeah! He had – he could put it over here.	
(278)	J:	*Ponla aquí* (helps J place the domino).	'Put it here.'
(279)	N:	It's just that you don't wanna lose because you don't got no three or four.	
(280)	J:	*Mira, si tú tienes un cuatro ponla aquí. Ya tú fuihte. Ehte eh tuyo.*	'Look, if you have a four put it here. You went already. This is yours.'
(281)	N-A:	Oh, that's right, he was putting it over there.	

One of the only two *Ud.* forms in the interviews or games is said by Ana to communicate distance and anger.[9]

J:	*Eso era mío.*	'That was mine.'
A:	*¡O no, eso no era suyo!*	'Oh no, that wasn't yours.'

This reflection of anger is usually conveyed by the use of English. Instead of distinctions in the pronouns and verbs, Spanish serves the *tú* (solidarity) function for Ana's relation with Juan, and English serves the *Ud.* (power) function (Brown and Gilman 1972).

Ana consistently speaks either English or Spanish to Juan; the only sentence internal code-switch directed to him is the English pronunciation of a cognate (English "zero" = Spanish *cero*). For the rest of the game, however, she only uses the Spanish pronunciation of "zero" when speaking Spanish. Nor is Juan the object of sentence internal code-switching from Nora more than once. One passage includes both Ana's and Nora's only sentence internal code-switches to Juan. One may have triggered the other. In lines 55 and 57 Nora initially uses an English discourse marker, "if," but replaces it for Juan's benefit. The passage also includes one of the English statements that Ana makes to Juan, a clarification of her preceding interpretation of how one wins the game (line 54):

(48)	J-N:	*Si tú tienes – velá si yo, si hay*	'If you have – right if I, if there is

[9] The other *Ud.* form is said by Juan to Nora: "No, ¡mire!" ('No, look!') It also communicates anger.

		así así así y aquí yo pongo uno, pue‡ yo gano, tranque.[10]	one like this, like this, like this, and I put one here, well I win, stalemate.'
49)	N-J:	*No, tú no puede‡ trancar.*	'No, you can't stalemate.'
50)	J-N:	*Sí.*	'Yes.'
51)	N-J:	*No.*	'No.'
52)	A-J:	*No. Eh que si alguien tiene algo así, tú pone‡ un zero así, si no tiene na†; tú no gana‡.*	'No. It's that if somebody has something like this and you put a zero like this, if you don't have none, you don't win.'
53)	N-J:	*Tú tiene†* – (interrupted)	'You have –
54)	A-J:	You have to get NUTTING.	
55)	N-J:	If *tú no* – if *tú pierdes toíto esto entonces tú ganah.*	'If you don't – if you lose all these then you win.'
56)	J-N:	*¿Ah?*	'Huh?'
57)	N-J:	*¡Cuando tú pierde‡ toito‡ loh domino‡ tú* entonces *tú gana‡!*	'When you lose all the dominoes you *then* you win.'
58)	A-N:	Go, hurry up, go.	

The teacher rated Nora English dominant, a judgment with which we might have agreed based on the interview but one not corroborated by the domino game. One obvious explanation for the different behavior can be considered domain effect, that is, domino games are related to the home domain where Spanish predominates, and the interviews are reminiscent of school and other institutional settings where English predominates (Fishman et al. 1971). However, the girls differ in the language of their general (G) or egocentric (E) remarks, that is, those that they make to themselves or for the group's benefit. Nora's general and egocentric remarks are in Spanish except when she counts to herself, which she does in English. This probably reflects the fact that she learned to count in English. Ana's general and egocentric remarks, on the other hand, are all in English. One exception in Spanish is triggered by Juan's persistent references to "tranque," a term unknown to her:

20)	J-G:	*Voy hacer tranque.*	'I'm gonna cause a stalemate.'
21)	N-G:	*Avanza, ¿quién va?*	'Hurry up, who goes?'
22)	J-G:	*Voy a hacer tranque.*	'I'm gonna cause a stalemate.'
23)	A-E:	*¿"Tranque, tranque," queh eso? Va a †cer tranque."*	'"Tranque, tranque," what's that? He's gonna cause a stalemate.'

Whereas both girls usually speak Spanish to Juan they usually speak English to each other. Nora addresses Ana in Spanish 24 percent of the time, however, despite the fact that Ana addresses her in English 70 percent of the time and in contradiction to ther claim in the interview that she did not speak Spanish to Ana. Although the numbers are too small to be significant, they give some indication of basic differences in Nora's

[10] *Trancar*, literally 'to block' in English, and *tranque* 'stalemate,' occur when no player has a domino that can be played.

use of Spanish with Ana and Ana's use of Spanish with Juan (see Table 5). Fifty percent of the older girl's Spanish to the younger consists of turn-taking commands, for example, *tú vas* 'you go' (4/8). Although this may have been learned at home as part of the game, in these specific cases they are continuations of the language of the previous utterance(s) (122–4), or refutations of Ana's previous utterance in English (158–60):

(122)	N-J:	*Avanza.*	'Hurry up.'
(123)	J-N:	*Yo no tengo na†.*	'I don't have anything.'
(124)	N-A:	*OK, tú vas.*	'OK, you go.'
(158)	A-N:	No, wait wait, look look look.	
(159)	N-A:	*¡O sí! Ahora tú vas.*	'Oh yes! Now you go.'
(160)	A-N:	*No,* tú *vah chica, chica, chica.*	'No, *you* go girl, girl, girl.'

Another passage includes the only adjective that is switched in either the interview or the domino game (9b) and a rhymed response in Spanish to an English word (98):

(94)	N-A:	You got twenty-eight points.	
(95)	A-N:	Who?	
(96)	N-A:	*Veintidós* points.	'Twenty-two points.'
(97)	A-N:	Who?	
(98)	N-A:	*Tú.*	'You.'

In lines 158–60, Nora's Spanish highlights her negative response to Ana and that in turn triggers a rare Spanish response from Ana that repeats the language and some of the form for an emphatic refutation. Ana breaks her "speak English only to Nora" pattern a total of three times. The remaining instances are both excited affirmations that contradict Nora's previous, short remonstrations, which might be either English or Spanish in Nora's phonological system, for example, "No," "Ana." In one case (lines 239–42) Ana continues to speak in the language she had been previously speaking (to Juan), but in the other it is an emphatic contrast with her previous utterance in English (lines 137–9):

(239)	J-A:	*Eso no es mío.*	'That's not mine.'
(240)	A-J:	*Eso no es mío tampoco, es de ella.*	'That's not mine either, it's hers.'
(241)	N-A:	*¡Ana!*	
(242)	A-N:	*¡O sí! ¡Ese es el tuyo!* (laughing)	'Oh yes, that's yours!'
(137)	A-N:	You go.	
(138)	N-A:	Noo.	
(139)	A-N:	*Sí sí sí.*	

These are examples of momentary inclinations that adept code-switchers follow that defy precise classification.

Although Ana does not speak much Spanish to Nora during the game, she employs another tactic that demonstrates that she knows Nora is bilingual and that also constitutes an affirmation of her own ability to speak two languages, that is, she changes languages within her own turn at speaking five times for various purposes, for example, emphasis, via repetition: (267) "That's not mine, *eso no es*–that's not mine," and elaboration, (182) "A 'T', can't you see, *mira lo que tú hiciste, Nora*" ('look what you made, Nora'). Her control of sentence internal switches, however, falls short of adult patterns. One, (269) "This is not mine either, *eso es* ('that is') yours," is of questionable acceptability; that is, switches between predicates and possessive pronouns are not usual, but the switch serves to give greater weight to the charge. Moreover, the word "yours" is in the customary language for addressing Nora and complements the previous "mine." A pattern similar to the triggering mentioned previously is obvious in the following exchange:

89)	N-J:	*Cuatro o uno.*	'Four or one.'
90)	A-N:	He has a *cuatro*!	'He has a four!'

Ana also switches what Valdés-Fallis would call a discourse marker. In contrast to Nora's "if *tú pierdes*" (line 55), Ana's "*Es que* [unintelligible] saves everything for nothing" is much more acceptable.

Ten-year-old Nora's three-sentence internal switches are also more varied in terms of syntax and purpose than her switches in the interview. One is a repetition of a false start to Ana (21) ("you could – tú puede‡ hacer eso") that may have been switched midstream as a concession to Juan. Another violates Gumperz's universal constraint against the switching of a lone adjective, (96) "Veintidós ('twenty-two') points," although switching for lone adjectives seems characteristic of younger children's code-changing; McClure's (1977, p. 100) data include thirteen lone adjectives. Nora's third sentence internal code-switch is a noun: (181) "No puede‡ ponerlo de ese way, Ana." ('You can't put it that way, Ana.')[11] When we compare the interviews with the domino game (see Table 6), we find that whereas only English NPs were switched in the interviews, the domino game provides examples of turn internal switches into both English and Spanish for discourse markers, full sentences, and NPs. The children obviously code-switch among themselves to a greater degree and with more variety than they did in the interview.

Juan still does not know enough English to be able to code-switch effectively, but he experiments with English in the domino game with four formulaic expressions, the crucial first step in second language learning (Wong Fillmore 1976). The fact that most are directed to Ana indicates Juan's recognition of her language preference in the game setting. One occurs in anger:

92)	A-J:	You shut up.	
93)	J-A:	No shut up.	
93)	J-N:	*¿Velá que yo iba?*	'Right I was supposed to go?'

[11] Although the Spanish would be "es*a* manera," the masculine is the usual borrowed form.

Table 6. *Comparison of turn-internal switches in interview and domino game: syntax*

Speaker	Language switch	Syntactic constituent switched	Switch
Ana			
Interview	1. S–E	preposition-noun	en Christmas
	2. S–E	pronoun-noun	mi half-sister
Game	1. S–E–S	determiner-noun-adjective	(52)
	2. E–S	conjunction-indep. clause	(103)
	3. E–S	indep. clause-indep. clause	(182)
	4. E–S	determiner-noun	(190)
	5. S–E	verb + relative-subordinate clause	(206)
	6. S–E–S	sent.-noun phrase + verb-sent.	(267)
	7. E–S–E	indep. clause-noun phrase + verb-pronoun	(269)
Nora			
Interview	1. S–E	verb-noun	es Christmas
	2. S–E	pronoun-noun	mi happy beldey (birthday)
	3. S–E	verb-noun	tiene shelves
	4. E–S	noun + verb-noun	She got altra presón [sic].
Game	1. E–S	false start-sent.	(21)
	2. E–S	conjunction-pronoun	(55)
	3. S–E	adjective-noun	(96)
	4. E–S	sent.-sent.	(112)
	5. S–E–S	determiner-noun-sent.	(181)

Note: S = Spanish; E = English. Numbers in parentheses refer to line numbers in the domino game transcript in Appendix.

As Juan triumphantly puts down the winning domino to the second game, he uses an English expression that turns out to be a pun on the end of the game, probably unintentionally:

(282) A-J: You go. Who goes?
(283) J-All: Go away! (puts down winning domino)

He had obviously learned to follow the trigger provided by Ana and elaborated on it for excellent effect.

Despite the fact that their switches are functionally and formally more limited than adult varieties, all the children call on their ability to code-switch as part of their repertoire with each other. It seems plausible to postulate that the constant demand on bilinguals to switch situationally with rapidity accustoms them to producing sentences in rapid alternation and that this skill is extended and exploited for its stylistic benefits, especially if sentence internal switching is a badge of community membership that is valued, albeit covertly. The existence of covert norms that produce linguistic behavior contrary to espoused norms is not an unusual linguistic behavior (Labov 1972).

Conclusion

The complexity of code-switching patterns, purposes, and syntactic constraints is already obvious in the speech of the eight- and ten-year-old bilinguals studied, although to a lesser degree than in the speech of adults. This study reaffirms other research concerning the ability of children to switch situationally with ease, the superior power/status of English versus Spanish, and the use of stylistic or conversational code-switching for emphasis, addressee specification, elaboration, and idiomatic expressions.

The analysis of the interviews and domino games also suggests that, as expected, bilinguals beyond the six-year-old "pre-operational stage" do not "only focus on one feature or variable of a situation at a time" (Genishi 1976, p. 166) but that their language choices often reflect awareness of several social, linguistic, and situational variables. These variables take on a particular configuration in specific interactions that either encourage or hinder code-switching, particularly within the boundaries of a sentence. Child-adult dyads in question-answer interactions constrain code-switching, and informal peer interactions stimulate it.

One implication for bilingual education is that the full range of a child's linguistic ability and code-switching patterns may not be obvious or exploited in formal classroom lessons or examinations. Because the form and function of code-switching is initially learned in various home and community interactions, an ethnographic approach (Mehan 1977; Hymes 1980; Heath 1977) that links the community to the school would enable us to understand why and how a child code-switches in the classroom in different ways at different times. Where the child and the teachers are members of the same speech community, we should expect a greater degree and variety of code-switching and less miscommunication, but this is jeopardized by two important factors: The first is that the teacher has been trained by another, often conflicting set of rules for appropriate linguistic behavior, for example, teachers may have learned to be ashamed of their variety of Spanish, as many Puerto Ricans have, or may be under orders never to mix English and Spanish in the classroom, or both (La Fontaine 1975). The other problem is that the speech community is heterogeneous and teacher and child may be caught in changing values due to language and culture shift, for example, teachers who were born and educated in Puerto Rico may be teaching U.S. Puerto Ricans, or U.S.

Puerto Rican teachers may have a classroom with island-born and reared children. Other factors that can affect the code-switching patterns in the classroom have to do with the organization of the program. One bilingual school may be run by parents, and another may be completely controlled by a different group; the philosophy of either may be transitional or maintenance.

The appropriate methodology for the study of the acquisition of code-switching and its role in the communicative competence of bilingual children must seek unity between quantitative and qualitative approaches. Children with differing linguistic ability and proficiency, contact with different class and racial groupings, access to monolinguals, opportunities for travel back to the island, and so on, make it impossible to have confidence in tabulated generalities about how the Puerto Rican community code-switches. This is especially true if some understanding is sought beyond a specification of intrasentential syntactic constraints, that is, about their interpretation in communication and their reaffirmation of the community's identity. Ultimately, both ethnography and quantification can be joined together with great profit (Sankoff 1972, Lavandera 1978, Zentella 1981b). Microanalyses of particular interactions can contribute to both.

Appendix: The domino game

Note: G = general remarks; E = to self, egocentric. J-A indicates that Juan is addressing Ana; XXX = unintelligible.

(1)	I-G:	*Uds. pueden empezar a jugar.*	(putting down box of dominoes) 'You can begin to play.'
(2)	J-A:	*Hay que ponerlos así. Tiene que ser así. Y ahora coge siete cada uno.* (*Uno-siete.*)	(taking out dominoes and laying them face down) 'You have to put them this way. And now each one take seven.' (counts from one–seven)
(3)	A-J:	I know how to play. (one-seven)	(counts from one to seven)
(4)	N-G:	*¿Quién tiene doble seis?*	'Who has double six?'
(5)	J-A:	*No, no chica.*	(changing the way A put away the rest of the dominoes) 'No, no girl.'
(6)	N-J:	*Déjalo así. ¿Quién va primero? Tú vah primero.*	'Leave it like that. Who goes first. You go first.'
(7)	J-N:	*No porque tú eres la más grande.*	'No, because you're the biggest.'
(8)	N-J:	No, no.	
(9)	N-A:	You go.	
(10)	J-G:	*Yo tiro. El que tenga –*	'I throw. Whoever has –' (interrupted)
(11)	N-A:	You have two six XXX put it down here.	

2)	J-G:	*Ajá, yo voy, yo voy, espérate.*	'Yeah, I go, I go, wait.' (they play in silence)
3)	J-A:	*No así, no, tiene que ser uno que sea igual, así.*	(challenging A's domino) 'Not like that, no, it has to be one just like it, like that.'
4)	A-N:	You could do it any way, right?	
5)	N-A:	Yeah, but you have to have the number.	
6)	A-N:	mmhm I know, 1-2-5-4-6-4.	(A looks through the remaining dominoes for an appropriate one)
7)	J-N:	*Ella no puede cogerlos así.*	'She can't take them like that.'
8)	N-A:	No you can't do that.	
9)	A-N:	You already know what I got.	
0)	J-A:	*Así, mira así.*	'Like this, look like this.'
1)	N-A:	If you don't got no more, you could come here, or yeah, you could – *tú puede‡ hacer eso. Yo voy.*	'– you can do that. I go.'
2)	J-A:	*Tiene‡ que tener el mismo.*	'You have to have the same one.'
3)	A-N:	Whoever finishes XXX after me, right?	
4)	J-G:	*Yo voy, yo voy.*	'I go, I go.'
5)	N-G:	*Allí †tá.*	'There it is.'
6)	J-N:	*No, así no.*	'No, not that way.'
7)	A-G:	Man! I was gonna put my zero there.	
8)	J-G:	*Yo voy.*	'I go.'
9)	A-J:	*No, ella va.*	'No, she goes.' (A plays, J puts down a wrong domino)
0)	N-J:	*Nooo.*	'Noo.'
1)	J-N:	*Sí.*	'Yes.'
2)	N-J:	*Tiene que tener uno o doh.*	'You(it) have(has) to have one or two.'
3)	J-N:	*¿Puede ser cuatro?*	'Can it be four?'
4)	N-J:	*Uno doh o uno.*	'One two or one.'
5)	A-N:	Uh, uh, you could put it there.	
6)	J-G:	*Yo no voy.*	'I don't go.'
7)	N-A:	No. Only here or here.	
8)	A-J:	*¿Tú no tiene‡?*	'You don't have?'
9)	A-N:	You go then.	
0)	J-G:	*Yo no voy.*	'I don't go.'
1)	N-J:	*Tiene† robar. Si tú robas y tiene† –*	'You have (to) steal. If you steal and you have' – (interrupted)
2)	J-N:	*No tengo. Va ella. ¿Este?*	'I don't have. She goes. This one?' (asks if a domino is OK)
3)	N-J:	Noo.	
4)	J-N:	*Va ella.*	'She goes.'
5)	A-N:	No, you go.	
6)	J-N:	*Mira, si, si yo tiro una que no*	'Look, if, if I throw one that

		tiene na†, yo gano.	doesn't have anything, I win.'
(47)	N-J:	No!	
(48)	J-N:	*Si tú tienes – velá‡ si yo, si hay así así así y aquí yo pongo uno, pue‡ yo gano, tranque.*	'If you have – right if I, if there is one like this, like this, like this and I put one here, well I win, stalemate.'
(49)	N-J:	*No, tú no puede‡ trancar.*	'No, you can't stalemate.'
(50)	J-N:	*Sí.*	'Yes.'
(51)	N-J:	No.	
(52)	A-J:	*No. Eh que si alguien tiene algo así tú pone‡ un* zero así, si no tiene na†; tu no gana‡.	'No. It's that if somebody has something like this and you put a zero like this, if you don't have none, you don't win.'
(53)	N-J:	*Tú tiene‡ –*	'You have –' (interrupted)
(54)	A-J:	You have to get NUTTING.	
(55)	N-J:	If *tú no* – if *tú pierdeh toíto‡ esto‡ entonces tú ganah.*	'If you don't – if you lose all these then you win.'
(56)	J-N:	*¿Ah?*	'Huh?'
(57)	N-J:	*¡Cuando tú pierde‡ toíto‡ loh domino‡, tú ENTONCES tú gana‡!*	'When you lose all the dominoes, you THEN you win.'
(58)	A-N:	Go, hurry up, go.	
(59)	J-?:	No XXX.	
(60)	A-N:	I gotta good one. No I don't, I got a TERRIBLE one. Shoot. Maan.	
(61)	N-A:	You go.	
(62)	A-N:	YOU go. He wen† an† then you go an† then I go, then he –	(J. interrupts re: direction of dominoes on the table)
(63)	J-G:	*Pero tiene que seguir pa† bajo! Hombre.*	'But it has to keep going down! Man.'
(64)	J-R:	*Mira, ¿velá† que tiene que seguir pa† bajo?*	'Look, right it has to keep going down?' (J calls over to researcher)
(65)	R-J:	*Pero no cuando no se puede por el tamaño de la mesa.*	'But not when you can't because of the size of the table.'
(66)	J-R:	*¿Velá que si yo hago así y aquí donde llega y yo pongo un dómino allí, hay tranque y gano?*	'Right if I go like this and here where it reaches and I put a domino there, there's a stalemate and I win?'
(67)	N-J:	No.	
(68)	A-N:	Make it longer so you could get there fast. He took one.	
(69)	N-J:	*No, tiene† ‡tener uno o cuatro.*	'No, you have (to) have one or four.'
(70)	A&N-J:	NO!	(J. puts down the wrong domino)
(71)	N-J:	*Uno o cuatro, cuatro va allí.*	'One or four, four goes there.'
(72)	J-N:	*Pue‡ míralo.*	'Well look at it.' (puts a four down)
(73)	A-G:	so so so fo fo go Go.	(squeals nonsense syllables)
(74)	A-N:	Go.	

5)	N-A:	No I already went.	
6)	A-N:	No, that's his.	
7)	N-A:	That's mine.	
8)	A-N:	That's yours? You can't put it –	
9)	N-A:	No, no. You could put it like that.	
0)	J-N:	*Tiene que ir pa†llá.*	'It has to go that way.' (J comments on the direction of the dominoes)
1)	N-J:	NO.	
2)	J-N:	*Sí, porque ése está así tendrá que ir así pa† que siga pa†lante.*	'Yes, because that one is like that it'll have to go like that so it can go forward.' (they play in silence)
3)	J-G:	*Ayy, un seis.*	'Ohh, a six.'
4)	A-N:	Only if you don't put yours in.	(N plays and A puts down her last domino; N challenges it.)
5)	N-A:	Nooo.	
6)	A & J:	Yes/*sí sí.*	(J agrees that A is right)
7)	N-G:	*Ana ganó.*	'Ana won.'
8)	J-N:	Uh uh.	(negation)
9)	A-J:	Yes, I don't got none, I won.	
0)	N-G:	*Ana ganó.*	'Ana won.'
1)	J-N:	*Ahora tenemos que contar to† esto. Tenemos que contar lo que tenemos juntos. Ella, porque ella fue la que ganó.*	'Now we have to count all this. We have to count what we have together. She [i.e., A gets the points] because she was the one who won.'
2)	N-J:	I know. Two, three, four, five . . .	(N counts in English)
3)	J-A:	*Ahora tú tiene‡ que hacer así Ana, tú tiene‡ que hacer así.*	'Now you have to go like this Ana, you have to go like this.' (J shows her how to mix up the dominoes for the next game)
4)	N-A:	You got twenty-eight points.	
5)	A-N:	Who?	
6)	N-A:	*Veintidós* points.	'Twenty-two points.'
7)	A-N:	Who?	
8)	N-A:	*Tú.*	'You.'
9)	A-N:	XXXX so boring, God.	
0)	J-mike:	*Tú soplah allí y la agujita – yup. ¡OLA!*	'You blow there and the little needle – yup. Hi!' (talks into microphone)

Game 2

1)	A-G:	Everybody take seven. I'm first.	
2)	N-A:	*Ahora tú puede‡ tirar cualquiera.*	'Now you can throw any one.'

(103)	A-G:	I'm first because – *yo soy primera.*	'I'm first.'
(104)	J-N:	*Sí, ella es la primera.*	'Yes, she's first.'
(105)	A-G:	Now, everybody be even.	
(106)	J-G:	*†Pérate, yo tengo siete.*	'Wait, I have seven.'
(107)	A-E:	One, two, three . . .	(counts 1–9 in English)
(108)	A-N:	How many you got?	
(109)	N-E:	One, two, three . . .	(counts 1–9 in English)
(110)	J-E:	*¡¡AVE MARÍA!! ¡Qué comida yo tengo!*	'Holy Mary! (whistles) What a meal (good deal) I have.'
(111)	A-G:	Now you got six?	
(112)	N-?:	Put it over here. *Pónelo pa†llá* (sic)	'Put it over there.'
(113)	A-G:	Oh no, I'm not gonna play. This is not mines. No no nono. Here take three XXX. I got three.	
(114)	N-G:	*Yo voy.*	'I go.' (J squeals)
(115)	N-J:	*Aquí hay otro.*	'Here's another one.'
(116)	J-N:	*No, si yosé.*	'No, I know.'
(117)	A-N:	How do you know, you're not supposed to peek at his.	
(118)	N-A:	I like to play this (A: Yeah) but not with big people.	
(119)	A-N:	My father plays XXX more than ten dollars.	
(120)	N-A:	My father –	
(121)	J-N:	*Mira, te voy a cambiar uno de éstos.*	'Look, I'm going to change one of these for/on you.'
(122)	N-J:	*Avanza.*	'Hurry up.'
(123)	J-N:	*Yo no tengo na†.*	'I don't have anything.'
(124)	N-A:	*OK, tú vas.*	'OK, you go.'
(125)	J-G:	*Era mío.*	'That was mine.'
(126)	A-J:	*O no, eso no era suyo.*	'Oh no, that wasn't yours.'
(127)	J-N:	*¿Velá† que se puede cambiar?*	'Right it can be changed?'
(128)	A-N:	I put that one down there. I go.	
(129)	N-J:	*Cuando tú no tienes, tú dices "paso." Dilo.*	'When you don't have any, you say "I pass." Say it.'
(130)	J-N:	*Pasa. Yo no tengo.*	'Pass. I don't have.'
(131)	N-G:	*OK yo voy.*	'OK I go.'
(132)	A-J:	*Tú no tienes uno, o si no tienes cero.*	'You don't have one, or maybe you have a zero.'
(133)	N-A:	*No, ya él fue y dijo paso.*	'No, he already went and said I pass.'
(134)	A-J:	*Mira el otro, mira.*	'Look at the other one, look.'
(135)	J-A:	*Mira tú.*	'You look.'
(136)	N-J:	*Yo miro aquel. No, tú vas.*	'I look at that one. No, you go.'
(137)	A-N:	You go.	
(138)	N-A:	Noo.	

39)	A-N:	*Sí, sí, sí.*	'Yes, yes, yes.'
40)	A-J:	*Yo vi, yo vi. Pasa.*	'I saw, I saw. Go ahead.'
41)	A-N:	Go ahead. He's gonna win so fast. XXX play.	
42)	J-G:	*Loh moví otra vez.*	'I moved them again.'
43)	N-J:	*¿Tieneh tres allí, los tres?*	'You have three there? The three of them?'
44)	J-N:	*Deja ver. Eso es un seis. Tengo el once.*	'Let's see. That's a six. I have the eleven.'
45)	A-N:	Ey, what's that? XX The little boy wants a XX tonight, I'll take it, right girl?	
46)	N-J:	*Yo lo que tengo eh cuatro.*	'What I have is a four.'
47)	A-J:	*¿Tú pasa‡? pasa.*	'You pass? Pass.'
	A-N:	Gimme that.	
48)	N-J:	*OK, pasa.*	'OK, pass.'
49)	A-J:	*Tú lo puede‡ poner aquí.*	'You can put it here.'
50)	N:	Noo.	
51)	J:	*†pérate.*	'Wait.'
52)	A-N:	Yes, you could make a design.	
53)	J-N:	*Tú vas.*	'You go.'
54)	N-J:	*Tú pasa?*	'Do you pass?'
55)	N&A-J:	NOO.	(N and A challenge a domino J puts down)
56)	A-J:	*Pasa.*	'Pass.'
57)	N-J:	*Pasa.*	'Pass.'
58)	A-N:	No, wait wait, look look look!	(J puts down an acceptable domino)
59)	N-A:	*¡O sí! Ahora tú vas.*	'Oh yes! Now you go.'
60)	A-N:	*No,* tú *vah chica, chica, chica.*	'No, you go girl, girl, girl.'
61)	J-G:	*Yo no quiero mah na†.*	'I don't want anymore.'
62)	A-N:	I got scared.	
63)	J-G:	*Yo no quiero tanto dómino†.*	'I don't want so many dominoes.'
64)	A-J:	You have to (repeat) take this.	
65)	N-J:	*Tiene‡ que cogerlo./Tú vas.*	'You have to take it. You go.'
66)	J:	*O-O.*	Oh-oh.
67)	N-J:	*¿Tiene‡ uno o tres?*	'Do you have a one or three?'
68)	A-N:	I got five left.	
69)	J-G:	*No miren.*	'Don't look.'
70)	N-E:	One, two, three . . .	(counts to five in English)
71)	A-N:	He got a lot.	
72)	N-A:	We have no paper.	
73)	A-N:	What?	
74)	J:	*¿Ese? ¿Puede ser?*	'That one? Can it be?' (can I play it)
75)	N&A-J:	NOO, o, sí, sí/no, sí.	(first they reject J's domino, then they accept it)
76)	N:	Aha.	
77)	J:	*Yo voy.*	'I go.'

(178)	N-J:	No. Ana.	
(179)	J:	*Deja ver aquí.*	'Let's see here.'
(180)	A-G:	I go.	
(181)	N-A:	*No puede‡ ponerlo de ese* way, *Ana. Voy yo.*	'You can't put it that way, Ana. I go.'
(182)	A-N:	A 'T', can't you see, *mira lo que tú hiciste, Nora.*	'look what you made, Nora.'
(183)	J-N:	*¿Puedo tener un do‡y un cuat – y un seis?*	'Can I have a two and a fo – and a six?'
(184)	N-J:	*Mira, tiene‡ que tener uno-cuatro o uno-uno.*	'Look, you have to have one-four or one-one.'
(185)	A:	*"Uno cuatro o uno-uno."*	(mimics the above; laughter)
(186)	N-A:	I always go through things like this.	
(187)	J-G:	*¿Este?*	'This one?'
(188)	N&A-J:	NOO.	
(189)	N-J:	*¡Cuatro o uno!*	'Four or one!'
(190)	A-N:	¡He has a *cuatro*!	'He has a four!'
(191)	J-G:	*¡Sí!*	'Yes.'
(192)	A-J:	You shut up.	
(193)	J-A:	No shut up.	
	J-N:	*¿Velá que yo iba? –*	'right I was supposed to go?
	J-A:	*Mija, cuando vaya ella voy yo –*	'Dear, when she goes I go.'
(194)	A-J:	*¡Yo no soy tu mi'ja!* (HHH)	'I am not your dear!' (laughter)
(195)	J-N:	*¿Puedo tener seis y doh?*	'Can I have six and two?'
(196)	N-J:	*¿Seis?* Noo.	'Six?'
(197)	A-J:	*Doh y cero.*	'Two and zero.'
(198)	N-J:	*Sí, así, va mejor.*	'Yes, like that, it goes better.'
(199)	A-J:	*Tiene‡ que tener –*	'You have to have –'
(200)	N-A:	Your turn!	
(201)	A:	No.	
(202)	J-A:	*Sí, tú vas.*	'Yes, you go.'
(203)	N-G:	*Yo tengo doh.*	'I have two.'
(204)	J-N:	*Después tú sigues así.*	'Then you follow like this.' (refers to placement of dominoes)
(205)	N-A:	Yeah yeah that's right.	
(206)	A-N:	*Es que* XX saves everything for nothing.	'It's that XX'
(207)	J-Mike:	*¡†Tate quieto!*	'Keep still!'
(208)	A-J:	Hurry up.	
(209)	J-A:	*Joyo.*	'Hole.' (imitation of "hurry up" sounds like a Spanish obscenity)
(210)	N-G:	*¿Quién va?*	'Who goes?'
(211)	A-J:	Shaddup, wait wait wait, hol‡ it, hol‡ it.	
(212)	N-A:	*No, así no.*	'No, not like that.'
(213)	A-N:	Yeah, so you could get here.	
(214)	N-A:	Das right.	

(15)	J-E:	*¡Ave María, que tranque yo voy a hacer!*	'Holy Mary! What a stalemate I'm going to cause.'
(16)	A-N:	Oh-oh, you're not right (four times)	
(17)	A:	Ana, that don't goes there.	
(18)	J-G:	*Voy a hacer tranque.*	'I'm gonna cause a stalemate.'
(19)	A-N:	XXX together.	
(20)	J-G:	*Voy a hacer tranque.*	'I'm gonna cause a stalemate.'
(21)	N-G:	*Avanza, ¿quién va?*	'Hurry up, who goes?'
(22)	J-G:	*Voy a hacer tranque.*	'I'm gonna cause a stalemate.'
(23)	A-E:	*¿"Tranque, tranque," queh eso? Va a †cer tranque.*	'"Stalemate, stalemate," what's that ? He's gonna cause a stalemate.'
(24)	J-N:	*¿Puedo tener cuatro y cero?*	'Can I have four and zero?'
(25)	N-J:	*Dame ver.* (sic)	'Give me see.'
(26)	J-N:	*No, uh, no tú no mira‡ así. Mira, este.*	'No, uh, no, you don't look like that. Look, this one.'
(27)	N-J:	No.	
(28)	J-N:	*¡DAMELO!*	'Give it to me!' (J screams as N takes a domino)
(29)	N-J:	*No ese e‡ mío, míralo allí.*	'No, that one's mine, look at it there.'
(30)	J-N:	ooo.	(accepts that N is correct)
(31)	N-J:	*Mira, este es.*	'Look, it's this one.'
(32)	J-G:	*El que tenga un – deja ver.*	'Whoever has a – let's see.'
(33)	A-J:	*Eso no se dice.*	'You're not supposed to say that.' (reference unclear)
(34)	N:	*¡Avanza!*	'Hurry up!' (silence)
(35)	A-N:	You wanna extra one? I got four.	
(36)	N-A:	No.	
(37)	J-N:	*¿Puedo tener un dos y un treh?*	'Can I have a two and a three?'
(38)	A-J:	*¿Qué tú hiceste?*	'What did you do?' (giggles)
(39)	J-A:	*Eso no es mío.*	'That's not mine.'
(40)	A-J:	*Eso no eh mío tampoco, es de ella.*	'That's not mine either, it's hers.' (giggles)
(41)	N-A:	¡Ana!	
(42)	A-N:	*¡O sí! ¡Ese es el tuyo!*	'Oh yes, that's yours!'
(43)	N-J:	*Avanza, ¿pasa?*	'Hurry up, do you pass?'
(44)	J-N:	*¿Puede ser este?*	'Can it be this one?'
(45)	N-J:	*Sí.*	'Yes.'
(46)	A-N:	*No, tuyo.*	'No, yours.'
(47)	N-G:	*Yo voy.*	'I go.'
(48)	A-N:	O yeah, you see –	(giggles)
(49)	N-G:	*Ya yo fui.*	'I went already.'
(50)	A-N:	That's yours.	
(51)	N-A:	That's yours, Ana.	
(52)	A-N:	No that's not.	

(253)	A-J:	*Voy yo.*	'I go.'
(254)	N-A:	*Tú vah, Ana.*	'You go, Ana.'
(255)	J-N:	*¡Voy yo!*	'I go!'
(256)	N-J:	No, Ana.	
(257)	J-N:	*¡NO, mire!*	'No, look!'
(258)	N-A:	*O, Ana, no* tú *vah.*	'No, you go.'
(259)	J-N:	*No va* – (interrupted)	'No X goes –'
(260)	N-J:	XXX *yo fui.*	'XXX I went.'
(261)	J-N:	*Yo voy primero, despues tú vah y dispueh* (sic) *ella va.*	'I go first, then you go and then she goes.'
(262)	A-J:	*Y yo que* XXXX.	'And I XXX.'
(263)	J-G:	piu piu	(noises)
(264)	A-J:	You shaddup.	
(265)	J-G:	piu piu piu	
(266)	N-A:	*Tú vah, avanza.*	'You go, hurry up.'
(267)	A-J:	Wait, c'mon man. That's not mine, *eso no es* – that's not mine.	'that's not –' (N gives back the dominoes that A tried to get rid of)
(268)	J-G:	*Yo sé que* XXX.	'I know that XXX.'
(269)	A-N:	This is not mine either, *eso es* yours.	'That's yours.'
(270)	N-A:	Yes, Ana, Ana, don't cheat.	
(271)	A-N:	No because you, you're cheating too, you people didn't let me have my chance.	(laughing)
(272)	N-J:	*No, Ana va.*	'No, Ana goes.'
(273)	N-A:	Ana, you should – you letting everybody see your cards.	
(274)	A-N:	I don't care.	
(275)	N-J:	NO.	(re: domino put down by J)
(276)	J-N:	*Sí.*	'Yes.'
(277)	A-N:	Yeah! He had – he could put it over here.	
(278)	J:	*Ponla aquí.*	'Put it here.' (helps J place domino)
(279)	N:	It's just that you don't wanna lose because you don't got no three or four.	
(280)	J:	*Mira, si tú tienes un cuatro ponla aquí. Ya tú fuihte. Ehte eh tuyo.*	'Look, if you have a four put it here. You went already. This is yours.'
(281)	N-A:	Oh, that's right, he was putting it over there.	
(282)	A-N:	You go. Who goes?	
(283)	J-G:	Go away!	(J puts down winning domino)
(284)	A-J:	So you get lemmee see.	
(285)	J-A:	*Yo tenía diez.*	'I had ten.'
(286)	A-N:	How much points you got?	
	R:	*Nos tenemos que ir.*	'We have to go.'

7)	N-E:	(Twelve–twenty)	(counts in English)
8)	J-N:	*Eso es pa† mí. Si yo lo tenía ya. Yo tenía to†.*	'That's for me. I had it/them already. I had everything.'
9)	N-G:	*Mi tío juega esto, mi tío juega esto mucho, y cartas.*	'My uncle plays this, my uncle plays this a lot.' (puts dominoes in box)
0)	A:	*Juega esto, juega esto.*	'Plays this, plays this.' (mimicking)
1)	J-mike:	*¡OLA! lalalala ¡BYE! turututu*	'Hi!' (blows into mike)

References

Alvarez, Celia, Litsa Marlos, Alicia Pousada, and Ana Celia Zentella. 1977. An analysis of Spanish and English formal and informal interviews in a Philadelphia Puerto Rican neighborhood. Manuscript, University of Pennsylvania.

Blom, Jan-Petter, and John J. Gumperz. 1972. Social meaning in linguistic structures: code switching in Norway.'' In *Directions in sociolinguistics: the ethnography of communication*, ed. John J. Gumperz and Dell Hymes, pp. 407–35. New York: Holt, Rinehart and Winston.

Brown, Roger, and A. Gilman. 1972. The pronouns of power and solidarity. In *Language and social context*, ed. Pier Paolo Giglioli, pp. 252–83. Harmondsworth: Penguin Books.

Bruck, Margaret, and Jeffrey Shultz. 1977. An ethnographic analysis of the language use patterns of bilingually schooled children. *Working Papers on Bilingualism/Travaux de recherches sur le bilinguisme* 13:59–61.

Cazden, Courtney. 1977. ''You all gonna hafta listen'': peer teaching in a primary classroom. Paper presented at the Minnesota Symposium on Child Development, October 1977.

Centro de Estudios Puertorriqueños. 1976. An initial study of the language use of five Puerto Rican children in a bilingual classroom. Mimeographed. New York: City University of New York, Language Policy Task Force.

Cohen, Roberta. 1976. Language use and code switching among six Spanish speaking children. Mimeographed. Manuscript, Hampshire College.

Elías-Olivares, Lucía. 1976. Language use in a Chicano community: a sociolinguistic approach. *Working Papers in Sociolinguistics* 30. Austin: Southwest Educational Development Laboratory.

Fishman, Joshua A., Robert Cooper, Roxana Ma et al. 1971. *Bilingualism in the barrio*. Bloomington: Indiana University Press.

Frahm, J. H. 1970. Verbal-nonverbal interaction analysis: exploring a new methodology for quantifying dyadic communication systems. Ph.D. dissertation, Michigan State University.

Genishi, Celia. 1976. Rules for code-switching in young Spanish-English speakers: an exploratory study of language socialization. Ph.D. dissertation, University of California, Berkeley.

Giles, Howard, and P. F. Powesland. 1975. *Speech style and social evaluation*. New York: Academic Press.

Good, T. L., and J. E. Brophy. 1970. Teacher-child dyadic interactions: a new method of classroom observation. *Journal of School Psychology* 8:131–7.

Gumperz, John J. 1976. The sociolinguistic significance of conversational code switching. In *Papers on language and context* (Working Paper 46), pp.

1–46. Berkeley: University of California. Language Behavior Research Laboratory.

Gumperz, John J., and Eduardo Hernández-Chávez. 1975. Cognitive aspects of bilingual communication. In *El lenguaje de los Chicanos*, ed. Eduardo Hernández-Chávez, Andrew Cohen, and Anthony Beltramo, pp. 154–64. Arlington, Va.: Center for Applied Linguistics.

Haugen, Einar. 1950. *The Norwegian language in America*. Philadelphia: University of Pennsylvania Press.

Heath, Shirley. 1977. An anthropological perspective on research in education: the view from ethnography. Paper prepared for Research for Better Schools, Philadelphia, Pennsylvania, October 1977.

Heller, Kenneth, 1972. Interview structure and interview style in initial interviews. In *Studies in dyadic communication*, ed. A. Seigman and B. Pope, pp. 9–28. Elmsford, N.Y.: Pergamon.

Hymes, Dell. 1974a. *Foundations in sociolinguistics: an ethnographic approach*. Philadelphia: University of Pennsylvania Press.

1974b. Ways of speaking. In *Explorations in the ethnography of speaking*, ed. Richard Bauman and Joel Sherzer, pp. 433–53. Cambridge University Press.

1980. Ethnographic monitoring. In *Language in education: ethnolinguistic essays*, pp. 104–18. Arlington, Va.: Center for Applied Linguistics.

Irvine, Judith T. 1978. Formality and informality in speech events. *Working Papers in Sociolinguistics* 52.

Labov, William. 1972. *Sociolinguistic patterns*. Philadelphia: University of Pennsylvania Press.

La Fontaine, Hernán. 1975. Bilingual education for Puerto Ricans: ¿sí o no? Paper presented at the National Conference on the Educational Needs of the Puerto Rican in the United States, Cleveland, Ohio.

Lance, Donald M. 1972. The codes of the Spanish-English bilingual. In *The language education of minority children*, ed. Bernard Spolsky, pp. 25–37. Rowley, Mass.: Newbury House.

Lavandera, Beatriz R. 1978. Code labels for speech events among bilinguals. Paper presented at the Georgetown University Roundtable on Languages and Linguistics, Washington, D.C., March 17, 1978.

Lewis, Michael, and Roy Freedle. 1973. Mother-infant dyad: the cradle of meaning. In *Communication and affect: language and thought*, ed. P. Pliner, L. Krames, and T. Alloway, pp. 127–55. New York: Academic Press.

Ma, Roxana, and Eleanor Herasimchuk. 1971. The linguistic dimensions of a bilingual neighborhood. In *Bilingualism in the barrio*, ed. Joshua A. Fishman, Robert Cooper, Roxana Ma, et al. pp. 347–465. Bloomington: Indiana University, Research Center for the Language Sciences.

Matarazzo, J. D., et al. 1963. Interviewer influence on duration of interviewee speech. *Journal of Verbal Learning and Verbal Behavior* 1:451–58.

McClure, Erica. 1977. Aspects of code-switching in the discourse of bilingual Mexican-American children. *GURT 1977*, ed. Muriel Saville-Troike, pp. 93–115. Washington, D.C.: Georgetown University Press.

Mehan, Hugh. 1977. Ethnography. In *Bilingual education: current perspectives*. Vol. 1. *Social science*, pp. 73–89. Arlington, Va.: Center for Applied Linguistics.

Pfaff, Carol. 1975. Constraints on code switching: a quantitative study of Spanish/English. Paper presented at the Linguistic Society of American meeting, Chicago, December 1975.

Poplack, Shana. 1977. On dialect acquisition and communicative competence: the case of Puerto Rican bilinguals. *Pennsylvania Working Papers on Linguistic Change and Variation* 2, no. 1. Philadelphia: University of Pennsylvania.

1978. Quantitative analysis of a functional and formal constraint on code switching. Paper presented at the National Conference on Chicano and Latino Discourse Behavior, Educational Testing Service, Princeton, New Jersey, April 18, 1978.

Sankoff, Gillian. 1972. Language use in multilingual societies: some alternative approaches. In *Sociolinguistics*, ed. J. B. Pride and J. Holmes, pp. 35–52. Harmondsworth: Penguin Books.

Seigman, A., and B. Pope, eds. 1972. *Studies in dyadic communication*. Elmsford, N.Y.: Pergamon.

Shultz, Jeffrey. 1975. Language use in bilingual classrooms. Mimeographed. Manuscript, Harvard University, Graduate School of Education.

Timm, Lenora A. 1975. Spanish-English code switching: el porqué and how not to. *Romance Philology* 28:473–82.

Valdés-Fallis, Guadalupe. 1976. Social interaction and code switching patterns: a case study of Spanish/English alternation. In *Bilingualism in the Bicentennial and beyond*, ed. Gary Keller, Richard V. Teschner, and Silvia Viera, pp. 53–85. Jamaica, N.Y.: Bilingual Press.

Weinreich, Uriel. 1953. *Languages in contact*. New York: Linguistic Circle of New York.

Wong Fillmore, Lily. 1976. Cognitive and social strategies in second language acquisition. Ph.D. dissertation, Stanford University.

Zentella, Ana Celia. 1981a. "Tá bien, you could answer me en cualquier idioma": code switching in two New York Puerto Rican bilingual classrooms. *Latino Language and Communicative Behavior*, ed. Richard Durán, pp. 109–31. Norwood, N.J.: Ablex Publishing Corp.

1981b. "Hablamos los dos, we speak both": growing up bilingual in el barrio. Ph.D. dissertation, University of Pennsylvania.

17

The use of Spanish and English in a high school bilingual civics class

ALEXANDER SAPIENS

Introduction

For the past decade, advocates of bilingual education have been under pressure to demonstrate that bilingual education is as effective or more effective than monolingual English education. Hence, the bulk of research in bilingual education has been product-oriented. There are few studies of bilingual teaching strategies or practices conducted in the classroom; little process-oriented research in bilingual education has been done. Because of this lack, very little is known about which bilingual practices are most effective with different types of linguistic minority students.

Although several models of bilingual education programs exist, no one really knows what goes on within bilingual classrooms. Present typologies of bilingual education programs rest on a weak empirical basis (Trueba 1977). No one knows the consequences of different bilingual teaching practices. How are two languages used in a bilingual classroom? What functions does language serve in the classroom? What kinds of interaction patterns can be observed? A whole tradition of research has addressed these questions through analysis of classroom language. Such questions need to be answered if we are to train teachers effectively, in particular bilingual teachers.

This chapter analyzes teacher talk in a bilingual classroom in order to answer some of these questions. The verbal context of a bilingual classroom is examined to find systematic patterning in the teacher's oral use of Spanish and English. A combined quantitative/qualitative approach is employed in an effort to build on the strengths of both research methodologies. The basic questions asked are: How are Spanish and English used in a bilingual classroom by a bilingual teacher with students whose linguistic skills range from Spanish only to Spanish and English to English only? Does the instructor meet the instructional and social needs of all students?

Critique of classroom studies of bilingual discourse analysis

A few studies of the verbal interaction in bilingual classrooms have been conducted. These systematic observations have focused primarily upon young children and student-initiated interaction. The instruments that are used to record and analyze classroom behavior determine the verbal patterns that will be captured and later analyzed. The categories of the instruments are easy to distinguish and reflect aspects of classroom interaction that relate to the teaching behaviors under study. Such pedagogical behaviors are based on theoretical constructs and not necessarily upon the actual teaching observed (Townsend 1976). Can these previous studies of bilingual interaction adequately capture the key elements of discourse analysis in a secondary bilingual classroom?

Studies of bilingual classrooms have been summarized in Table 1. Note that all have been done at preschool or early elementary grade levels. Most of the studies looked at both teacher and student talk. The student-oriented studies were limited to preselected individuals and did not include the entire class. For other studies on bilingual children where the focus was not on the classroom, see Carrasco (1979), Carrasco, Vera, and Cazden (in press), Genishi (1976), and Zentella (1978). Only Phillips and the three Shultz studies looked at code-switching. Few studies considered the use of different varieties of the same language. The three Shultz studies were the only analyses based on actual classroom language. The other studies were based on codings rather than recordings and transcriptions of the language. All the studies noted the social context in which the data were collected, yet little or no data were provided to check the interpretations of the researcher. For most of the studies, there is no way to check the validity or reliability of the researcher's coding or data gathering. For the most part, these last two issues were not discussed in great detail. Most of the investigators addressed some qualitative questions that go beyond dealing only with observable data. The Phillips and the three Shultz studies addressed sociolinguistic aspects of language use. Background information on the students and teachers in terms of academic and linguistic experience was varied. It is evident from this survey of bilingual classroom studies that the underlying assumptions of the particular approach determined not only what was actually analyzed, but in large part, the type of conclusions drawn from the data.

The Rodríguez-Brown et al. (1976) study examined three bilingual first-grade children in a bilingual and regular classroom setting three times during the school year. They examined code-switching, the time devoted to each language, and the functions employed by each language. They also compared peer interaction in the bilingual and English-language classrooms. What is unique about this study is the different analyses conducted by different pairs of researchers on the same subjects. The principal finding was that different settings resulted in distinct language patterns.

Table 1. *Analysis of bilingual classroom studies*

	Rodríguez-Brown, Bruck, Walcer, and Shultz (1976)	Shultz (1975)	Bruck and Shultz (1977)	Phillips (1975)	Legaretta (1977)	Townsend[a] (1976)	Townsend and Zamora (1975)
1. Grade level	1	K-2	1	K-3	K	N/A	Preschool
2. Study focus	Ss	Ss, Tchrs	Ss	Ss, Tchrs	Ss, tchrs, aides	Tchr	Tchrs, aides
3. Analysis of code-switching	Yes	Yes	No	Yes	No	No	No
4. Analysis of language varieties of Spanish and English	No	Yes (only Spanish)	No	No	No	No	No
5. Analysis based on classroom language	Yes	Yes	Yes	No	No	No	No
6. Data collection	Videotape	Audiotape	Videotape	On-site coding	On-site coding	On-site coding	On-site coding
7. Social context	Yes	Yes	Yes	Yes	Yes	Yes	Yes
8. Presentation of data permits reanalysis	No	Some	Some	No	No	No	No
9. Qualitative questions addressed	Yes	Yes	Yes	Yes	Yes	No	No
10. Sociolinguistic issues considered	Yes	Yes	Yes	Yes	No	No	No
11. Background notes	Yes	Yes	Yes	Yes	No	No	No

Note: K = kindergarten; N/A = not applicable; Ss = students; Tchr(s) = teacher(s)

[a] Townsend (1976) is not actually a research study, but it does provide a procedure for studying bilingual classroom interaction.

Although changes in language use were attributed to differences in setting, divergent language behaviors could have been the result of different teachers, peers, and/or topics. Although the investigators tried to address developmental aspects of language use over time, the differences in classroom activities, subject matter, and participants precluded accurate interpretation of the data.

Shultz (1975) studied the bilingual verbal interaction of students in a combined first- and second-grade classroom. His primary concern was the use of code-switching by children: Under what conditions and in what contexts are the two languages used? Code-switching was viewed in terms of the alternate use of two languages by one person. This severely limited the scope and usefulness of the study by not including switches in language between speakers. Only code-switching between students was examined because the investigator discounted all teacher-initiated exchanges on the assumption that "the child was usually not in a position to choose which language he was to use" (Shultz 1975, p. 6). The students demonstrated the concept of language appropriateness by their conscious choice of Spanish and English based on setting, topic, and person.

In a subsequent analysis of teacher talk, Shultz found that the teachers spoke standard Spanish rather than vernacular Spanish. In other words, they did not try to reduce the mismatch between the language of the school and the language of the child. This language strategy had the effect of subordinating the child's language while at the same time not providing a strong communicative link to the school. By presenting the lessons in English, the teachers gave the students the impression that English was the more useful language. This was evidenced in the students' more frequent use of English despite their Spanish dominance.

The Bruck and Shultz (1977) study of language-use patterns in two first-grade bilingual classrooms employed an ethnographic approach to the study of bilingual classroom interaction through the use of videotape. Although such an approach can accurately record verbal interaction, the videotape equipment can affect the conversation that occurs "under the lights." The time, training, and money needed to operate videotape equipment places it out of the reach of most researchers. This approach permits reexmination of actual language data, whereas most studies only refer to the coding categories employed. This longitudinal study compared the language use of two students with different teachers. Although the researchers examined the student-teacher interaction of both students, they ignored the influence of other students. The role and status of Spanish and English in the community was assessed but not in terms of the varieties of Spanish and English used. Differential use of distinct varieties, as well as community attitudes toward their use, influence when, where, and with whom these language varieties are used.

Phillips (1975) examined code-switching in eight bilingual education classrooms, kindergarten through third grade. The study was restricted to the Spanish and English language-development lessons. Data collection was limited to instances of code-switching which were coded on site. Unfortunately, the language proficiency of the students was based upon self-assessment, which is very unreliable with young children. She also failed to note the direction of the switches. The most significant finding was the high use of code-switching during the Spanish lessons and lack thereof during the English lessons. This is indicative of a language shift toward English. Code-switching by the teacher did not stimulate a similar response in students.

Legarreta (1977) looked at five bilingual kindergarten classrooms, comparing the concurrent translation model with the alternate days model, in which she did a quantitative study of the functional use of Spanish and English. She tried to demonstrate that the concurrent translation model did not achieve balanced use of Spanish and English whereas the alternate days model did. Close examination of the data did not substantiate this dichotomy. The students spoke very little in comparison with the teachers. English was definitely favored over Spanish. Anglo English-speaking children in the classrooms, who spoke little if any Spanish, were not included in the data collected. Although this would have skewed her results even more toward English language use, by not including these children, a more accurate assessment of the verbal interaction that occurred in these classrooms could not be and was not made. This study was quantitative in nature. Student language proficiency was ignored, which limited the usefulness of this study. Language dominance and proficiency influences language-use patterns (Valdés-Fallis, 1976). By not looking at language and cultural background, all the Spanish-speaking students were treated as belonging to the same ethnic group. Hispanics comprise many nationalities and ethnic groups. This is especially true in the San Francisco Bay area, where this particular study was conducted. This factor could lead to misinterpretation of the data.

Townsend (1976) developed an instrument for the purpose of analyzing bilingual classroom interaction called SCIMP (System for Coding Interaction with Multiple Phases). SCIMP consists of five instruments with four overlays. The challenge posed by SCIMP is to learn the different categories of each instrument as well as those of each overlay and to be able to record the observed verbal behaviors observed in the classroom. Although this was developed for on-site analysis, it could be employed more effectively if used with a videotape. SCIMP is basically a Flanders-type system. Overlay A, used for bilingual interaction, can account for the amount of Spanish and English spoken but not for the different functions served by each language, nor can it adequately deal with code-switching.

Townsend and Zamora (1975) studied the verbal (Townsend) and nonverbal (Zamora) interaction patterns that occur between preschool children and teachers/teacher aides. Their purpose was to look at and compare the linguistic behaviors of the bilingual teachers and the bilingual teacher aides with their students. Townsend and Zamora found significant differences between teacher-student and teacher aide-student verbal and nonverbal interaction. Nonverbal behavior is important in contextualizing verbal interaction.

Setting of present study

The high school in which the classroom observation took place was located in a predominantly minority residential neighborhood of San Jose, California. The ethnic composition of the school was approximately 50 percent Hispanic, 35 percent Anglo, 10 percent black, and 5 percent Asian. The Hispanics were very diverse in origin and primarily included Chicanos (native-born of Mexican origin) and Mexicans.

The teacher, a Chicano, was fluent in Spanish and English. Equally expressive in both languages, a formal classroom register was rarely used in Spanish. This was not surprising because most bilinguals do not possess the same registers (situationally specific speech) nor the same number of registers in both languages. In their study of a Puerto Rican community in New York City, Ma and Herasimchuk (1971, p. 355) found that bilinguals who

> use Spanish more frequently over a wider range of social interactions . . . reflect this fact linguistically by having more varieties of Spanish than in English. Similarly, the reverse should hold for speakers who are closer on the bilingualism scale to English usage and dominance.

A distinction should be made between a trained bilingual teacher and a teacher who is bilingual. Although this teacher was bilingual, formal training, including in-service workshops on bilingual education, had been in English. Considered a bilingual teacher, he possessed neither a bilingual specialist credential nor a bilingual certificate of competence. Neither is required in California bilingual education programs at the secondary level.

The rapport that the teacher had developed with his students was exceptional. There were no evident discipline problems or personality conflicts. Communication between teacher and students flowed easily and naturally. Everyone appeared to be cheerful and interested. The teacher used a great deal of humor in controlling and directing the classroom discussion. Constantly moving from side to side and back and forth, he lectured from notes placed on a metal music stand. The teacher employed a technique of scanning the classroom from left to right, right to left, not unlike an oscillating fan, thereby engaging the entire class. No one escaped his perpetually moving gaze.

The classroom was set up in rows, aligned obliquely. Almost everyone directly faced the teacher as he moved within the imaginary boundaries of an invisible triangle formed by the blackboard, the music stand (with

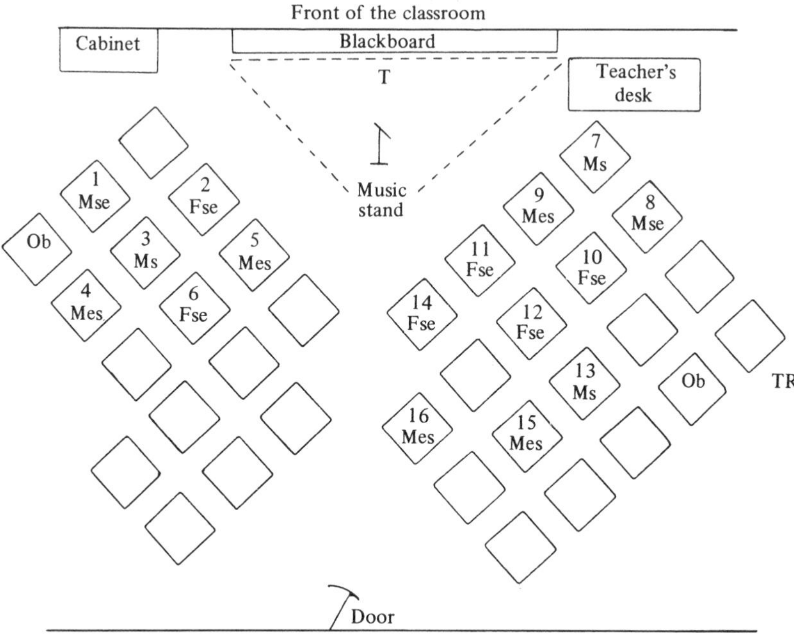

Figure 1. Classroom setting

lecture notes), and his desk. The students were evenly dispersed throughout by language and sex. An earlier classroom arrangement with all the English-dominant speakers on one side and all the Spanish-dominant speakers on the other side appeared to aggravate antagonisms that developed between both groups. The present seating pattern reduced many of the classroom control problems encountered earlier.

The students in this bilingual civics class were all high school seniors. All Hispanic, they were culturally and linguistically diverse. All were either Spanish monoliguals or bilinguals. Approximately one-third were English-dominant bilinguals, some with limited proficiency in Spanish. Approximately one-third were Spanish monolinguals. Six of the students were classified as limited English speaking or non-English speaking by the school. No assessment was made of the students' competence in Spanish. The teacher always addressed the students in their dominant language. The use of names by the teacher was also an indicator of language dominance: "Frank" was invariably an English-dominant speaker, whereas "Francisco" was a Spanish-dominant speaker. (See Table 2.)

Their receptive competence (listening and understanding) exceeded their productive competence (speaking). The following exchange is illustrative of this phenomenon.

Table 2. *Student profiles*

Student	Nationality or ethnicity	Sex	Years in U.S.A.[a]	Language dominance: As rated by the teacher	Language dominance: As rated by the school
1	Mexican	Male	6	Spanish–English	Bilingual
2	Mexican	Female	6	Spanish–English	Limited English speaking
3	Mexican	Male	.5	Spanish	Limited English speaking
4	Chicano	Male	—	English-Spanish	Bilingual
5	Chicano	Male	—	English-Spanish	Bilingual
6	Mexican	Female	6	Spanish-English	Bilingual
7	Mexican	Male	1	Spanish	Limited English speaking
8	Mexican	Male	3	Spanish-English	Non-English speaking
9	Chicano	Male	—	English-Spanish	Bilingual
10	Mexican	Female	6	Spanish-English	Bilingual
11	Mexican	Female	4	Spanish-English	Limited English speaking
12	Puerto Rican	Female	—	Spanish–English	Bilingual
13	Salvadoran	Male	1.5	Spanish	Non-English speaking
14	Mexican	Female	4	Spanish-English	Bilingual
15	Chicano	Male	—	English–Spanish	Bilingual
16	Chicano	Male	—	English–Spanish	Bilingual

[a] Dashes mean U.S.–born.

Teacher: *Cuatro . . . ¿serían quién? ¿María? Digo, en tu vista, ¿No?*
María: (Silence. Blushes)
Larry: The people who make up all this . . . (inaudible)

Although Larry understood Spanish, he felt much more at ease speaking in English.

The students were given the regular government textbook printed in English. The instructor did use some bilingual dittos to present material. However, because of the limited English skills of the majority of the class and the advanced reading level of the text, few reading assignments were ever given. Reading assignments were limited to specific lessons. Most of the course content was conveyed by means of class lectures and not through reading. The students were encouraged to take notes during the lectures.

The teacher was unique in his attitude toward code-switching. His principal concern was transmission of knowledge, regardless of the mode of transmission. Because of the diverse language skills of the students, the instructor had to use both languages alternately. Literal translations were rare. Most repetitions in the other language were limited to occasional words or idiomatic expressions.

Collecting the data

The fifty-minute class was tape-recorded with a Panasonic RQ-323S portable tape recorder with a built-in microphone. Inconspicuous placement of the tape recorder at the back of the room resulted in a clear recording of the teacher. However, some of the student talk was inaudible.

The two observers, each seated in the back of a row on the sides of the classroom, took field notes during the entire class. These notes enabled them to include nonverbal actions in the transcription of the recording. The observers tried to maintain a low profile and remain as unobtrusive as possible in order that the lesson be taught in a natural fashion.

Prior to the lesson, an interview permitted the observers to know what subject matter was to be presented. The teacher's attitude and views relevant to language use, subject matter, and teaching style were solicited. The teacher noted that more English than Spanish was spoken in the classroom. He considered his class unconventional in the sense that he presented the content in terms of the students' experience. His goal was to relate events in the past to the present, to the "here and now." In doing so, he "spoke at their level."

A series of interviews was conducted with the classroom teacher, the school ESEA (Elementary and Secondary Education Act) Title I coordinator, and the bilingual school counselor prior to and subsequent to the classroom observation. These interviews were the source of much of the demographic data collected.

Quantitative analysis of classroom language

One way of comparing the status of Spanish and English in a bilingual classroom is to determine the amount of time allocated to each. This is but one dimension of language use, and it indicates only how much each language is used. It is not the amount of time that determines the status of the two languages but, rather, the functional allocations assigned to each language. Many studies have looked at how much each language is spoken in order to establish linguistic parity. The common belief is that if the time or content is presented equally in Spanish and English, then parity will be achieved. Many bilingual education programs with professed goals of language maintenance try to establish such a balance in the use of the two languages based upon the number of courses taught in Spanish and English.

Table 3. *Language use in classroom*

	Teacher		Students		Class	
Language	Time	% of total time	Time	% of total time	Time	% of total time
Spanish	17′ 50″	79	4′ 40″	21	22′ 30″	100
English	22′ 10″	81	5′ 20″	19	27′ 30″	100
Total time	40′	80	10′	20	50′	100

Note: ′ = minutes; ″ = seconds

The first part of this analysis deals with the actual amount of Spanish and English spoken during the lesson, estimated in minutes and seconds. The teacher spoke 80 percent of the time, which is not unusual in a lecture course. (See Table 3.) This makes the students, especially those who have limited access to reading materials, more dependent upon the teacher for course content. If the students are speaking only 20 percent of the time, is the teacher getting enough feedback from the students? What effect does this teaching strategy have upon student learning? Although the teacher elicited responses from nearly every student, one-third of the class accounted for most of the student talk. The teacher viewed himself as the sole purveyor of knowledge. The students were viewed as empty vessels lacking the knowledge dispensed by the instructor.

The teacher spoke Spanish 45 percent of the time and English 55 percent of the time, as did the students. At first glance, the lesson was taught about equally in both languages. Note that the teacher and students spoke almost the same amount of Spanish and English even though two-thirds of the class was composed of Spanish-dominant speakers. English was clearly treated as the more advantageous and more commonly spoken language, a sociolinguistic fact that holds in the school as well as in the community. Or did the greater use of English merely reflect student response to teacher elicitation? In order to answer this question, verbal exchanges were examined in terms of who initiated an exchange and in which language. The analysis of exchanges was limited solely to the interaction between the teacher and the students and did not include student-student interaction.

The classroom language was analyzed in terms of teacher-student verbal exchanges. Verbal exchanges are utterances from two or more speakers directed at one another in temporal and contextual juxtaposition. An utterance is everything said by one speaker before another speaks. Teacher-student exchanges were analyzed in terms of language and interlocutors. The data in Table 4 supported the assumption that the speakers responded in the same language in which they were addressed. The

Table 4. *Verbal exchanges*

Language	Teacher-initiated exchanges		Student-initiated exchanges		Total exchanges	
	No.	%	No.	%	No.	%
Spanish–Spanish exchanges	35	92	3	8	38	100
Spanish–English exchanges	3	75	1	25	4	100
Total Spanish-initiated exchanges	38	90	4	10	42	100
English–English exchanges	32	80	8	20	40	100
English–Spanish exchanges	6	86	1	14	7	100
Total English-initiated exchanges	38	81	9	19	47	100
Total exchanges	76	85	13	15	89	100

teacher responded in the same language in which he was addressed 85 percent of the time and the students did so 88 percent of the time.

Eight-five percent of the verbal exchanges were initiated by the teacher, indicating that he controlled the flow of discourse in this classroom. The analysis of verbal exchanges corroborated the earlier analysis, which found that the teacher spoke more than 80 percent of the time and that each language was used about half the time. The teacher elicited responses from the students equally in Spanish and English.

What is more significant with regard to the students' English language development is that 70 percent of the student-initiated verbal exchanges were initiated in English. More than twice as many elicitations were made by the students in English than in Spanish. The differential language use of Spanish and English by the students seems to indicate that English is more useful than Spanish in the classroom. Although this was not explicitly communicated to the students, they still got the message. "Speakers have asymmetrical linguistic systems: they can perceive and understand linguistic distinctions which they do not (or cannot) themselves make" (Stubbs 1976, p. 31). The more frequent use of English is further evidence that the students comprehend much more English than they can speak.

Qualitative analysis of classroom language

The most salient language patterning found in this classroom was code-switching. Code-switching is the alternate use of two languages in which one language is interspersed in the context of the other without phonological or morphological modification. Code-switching "can be characterized by the following features: (1) Each switch into Spanish or English consists of *unchanged Spanish or English words*, and (2) these words are pronounced by the speaker *as a native speaker of that language would pronounce them*" (Valdés-Fallis 1978, p. 2). This definition of code-switching refers to intrapersonal code-switching, that which occurs within a single speaker's utterance. It was actually the more common type of code-switching found in the data. This type of code-switching has been the subject of most studies concerning code-switching and bilingualism.

In California, the English monolingual and Spanish monolingual speech communities are linked by Spanish-English bilinguals. Hispanics have been undergoing a rapid intra- and trans-generational language shift to English. The prevalent use of code-switching among bilinguals is characteristic of language contact and language shift.

Herein lies the problem for educators. How does one teach children whose linguistic repertoires include both languages and whose linguistic range is restricted in both because of the differences in the functional roles played by both languages? The resolution of this problem necessitates an understanding of what code-switching is, how different types of code-switching are societally motivated, and what functions code-switching may serve.

Several investigators have studied the social aspects of code-switching. Most adult code-switching is not motivated by lack of the appropriate term in one language (Lance 1975). Topic, setting, and interlocutors may influence the alternate use of languages (Blom and Gumperz 1972). Code-switching is further influenced by the roles played by the languages as well as by the status of the speakers within the speech community. Code-switching may be employed for stylistic purposes or for solidarity (Gumperz and Hernández-Chávez 1972). Code-switching is not a haphazard mixing of two codes but follows certain patterns that most bilinguals find intuitively acceptable. It is governed by grammatical rules. Code-switching is utilized by bilinguals for specific functions such as to convey meaning. It serves little purpose in communication with monolinguals. The use of code-switching is normally restricted to ingroup or "we" communication.

The teacher accounted for all of the intrapersonal code-switching, that which occurred within an utterance, which confirmed that switching languages was a strategy employed to provide the students with equal access to information. No student code-switched with the teacher. The students, by limiting their responses to one language, had not demonstrated sufficient solidarity with the teacher to code-switch with him. The difference in role relationships served to maintain distance between the teacher and students. This was corroborated by work on pronouns of power and solidarity, which accounted for nonreciprocal patterns of address in terms of higher status or greater power (the teacher) may use the T-form of address with a lower-status person (the student), but the student must use the V-form of address when speaking to the teacher. In this situation, the T-form of address is code-switching, whereas the V-form is the use of one language. Had solidarity been established, both teacher and student would have code-switched. The bilingual students refrained from code-switching with the teacher, indicating that solidarity was not established even though an appearance of solidarity prevailed. The nonreciprocal role relationships between teacher and students were maintained by the students' not accepting the teacher as a peer or an equal even though he tried to present himself as one.

Code-switching has been viewed by many educators as indicative of a poor command of both languages. This simply was not the case in this study. Contrary to popular belief, the use of code-switching as a mode of communication requires a good command of the grammatical systems of both languages (Aguirre 1977). When questioned, many students responded that they did indeed code-switch among themselves.

One of the motivating reasons for using both languages as media of instruction was to maintain the use of Spanish. Interpersonal or conversational code-switching was examined to determine whether both languages were maintained equally by the students. Conversational code-switching is the juxtaposition of two languages in a verbal exchange (Gumperz 1976). Whereas most definitions of code-switching are limited to one speaker, conversational code-switching captures shifts in language between speakers. It also incorporates utterances that may be greater or less than a sentence. This broader definition permits analysis of more data. (See Table 5.)

Conversational code-switching occurred only 12 percent of the time. The teacher or student almost always responded in the language in which addressed. This was especially true for the teacher. The students switched from English to Spanish twice as often as from Spanish to English. The direction of the switching reflected the linguistic composition of the class, which included mostly Spanish-dominant speakers. They were able to express their views and support their arguments in their stronger language. This language alternation demonstrated that the Spanish-dominant students understood far more English than they actually spoke. Conversely, the English-dominant bilinguals understood more Spanish than they spoke.

Although code-switching conveys information about roles and role relationships and indicates a language shift in a language contact situation, it reveals little about the content conveyed by each language. What functions did each language serve? Did the teacher's bilingual teaching strategy include full development of each language across the full range of classroom functions? Consistent failure to use one of the languages for major classroom functions should result in a restricted range of usage.

Table 5. *Interpersonal conversational code-switching*

	Teacher-initiated exchanges		Student-initiated exchanges		Total exchanges	
	No.	%	No.	%	No.	%
Common-language exchanges	67	86	11	14	78	100
Mixed-language exchanges	9	82	2	8	11	100
Total exchanges	76	85	13	15	89	100

The principal methodological problem was to discover the set of categories that would provide the most meaningful basis for comparison of the functions for which the two languages were being utilized. Several coding systems were considered, but none seemed to capture the meaningful distinctions that could lead to a cross-language comparison of functions. After examining the data several times, the analysis of language use in instruction, classroom control, and social relations was pursued. Each category was divided into topically related moves. The instructional category included key concepts and expansion. Key concepts refer to informatives that express one of the basic concepts presented in the lesson: political groups, hierarchy of political power, and modes of political power change. Expansions refer to elicitations, informatives, and responses. Teacher informatives include explanations, examples, interpretations, and translations. Teacher elicitations refer to substantive or content questions. Teacher evaluations or responses involve repeating, correcting, or confirming student responses. The category of control includes discipline and procedural language. Discipline consists of directives, commands, and requests used to control student behavior or to maintain order. Procedural language refers to directives that structure student activity related to the progress of the lesson, such as taking notes, requesting papers, and assigning homework. The social category includes personal and noninstructional talk. Social language includes all teacher elicitations, informatives, and evaluations not categorized as instructional or control. This category consists primarily of humor, praise, ritual, and personal nonacademic topics. Ritual refers to such words or utterances as "huh," "so," "OK," and "all right." Noninstructional talk refers to any verbal interaction that is not related to the lesson or instruction at hand and that does not apply to the other categories.

The three categories refer to the instructional or topical intent of discourse moves. Exchanges and utterances are composed of moves. Moves are basic discourse units of analysis based on language function rather than language form. The structure of classroom dialogue can be examined in terms of moves in order to determine *what is done* with language as opposed to *what is said*. The moves used in this study are informatives, elicitations, evaluations, and directives. Informatives provide information; elicitations evoke verbal responses; evaluations appraise student responses; and directives request verbal or nonverbal responses. Because of the exploratory nature of this study, the analysis of language use examined the communicative aspects of the moves (instruction, control, and social) but not their discourse function (informative, elicitation, evaluation, and directive).

The analysis of Spanish and English language use was limited to teacher talk. Instruction accounted for about 60 percent of the moves, whereas control accounted for only 10 percent of the moves. Social language, which was used equally in Spanish and English, accounted for approximately 30 percent of the teacher talk. English was the preferred language in all three categories. In this lesson, English was overwhelmingly selected as the language of instruction and classroom control. Based on the teacher's bilingual teaching strategy, English is functionally the more important language. (See Table 6.)

If transmission of knowledge is the instructor's principal concern, more time or talk should have been focused on instruction and less on the social uses of language. English was used to convey key concepts twice as often as Spanish. The basic concepts, the glue that binds the facts, opinions, and interpretations into a meaningful entity, should have been presented in the dominant language of the students and elaborated in their weaker language, not the reverse, as was the case in this lesson. The Spanish-dominant students could have missed the point of the lesson. The preferred strategy would have been to present the new information in Spanish and to integrate it into the students' existing knowledge through Spanish and English and vice versa for the English speakers.

Analyses of classroom interaction incur an obligation to link such descriptions to pedagogical issues. This analysis of the concurrent method of bilingual instruction at the secondary level puts forth an integrated quantitative and qualitative approach to the study of bilingual classroom interaction. The use of two languages enables the researcher to examine more clearly communicative strategies with regard to transmission of knowledge and language maintenance. Although validity and reliability of the categories described and used were not discussed, part of the coded transcription has been included in the Appendix.

Mehan (1979) proposed that the structure of a lesson had a sequential organization of three stages: an opening phase, an instructional phase, and a closing phase. Excerpts from each phase of this lesson were included in the Appendix. Like the Mehan study, the language strategies employed by the teacher in each phase were distinct. The opening and closing phases were characterized by directives (control and social), whereas the instructional phase was characterized by informatives, elicitations, and

Table 6. *Communicative aspects of teacher language*

Use of language	Spanish No. of moves	Spanish % of moves	English No. of moves	English % of moves	Total No. of moves	Total % of moves
Instruction						
Key concepts	15	2	15	4		
Expansion	130	21	196	31		
Total	145	23	219	35	364	58
Control						
Discipline	1	0	3	0		
Procedural	14	2	48	8		
Total	15	2	51	8	66	10
Social						
Personal	70	11	79	13		
Noninstructional	22	4	28	4		
Total	92	15	107	17	199	32
Total	252	40	377	60	629	100

evaluations (instruction and social). The differences in language function reflect the different purposes or objectives of each phase.

Conclusion

Many bilingual teachers are daily confronted with a linguistically heterogeneous classroom. How does the teacher convey the content, develop and validate the students' language, and maintain a disciplined, yet viable learning environment? The teacher in this study employed the concurrent method by continually code-switching in an effort to communicate equally in both languages.

A quantitative analysis of language use revealed that although both languages were spoken nearly the same amount of time, English was favored over Spanish. The functional analysis of language use showed that English was particularly favored over Spanish for instruction and classroom control. The hidden message of the lesson was that English was the more advantageous language. This was borne out by student mixed-language response, in which English was favored over Spanish.

Although the strategy of code-switching helped motivate the students and maintain rapport with them, it did not serve as a good language model in either Spanish or English. The linguistic repertoires of the students were not developed equally in both languages because English was clearly favored in instruction, classroom control, and solidarity. From a quantitative and qualitative perspective, it was apparent that the students' language skills were shifting from Spanish to English and that Spanish was not being maintained in the classroom. Although there was an appearance of learning in both languages, complete presentation of the key concepts and their relationship to student experience was provided primarily in English even though most of the students were Spanish dominant. The teacher met with partial success in the goals of language maintenance and transmission of knowledge.

The teacher controlled the talk in the classroom. He determined when and what was said to whom. Since the teacher accounted for 80 percent of the talk, the main communicative role of the students was to listen. To provide access to knowledge and to establish solidarity with the students, the teacher had to code-switch. The students did not code-switch, although several did outside of class. Interlocutors almost always responded in the same language in which they were addressed. The nonreciprocal pattern of address employed by the students revealed that the social distance between the teacher and students was not significantly reduced.

If transmission of knowledge is the primary goal, code-switching can be a viable approach in a linguistically diverse class. If language maintenance is a primary goal, perhaps an alternate periods model would be more effective because code-switching is symptomatic of language shift. Bilingual teachers must become more conscious of their language-use patterns and the effect of their communicative strategies.

Appendix: excerpts from the transcription of the lesson with coding

Key:

	Exchange		*Move*
T–S	Teacher–student exchange	Ik	Instruction – key concept
S–S	Student–student exchange	Ie	Instruction – expansion
Eng–Eng	English–English exchange	Cd	Control – discipline
Eng–Span	English–Spanish exchange	Cp	Control – procedural
Span–Span	Spanish–Spanish exchange	Sp	Social – personal
]	Exchange	Sn	Social – noninstructional
}	Part of exchange omitted	*	Student response not coded

Tape recorder counter	*Interlocutors*	*Discourse*	*Exchange*	*Move*
		OPENING PHASE of the lesson		
1	Teacher	I want you guys to take that out and hand it up to the front and hand it up this way . . .		Cp–Eng
		OK? (referring to homework assignment)	T–S Eng–Eng	Sp–Eng
	Student 1	Hope we did good! Hope I aced it!		*
	Student 2	You better believe it!	S–S Eng–Eng	*
	Student 1	Hey, I was working hard, *ese*. (inaudible)		*
	Student 3	*Todavía me falta.*		*
14	Teacher	(Raps on the music stand that holds lecture notes) The next thing that I would like you to do . . .		Cp–Eng

Tape recorder counter	Interlocutors	Discourse	Exchange	Move
		Would you please take out a sheet of paper for		Cp–Eng
		some notes?	T–S	
			Eng–Eng	
	Student	Aw, man! It's Tuesday! (emphatic)		*
			S–T	
	Teacher	*Vámonos, luego, luego. De cuete.*	Eng–Span	Cd–Span
		I hope everyone had a good three-day weekend,		Sp–Eng
		'course, yesterday, I gave everyone the day off.		Sp–Eng
		INSTRUCTIONAL PHASE of the lesson		
71	Teacher	Joe. Who should have the political power?		Ie–Eng
		Who should have the ultimate concentrated political		Ie–Eng
		power?	T–S	
			Eng–Eng	
		Who should be the boss? (emphatic)		Ie–Eng
75	Joe	(Inaudible)		*
76	Teacher	The people! huh! The people.		Ie–Eng, Ik–Eng
		Nice (writing on the blackboard).		Sp–Eng
		Now if we shoot it down from the people, Joe . . .	T–S	Sp–Eng
			Eng–Eng	
		Who else should . . . who would be second in command		Ie–Eng
		to the people as far as political power or relegated		
		authority . . . (inaudible) . . . people.		
79	Joe	Elected . . . Elected individuals . . . elected . . .		*
		people . . . individuals elected by the people.		*
80	Teacher	OK? So . . .		Ie–Eng, Sp–Eng
		Sería gente elegida, ¿no?		Ik–span
		(Writes on the blackboard) . . . *elegida* . . . All right . . .		Sp–Eng, Ik–Eng
		So . . . First you have the people,		

		Luego tenemos a la gente elegida que tienen el poder . . . por tal de que la gente le ha dado el poder político a ésos, a esa gente que han elegido ellos. Sus representantes . . . , gobernales.		Ik–Span
		After those elected individuals, who should have political power? (door slams)		Ie–Eng
		So we're saying . . . Number one.		Ie–Eng
		And these guys are number two. And number three . . .		Ie–Eng, Ie–Eng
		¿Quién sería terceros?	T–S Span–Span	Ie–Span
	Student	(Inaudible)		*
88	Teacher	Huh? Who should be the third ones? Huh?	T–S Span–Span	Sp–Eng, Ie–Eng, Sp–Eng
		Francisco. ¿Quién, pues quién?		Ie–Span
89	Francisco	*Los grupos.*		*
	Teacher	*Los grupos. Como ¿quién?* (door slams)	T–S Span–Span	Ie–Span, Ie–Span
	Francisco	*Como los cantantes.* (Francisco laughs)		*
90	Teacher	*No. No son los Solitarios, no los Bellos, ni los Babys, ni los grupos de* soccer.		Sp–Span
		¿Grupos como quién?		Ie–Span
92	Francisco	*Los que son elegidos para la . .* (inaudible) (laughter)	T–S Span–Span	*
93	Teacher	*Grupos representantes*		Ie–Span
		¿Qué bueno es decir eso? *¿No? O sea que . . .*		Sp–Span, Sp–Span
		Representative groups. (Writes on the blackboard) OK!		Ik–Eng, Sp–Eng
		So these guys are three. You know . . .		Ie–Eng, Sp–Eng
		The three guys that we had.		Ie–Eng
96		*Serían los terceros . . . en esta escalera de poder político*, OK?		Ik–Span Sp–Eng

Tape recorder counter	*Interlocutors*	*Discourse*	*Exchange*	*Move*
98		*Cuatro, ¿serían quién? ¿María? Digo en tu vista, ¿No?*	T–S	Ie–Span, Sp–Span
			Span–Eng	
	María	(Silence. Blushes)		*
	Larry	The people who make up all this . . . (inaudible)		*
100	Teacher	Ideally, we started out . . .		Ie–Eng
		empezamos con la gente, ¿verdad? Y entonces de la gente		Ik–Span
		nos estamos yendo a los . . . a la gente que nosotros		Ik–Span
		elegimos que le damos ese poder que nos representen.		
		Y luego, nos vamos con los grupos que esta gente elegida		Ik–Span
		construye para poder dirigir este poder político . . . ¿No?		
103		And then . . . who should be the fourth guys under here?		Sp–Eng, Ie–Eng
		Yeah, Joe?	T–S	
			Eng–Eng	Ie–Eng
104	Joe	The people . . . that are . . . elected by the representative groups, I guess.		*
105	Teacher	The speakers for these groups.	T–S	Ie–Eng
			Eng–Eng	
	Joe	The speakers for the groups.		*
106	Teacher	Fine, ummmmm (clears throat)		Sp–Eng
		The speakers . . . (writes on the blackboard)		Ie–Eng
		O los representantes de ese grupo . . . , quien hablan		Ik–Span
		por el grupo. ¿No? Porque no es bueno de tener un grupo		Ie–Span
		de cien personas y que todos hablen al mismo tiempo.		
		Tiene que haber . . . tener un representante.		Ik–Span

		Does this represent . . .		Ie–Eng
		Why not? Why are you saying no?	T–S	Ie–Eng
			Eng–Eng	
137	Joe	Because this is . . . because that . . . oh, there are		*
		kings and stuff. And that's one individual. (inaudible)		*
140	Teacher	(inaudible) kings, queens . . .		Ie–Eng
		¿Tenemos reyes todavía? ¿Hay reinas? Digo,		Ie–Span, Ie–Span
		aparte de tu novia? (laughter)	T–S	Sp–Span
			Span–Eng	
		¿Hay reinas?		Ie–Span
143	Rafael	Queen Elizabeth.		*
	Teacher	Queen Elizabeth.		Ie–Eng
			T–S	
	Rafael	*Hay la reina de Inglaterra.* (inaudible)	Eng–Span	*
	Teacher	OK. *Inglaterra.* OK. Now.		Ie–Eng, Ie–Span
				Sp–Eng
145		Probably today you can argue and say, Wow, she doesn't		Ie–Eng
		even have no political power!		
		That's true!		Ie–Eng
203		*A través de la historia . . .*		Ie–Span
		Through our history . . .		Ie–Eng
		A mí se me hace que hay dos modos . . . ¿no? de que		Ik–Span
		puede pasar el poder político cambie manos		
210		or the changing of the guard. *¿No?*		Ie–Eng, Sp–Span
		(Writes on the blackboard)		
		. . . of the guard, that's another expression, *¿No?*		Sp–Eng, Sp–Span
		O sea cuando el poder político va a cambiar manos.		Ie–Span
213		Let's take two.		Ie–Eng
234		I think this is what has happened throughout history is		Ie–Eng
		political power.		
		But then soft modes and hard modes have taken political		Ik–Eng
		power away from the people.		

Tape recorder counter	*Interlocutors*	*Discourse*	*Exchange*	*Move*
		Now, how do you take power away from a person?		Ie–Eng
		Like, let's say that I was a king		Ie–Eng
236		*y ahorita estamos en Inglaterra en los 1700s, 1600s,*		Ie–Span
		1400s, y quería yo . . . ¿Cómo les diré? . . .		Ie–Span
		más o menos convencerlos a ustedes, Raquel, que ustedes deberían de darme a mí un poder político para yo gobernarlos a ustedes para que ustedes no tengan tanta apuración y viven muy bien y yo me encargo de estos problemas políticos, económicos y sociales también.		Ie–span
		So! *¿Cómo varían en . . .*		Sp–Eng, Ie–Span
		¿Qué cosas haría yo para convencerte de que es para tu beneficio que tu mereces . . . para darme tu poder		Ie–Span
		político? ¿Qué haría yo?	T–S	Ie–Span
			Span–Span	
246	Raquel	*Este . . .*		*
	Teacher	One, one, go!		Sp–Eng
			T–S	
	Raquel	*Este, mejores situaciones económicas que le daba.*	Eng–Span	*
		Más alimentos que tenían antes . . . o mejor viviendas.		*
250	Teacher	OK. *Yo les daría a ustedes más alimentos y mejores*		Ie–Eng, Ie–Span
		viviendas, ¿Verdad?		Sp–Span
		So what would we call it in English? What would we say		Ie–Eng, Ie–Eng
		then? Social conditions . . .		Ie–Eng
		o condición social. ¿No?		Ie–Span, Sp–Span
		OK. Social condition. (Writes on the blackboard)		Sp–Eng, Ie–Eng
			T–S	
333	Student	*Paternalismo.* (laughter)	Span–Span	*
	Teacher	*¡Soy su padre! ¡Los cuido!* (laughter)		Sp–Span
		Y de eso sale otras variedades de paternalismo y eso . . .		Ik–Span

		tenemos para explicar . . .	
		The idea of being a father figure to all of the people	Ie–Eng
		in the country . . . *Paternalismo.*	Ik–Span
		Porfirio Díaz, en serio . . . ese hombre estaba allá casi,	Ie–Span
		como les diré, ya al último, ya estaba loco de pensar quien	
		era el padre de todos los mejicanos; cuidaba a sus hijos,	
		eran sus hijos y sus hijas . . .	
		pués eran sus hijas . . . (laughter)	Sp–Span
		Andaba haciendo y deshaciendo con el mejicano que le	Ie–Span
		daba la gana.	
		But he really felt, *Rafael.* He really felt that	Ie–Eng
346		he was a father figure in *Méjico.*	
365		(Role playing a peasant with hat in hand) *No pués,*	Sp–Span
		fíjese patrón que . . . , (laughter) *El señor Díaz*	Sp–Span
		es nuestro padre . . . así nos ha dicho . . .	
		And then, *y luego que hacemos . . .*	Sp–Eng, Sp–Span
		That's soft mode. Are there any other ways to convince	Ik–Eng, Ie–Eng
		people to give you power willingly?	
		And then, you gain it?	Ie–Eng
		How did Richard Nixon do it?	Ie–Eng
		Was he . . . he did it in a soft mode, didn't he?	Ie–Eng
		I don't think he did it in a hard mode because hard mode,	Ie–Eng
		you know where that's coming from . . . like take out the	
		guns!	
Side two		CLOSING PHASE of the lesson	
203	Teacher	OK, so listen.	Cd–Eng
		Tomorrow what I wanna do the second part of this.	Cp–Eng
		Listen, everybody.	Cd–Eng
		I want both, about five examples on each one.	Cp–Eng

Tape recorder counter	*Interlocutors*	*Discourse*	*Exchange*	*Move*
		We're gonna have five examples that . . .		Cp–Eng
		In fact, why don't you guys do that tonight?		Cp–Eng
			T–S	
207	Student	Nooo.	Eng-Eng	*
208	Teacher	You guys do that tonight.		Cp–Eng
		I'll relax tonight.		Sp–Eng
		You guys come tomorrow prepared with five examples of soft mode of . . . ah . . . conditions or, . . . ah . . . examples of a soft mode way of gaining political controls taken away from the people.		Cp–Eng

References

Aguirre, Adalberto, Jr. 1977. Acceptability judgment of grammatical and ungrammatical forms of intrasentential code alternation. Ph.D. dissertation, Stanford University.

Blom, Jan-Petter, and John J. Gumperz. 1972. Social meaning in linguistic structures: code-switching in Norway. In *Directions in Sociolinguistics*, ed. J. J. Gumperz and Dell Hymes, pp. 407–34. New York: Holt, Rinehart and Winston.

Brown, Roger, and Albert Gilman. 1970. The pronouns of power and solidarity. In *Psycholinguistics*, ed. R. Brown, pp. 302–35. New York: Free Press.

Bruck, Margaret, and Jeffrey Shultz. 1977. An ethnographic analysis of the language use patterns of bilingually schooled children. *Working Papers on Bilingualism* 13:59–91.

Carrasco, Robert L. 1979. Expanded awareness of student performance: a case study in applied ethnographic monitoring in a bilingual classroom. *Working Papers in Sociolinguistics* 60:1–49.

Carrasco, Robert L., Arthur Vera, and Courtney B. Cazden. In press. Aspects of bilingual student's communicative competence in the classroom: a case study. In *Latino language and communicative behavior*. Vol. 4. *Discourse processes: advances in research and theory*. Norwood, N.J.: Ablex Publishing Corp.

Genishi, Celia S. 1976. Rules for code-switching in young Spanish-English speakers: an exploratory study of language socialization. Ph.D. dissertation, University of California, Berkeley.

Gumperz, John J. 1976. The sociolinguistic significance of conversational code-switching. *Working Papers of the Language Behavior Research Laboratory* 46:1–46.

Gumperz, John J., and Eduardo Hernández-Chávez. 1972. Bilingualism, bidialectalism, and classroom interaction. In *Functions of language in the classroom*, ed. C. B. Cazden, V. P. John, and D. Hymes, pp. 84–108. New York: Teachers College Press.

Lance, Donald M. 1975. Spanish-English code-switching. In *El lenguaje de los Chicanos*, ed. E. Hernández-Chávez, A. D. Cohen, and A. F. Beltramo, pp. 138–53. Arlington, Va.: Center for Applied Linguistics.

Legarreta, Dorothy. 1977. Language choice in bilingual classrooms. *TESOL Quarterly* 11:9–16.

Ma, Roxana, and Eleanor Herasimchuk. 1971. The linguistic dimensions of a bilingual neighborhood. In *Bilingualism in the barrio*, ed. J. A. Fishman, R. L. Cooper, R. Ma, et al. pp. 347–464. Bloomington, Ind.: Indiana University, Research Center for the Language Sciences.

Mehan, Hugh. 1979. *Learning lessons*. Cambridge, Mass.: Harvard University Press.

Phillips, Jean M. 1975. Code-switching in bilingual classrooms. Master's thesis, California State University, Northridge.

Rodríguez-Brown, Flora V., Margaret Bruck, Carol S. Walcer, and Jeffrey Shultz. 1976. Language interaction in a bilingual classroom: an observational study. Paper presented at the Sixtieth Annual Meeting of the American Educational Research Association, San Francisco, April 1976.

Shultz, Jeffrey. 1975. Language use in bilingual classrooms. Paper presented at the annual meeting of Teachers of English to Speakers of Other Languages, Los Angeles, March 1975.

Stubbs, Michael. 1976. *Language, schools and classrooms*. London: Methuen.

Townsend, Darryl R. 1976. Bilingual interaction analysis: the development and status. In *The bilingual child*, ed. A. Simões, Jr., pp. 189–226. New York: Academic Press.

Townsend, Darryl R., and Gloria L. Zamora. 1975. Differing interaction patterns in bilingual classrooms. *Contemporary Education* 46:196–202.

Trueba, Henry T. 1977. Ethnographic research in bilingual education. Paper presented at the National Policy Conference on Bilingualism in Higher Education, San Francisco, February 1977.

Valdés-Fallis, Guadalupe. 1976. Social interaction and code-switching patterns: a case study of Spanish/English alternation. In *Bilingualism in the bicentennial and beyond*, ed. G. D. Keller, R. V. Teschner, and S. Viera, pp. 53–85. Jamaica, N.Y.: Bilingual Press.

1978. *Code switching and the classroom teacher*. Arlington, Va.: Center for Applied Linguistics.

Zentella, Ana C. 1978. Code switching and interactions among Puerto Rican children. *Working Papers in Sociolinguistics* 50:1–34.

18

Marble terminology in a bilingual South Texas community: a sociolinguistic perspective on language change

JOSÉ L. GALVÁN

The language of children's games is of interest to linguists from a variety of perspectives. For instance, it is claimed that the child's acquisition of language is the very mechanism of language change (Bar-Adon 1971, King 1969). Children's games provide ample data with which to trace such development (see, for example, Bar-Adon 1971). Language change in turn governs the formation and spread of dialects. Games seem to follow dissemination patterns much like those of language change phenomena (Sutton-Smith 1972, Stone 1971, Ariès 1962). Related to these questions is the inquiry into language maintenance in multilingual societies (see Haugen 1973). Although less is known about the nature of bilingualism or about how to deal with degrees of bilingualism than one would want, still it is relevant to investigate bilingual communities for such things as attitudes toward languages, monolingualism, and bilingualism and incidence of bilingualism in adults versus children. The language of children's games would seem less likely to show effects of influence from printed materials, the media, or school authority figures than other linguistic domains; thus it provides an interesting potential base from which to begin searching out answers to some of these questions.

The present study grew out of a previous attempt to describe the Mexican-American marble folkgame milieu (for the folkloric analysis, see Galván 1974). One of the major conclusions of the folkloric study concerned a highly pronounced trend from Spanish to English noted in the language of marble games in a bilingual community of South Texas. The present chapter considers those data from a sociolinguistic framework and supplements them with additional data aimed at verifying aspects of it.

The writer is indebted to Gary N. Underwood and Américo Paredes for their helpful comments and suggestions on earlier versions of this paper. Of course, they are not responsible for the contents.

Description of data

The data collection for this study was begun in the spring of 1974 in two South Texas communities and continued in the fall of 1974 in one of them.[1] Because the continuation study was conducted in order to verify the generality of specific findings from the original study, the results will be presented in that order.

Informants for the original study were drawn from two distinct neighborhoods in City I and represented at least two generations.[2] Two boys, aged nine and eleven, and a forty-four-year-old adult male, all from Neighborhood A, and two boys, aged nine, both from Neighborhood B, were interviewed in City I. The adult, who provided by far the most complete data, reported on games that he knew during 1935–45 when he was between five and fifteen years old. In addition, one twelve-year-old boy was interviewed in City II. (Henceforth, reference to the cities and neighborhoods will be in the form of IA, IB, and II, for City I-Neighborhood A, City I-Neighborhood B, and City II, respectively.) The youngsters were each interviewed immediately after school during the afternnon in a play setting located in their respective neighborhoods. The youngsters from IA were tape-recorded. The adult was interviewed in his home. All are Mexican-Americans and bilinguals.

The continuation study is based on random samples of the entire fifth- and sixth-grade populations in City I. Sixty fifth-graders and fifty-four sixth-graders were interviewed individually by means of a questionnaire based on the findings of the original study. The interviews were brief, no more than five minutes each, and were conducted at school either during physical education period or (in the case of fifteen sixth-graders) in a school corridor during regular academic periods. Tables 1 and 2 present summary information about the two samples, which were chosen on the basis of a table of random numbers.

Some limitations can be cited for the data. Sutton-Smith and Rosenberg (1972) are critical of historical comparative analyses of children's games that involve reminiscence data. The adult informant, of course, reported what he remembered from his childhood. A related objection is that the youngsters in both studies were queried out of the season for marbles in their locale. However, despite these difficulties with the data, there is reason to pursue the analysis. Most significantly, the comparative analysis shows gross differences between sets of data that are not likely the product of chance. As for the Sutton-Smith and Rosenberg objection to reminis-

[1] The writer appreciates the help of Amparo Galván Cárdenas, Pauline Downing, Gilberto Narro García, George Morley, Rudy Reyes, Tony N. Rico, and Sylvia Cantú Salinas in locating the informants for this study.

[2] Bar-Adon (1971) defines a child generation as a school year or a play season, as opposed to the traditional view of generation as a 20- to 30-year span. Viewed in these terms, there are of course more than two generations represented here.

Table 1. *Characteristics of random samples, fifth and sixth grades*

	Fifth grade				Sixth grade			
	Total population	Sample population	% of total	% of sample	Total population	Sample population	% of total	% of sample
Totals	606	60	9.9		587	54	9.2	
Males	318	32	52.5	53.3	302	28	51.4	51.9
Females	288	28	47.5	46.7	285	26	48.6	48.1
Spanish speakers	490[a]	56	88.9	93.3	460[a]	47	87.5	87
Non-Spanish speakers	61[a]	4	11.1	6.7	66[a]	7	12.5	13
Bilinguals		56[b]		93.3		45		83.3

[a] These figures are from a government report prepared in September 1974 and thus reflect a different total population.
[b] This number includes one Italian-English bilingual. All others are Spanish-English bilinguals.

Table 2. *Distribution of sample by age*

Grade and age	Males	Females	Total
Fifth grade			
9	1	0	1
10	14	11	25
11	17	15	32
12	0	1	1
13	0	1	1
Sixth grade			
10	1	1	2
11	14	14	28
12	9	8	17
13	4	3	7

cence data, two answers can be posited. Within limits, the language of games seems to linger into adulthood. Sutton-Smith and Rosenberg's concern with such data is understandable, given the extensive collections of children's games now readily available. It could be argued that these collections may possibly influence a person's memories. Nevertheless, until very recently there was no such collection devoted exclusively to marble lore. Ferretti (1973) describes the New York marble milieu in a paperback volume written for the general reader, but his data are taken strictly from monolingual English speakers. Several key examples can be cited in comparing the New York and South Texas data to argue against the probability of direct influence.[3] Also, it will become clear when the present data are described that the adult informant in this study provides a remarkably complete set of information.[4] Significantly, it is entirely in Spanish. The second answer to the Sutton-Smith and Rosenberg criticism is a practical one. No descriptive account of marble playing in South Texas from an earlier period is available; hence it is more economical to use reminiscence data. To be sure, the comparative analysis presented here should be verified, in time, by revisiting City I and obtaining subsequent samples.

Initial study

Ten marble games were described by the original six informants. One of these ten games actually covers five reported variants that, when ana-

[3] For example, ringer, or ring taw, is one of the more popular games played in New York, yet neither the terms nor the game was seen in South Texas. Also, Ferretti describes several sidewalk and indoor marble games. These were not seen either.

[4] During the interview, he stopped at one point to search for a particular marble that he described in detail as he remembered it. After going through several hundreds of marbles that he kept in a cloth sack, he produced the very marble he had described.

Table 3. *Marble games distribution by neighborhood*

1935–45 IA (adults)	1974 IA (children)	IB	II
1. *la chuza*	*la lechuza, el pocito*	*el pocito*	*el pocito*
2. *el tirito*	*el tirito*	*el tirito*	*el tirito*
3. —	—	—	*bombas*
4. *el soldadito*	—	—	—
5. *el sense*	—	—	—
6. *el ahogado*	*el* triangle, *el blanquillo, el pescado*	*el* triangle, *la* $rueda_2$	*la* $rueda_1$
7. —	*el codo*	—	—
8. —	—	*el posito linea*	—
9. *las nacas*	—	—	—
10. —	—	*los cinco positos*	—

lyzed, are clearly the same type. Another is known to different players by different names, but because there is no difference in the playing scenario or the rules and skills involved it is treated as one game. Table 3 summarizes the game names presented. Notice that the order in which the various games are described is retained in the tables for ease of reference in the text. The descriptions of the games are followed by a brief discussion of the marble names elicited from the same informants. These data are summarized in Table 4. The last part of the data presentation for the original study is a collection of miscellaneous terms and expressions heard in connection with marble play.

Marble games

1. *La chuza, la lechuza, el pocito.* This game is played by two players. The challenger begins the play by stating the stakes in terms of an arbitrary number of marbles. If the challenged player accepts the challenge, he hands over the specified number of marbles. The challenger matches that number from his store of marbles and, placing all of the marbles in his cupped hand, drops them into a circular hole in the ground. The winner is determined by the numbers of marbles landing in and out of the hole. Evens (*pares*) win for the challenger, odds (*nones*) for the challenged. When the players put up only one marble apiece, the challenger's marble alone must land in the hole in order for him to win.

This game was known by all of the informants interviewed initially but by different names. The adult knew it only by the name *la chuza,* which translates in Velázquez, Gray, and Iribas (1967) as "a stroke in the game of pigeon-holes knocking all at once with one ball" and in Williams (1968)

Table 4. *Names of marbles by neighborhood*

1935–45 IA (adult)	1974 IA (children)	IB	II
AGUE[a]	*CANICA*[a]	*CANICA*[a]	*CANICA*[a]
canica	—	—	—
ague$_1$[b]	cat-eye	cat-eye	cat-eye
puro	crystal	judies[c]	regular, clear one
plomo	steely	—	—
ague$_2$[b]	—	—	tiger
ague$_3$[b]	—	—	beauty
pelotón	*canicón*	*canicón*	*canicón*

[a] Generic term used to refer to all marbles regardless of type.
[b] To the adult informant, this is one and the same category.
[c] Only the plural form was elicited.

as "strike (in bowling)." The youngsters from IA knew this game as either *la lechuza* 'the owl' or *el pocito* 'the small hole.' All the others called it only *el pocito.*

Play is begun with the challenger stating his challenge in the form of *Échame x* 'Give me x,' where *x* represents the number of marbles to be wagered.

2. *El tirito.* This game, which was known to all informants by the same name, meaning 'the shooter,' (the marble used in shooting), also involves two participants. The challenger begins play by shooting his marble and challenging the other player to follow. The challenge is usually in the form of *Te juego al tirito. Andale, ya tiré.* 'I'll play you a game of *el tirito.* Come on, I've already shot.' The second player accepts the challenge by shooting toward the challenger's marble, attempting to hit it.

3. *Bombas.* Known only to the informant from II, this game is identical to *el tirito* except that the shooting is done from the air. *Bombas* translates simply as 'bombs.'

4. *El soldadito.* This game, known only to the adult informant, is played by two players as well. The name translates as 'the young soldier.' Two parallel lines are drawn on the ground, each player assuming control of one of them. Each player then places five marbles on his line, the object being to hit the other player's marbles while shooting from the "home" line. Order of play is determined by a procedure known as *a la raya* 'to the line,' in which both players shoot or toss a marble toward one line from the same distance. The one whose marble lands closest to the line is first to shoot.

5. *El sense.* Two or more players can participate in this game, which

is played with an oblong and a line etched into the ground. As with *el soldadito,* there is no usual distance between the oblong and the line; the distance, which affects the difficulty of play, is agreed upon by the players prior to the beginning of play. The procedure of *a la raya* determines the order of play, which begins after each participant places an equal number of marbles (the ante) on the outline of the oblong. The object is twofold: to capture as many marbles from the oblong as possible and to hit an opponent's shooter. The marbles are captured by hitting them with the shooter, but any player whose shooter is hit by another player's shooter is immediately out of the game. In addition, a player is given an extra shot if (1) he shoots his shooter into the oblong, or (2) he shoots his shooter back across the line. A player can thus land his first shot inside the oblong, and, if his shooting skill is well developed, he can continue capturing marbles as long as his shooter remains inside the outline. Play cannot be terminated, however, until only one shooter (i.e., one player) remains in play. Therefore, at least one marble must be left on (or in) the oblong until all but one player have been removed from the game.

This game was known only to the adult informant, who said that it was considered the hardest game, one that favored the accurate shooter. Whoever reigned as the current champion of *el sense* held title to the best shooter designation as well.

6. *El ahogado*. The term *el ahogado* 'the drowned one' is used here to refer to five variants of the same game. As in *el sense,* the game is played with a connected geometrical shape and a straight line and involves two or more players. The five variations differ for the most part in the geometrical shape used. The adult informant, whose game involves a triangle and a line, is the only one who calls it *el ahogado*. This same game was known to the players from IA and IB as *el* triangle. The IA players in addition played *el blanquillo* 'the egg' and *el pescado* 'the fish' with identical sets of rules. The shapes here are, of course, an oval and a fish (an oval with a triangle for a tail). The IB players did not know these two but did play a variant they called *la rueda* 'the circle.' This variation was played with two circles, one within the other in target fashion, and a line. The II player reported knowing *la rueda,* but his version used only one circle. For clarity, the II version will be *la* $rueda_1$ and the IB version *la* $rueda_2$.

The game follows the general pattern of *el sense* in that each player contributes a specified number of marbles that are then placed on the outer outline of the connected figure (in *la* $rueda_2$ it is the outer circle). *A la raya* again determines the order of play, and the players shoot from the line toward the geometrical figure with the object of getting as many marbles as possible out of the figure. However, *el ahogado* gets its name from the verb *ahogarse* 'to drown oneself,' which is the term for having a marble left inside the outline, and this is the principal difference from *el sense*. When a shooter is left inside, whether by oneself or by an opponent's shot, that marble becomes part of the ante. That player then takes his turn when it comes up again, with a new shooter, from the line. In *la rueda*$_2$, it is the inner circle that one must avoid. Unlike *el sense,* there are no free shots in *el ahogado.*

7. *El codo.* This game might be considered a sixth variant of *el ahogado* because the rules for play are identical to it. However, it is treated here as a separate game because the shooting skill involved differs significantly. *El codo,* which translates as 'the elbow,' probably gets its name from the fact that the players shoot from the air but with their elbow touching ground. It involves a hole like that used in *la chuza* and a line. The ante is placed in the hole, the order of play determined *a la raya,* and the rules of play are those described for *el ahogado.* The difference, of course, is that the player must shoot strongly enough to bounce a marble out of the hole. This game was reported only by the IA informants.

8. *El pocito línea.* Two or more players can participate in this game, which means the 'small-hole/line.' As the name implies, one circular hole and a straight line define the playing area. Again, the order of play is determined by *a la raya.* The players then shoot toward the hole from the line. If a player is successful in sinking his marble, he moves his marble to wherever another player's marble might be and attempts to shoot the opponent's marble into the hole, at which point he would win that marble. If he is unsuccessful in sinking his opponent's marble, he must wait his turn and attempt to get his marble in the hole once more before he can try again to sink his opponent's marble. Another way to win this game is to hit the opponent's marble back across the line. This game was reported only by the IB players.

9. *Las nacas.* The playing area for this game includes a row of five circular holes parallel to a straight line. The name *las nacas* appears to be a colloquialism that is used to refer to a slap on the arm made with the extended third and fourth fingers. A good *nacas* (the informant reports that only a plural form is possible) is one that makes a loud slap sound, thus the two fingers are usually wet before striking. As one would expect, the winner of the game earns the right to give *las nacas* to the rest of the players, hence the name.

The game is played by each player shooting in turn (order by *a la raya*) from the line toward the first hole. The holes are numbered from left to right as one faces them from the line. When a player sinks his marble, he is entitled to move his marble out of the hole a distance of one outstretched hand and attempts to sink the next hole in the row. Once he reaches the fifth hole, the player proceeds back, in order, toward the first hole. Whoever completes the cycle first wins the game and gives *las nacas* to the rest. This was the only game reported in which marbles are not won or lost. It was known only to the adult informant.

10. *Los cinco pocitos.* This game, which translates as 'the five small holes,' was reported only by the players of IB. It is played with five

circular holes and a line. However, the holes are arranged with four holes to form a square and the fifth in the center. They are numbered counterclockwise beginning with the righthand hole closest to the line. The center hole, of course, is the fifth hole, and it is the crucial one because it can give a player *la ponzoña* 'the poison' with which he can capture his opponents' marbles. After establishing the order by *a la raya,* the players begin the game by attempting to sink the five holes in sequence, using the procedure outlined for *las nacas*. That is, if a marble is successfully sunk, its owner is entitled to shoot toward the next hole from a hand's length out of the made hole. Once a player makes the fifth hole, in sequence, he is the possessor of *la ponzoña* and begins trying to hit his opponents' marbles. Again, each time he is successful, he earns a free shot as well as the marble he has hit. Unlike *las nacas,* though, a player whose marble lands in a hole out of sequence is out of the game (but he keeps his marble).

Marble names

Seven distinct marble types were identified, although no single group of informants reported all types. In fact, even when more than one group identified a single type, they never agreed entirely on the appropriate name. There were two cases in which all of the contemporary players (the children in this study) agreed on a name, but in both cases the adult informant's name differed. Even in the generic label for marbles, the difference in names was between the children and the adult. *Canica* is the current term used for marbles in general and for marble games in general. For instance, the youngsters might say, *Vamos a jugar a las canicas* 'Let's play marbles' or *Compré veinte canicas* 'I bought twenty marbles.' The adult recognized the term *canica,* but for him it was the name of a specific marble type. His generic term for marbles was *ague* 'agate.' In addition, though, *ague* could be used for a specific type. For example, he could say, *Te juego a agues* 'I'll play you a game of marbles' or *Te cambio una ague por una x* 'I'll exchange with you an agate for an *x*.' In the former case the use is clearly generic, whereas in the latter it is unquestionably specific. But the degree of specificity is not as large with *ague* as with any of the other names. Therefore, in comparing the names between the adult and the children, it was necessary to establish three *ague* categories for the adult (who does not distinguish among them) in order to compare them properly with the current groups' names. I have arbitrarily labeled them $ague_1$, $ague_2$, and $ague_3$ merely for ease of reference, but it should be remembered that they are the same category for the adult.

1. *Canica*. The contemporary marble players use this term in the generic sense; therefore, as a marble type it is restricted to the adult informant. He defined a *canica* as a marble made of ceramic or baked clay. Nothing else could be called by this label. When asked if he had had any

marbles of this type, he said he had discarded them long ago in preference for the newer glass types. None of the youngsters had even heard of ceramic or baked clay marbles.

2. Cat-eye, *ague*$_1$. This is one of three marble types known to all of the groups interviewed, although they used different names. The adult's *ague* category subsumes this type, which all of the children knew as cat-eye. It is made of transparent glass in a variety of tints with a band of opaque coloration in the center. This bank is tapered at either end, giving a realistic impression of a cat's eye.

3. *Puro,* crystal, judies, regular, clear one. This is the only category that produced different names from each of the groups questioned. These are the transparent glass marbles with no visible pattern. To the adult they were *puro* 'pure' or 'clear'. They were crystal to the children from IA, judies to those from IB (this term was elicited only in its plural form), and either regular or clear one to the one from II. Incidentally, the adult had defined his *ague* type as being any glass marble, cat-eyes and all, except the *puro*.

4. *Plomo,* steely. This type was known only to the adult and the children from IA. It is a name applied to ball bearings used to play marbles. As might be expected, the adult informant used the term *plomo,* and the children "steely." In standard dictionaries, the word *plomo* is defined as 'lead,' the heavy metal; however, in the regional dialect it can also refer to a heavy ball made of either lead or steel. Thus, lead fishing weights as well as steel ball bearings are called *plomo*.

5. Tiger, *ague*$_2$. Tigers were described specifically only by the II informant. The adult's *ague* definition, though, includes this type even though it does not define it precisely. The youngster from II defined tigers as transparent marbles with striped centers. They differ from cat-eyes in that the tigers' stripes are narrower and more numerous.

6. Beauty, *ague*$_3$. Beauties also were described in detail only by the II informant. He defined them as opaque marbles of two or more colors in no particular pattern. As with the previous category, the adult's *ague* class would by definition include this type.

7. *Pelotón, canicón.* This type merely refers to size. Thus any marble of any color or other description that is large in comparison to the usual marble is called a *pelotón* by the adult informant and *canicón* by the youngsters. Asked if this description also included large ball bearings, the adult said it did not and the youngsters that they did not think so (none of them was absolutely certain).

Miscellaneous

In the course of collecting the data, some miscellaneous expressions and terms were noticed and recorded for comparison. These include, for example, the expressions used in starting games, in declaring the losers, and in performing various moves within a game. Also included is a comparison of terms used to refer to a player's shooting marble.

There was general agreement on the pattern for starting games. All informants agreed on the form, *Te juego x* 'I'll play you a game of *x*,' where *x* is replaced by any marble game known to the parties involved. In addition, when playing Game 2, the challenger adds the cue for his opponent to take his turn. Thus it becomes, *Te juego al tirito. Ándale, ya tiré.* 'I'll play you a game of *el tirito*. Come on, I've already shot.' The only exception is Game 1, which uses the pattern *Échame x* 'Give me *x*.'

Two verbs, *pelar* and *pelucar,* which translate roughly as 'to strip' (of marbles), were used to declare the loser(s). For example, *Lo pelamos* means 'We stripped him [of his marbles],' and *Me pelucaron* means 'They [or all of you] stripped me [of my marbles].' There are no pronoun restrictions in the use of these two verbs.

In the description of Games 9 and 10, a procedure was detailed by which a player removes his marble from a hole. This procedure is in fact more general than that, although it does not play a crucial part in any of the other games. Most games will include a provision for moving a marble from behind an obstacle or a trap, and this move is executed in the same manner as the procedure of Games 9 and 10. That is, the marble is moved the distance of one outstretched hand in any direction. The adult informant calls this procedure *sacar la cuarta* 'to mark a quadrant of a circle' (referring to the motion of the hand as it pivots on the thumb to mark off the distance). The youngsters from IA and II call this same procedure "movies" (from the verb "to move"). In IB, "movies" is a secondary label; "handsies" is the preferred term. The youngsters from IB additionally can declare "cleanies," which entitles them to clear the ground of twigs and other debris; "uppies," which entitles them to shoot from an elevated position (as in *bombas*); or "downies," which enables them to bring the marble down from an elevated place (as from a curb down to the street level, for example). Neither the adult nor the IA informants reported these variations. The II informant, though, did report both cleanies and *bombas,* which corresponds to uppies.

Finally, there were differences in names used by the players to refer to the shooting marble. The adult informant, for instance, described *el tiro* 'the shooter' as being a perfectly round and accurate marble, and he distinguished between just any *tiro* and *el tiro para el ahogado* 'the shooter for the game of *el ahogado*.' The latter was somehow more perfectly round and more accurate. The IB players surprisingly reported that they do not use special terms for the shooting marble. The IA children called it *el tirito,* whereas the II informant called it the shooter.

Discussion

Perhaps the most significant characteristic of the data is the obvious shift in language emphasis in marble games from Spanish to English. Table 4 demonstrates this change. Whereas the adult identified five marble categories in Spanish, the children supplied only one. The generic term in all cases was a Spanish word, and it is interesting that the only marble class for which the young players gave a Spanish term, *canicón* (the class of large marbles), is in some sense a generic term as well. The term identifies a large marble of any design, opaqueness, or material. A second example, though not as convincing, is seen in Table 3. The children from IA and IB gave the name *el* triangle for one of the games, not only using the English word but also pronouncing it with an English-like phonology.

However, although the present data are suggestive, they are incomplete for a historical linguistic analysis. For instance, it is impossible at present to determine whether this trend is merely a lexical phenomenon brought about through phonological transfer or whether it is reflective of a more far-reaching linguistic change. Beyond the identification of a noticeable shift in the language of marble play, it remains to be shown whether this shift signals a fundamental change in the linguistic character of the bilingual population in question. Lehmann (1974) and others reject isolated lexical data as insufficient by themselves to identify significant historical changes in a grammar. Not enough data are available from the 1935–45 period to formulate a reliable grammatical model on any level with which to compare the contemporary data. Despite this objection, there is sufficient interest in such language-change phenomena as code-switching among bilinguals to warrant an examination of specific examples.

The lexical data suggest that one way at least in which marble terminology has been affected in time has been in the replacement of numerous Spanish lexemes by English. In addition, the data offer some examples of re-creations by way of phonological changes, morphological simplifications, and extensions of semantic ranges. Bar-Adon (1971) has identified this as one of two principal tools for investigating the processes of language transmission and linguistic continuity (i.e., language change). The other one is the analysis of children's naively consistent linguistic theories, of which none has as yet been detected in this data. Consider the following examples in reference to the questions of language change and language transmission.

1. As was already seen in Table 3, *la chuza* 'the strike' (as in bowling) becomes either *la lechuza* 'the owl' or *el pocito* 'the small hole'. Clearly, the original term has been lost to these informants. It is safe to assume, then, that *el pocito* is the latest of the three terms and that it is likely to replace *la lechuza* in the future as the name for this game. In fact, this re-creation (*la lechuza*) is easily explained in terms of both phonological changes and semantic range extension. Historically, *la chuza* is interpreted phonologically as being homophonous with *lechuza,* and the semantic range of *lechuza* is extended to accommodate the name of this game. The second step was verified by one IA informant when he stated that the hole might represent the owl's eye, in response to the question of how the game was named.

2. The IB informants reported the name "judies" for the clear marbles,

whereas the II informant gave "beauties" as the term for opaque marbles having two or more colors in no particular pattern. Notice that the IB youngsters did not specify the latter category or term (see Table 4). Because there is no apparent explanation for the term "judies" (i.e., it is not a familiar term in marble lore nor is it a term found on commercial packages of marbles), we are assuming it to be a re-creation. One interpretation would be that the two terms, "judies" and "beauties," are related historically. Following this argument, the difference is a result of language interference during the language transmission process. The child who is English dominant easily maintains the term "beauties," just as any child will display little variance with his linguistic mentors. The distortion, then, might first have occurred when the Spanish-dominant hearer received the phonetic sequence [byudiys]. In aggressive game situations such as marble playing often is, code-switching is a common occurrence. Consequently, it is possible that the Spanish-dominant hearer would misinterpret the [byu] cluster for the [ju] cluster due to phonological transfer from Spanish, where intervocalic /b/ (as in "*una* beauty", a beauty) becomes the fricative [ƀ] and may even be dropped in fast speech and where initial [y] becomes the affricative [ǰ]. Hence "beauties" becomes "judies."

3. The IA informants gave the term "steelies" for ball bearings used as marbles. They did not own any of this type of marbles, and thus the term had come in response to a general question for names of marbles. At one point during the interview, one of the youngsters asked, "¿Otras con nombre?" ('Do you want others with names?') Seeing the puzzled response to his question the child continued, "Como Mrs. Steele" ('Like Mrs. Steele'). Clearly, this example illustrates a case of overextension that follows much the same pattern as the previous one. The term "steelies" must have been received as a totally foreign form that had no meaning other than as the name for ball bearings and that only later was associated with the monophonous name of their teacher, Mrs. Steele.

Follow-up study

The continuation study was undertaken in order to verify the incidence of the two re-creations, *lechuza* and "judies," in the general school population of City I and to attempt to establish the extent of English-influenced or borrowed English terms for marbles and marble games. In addition, the questionnaire was designed to yield a limited range of social information in order to determine potential correlations with sex, social class, position in the family, neighborhood, and bilinguality (see sample form in the Appendix). This paper reports only on the verification aspect and the correlation of the re-creations with sex and bilingualism. It should be noted that the measure of bilingualism given here is a rough one. Bilinguals were classified subjectively by the investigator as English dom-

Table 5. *Subjective dominance assessment of sample by grade and sex*

	Fifth grade			Sixth grade		
	Male	Female	Total	Male	Female	Total
English dominant	0	3	3	2	3	5
Balanced	6	14	20	2	5	7
Spanish dominant	24	8	32	20	13	33
Undetermined	1	0	1	0	0	0
Italian–English	0	1	1	0	0	0
English monolingual	1	2	3	4	3	7
Spanish monolingual	0	1	1	0	2	2

inant, balanced, or Spanish dominant. This informal classification was based on gross differences that emerged during the interviews, such that an individual was termed a balanced bilingual only if his performance in both languages did not violate the rules of syntax, morphology, and phonology. No attempt was made at validating this method of classification, which no doubt would be found to be overinclusive in the two dominance categories. Nevertheless, the results of the dominance measure are summarized in Table 5, and the distribution of the re-creations across the sample population is shown in Tables 6 and 7. Notice that one Italian-English bilingual was identified in the fifth-grade sample. She was classed as English dominant on the basis of self-evaluation; the investigator does not know Italian. Incidentally, she is the only student enrolled in City I schools of her linguistic background.

The interviews were brief, rarely taking more than five minutes. In most cases, the randomly selected children were interviewed individually during physical education class in an isolated but sheltered part of the playground. Some sixth-grade students attended band class instead of physical education, and they were interviewed in a school corridor during regular academic classes. The interview procedure was simple: students were first asked sociological information, then they were asked to identify marbles by name from a set of real marbles shown to them, and finally they were asked to name the games played. A set of cards showing a variety of geometrical shapes was prepared to aid in recalling game names, but it was not needed in most cases. Interviews were conducted in both languages whenever possible. The language-dominance assessment was made at the conclusion of each session.

Results of the questionnaire demonstrate that the re-creations identified in the initial study were not idiosyncratic. Consider Tables 6 and 7. *Lechuza* was identified in both grades by about 13 percent of the total samples and by 25 percent of the total males. None of the females used

Table 6. *Distribution of re-creations, fifth grade*

	Total		English dominant			Balanced			Spanish dominant		
	M	F	M	F	Total	M	F	Total	M	F	Total
Lechuza	8	0	0	0	0	1	0	1	7	0	7
Chuza	5	0	0	0	0	0	0	0	5	0	5
Both	0	0	0	0	0	0	0	0	0	0	0
Judies	27[d]	16[e]	0	2[f]	2	4	6	10	22	7	29
Judies/beauties[a]	24[d]	7	0	1[f]	1	3	2	5	20	4	24
Judies = beauties[b]	15[d]	3	0	0	0	2	1	3	13	2	15
Judies ≠ beauties[c]	8	4	0	1	1	1	1	2	7	2	9

[a] Both terms are used.
[b] Both terms are used as synonyms.
[c] Both terms are used but not as synonyms.
[d] Includes one bilingual who spoke too little to determine dominance.
[e] Includes one monolingual English speaker.
[f] Includes one Italian-English bilingual.

either *lechuza* or *chuza*. In both grades, the highest proportions of children who recognized either one or both of these terms were found in the Spanish-dominant groups, as can be seen in Tables 6 and 7. In fact, only one balanced bilingual in each grade, and none of the English-dominant bilinguals, reported *lechuza*. The results for *el pocito* have not been tabulated.

The term "judies" is much more common in both grades, and it shows up for both sexes. In fact, 71.1 percent of the fifth-grade sample and 61.1 percent of the sixth-grade sample reported it. More males used it in both grades, 84.4 percent as compared with 57.1 percent in the fifth grade and 75 percent as compared with 46.2 percent in the sixth. A significant number of students used both "judies" and "beauties": 51.7 percent of the fifth grade and 37 percent of the sixth. Interestingly, the two terms were synonymous for about 30 percent of both grades, whereas 20 percent of the fifth-grade sample and 7.4 percent of the sixth reported them as distinct marble types. Again, the Spanish-dominant categories show the largest percentages for incidence (1) of "judies," (2) of both "judies" and "beauties," and (3) of both terms as synonyms. A larger percentage of the English-dominant group in the fifth grade, about 33.3 percent, reported them as distinct types. In the sixth grade the only students to identify them as separate types were in the Spanish-dominant group.

The inevitable conclusion is that both re-creations are used by significant numbers of the school population. The term "judies" apparently

Table 7. *Distribution of re-creations, sixth grade*

	Total		English dominant			Balanced			Spanish dominant		
	M	F	M	F	Total	M	F	Total	M	F	Total
Lechuza	7	0	0	0	0	1	0	1	6	0	6
Chuza	4	0	0	0	0	0	0	0	4	0	4
Both	1	0	0	0	0	0	0	0	1	0	1
Judies	21	12	1	0	1	1	4	5	19	8	27
Judies/beauties[a]	15	5	0	0	0	0	2	2	15	3	18
Judies = beauties[b]	13	3	0	0	0	0	2	2	13	1	14
Judies ≠ beauties[c]	2	2	0	0	0	0	0	0	2	2	4

[a] Both terms are used.
[b] Both terms are used as synonyms.
[c] Both terms are used but not as synonyms.

is so widely used that even monolingual English speakers can adopt it.[5] Questionnaire results showed two non-Spanish speakers reporting the term, the Italian-English bilingual and a monolingual English speaker.

Larger proportions of the Spanish-dominant students than of any other dominance group use each of the re-creations. But it is not clear why this is so. If it is the case that Spanish-dominant bilinguals use Spanish more often than balanced or English-dominant bilinguals, then this finding is consistent with the interpretation of *lechuza* given in the initial study. However, this would not support the interpretation of the re-creation of "judies" unless we assume that Spanish-dominant bilinguals are more vulnerable to linguistic interference than other bilinguals. This assumption appears groundless. Notice that in the fifth grade, more of the English-dominant students than of any other class maintain a distinction between "judies" and "beauties." This would appear to indicate that the re-creation did not occur within this group initially but was borrowed from

[5] The phenomenon of monolingual English speakers in this community adopting language features that originated in the bilingual portion of the population can be explained in terms of (1) the population statistics given in Table 1 and (2) the domain under investigation. That is, the economic power of the monolingual English speakers in the wider community evidently promotes a higher status role for English than for Spanish in the business and political domains, but this relationship appears to be reversed in the playground domain. Notice in Table 1 that nearly 90 percent of both grade levels are classified as Spanish speaking. In fact, several monolingual English-speaking youngsters were observed using Spanish-accented English while engaged in active play. This apparent status role reversal in the playground suggests the need for the longitudinal study of language attitudes. For instance, it would be valuable to understand not only how an individual's attitudes evolve during childhood but also how they affect and are affected by the attitudes of other members of the community. In addition, it would be valuable to study the factors associated with changes in a community's attitudes. These are important questions in view of the social, ethnic, and linguistic segmentation characteristic of societies throughout the world.

either the balanced or the Spanish-dominant bilinguals. In any case, more statistical analysis is needed to determine the significance, if any, of the Spanish-dominant category with respect to the two terms.

Appendix: Sample questionnaire form

Name: ______________________________ No.: _______

1. (English Dominant) (Balanced) (Spanish Dominant)
2. Sex: _________ 3. Age: _________
4. a. Older bros. ___ sisters ____ b. Younger bros. ___ sisters ____
5. a. Father's occup. __________ Mother's occup. _______________
6. Address: ____
7. Language spoken with
   a. Father: _______________ b. Mother: _______________
   c. Siblings: _______________ d. Friends: _______________
   e. Grandmother: ___________ f. Grandfather: ____________
   g. At Play: _______________ h. Mostly: _______________
   i. Marbles: _______________
8. Marble Identification
   (marbles) (canicas) (agues) (puro) (plomo) (cat-eye)
   (crystal) (judies) (regular) (clear one) (steely) (tiger)
   (beauty) (pelotón) (canicón)
9. Game Name Identification
   (la chuza) (la lechuza) (el pocito)
   (el tirito) (bombas) (el soldadito) (el sense)
   (el ahogado) (el triangle) (el blanquillo) (el pescado) (la rueda)
   (el codo) (el pocito linea) (las nacas) (los cinco pocitos)

References

Ariès, P. 1962. *Centuries of childhood.* New York: Knopf.

Bar-Adon, A. 1971. Child bilingualism in an immigrant society: implications of borrowing in the Hebrew "language of games." In Preprints of the Chicago Conference on Child Language, pp. 264–318.

Ferretti, F. 1973. *The great American marble book.* New York: Workman.

Galván, J. 1974. Marble games of south Texas: a study in language change. Manuscript. University of Texas, Austin.

Haugen, E. 1973. Bilingualism, language contact, and immigrant languages in the United States: a research report, 1956–1970. In *Current trends in linguistics,* ed. T. Sebeok, vol. 10, pp. 505–91. The Hague: Mouton.

King, R. 1969. *Historical linguistics and generative grammar.* Englewood Cliffs, N.J.: Prentice-Hall.

Lehmann, W. 1974. Subjectivity. *Language* 50:622–9.

Stone, G. 1971. The play of little children. *Child's play,* ed. R. Herron and B. Sutton-Smith, pp. 1–14. New York: Wiley.

Sutton-Smith, B., ed. 1972. *The folkgames of children.* Austin: University of Texas Press.

Sutton-Smith, B., and B. Rosenberg. 1972. Sixty years of historical change in the game preferences of American children. In *The folkgames of children,* ed. B. Sutton-Smith, pp. 258–94. Austin: University of Texas Press.

Velázquez, M., E. Gray, and J. Iribas, eds. 1967. *New revised Velázquez Spanish and English dictionary.* Chicago: Follett.

Williams, E. ed. 1968. *The Bantam new college Spanish and English dictionary.* New York: Bantam.

Index